The Ad Hoc Committee to Oversee the Use of the Catechism of the National Conference of Catholic Bishops has found this catechetical series to be in conformity with the *Catechism of the Catholic Church.*

Series Authors: **Janaan Manternach**
Carl J. Pfeifer

Teacher Edition Authors: **Jeannine Wadoz Goggin**   **Kate Sweeney Ristow**
Stephanie Spence, A.N.G.   **James Bitney**

Contributing Authors: **Susan G. Keys**   **Paula Lenz**
Maureen Shaughnessy, S.C.   **Barbara Carol Vasiloff**

Student Edition Authors: **Jeannine Wadoz Goggin**   **Maureen Gallagher**
Stephanie Spence, A.N.G.   **Jean Marie Weber**
Joan R. DeMerchant

SILVER BURDETT GINN
PARSIPPANY, NJ

Contents . . . .

Consultants
Linda Blanchette, Anita Bridge, Fred Brown, Rod Brownfield, Sister Mary Michael Burns, S.C., Patricia Burns, Bernadine Carroll, Mary Ellen Cocks, Sister Peggy Conlon, R.S.M., Mary Ann Crowley, Pamela Danni, Sister Jamesetta DeFelice, O.S.U., Sister Mary Elizabeth Duke, S.N.D., Mary M. Gibbons, Yolanda Gremillion, Sister Angela Hallahan, C.H.F., Alice J. Heard, Sister Michele O'Connoll, P.B.V.M., Sister Angela O'Mahoney, P.B.V.M., Sister Ruthann O'Mara, S.S.J., Sandra Okulicz-Hulme, Judy Papandria, Rachel Pasano, Sallie Ann Phelan, Sister Geraldine M. Rogers, S.S.J., Mary Lou Schlosser, Patricia Ann Sibilia, Margaret E. Skelly, Lisa Ann Sorlie, Sister Victorine Stoltz, O.S.B., Sister Nancy Jean Turner, S.H.C.J., Christine Ward, Judith Reidel Weber, Kay White, Elizabeth M. Williams, Catherine R. Wolf, Florence Bambrick Yarney, Kathryn K. Zapcic

Advisory Board
Rev. Louis J. Cameli, Philip J. Cunningham, Sister Clare E. Fitzgerald, William J. Freburger, Greer G. Gordon, Sister Veronica R. Grover, S.H.C.J., Rev. Thomas Guarino, Rev. Robert E. Harahan, Rev. Eugene LaVerdieré, S.S.S., Rev. Frank J. McNulty, Rev. Msgr. John J. Strynkowski

National Catechetical Advisor
Kathleen Hendricks

Nihil Obstat
Kathleen Flanagan, S.C., Ph.D., Censor Librorum
Ellen Joyce, S.C., Ph.D., Censor Librorum

Imprimatur
✠ Most Reverend Frank J. Rodimer,
    Bishop of Paterson
    November 8, 1996

The *nihil obstat* and *imprimatur* are official declarations that a book or pamphlet is free of doctrinal and moral error. No implication is contained therein that those who have granted the *nihil obstat* and *imprimatur* agree with the contents, opinions, or statements expressed.

ISBN 0-382-30503-5

[Acknowledgements and Credits appear on end page of book.]

345678910–0504030201009998

Dear Catholic School Teacher,

The teaching of religion is an important responsibility for all Catholic School teachers. We commend you for assuming this responsibility and are proud to be your partner in sharing the Catholic faith with children.

We are especially pleased to announce that the National Conference of Catholic Bishops' Ad Hoc Committee to Oversee the Use of the Catechism has found this new edition of *This Is Our Faith* to be in conformity with the *Catechism of the Catholic Church*. This means that *This Is Our Faith* has a breadth and depth of content wherein the presentation of Catholic doctrine is authentic and therefore suitable for catechetical instruction.

This sharing of faith includes many dimensions: the instruction in doctrine, Scripture, and morality; the experience of prayer and liturgy; the building of a value system; the ability to relate teaching to life; the knowledge of the rich heritage we share in time, place, and people; and the profound respect for and love of the Catholic Church. *This Is Our Faith* addresses each of these dimensions.

We take our responsibility to Catholic education seriously and once again we have consulted you, the classroom teacher, at every step along the way of the development of this revision. The next few pages will give you an overview of the new *This Is Our Faith*. We know that you will find in this program everything that a publisher can provide to support you in your important work.

Your commitment to Catholic education and to the children whom you teach is one that we share. This program has been created to be the best for you and for your class. It is to you that we dedicate this edition of *This Is Our Faith*.

Sincerely,

Raymond T. Latour

Raymond T. Latour
Vice President & Director
Religion Division

Content is important to Catholic identity.

What content is included?

THIS IS OUR FAITH is a developmental program, based on Scripture and rooted in the teachings of the *Catechism of the Catholic Church*. While the content for each year centers on one particular theme, strands on Church, Sacraments, Trinity, and Morality are interwoven throughout the program. The presentation of doctrine has been increased in each chapter of this new edition.

Plus—chapter reviews and **expanded unit reviews** help you to evaluate student progress as you teach!!

The chart to the right outlines the doctrinal content of Grade 2.

TRINITY — THREE PERSONS ONE GOD

CREATOR/FATHER	JESUS
God's love gives us the freedom to make choices.	Jesus brings us God's forgiveness.
We profess our belief in God the Father during Mass.	Jesus is the Son of God and began God's Church on earth.
God is always willing to forgive us.	Jesus died for us on the cross.
	Jesus rose from the dead to save us and give us new life.
	At Baptism, our lives are joined to Jesus.
	Jesus gives us himself in the Eucharist.
MORALITY	THE BIBLE
As Christians we are called to lead just and peaceful lives in the service of God, ourselves, and others.	God speaks to us during the Liturgy of the Word through the Bible.
We have a responsibility to respect all of God's creation.	The Bible is divided into two parts: the Old Testament and the New Testament.
We are responsible for the choices we make and the actions we take.	The readings we listen to at Mass are from the Old Testament and the New Testament.
	The Amen Section in each text contains special lessons on Church feasts and seasons and on honoring Mary, saints, heroes, and heroines. These topics also appear as part of various lessons throughout the text.

262   263

Our Amen Section of Saints, Feasts and Seasons is still conveniently located in the back of the student book and has been expanded just as you requested. Every year your students will have the opportunity to celebrate the holy seasons of Advent, Lent, Christmas, and Easter in addition to other special feasts.

THE HOLY SPIRIT

The Holy Spirit helps us make good choices.

The Holy Spirit was sent by Jesus to be with us.

The Holy Spirit first comes to us in the sacrament of Baptism.

At Confirmation, the Holy Spirit makes us strong to live and share our faith in Jesus.

SACRAMENTS

At Baptism, we become members of the Church.

The Eucharist was instituted by Jesus at the Last Supper.

At Baptism, Jesus gives us new life.

The Eucharist is a sacrament of thanksgiving, sacrifice, unity, peace, and justice.

In the Eucharist, bread and wine are changed into the body and blood of Jesus.

In the sacrament of Reconciliation, we express sorrow for our sins.

In the sacrament of Reconciliation, we celebrate God's forgiveness.

Sacraments are celebrations of Jesus' love and presence.

Confirmation is a sacrament of initiation.

About the Mass

About Reconciliation

A complete chapter reviewing the basics of these sacraments.

CHURCH

The Church is the people of God.

The Church is the community of Jesus' followers.

We become members of the Church at Baptism and participate in the life of the Church through the sacraments of Eucharist and Reconciliation.

The Catholic Church is a sacramental Church.

The Church gathers at Mass to celebrate the life of Jesus with us.

PRAYERS AND PRECEPTS

Sign of the Cross

The Lord's Prayer

Hail Mary

Glory Be to the Father

Morning Prayer

Evening Prayer

Grace Before Meals

Grace After Meals

Prayer to My Guardian Angel

Prayer of Sorrow

Prayers and precepts of the Church are used in lessons throughout the texts. Selected traditional prayers also appear in the front of the text in a section called Let Us Pray. Precepts also appear in a special end-of-text section designed to encourage their memorization.

RELIGIOUS VOCABULARY

Absolution
Anointing
Baptism
Catholic Church
Celebration
Christian
Church
Communion
Community
Confess
Confirmation
Contrition

Eucharist
Eucharistic Prayer
Godparent
Gospel
Homily
Hosts
Liturgy of the Eucharist
Liturgy of the Word
Mass
Penance

Prayer of the Faithful
Presence
Reconciliation
Respond
Responsibility
Resurrection
Sacraments
Sacrifice
Serve
Sin
Sponsor
Unite

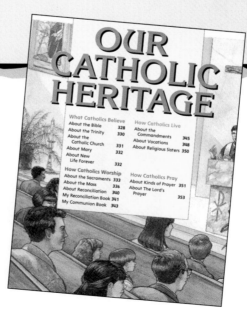

OUR CATHOLIC HERITAGE

What Catholics Believe		How Catholics Live	
About the Bible	328	About the Commandments	345
About the Trinity	330	About Vocations	348
About the Catholic Church	331	About Religious Sisters	350
About Mary	332		
About New Life Forever	332		
How Catholics Worship		How Catholics Pray	
About the Sacraments	333	About Kinds of Prayer	351
About the Mass	336	About The Lord's Prayer	353
About Reconciliation	340		
My Reconciliation Book	341		
My Communion Book	343		

Our Catholic Heritage, a special doctrinal section organized according to the four pillars of the *Catechism of the Catholic Church,* is included in each grade-level student book to provide you with the opportunity and resources necessary to teach and review basic Catholic teachings every year.

What about prayer?

THIS IS OUR FAITH emphasizes prayer in all forms from traditional to spontaneous, from music to meditation, from the spoken word and formal liturgical prayer to the psalms and prayers of the heart. Children learn not only prayers, but how to pray alone, in a small group, within the classroom or school or in the church assembly. **Among other resources within THIS IS OUR FAITH, you will find the following:**

Praying with a Procession

Teacher: Today we will have a procession to praise God. Let us process to the prayer table, remembering that God is here with us.

Teacher: The Lord be with you.

All: And also with you.

Teacher: O great and wonderful God, you always listen to our prayers. Let our procession today be our prayer. May it give you glory. We pray this prayer and all our prayers in the name of Jesus, your Son.

All: Amen.

120   Prayer

▲ Prayer pages in each chapter of the student book provide instruction on and an experience of prayer each week.

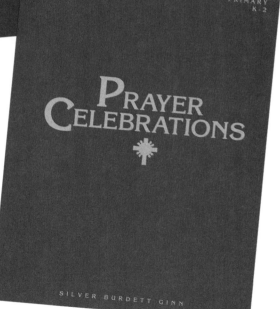

PRIMARY
K-2

PRAYERS FOR EVERY DAY

SILVER BURDETT GINN

PRIMARY
K-2

PRAYER CELEBRATIONS

SILVER BURDETT GINN

▲
Prayers for Every Day is a wonderful resource for you. In it you will find prayers for every day of the year, as well as additional prayers to be said during special times and seasons.

◄
Prayer Celebrations are resource books full of complete grade-level-specific prayer services ready to use with your class. Everything is done for you. All you need to do is read the special preparation page, duplicate the master sheet, and begin the celebration!

What about Sunday?

This brand-new supplemental program helps prepare children to better understand the Sunday readings. It provides ways to help children participate more fully in the Sunday liturgy—a need expressed by many teachers. Here's how to do it!

Each week, perhaps on Friday, distribute the student leaflets for Sunday. Then together, listen to the Word of God and follow the specific activities that will help the Word take on real meaning for children. They will be ready to listen and pray on Sunday!

This is indeed a true liturgical-year program! Each leaflet is brand-new and developed for each liturgical cycle!

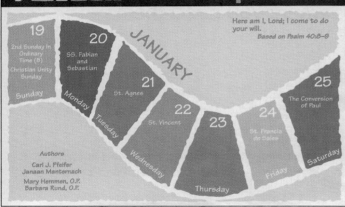

◄ Background for the Teacher and a session outline are clearly and simply presented on each teacher folder—which also provides a handy storage unit for the student leaflets.

THIS IS OUR FAITH has always provided the best in Teacher Editions.

What's new in this one?

Chapter Organizers keep you on target and make planning quick and easy.

All content is correlated with the *Catechism of the Catholic Church*

We Belong to the Catholic Church

1

Objectives

To help the children
■ Recognize that they belong to the Catholic community.
■ Understand that the Church is a community of people.
■ Discover special objects used in the parish church.
■ Discover special objects used at Mass.
■ Pray in the presence of God and review the chapter.

Correlation to the **C**atechism of the Catholic Church
Paragraphs
751, 771, 775, 777, 1181, 1267

Chapter Outline

	Step 1 Learning About Our Lives	Step 2 Learning About Our Faith	Step 3 Learning How to Live Our Faith
Day 1	■ Introduce community. ■ Read a poem. *ABOUT 10 MINUTES*	■ Read about communities. ■ Define the new words. ■ Present the doctrine. *ABOUT 15 MINUTES*	■ Complete an activity. *ABOUT 5 MINUTES*
Day 2	■ Review Day 1. *ABOUT 5 MINUTES*	■ Enthrone the Bible. ■ Proclaim and dramatize the Scripture story. ■ Discuss the Scripture story. *ABOUT 20 MINUTES*	■ Complete an activity. ■ Pray together. *ABOUT 5 MINUTES*
Day 3	■ Name the parish and pastor. *ABOUT 2 MINUTES*	■ Read about discovering and exploring parish churches. ■ Explore the parish church. ■ Review the new words. *ABOUT 22 MINUTES*	■ Sing and pray together. *ABOUT 6 MINUTES*
Day 4	■ Review Day 3. *ABOUT 5 MINUTES*	■ Explore the sacristy. ■ Present the new words. *ABOUT 20 MINUTES*	■ Complete a drawing activity. *ABOUT 5 MINUTES*
Day 5	**Prayer** Gather for prayer and pray together. **Review** Review the chapter and read the Scripture verse.		

Plan Ahead

	Preparing Your Class	Materials Needed
Day 1	Read over the lesson. Prepare a discovery table. Make a paper doll chain. Print *community* on a card.	■ symbols of communities ■ paper doll chain ■ Bible, candle
Day 2	Read over the lesson. Prepare simple props for dramatizations of Bible stories. Prepare a prayer table.	■ cloth or scarf ■ paper doll chain ■ Bible, candle
Day 3	Arrange for partners to explore church. Prepare church for visit. Print five 2" × 4" cards per child, naming items found in church.	■ 2" × 4" item cards ■ score or recording of a familiar song
Day 4	Contact parish leader for visit to sacristy. Print four 2" × 4" cards per child, naming items found in the sacristy.	■ textbooks ■ 2" × 4" item cards
Day 5	Read over the lesson. Prepare for prayer in church. Select an easy setting of a "Holy, Holy, Holy."	■ votive candle ■ paper strips or paper footprints

Additional Resources

As you plan this chapter, consider using the following materials from The Resourceful Teacher Package.

■ *Classroom Activity Sheets 1 and 1a*
■ *Family Activity Sheets 1 and 1a*
■ *Chapter 1 Test*
■ *Prayers for Every Day*
■ *Projects: Grade 2*

You may also wish to refer to the following Big Book.

■ *We Celebrate God's Word,* page 22

In preparing the children for the Sunday readings, you may wish to use Silver Burdett Ginn's *Getting Ready for Sunday* student and teacher materials.

Chapter Organizer 11b

11a Chapter Organizer

Also in each chapter you will find special feature boxes, giving you additional tips where you need them.

Focus On
provides background information for you on specific topics.

Curriculum Connection
helps you tie in what is being taught in Religion with other content areas.

Enriching the Lesson
includes extras—additional ideas to expand and enrich the lesson.

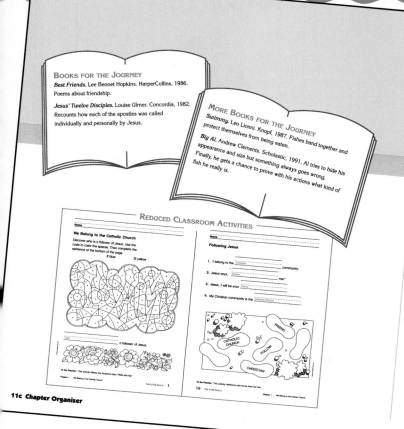

BOOKS FOR THE JOURNEY
Best Friends. Lee Bennet Hopkins. HarperCollins, 1986. Poems about friendship.

Jesus' Twelve Disciples. Louise Ulmer. Concordia, 1982. Recounts how each of the apostles was called individually and personally by Jesus.

MORE BOOKS FOR THE JOURNEY
Swimmy. Leo Lionni. Knopf, 1987. Fishes band together and protect themselves from being eaten.

Big Al. Andrew Clements. Scholastic, 1991. Al tries to hide his appearance and size but something always goes wrong. Finally, he gets a chance to prove with his actions what kind of fish he really is.

REDUCED CLASSROOM ACTIVITIES

11c Chapter Organizer

Background for the Teacher

CHARACTERISTICS OF COMMUNITY
The distinguishing characteristics of the Christian community are faith, hope, love, and commitment to Jesus Christ. To be a Christian is simply to be a friend and follower of Jesus. We name ourselves with his name (Christian), and we mark ourselves with his sign, the cross. We accept his teachings and try to live a life of commitment to God in the Catholic Church, whose members are bonded in Christ Jesus. The *National Catechetical Directory* (NCD) states: "In the Catholic Church are found the deposit of faith, the sacraments, and the ministries inherited from the apostles. Through these gifts from God, the Church is able to grow and act as a community in Christ, serving human beings and mediating to them His saving word and activity" (#93).

EXPERIENCING THE CATHOLIC CHURCH
Although the family is still the primary community for most children at this age level, these children are beginning to feel a real sense of belonging to other groups and organizations. They are part of communities that share common interests, such as Scout groups or sports teams; communities that share common goals, such as classroom communities; or communities that share common experiences, such as circles of friends. These broadened experiences deepen the children's experiences of what it means to belong. During this year, the children will explore what it means to belong to the Catholic Church and will come to a better understanding of their roles within the Church.

The children's understanding of the word *catholic* may come from their experiences of attending their parish church, where they worship with the Catholic community. Through their experiences in class, you can help the children develop a sense of pride in being at home within the Catholic Church. In effect, your group can become a microcosm of the Catholic community, a family that gathers together to practice its faith.

Chapter Organizer **11d**

Background for teachers provides excellent information for you on what is to be taught as well as insights into how to teach it.

Cultural Awareness
gives you needed information to aid students in their appreciation of other cultures.

Teaching Tips
provides just what you need—an extra idea, project, or help - just when you need it.

These new features plus our new size and easier to use format, along with our proven method of teaching—our three-step lesson plan—and a complete lesson every day makes this the best teacher edition ever!

You've always had great additional teacher resources.

What's new in this edition?

We've already told you about the *new* **Prayer Celebrations Book,** the *new* **Prayers for Every Day,** and the *new* **Getting Ready for Sunday** program.

Here's more!

▶ **Project Books**
One per grade give ideas and opportunities to enhance and expand learning.

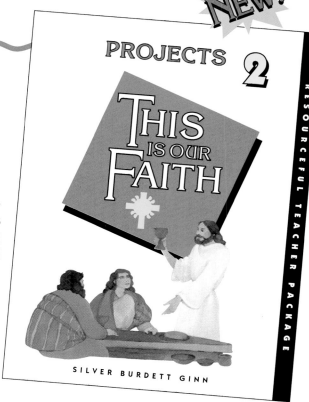

▲ **Saints and Other Holy People**
provide excellent role models for students.

▶ **Saints Cards**
(32 of 6 Saints for each year)
Take-home cards for each child to treasure.

Saint Elizabeth of Hungary

Saints Francis and Clare

NEW!

Videos
One per grade,
correlated to each unit!
(Ready in 1998)

NEW!

▲ **Teacher Resource Package**
Includes Project Booklet,
Classroom Activities, Family
Activities and Letters in English
and Spanish, and Tests as well as
a handy tote to keep all your
resources together.

Familiar Resources Designed Especially for the 1998 Edition!

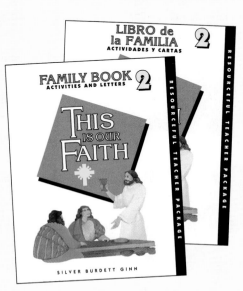

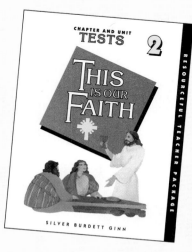

▲ **Classroom Activities**
Two sheets for every chapter!

▲ **Family Activities and Letters**
(in English and in Spanish)
Ready to duplicate and send home!

▲ **Tests**
Both Chapter and Unit

And, as your students would say,

"What does THIS IS OUR FAITH have to do with real life?"

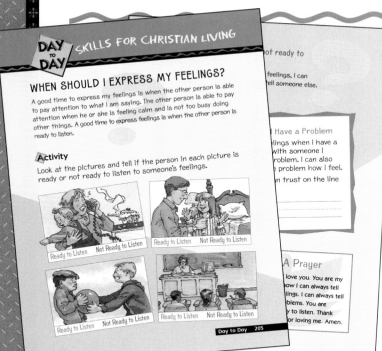

DAY TO DAY SKILLS FOR CHRISTIAN LIVING

WHEN SHOULD I EXPRESS MY FEELINGS?

A good time to express my feelings is when the other person is able to pay attention to what I am saying. The other person is able to pay attention when he or she is feeling calm and is not too busy doing other things. A good time to express feelings is when the other person is ready to listen.

Activity

Look at the pictures and tell if the person in each picture is ready or not ready to listen to someone's feelings.

Ready to Listen   Not Ready to Listen
Ready to Listen   Not Ready to Listen
Ready to Listen   Not Ready to Listen
Ready to Listen   Not Ready to Listen

Day to Day 205

Living our faith goes well beyond the classroom experience into the everyday challenges and opportunities faced by each of our children every day. Each class begins with a life experience and ends with an integration of what has been learned into the child's life.

◀ Day to Day: Skills for Christian Living

At the end of each unit, two pages focus on the development of personal and moral skills in a sensitive and constructive way consistent with our Gospel values and Christian life. This is an infinitely practical feature that will help the faith and life to emerge as one.

I am a follower of Jesus.
This year I want to learn more about my Catholic faith.
This is my journey.
Many people will help me along the way.

◀ For each grade-level the gatefold invites students to journey together as a school community through faith and life!

THIS IS OUR FAITH provides a complete and comprehensive coverage of Doctrine, Scripture, Morality, Prayer and Review, all taught in age-appropriate and proven ways.

Including all of the resources you've used and loved—and many new ones that you've wanted.

Written with you in mind and backed by the very best service in publishing for Catholic schools.

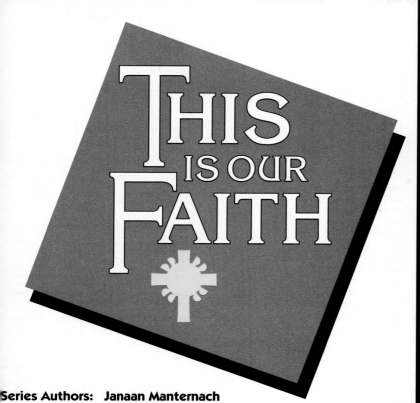

This Is Our Faith

Series Authors: **Janaan Manternach**
                     Carl J. Pfeifer

Authors: **Philip Cunningham**
             Joan R. DeMerchant
             Maureen Gallagher

Consulting Editor: Jean Marie Weber

Contributing Authors: Robert Hamma
                        Kate Sweeney Ristow

SILVER BURDETT GINN
PARSIPPANY, NJ

THIS IS OUR FAITH
SCHOOL PROGRAM

Contributing Authors: James Bitney, Robert Hamma, Paula A. Lenz, Judene Leon, Yvette Nelson, Sister Carolyn Puccio, C.S.J., Anna Ready, Kate Sweeney Ristow, Barbara Carol Vasiloff, Sister Maureen Shaughnessy, S.C., Sister Cecilia Maureen Cromwell, I.H.M., Patricia Frevert, Mary Lou Ihrig, Sister Arlene Pomije, C.S.J., Sister Mary Agnes Ryan, I.H.M., Brother Michael Sheerin, F.M.S.

Opening Doors: A Take-Home Magazine: Peter H.M. Demkovitz, Janie Gustafson, Margaret Savitskas

Day to Day: Skills for Christian Living: Susan G. Keys

Advisory Board:

Rev. Louis J. Cameli

Philip J. Cunningham

Sister Clare E. Fitzgerald

William J. Freburger

Greer J. Gordon

Sister Veronica R. Grover, S.H.C.J.

Rev. Thomas Guarino

Rev. Robert E. Harahan

Kathleen Hendricks

Rev. Eugene LaVerdieré, S.S.S.

Rev. Frank J. McNulty

Rev. Msgr. John J. Strynkowski

Consultants: Linda Blanchette, Anita Bridge, Fred Brown, Rod Brownfield, Sister Mary Michael Burns, S.C., Pat Burns, Bernadine Carroll, Mary Ellen Cocks, Sister Peggy Conlon, R.S.M., Mary Ann Crowley, Pamela Danni, Sister Jamesetta DeFelice, O.S.U., Sister Mary Elizabeth Duke, S.N.D., Mary M. Gibbons, Yolanda Gremillion, Sister Angela Hallahan, C.H.F., Alice T. Heard, Sister Michele O'Connoll, P.B.V.M., Sister Angela O'Mahoney, P.B.V.M., Sister Ruthann O'Mara, S.S.J., Sandra Okulicz-Hulme, Judy Papandria, Rachel Pasano, Sallie Ann Phelan, Sister Geraldine M. Rogers, S.S.J., Mary Lou Schlosser, Patricia Ann Sibilia, Margaret E. Skelly, Lisa Ann Sorlie, Sister Victorine Stoltz, O.S.B., Sister Nancy Jean Turner, S.H.C.J., Christine Ward, Judith Reidel Weber, Kay White, Elizabeth M. Williams, Catherine R. Wolf, Florence Bambrick Yarney, Kathryn K. Zapcic

Nihil Obstat

Kathleen Flanagan, S.C.
Censor Librorum

Ellen Joyce, S.C.
Censor Librorum

Imprimatur

✠ Most Reverend Frank J. Rodimer
  Bishop of Paterson

November 8, 1996

The *nihil obstat* and *imprimatur* are official declarations that a book or pamphlet is free of doctrinal and moral error. No implication is contained therein that those who have granted the *nihil obstat* and *imprimatur* agree with the contents, opinions, or statements expressed.

ACKNOWLEDGMENTS

Scriptural texts used in this work are taken from the *New American Bible with Revised New Testament*, Copyright © 1970, 1986 by the Confraternity of Christian Doctrine, Washington, DC, and are used by permission of copyright owner. All rights reserved.

All adaptations of Scripture are based on *the New American Bible with Revised New Testament*.

"Blessings of a Pet" reprinted with permission from the *New St. Joseph's People's Prayer Book* (page 1037), copyright © 1980 by Catholic Book Publishing Co., New York, NY. All rights reserved.

Excerpts from the English translation of *Rite of Baptism for Children* © 1969, International Committee on English in the Liturgy, Inc. (ICEL); excerpts from the English translation of *Rite of Christian Initiation of Adults* © 1988, ICEL; excerpts from the English translation of *The Roman Missal* © 1973, ICEL; excerpts from the English translation of *Rite of Penance* © 1974, ICEL; excerpts from the English translation of *Rite of Confirmation*, Second Edition © 1975, ICEL; excerpts from the English translation of *Pastoral Care of the Sick: Rites of Anointing and Viaticum* © 1982, ICEL; excerpts from the English translation of Eucharistic Prayers for Masses with Children © 1975, ICEL. All rights reserved.

Contents ~~~~~~~~~~

Catechism of the Catholic Church

Since its publication in June 1994, the English translation of the *Catechism of the Catholic Church* has enjoyed a wide readership among Catholics throughout the United States. Parents and teachers will want to know how the chapter themes in THIS IS OUR FAITH relate to the content of the *Catechism*.

As a service, we have included a Catechism Reference Box at the beginning of each chapter in the Teacher Edition. We suggest that in preparing to teach the chapter, teachers first read the section "Background for the Teacher." For additional enrichment, you may wish to refer to the paragraphs in the *Catechism* that are indicated in the Reference Box.

Although the *Catechism of the Catholic Church* is not the only source of enrichment regarding doctrine, it can be most helpful in broadening our understanding of faith. We are encouraged to use it as a reference in our ongoing study of our Catholic tradition.

Learning Prayers

The children at this age probably have learned most of the prayers on this page. You may want to review these prayers by discussing the meaning of each line of every prayer and the meaning of each prayer in our daily lives.

Introducing the Prayers

Ask the children to look at the prayers on page 1. They are placed here as an easy-to-find reference for the children. You might use one of more of these prayers to open and close each class session.

Challenge the children to commit these prayers to memory and to pray them often. Suggest that they pray one or more of these prayers each night before falling asleep. Ask the children to suggest other times when they might say the prayers on this page.

Let Us Pray

Sign of the Cross
In the name of the Father
   and of the Son,
   and of the Holy Spirit.
Amen.

The Lord's Prayer
Our Father, who art
   in heaven,
     hallowed be thy name;
thy kingdom come;
thy will be done on earth
   as it is in heaven.
Give us this day
   our daily bread;
and forgive us
   our trespasses
   as we forgive those
   who trespass against us;
and lead us not
   into temptation,
   but deliver us from evil.
Amen.

Hail Mary

Hail Mary, full of grace,
   the Lord is with you.
Blessed are you among
   women,
   and blessed is the fruit
   of your womb, Jesus.
Holy Mary,
   Mother of God,
   pray for us sinners,
   now, and at the hour
   of our death.
Amen.

Glory Be to the Father

Glory be to the Father,
   and to the Son,
   and to the Holy Spirit.
As it was in the
   beginning, is now,
   and ever shall be,
   world without end.
Amen.

3

Let Us Pray

A Morning Prayer
My God, I offer you today
  all I think and do and say,
  uniting it with what was
  done on earth,
  by Jesus Christ, your Son.
Amen.

Evening Prayer
Dear God, before I sleep
  I want to thank you
  for this day
  so full of your kindness
  and your joy.
I close my eyes to rest safe
  in your loving care.
Amen.

Grace Before Meals
Bless us, O Lord, and these your gifts,
   which we are about to receive
   from your goodness,
   through Christ our Lord.
Amen.

Grace After Meals
We give you thanks for all your gifts,
   almighty God,
   living and reigning
   now and forever.
Amen.

Let Us Pray

Prayer to My Guardian Angel

Angel of God, my guardian dear,
    to whom God's love commits me here.
Ever this day be at my side
    to light and guard, to rule and guide.
Amen.

Prayer of Sorrow

My God,
I am sorry for my sins with all my heart.
In choosing to do wrong
and failing to do good,
I have sinned against you
whom I should love above all things.
I firmly intend, with your help,
to do penance,
to sin no more,
and to avoid whatever
leads me to sin.
Our Savior Jesus Christ
suffered and died for us.
In his name, my God,
have mercy.
Revised Rite of Penance

6

Beginning the Journey

Introductory Lesson

Objectives

To help the children
- Experience a sense of welcome.
- Make a commitment to the journey of faith.
- Want to learn to know and love Jesus better.

Lesson Outline

- Welcome the children.
- Play a get-acquainted game.
- Introduce the student text.
- Pray together.
- Make a commitment to the faith journey.
- Conclude the session.

Plan Ahead

Make an Answer Chart to help the children get acquainted with one another. Draw a large circle on a sheet of posterboard. Divide the circle into eight pie-shaped segments. Label each segment with an incomplete sentence, such as "When I grow up, I want to be . . ."; "My favorite food is . . ."; "My favorite TV show is . . ."; "I like to play with . . ."; "If I could be an animal, I would be a . . ."; and so on.

Make an arrow from posterboard and attach it to the center of the circle with a brad fastener.

As an alternative, make an Answer Box, putting slips of paper with the incomplete sentences printed on them in a brightly decorated box from which the children can draw.

Prepare a name tag for each child. These tags should be large enough for the children's first names to be clearly visible. Arrange the name tags on a table located near the entrance to the room.

Prepare a special area in your room for prayer. This need not be elaborate. Cover a table or desk with a cloth and place a Bible and candle on the cloth. You might also add flowers to decorate the table.

Materials Needed

- crayons or felt-tip markers
- recording of a welcome song
- record player, tape player, or CD player
- posterboard
- a Bible
- flowers (optional)
- a candle and matches
- an Answer Chart (See Plan Ahead.)
- name tags (See Plan Ahead.)
- *Parent Preview Magazine*

Becoming a Community

An ancient Chinese proverb tells us that "a journey of a thousand miles must begin with a single step." You and your second graders are about to begin an exciting journey together. The introductory session provides you, the teacher, with the opportunity to greet the children and to help them begin to know one another. Your goals for the year should be not only to teach the children to understand and appreciate the Catholic community, but also to help them become a community of faith. Helping the children to get acquainted, to learn one another's names, and to feel comfortable with each other and their surroundings will help to ensure that your group is on the way to becoming a community.

During this session, invite the children to participate in the journey of faith. As Christians, we are like pilgrims on a long journey. Our ultimate destination, of course, is everlasting life and being happy with God and with all those who have tried to love God in this life. While this concept is beyond the understanding of seven- and eight-year-old children, you can help them appreciate that they are called to grow closer to God and Jesus while they are learning more about the beliefs and traditions of our faith.

Jesus Is with Us

The journey theme is meant to help focus the attention of the young people and to illustrate in a memorable way this fact: The loving Jesus they meet in their studies is with them in all their life experiences. The world they find so interesting, so demanding, and sometimes so thrilling is *God's* world, made a new creation through Jesus and the Spirit.

The session concludes with a prayer experience in which the children will dedicate themselves to the challenging faith journey. They are invited to sign their names on the commitment page located on the inside front cover panel of the student text. They will also hear encouraging words from Scripture. These promises will assure the children that Jesus' presence and care will continue as they journey through life.

Starting the Year Right

Having a successful year begins long before the children arrive for the first session. To help you succeed, The Resourceful Teacher section of this book, beginning on page 365, includes

- notes on catechesis, faith, the role of the teacher, the *National Catechetical Directory,* and the *Catechism of the Catholic Church*

- a profile of the second-grade child

- tips on creating a healthy classroom environment

- suggestions for helping the children develop social skills

- tips on good planning strategies

- ideas on using learning activities

- suggestions for assessing learning

- ideas for using prayer within the session

- tips on involving the community

Refer to The Resourceful Teacher section before planning your first session and whenever you need help throughout the year.

Beginning the Journey

We are starting a journey. Where are we going on our journey? Who will go with us?

My teacher's name is

_____

Many children will go with me on the journey. Here are some of their names.

_____

_____

_____

_____

My family will join me on this journey, too. Here is a picture of my family.

Welcoming the Children

Using a welcome song as background music, greet the children individually as they arrive. Tell them how happy you are to have them in your group. Help them find their name tags and put them on.

or...

Have materials on hand (construction paper, scissors, glue, crayons, stickers, and safety pins) for the children to create their own personalized name tags.

Seat the children in a circle so that they can see one another. Have each child introduce himself or herself to the group. Point out that although each one of us is unique, we all share something important. Explain that this year we will discover together what it is that we share.

Playing a Get-acquainted Game

Show the children the Answer Chart and tell them that it will help them get to know one another better. Ask for a volunteer to spin the arrow and complete the indicated sentence. Continue until every child has had an opportunity to participate.

Introducing the Student Text

Distribute the student texts to the children. Give the children the opportunity to look through the books and to comment on them.

Ask the children to turn to page 7. Read the first sentence and the two questions aloud. Discuss how this religion class is like a journey. Help the children appreciate that on this journey they will all come to know and love Jesus better.

Work with the children to complete the activities on the page. Tell the children that, as their teacher, you will help them learn about Jesus Christ and the Church. Print your name on the chalkboard for them to copy.

Allow time for the children to share their answers and drawings with the group.

Praying Together

Gather the children around the prayer table. Direct them to bring their books with them. Light the candle and explain that the lighted candle is a sign that Jesus is with us.

Read the Leader's greeting aloud and invite the children to make the sign of the cross with you. Before you read the gospel story, lift the Bible reverently as if offering it to the children. Then read Jesus' words aloud slowly. Encourage the children to pray the gospel response together.

Ask the children to return to their seats as you read aloud the final paragraph. Define the word *commitment* as "a promise." Help the children understand that they are promising to follow Jesus and to learn more about their faith. Read aloud the commitment statement on the inside cover panel. Allow a moment for the children to think silently about the promise they are making. Then encourage them to sign their baptismal (first) names with felt-tip markers on the line provided.

Concluding the Session

Tell the children how pleased you are with their participation. Remind them of their commitment to know and love Jesus better. Express your eagerness to be with them at your next session. Remember to send the children home with the *Parent Preview Magazine* from the student text. Collect the children's name tags and save them for future sessions.

Prayer for the Journey

Leader: We begin our journey with prayer. In the name of the Father, and of the Son, and of the Holy Spirit.

All: Amen.

Leader: God, you care for us like a loving father. Be with us as we begin our journey. Help us to be good friends and followers of Jesus, your Son.

All: Amen.

Leader: The Bible is a very special book. It is a holy book. Through the words of the Bible, God speaks to us. In the Bible, Jesus says, "Come, follow me. I am the way. I will lead you to life and happiness. Walk in my light. I will be with you." [pause] The gospel of the Lord.

All: Praise to you, Lord Jesus Christ.

Leader: Let us now show that we want to start on our journey to know and love Jesus better by signing our names on the inside front cover of our books.

8

Enriching the Lesson

To emphasize the journey theme, ask the children to make footprints. Have the children work in pairs, each partner in turn tracing the other's shoe on construction paper. Direct the children to use scissors to cut out their paper footprints. Invite the children to write, "I will walk with Jesus" on their footprints. Encourage them to display their footprints where they will see them at home and be reminded of their promises.

THIS IS OUR FAITH ✦

A Preview of Grade 2

2

SILVER BURDETT GINN • SCHOOL PROGRAM

OPENING DOORS
A Take-Home Magazine

You are cordially invited...

Second-Grade Child

No one knows your seven-year-old better than you! It may be helpful and interesting to you as a parent or guardian, however, to explore some of the characteristics of the second grader.

Second Graders

- are active.
- are inquisitive.
- are full of life.
- are more sure of themselves.
- are still dependent on the guidance of their parents, teachers, and other adults.
- need activities of short duration, perhaps no more than eight to ten minutes.
- need a variety of different kinds of activities.
- learn best when involved in doing something, such as drawing or singing.
- need to be involved in real objects and experiences.
- need lots of reminders.
- need to experience success at simple tasks.
- need acceptance of their feelings of joy, fear, sadness, and anger.
- need to be encouraged to share.
- need a model of someone who shares.
- think more easily about the concrete (a peanut butter and jelly sandwich) than about the abstract (nutrition).

> THIS IS OUR FAITH Grade 2 Program has been designed to reflect the doctrine presented in the *Catechism of the Catholic Church* at a level that is appropriate for the second-grade child.

4

© 1994 Silver Burdett Ginn, Inc.

Parent Preview ∼

A Preview of Grade 2

The purpose of the *Parent Preview Magazine* is to introduce the parents of your children to THIS IS OUR FAITH, Grade 2. This preview invites the family to join their child on this year's journey of faith, while providing a brief summary of the material taught in Grade 2. Special emphasis is given to describing *Opening Doors: A Take-Home Magazine,* as well as to profiling the second-grade child.

Sending the Magazine Home

At the end of the first session, help the children carefully remove the *Parent Preview Magazine* from their texts. Explain to the children that this preview magazine will introduce their families to THIS IS OUR FAITH, Grade 2. Demonstrate how to fold the page, forming a four-page booklet. Encourage the children to bring the preview magazine home and to share it with their families.

...embarked on the day you presented your son or daughter for Baptism. Throughout the years you have been and continue to be the most important person of faith for your child. As your second-grader commits to this year's faith journey, you are invited as the primary educator in faith to journey along with your child, in whatever way is most comfortable for you. This Is Our Faith is privileged to assist you in this important task.

This Year in Grade 2

This year your second grader will be introduced to some of the basic teachings about the sacramental life of the Catholic Church as he or she discovers what it means to belong to the Christian community.

In Unit 1 your child will be reminded of the communities to

which he or she belongs: your family, your town, your child's school, and your parish. This first unit will remind your child that we respond to our membership in the Catholic Church by embracing Jesus' values and teachings and by accepting our responsibilities as members of this community.

OPENING DOORS
A Take-Home Magazine™

As your child completes each unit of This Is Our Faith, you will receive a take-home magazine entitled, *Opening Doors: A Take-Home Magazine*. Each magazine will include the following features to help you grow in your own faith and to help you share that faith with your child.

A Closer Look

includes an article relating the unit theme to a particular aspect of the Mass and family interactive pages for you and your child to enjoy together.

Being Catholic

highlights a particular aspect of our Catholic heritage.

Growing Closer

suggests activities to help you and your family integrate your faith into everyday life.

And also . . .

Looking Ahead

previews the next unit of This Is Our Faith.

UNIT 1

Our Church Celebrates Sacraments

What is your favorite celebration?

Introducing the UNIT

Invite a child to read the unit-focus question on page 11. Elicit from the group that the picture shows a Fourth of July celebration. Ask the children to name their favorite celebrations. Tell them that in Unit 1 they will learn how Jesus' friends and followers celebrated special times.

New Words

community	hosts
Christians	lectionary
faith	chalice
Catholic	celebrations
Church	presence
Catholics	seven
parish	sacraments
church	anointing
pastor	disciples
baptismal font	Baptism
altar	godparents
ambo	Confirmation
crucifix	Holy Spirit
vestments	guide
paten	sponsor

Unit Aim

To help the children identify their membership in the Catholic Church and parish community through the celebration of the sacraments, especially the initiation sacraments of Baptism and Confirmation.

Doctrinal Summaries

CHAPTER 1
We are friends and followers of Jesus Christ. We belong to the Christian community called the Catholic Church.

CHAPTER 2
Catholics have special celebrations called sacraments. Sacraments are signs of the loving presence of Jesus with us now.

CHAPTER 3
The Catholic community welcomes new members at Baptism, and our lives are joined to Jesus. At Baptism, Jesus gives us new life, the life of the Holy Spirit. Baptism is one of the seven sacraments.

CHAPTER 4
At Confirmation, God sends the Holy Spirit to us. The Holy Spirit makes us strong to live and share our faith in Jesus.

Note:
As you prepare this unit, you may wish to refer to the reference section, *Our Catholic Heritage,* beginning on page 327.

Additional resources for Unit 1 include a Unit Test and a Family Letter as well as a video and selections from THIS IS OUR FAITH Music Program. You might also find it helpful to preview *Saints and Other Holy People* and *Prayer Celebrations* for possibilities to enhance the unit.

We Belong to the Catholic Church

Objectives

To help the children
- Recognize that they belong to the Catholic community.
- Understand that the Church is a community of people.
- Discover special objects used in the parish church.
- Discover special objects used at Mass.
- Pray in the presence of God and review the chapter.

Chapter Outline

	Step 1 **Learning About Our Lives**	Step 2 **Learning About Our Faith**	Step 3 **Learning How to Live Our Faith**
Day 1	■ Introduce community. ■ Read a poem. *ABOUT 10 MINUTES*	■ Read about communities. ■ Define the new words. ■ Present the doctrine. *ABOUT 15 MINUTES*	■ Complete an activity. *ABOUT 5 MINUTES*
Day 2	■ Review Day 1. *ABOUT 5 MINUTES*	■ Enthrone the Bible. ■ Proclaim and dramatize the Scripture story. ■ Discuss the Scripture story. *ABOUT 20 MINUTES*	■ Complete an activity. ■ Pray together. *ABOUT 5 MINUTES*
Day 3	■ Name the parish and pastor. *ABOUT 2 MINUTES*	■ Read about discovering and exploring parish churches. ■ Explore the parish church. ■ Review the new words. *ABOUT 22 MINUTES*	■ Sing and pray together. *ABOUT 6 MINUTES*
Day 4	■ Review Day 3. *ABOUT 5 MINUTES*	■ Explore the sacristy. ■ Present the new words. *ABOUT 20 MINUTES*	■ Complete a drawing activity. *ABOUT 5 MINUTES*
Day 5	**Prayer** Gather for prayer and pray together. **Review** Review the chapter and read the Scripture verse.		

Plan Ahead

Preparing Your Class

Day 1 Read over the lesson. Prepare a discovery table. Make a paper doll chain. Print *community* on a card.

Day 2 Read over the lesson. Prepare simple props for dramatizations of Bible stories. Prepare a prayer table.

Day 3 Arrange for partners to explore church. Prepare church for visit. Print five 2" × 4" cards per child, naming items found in church.

Day 4 Contact parish leader for visit to sacristy. Print four 2" × 4" cards per child, naming items found in the sacristy.

Day 5 Read over the lesson. Prepare for prayer in church. Select an easy setting of a "Holy, Holy, Holy."

Materials Needed

Day 1
- symbols of communities
- paper doll chain
- Bible, candle

Day 2
- cloth or scarf
- paper doll chain
- Bible, candle

Day 3
- 2" × 4" item cards
- score or recording of a familiar song

Day 4
- textbooks
- 2" × 4" item cards

Day 5
- votive candle
- paper strips or paper footprints

Additional Resources

As you plan this chapter, consider using the following materials from The Resourceful Teacher Package.

- *Classroom Activity Sheets 1 and 1a*
- *Family Activity Sheets 1 and 1a*
- *Chapter 1 Test*
- *Prayers for Every Day*
- *Projects: Grade 2*

You may also wish to refer to the following Big Book.

- *We Celebrate God's Word,* page 22

In preparing the children for the Sunday readings, you may wish to use Silver Burdett Ginn's *Getting Ready for Sunday* student and teacher materials.

BOOKS FOR THE JOURNEY

Best Friends. Lee Bennet Hopkins. HarperCollins, 1986. Poems about friendship.

Jesus' Twelve Disciples. Louise Ulmer. Concordia, 1982. Recounts how each of the apostles was called individually and personally by Jesus.

MORE BOOKS FOR THE JOURNEY

Swimmy. Leo Lionni. Knopf, 1987. Fishes band together and protect themselves from being eaten.

Big Al. Andrew Clements. Scholastic, 1991. Al tries to hide his appearance and size but something always goes wrong. Finally, he gets a chance to prove with his actions what kind of fish he really is.

REDUCED CLASSROOM ACTIVITIES

Name

We Belong to the Catholic Church

Discover who is a follower of Jesus. Use the code to color the spaces. Then complete the sentence at the bottom of the page.

X blue   **O** yellow

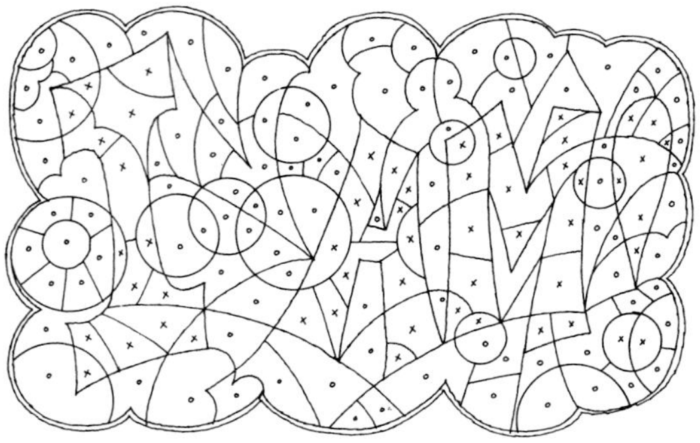

I am _____ a follower of Jesus.

To the Teacher: This activity follows the Scripture story "Walk with Me."

Chapter I   We Belong to the Catholic Church   THIS IS OUR FAITH 2   **I**

Name

Following Jesus

1. I belong to the _Christian_____ community.

2. Jesus says, "_Follow_____ me!"

3. Jesus, I will be your _friend_____.

4. My Christian community is the _Catholic Church_____.

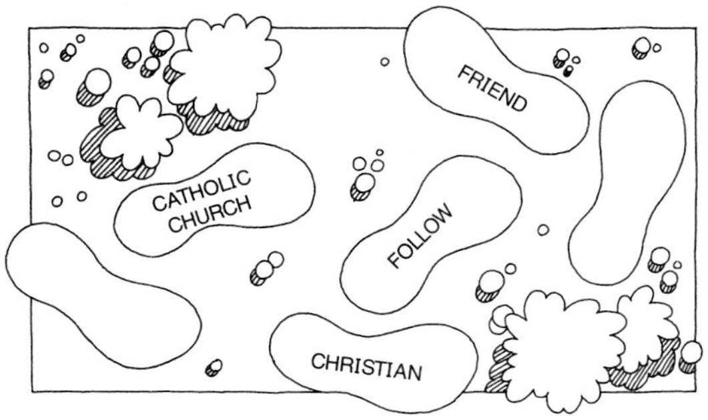

To the Teacher: This activity reinforces new words from the text.

Ia THIS IS OUR FAITH 2   Chapter I   We Belong to the Catholic Church

11c Chapter Organizer

CHARACTERISTICS OF COMMUNITY

The distinguishing characteristics of the Christian community are faith, hope, love, and commitment to Jesus Christ. To be a Christian is simply to be a friend and follower of Jesus. We name ourselves with his name (Christian), and we mark ourselves with his sign, the cross. We accept his teachings and try to live a life of commitment to God in the Catholic Church, whose members are bonded in Christ Jesus. The *National Catechetical Directory* (NCD) states: "In the Catholic Church are found the deposit of faith, the sacraments, and the ministries inherited from the apostles. Through these gifts from God, the Church is able to grow and act as a community in Christ, serving human beings and mediating to them His saving word and activity" (#93).

EXPERIENCING THE CATHOLIC CHURCH

Although the family is still the primary community for most children at this age level, these children are beginning to feel a real sense of belonging to other groups and organizations. They are part of communities that share common interests, such as Scout groups or sports teams; communities that share common goals, such as classroom communities; or communities that share common experiences, such as circles of friends. These broadened experiences deepen the children's experiences of what it means to belong. During this year, the children will explore what it means to belong to the Catholic Church and will come to a better understanding of their roles within the Church.

The children's understanding of the word *catholic* may come from their experiences of attending their parish church, where they worship with the Catholic community. Through their experiences in class, you can help the children develop a sense of pride in being at home within the Catholic Church. In effect, your group can become a microcosm of the Catholic community, a family that gathers together to practice its faith.

Objective

This lesson helps the children recognize that they are friends of Jesus and that they belong to the Catholic Church.

Step 1 / INTRODUCTION

Learning About Our Lives

Introducing Community

Begin by having the children pray the prayer that marks them as Christians, the Sign of the Cross.

Show the children a paper doll chain with the word *community* printed on each doll. As the children name a community to which they belong, print the names of the communities on the legs of the paper dolls. Use this paper chain as a focal point for reviewing the meaning of the word *community* and the goal of this chapter. You might choose to display the paper chain by attaching it to a discovery table or by pinning it to a bulletin board.

Reading a Poem

Ask a child to read the poem "A Group of Friends" aloud. Print the word *community* on the chalkboard or show a prepared card with the word *community* printed on it. Say the word and have the children repeat it. Then bring the children to the discovery table, on which you have displayed items such as a Cub Scout/Brownie handbook, a family name sign, a baseball glove, a church bulletin, and so on. Refer to the communities represented on the discovery table (families, organizations, teams, and so on). Then invite a child to read the focus question on page 12. What kind of community is shown in the picture at the top of page 12? (*Friends*)

We Belong to the Catholic Church

What is the name of a group of people you like to do things with?

A Group of Friends

As I was walking to the park,
I met a boy whose name was Mark.
I asked him, "Would you like to play?"
He smiled and said, "Well, yes! Okay."

We played that day and many more.
Then two more joined, and now we're four.
Different, yet the same are we,
We have all become a group you see,
A group that is **community**.

★ ★★★ ★
Enriching the Lesson ★

Invite the children to bring in other symbols of communities to which their families belong. Add these items to the discovery table. Invite the children to draw a picture of themselves sharing or doing something with the community symbolized by the items they brought in. Allow time for the children to tell about their pictures or community symbols. Place the drawings on the discovery table or on a bulletin board.

Jesus Calls Us to Be Friends

Jesus calls us to be friends with each other and with him. Friends and followers of Jesus are called **Christians**.

Jesus also calls us to be a **community**. A community is a group of people who shares something important together.

We belong to the Christian community called the **Catholic Church**. The Catholic Church shares our **faith** in Jesus.

Activity

Fill in the name of the Catholic Church where you and your family share faith.

New Words

Christians	friends and followers of Jesus Christ
community	a group of people who share something important together
Catholic Church	the Christian cpommunity to which we belong
faith	Faith in Jesus means that we have come to know him and trust him.

We Believe

We are friends and followers of Jesus Christ. We belong to the Christian community called the Catholic Church.

Doctrine 13

Teaching Tips

Print the words shown in the New Words box on half-sheets of posterboard, using a half-sheet for each word. Label each poster by unit and chapter. Print the definitions of the new words on the back of each half-sheet. Continue to assemble all the new words for this unit into a poster book of vocabulary terms. Use the poster book for review or in a learning center.

Step 2 / DEVELOPMENT

Learning About Our Faith

Reading About Communities

Read "Jesus Calls Us" on page 13. Emphasize that families, Churches, and schools are all communities that can share faith in Jesus. Share a story about a faith community in which you were a member, as a child or as an adult, such as your family, school, or parish. Mention community activities such as parish picnics, family gatherings, and so on.

Defining the New Words

Direct the children's attention to the New Words box at the bottom of page 13. Read the definition of *community* together. Now read aloud the definitions of *Christians* and *faith*. Help the children learn the definitions by repeating them together several times.

Presenting the Doctrine

Read with the children the We Believe statements. Tell them it is important to remember that they are friends and followers of Jesus Christ and that they belong to the Catholic Church. Gather the children together at the prayer table, on which you have placed a Bible and a lighted candle. Pray aloud together The Lord's Prayer, the prayer prayed by all followers of Jesus.

Step 3 / CONCLUSION

Learning How to Live Our Faith

Completing an Activity

Focus the children's attention on the activity on page 13. Invite the children to print the name of the Catholic Church to which they belong. Have on the chalkboard the names of the parish church or churches and the school for the children to copy.

Objective

This lesson helps the children understand that the Church is a community of people as well as a place where people gather as members of Jesus' family.

Step 1 / INTRODUCTION

Learning About Our Lives

Reviewing Day 1

Review the concept of community, using the items on the discovery table or the paper doll chain. Ask if anyone can think of another community to which he or she belongs. Then draw the children's attention to the new words from Day 1, which you printed on the chalkboard or poster book prior to class. Ask the children if they remember what *community*, *Christians*, and *faith* mean. If necessary, repeat the definitions of the words.

Step 2 / DEVELOPMENT

Learning About Our Faith

Enthroning the Bible

Encourage the children to recognize the presence of God in the Scriptures with an enthronement of the Bible. Place the Bible on a simple bookstand on the classroom prayer table. Cover the table with a cloth or scarf that can be changed seasonally. A candle may be lighted on the prayer table if fire regulations allow. Then seat the children near the prayer table. Tell the children that we light the candle to remind us of Jesus, the Light of the World.

Proclaiming the Scripture Story

Introduce the Scripture story on pages 14–15 by telling the children that this story found in the Bible tells about the community that Jesus and his friends belonged to.

Proclaim the Scripture story. Then print on the chalkboard the names of the followers whom Jesus called—Peter, James, Andrew, and John. Select five volunteers to dramatize the Scripture story as you read it a second time.

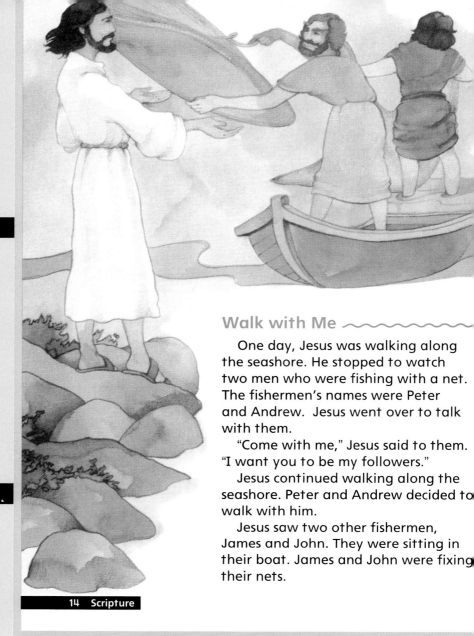

Walk with Me

One day, Jesus was walking along the seashore. He stopped to watch two men who were fishing with a net. The fishermen's names were Peter and Andrew. Jesus went over to talk with them.

"Come with me," Jesus said to them. "I want you to be my followers."

Jesus continued walking along the seashore. Peter and Andrew decided to walk with him.

Jesus saw two other fishermen, James and John. They were sitting in their boat. James and John were fixing their nets.

14   Scripture

Enriching the Lesson

Invite a guest speaker to give a short talk about your school community. If the speaker is someone other than a school administrator, provide ideas for a topic and specific guidelines, such as length of talk, kinds of visual aids to use, and opportunity for interaction with the children. Coach the children on greeting the speaker and using appropriate listening etiquette. Thank the speaker for coming.

Teaching Tips

The children may ask: Did the followers of Jesus use fishing poles? Tell the children that Jesus' followers fished in a way similar to how commercial fishers fish today. They caught fish in nets, dragged the nets into boats, and then sorted the fish. Most of the fish were sold fresh, some were dried and sold later. There were no freezers to preserve the fish.

"Come," Jesus called to them.
"Be my followers. Walk with me."
So James and John joined Jesus,
Peter, and Andrew. Together they
walked and talked on the shore.
They became friends.

Based on Matthew 4:18–22

Activity

1. Circle three things you like to talk about when you
   walk with your friends.

   my family   games and sports   school

   my favorite things   my pets   my friends

2. Name something you think Jesus and his friends
   talked about.

   _____

   _____

3. Jesus and his friends formed a

   community_____ .

Teaching Tips

Collect items to use as simple props or costumes for dramatizing Scripture stories. Large pieces of material can be draped over shoulders, decorative ropes used as belts, plain dish towels for head coverings, old pieces of netting for fishermen, and a few canes for shepherds or walkers. Costumes allow shy children to participate with greater confidence.

Discussing the Story

Discuss the story with the children. Ask:

- Where was Jesus walking? (*Along the seashore*)

- What were Peter and Andrew doing? (*Fishing*)

- What did Jesus say to them? (*"Come with me. I want you to be my followers."*)

- What did Peter and Andrew do? (*Followed Jesus*)

- What happened next? (*Jesus asked James and John to be his followers.*)

- What did Peter, Andrew, James, and John become? (*Friends and followers of Jesus*)

Remind the children that Peter, Andrew, James, and John wanted to get to know Jesus so that they could be good friends and followers. We too want to know more about Jesus so that we can be better friends and followers of him.

Step 3 / CONCLUSION

Learning How to Live Our Faith

Completing an Activity

Direct the children's attention to the activity at the bottom of page 15. When the children have completed the activity, take some time to listen to the children's responses.

Praying Together

Call the children by name to join you around the prayer table. Invite them to thank Jesus silently for calling them to be his followers. When they are ready, instruct the children to respond "I will follow you, Jesus" after each of the following phrases.

When I play with my friends, . . .

When I learn in school, . . .

When I help at home, . . .

When I go to church, . . .

Ask the children to join hands and follow you around the room as you sing a song they know about Jesus. (You might want to use "Best Friends" or "Children of God," found in the THIS IS OUR FAITH Music Program, Grade 2.)

15

Objective

This lesson helps the children discover special objects in their parish church.

Step 1 / INTRODUCTION

Learning About Our Lives

Naming Your Parish and Pastor

Ask the children to name their Catholic Church or parish. Print the name(s) on the chalkboard. Name the pastor, or leader, of the parish, and print this name on the chalkboard.

Step 2 / DEVELOPMENT

Learning About Our Faith

Reading "Discovering Our Parish"

Ask a volunteer to read "Discovering Our Parish" on page 16. Elicit the names of other parishes in town or perhaps other churches that the children have attended when visiting relatives. Accept all answers, even if a church mentioned is not Catholic.

Reading "Maria Explores Her Parish Church"

Read aloud with the children "Maria Explores Her Parish Church." Answer any questions the children may have about the things Maria discovered in her church.

Exploring Your Parish Church

Prior to class, invite a class of older children to join your class as partners to explore your church. Have prepared five 2" × 4" cards for each child; on each card have the name of one item from the five items explained in "Maria Explores Her Parish Church" on pages 16–17. Welcome the older students and ask each child in your class to sit with an assigned partner. Direct the children to bring their cards, line up with their partners, and walk to church with you. Inside the church, have the children find the items listed on their cards: *altar, baptismal font, candles, ambo,* and *crucifix.*

Discovering Our Parish

Catholics gather together in communities called **parishes.** The leader of a parish is called a **pastor.** There is usually more than one Catholic parish in a large town or city. Can you name another Catholic parish that you have visited?

Maria Explores Her Parish Church

1. "This **parish church** is a special place, where the people of God meet," Dad said.

   "This font of water is called the **baptismal font**," Maria said. "This is where the new members of the Church are baptized."

2. "And this is the **altar**," Dad said. "The altar is a table where the second part of the Mass is celebrated."

Genuflecting We touch our right knee to the floor and bow our heads to show respect for God. *To genuflect* means "to bend the knee." When the Blessed Sacrament is kept in a special chapel, it is customary to pause, stand, and bow one's head to the altar before entering a pew.

Teaching Tips

Before teaching the lesson, check that the church will not be used during the time you wish your class to explore it. Place large ribbon bows near all the items children are to identify. Print item cards for each child. Arrange with the teacher of the older students (Grades 5–8) to review the church items with his or her students. Assign partners for each second grader.

. "This is called the **ambo**," Dad told Maria. "This is where the word of God is read and explained."

4. "I know what this is!" Maria said with excitement. "This is a **crucifix**. It's Jesus' cross." Maria and Dad prayed a quiet prayer and then walked home.

New Words

Catholics	followers of Jesus who belong to the Catholic Church
parish	another name for our Christian community
pastor	the leader of a parish
parish church	a place where Catholics gather to pray with other members of the Catholic Church
baptismal font	the water font where new members of the Church are baptized
altar	the table at which the Mass is celebrated
ambo	the reading stand where the word of God is read
crucifix	a cross that holds the body of Jesus

Doctrine 17

Then allow them to spend a few more minutes exploring the church before returning to the classroom.

Reviewing the New Words

Add the word *Church* to the word list. Help the children understand that the word *Church*, with a capital or uppercase *c*, means a "community of Christians." Explain that when we spell the word *church* with a small or lowercase *c*, we mean a building.

Introduce the word *Catholics* by writing it on the chalkboard or posterboard and asking the children to repeat it. Emphasize that the Christian community to which we belong is the Catholic Church.

Explain that a parish church is a place where Catholics gather to pray with other members of the Catholic Chruch.

Direct the children's attention to the words you have written on the chalkboard or posterboard during this session. Review all the new words. Ask the children to read the definitions in their books on page 17.

Step 3 / CONCLUSION

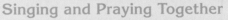

Learning How to Live Our Faith

Singing and Praying Together

Have the children sing a familiar song of thanks. Then pray this prayer: "Good God, we are friends and followers of Jesus. We belong to this Christian community of _____ Parish. We are members of the Catholic Church. We thank you for this time to explore our church. Help us to become your holy people. Amen." Conclude by singing together another verse of the song.

Teaching Tips

Some Catholic churches have no resident priest or pastor. Other church leaders are appointed—religious sisters, deacons, or laypersons. This is especially true in Latin America and will become truer in North America as the number of older priests retire. In some areas of the United States, the same pastor serves several parishes. Ask the children who the parish leader is in your church.

Enriching the Lesson

When you and the children return from the church tour, divide the class into small groups with partners. Have the older children draw a simple outline of the floor plan of your church on a large roll of paper. Ask each group to draw the five items that they found in church. Other discovered items may be added to each drawing.

Objective

This lesson helps children discover special objects used at Mass.

Step 1 / INTRODUCTION

Learning About Our Lives

Reviewing Day 3

Review the new words on page 17. Ask: What things did you discover yesterday in your exploration of the church? Which things are listed in the New Words box on page 17? What did you like about exploring the church?

Step 2 / DEVELOPMENT

Learning About Our Faith ✝

Exploring the Sacristy

Read aloud with the children "Special Objects Used at Mass" on page 18. Distribute 2" × 4" item cards with the names of the four objects described in the pupil text. Then take the children to the church to explore the sacristy. Review the sign of the cross and genuflecting as the children enter the church. Remind the children that the sacristy is a small room where things used during Mass are kept. Show the children the vestments, paten, chalice, and lectionary as each child holds up the matching item card. You might want to show more than one example of some objects, such as the priest's vestments. Summarize the visit by stating that all these things are holy because we use them to worship God; we treat all these holy things with respect. Remind the children that all things used in the church are holy and that all people gathered to praise God are holy.

Special Objects Used at Mass

A sacristy is a small room inside a church where the objects that are used during Mass are kept.

▲ **Vestments** are the special garments the priest wears during Mass.

▲ The **paten,** or plate, holds bread or **hosts** that will become Jesus.

◀ The **chalice,** or cup, holds the wine that will become Jesus.

▲ The large book of Bible readings used during the first part of the Mass is called the **lectionary.**

18   Doctrine

🍎 Teaching Tips

Establish a three-part form to spontaneous prayer that starts with a greeting, includes a petition or statement of gratitude, and ends with a consistent closing statement. Cue children to respond "Amen" whenever they hear the closing statement that will always be either "We ask this in the name of Jesus," or "We ask this in the name of the Father, and of the Son, and of the Holy Spirit."

Draw a picture of one special object that you have discovered in your church. Then tell the story of how it is used.

New Words

vestments	special garments worn by the priest during Mass
paten	the plate that holds the bread or hosts at Mass
hosts	bread that becomes the Body of Christ at Mass
lectionary	the book where all the Bible readings used at Mass are found
chalice	the cup that holds the wine at Mass

Doctrine 19

---

or...

Invite the parish priest, parish council member, or deacon to host this tour of the sacristy. Be sure to give him or her a list of the objects presented in the student text. Additional items to show are the monstrance, servers' vestments, ushers' baskets, censer, and so on.

Presenting the New Words

When you have returned to the classroom, direct the children's attention to the New Words box on page 19. Ask them to read aloud and repeat several times the definition of *vestments, paten, hosts, chalice,* and *lectionary.*

Step 3 / CONCLUSION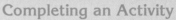

Learning How to Live Our Faith

Completing an Activity

Direct the children's attention to the activity on page 19. Have them draw a picture in their books of one object they discovered in church. When the children have completed their drawings, allow sufficient time for each child to tell how his or her object is used.

CURRICULUM CONNECTION

Art Distribute large sheets of colored craft paper. Invite the children to use the church item cards identifying objects named in Day 3 and Day 4 to form the outline of a church. Have the children paste these cards with the item name side up on the craft paper. The children may draw or add pictures of people praying within the church frame.

DAY 5
PRAYER/REVIEW

Objective

This lesson helps the children learn that God is with us now and, by praying together, provides them with a shared faith experience.

Gathering for Prayer

Return with the children to the parish church. Gather the children in front of the altar. Place a lighted votive candle in the center of the altar. As you light the candle, remind the children that a lighted candle is a sign of Jesus, the Light of the World.

Praying Together

Before beginning the prayer experience, tell the children that they will be saying or singing together *Holy, holy, holy Lord, God of power and might.* Practice saying or singing it with the children until it is familiar.

Begin the prayer experience by reading aloud the first paragraph on page 20. Then lead the children in saying or singing the "Holy, Holy, Holy" that you practiced earlier.

Continue the prayer experience by moving from child to child, placing your hands in blessing on each child's head, while saying "(*Name*), God lives in you." Invite each child to respond "Amen."

Conclude the prayer experience by praying aloud the last paragraph on page 20. Encourage the children to respond "Amen."

Praying in the Presence of God

Teacher:	God is here in this church. We light a candle to remember that God is with us. There are many other things that remind us that God is present. Now let us pray a song of praise.
All:	Holy, holy, holy Lord, God of power and might.
Teacher:	God is also present in each one of us. (Name), God lives in you.
Each child:	Amen!
Teacher:	Let us go forth from this holy place and live as God's holy people. We remember that God calls us sons and daughters. Let us live together in peace. Let us love one another.
All:	Amen!

Focus on

Sacred Space   Take time to develop in the children a respect for sacred space. This respect for external sacred space will soon develop into a respect for *internal* sacred space. A realization that God dwells within our own person and within each human person leads us into an abiding sense of respect for all people and all living things because God dwells there.

Teaching Tips

For the music to the "Holy, Holy, Holy" you may want to use one of the settings found in *Young People's Glory & Praise,* NARL, 1991, available from OCP (Oregon Catholic Press), 5536 N. E. Hassalo, Portland, OR 97213. Extract, teach, and use just the four-measure phrase of music to which the words *Holy, holy, holy Lord, God of power and might* have been set rather than the entire composition.

Chapter Review

Use the clues to fill in the crossword puzzle.

Down

1. Our special sign is the _____ .
2. We _____ to God, our Father.

Across

1. Catholics _____ about and love everyone in the world.
2. Our parish is a community of _____ who belong to the Catholic Church.

(crossword: **Care** across top; **People** across middle; down word **Cross**; down word **Pray**)

3. What do we call a group of people who share something important together?

community

4. To which Christian community do we belong?

Catholic Church

5. Talk about something we do that shows we are Catholic Christians.

> **Jesus says,**
> **"I want you to love one another as I love you."**
> **Based on John 15:14**

Reviewing the Chapter

Begin the chapter review by asking a volunteer to read aloud the directions at the top of page 21. Help the children complete the word puzzle by printing each answer word on the chalkboard or posterboard.

Then take time to go through the three review items aloud with the children. Ask the first two questions and give the children time to fill in the blanks. Be supportive of each child who participates in the discussion of item 3.

Reading the Scripture Verse

Read the Scripture verse on page 21. Ask: What does Jesus ask us to do? How can we be like Jesus? Then ask the children to name ways they can treat others more kindly in the classroom, in the cafeteria, and on the playground. Ask: How does Jesus want us to treat members of our family? What can you do as a favor for someone in your family? Distribute paper strips or paper footprints. Direct the children to print the name of a family member for whom they will be a "secret favor pal." Then ask the children to print a favor that they will do on the back of the paper strip or footprint. Encourage the children to put their paper strips or footprints in a place at home where they will remind them to do their special favors.

★ Enriching the Lesson ★

Use the poster book you have prepared to review all the new words with the children. Direct them to work in pairs. Ask each pair to create sentences using all of the new words learned in Chapter 1. Each sentence may contain more than one new word.

21

2 We Celebrate Special Times

Objectives

To help the children
- Understand that the sacraments are special celebrations of the Church.
- Reflect on the deeper meanings of and use of the signs of love.
- Recognize the seven sacraments as celebrations of God's love.
- Act as friends and disciples of Jesus by giving signs of love.
- Celebrate God's love by praying together and review the chapter.

Chapter Outline

	Step 1 Learning About Our Lives	**Step 2** Learning About Our Faith	**Step 3** Learning How to Live Our Faith
Day 1	■ Introduce the chapter. ■ Introduce the word *celebrations*. ■ Interpret photographs. ■ Complete an activity. *ABOUT 15 MINUTES*	■ Discuss celebrations. ■ Present the new words. ■ Present the doctrine. *ABOUT 10 MINUTES*	■ Pray together. *ABOUT 5 MINUTES*
Day 2	■ Review Day 1. *ABOUT 5 MINUTES*	■ Read and discuss a Scripture story. ■ Present the new word. *ABOUT 15 MINUTES*	■ Complete an activity. ■ Pray together. *ABOUT 10 MINUTES*
Day 3	■ Review Day 2. *ABOUT 5 MINUTES*	■ Present the seven sacraments. ■ Present the doctrine. ■ Discuss the seven sacraments. *ABOUT 15 MINUTES*	■ Complete an activity. *ABOUT 10 MINUTES*
Day 4	■ Give signs of love. *ABOUT 10 MINUTES*	■ Be a disciple. ■ Introduce the new word. ■ Complete an activity. *ABOUT 10 MINUTES*	■ Brainstorm. ■ Create an acrostic. ■ Pray with joy. *ABOUT 10 MINUTES*
Day 5	**Prayer** Pray together responsorially with rhythm instrument accompaniment. **Review** Complete a word puzzle; review the chapter; and read the Scripture verse.		

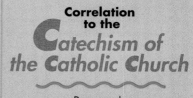
Plan Ahead 〰〰〰〰〰〰

	Preparing Your Class	**Materials Needed**
Day 1	Read over the lesson plan. Decorate the room for a celebration before the children arrive. Select lively music. Create a party atmosphere.	■ magazine, scissors, glue ■ large sheets of construction paper ■ music tape and tape recorder
Day 2	Read over the lesson plan. Prepare prayer table. Prepare expressive reading of the Scripture story.	■ pencils ■ Bible
Day 3	Read over the lesson plan. Create seven posters, one for each sacrament, prior to the session.	■ seven sacraments posters ■ pencils
Day 4	Read over the lesson plan. Think of a personal story to tell about someone who has helped you.	■ pencils
Day 5	Read over the lesson plan. Gather rhythm instruments to accompany children's prayer responses. Prepare prayer table.	■ rhythm instruments

Additional Resources

As you plan this chapter, consider using the following materials from The Resourceful Teacher Package.

■ *Classroom Activity Sheets 2* and *2a*

■ *Family Activity Sheets 2* and *2a*

■ *Chapter 2 Test*

■ *Prayers for Every Day*

■ *Projects: Grade 2*

You may also wish to refer to the following Big Book.

■ *We Celebrate the Sacraments,* pages 2–24

In preparing the children for the Sunday readings, you may wish to use Silver Burdett Ginn's *Getting Ready for Sunday* student and teacher materials.

Books for the Journey

I'm in Charge of Celebrations. Byrd Baylor. Charles Scribner's Sons, 1986. A poetic narrative describing celebrations that the author chooses and delights in.

The Clown of God. Tomie dePaola. Harcourt Brace Jovanovich, 1978. A story about a juggler's gift to Mary and the Christ Child.

More Books for the Journey

Mr. Rabbit and the Lovely Present. Charlotte Zolotow. Harper-Collins, 1977. Reveals a child's thoughtfulness and care in the selection of a gift to celebrate her mother's birthday.

Through Grandpa's Eyes. Patricia MacLachlan. Harper-Collins, 1983. Life is celebrated more fully by a young child as he experiences aspects of it in a different way during a visit with his blind grandfather.

Reduced Classroom Activities

Name _____

We Celebrate Special Times

Write a word on each balloon to name a special time we like to celebrate. Color the balloons.

 BIRTHDAY CHRISTMAS A NEW BABY A WEDDING THANKSGIVING

To the Teacher: This activity introduces the concept of celebration.

Chapter 2   We Celebrate Special Times   This Is Our Faith 2   **2**

Name _____

Signs of Jesus' Love

Start at the large letter "S" to find the hidden word. Go in the direction of the arrow and circle every third letter. (The next letter is circled for you.) Copy the letters in the blanks to complete the sentence.

S _ a _ c _ r _ a _ m _ e _ n _ t _ s

are celebrations of Jesus' love for us and signs of his presence with us now.

To the Teacher: This activity follows the chapter review.

2a   This Is Our Faith 2   Chapter 2   We Celebrate Special Times

Background for the Teacher

THE CHURCH AND THE SACRAMENTS

In our Catholic tradition we view the celebration of the sacraments as fundamental to our mission as Church and to our lives as disciples of Jesus. Sacraments are a unique and profound expression of our Catholic identity. As stated in the *Catechism of the Catholic Church*, catechesis is rooted in "the initial proclamation of the Gospel or missionary preaching to arouse faith; examination of the reasons for belief; experiences of Christian living; celebration of the sacraments; integration into the ecclesial community; and apostolic and missionary witness." (Prologue 6)

As a Catholic school religion teacher, you have the opportunity to provide your students with spirited insights into the sacraments. The sacraments are Christ's actions in and through us, his Church; are signs of God's love and grace in our lives; can strengthen our personal faith; and can help to form us into a believing, celebrating faith community.

We celebrate the presence of the risen Christ through the sacramental words, gestures, and symbols of each sacrament. Our actions express our faith, our love, and our response to the presence of Jesus among us, to his empowering each of us, to his healing touch, and to his forgiveness. We become signs of God's love when we show love to one another. Through sacramental experiences we are called to live more fully as disciples of Jesus, united to him and to one another in the Spirit of God. Increase in charity, witness to Gospel values, and service to others are signs that we are a sacramental people.

THE CELEBRATION OF THE SACRAMENTS

During this year, the four sacraments of Baptism, Confirmation, Eucharist, and Reconciliation will be presented as celebrations of belonging, caring, loving, and forgiving. This chapter builds on the children's appreciation of celebrations and introduces them to the special moments that we as Catholics celebrate and value in each of the sacraments. Second graders associate special moments with celebrations. They enjoy birthdays, anniversaries, holidays, and visits with friends and relatives. The presence of family and friends helps to make the celebrations joyful and meaningful.

You can heighten the children's appreciation for celebration in worship by finding opportunities for celebrating holy moments with them. The children's name days, saints' feasts, holy days, and the year's liturgical seasons provide opportunities for the children to make the connection between life experience and our Catholic tradition. Remind the children of Jesus' love for us and our love for him so that they will experience the sacraments as very special celebrations and gatherings of our Catholic community.

Objective

This lesson helps the children better understand celebrations and introduces them to the sacraments, the special celebrations of the Church.

Step 1 / INTRODUCTION

Learning About Our Lives

Introducing the Chapter

On the day of the lesson and before the children arrive, decorate the room for a celebration. Use paper streamers and balloons; play lively music to create a party atmosphere. After the children are seated, explain that today's lesson is about special celebrations.

Introducing the Word *Celebrations*

Print the word *celebrations* on the chalkboard or posterboard. Read the word aloud and have the children repeat it. Tell the children that parties are celebrations of special events.

Encourage the children to respond to the following questions.

- What kinds of celebrations or parties have you been to? (*Birthdays, Halloween, christenings*)

- What did you do at these celebrations? (*Eat, play games, talk, sing*)

Then ask the chapter-focus question, "What are some ways you and your family celebrate people and things that are important to you?" (*Answers will vary.*)

Interpreting Photographs

Invite the children to open their books to page 22. Read "Celebrations" aloud, then direct the children's attention to the photographs. Ask the children to name what is being celebrated in each picture. (*Birthday, Fourth of July*) Ask them to tell about these celebrations.

Completing an Activity

Encourage each child to think of one celebration that is very important to him or her. Ask each one to draw a picture of this celebration in the space provided on page 23.

What are
some ways
you and your
family
celebrate
people and
things that
are important
to you?

We Celebrate Special Time

Celebrations

Almost everyone celebrates special people or special times. It is good to be together when we are happy and when we are sad. We sometimes use special actions, sing special songs, eat special foods, or wear special clothes when we celebrate. **Celebrations** are important times of being together.

What are the people in the photographs celebrating? What special actions, signs, and words are they using?

★ ★★★ ★ Enriching the Lesson ★

Prior to this lesson, write a note to each child's family telling of plans for a special party to celebrate the class as a community. Ask that the child bring in a photograph of a family celebration to place on a large poster entitled "We Celebrate." During class, glue the pictures to the poster, print each child's name under the photographs, and have each child describe how they and their families celebrate important occasions.

22

Activity

Draw a picture of you celebrating a special day.

Signs of Celebration

Some celebrations help us feel special. Some celebrations help us remember someone who is important to us. Most celebrations help us feel that we belong to each other.

We are also invited to take part in celebrations that use special signs to celebrate Jesus' friendship and **presence** with us. We call these special signs and celebrations the **seven sacraments**.

We Believe

Catholics have special signs and celebrations called the seven sacraments. Sacraments are signs and celebrations of Jesus' lovefor us that make him present to us now.

New Words

celebrations	special times of being together to show how important someone or something is to us
presence	being with someone
seven sacraments	special signs and celebrations of Jesus' love for us that make him present to us now

Cultural Awareness

Help the children appreciate that our Catholic community is made up of people from different lands and traditions who have special ways of celebrating together. Ask the children to name other cultural celebrations. (Saint Patrick's Day, Kwanzaa, La posada, Chanukah, Powwow) Emphasize that Jesus calls us to respect the different ways the people of our world celebrate special times.

or . . .

Invite the children to make celebration montages. Provide magazines, large sheets of construction paper, scissors, and glue. Encourage the children to look through the magazines to find pictures of people celebrating together. Help them to cut out the pictures and glue them to the construction paper. After the children have finished, discuss the pictures they have chosen. You might have the children do this activity in small groups rather than independently. This will help them continue the process of community building.

Step 2 / DEVELOPMENT

Learning About Our Faith

Discussing Celebrations

Ask volunteers to read aloud "Signs of Celebration" on page 23. Help the children make the connection between family celebrations and the sacraments. Emphasize the idea that celebrations give us a sense of belonging. Invite the children to suggest ways we can show our happiness and love for our families and friends during celebrations.

Presenting the New Words

Focus the children's attention on the New Words box. Ask them to repeat the new words and their definitions after you.

Presenting the Doctrine

Read aloud the We Believe statements. Then review them with the children by saying the two sentences again, but leaving out some words. Invite the children to complete the sentences verbally.

Step 3 / CONCLUSION

Learning How to Live Our Faith

Praying Together

Gather the children at the prayer table. When the children are ready, pray:

Jesus, thank you for celebrations that help us feel special. Thank you for celebrations that help us show our love for one another. Help us to remember that whenever we celebrate together, you are with us. Amen.

DAY 2
SCRIPTURE

Objective

This lesson helps the children understand that signs can have deeper meanings, that they need signs of love in their lives, and that they use signs to celebrate their love.

Step 1 / INTRODUCTION

Learning About Our Lives

Reviewing Day 1

Briefly review the kinds of celebrations the children identified on Day 1 by naming them and by recalling that these celebrations happen within a community (family, friends, school team, and so on). The celebrations may occur on a special event (Fourth of July, birthday, Baptism) and usually involve enjoyable activities (eating, playing, singing).

Point out to the children that our Church has special celebrations that remind us that Jesus is in our lives now. Ask: What do we call these celebrations? (*Sacraments*)

Step 2 / DEVELOPMENT

Learning About Our Faith

Reading a Scripture Story

Explain that just as we enjoy celebrating with friends, Jesus enjoyed celebrating with his friends. Tell the children that you will now read a story about a visit Jesus had with his friends Mary, Martha, and Lazarus. Invite the children to move to the prayer table. When the children are ready, read aloud the Scripture story on pages 24–25.

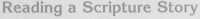

A Sign of Love

One day, Jesus visited his friends Martha, Mary, and Lazarus. They were glad to see Jesus and prepared a special meal to celebrate his visit. Martha, Mary, Lazarus, and some other guests sat with Jesus at the table.

After the meal, Mary showed her love for Jesus in a special way. She brought out some expensive perfume and poured it over the feet of Jesus. Then she dried his feet with her hair.

Another guest saw what Mary had done. He got very angry. "She could have sold the perfume for a lot of money," said the guest. "Instead, she wasted it."

24   Scripture

🍎 Teaching Tips

Proclaiming the Scriptures means to read the Scriptures with conviction and expression. Help the children's understanding of the Scripture story by creating the scene: Jesus is in a village, on a boat, in the synagogue. Set the mood by explaining to whom Jesus is speaking: friends, a crowd, a needy person. Be expressive. Use dramatic pauses. Prepare the story in advance so that you can look at the children as you read.

★ Enriching the Lesson

Write out the key events in the story "A Sign of Love" on craft paper. Write each sentence on a separate sheet. For example: Jesus was visiting friends; the friends prepared a special meal for Jesus, and so on. Scramble the sentences on the floor. Ask the children to unscramble them and place them in the proper order. Praise the children for listening attentively to the story.

24

Jesus replied, "Leave Mary alone. She is not wasting her gift. **Anointing** me with perfume is a sign of her love for me. She is celebrating my being here."

Based on John 12:1–8

Activity

If Jesus was coming to your home today, what would your special celebration look like? Draw a picture of your special celebration.

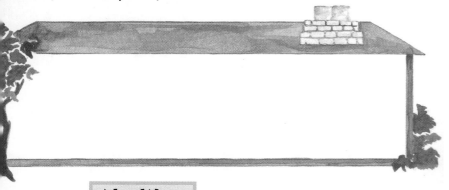

New Word

★
★   **anointing**   putting blessed oil on a person's body as a sign
★   of love, respect, honor, or healing
★

Scripture   25

Enriching the Lesson

You might want to deepen the children's experience of anointing by prayerfully anointing them with oil you've prepared beforehand. Mix perfume and olive oil to create a scented oil. Place in a small dish on the prayer table. Gather the children around it. Begin the anointing ritual by dipping your finger into the oil and rubbing the oil into a child's hands, saying, "(Name), may this oil remind you that Jesus loves you." Continue around the circle until each child has been anointed.

Discussing the Story

Use the following questions to discuss the story.

■ Who was Jesus visiting? (*Martha, Mary, and Lazarus*)

■ How did Martha, Mary, and Lazarus welcome Jesus? (*They prepared a special meal for him.*)

■ How did Mary show her love for Jesus? (*She poured expensive perfume over Jesus' feet.*)

■ Why did another guest get angry? (*He thought that Mary wasted the perfume.*)

■ What did Jesus say about what Mary did? (*Jesus said that Mary was showing him a sign of her love.*)

Help the children value Jesus' appreciation for the love people showed him. Encourage them to conclude that Lazarus, Martha, and Mary were celebrating their friend's presence.

Presenting the New Word

Discuss with the children the meaning of the word *anointing*. Read the definition on page 25 aloud together.

Step 3 / CONCLUSION

Learning How to Live Our Faith

Completing an Activity

Invite a volunteer to read aloud the directions for the activity on page 25. Have the children draw a picture of a celebration in their homes that shows Jesus as an invited guest. Take sufficient time to discuss what they have drawn.

Praying Together

Gather the children at the prayer table. Pray a litany with the children. Invite them to respond with the words *I will show my love for you, Jesus.*

When I see someone who is lonely, _____ .

When I see someone who needs help, _____ .

When I see someone who is sad, _____ .

When I see someone who is ill, _____ .

DAY 3
DOCTRINE

Objective

This lesson helps the children recognize that the sacraments are celebrations of God's love.

Step 1 / INTRODUCTION

Learning About Our Lives

Reviewing Day 2

Talk with the children about the Scripture story on pages 24–25. Help the children recall that because Jesus was with his friends, they needed to celebrate and to show their love for him.

Tell the children that today's lesson will remind them that Jesus is with us every day and in many different ways. Explain that Catholics also have special ways of being with Jesus. Ask: Does anyone know what we call these special celebrations? (*Sacraments*)

Step 2 / DEVELOPMENT

Learning About Our Faith

Presenting the Seven Sacraments

Create seven posters, one for each sacrament. Print each sacrament's name in a different color and use photographs or art work for the signs and symbols of the sacraments. Point to the name of each sacrament, say it aloud, and invite the children to echo each sacrament's name after you.

Presenting the Doctrine

Explain that now the children are going to read about the seven sacraments. Instruct the children to open their books to page 26 and invite a volunteer to read aloud the first paragraph of "Celebrations of God's Love." Assign the remaining paragraphs to seven different children. Each child should stand or come forward individually to read his or her paragraph about one of the seven sacraments.

Celebrations of God's Love

Jesus is with us every day and in many different ways. Catholics also have special ways of being with Jesus. We call these celebrations the seven sacraments.

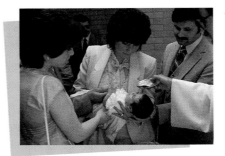

◀ Baptism is a sacrament that joins us to Jesus and welcomes us into the Church. We are baptized with water. Water is a sign that we share Jesus' new life.

In the sacrament of ▶ Confirmation, we receive the Holy Spirit in a special way. The Holy Spirit helps us to tell everyone the good news about Jesus.

◀ At Mass we share a special meal with Jesus. The Eucharist is another sacrament of Jesus' love.

26 Doctrine

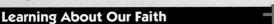

Focus on

As you present the seven sacraments to the children, you might wish to focus on these key elements common to all the sacraments. The sacraments

■ are celebrated at special times in our lives.

■ use special signs to show us Jesus' love.

■ show us that Jesus is present with us now.

◀ In the sacrament of Reconciliation, we say we are sorry for our sins. We celebrate God's forgiveness.

In Anointing of the Sick, ▶ Jesus brings his peace and help to people who are sick.

◀ In the sacrament of Holy Orders, men become deacons, priests, and bishops. They join Jesus' work in a special way.

In the sacrament of ▶ Matrimony or Marriage, a man and a woman promise to love each other. They celebrate their love in this sacrament.

Activity
Which sacrament have you already celebrated?

Baptism

Doctrine 27

Teaching Tips

You might have a child in your class who has not been baptized. Be sensitive to this child's feelings about being "different" from the other children. Assure the child that he or she is loved by God just as much as the children who are baptized. Don't allow the other children to dwell on the reasons why the child is not baptized. Assure all the children that each one of them is a child of God.

Discussing the Seven Sacraments

Take time to discuss each of the seven sacraments with the children. Use these questions to encourage discussion.

- Which sacrament(s) have you celebrated?
- Have you ever gone to a Baptism celebration? What happened there?
- Do you know anyone who has celebrated the sacrament of Confirmation?
- What is the sacrament of Eucharist?
- When might someone want to celebrate the sacrament of Reconciliation?
- Do you know anyone who has celebrated the sacrament of Anointing of the Sick?
- Name someone in our parish who celebrated Holy Orders.
- What do a man and a woman promise to do in the sacrament of Matrimony?

Step 3 / CONCLUSION

Learning How to Live Our Faith

Completing an Activity

Invite a volunteer to read aloud the activity question on page 27. Have the children write their answers on the lines provided. When they have completed the activity, ask volunteers to read aloud their responses to the question. Remind the children that Baptism is always the first sacrament of welcome into the Christian community. Allow the children to tell why they are looking forward to celebrating the other sacraments.

DOCTRINE/MORALITY

Objective

This lesson helps the children recognize that when they give signs of love to others, they are acting as friends and disciples of Jesus.

Step 1 / INTRODUCTION

Learning About Our Lives

Giving Signs of Love

Tell a personal story about someone who has helped you. Invite a few of the children to tell a story about someone who has helped them. Connect the persons' acts of kindness to Jesus' care for others. Ask the children to tell about something good or helpful that they have done for another person. Explain that their good actions were signs of love and that they were acting as friends of Jesus.

Step 2 / DEVELOPMENT

Learning About Our Faith +

Being a Disciple

Instruct the children to open their books to page 28. Invite a volunteer to read the text. Discuss what the men and women did to show they were friends of Jesus. (*Traveled together, ate meals together, celebrated happy times, and prayed together*) Tell the children that these friends of Jesus are called disciples.

Introducing the New Word

Introduce the word *disciples* by reading aloud the definition on page 29. Then have the children echo you as you say the word and its definition once again. Discuss what it means to be a disciple of Jesus today.

Completing an Activity

Guide the children through the activity on page 28. Instruct them to circle the sentences that show how they can be disciples of Jesus. Tell the children to draw a line through the sentences that show that they are not trying to be disciples. Discuss with them why certain actions show that they are being friends and disciples of Jesus, while other actions do not.

28

Friends and Disciples

Some of Jesus' first friends were called **disciples**. They traveled together and ate meals together. They celebrated happy times together. They prayed together. The disciples learned many important things from Jesus.

Jesus' disciples told other people about Jesus. They taught others the same important things that Jesus had taught them.

Jesus invites us to be his disciples, too. He asks us to celebrate with others. He asks us to pray with each other and to listen to each other. Whenever we live and love like Jesus, we are being his disciples.

ctivity

Circle some of the ways you can be a disciple of Jesus. Draw a line through actions that show how a person is not trying to be a disciple.

> I can celebrate happy times with others.
>
> I can be selfish with my toys.
>
> I can invite friends to play with me.
>
> I can fight with my brothers and sisters.
>
> I can forgive someone who hurts me.

28   Doctrine

Focus on

Disciples Explain to the children that a disciple is a pupil or follower of any teacher. The early followers of Jesus, including the Twelve Apostles, and Jesus' friends were his disciples, or students. Jesus was their teacher; he was their master. The disciples believed in Christ as the Messiah and learned from him the new message of love and justice, hope, trust, obedience, and life everlasting. A person is a disciple of Jesus when he or she is committed to him and his work.

What Can You Do?

In the seven sacraments, we celebrate the special ways that Jesus is with us. We can become signs of Jesus' love when we show love to others. We show our love for other people by doing special things for them. What we do is a sign of our love.

Read the story below each picture. Talk about all the things you could do to show your love.

1. Your grandmother lives far away. You haven't seen her all summer. She is coming to visit tomorrow.

2. You have a friend who helps you. This friend is always there to play and talk with. Next week is your friend's birthday.

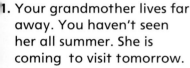

New Word

★
★ **disciples**   people who live and love as Jesus did
★

Teaching Tips

Print the term *signs of love* on the chalkboard. Brainstorm this term for two minutes. (Brainstorming is a technique that involves asking the whole class for ideas and words and making a list of all responses for the entire group to see. All ideas or answers are accepted and become part of the list.) Call on volunteers to role-play ways of showing signs of love. Afterward, ask them to sum up what the term *signs of love* means.

Enriching the Lesson

Arrange to have your class visit the preschool or kindergarten children. Decide before the visit what your class might do to help these children. (Sing "Best Friends," a song from This Is Our Faith Music Program, Grade 2, or help them play a game on the playground.)

Learning How to Live Our Faith

Brainstorming

Tell the children to follow in their books on page 29 as you read aloud the first paragraph of "What Can You Do?" Then ask volunteers to read the stories below the photographs. Brainstorm with the children about ways to show signs of love in each situation. Lead them to conclude that showing love for others means more than just doing what we are asked. Remind the children that Jesus wants us to try to find ways to make others feel loved.

Creating an Acrostic

Have students create an acrostic for the word *disciples*. These are some suggestions.

D — Doing good

I — Inviting

S — Special

C — Caring

I — Including

P — Praying

L — Loving

E — Enjoying

S — Sharing

Praying with Joy

Explain to the children that celebrations usually are joyful; therefore, today your shared prayer will be "jumping for joy." Invite the children to say, "For _____ (Name a celebration, for example, a swim party, a Fourth of July picnic, a soda after our soccer game, and so on), I jump for joy!" The children can jump in place or reach up high as a sign of their joy. Conclude by praying, "We thank you, Jesus, for all the celebrations in our lives and for all the people who have helped us to be happy. We pray this in Jesus' name. Amen."

DAY 5

PRAYER/REVIEW

Objective

This lesson helps the children express their joy in celebrating the reality of God's love by praying together.

Praying Together

Gather the children at the prayer table. Invite the children to put themselves in the spirit of prayer. When they are quiet, introduce the psalm response, "Sing a new song to the Lord." When the children are familiar with the response, continue by leading them in prayer, using the invocations on page 30.

Enhance the children's prayer experience by using appropriate rhythm instruments such as claves, maracas, finger cymbals, drums, tambourines, bells, sand blocks, tone blocks, and rhythm sticks to accompany their responses.

Before continuing and praising God for the gift of each other, pause and invite the children to become quiet. Then say, "Now let us praise God for the gift of each other." Walk around to each child and say: "We praise you, God, for creating (*Name*)." Encourage the class to respond, "Sing a new song to the Lord!" After you have prayed for all the children, pause and ask them to return quietly to their seats.

Praying in Celebration of God's Love

Teacher: We gather to sing praise to our God. Play beautiful melodies!
All: Sing a new song to the Lord!

Teacher: Sound the trumpets and horns! Celebrate God with joyful songs.
All: Sing a new song to the Lord!

Teacher: Let the sea roar with its creatures. Let the rivers clap their hands.
All: Sing a new song to the Lord!

Teacher: Let all the hills ring out their joy. God loves us and all the earth.
All: Sing a new song to the Lord!

Teacher: Now let us praise God for the gift of each other. We praise you, God, for creating (*Name*).

All: Sing a new song to the Lord!

Based on Psalm 149

30 Prayer

Focus on

Praise To praise God means to tell God simply and honestly that God is great! Praise is, perhaps, the prayer least prayed. When we praise God, we focus completely on *God*—not on our ourselves nor even on others. To praise God means to turn our attention away from ourselves and to focus on the One who brought us into life and sustains us throughout our lives. We become people of praise when we acknowledge that everyone and everything comes from God and belongs to God.

Chapter Review

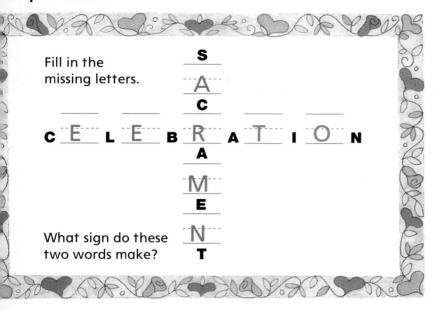

Fill in the missing letters.

```
                    S
 _  _  _  _        A
                    C
C E L E B R A T I O N
                    R
                    A
                    M
                    E
What sign do these   N
two words make?      T
```

1. What do we call a special time when we show how important someone or something is to us?

   ___celebration___

2. What name do Catholics give to special celebrations of Jesus' love for us and our love for him?

   ___sacraments___

Jesus says,
"Live on in
my love."
Based on
John 15:9

3. Talk about what we can do to follow Jesus as his disciples.

★ ★★★ ★
Enriching
the Lesson ★

Invite the children to role-play situations in which they have the opportunity to show love for others. Then divide the class into two groups and have the children in each group work in pairs. Instruct each group to read a different story on page 29 and have the pairs in the group act out "their" story and supply endings for it.

Completing a Puzzle

Explain the directions to the word puzzle on page 31. You may want to tell the children that the puzzle words are two of the new words in this chapter. After the children have completed filling in the letters, ask them to read their answers aloud. Then ask what sign is formed by the two words. (*Cross*)

Reviewing the Chapter

Take time to go through the three-part review. Be supportive of each child who participates in the discussion of item 3.

Praying the Scripture Verse

Read aloud the Scripture verse based on John 15:9. Then call each child forward individually. Trace the sign of the cross on each child's forehead and say the following to each child, addressing him or her by name: (*Name*), live on in Jesus' love." When all the children have returned to their seats, say a short spontaneous prayer.

Remind the children to look for ways to show signs of love and care toward everyone they meet this week.

We Celebrate Baptism

Objectives ~~~~~~

To help the children

■ Identify signs of welcome and be introduced to the sacrament of Baptism.

■ Learn about the signs of the sacrament of Baptism.

■ Learn how the sacrament of Baptism is celebrated.

■ Renew their baptismal promises of faith.

■ Pray with gratitude for the gift of Baptism and review the chapter.

Chapter Outline ~~~~~~~~~~~~~~~

	Step 1 Learning About Our Lives	**Step 2** Learning About Our Faith ✚	**Step 3** Learning How to Live Our Faith ✚
Day 1	■ Review Chapter 2. ■ Discuss a photograph. ■ Read and discuss a poem. *ABOUT 15 MINUTES*	■ Discuss a Scripture story. ■ Introduce Baptism. ■ Present the new word. ■ Present the doctrine. *ABOUT 20 MINUTES*	■ Pray together. *ABOUT 10 MINUTES*
Day 2	■ Introduce the chapter. ■ Read about signs. ■ Interpret signs in an activity. *ABOUT 10 MINUTES*	■ Present the signs of Baptism. *ABOUT 10 MINUTES*	■ Become like Jesus. *ABOUT 10 MINUTES*
Day 3	■ Welcome a new baby. *ABOUT 5 MINUTES*	■ Read a story. ■ Dramatize the story. ■ Discuss baptismal ceremonies. ■ Present the new word. *ABOUT 20 MINUTES*	■ Complete an activity. ■ Pray together. *ABOUT 5 MINUTES*
Day 4	■ Think about promises. *ABOUT 5 MINUTES*	■ Explain baptismal promises. ■ Renew baptismal promises. *ABOUT 10 MINUTES*	■ Complete an activity. ■ Complete a baptismal certificate. *ABOUT 15 MINUTES*
Day 5	**Prayer** Pray together with water and the cross. **Review** Review the signs of Baptism and read the Scripture verse.		

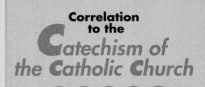

Correlation to the
Catechism of the Catholic Church
Paragraphs
1234, 1238, 1243, 1255

Plan Ahead ~~~~~~

	Preparing Your Class	**Materials Needed**
Day 1	Read over the lesson plan. Prepare the prayer table. If enriching the lesson, create a Welcome poster prior to class.	■ pencils
Day 2	Read over the lesson plan. If enriching the lesson, ask the children to bring in baptismal keepsakes prior to the class.	■ pencils
Day 3	Read over the lesson plan. Bring in props needed for dramatization of a baptismal ceremony. If enriching the lesson, make the necessary preparations.	■ a doll and a candle ■ small cruet of water ■ cotton ball dipped in oil ■ white garment or bib ■ crayons or felt-tip markers
Day 4	Read over the lesson plan. If enriching the lesson, make sure all the necessary materials are available for the session.	■ pencils or pens
Day 5	Read over the lesson plan. Prepare the prayer table.	■ large bowl of water ■ candle

Additional Resources

As you plan this chapter, consider using the following materials from The Resourceful Teacher Package.

■ *Classroom Activity Sheets 3 and 3a*

■ *Family Activity Sheets 3 and 3a*

■ *Chapter 3 Test*

■ *Prayers for Every Day*

■ *Projects: Grade 2*

You may also wish to refer to the following Big Book.

■ *We Celebrate the Sacraments,* pages 4–6

In preparing the children for the Sunday readings, you may wish to use Silver Burdett Ginn's *Getting Ready for Sunday* student and teacher materials.

BOOKS FOR THE JOURNEY

The Long Way to a New Land. Joan Sandin. Harper & Row, 1986. Reveals what being welcomed means through a story of a family who says goodbye forever to their homeland and travels to a new land, America.

Hi. Ann Herbert Scott. Philomel, 1994. A small child's "Hi" is finally welcomed by a "post office lady" who gives her a warm response.

MORE BOOKS FOR THE JOURNEY

Geraldine's Baby Brother. Holly Keller. Greenwillow/Morrow, 1994. Geraldine, upset by the arrival and attention her new baby brother is receiving, finally accepts and welcomes him in her own way and on her own terms.

A Good and Perfect Gift. Drew Bacigalupa. Our Sunday Visitor, 1978. A small child's wish for the gift of a daddy is granted when a special man is welcomed to spend Christmas with her mama and her.

REDUCED CLASSROOM ACTIVITIES

Name

We Celebrate Baptism

Cut out the six boxes. Glue them to strips of construction paper to make a wall hanging.

Lighted candle

White garment

Christian community

Godparents

Oil

Water

To the Teacher: This activity follows the story "Mark's Baptism." Precut 3"-x-18" strips of paper for hanging.

Name

About My Baptism

Color each picture below. Write your own special answers under each box.

Who are your godparents?

What is the name of the church where you were baptized?

Who baptized you?

Who celebrated with you?

To the Teacher: Use this page as a parent-and-child activity.

BAPTISM AS A SACRAMENT OF INITIATION

Initiation means "to begin or start." In the Catholic Church there are three sacraments of initiation: Baptism, Confirmation, and Eucharist. Baptism is the beginning of new life; Confirmation is the strengthening of that new life; and the Eucharist nourishes the Christian with the body and blood of Jesus. *To baptize* means "to plunge" or "to immerse." Immersion into the baptismal water symbolizes burying sin in the water and rising up in the new life of Jesus. Baptism also is the sacrament of faith.

It is a traditional practice of the Roman Catholic Church to baptize infants. The community celebrates the infant's membership in the Catholic Church and ritually initiates the child. This chapter uses the story "Mark's Baptism" to explain the Baptism of infants. The rich symbolism of the Baptism of adults and its roots in the Easter Vigil will be explained at the older grade levels.

Water is a sign in the sacrament of Baptism. It is a sign of new life in Jesus. As the water is poured over the person's head, the priest or deacon says, "I baptize you, in the name of the Father, and of the Son, and of the Holy Spirit." The water and the words are signs that God is present with us. Other sacramental signs of Baptism are anointing with oil, lighting of the baptismal candle, and placing the white garment on the candidate.

EXPERIENCES OF INITIATION

Second graders have experienced various types of welcome and initiation. Many know what it's like to be welcomed home after school, to be welcomed into a new class, to be initiated into a club, or to be welcomed on a team. They can identify a birthday celebration as the remembrance of their welcome into their family. And they can see how, at Baptism, they were welcomed into the Christian family.

After reading "Mark's Baptism," the children will have the opportunity to learn about the baptismal promises that were made for them at Baptism. The activity provided will help the children recall these promises and make a personal statement of belief. The activity will also help the children realize the responsibilities they have as baptized Catholics. The *National Catechetical Directory* reminds us: "In response to their call to share in Christ's priesthood, the baptized are to minister both to the community of faith and to the whole world." (#116)

Objective

This lesson helps children identify signs of welcome and introduces them to the sacrament of Baptism.

Step 1 / INTRODUCTION

Learning About Our Lives

Reviewing Chapter 2

Help the children recall that sacraments are celebrations of Jesus' love for us and a sign of his presence with us now. Explain to the children that today they are going to learn about a sacrament of welcome.

Introducing the Chapter

Ask the children to open their books to page 32. Read aloud the chapter-focus question and invite the children's responses.

Discussing a Photograph

Ask the children to look at the photograph on page 32. Then ask the following questions.

■ Whom might the children be welcoming? (*Another child, a teacher*)

■ Why would that person feel welcome to join the group? (*Everyone looks happy.*)

Reading and Discussing a Poem

Invite the children to read "Come and Join Us." Ask the following questions.

■ What does it mean when you promise to do your part as a member of a group? (*To cooperate, to be helpful*)

■ How can you welcome someone into your class, your team, or your group of friends? (*By shaking hands, by smiling, by asking the person to join in, by saying "Welcome"*)

Step 2 / DEVELOPMENT

Learning About Our Faith

Listening to and Discussing a Scripture Story

Ask the children to listen carefully as you read aloud "Jesus Welcomes Us" on page 33. Elicit from the children what the followers and friends of Jesus are called. (*Disciples*)

We Celebrate Baptism

▲ What are the children doing that makes you feel they welcome one another?

What happens when we are welcomed into a group or family?

Come and Join Us

Say your name and where you live,
And promise, cross your heart,
That as a member of our group
You, too, will do your part.

And now that you have done all this,
We'll sing a welcome song.
For you are now a part of us,
To us you now belong.

32   Doctrine

Cultural Awareness

If you have children in your class for whom English is a second language, invite them to write the word for *welcome* in their native language. If the children need help doing this, encourage them to ask their families for help.

Prepare a chart of words that say welcome in different languages (or print them on the chalkboard.) Help the students to name the language of each word.

Enriching the Lesson

Ask the children to read the Welcome poster you have created prior to class:
WELCOME TO OUR CLASS.
WE . . .

W — work, whisper, and write.
E — enjoy each other.
L — listen to, look at, and love one another.
C — care about our class community.
O — open our doors, open our minds, and our book.
M — make many special things.
E — express signs of welcome.

Jesus Welcomes Us

Jesus told his disciples to <u>tell others about him</u>. He told his disciples to <u>invite all people who love him into his community</u>.

"Go out and <u>welcome people of all nations</u>," Jesus said to them. "<u>Baptize them</u> in the name of the Father, and of the Son, and of the Holy Spirit. <u>Teach them</u> all that I have taught you. And know that I am with you always."

Based on Matthew 28:18–20

Activity

Underline the things in the story that Jesus asks his followers to do.

Our Church Welcomes Us

Our Church welcomes new members at the sacrament of **Baptism**. At Baptism we become members of the Church and share new life with Jesus.

We Believe

The Catholic community welcomes new members at Baptism, and our lives are joined to Jesus. At Baptism, Jesus gives us new life, the life of the Holy Spirit. Baptism is one of the seven sacraments.

New Word

★ **Baptism**   Baptism is a sacrament of welcome. At Baptism, our lives are joined to Jesus and the Church welcomes us as new members.

Scripture   33

Teaching Tips

I am significant is an important perception for children to have about themselves. To build self-esteem consider these suggestions.

■ Call a student by name as often as possible.
■ Say: I thank you for your _____ . (Name the gift the child shares with the class community, such as friendliness, patience, kindness, and so on.)
■ Note when a child returns from an absence that he or she was missed.

Completing an Activity

Instruct the children to read silently "Jesus Welcomes Us" on page 33. Invite them to underline the things in the story that Jesus asks his followers to do. (*Tell others about him; invite all people who love him into his community; welcome people of all nations; baptize them; teach them.*) Clarify each action and phrase of the answer.

Then ask:

■ How would you invite all people to become disciples?
■ How do you know that Jesus is always with you? (*Jesus promised that he would be. The Church celebrates sacraments that are signs of his presence with us now.*)

Introducing the Sacrament of Baptism

Ask a volunteer to read "Our Church Welcomes Us" on page 33. Ask the children how the Catholic Church welcomes new members. (*We welcome new members through a special celebration called the sacrament of Baptism.*)

Presenting the New Word

Present the new word *Baptism*. Read the sentences, one at a time, having the children repeat them after you.

Presenting the Doctrine

Direct the children's attention to the We Believe statements on page 33. Ask them to study the paragraph. Then read it aloud, omitting key words. Ask the children to supply the missing words.

Step 3 / CONCLUSION

Learning How to Live Our Faith

Praying Together

Gather the children at the prayer table. Remind them that to be friends and disciples of Jesus we must be willing to welcome one another.

Ask the children to quiet themselves. Then pray: "Jesus, we want to be your disciples, but it's not always easy to welcome one another. Help us to remember how you always welcomed children, those who were sick, and those who were lonely. Teach us how to welcome one another, even when it is difficult. Amen."

Invite the children to welcome everyone they meet today with a special sign of welcome.

33

Objective

This lesson helps the children learn about everyday signs and the signs of the sacrament of Baptism.

Step 1 / INTRODUCTION

Learning About Our Lives

Introducing the Chapter

Invite children to share what they said or did to welcome someone since yesterday. Ask how they felt as they welcomed others.

Explain that today you and the children are going to talk about everyday signs and the signs used in Baptism.

Reading About Signs

Read together the paragraph at the top of page 34. Lead a brief discussion about the signs that are familiar to the children.

Interpreting Signs in an Activity

Invite the children to gather with their books in a story circle. Explain that each day as we come to school we see certain signs along the way and that these signs help us remember the route. Then tell the children to open their books to page 34. Before you read aloud the activity story about following certain signs on the way to school, explain that you will pause whenever a picture of a sign appears in place of the words. Each time you pause, the children should name the sign pictured. Demonstrate by reading the first two sentences. (The children should respond, "Bus stop" and "Stop light.") Affirm their responses, then continue telling the story.

34

Signs Are All Around Us

Our world is full of signs. There are signs that remind us of people and events. There are signs that remind us of special places and things.

 Activity

Find your way to school by using the signs in the map below.

Go past the . At the corner, watch the .

You can safely cross the street when the is lighted.

Next you'll pass the . Then you'll pass the

 . You're almost there! Look up ahead. Do you

see the  ? That's your school!

🍎 Teaching Tips

Tell the children that they can find signs in different subjects that they are learning. Have them identify the signs in arithmetic for addition, subtraction, division, and multiplication. In music, have them look for the treble clef on the staff, the key signature, the time signature, the directions for how fast or slow the music will be performed.

Have the children draw as many of these signs as they can find.

Signs of New Life

Just as there are signs all around us in our world, the sacrament of Baptism has signs, too. These signs remind us of our new life in Jesus.

◄ **Water**
The priest pours water over our heads to remind us that Baptism washes away our old life. We are now new people who live in Jesus' love.

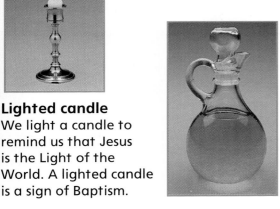

◄ **White garment**
The garment reminds us that it is Jesus' new life we put on when we are baptized.

Lighted candle
We light a candle to remind us that Jesus is the Light of the World. A lighted candle is a sign of Baptism.

◄ **Oil**
At Baptism, we anoint the person's head with oil as a sign that God calls us to live special lives. We are called to live as Jesus lived.

Doctrine 35

★ **Enriching the Lesson** ★

A day or two before this lesson, invite the children to bring in one keepsake from their Baptism such as the candle, the white garment, or a photograph. When the items are brought in, place them on the discovery table. Complete the display by adding a dish of oil and a bowl of water. Invite the children to gather around the discovery table. Each child shows and tells what he or she brought.

Step 2 / DEVELOPMENT

Learning About Our Faith

Presenting the Signs of Baptism

Read the introductory paragraph on page 35 to the children. Invite four volunteers to read aloud the paragraphs about the signs of Baptism. When the volunteers have finished reading, invite all of the children to echo each line of the following prayer.

Jesus, the light of the world.

Thank you for the water of Baptism.

Water reminds me of my new life in Jesus.

Thank you for the lighted candle of Baptism.

Help me to be a light to others.

Thank you for the oil of Baptism.

I promise to be your disciple.

Thank you for the white garment of Baptism.

The white garment reminds me that it is Jesus I've put on at Baptism.

Amen.

Step 3 / CONCLUSION

Learning How to Live Our Faith

Becoming like Jesus

Explain that in the sacrament of Baptism, we are called to live as Jesus did and to be his disciples. Invite the children to complete the following statements. (*Answers will vary.*)

I listen as Jesus listened to others when I . . .

I love as Jesus loved Martha, Mary, and Lazarus when I . . .

I am the light of Jesus for others when I . . .

I share as Jesus shared with others when I . . .

DAY 3
DOCTRINE

Objective
This lesson helps the children learn how the sacrament of Baptism is celebrated.

Step 1 / INTRODUCTION

Learning About Our Lives

Welcoming a New Baby
Invite discussion about what happens when a new baby is born and joins the family. Ask anyone who has a younger brother or sister to describe the excitement of having a new baby in the family. Ask: What did the family do to prepare? How did the family select a name for the new baby? Conclude with the concept that one way parents show their love for the new child is to bring the baby to church for the sacrament of Baptism.

Step 2 / DEVELOPMENT

Learning About Our Faith

Reading a Story
Read aloud the story "Mark's Baptism" on pages 36–37, or ask volunteers to read the story aloud. As each paragraph is read, refer to the illustrations that accompany the text. As the word *godparents* is introduced, print it on the chalkboard.

Dramatizing the Story
Encourage the children to dramatize the story using the props you have arranged beforehand on the discovery table. These items should include a doll, a small cruet of water, a cotton ball dipped in oil, a white garment or bib, and a candle. Select children to play the roles of Mark's parents, Uncle Peter, Aunt Ruth, and Father Adams. Choose a narrator and invite the rest of the group to serve as relatives or friends.

Mark's Baptism
as told by his sister, Lisa Ann

Today is a wonderful day for my family. My new baby brother, Mark, is being baptized at Sunday Mass. All of our family and friends are here. And s♦ is the rest of our parish family.

1. Father Adams welcomes everyone, especially Mark. Then the Mass begins.

3. Father Adams asks everyone if we believe in God the Father, and in Jesus, and in the Holy Spirit. We all answer, "I do."

2. Soon it is time for Mark to be baptized. Father Adams makes the sign of the cross on Mark's head. Then Mom and Dad do the same. And so do Uncle Peter and Aunt Ruth, who are so proud to have been chosen to be Mark's **godparents**.

4. Father Adams pours water ove♦ Mark's head. He says, "I baptiz♦ you, Mark, in the name of the Father, and of the Son, and of the Holy Spirit."

36 Doctrine

Immersion The baptismal ritual of immersion has been reclaimed from the early Church. A candidate stands in a baptismal font. The candidate may be completely immersed or abundant water may be poured over his or her head. This ritual usually is integrated into the Easter Vigil service. We situate baptismal fonts prominently in our churches to remind the faith community to prepare, sustain, and celebrate with new members.

Cultural Awareness
Godparents are very important to every Catholic. This is especially true in the Hispanic, Creole, Haitian, and African-American communities. If you have children from these cultures in your class, you might wish to invite one of the parents, other family members, or perhaps one of the children's godparents to talk with the children about the special role and responsibility godparents have in their cultures.

5. Father Adams makes the sign of the cross on Mark's head with blessed oil. He puts a white robe on Mark. He prays that Mark will live as a friend of Jesus.

6. Mark looks up at the lighted candle. Father Adams says, "Mark, receive the light of Christ." Then he gives the special candle to Mom and Dad.

7. Father Adams blesses Mom and Dad. Then he blesses all of us. And that's when Mark falls asleep.

Activity

Color the signs of Baptism. Draw a line through the objects that are not signs of Baptism.

New Word

★
★ **godparents** two people chosen by our parents to help us
★ grow as friends and followers of Jesus
★

Doctrine 37

★ ★ ★ ★ ★
Enriching the Lesson
★ ★ ★

Ask if any child in your class has a new brother or sister who soon will be baptized. If so, ask the child's parents for permission to attend the Baptism with your class. Or check with the parish office for the date and time of the next scheduled Baptism. Contact the parents of the child or children to be baptized and ask permission for your class to witness the ceremony.

Discussing Baptismal Ceremonies

Ask the children if they have ever been to a baptismal celebration. Ask them to share the details of the ceremony. At this time you may wish to explain that people may be baptized at any age. Explain that the ceremony is a little different when an older child or adult is baptized.

or . . .

Arrange for the children to visit your parish church and tour the baptismal area. Point out the font or immersion pool. Poll the children to see how many of them were baptized in your parish. If there is water in the font, invite the children to use it to sign themselves with the sign of the cross.

Presenting the New Word

Invite the children to read the definition of *godparents* aloud. Ask volunteers to use the word in a sentence. Then challenge the children to locate the word within the text. If time permits, help the children to create and send a thank-you letter to their godparents.

Step 3 / CONCLUSION

Learning How to Live Our Faith

Completing an Activity

Invite the children to color the signs of Baptism found in the activity on page 37. Tell them that not every picture in the activity is a sign of Baptism. Have them draw a line through the objects that are not signs of Baptism. Praise their efforts.

Praying Together

Lead the children in the following prayer. "Let us give thanks for our godparents. (Pause)

Dear Jesus, at Baptism our parents selected two special people to be our godparents. We thank you for their presence in our lives. We name them now." (Invite each child to say the names of his or her godparents if they know the names.) Continue. "May God bless these special people. (Invite all to make the sign of the cross as you conclude the prayer.) "In the name of the Father, and of the Son, and of the Holy Spirit. Amen."

DAY 4
DOCTRINE

Objective

This lesson helps the children to discover their growing faith and to renew the faith promises made for them at Baptism.

Step 1 / INTRODUCTION

Learning About Our Lives

Thinking About Promises

Discuss with the children the concept of promises. Ask:

- What kinds of promises have you made to your parents?
- How has a friend asked you to make a promise to him or her?

Tell the children that the lesson is about the promises of Baptism. Stress that when we were welcomed into the Catholic Church, our parents and godparents spoke these promises for us. Tell the children that now that they are older, they can make the promises themselves.

Step 2 / DEVELOPMENT

Learning About Our Faith

Explaining Baptismal Promises

Choose a volunteer to read aloud the introductory text of the activity on page 38. You may want to explain that all Catholics renew their baptismal promises every year at Easter. Read the priest's questions printed in the speech balloons. Distribute pencils or pens. Instruct the children to write the words *I do* in each empty speech balloon.

What We Believe

The Catholic Church welcomed us at Baptism. We celebrated becoming members of the Christian community.

At Baptism, the priest asked some questions and our parents and godparents answered for us. The priest asked them what they believed as Catholics. Here are some questions the priest asked. Now you can answer for yourself. Write the words **I do** in each speech balloon.

Focus on

Promises Explain to the children that a promise is an agreement to do or not to do something. A person can make a promise orally or in writing. Discuss some of the promises people make to each other. A man promises to marry a woman and gives her a sign of his love (engagement). Husbands and wives promise to love and be true to each other (vows). Business people promise to uphold the terms of a business agreement (written contract). Borrowers promise to pay back money (promissory note).

Activity

You are a member of the Catholic Church. Name something you now know about Jesus that you did not know when you were baptized.

_____

- -

_____

Then ask your family to help you complete this certificate.

My Baptism

_____

My name is _____

_____

I was baptized on _____

           (month)   (day)   (year)

_____

My godmother is _____

_____

My godfather is _____

Doctrine 39

Enriching the Lesson

Help the children make welcome cards for the newly baptized in the parish. Distribute light-colored construction paper cut to greeting card size. Ask the children to draw decorations on the cards, using crayons or felt-tip markers. Then ask the children to write messages of welcome on their cards. Collect the completed cards.

Arrange to have the cards distributed after parish Baptisms.

PRAYER/REVIEW

Objective

This lesson helps the children thank God for the gift of Baptism and the gift of water.

Praying with Water and the Cross

Gather the children, with their books, around the prayer table, on which you have placed a large bowl of water and a candle. Explain to the children that in their study of the sacrament of Baptism, they have talked often about water, a sign of new life in Jesus. Tell them that today they are going to thank God for the gift of water. Ask the children to put their books in front of them on the floor. Light the candle as you read aloud the first paragraph on page 40.

Then read the next paragraph aloud. When you have finished, invite the children to approach the prayer table, one by one, dip the fingers of their right hand into the bowl of water, and make the sign of the cross.

When you and the children have signed yourselves with water and the cross, ask the children to pick up their books and open them to page 40. Read with the class the prayer at the bottom of the page.

Praying with Water and the Cross

Teacher: Let us gather together around this candle in the name of Jesus, in whom we are baptized.

Teacher: We have been signed with the waters of Baptism. Let us remember our new life in Jesus by marking ourselves with water and the cross.

All: Jesus, we are happy to be called your friends. Thank you for welcoming us into the Christian community through the waters of Baptism. Amen.

40   Prayer

Teaching Tips

Our Catholic heritage is rich in its use of symbols as aids in worship and prayer. Our churches are filled with symbols of faith—crosses, crucifixes, holy water, baptismal fonts, statues, and candles. Many of these faith symbols are called *sacramentals* because they help us focus on Jesus as we pray and worship. When praying with children, put before them symbols such as the cross, water, and light. These symbols will engage their senses and will make their prayer more meaningful.

Enriching the Lesson

Ask the children to stand. Invite them to repeat the following promises by echoing your words after each line.

Dear Jesus, (echo)
I promise to trust you. (echo)
I promise to accept others. (echo)
I promise to make up when I hurt others. (echo)

I make these promises in the name of the Father, and of the Son, and of the Holy Spirit. Amen. (Make the sign of the cross during the last sentence.)

Chapter Review

Circle signs of new life that we see at Baptism.

- oil
- water
- table
- lighted candle
- food
- window
- fish
- white garment

1. What do we call the first sacrament of welcome into the Christian community that joins our lives with Jesus?

Baptism

2. What does Jesus give us at Baptism?

new life

3. Talk about what happens at a Baptism that makes it a special celebration for each of us.

Welcome one another just as Jesus welcomes you.
Based on Romans 15:7

ℱ𝑜𝑐𝑢𝑠 𝑜𝑛

The Sign of the Cross Remind the children that the Sign of the Cross is both a prayer and an action. Explain that when we pray the Sign of the Cross, we are saying what we believe about the Trinity—that God is our Father, Jesus is the Son of God, and the Holy Spirit is the Spirit of God.

Reviewing the Signs of Baptism

Remind the children that when they were welcomed into the Catholic community at Baptism, they received new life from Jesus. Tell the children that the sacrament of Baptism has many signs of new life. To help the children discover these signs, direct their attention to the first part of the review at the top of page 41. Invite them to read the list of words that include four signs of new life that are seen at Baptism. Give the children sufficient time to circle their answers. When the children are ready, invite a volunteer to read his or her answers. (*Oil, water, lighted candle, white garment*)

Now ask the children to fill in the blanks for the first two questions. Invite volunteers to read the questions aloud and give their answers. (*Baptism, new life*) Read aloud item 3 and discuss it with the class. Be supportive of each child who participates in the discussion.

Reading the Scripture Verse

Read the Scripture verse from Romans 15 found on page 41. Ask: What does Jesus want us to do? How should we welcome one another?

We Celebrate Confirmation

Objectives

To help the children

■ Recognize that Confirmation is another sacrament of welcome.
■ Understand that the Holy Spirit comes to them in Confirmation.
■ Learn about the sacrament of Confirmation.
■ Discover that the Holy Spirit will help them live as Christians.
■ Pray to the Holy Spirit and review the chapter.

Chapter Outline

	Step 1 Learning About Our Lives	**Step 2** Learning About Our Faith	**Step 3** Learning How to Live Our Faith
Day 1	■ Introduce the chapter. ■ Read and discuss a story. *ABOUT 10 MINUTES*	■ Review baptismal promises. ■ Introduce the sacrament of Confirmation. ■ Define the word *Confirmation*. *ABOUT 15 MINUTES*	■ Make a promise to the Holy Spirit. ■ Make a promise to follow Jesus. *ABOUT 5 MINUTES*
Day 2	■ Share fears. *ABOUT 8 MINUTES*	■ Present the doctrine. ■ Recognize the signs of Confirmation. ■ Define *Holy Spirit* and *guide*. *ABOUT 18 MINUTES*	■ Pray to the Holy Spirit. *ABOUT 5 MINUTES*
Day 3	■ Introduce the lesson. *ABOUT 3 MINUTES*	■ Read and discuss a story. ■ Review the signs of the Holy Spirit. ■ Define the word *sponsor*. *ABOUT 12 MINUTES*	■ Complete an activity. ■ Hear a speaker on Confirmation. ■ Pray together to the Holy Spirit. *ABOUT 15 MINUTES*
Day 4	■ Review Day 3. ■ Read and discuss a story. *ABOUT 10 MINUTES*	■ Discover ways of doing good. *ABOUT 15 MINUTES*	■ Identify Christian actions. *ABOUT 5 MINUTES*

Day 5   **Prayer**   Pray to the Holy Spirit and consider ways to make the world a better place.
　　　　　　 Review   Review the chapter and read the Scripture verse.

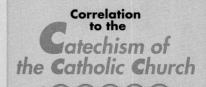
Plan Ahead ~~~~~~~~~~

Preparing Your Class

Day 1   Read over the lesson. Make a welcome banner prior to the session. Prepare the prayer table.

Day 2   Read over the lesson. If enriching the lesson, make a Pentecost poster and gather materials for stick figures.

Day 3   Read over the lesson. Prepare the prayer table. If enriching lesson, prepare props for a dramatization.

Day 4   Read over the lesson. Prepare the discovery table. Bring in parish bulletin.

Day 5   Read over the lesson. Prepare the prayer table. Select a familiar, joyful song from THIS IS OUR FAITH Music Program, Grade 2.

Materials Needed

Day 1
- welcome banner
- pencils, candle

Day 2
- candle
- pencils

Day 3
- cruet of olive oil
- picture of the local bishop

Day 4
- lined paper
- parish bulletin
- bottle caps, paper plates, cans, bottles

Day 5
- cruet of oil, candle
- music recording of a joyful song
- drawing paper

Additional Resources

As you plan this chapter, consider using the following materials from The Resourceful Teacher Package.

- *Classroom Activity Sheets 4* and *4a*
- *Family Activity Sheets 4* and *4a*
- *Chapter 4 Test*
- *Prayers for Every Day*
- *Projects: Grade 2*

You may also wish to refer to the following Big Book.

- *We Celebrate the Sacraments,* pages 10–12

In preparing the children for the Sunday readings, you may wish to use Silver Burdett Ginn's *Getting Ready for Sunday* student and teacher materials.

BOOKS FOR THE JOURNEY

Amelia's Road. Linda Jacobs Altman. Lee & Low, 1993. Amelia, the young daughter of migrant workers, creates her own sense of belonging in spite of not having a permanent home.

Jacob's Rescue: A Holocaust Story. Malka Drucker and Michael Halperin. Bantam, 1993. A story that a child hears at Passover about her father and her uncle's childhood during the Holocaust.

MORE BOOKS FOR THE JOURNEY

Christopher: The Holy Giant. Tomie dePaola. Holiday House, 1994. A legend of a man who sets out to serve royalty and ends up serving Jesus.

A Light in the Attic. "Somebody Has To," p. 28. Shel Silverstein. HarperCollins, 1981. A poem that delightfully picks up on the call to serve.

The Heart of the Wood. Marguerite W. Davol. Simon & Schuster, 1992. Each one's giftedness can be found in the heart of the wood.

REDUCED CLASSROOM ACTIVITIES

Name _____

We Celebrate Confirmation

Adults help children in many ways. Adult Christians help children at Confirmation by being their sponsors. Draw lines to match the children below with the adults who helped them. Write one of these three titles next to the picture of each adult: scout leader, teacher, coach.

coach _____

scout leader _____

teacher _____

To the Teacher: This activity will help second graders connect the role of sponsor with other familiar adult roles in their lives.

Name _____

Confirmation and Baptism Are Alike

Make a "Sacraments Quilt" from the boxes below. Choose one color crayon to shade in the squares about Confirmation. Choose another color crayon to shade in the squares about Baptism. One box should be shaded in with both of your colors. Read the squares about Baptism aloud to a partner. Your partner will read the squares about Confirmation to you.

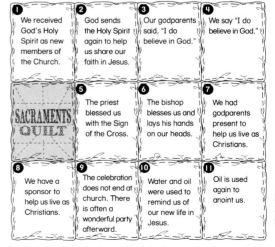

❶ We received God's Holy Spirit as new members of the Church.	❷ God sends the Holy Spirit again to help us share our faith in Jesus.	❸ Our godparents said, "I do believe in God."	❹ We say "I do believe in God."
SACRAMENTS QUILT	❺ The priest blessed us with the Sign of the Cross.	❻ The bishop blesses us and lays his hands on our heads.	❼ We had godparents present to help us live as Christians.
❽ We have a sponsor to help us live as Christians.	❾ The celebration does not end at church. There is often a wonderful party afterward.	❿ Water and oil were used to remind us of our new life in Jesus.	⓫ Oil is used again to anoint us.

To the Teacher: This activity reviews Chapters 3 and 4 by describing the many similarities between the two sacraments.

Background for the Teacher ~~~~~~~~~~~~~~~~

CONFIRMATION AND THE HOLY SPIRIT

Jesus challenges us to live as Christians in the world. We may be hesitant at times to practice our faith or share it with others. Our belief in the powerful presence of the Holy Spirit in our lives gives us the courage to live as disciples. The Pentecost event (Acts 2:1–4) relates the conversion of the disciples from being the hidden ones to being witnesses. The Holy Spirit imparts courage and strength to proclaim the good news. The fruits of the Spirit—love, joy, peace, patience, kindness, generosity, faithfulness, gentleness, and self-control—are released in those who are confirmed.

During this session you have the opportunity to help the children understand that their initiation, or, to use the children's term, their welcome, into the Catholic Church community is ongoing. They will begin to appreciate the presence and the strengthening gift of the Holy Spirit, who will help them live out their baptismal call. You can also help the children begin actively to search out ways to live as Christians and to share with others their faith in Jesus.

HISTORY OF CONFIRMATION

Prior to the fifth century, Confirmation was part of the sacrament of Initiation in which adults were baptized, confirmed, and received the Eucharist in the same ceremony. The bishop was the ordinary minister of this sacrament. Initiates spent a period of time learning about the Catholic faith and practicing it with the assistance of a sponsor. This period of learning was called the *catechumenate* and the initiates were called *catechumens.*

The separation of Baptism and Confirmation began during the fifth century. At that time, bishops, physically unable to preside at all the sacramental initiations throughout their dioceses, retained their role in the reception of candidates by presiding at that part of the ritual that had formerly concluded the original baptismal rite. Thus, they anointed the new members and "confirmed" their initiation into the Church. But it was not until the Middle Ages, when the practice of infant Baptism had become the norm, that Confirmation was identified as a separate and distinct sacrament.

The Rite of Christian Initiation of Adults (RCIA) has restored the ancient initiation rituals of the early Church. The official sequence was Baptism, Confirmation, and Eucharist.

Contemporary Confirmation practices—preparation and celebration—differ by diocese. Some dioceses have restored the original order of Baptism, Confirmation, and Eucharist with the emphasis on initiation. Others confirm candidates after they have received the Eucharist. The emphasis is on the strengthening of faith and virtue. Many parishes confirm students as teenagers to stress an adult commitment to the faith.

Objective

This lesson helps the children learn how to make someone feel welcome and recognize that Confirmation is another sacrament of welcome.

Step 1 / INTRODUCTION

Learning About Our Lives

Introducing the Chapter

Display a welcome banner or sign you have made or brought from home. Invite the children to think of ways they can make others feel welcome. Print the answers on the chalkboard.

Gather the children into a sharing circle. Ask a child to read the focus question on page 42. Stress those gestures, words, and actions that make people feel welcome. Ask: How do we make others feel welcome in our classroom? (*Answers will vary.*)

Reading and Discussing a Story

Allow the children to take turns reading aloud the story "Miguel Feels More Welcomed." Ask:

■ What did Miguel have to do before he earned his uniform? (*Learn the Cub Scout promise*)

■ How did Miguel feel when he received his uniform? (*Proud and happy*)

Assist the children in understanding that for Miguel to be a Cub Scout, he had to do more than wear a uniform. He also had to keep the promises he had made to the group.

Step 2 / DEVELOPMENT

Learning About Our Faith ✝

Reviewing Our Baptismal Promises

People make promises to God. Your parents made promises for you at your baptism. Ask:

■ Who remembers the promises at Baptism? (*To believe in God and live as disciples*)

■ How can you help your parents keep these promises? (*Answers will vary.*)

■ Who also promises to help them? (*The parish community*)

---

4 We Celebrate Confirmation

How do you make someone feel welcomed to your home or to your group of friends?

Miguel Feels More Welcomed

Miguel wanted to join the Cub Scouts. The first time he went to a meeting he felt afraid because he did not know anyone in the troop.

The scoutmaster welcomed Miguel warmly. He introduced him to the troop. By the end of the meeting, Miguel began to feel welcomed.

"You need to learn the Cub Scout promise before the next meeting," the scoutmaster told him. "If you can say it at the next meeting, you'll receive your uniform."

Miguel studied the promise. He said it over and over to anyone who would listen.

Focus on

Make the connection between Confirmation and Baptism as sacraments of welcome into the Christian community. Confirmation gives us the strength needed to live as Christian disciples. Present the gifts of the Holy Spirit as prayerfulness, courage, strength, kindness to others, and doing the right thing. Teach the children that their sponsors and the Christian community provide a model to support them as they strive to witness the good news.

Enriching the Lesson

Invite a Cub Scout and Brownie (young Girl Scout) to recite their promises. The Cub Scout promise is "I, *name*, promise to do my best, to do my duty to God and my country, to help other people, and to obey the law of the pack." The Brownie promise is "On my honor, I will try to serve God and my country, to help other people at all times, and to live by the Girl Scout law." Note the similarities: service to God, country, and others; a promise to obey the rules.

The night of the meeting finally came. Now it was Miguel's turn to say the promise.

"Are you ready, Miguel?" the scoutmaster asked.

"I sure am!" Miguel responded.

Miguel recited the promise without any mistakes. The other scouts cheered. The scoutmaster congratulated Miguel and gave him his uniform.

Everyone was very proud of Miguel.

Welcomed Again

When most of us were babies, our parish community welcomed us at Baptism. We are welcomed again as members of the Church in the sacrament of **Confirmation**. The Holy Spirit promises to make us strong in faith. We share the gifts of the Holy Spirit with others.

Activity

The Holy Spirit promises to be with you. The Holy Spirit will help you to be brave and kind. What promise do you make to the Holy Spirit?

I promise to _____

_____

New Word

★
★
★ **Confirmation**   Confirmation is another sacrament of
★   welcome into the Catholic Church through
★   which the Holy Spirit makes us strong to live
★   and share our faith in Jesus.
★
★

`Doctrine  43`

🌐 ***Cultural Awareness***

Discuss with the children how people make different gestures to show the sincerity of their promises. A handshake seals a promise or contract. In some cultures, a special object is exchanged as a sign of a promise. The exchange of rings in a wedding ceremony in our culture reflects this practice. Children sometimes cross their hearts to show a promise of sincerity.

Introduce the sacrament of Confirmation as the sacrament that welcomes us again into the Christian community. Tell the children that the Holy Spirit gives us the strength to love one another and to fulfill the baptismal promise to live as disciples. Read and discuss "Welcomed Again" on page 43.

Defining the New Word

Read the definition of *Confirmation*. Ask: Who has heard this word before? Does anyone know someone who has been confirmed? What promises is he or she making to God in Confirmation? (*To be followers and disciples of Jesus*) Have the children repeat the new word and its definition several times.

Step 3 / CONCLUSION

Learning How to Live Our Faith

Making a Promise

Ask a child to read the paragraph inside the activity box on page 43. Ask: What promises have you made this week? (*To do homework, to make the bed, to be good, and so on*) Guide the children in printing a promise to the Holy Spirit on the lines provided.

Praying to Jesus

Place the welcome banner or sign on the prayer table. Light the candle. Read this promise from God based on Isaiah 41:10: "I am your God. I will strengthen you and help you." Say to the children: "Bow your heads and close your eyes. Imagine that Jesus is here in the circle next to you. Jesus asks you to promise to follow him today. Silently tell Jesus how you will do that (pause). Open your eyes now and say or sing 'Amen.'" (Choose a sung "Amen" familiar to the children.)

SCRIPTURE/DOCTRINE

Objective

This lesson helps children understand that the Holy Spirit comes to them in Confirmation to make them strong to live and share their faith in Jesus.

Step 1 / INTRODUCTION

Learning About Our Lives

Sharing Fears

Share a childhood story of fear, for instance, fear of the dark, fear of strange places, fear of making new friends, and so on. Ask a volunteer to read the activity directions on page 44. Invite the children to share what they are afraid of. Then have the children write on the lines provided something that frightens them.

Step 2 / DEVELOPMENT

Learning About Our Faith

Presenting the Doctrine

Ask for volunteers to read "The Disciples Receive the Holy Spirit" on page 44. Explain that the disciples were afraid after Jesus died because he was no longer with them. Direct the children to close their eyes and imagine what it was like when the disciples received the Holy Spirit. Ask the following questions.

- Why were the disciples afraid? (*Jesus was no longer with them.*)
- Where were they hiding? (*In an upper room*)
- What did they hear? (*A noise like a strong wind blowing*)
- What appeared above each disciple? (*Tongues of fire*)
- What were the tongues of fire and the rushing wind signs of? (*The Holy Spirit*)
- How did they know the Holy Spirit had come? (*They were filled with courage.*)
- What did they do? (*They spoke in many languages about Jesus.*)

ctivity

Everyone is afraid of something. Name something that frightens you.

_____

The Disciples Receive the Holy Spirit

The disciples of Jesus were afraid because Jesus was no longer with them. They hid in an upper room. Suddenly they heard a noise, like a strong wind blowing. Tongues of fire appeared over each of them. The **Holy Spirit** filled them with courage. They began to speak in many languages. They told the people to believe in Jesus.

Based on Acts 2:1–4

44 Scripture

Teaching Tips

We can recall father/son images to describe God the Father and God the Son. But what do we say to children about the Holy Spirit, the intangible, the image-less Spirit of God? Draw heavily on the tangible symbols of the Spirit—breath, wind, fire—to create a sense of God as Spirit. We don't know what the Holy Spirit *looks* like, but we do know how the Spirit *acts* in our lives—breathing new life into us, blowing through our lives with peace and joy, and engulfing us with strength to live as Christians.

Signs of Confirmation

Jesus sent the Holy Spirit to his disciples to help make them strong. The Holy Spirit can help us become strong friends and followers of Jesus.

At Confirmation we celebrate the presence of the Holy Spirit. The signs below remind us that the Holy Spirit comes to us in this sacrament.

With hands stretched out, ▶ the bishop and priest pray to the Holy Spirit. They ask the Holy Spirit to help us and **guide** us. This sign is called the laying on of hands.

◀ The bishop anoints our foreheads with blessed oil. The bishop says, "Be sealed with the Gift of the Holy Spirit." That means "May you be filled with God's Spirit." Anointing with oil is another sign of Confirmation.

We Believe

Confirmation is another sacrament of welcome into the Catholic Church. We believe that the Holy Spirit is God's Spirit. The Holy Spirit helps us to follow Jesus and live holy lives.

New Words

★ **Holy Spirit** the Spirit of God who helps us follow Jesus
★ **guide** to show the way

Doctrine 45

★ Enriching the Lesson ★

Make a contemporary Pentecost poster. On a large sheet of craft paper, draw simple stick figures representing each child in the class. Invite the children to complete the heads and bodies of the stick figures to identify the figures as themselves. They may use crayons, markers, or pieces of material. Cut out of red craft paper flames, or tongues, of fire and paste them above the stick figures.

Have the children follow in their books as you read "Signs of Confirmation" on page 45. Help the children recognize that in Confirmation the Holy Spirit gives us the strength to live and share our faith in Jesus. Ask the children to name the two signs of the Holy Spirit's presence. (*The anointing with oil and the laying on of hands*)

Ask the following questions.

- Who came to the disciples when they were afraid? (*The Holy Spirit*)
- Who comes to us in Confirmation to make us brave and strong? (*The Holy Spirit*)
- What does the bishop say as he signs our foreheads with oil? (*"Be sealed with the Gift of the Holy Spirit."*)

Defining the New Words

Tell the children to look at the New Words box. Have them read aloud the definitions of the words *Holy Spirit* and *guide*. Challenge them to locate these words in the explanatory passage you have just read. Ask: Who is the Holy Spirit? (*The Spirit of God*) What does *guide* mean? (*To show the way*)

Presenting the Doctrine

Read together the We Believe statements on page 45. Challenge the children to express in their own words how the Holy Spirit helps us in the sacrament of Confirmation.

Step 3 / CONCLUSION

Learning How to Live Our Faith

Praying to the Holy Spirit

Direct the children to bring their books and gather around the prayer table. Light the candle. Point out to the children that the flame is a tongue of fire. Make the sign of the cross, and say, "Holy Spirit, come to us. Help us to be strong and brave."

45

Objective

This lesson helps the children understand what takes place during Confirmation and what the signs of the Holy Spirit's presence are.

Step 1 / INTRODUCTION

Learning About Our Lives

Introducing the Lesson

Place a cruet of olive oil on the discovery table. Tell the children that the oil of Confirmation is called *chrism*. Also place a picture of you local bishop on the table. (Check your diocesan newspaper for a picture of your bishop.) Tell the children that they will learn about the use of oil in Confirmation and the role of the bishop.

Step 2 / DEVELOPMENT

Learning About Our Faith

Reading and Discussing a Story

Read with the children the story "Maria's Confirmation," on pages 46–47. As the word *sponsor* is introduced, print it on the chalkboard. Before asking the questions below, explain to the children that a bishop is the leader of many local parishes. Tell the group that a bishop usually comes to the parish to celebrate the sacrament of Confirmation.

- What did Bishop Lee say the Holy Spirit would do through the sacrament of Confirmation? (*Unite Maria and her friends more closely with Jesus and his followers*)

- Why did Bishop Lee sprinkle Maria and her friends with holy water? (*To remind them of their baptism*)

- Who is Mrs. López? (*Maria's sponsor*)

- Why did Bishop Lee sign Maria with blessed oil? (*As a sign of the Holy Spirit's presence*)

Maria's Confirmation

as told by her brother, Alex

1. Father Adams presented Maria and her friends to the bishop. "Welcome," Bishop Lee said. "Today God will send the Holy Spirit to you in the sacrament of Confirmation. The Holy Spirit will unite you more closely with Jesus and with all his friends and followers."

2. Then the bishop asked Maria and the others to please stand. He asked, "Do you believe in God the Father, Jesus, and the Holy Spirit?" Each of them answered, "I do." Then Bishop Lee sprinkled them with holy water to remind them of their Baptism.

3. Bishop Lee and Father Adams stretched out their hands over Maria and the others being confirmed. They prayed that the Holy Spirit would make them stronger friends and followers of Jesus.

4. Then Maria and Mrs. Lopez, Maria's **sponsor**, stood before the bishop. Mrs. Lopez placed her hand on Maria's shoulder and told Bishop Lee that Maria had chosen Angela as her Confirmation name.

46 Doctrine

★ Enriching the Lesson ★

Invite an older student who has been confirmed to speak to the class. Encourage him or her to bring pictures of Confirmation. Also invite the student's sponsor. Ask the sponsor to tell the story of how he or she helped the candidate to understand and live the Catholic faith.

Teaching Tips

In some dioceses the Confirmation candidates choose a Confirmation name. This biblical or saint's name signifies a Christian virtue that the candidate wishes to receive or exemplify. Remind the children that when they were baptized they received a baptismal name.

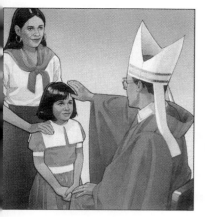

5. Bishop Lee dipped his thumb into a dish of blessed oil. Then he put his hand on Maria's head and made the sign of the cross on her forehead with his thumb. As he anointed her forehead, he said, "Angela, be sealed with the Gift of the Holy Spirit." She answered, "Amen."

6. The celebration did not end at church. Everyone went home and had a wonderful party.

Activity

Unscramble the words. Then write them on the lines below.

yaM   oyu   eb   flledi   ithw   'sdGo   Siprit

May you be filled with

God's Spirit.

New Word

★ **sponsor**   someone we choose at Confirmation to help us
★   live as a friend and follower of Jesus

Doctrine 47

Enriching the Lesson

To help the children understand the story "Maria's Confirmation," invite them to dramatize it. You will need a bowl of water and a small container of oil. Choose two children to take the parts of Father Adams and Bishop Lee. Half of the remaining children can be those who are going to be confirmed; the others can serve as their sponsors.

Focus on

Chrism   Chrism is a mixture of oil (often olive oil) and balsam (or balm), an aromatic resin obtained from various plants. Chrism is used in the sacraments of Baptism, Confirmation, and Holy Orders. It is also used to consecrate the walls of a new church building, altars, chalices, and patens. Chrism is blessed by the local bishop at the Chrism Mass during Holy Week.

Reviewing the Signs of Confirmation

Review with the children what the signs of the Holy Spirit's presence are. (*Laying on of hands and anointing with oil*) Ask:

- Find the picture of the laying on of hands on page 46. How does the bishop accomplish this? (*He stretches out his hands and prays over the ones being confirmed.*)

- For what does he pray? (*That the Holy Spirit would make the candidates stronger followers of Jesus*)

- How does the bishop anoint with oil? (*With the sign of the cross on the forehead*)

- What does the bishop say? (*"Be sealed with the Gift of the Holy Spirit."*)

- How does the Holy Spirit make us strong to live our faith in Jesus? (*Answers will vary.*)

- Who helps us prepare for the sacrament of Confirmation? (*Our sponsor*)

Defining the New Word

Have the children repeat the word *sponsor* and its definition after you. Ask them to use the word orally in a sentence, such as "My sponsor for Confirmation is (*Name.*)"

Step 3 / CONCLUSION

Learning How to Live Our Faith

Completing an Activity

Read aloud the directions for the activity on page 47. Help the children unscramble the words to create the sentence "May you be filled with God's Spirit."

Praying Together

Remind the children that the Holy Spirit comes to us when the bishop signs us with holy oil. Tell them that we ask the Spirit to help us become signs of God's presence to each other. Invite the children to make the response "Come, Holy Spirit!" after each phrase below.

As we remember our Baptism, . . . (*Response*)

As we become members of the Church, . . . (*R.*)

As we welcome others, . . . (*R.*)

As we become signs or your presence, . . . (*R.*)

We ask this in Jesus' name. Amen.

DAY 4
MORALITY

Objective

This lesson helps the children to understand that through Confirmation the Holy Spirit will help them to live as Christians.

Step 1 / INTRODUCTION

Learning About Our Lives

Reviewing Day 3

Review how we are signs of the presence of the Holy Spirit when we do acts of kindness. Focus the children's attention on the discovery table, on which you have placed bottle caps, paper plates, cans, and bottles for recycling. Ask: What do we do with these things? (*Throw them away or recycle them*)

Reading and Discussing the Story

Ask a volunteer to read the story "Martin Learns to Help Others" on page 48. Ask:

- Why did Martin and his friends clean the lot? (*To make a place to play, to do something good for the neighborhood*)

- Why did Martin want to do a good thing? (*He was confirmed and had received the Holy Spirit.*)

- Who gave Martin and his friends the strength to do something good? (*The Holy Spirit*)

Step 2 / DEVELOPMENT

Learning About Our Faith

Discovering Ways of Doing Good

Read the paragraph "With the Holy Spirit's Help" on page 49. Ask: Who helps us do the right thing? (*The Holy Spirit and the Christian community*) Show a copy of your parish bulletin. Read about some of the good things that people in your parish are doing for others, such as collecting food or making sandwiches for the hungry, raising money for charity, hosting meetings for the elderly, and so on.

48

Martin Learns to Help Others

Martin celebrated Confirmation this year. Martin decided to do something good for others. He knew that his younger sister, Meg, and her friends had no place to play. Martin felt bad but didn't know what he could do about it. Then Martin had an idea!

The next afternoon, Martin asked his friends to help him clean up the empty lot near their apartment house. It took a long time for Martin and his friends to pick up all the cans, broken glass, and garbage, but they didn't give up. They also cleaned the walls that were covered with spray paint.

Soon the little children had a safe and clean place to play. Meg and her friends were so happy. Martin was happy, too! The Holy Spirit gave Martin and his friends the strength to do something good for their neighborhood.

Enriching the Lesson

Invite the children to suggest ways to make the school grounds more beautiful. Use class time to collect litter and find things that are unsafe because they need repair. Present a list of suggestions to the principal or school administrator.

Talk about how we frequently waste paper in the classroom. Remind the children that using paper wisely saves trees. Collect used white paper in a special box for recycling.

With the Holy Spirit's Help

The Holy Spirit helped Martin know what he could do to help others. The Holy Spirit helps those who are confirmed live as Christians. We pray to the Holy Spirit to give us the strength to do the right thing. Our Christian community will help us as we make our world a better place in which to live.

Activity

What do you see the people doing that shows they are followers of Jesus?

CURRICULUM CONNECTION

Art and Science Confer with the art teacher about using recyclables and junk in an art project. Children can use foam trays, bottle caps, egg cartons, paper rolls, and so on to make funny self-portraits.

This lesson also correlates with a science lesson on conservation and preservation of natural resources. Review the three "R's": reduce, recycle, reuse.

Ask the children to think of something good that they can do. Print on the chalkboard "Holy Spirit, please help me to _____. Amen." Distribute sheets of lined paper. Direct the children to copy and finish this prayer. Collect these prayers and place them on the prayer table.

Step 3 / CONCLUSION

Learning How to Live Our Faith

Identifying Christian Actions

Ask the children to look at the pictures on page 49 of the text. Give them sufficient time to study the photographs. Ask them to describe what is happening in each picture. Ask:

- How are the people in each photograph acting as followers of Jesus?
- What can we do to help other people and to make the world a better place?
- Have you ever cleaned a street, recycled paper or cans, or walked for hunger?

Remind the children of the school's efforts to clean up litter, recycle refuse, or feed the hungry. Help the children appreciate that Jesus wants us to help others and to make our world a better place.

Objective

This lesson helps the children to pray responsorially so that they may be filled with the joy of the Holy Spirit.

Praying to the Holy Spirit

Invite the children to gather around the prayer table. Place a cruet of oil in the center of the table and light the candle. Practice with the children the response "Holy Spirit, fill our hearts with joy." When the children are comfortable with the response, lead them in the prayer to the Holy Spirit on page 50.

Explain to the children that one of the uses of oil is for anointing or blessing. Tell them that you will now bless them with oil and ask that the Holy Spirit fill their hearts with joy. While signing the foreheads of the children say this blessing: "(*Name*), may the Holy Spirit fill your heart with joy." Invite each child to respond "Amen."

You might wish to have the children sing a joyful song as they process back to their desks.

Making the World a Better Place

When the children have returned to their desks, ask:

- What did you do this week to make the world better for others? (*Answer will vary, but might include acts of kindness toward people or animals, or care of the environment, such as recycling.*)

- Who helped us do these good things? (*The Holy Spirit*)

- Who else do you know who does good things? (*Family members, parishioners, friends, classmates, and teachers*)

- How else does the Holy Spirit help us? (*The Holy Spirit helps us to pray, to be strong and brave, to be kind to others, to do the right thing.*)

Praying to the Holy Spirit

Teacher: Children, let us gather around this candle. Today we celebrate God's Spirit the Holy Spirit.

Teacher: When we wake up in the morning...

All: Holy Spirit, fill our hearts with joy.

Teacher: When we learn new things...

All: Holy Spirit, fill our hearts with joy.

Teacher: When we play with our friends...

All: Holy Spirit, fill our hearts with joy.

Teacher: When we get ready for bed...

All: Holy Spirit, fill our hearts with joy.

50   Prayer

Focus on

Praying to the Spirit Tell the children that when we pray to the Holy Spirit, we pray for the gifts that the Spirit gives—joy, love, peace, courage, and strength. The Holy Spirit is the Spirit of God and can be found in each of us. When we pray to the Spirit, we pray with joy and expectation, knowing that the Spirit of God is within us, urging us to pray, to ask of God what we need for ourselves and others.

CURRICULUM CONNECTION

Music You may want to have the children join in singing "Pentecost Prayer" along with the instrumental recording as they process back to their seats. The music is found on page 141 in the Program Director's Manual, Grade 1, of THIS IS OUR FAITH Music Program.

Chapter Review

Draw yourself doing something that shows you are a Catholic Christian, a friend and follower of Jesus.

1. What is another sacrament of welcome in which God sends us the Holy Spirit to make us strong friends and followers of Jesus?

Confirmation

2. At Confirmation, whom do we choose to help us live as friends and followers of Jesus?

sponsor

3. Talk about what happens at Confirmation that makes us feel even more a part of the Catholic community.

"You are signed with the seal of the Holy Spirit."
Based on Ephesians 1:13

Review 51

Enriching the Lesson

If older students are soon to celebrate Confirmation in your parish, invite the children to make congratulations cards for them. Print "Blessings on Your Confirmation" on the chalkboard. Encourage the children to draw a picture about Confirmation on the front of the card and print their own wish or message or copy the one on the chalkboard. Distribute the name of one Confirmation candidate to each child so that the children may personalize their cards.

Reviewing the Chapter

Read the directions for the drawing activity at the top of page 51. Ask the children to suggest actions they might draw. As the children are drawing, talk with them individually about their work.

Assist the children in writing the answers to questions 1 and 2 of the chapter review on the lines provided. Then gather the children into a sharing circle to discuss item 3. Be supportive of each child who participates in the discussion.

Reading the Scripture Verse

Read the Scripture verse based on Ephesians 1:13. Ask: Who says words like these during Confirmation? (*The bishop*) When does he say them? (*When he makes the sign of the cross on each candidate's forehead.*)

Using the Unit Organizer

Completing a graphic organizer such as a chart or table can help the children to organize information that has been presented in the unit. Organizers can enable the children to visualize their thinking and recognize relationships among ideas. This will give the children the opportunity to understand more completely the materials they have been studying.

Completing the Organizer

Have the children turn to page 52 in their books. Direct the children's attention to the Unit Organizer. Tell the children to read silently the incomplete statements in the balloons and write their answers on the lines provided. Tell them to draw the signs of Baptism on the banner and then read the statement about Confirmation and complete it on the lines in the gift boxes. Point out where to start. Then ask the children to complete the activity independently. If necessary, tell them that they may look back through the previous four chapters for help. When everyone has finished, have the children compare their responses with the class.

Looking Back: Self-Assessment

The critical reflection questions below give the children an opportunity to sharpen their thinking skills. The questions can be used as a class discussion or independent writing activity.

- Which was your favorite Scripture story in this unit? What did you like most about it?
- Which activity in this unit did you most enjoy? Why?
- Which picture in this unit did you like best? What did you like about it?

Start **Unit 1 Organizer**

Some communities I belong to are

Three of the seven sacraments are

Baptism has special signs. Here is picture of them.

Some important words about the sacrament of Confirmation are

52   Unit Organizer

Unit 1 Review

Choose a word in the box to finish each sentence.
Write the word on the line below the sentence.

> Catholic   Christians   community
>
> Confirmation   sacraments

1. Followers of Jesus are called *Christians* .

2. We belong to the Christian community called the

   Catholic Church.

3. Special signs and celebrations of Jesus' love for us that make him present to us now are called

   sacraments .

4. Another sacrament of welcome is called

   Confirmation .

Reviewing the Unit

The purpose of the Unit Review is to reinforce concepts presented in the preceding four chapters and to check the children's understanding. After explaining the directions, give the children sufficient time to complete the two-page review. Answer any questions they may have as you check their work.

Testing

After the students have completed the Unit Review, you may wish to distribute copies of the Unit 1 Test from the Test Booklet.

Project

If time permits, you may wish to do the following project with the children.

Before the session, use a long sheet of newsprint or white shelf paper to make a scroll. Print the words *We Belong* at the top. Then invite some of the adult members of your parish community to sign the scroll.

Show the scroll to the children. Read the signatures. Then explain that the scroll reminds us that we belong to God's family.

Invite the children to sign their names on the scroll. When all have signed the scroll, say a short spontaneous prayer telling God how happy we are to be a part of the Catholic community.

Unit **1** Review

5. Think about the story "Mark's Baptism." Number the pictures in the right order. Use the numbers **1** through **5.**

2

4

5

1

3

BEING A GOOD LISTENER

A good listener tunes in to the person who is speaking. What's wrong with the two pictures at the top of the page?

How can I tune in to someone who is speaking?

I can tune in to the person who is speaking by using eye contact, by paying attention, and by being quiet.

Day to Day   55

Day to Day ~~~

Introducing Day to Day: Skills for Christian Living

The five lessons of this feature focus on different skills for communicating about feelings. The first lesson focuses on how to be a good listener. Subsequent lessons look at specific ways in which listeners respond, how and when to express their feelings, and what to do when a message is communicated, but is misunderstood or is not heard.

Objective

This lesson helps the children appreciate that listening is a sign of respect for the person who is speaking and helps them become aware of three skills for effective listening: eye contact, paying attention, and remaining quiet.

Introducing the Lesson

Read aloud the sentence on page 55. Ask the children what the words "tunes in" mean. Explain that this lesson will focus on skills for tuning in to someone who is talking. (Don't identify the skills until later in the lesson.)

Preparing to Use Role-Plays

Ask six children to volunteer for role-playing. Pair three speakers with three listeners. Speakers will talk for about one minute on topics such as summer activities, Saturday events, family interactions, and so on. Each listener is given a specific role to enact in turn. Do not let the rest of the group know what the listeners will demonstrate. While the speakers are speaking in turn, listener 1 will look out the window; listener 2 will tie shoe laces; listener 3 will interrupt the speaker and talk at the same time.

Enacting and Discussing the Role-Plays

Have each pair act out their particular role-play. Follow each role-play with discussion guided by the following questions.

- Who was the speaker and who was the listener in this situation?

- What happened in this role-play? Did the listener really listen to the person who was speaking? What was the listener doing that

Lesson continues on page 56.

made it difficult to really listen to what was being said?

- How did the person feel who was doing the talking, but not really being listened to?
- What would the listener have to do to demonstrate better listening? (*Maintain eye contact; pay attention; remain quiet while the other person is speaking.*)

Reenacting the Role-Plays

After identifying what the listener would have to do to demonstrate better listening, have the children reenact the role-plays, this time substituting the more appropriate listening skill. Ask the class to identify what was different, in terms of listening behavior and how the person being listened to felt.

Analyzing Pictures

Direct the children's attention to the pictures on page 55. Reinforce what was introduced by the role-plays by having the class identify the behaviors in the pictures. Summarize by having the children name the three things they can do to demonstrate good listening: maintain eye contact, pay attention, and remain quiet while the other person is speaking. Read with the class the answer to the question "How can I tune in to someone who is speaking?"

Completing an Activity

Ask the children to draw a picture in the space provided on page 56 that shows them tuning in to someone who is speaking. Have the children share their drawings when completed.

Following Jesus

Read aloud the statements in the Following Jesus box. Ask the children to explain how being a good listener might help us to be a follower of Jesus. (*Being a good listener shows that we care about and have respect for the person who is speaking. Jesus asks us to care about each other.*)

Concluding the Lesson

Reinforce the concepts presented in this lesson by calling the children's attention to the use, or nonuse, of these skills in daily interactions. Give examples of effective and poor listening behavior to the children.

Invite a volunteer to pray the prayer in the prayer box. Then have the entire class pray it together.

56

Activity

Draw a picture of you tuning in to someone who is speaking.

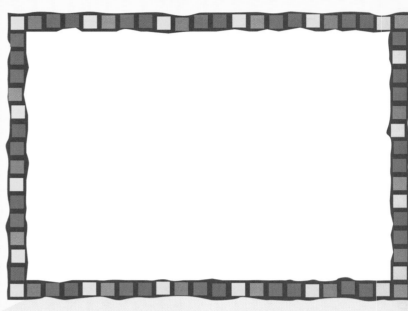

Being a good listener shows respect for the person who is speaking.

Following Jesus

Jesus asks us to care about each other. Listening to someone is a special way to say, "I care about you." By being a good listener, I show care for the other person.

A Prayer

Jesus, you always listened well to others. Help us to be good listeners, too. Help us show our care for others by listening carefully to one another. Amen.

OPENING DOORS
A Take-Home Magazine™

Growing Closer

A FAMILY COAT-OF-ARMS is a symbol of what makes a family special. Your family is special, too! Make a family coat-of-arms. Draw a symbol of your family. Then ask your family to add their own symbols.

EVERYONE LIKES TO LOOK at family photos! Ask your family to look at photos with you. Remember that photos remind us of special people, places, and times. Enjoy this special time with your family!

Looking Ahead

Unit 2 will focus on the process of reconciliation. In the Scripture story of the Prodigal Son, the children will learn that God will always forgive us when we are sorry. And we, in turn, are called to forgive others. As Catholics we can celebrate God's forgiveness in a special way in the sacrament of Reconciliation.

8   Answers for page 5: holy water, Baptism; Eucharist, Jesus; © 1994 Silver Burdett Ginn, Inc.
    Bible, God; lighted candle, pray

Opening Doors

A Take-Home Magazine

The five removable, family-directed supplements entitled *Opening Doors: A Take-Home Magazine* provide you, the teacher, with a unique opportunity to involve parents or guardians more fully in their child's catechetical program. Each magazine will include the following features.

A Closer Look
An article relating the unit theme in the text to a particular aspect of the Mass

Being Catholic
An article explaining a particular aspect of our Catholic heritage

Growing Closer
Suggested activities to help the family integrate faith into everyday life

Looking Ahead
A preview of the next unit in THIS IS OUR FAITH, Grade 2

Sending the Magazine Home

As you complete Unit 1 with your class, assist the children in carefully removing *Opening Doors: A Take-Home Magazine* (two pages) from their texts by separating the magazine pages from the book along the perforations. Demonstrate how to fold the two pages, forming an eight-page booklet.

When the magazines are folded, take time to explain each section of the magazine to the children. Allow the children to ask any questions they may have. Ask the children to take the magazine home and encourage their families to read it with them and participate in the suggested activities. You may wish to attach a letter of your own, encouraging the family to use the magazine each time their child brings it home.

Follow the same procedure in sending home the remaining magazines for Units 2, 3, 4, and 5.

parishioners are and where they live, but how much do you know about your Catholic brothers and sisters outside the parish?

According to the *1989 Official Catholic Directory*, there are 54,918,989 Catholics in the United States today. This number makes up 22.48% of the total U.S. population. These Catholics live in 34 archdioceses and 154 dioceses throughout the country.

If you look at the chart, you will see how many Catholics live in each state and what percentage of the state's total population is Catholic.

State	Total Pop.	Catholic Pop.	Cath. %
Missouri	4,954,295	788,048	16
Montana	766,553	130,194	17
Nebraska	1,567,902	329,925	21
Nevada	1,002,570	147,000	15
New Hampshire	1,027,008	295,930	29
New Jersey	7,595,800	3,072,758	40
New Mexico	1,543,585	459,868	30
New York	18,047,118	6,771,854	38
North Carolina	6,230,946	140,288	2
North Dakota	677,689	173,436	26
Ohio	10,764,839	2,219,167	21
Oklahoma	3,106,100	143,226	5
Oregon	2,690,550	282,390	10
Pennsylvania	11,979,366	3,579,707	30
Rhode Island	986,000	625,170	63
South Carolina	3,425,000	75,382	2
South Dakota	698,316	146,906	21
Tennessee	4,745,400	127,220	3
Texas	16,621,406	3,227,019	19
Utah	1,678,000	69,944	4
Vermont	541,000	147,816	27
Virginia	5,856,990	347,490	6
Washington	4,400,826	434,606	10
West Virginia	1,919,000	107,379	6
Wisconsin	4,890,364	1,531,706	31
Wyoming	482,088	60,120	12

Fishes, asking what water is, went to a wise fish. He told them that it was all around them, yet they still thought that they were thirsty.

—a Sufi saying

The Sacred Around Us

From early on, we teach our children to make the sign of the cross, saying, "In the name of the Father, and of the Son, and of the Holy Spirit." It reminds us of the special nature of our Christian belief in the Trinity — three persons yet one God. We believe in a God who created us out of pure love that decided to share itself in abundance. We believe in a God who loved us so much that becoming one with us in Jesus was a complete expression of that love. We believe in a God who remains with us in the Spirit.

The sign of the cross also reminds us of one of our most distinctive characteristics as Catholics: our appreciation for and use of symbols.

Our faith gives us a kind of spiritual sight that transforms what we see and enables us to see more than the obvious. Symbols represent something beyond the obvious. (A cross is more than a horizontal and vertical beam; Eucharist, more than bread and wine.) Symbols also reveal, or make really present. We believe, for example, that God's grace is revealed in the sacraments. We don't simply receive an explanation of what is represented in a sacrament. We experience and receive as gift the actual, or real presence of God in these special moments.

Why don't we always "see" it this way? For one reason or another, we all seem to forget at times that all life is sacred, that God is present everywhere. We know God's love through persons, places, events, nature, and even history. But we must make a deliberate choice to see our world in this way, through eyes of faith. And though faith is a gift, without the help of those special persons, places, and events in our lives that have helped us "see," we may never have recognized the gift.

Perhaps, then, the greatest gift we can give our children is the gift of a "sacra-mentality," a way of seeing and thinking that recognizes the sacred all around us.

Take the time to look around at the people in your home, at the people in church, at the movements and the actions of the various liturgical ministers at Mass. Take a good look at the symbols of our faith that reveal to us and to our children that indeed we live in a world of grace and that all of life is a gift that is ours to receive.

U.S. Catholics Today

In religious education classes, your child is being taught that the Catholic Church is a community — a group of people much like a family. Most families have a pretty good idea who the family members are and where they live. If you have participated for a while in your

Percentage of Catholics in U.S. Population

State	Total Pop.	Catholic Pop.	Cath. %
Alabama	3,464,335	126,774	4
Alaska	401,769	45,940	11
Arizona	3,121,200	577,920	19
Arkansas	2,360,000	69,416	3
California	27,538,436	6,137,006	22
Colorado	3,239,671	485,236	15
Connecticut	3,242,500	1,362,970	42
Delaware	814,300	134,598	17
District of Columbia	2,188,000	395,016	18
Florida	11,748,250	1,494,360	13
Georgia	6,630,555	216,368	3
Hawaii	1,062,344	191,520	18
Idaho	1,002,000	70,642	7
Illinois	11,490,981	3,535,524	31
Indiana	5,360,025	695,551	13
Iowa	2,895,039	510,388	18
Kansas	2,407,652	373,770	16
Kentucky	3,697,674	376,688	10
Louisiana	4,444,421	1,404,411	32
Maine	1,124,660	279,000	25
Maryland	2,548,947	438,016	17
Massachusetts	5,679,393	2,842,040	50
Michigan	9,010,107	2,281,181	25
Minnesota	4,072,371	1,097,821	27
Mississippi	2,548,981	99,197	4

Symbols All Around Us

Your child is already aware of many common symbols. Use the material on these two pages to help your child reflect on the importance of symbolism. Together, discover the Catholic Christian meaning behind some symbols used in church.

Symbols point the way to a place or a person. Symbols remind us of special people, places, or things.

4

these symbols you already know. More symbols are on this page. Can you name them? Then finish each sentence.

Holy water reminds us of our

_____.

The Eucharist is a very special meal that _____ shares with us.

A Bible reminds us of one way _____ speaks to us.

A lighted candle reminds us that God is with us when we _____.

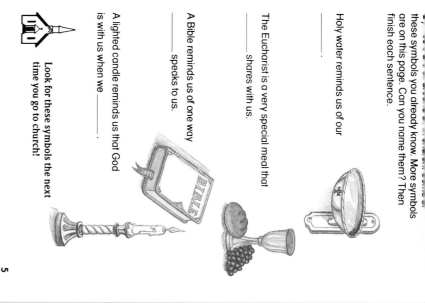

Look for these symbols the next time you go to church!

5

60

UNIT 2

Our Church Celebrates Reconciliation

Have you ever said you're sorry and been forgiven?

Introducing the UNIT

Read aloud the unit-focus question on page 61. Invite the children to share their experiences of sorrow and forgiveness. Tell the children that in Unit 2 they will learn about the sacrament that celebrates God's forgiveness.

New Words

right
responsibility
sin
reconciliation
grace
sacrament of
 Reconciliation
confess
penance
contrition
absolution

Unit Aim

To help the children recognize daily acts of reconciliation and the sacrament of Reconciliation as opportunities to express sorrow and to ask God's forgiveness for our sins.

Doctrinal Summaries

CHAPTER 5
God calls us to be responsible for and to care for others, especially people in need. We are also called to care for the earth.

CHAPTER 6
God gives us the freedom to make choices. When we choose to do what we know is wrong or when we choose to hurt someone on purpose, we sin.

CHAPTER 7
God always loves us, even when we hurt others and do wrong. God will always forgive us when we are sorry. God wants us always to be willing to forgive others, too.

CHAPTER 8
In the sacrament of Reconciliation, we say we are sorry to God. We ask God to forgive us for our sins. We tell God that we will try not to sin again. God forgives us through Jesus Christ and the Church.

Note:
As you prepare this unit, you may wish to refer to the reference section, *Our Catholic Heritage*, beginning on page 327.

Additional resources for Unit 2 include a Unit Test and a Family Letter as well as a video and selections from THIS IS OUR FAITH Music Program. You might also find it helpful to preview *Saints and Other Holy People* and *Prayer Celebrations* for possibilites to enhance the unit.

5

We Have a Responsibility to Care

Objectives ～～～～～

To help the children

■ Recognize that Christians have a responsibility to care about others.

■ Understand that Jesus teaches us to be generous in our caring.

■ Identify Saint Elizabeth of Hungary as a model of Christian caring.

■ Discover ways to be thoughtful, generous, and caring.

■ Pray to become a caring community and review the chapter.

Chapter Outline ～～～～～～～

	Step 1 **Learning About Our Lives**	**Step 2** **Learning About Our Faith**	**Step 3** **Learning How to Live Our Faith**
Day 1	■ Review meaning of *community*. ■ Introduce the chapter. *ABOUT 5 MINUTES*	■ Interpret photographs. ■ Discover our call to care. ■ Present the doctrine. ■ Introduce new words. *ABOUT 20 MINUTES*	■ Complete an activity. *ABOUT 5 MINUTES*
Day 2	■ Review new words. *ABOUT 5 MINUTES*	■ Present a Bible story. ■ Dramatize the Bible story. ■ Understand generosity. *ABOUT 15 MINUTES*	■ Complete an activity. ■ Show how we share. *ABOUT 10 MINUTES*
Day 3	■ Decode a message. *ABOUT 5 MINUTES*	■ Introduce the theme. ■ Read and interpret the play. ■ Complete an activity. *ABOUT 20 MINUTES*	■ Pray together. ■ Connect with family caring. *ABOUT 5 MINUTES*
Day 4	■ Respond by acts of caring. *ABOUT 10 MINUTES*	■ Become friends of Jesus. *ABOUT 10 MINUTES*	■ Complete an activity. ■ Share examples of caring. ■ Pray together. *ABOUT 10 MINUTES.*
Day 5	**Prayer** Prepare for prayer; pray a litany; and offer gifts for the poor and needy. **Review** Complete a cartoon; review the chapter; and explain the Scripture verse.		

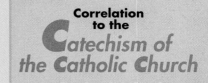

Plan Ahead ∿∿∿∿∿∿∿

Preparing Your Class	Materials Needed
Day 1 Read over the lesson prior to class. If enriching the lesson, gather clothesline, clothespins, and colored paper and draw a New Word poster.	■ pencils
Day 2 Prepare coins and props for Scripture story. Gather magazine and calendar pictures of people caring. If enriching the lesson, gather all necessary items.	■ basket ■ quarters, dimes, pennies ■ Bible prop box ■ magazine, calendar pictures ■ drawing paper, paste or tape
Day 3 Write a secret code message on chalkboard. Make paper "gold coins" for each child. Place basket on prayer table.	■ paper circles, three inches in diameter ("gold coins") ■ basket ■ posterboard
Day 4 Read over the lesson prior to class. Prepare posterboard on which to place family photos or drawings.	■ posterboard ■ glue or tape
Day 5 Read over the lesson prior to class. Decorate the prayer table. Get recorded cassette or printed music for "Gifts in My Heart" or a familiar song of thanksgiving.	■ pictures of people caring ■ basket ■ crayons, felt-tip markers ■ gifts from home for poor ■ recorded or printed music

Additional Resources

As you plan this chapter, consider using the following materials from The Resourceful Teacher Package.

■ *Classroom Activity Sheets 5* and *5a*

■ *Family Activity Sheets 5* and *5a*

■ *Chapter 5 Test*

■ *Prayers for Every Day*

■ *Projects: Grade 2*

You may also wish to refer to the following Big Book.

■ *We Celebrate the Sacraments,* pages 13–15

In preparing the children for the Sunday readings, you may wish to use Silver Burdett Ginn's *Getting Ready for Sunday* student and teacher materials.

Books for the Journey

Frederick. Leo Lionni. Knopf, 1973. Poetically and imaginatively reveals the truth that everyone has a responsibility to do what she or he does best for the community's well-being.

The Giving Tree. Shel Silverstein. HarperCollins, 1964. To never give up caring is the essence of responsibility.

More Books for the Journey

The Happy Prince. Oscar Wilde. Simon & Schuster, 1992. Tells how the beautiful, golden, jewel-studded statue and the little swallow give all they have to the poor.

The Letter on Light Blue Stationery. Joy Berry. Kids Media Group, 1991. A story to help teach children that everyone has value and different gifts.

Reduced Classroom Activities

Name

We Have a Responsibility to Care

In each box below, draw a picture that shows how you were responsible and showed your care. Let someone who knows about your good deeds sign the coupons. Return your finished pictures for use in the class graph.

I made my home a better place by . . .	I showed responsibility for God's earth by . . .
Signature:	Signature:
I respected another's rights at school by . . .	To practice being responsible, I . . .
Signature:	Signature:

To the Teacher: This activity follows the story "A Woman's Generous Gift." Create a class graph by providing headings labeled HOME, SCHOOL, EARTH, and OTHER.

Chapter 5   We Have a Responsibility to Care   This Is Our Faith 2   **5**

Name

Love One Another

Color this banner and then cut along the heavy black lines. Hang the banner in your room. The words will remind you to love and care for others.

To the Teacher: This activity could be used as an introduction, a reinforcement, or a review of the chapter.

5a   This Is Our Faith 2   Chapter 5   We Have a Responsibility to Care

61c Chapter Organizer

Background for the Teacher

CALL TO CHRISTIAN RESPONSIBILITY

Jesus calls his disciples to a new kind of responsibility. Christian responsibility surpasses the normal duty to respect the rights and needs of others. It is rooted in love of God and love of neighbor. In the Acts of the Apostles, Christians were recognized by their love for one another. "Charity is the greatest social commandment. It respects others and their rights. It requires the practice of justice, and it alone makes us capable of it." (*Catechism of the Catholic Church*, #1889) Our charity must extend to more than friends and acquaintances; it must extend to strangers, enemies, and those persons less fortunate than ourselves.

The gospels clearly tell us that in response to God's love for us, we must look beyond ourselves as individuals and as a Christian community and be responsive to the needs of others.

The hallmark of the early Christian communities was the members' obvious love for and sense of responsibility to all. Their example verified the words of Jesus before he died: "This I command you: love one another" (John 15:17). It is our Church's traditional teaching to give all that we have and all that we can offer to others. We cannot set limits on our Christian commitment. We should adopt a lifestyle that reflects a generosity of spirit. The chapter's Scripture story "A Woman's Generous Gift" (based on Mark 12:41–44) provides an example of such generosity.

MODELS OF RESPONSIBILITY

Second graders have begun to understand that people have responsibilities to one another. Their family, school, and peer-group experiences have made them increasingly aware that everyone has needs and is needed. The children have begun to realize that we all have rights and responsibilities and that we all need to give and receive love.

You can heighten the children's awareness of individual responsibility to God and of group commitment by treating each child as a responsible individual. At this age, children have limited abilities to reach out to those in need. However, you can continue to provide role models for them by pointing out people who care for and help others.

Traditionally, the saints have been models of that Christian responsibility and charity required of the disciples of Jesus. Small children also need to see the daily examples of Christian caring. They need to recognize familiar people engaged in living the mandate of love of God and neighbor. It is important to give and discuss specific examples of caring, thoughtfulness, and generosity.

Objective

This lesson helps the children recognize that as members of a Christian community they have a responsibility to care for others.

Step 1 / INTRODUCTION

Learning About Our Lives

Reviewing the Meaning of Community

Help the children recall that in Unit 1 they learned that a community is a group of people who share something important together. Explain that each member of a community has certain responsibilities.

Introducing the Chapter

Ask the children to open their books to page 62. Invite a volunteer to read aloud the chapter title. Print the word *responsibility* on the chalkboard. Show that the word *response* is part of the word *responsibility*. Ask: What is a response? (*An answer, a reply, a reaction*) Print the words *response* and *ability* under the word *responsibility*. Stress that we all have the ability to respond to something if we choose to do so.

Invite a child to read the chapter-focus question on page 62. Accept all answers. (*Help out, watch my little sister, pick up my toys, do my school work, feed my pet, and so on*) Ask the children to think of other ways their families need them.

Step 2 / DEVELOPMENT

Learning About Our Faith

Interpreting Photographs

Direct the children to look at the photograph at the top of page 62. Ask a volunteer to describe what is happening in the picture. Ask: What can we do to help physically challenged children? Encourage the children to look at and speak respectfully to all persons. When people are treated with respect and courtesy, they will tell us their stories, indicate their needs, and share their gifts. Read the first sentence aloud and ask: How are you needed in our school? By your friends? (*Answers will vary.*)

62

---

5 We Have a Responsibility to Care

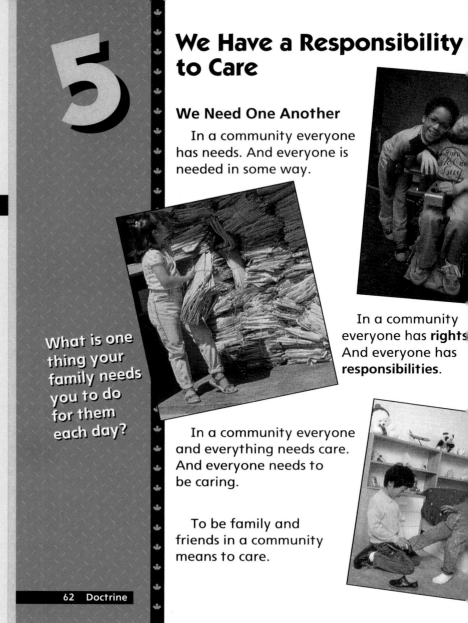

We Need One Another

In a community everyone has needs. And everyone is needed in some way.

What is one thing your family needs you to do for them each day?

In a community everyone has **rights** And everyone has **responsibilities**.

In a community everyone and everything needs care. And everyone needs to be caring.

To be family and friends in a community means to care.

62 Doctrine

 Cultural Awareness

Redirect attention to the photograph on page 62 of the boy who is using the wheelchair. Ask the children if they know anyone who uses a wheelchair. Help the children appreciate that people with disabilities are not different. Like everyone else, they have rights and responsibilities. They have needs and they want to be needed. They need care and they want to be caring.

Enriching the Lesson

Distribute sheets of colored paper (about $8^1/_2$ inches by $5^1/_2$ inches). Direct the children to trace a hand on the paper and cut out the handprint. Have them print on the handprint one way they help their families. Assist the children in attaching the handprints with clothespins to a sturdy string. On a strip of paper, print with a marker "We have a responsibility to care" and attach it to the line of caring handprints.

We Care for Others

Jesus teaches us that we must care for others. He asks us to help others when they are in need. Jesus wants his friends to become a community of people who care.

Activity

Draw a circle around the people who are showing care.

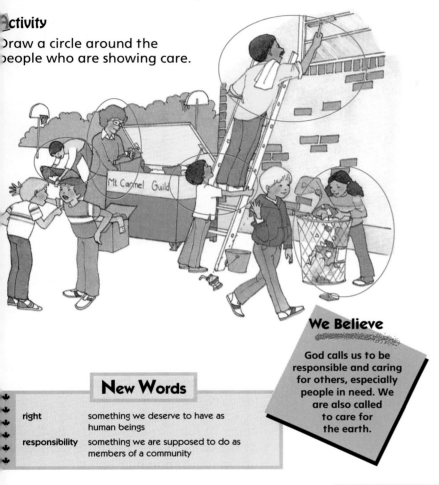

Mt Carmel Guild

We Believe

God calls us to be responsible and caring for others, especially people in need. We are also called to care for the earth.

New Words

right something we deserve to have as human beings

responsibility something we are supposed to do as members of a community

Doctrine 63

Discuss the second photograph by asking: What is this girl doing? Is she responsible? Stress that we all can do something to help recycle and use our natural resources wisely. Have a volunteer read the sentences opposite the photograph.

Direct attention to the third photograph. Ask: Who needs care and who is being responsible? What are some ways we are responsible for younger children? (*We help them pick up toys, babysit them, play with them.*) Read the sentences opposite the photograph aloud with the children.

Discovering Our Call to Care

Invite a volunteer to read the paragraph at the top of page 63. Recall earlier responses to caring for others in community. Ask: How does Jesus ask us to be responsible for people in the community? (*Help others in need, care for others*)

Presenting the Doctrine

Present the We Believe statements. Stress that because of God's love for us, all Christians have a responsibility to care for others.

Introducing the New Words

Introduce the new word *right* on page 63. Read aloud the definition. Read aloud the definition of *responsibility*. Help the children learn the definitions of the words by asking them to repeat the words and sentences aloud several times.

Step 3 / CONCLUSION

Learning How to Live Our Faith

Completing an Activity

Instruct the children to look at the illustration on page 63. Read the directions and allow the children time to circle the pictures of people who are showing care. Ask them to explain their reasons for not circling some people and their activities.

Enriching the Lesson

Show a poster on which you have drawn a scroll with the words *responsibility* and *rights* printed on it. *Life, freedom, health, education, safety,* and *happiness* are printed around *rights* in pastel colors. Ask: Who can name a right? Can you name any other rights you have as members of your family or as students? Around the word *responsibility*, print some things second graders are supposed to do.

Focus on

Human Rights Catholic social teaching lists human rights as the right to life, liberty, security, food, clothing, shelter, health care, leisure, free speech, education, religion, family life, work, property, just wage; also, the right to participate in government, to assemble, and to vote. These are political, economic, and social rights granted to all regardless of age, color, or race.

Objective

This lesson helps children understand that God asks us to be responsible and generous in our caring for others.

Step 1 / INTRODUCTION

Learning About Our Lives

Reviewing the New Words

Review the meaning of *right* and *responsibility*. Ask: Have you thought of any other ways you can be a responsible, caring, and generous person? If you have made an optional New Words poster, add these responses to the poster.

Step 2 / DEVELOPMENT

Learning About Our Faith

Presenting a Bible Story

Invite the children to follow along silently as you read aloud the story "A Woman's Generous Gift." When you have finished, ask the following questions as you discuss the story with them.

- Where did Jesus and his friends go to pray? (*The Temple*)
- What did they see people doing? (*Putting money in collection boxes*)
- Whom would this money help? (*The poor*)
- What did the rich people give? (*Gold coins*)
- What did the working people give? (*Silver coins*)
- What did the woman who had little money give? (*Two pennies*)
- What did Jesus say to his friends? (*"Look at the woman who has little money. She put in more than all the rest."*)
- Why were Jesus' friends surprised at what Jesus said? (*The other people gave gold and silver.*)
- Why did Jesus think the poor woman's gift was the greatest gift? (*She gave everything she had.*)

A Woman's Generous Gift

One day, Jesus and his friends went to the Temple in Jerusalem to pray. They saw many people putting money in the collection boxes for those in need.

Rich people dressed in beautiful clothes put in gold coins. Other people dressed in working clothes put in silver coins.

Then another woman walked by. She was dressed in old clothes. The woman put two pennies in the box.

Jesus and his friends watched the woman. Jesus said to his friends, "Look at the woman who has little money. She put in more than all the rest."

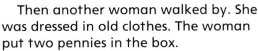

64   Scripture

🍎 Teaching Tips

Children will grow in self-esteem if they feel that they can influence what happens in their lives. When children act responsibly, they *do* make a difference. They need to experience making a contribution that is appreciated or viewed as significant by others. Expressing your approval or appreciation of the children helps to increase their self-esteem.

★ Enriching the Lesson ★

Distribute paper "gold coins" about 3 inches in diameter to each child. Encourage the children to print on their coins one way they will be generous today. Invite each child to place the coin in the basket you have put on the discovery table and say, "I give everything today." All sing "Children of God" from THIS IS OUR FAITH Music Program, Grade 1, after all have placed the gold coins of caring in the basket.

"What do you mean?" his friends asked. "She put in just two pennies. The others put in gold and silver."

"But they gave just a little bit of what they had," Jesus said. "The last woman gave everything she had."

Based on Mark 12:41–44

Activity

Draw or find a picture of someone who is responsible and shares with others in need.

Teaching Tips

For centuries, Christian artists have represented Christianity in action through stained glass windows, statues, and paintings. Children are comfortable expressing their responses to Christian actions through drawings or other images. Having children apply concretely what they have learned through visual representation helps them to relate their learning experience to real-life situations.

Dramatizing the Story

Invite the children to act out the Scripture story as you narrate it. Assign the parts: a child to hold a large basket to collect the coins; several children to be workers; a girl to be the generous woman; a boy to be Jesus; and the remainder of the class to be Jesus' disciples. Simple props needed are a basket, quarters wrapped in gold foil, dimes, two pennies, and costumes from the Bible prop box.

Understanding Generosity

Explain to the children that the woman who had little money showed how much she cared for others by giving all she had to those who had even less. It may be natural to want to keep for ourselves the little that we have. But Jesus calls all of us to be responsible and to care. We show our care by sharing what we have. It did not matter to Jesus that some people gave more because they were wealthy. Jesus wants us to give generously no matter how much or how little we have. Jesus wants us to care for others, as well as for the earth, from which we receive many gifts.

Step 3 / CONCLUSION

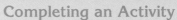

Learning How to Live Our Faith

Completing an Activity

Provide magazine pictures or calendar photographs that depict people caring. Distribute small sheets of drawing paper. Invite the children to choose a photograph or draw a picture showing people who care and share with others in need. Use paste or tape to attach these pictures to the space provided on page 65.

Showing How We Share

Ask the children to think quietly about how they give generously. Ask: What if you had three friends over to play and had only one apple? One video game for two players? One soccer ball? Invite oral responses. Comment on creative ways of sharing. Ask: What would Jesus expect you to do as one of his followers? (*To share generously and care for others*)

65

Objective

This lesson helps the children identify Saint Elizabeth of Hungary as a model of the Christian responsibility to care.

Step 1 / INTRODUCTION

Learning About Our Lives

Decoding a Message

To review the main theme of this chapter, challenge the children to break the code and decipher the hidden message. (Number the letters of the alphabet: 1=a, 2=b, 3=c, 4=d, 5=e, and so on.) Assist the class by printing the alphabet on the chalkboard. Call on volunteers to print the numbers above the letters as the class prompts them. Code "to love" as 20 15 12 14 22 5. Invite half of the class to code "to share." (20 15 19 8 1 18 5) and the other half to code "to be friends." (20 15 2 5 6 18 9 5 14 4 19)

or . . .

Encourage the children to think of a person who is very good to them or who cares for them. Ask: What is this person like? (*Is nice, loves me, gives me things, takes care of me, makes me happy*) On a posterboard, print "A Recipe for Caring." List the qualities that the children offer in their responses. Other qualities may be added during the week.

Step 2 / DEVELOPMENT

Learning About Our Faith

Introducing the Theme

Explain to the children that being responsible and caring for others is not always easy. Some people are jealous of good works and can say things that hurt or discourage us.

Reading the Play

Tell the children that "A Saint Who Cared" is about a special queen who continued to care even when it was difficult. Read the play with the children. Individual parts may be assigned to single readers or to groups of children.

A Saint Who Cared

Narrator: A long time ago, a woman named Elizabeth married a king named Ludwig. They lived in a country called Hungary.

Ludwig: I am happy we built a hospital to care for sick people. The hungry people are grateful when we give them baskets of food.

Narrator: Soon King Ludwig had to go to war. While he was away, he became very sick.

Messenger: My Queen, I'm so sad to tell you that your husband has died.

Elizabeth: What terrible news. My heart is broken. Let us pray for King Ludwig and for all the soldiers who have died.

Narrator: In her sadness, Elizabeth continued to care for her family, as well as for those who were poor or sick.

Enriching the Lesson

Invite someone from the parish Saint Vincent De Paul Society or a local food pantry to speak to the children about the work the helpers or volunteers do in the organization and the people they help. Request that the speaker suggest some ways small children can be involved; for example, by contributing a box of cereal or a can of food or by recycling used paper or plastic bags.

CURRICULUM CONNECTION

Social Studies Explain to the children how many communities offer services to people in need. Firefighters, police officers, clergy members, merchants, teachers, tutors, nurses, first aid volunteers, doctors, and social workers are involved in the welfare of the community. Many donate their time and resources to all in the community, especially the poor and disadvantaged, the homeless and unemployed.

Enemy #1: Elizabeth gives too much money to the poor. She is spending all the money of the kingdom.

Enemy #2: We must send her away from the castle and take over the king's treasury.

Narrator: Elizabeth and her four children were forced to leave the castle.

Elizabeth: Do not worry, children. God will take care of us. We will continue to care for the sick. Somehow we will fill these baskets with food for the poor.

Narrator: Elizabeth spent the rest of her life caring for those who were sick or hungry. She is a saint who really cared for others.

Activity

Choose a word to complete each sentence. Put a check (✔)by the things that you will try to do.

| smile | pray |
| help | share |

Pray
for others.

Smile
at someone.

Help
at home.

Share
food or toys.

Interpreting the Story

Ask the following questions.

- How did Queen Elizabeth show her responsibility to care? (*She cared for the sick and fed the poor.*) What happened to her husband? (*While away at war, he became sick and died.*)

- Who did not like Queen Elizabeth's good works? (*Her enemies*)

- Why did they not want her to care for the sick and feed the hungry? (*They thought she was spending too much money.*)

- Who helped Queen Elizabeth and her children continue to care for the sick and the hungry? (*God*)

- Who helps you to continue to do good works? (*God, parents, grandparents, teachers, friends*)

Completing an Activity

Ask the children to use the words above the baskets on page 67 to complete the sentences in the baskets. When all have finished, invite the class to complete the sentences orally.

Step 3 / CONCLUSION

Learning How to Live Our Faith

Praying Together

Distribute another paper gold coin to each child. Invite the children to print the name of a person who, like Queen Elizabeth, helps them to care for others in need. When all have finished, invite the children to bring their coins and gather around the prayer table. Ask them to share the person's name or story with the group as they drop the gold coin into the basket on the prayer table. (*My mother helps me to care for my little sister, my dad takes me to Grandma's house to visit because she is lonely, and so on.*) Close by reciting the "Glory Be to the Father" together or as an echo prayer.

Connecting with Families

Invite the children to ask family members to share how they care about other people. Have the children bring to the next session a photograph or a drawing of their family members helping others.

🍎 Teaching Tips

If you have invited a guest speaker, integrate the speaker's message with the content of this chapter. Follow up that message with an action. Suggest ways that the children and their families may become involved in the speaker's ministry or service.

DAY 4
MORALITY

Objective

This lesson helps the children discover examples of thoughtfulness, generosity, and caring.

Step 1 / INTRODUCTION

Learning About Our Lives

Responding by Acts of Caring

Invite the children to share how they or family members show Christian responsibility to care. They may show photographs, drawings, or recount stories. Affirm all the wonderful ways that second graders can become involved. Tape or paste the pictures to posterboard or pin to a bulletin board. Entitle the poster "Our Family Cares."

Step 2 / DEVELOPMENT

Learning About Our Faith

Becoming Friends of Jesus

Invite a volunteer to read the first paragraph of "Friends of Jesus" on page 68. Allow time for the children to place the letter *G* beside the picture of the boys sharing raisins. Ask: When are we generous? (*When we share everything, even the things we save for ourselves*) Call on another volunteer to read the second paragraph. Allow time for printing the letter *T* near the picture of the child and his grandmother. Ask: How can we be thoughtful of others in our home? (*Answers will vary.*) Invite a volunteer to read the last paragraph on page 68. Allow time for placing the letter *C* near the picture of a child including another at play. Ask: What are some ways we can care about others at school? (*Answers will vary.*) Stress that to be good disciples of Jesus, we need to be generous, thoughtful, and caring.

Step 3 / CONCLUSION

Learning How to Live Our Faith

Completing an Activity

Read aloud the directions for completing the poem on page 69. Circulate around the room to assist the children in writing their responses

Friends of Jesus

As friends and followers of Jesus, we have a responsibility to be generous, thoughtful, and caring. Jesus teaches us how to give to others. Sometimes we are willing to share what we don't need or want. Jesus asks us to be willing to share everything, even the things we have saved just for ourselves.

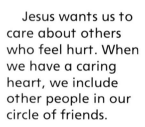

As Jesus' followers, we are asked to be thoughtful. Jesus encourages us to think of other people and their needs. We try to see the needs of others before someone has to ask for our help.

Jesus wants us to care about others who feel hurt. When we have a caring heart, we include other people in our circle of friends.

68 Morality

Teaching Tips

When teaching children about Jesus' call to be generous, thoughtful, and caring, be realistic about a seven-year-old's ability to follow closely the teachings of Jesus. Children of this age are still developing in their awareness of others and will often tend to be self-centered. Remind the children that Christians of all ages sometimes fail at following Jesus' teachings. Tell them that Baptism marks us as a Christian but becoming a true Christian is a lifelong effort.

Activity

Complete the poem by using the words in the box. Then read the poem alone or with others.

done   sad
glad   me
none
Responsibility

I Can Care

I'll share some of my money
With someone who has <u>n o n e</u>.

I've always time for helping
Get another's work all <u>d o n e</u>.

And when I'm full of laughing,
I'll look for someone <u>s a d</u>.

And share with them my laughter
Until they're feeling <u>g l a d</u>.

I like to care for others
As others care for <u>me</u>.

There is a word for all of this—
<u>R e s p o n s i b i l i t y</u>.

---

on the lines provided. Then read the poem aloud. Ask: Who can name one way the speaker in the poem shows care for others? (*Will share money, help with work, cheer up someone*) What are other ways of helping that are not mentioned in the poem? (*Affirm all answers.*) Help the children understand that when we show love and care for one another, we are living as Jesus wants us to live. We are showing others that we are friends of Jesus because we are doing what he asks.

Sharing Examples of Caring

Invite the children to form a sharing circle and share examples of thoughtful acts they have noticed, without mentioning specific names. (*Yesterday, I saw a boy help another student who was feeling sick find the correct page in the math book. I heard someone ask another if she needed help.*) Give examples to the children of where generosity is needed. (*Sometimes it takes some people longer to finish their work or to line up. We are generous when we wait patiently. I noticed that when someone forgot to bring lunch, others offered to share their lunches.*) Point out instances of caring (*offering to care for the hamster during a school vacation; telling a friend who was absent that he was missed, and so on*). Encourage the children to tell about other generous, thoughtful, and caring acts.

Praying Together

Encourage the children to clear their desks and sit quietly. (Say this slowly and in a quiet voice.) Ask them to close their eyes and become quiet inside. Ask the children to picture someone they have a responsibility to care for: a friend, a family member, maybe a child in another land who is in need. Have the children ask God to help them think of a way to be generous, thoughtful, and caring to the persons they are thinking of. Allow a few moments of quiet time for the children to pray. Close the prayer by saying, "Jesus, thank you for helping us to be responsible and caring. Thank you for calling us to be generous, thoughtful, and caring. Amen." Invite the children to bring something from home to share with those in the community who are hungry or poor (canned food, articles of clothing, games, money).

Teaching Tips

Prayer comes to children naturally. They continue their inner conversation with God through simple prayers and rituals. Small children are comfortable praying through symbols or motions. Simple rituals express the wonder that children see and feel in the presence of love, peace, harmony, and mystery. Help the children create rituals that use lighting, objects, music, and actions. Let the rituals speak for themselves.

Objective

This lesson helps the children pray to Jesus for help in caring for others.

Preparing for Prayer

Decorate the prayer table with the caring pictures and with the string of caring handprints, if you opted to make them. In the center of the table, place a basket as a symbol for responsibilities. The basket also reminds us of Saint Elizabeth, who gave when it was difficult, and of the generous woman who gave everything she had—her two pennies. Invite the children to bring their books and their gifts for the poor and needy of the community to the prayer table.

Praying a Litany

Have the children open their books to page 70 and follow along as you read aloud the introductory paragraph. Review the prayer with them. Then assign five children to take the readers' parts and invite the rest of the class to respond all together. Explain that each child will place a gift in the basket at the end of the litany. Allow sufficient time for the students to print on the line provided what their gifts are. Pause for a few moments of quiet before beginning the prayer. Sing with the children "Gifts in My Heart" from THIS IS OUR FAITH Music Program, Grade 3, or another familiar song of thanks to complete the prayer service.

Praying to Become a Caring Community

Teacher: This is a reading from the Bible about how we should care about one another.

> Followers of Jesus, let us show love in our actions and not only talk about it. Let us love one another because love is from God. Everyone who loves is a child of God and knows God, for God is love.
>
> Based on 1 John 4:7–8

Reader 1: When someone needs help,
All: Jesus, help us care for others.
Reader 2: When someone is hurt and sad,
All: Jesus, help us care for others.
Reader 3: When someone is lonely,
All: Jesus, help us care for others.
Reader 4: When someone is sick,
All: Jesus, help us care for others.
Reader 5: When someone is poor and hungry,
All: Jesus, help us care for others.
Each Child: Here is my gift of

_____

70   Prayer

Focus on

Litany A litany is a form of prayer that has been popular in the Church for thousands of years. A litany is usually prayed aloud, requiring a leader and a congregation. Many litanies call upon the saints, repeatedly asking them to "pray for us." Litanies, however, can take on many forms, but usually have the repeated response. Introducing children to the litany form of prayer is a way of introducing them to the formal prayers of the Church and developing in them a variety of ways to pray.

Enriching the Lesson

You might want to begin this lesson by reading a story about caring for others. Stress the thoughtfulness, generosity, and caring shown by the characters in the story. Some titles you might wish to consider are *Mrs. Katz and Tush.* Patricia Polacco. Bantam Books, 1992; *Wilfred Gordon McDonald Partridge.* Mem Fox. Kane/Miller, 1985.

Chapter Review

In the speech balloon, write words that say how you, as a friend of Jesus, can help. Then color the cartoon.

I can't carry this. It's too heavy!

1. What are two things everyone in a community has?

rights

responsibilities

2. What is one word that describes the woman in the gospel story who gave everything she had?

generous

3. Talk about what we can do to show we care for people and the earth.

Jesus says, "People will know you are my friends by your love for one another."
Based on John 13:35

Review 71

Enriching the Lesson

Encourage the children to write a few sentences about the caring things they did this past week. Collect their stories and create a "Caring Chronicle." Encourage the children to submit drawings of generosity, thoughtfulness, or caring. Original prayers and poems may also be included. Children can work as partners; one to create a poem or prayer, the other to draw a picture. Allow the children to bring the Caring Chronicle home, each on his or her turn.

Completing a Cartoon

Distribute crayons or felt-tip markers. Call attention to the drawing on page 71. Read the directions for this activity. Invite the children to print the older boy's response in the balloon, then color the cartoon. Encourage them to work independently. After they have finished, ask volunteers to share their responses.

Reviewing the Chapter

Take time to go through the three review questions aloud with the children. Ask the first two questions and give the children sufficient time to write their answers. Be supportive of each child who participates in the discussion of the third item.

or...

Ask the following questions.

- What are two things that everyone in a community has? (*Rights and responsibilities*)
- For what are you responsible? (*Answers will vary.*)
- What word do we use to describe the woman in the gospel story who gave everything she had? (*Generous*)
- Name a saint who cared for the sick and the hungry. (*Saint Elizabeth of Hungary*)

Explaining the Scripture Verse

Ask the children to read aloud the Scripture verse at the bottom of page 71. Review that Jesus calls us to be friends to others by caring about them and treating them generously and thoughtfully. When we love and care for others, we are doing what Jesus asks of us. We become his disciples and live as Jesus did.

6

We Have Choices to Make

Objectives

To help the children

- Know that God gives them the freedom to make caring or selfish choices.
- Choose to forgive as Jesus forgives.
- Call on the Holy Spirit to help them make good, caring choices.
- Distinguish between accidents, mistakes, and sins.
- Pray to a forgiving, merciful God and review the chapter.

Chapter Outline

	Step 1 Learning About Our Lives	**Step 2** Learning About Our Faith	**Step 3** Learning How to Live Our Faith 
Day 1	■ Introduce the chapter. ■ Discuss choices we've made. ■ Complete an activity. *ABOUT 10 MINUTES*	■ Present the doctrine. ■ Present the new word. *ABOUT 15 MINUTES*	■ Role-play and discuss a situation. *ABOUT 5 MINUTES*
Day 2	■ Make puppets. ■ Make a choice with puppets. *ABOUT 10 MINUTES*	■ Read a story. ■ Dramatize the story. ■ Understand the story. *ABOUT 15 MINUTES*	■ Complete an activity. ■ Use puppets. *ABOUT 5 MINUTES*
Day 3	■ Introduce the lesson. *ABOUT 5 MINUTES*	■ Make choices. ■ Read a poem. ■ Pray together. *ABOUT 15 MINUTES*	■ Complete an activity. ■ Discuss the activity. ■ Write a prayer. *ABOUT 10 MINUTES*
Day 4	■ Pray together. ■ Review the chapter theme. *ABOUT 5 MINUTES*	■ Introduce accidents, mistakes, and sins. ■ Review the vocabulary. ■ Complete an activity. *ABOUT 15 MINUTES*	■ Draw alternate choices. ■ Recognize help in making choices. *ABOUT 10 MINUTES*
Day 5	**Prayer** Prepare for prayer and pray together the Jesus Prayer. **Review** Review the chapter and read the Scripture verse.		

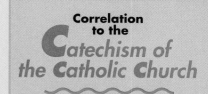
Plan Ahead ~~~~~~~~~~~

	Preparing Your Class	**Materials Needed**
Day 1	Read over the lesson prior to class. Prepare word poster. If enriching the lesson, gather necessary materials for stringing colored beads.	■ poster
Day 2	Read over the lesson. Gather materials for puppets. Prepare Bible prop box.	■ paper lunch bags ■ markers ■ crown, robe, apron, cloak
Day 3	Read over the entire lesson prior to class. Prepare for prayer writing. If enriching the lesson, gather art materials for drawing.	■ pencils ■ lined paper
Day 4	Read over the lesson prior to class. If enriching the lesson, select a story to read.	■ children's prayers ■ drawing paper ■ markers
Day 5	Read over the lesson prior to class. Prepare a poster.	■ children's drawings

Additional Resources

As you plan this chapter, consider using the following materials from The Resourceful Teacher Package.

■ *Classroom Activity Sheets 6* and *6a*

■ *Family Activity Sheets 6* and *6a*

■ *Chapter 6 Test*

■ *Prayers for Every Day*

■ *Projects: Grade 2*

In preparing the children for the Sunday readings, you may wish to use Silver Burdett Ginn's *Getting Ready for Sunday* student and teacher materials.

BOOKS FOR THE JOURNEY

The Empty Pot. Demi. Henry Holt & Co., 1990. A child's choice to do everything he can to make the seed that he was given grow with remarkable consequences.

Babushka's Doll. Patricia Polacco. Simon & Schuster, 1990. Rambunctious Natasha learns the consequences of playing just once with a naughty doll that comes to life.

MORE BOOKS FOR THE JOURNEY

Hope for the Flowers. Trina Paulus. Paulist Press, 1972. A caterpillar chooses to do what he has to do to become all that he might be.

I Can Say No: A Child's Book about Drug Abuse. Doris Sanford. Questar, 1987. This story helps children recognize that there are no right reasons for using drugs.

REDUCED CLASSROOM ACTIVITIES

Name _____

We Have Choices to Make

Color the stepping stones that tell about loving choices. Talk about how each choice is a sign of love.

To the Teacher: This activity follows the We Believe section of the chapter.

Chapter 6   We Have Choices to Make   THIS IS OUR FAITH 2   **6**

Name _____

Help Us, Holy Spirit

Finish the prayer to the Holy Spirit by filling in the blanks.

Help us, Holy Spirit, to make loving choices.
Help us, Holy Spirit, to make loving choices with brothers and sisters.

_____ _____

_____ , _____ , to make

loving choices with baby sitters.
Help us, Holy Spirit, to make loving choices with friends.

_____ _____

_____ , _____ , to make

_____

loving choices with _____

_____

_____ .

To the Teacher: This activity follows "Choices to Make."

6a   THIS IS OUR FAITH 2   Chapter 6   We Have Choices to Make

MAKING MORAL CHOICES

As disciples, we are called to consistently choose to love God and love our neighbor as ourselves. Discerning how best to love our neighbors is often difficult. We look to Jesus in the gospels as our model. Jesus is just and merciful; Jesus is forgiving and chastising; Jesus loves faithful friends and includes the outcasts. Jesus continually calls us to go beyond the boundaries of what is expected to what is generous. Knowing our weaknesses, Jesus sent the Holy Spirit to enlighten our minds that we might make good, moral decisions. Disciples of Jesus are known by their love for and service to all, especially the needy and the rejected persons of society.

Human freedom is the basis of all moral life. "Freedom is the power, rooted in reason and will, to act or not to act, to do this or that, and so to perform deliberate actions on one's own responsibility. By free will one shapes one's own life" (*Catechism of the Catholic Church*, #1731). Freedom then is the source of our goodness and our happiness. But moral choice is more complex. It demands the distinction between two goods—between the choice to act or not to act. It requires that we learn the difference between love of self and selfishness. As Christians, we must reflect on the consequences of our choices and pray for guidance in making our decisions according to a well-formed conscience.

LEARNING HOW TO CHOOSE

Some choices for second graders are regulated by adults who are responsible for them. But there are many daily choices that children make for themselves—such as the choice between selfish words and actions or loving ones. Second graders can understand that they are responsible for their choices and the consequences of those choices. Sometimes children judge the gravity of their choices by the response of adults. It is important that we make the distinction between accidents, mistakes, and sin. Sin is presented as a deliberate doing of wrong or refusal to do what is right. Accidents and mistakes are unplanned, even though they can produce similar undesired consequences.

Since second graders have a natural tendency to act out of self-interest, they need to know that they will not always choose wisely or correctly. Do not give them the impression that choosing to lead a life of love is always easy. They should not be made to feel needless guilt about wrong choices they have made in the past or will make in the future.

You can explain that God wants us to direct our best efforts toward choosing a life of love. Continue to use examples from Scripture like "The King and the Servant" to teach children about good, caring choices. Always affirm the children's attempts to make good decisions.

___MORALITY/DOCTRINE___

Objective

This lesson helps the children know that God gives them the freedom to make caring or selfish choices.

Step 1/INTRODUCTION

Learning About Our Lives

Introducing the Chapter

Review the meanings of *responsibility* and *right* from the previous chapter. Tell the children that when we live responsibly and care for others, we are making choices that are helpful for ourselves and others. But sometimes, we all make choices that are selfish or hurtful.

Discussing Choices We've Made

Invite a volunteer to read the chapter title and focus question on page 72. Discuss the various choices that the children suggest. Some choices take more thought than others. (Deciding what to do on Saturday takes more thought than deciding what to have for breakfast.) Stress that making choices involves thinking about many possibilities and deciding on the one that seems best.

Completing an Activity

Invite a volunteer to read the paragraph "Making Choices." When we think about choices, we have to remember what might happen when we make a choice.

Read the directions for the activity and ask the children to complete it. When they have finished, explore with them whether the choices were easy or difficult. Discuss the consequences of their choices.

■ What might happen if Luke tells a lie? (*Anne might find out and tell her father about the lie.*)

■ What might happen if John copies Kim's homework? (*He could get in trouble.*)

■ What will happen if Sarah keeps the money? (*The rightful owner will be denied the opportunity of getting the money back.*)

What was the hardest choice you ever made?

We Have Choices to Make

Making Choices

Life is full of choices. We make choices every day. Some choices are easy to make. Others are more difficult.

Activity

Read the stories and answer the questions.

1. Luke's father gives him a whole pack of gum. Later, his sister Anne asks Luke if he has any gum. Luke thinks to himself, "Anne doesn't know Dad gave me that gum." If you were Luke, what would you choose to tell Anne?

_____

2. John didn't do his homework. He sees Kim's homework on the table. Everyone else is busy playing. John could do his homework now, or he could copy Kim's work. What would you choose to do if you were John?

_____

Focus on

Making Choices In our fast-paced world, people may act on impulse. Choices made without forethought may or may not be beneficial. Reflection before an action is a skill that needs to be developed. Point out the steps of decision making: think or reflect on alternatives, consider consequences, choose to act, and acknowledge the outcome. It takes time to form a habit of making good choices.

Teaching Tips

Help the class recognize the difference between thinking and choosing. Offer these sentences for practice.
1. Should I wear a coat or not? (*Thinking*)
2. I'll have chocolate-marble ice cream. (*Choosing*)
3. I wonder what is on television. (*Thinking*)
4. What will happen if I don't eat my vegetables? (*Thinking*)
5. I won't go to bed now. (*Choosing*)
6. I'll give my friend my favorite rock. (*Choosing*)

3. Sarah and Jason see a wallet laying beside the path. Sarah thinks they should keep it and the money inside. Jason thinks they should try to find the owner. What would you choose to do?

_____

- -

_____

- -

_____

Free to Choose

God gives us the freedom to choose. We can choose to do what is helpful and good for ourselves and others, or we can choose to do what hurts ourselves and others.

Jesus teaches us to choose what is helpful and loving. When we do something we know is wrong or hurt someone on purpose, we **sin**. When we don't do something we know we should do, we might also sin.

We Believe

God gives us the freedom to make choices. When we choose to do what we know is wrong, or when we choose to hurt someone on purpose, we sin.

New Word

sin Sin means to hurt someone on purpose or to do something we know is wrong. When we don't do something we know we should do, we might also sin.

Doctrine **73**

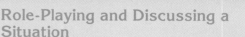
Learning About Our Faith

Presenting the Doctrine

Direct the children's attention to "Free to Choose" on page 73. Read aloud the first paragraph. Ask: What are the two kinds of choices we make? (_Helpful or good, hurtful or wrong_) Print these words on the chalkboard. Which of these choices would Jesus want us to make? (_Helpful or good_) Read the second paragraph and discuss it.

Read together the We Believe statements. Emphasize that God makes us free to choose. God wants us to become loving disciples because we choose to be, not because God forces us.

Presenting the New Word

Introduce the new word _sin_. Print the word on a poster surrounded by the words "wrong," "on purpose," "not doing what I should." Ask a volunteer to read the definition of _sin_ in the New Word box. Ask:

- What are the choices we can make? (_Helpful, good; hurtful, bad_)
- What do we call doing wrong on purpose? (_Sin_) What do we call not doing something we should do? (_Sin_)
- How does Jesus want us to act? (_In a helpful, caring way_)

Step 3 / CONCLUSION

Learning How to Live Our Faith

Role-Playing and Discussing a Situation

Ask the children to role-play the following situation.

Glenn's dad wants him to come right home from school. Glenn's friends want him to play soccer. What choices can Glenn make? (_To go right home or to play soccer_)

After you have discussed with the children the choices that Glenn could make, discuss the consequences of each choice.

Objective

This lesson teaches the children to choose to forgive as Jesus forgives.

Step 1 / INTRODUCTION

Learning About Our Lives

Making Puppets

Distribute small paper lunch bags, two per child. Distribute colored markers. Help the children make two simple hand puppets. Open the bag, draw a large circle for the head at the top or closed end of the bag. Draw a shirt under the circle. Make one puppet's face happy and smiling, the other sad. Be sure to color the shirts differently. When all have finished making their puppets, ask them to put their hands inside the puppet bags and place them on the top of their desks.

Making a Choice with Puppets

Direct the children to raise up the appropriate puppet in response to these situations.

- There was only one seat left on the bus, and Joey pushed Peter out of his way to get the seat. How did Peter feel? (*Sad puppet*)

- Yesterday I assigned homework. Five people in the class decided not to do it. How do I feel? (*Sad puppet*) Those five people have to do their homework during recess. How do they feel? (*Sad puppet*) How do the other children feel who did their homework? (*Happy puppet*)

- Kaylyn ignored her friend Tasha at recess. How did Tasha feel? (*Sad puppet*) After school Kaylyn told Tasha she was sorry. How did Tasha feel? (*Happy puppet*) Tasha forgave her friend. How did Kaylyn feel? (*Happy puppet*)

Step 2 / DEVELOPMENT

Learning About Our Faith +

Reading a Story

Before reading "The King and the Servant," recite the servant's response on page 74,

The King and the Servant

There was once a servant who owed a king a lot of money. One day the king said to the servant, "You must pay back the money you owe me."

"Please give me a little more time," the servant begged.

The king felt sorry for the servant. So he said, "That's all right. I forgive your debt. There's no need to pay me or to worry anymore."

The servant was so relieved! But as he was walking home, he met a man he knew. This man owed him a dollar. The servant said, "Pay back the money you owe me, now."

"Please give me a little more time," the man begged.

Focus on

Mercy The Scripture story centers on the king's act of forgiving a debt. Justice demands that all debts be paid. Even when the debtors are not able to pay their debts, the collector would have a right to take what rightfully belongs to him or her. Jesus calls us beyond justice to mercy. Understanding the financial situation of the debtor, the collector forgives the debt. Encourage the children to go beyond what is fair to what is a loving or merciful response.

Enriching the Lesson

Read the story about Jesus teaching us how to pray The Lord's Prayer from Matthew 6:9–15. Invite the children to reflect on Jesus' words to forgive others as we are forgiven by responding "Forgive us as we forgive others" in the pauses. Jesus, when someone calls us names . . . Jesus, when someone gets angry and shoves us . . . Jesus, when someone tells lies about us . . . and so on. Close by praying The Lord's Prayer.

The servant got very angry and grabbed the man. "I want my money now!" he shouted.

"Please," said the man. "I don't have it right now." But the servant didn't care, and he put the man in jail until he paid back the dollar.

When the king heard what his servant had done, he punished him for his selfishness and lack of care.

Based on Matthew 18:23–30

Activity

Help the children in the stories below choose to care and forgive.

Sammy took Tong's favorite baseball cards. Sammy lost them at the park. When he told Tong what happened, Tong said,

" _____ "

I forgive you _____ .

Ashley called Sammy a big bully and hurt Sammy's feelings. Later, Sammy told Ashley,

" _____ "

I forgive you _____ .

Teaching Tips

Puppets spark the imagination and creativity of children and allow shy children to express themselves more easily. A puppet is any object that is manipulated to convey a message. Simple paper circles on sticks are puppets. Paper plates with happy and sad faces may be used in this lesson instead of paper bags. Encourage the children to move a hand puppet up and down and side to side.

"Please give me a little more time." Invite the children to repeat this response, then have them follow along silently as you read the story aloud.

Dramatizing the Story

Invite volunteers to be the narrator, the king, the servant who owed the king a large amount of money, and the man who owed the servant a small amount of money. From the Bible prop box, gather a crown and robe for the king, an apron for the servant, and a cloak for the man who owed the servant money.

Understanding the Story

Ask the following questions.

- How did the king in the story make the right choice? (*He chose to forgive the servant.*)
- How did the servant make a choice that was hurtful? (*He got angry and did not forgive; he put the man who owed him money in jail.*)
- What do we call something we know we should do, but we don't do it ? (*Sin*)
- What did the king do that the servant did not choose to do? (*Forgive*)

Step 3 / CONCLUSION
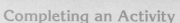

Learning How to Live Our Faith

Completing an Activity

From the story of the king and the servant, the children learn that Jesus wants us to forgive others. Invite a volunteer to read about Sammy and Tong on page 75. Complete the sentence with "I forgive you." Read about Ashley and Sammy and complete the sentence. Suggest that the children remember a time when someone did something to them that was hurtful. Assist them in completing the sentence.

Using the Puppets

Use the happy/sad paper bag puppets to show how the king, the servant, and the man who owed the king money felt in the Scripture story. Then show how Sammy and Ashley feel in the activity. Invite volunteers to share the situations that prompted the "I forgive you" lines they wrote. Use the puppets to show how at first the people are sad, but later are happy when they forgive or are forgiven.

Objective

This lesson encourages the children to pray to the Holy Spirit for help in making good, caring choices.

Step 1 / INTRODUCTION

Learning About Our Lives

Introducing the Lesson

Help the children recall what they have learned about the Holy Spirit. Ask:

- Who sends the Holy Spirit to help us make choices? (*Jesus*)

- How does the Holy Spirit help us? (*Helps us to notice those in need; helps us to choose to care; strengthens us when we have hard choices to make*)

- What happens if there is more than one way to help? (*We ask the Holy Spirit to help us make the most loving choice.*)

Step 2 / DEVELOPMENT

Learning About Our Faith

Making Choices

Read with the class the explanatory paragraph "Choices to Make" on page 76. Explain that many times our choices are not between good and bad, but between greater and lesser goods. For example, we can choose to answer our mother's call for help or finish helping a little sister. Both choices are good. We have to choose the better good. The Holy Spirit helps us to decide the most loving choice. Encourage the children to pray to the Holy Spirit when they face difficult decisions.

Reading a Poem

Read aloud the poem on page 76 as the children follow along. Ask:

- Who is the speaker? (*A child*)

- Who wants us to choose to do good things? (*God, our parents, we ourselves*)

- Who can help us make good choices? (*Our families, our friends, Jesus, the Holy Spirit*)

Choices to Make

Jesus gives us the Holy Spirit to help us make choices. With the Holy Spirit's help, we can choose to care for other people. The Holy Spirit can help us decide how to act in the most loving way. We can then choose the best way to help others rather than hurt them. We can choose to be kind rather than to be mean.

What's Best for Me

The choice I make
Might not always be
The one that you
Expect of me.

But sometimes I
Will choose to do
The good things that
You want me to.

Help me, Jesus,
to be free
To mostly choose
What's best for me.

76 Doctrine

![CURRICULUM CONNECTION]

Physical Education In physical education class children are taught the skills of team playing and courtesy. Ask: What is the proper way to act when another team is winning and your team is losing? What actions show we are not good team players? Stress with the children that respect for others extends to the way we choose to play our games. Invite a coach to speak to the class about playing fair, taking losses well, and respecting others.

Enriching the Lesson

Play "Stand Up, Sit Down" with the children. Tell them that you are going to read a list of selfish actions and caring actions. Instruct the children to stand when they hear a caring action and to sit when they hear a selfish action. Add other actions to lengthen the game.

- Helping a neighbor
- Hitting your brother
- Going to church
- Stealing candy
- Loving your parents
- Telling lies
- Sharing your toys

Activity

Look at the pictures and read the sentences. Complete the missing words. Then circle the pictures that show someone choosing to care.

1. Greg chooses to

steal.

2. Nancy chooses to

share.

3. Tony chooses to

fight.

4. Joan chooses to

obey.

5. José chooses to

pray.

Praying Together

Have the children think of all the choices they make each day. Invite them to name choices that are caring and loving (*obeying parents, being good to friends, talking to grandparents*). Lead the class in asking Jesus and the Holy Spirit to help them make loving choices. Pray the poem together.

Step 3 / CONCLUSION

Learning How to Live Our Faith

Completing an Activity

Read aloud the directions for the picture clue activity on page 76. Ask the children to complete the words independently. Help the children with the spelling of the words. After they have completed the words, check their answers. Then have the children circle the pictures that show someone choosing to care.

Discussing the Activity

Allow the children time to explain their reasons for circling particular pictures. Ask for volunteers to "tell the story" of the good choices. Guide the children with the following questions.

- What is Nancy doing in the picture? (*Sharing popcorn*)
- Why is she doing that? (*To be a friend*)
- What else could she have chosen to do? (*Kept it for herself, be selfish*)
- What is Joan's mother doing in the picture? (*Calling her back home*)
- What is Joan going to do? (*Listen to her mother*) Why? (*To obey*)
- What is José going to do? (*Pray in church*)

Writing a Prayer

Distribute sheets of lined paper. Ask the children to copy from the board as you print "Holy Spirit, please help me to choose to ____." Encourage the children to think of a choice that they need to make. (*Please help me to choose to play fairly with my brother; to be kind to my friends; to do what my mother asks, and so on.*) Have them print that choice as part of their prayer. Invite volunteers to share what they have written. Assemble the prayers into a notebook and place it on the prayer table.

DAY 4
MORALITY

Objective

This lesson helps the children make the distinction between accidents, mistakes, and sins.

Step 1 / INTRODUCTION

Learning About Our Lives

Praying Together

Gather the children around the prayer table. Recall yesterday's activity of writing a prayer to the Holy Spirit. Ask for volunteers to read the prayers they wrote. Have the class echo this response to each child's prayer: "Holy Spirit, help us to choose to love."

Reviewing the Chapter Theme

Instruct the children to turn to page 72. Ask:

- What is the theme of this chapter? (*We have choices to make.*)
- Who remembers what we call a choice to do something wrong on purpose? (*Sin*)
- Who remembers what we call a choice not to do something we should do? (*Sin*)
- Who give us the freedom to make choices? (*God*)
- Who helps us make choices that are loving and caring? (*Parents, teachers, friends*)
- Who did Jesus send to help us make loving choices? (*The Holy Spirit*)

Step 2 / DEVELOPMENT

Learning About Our Faith

Introducing Accidents, Mistakes, and Sins

Read the introductory lines of "Which Is It?" at the top of page 78. Ask: What is an accident? Ask the children for an example of an accident. (*Answers will vary.*) Invite a volunteer to read the paragraph about mistakes on page 78. Ask: What is a mistake? Is it easy to know when something is an accident, a mistake, or a sin?

Which Is It?

It is important to know the difference between something that might be a sin and something that is only an accident. When we have an accident, it is not our fault. We don't have accidents on purpose. Accidents are things that just happen to us. Even if we break something that costs a lot of money, it is not a sin. It is an accident because we didn't do it on purpose.

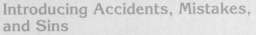

It is just as important to understand the difference between a mistake and a sin. Everyone makes mistakes. In Math class, we might make mistakes when we add or subtract. At home, we might give the dog some cat food instead of dog food. We didn't do it on purpose. We made a mistake. Making mistakes is okay. Only when we do something wrong on purpose can we call it a sin.

78 Morality

Enriching the Lesson

Select a story from the books suggested in "Books for the Journey and More Books for the Journey" on page 71c. Read the story to the children and ask them to identify the choices in the story.

Activity

Now try these examples. Write **A** for accident, **M** for mistake, or **S** for sin.

You wanted to give everyone in your class an invitation to your birthday party. You forgot to give the invitations to three classmates.

_____
A or M

You scribbled all over your brother's homework paper because you thought it was scrap paper.

_____
M

You wanted to watch your favorite TV show. Your older sister changed the channel. You hit her.

_____
S

Your teacher is sick and is not in school today. You decide to misbehave for the substitute teacher. You make the day very difficult for him.

_____
S

Morality   79

Teaching Tips

Help the children develop self-esteem. Reassure them that it is all right to say, "I am not perfect and it's okay." Some children get very upset with themselves when they make mistakes. They feel pressure to be perfect. Adult reactions to accidents or mistakes often give the message that great wrong has been done. As teachers, it is good to assure the children that accidents happen and can be rectified. Mistakes are a part of life, and learning from mistakes is how we grow.

Reviewing the Vocabulary

Write the words *accident*, *mistake*, and *sin* on the chalkboard. Assist the children in copying the words. Allow time for the children to review the definition of *sin* in the New Word box on page 73.

Completing an Activity

Instruct the children to read the directions for the activity on page 79. Then read aloud each of the five situations. Ask the children to decide independently if each situation is an example of an accident, a mistake, or a sin. Stress that a sin is something wrong that is done on purpose. After the children have written their answers in their books, check the answers. Have them explain the differences between an accident, a mistake, and a sin.

Step 3 / CONCLUSION

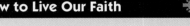

Learning How to Live Our Faith

Drawing Alternate Choices

Distribute drawing paper and markers. Have the children fold the paper in half. Invite the children to draw on one side pictures of themselves having an accident or making a mistake. On the other side, have them draw a picture of something that is a sin, something wrong that is done on purpose. When all have finished their drawings, gather the children into a sharing circle and ask them to talk about their drawings. Stress that accidents happen by chance. Mistakes are not meant to be. Only sin is a deliberate wrongdoing. It is something we know is wrong and do on purpose anyway.

Recognizing Help in Making Choices

Suggest this question for discussion, "Who helps us when we make choices?" Begin by sharing some recent decision you made and how someone helped you with that decision. Stress that you pray for assistance in making your choices. Ask for volunteers to share some of the choices they made this week in which they received help from the Holy Spirit, their parents, their teachers, or others.

PRAYER/REVIEW

Objective

This prayer teaches children that God is forgiving and allows them to celebrate the Lord's mercy.

Preparing for Prayer

Invite the children to bring the pictures they have drawn about accidents or mistakes and sins to the prayer table. Also display a poster of Jesus forgiving sins. Invite the children to recall that the theme of Chapter 6 is "We Have Choices to Make."

Tell the children that Jesus wants us to make choices that are loving and helpful. Sometimes we fail. We make mistakes, have accidents, or choose to do wrong or fail to do right on purpose. We need to know that God still loves us. We need to forgive others and to be forgiven. Today we will pray to be generous in our forgiveness of others.

Praying the Jesus Prayer

Ask the children to open their books to page 80 and to follow in their books as you read the opening paragraph. Have them repeat after you the Jesus Prayer: "Jesus, Son of God, have mercy on me." Stress that Jesus takes away our sins and has mercy on us. Invite the children to make this response as indicated after each invocation on page 80. Pause for a moment of quiet, then begin the prayer. At the end of the prayer, have the children offer each other a sign of peace. Instruct the children to say to the persons on their right and left, "I give you peace."

Praying the Jesus Prayer

Teacher: We follow Jesus by making good choices, by listening to Jesus in prayer, and by treating one another with respect and care. One way we can listen to Jesus in prayer is by praying the Jesus Prayer:
Jesus, Son of God, have mercy on me.

Teacher: When I am hurting or sad,
All: Jesus, Son of God, have mercy on me.

Teacher: When I have hard choices to make,
All: Jesus, Son of God, have mercy on me.

Teacher: When I feel lonely or lost,
All: Jesus, Son of God, have mercy on me.

Teacher: When others ask me to forgive them,
All: Jesus, Son of God, have mercy on me.

Teacher: When I'm not sure what to do,
All: Jesus, Son of God, have mercy on me.

80 Prayer

Teaching Tips

Show the children how making a choice can result in multiple consequences. Choosing not to learn to read would mean failure in school and inability to enjoy reading the funnies, playing board games (Monopoly), following directions for making things, and so on. One bad act can have many consequences. In the same way, a good act can have a long-lasting result, such as a lifetime friendship.

Chapter Review

Write **yes** next to the sentences that are choices to care about God and others. Write **no** next to the sentences that are choices to act selfishly.

yes   I forgive you.

yes   I will pray for you.

_no_   I hate you.

yes   Be my friend.

yes   I'm sorry.

1. What special freedom does God give each of us?

the freedom to make choices

2. What happens when we selfishly choose not to care?

We sin.

> **God says,**
> **"Choose a life**
> **of love."**
> **Based on**
> **Deuteronomy 30:19**

3. Talk about some things that we can do when we have to make a choice between caring or not caring.

Reviewing the Chapter

Read aloud the directions for the review. Allow sufficient time for the children to read the six sentences and to write their answers on the lines provided. Go over the answers orally. Take time to go through the three review questions that follow. Allow the children time to answer questions 1 and 2. Be supportive of each child who participates in the discussion of item 3.

Reading the Scripture Verse

Direct the children to the reading based on Deuteronomy 30:19. Explain to the children that Jesus wants us to do the loving thing. He promises us we will be happy if we choose his ways. How do you feel when you do something that is kind or loving? (*Affirm any answer.*)

★ ★ ★ ★ Enriching the Lesson ★

Read or tell the children a story of a missionary whose choice to serve God affects many people. Maryknoll Missionaries and Holy Childhood Associations publish free magazines with many stories about the effects of others' caring. Point out that poverty is often the result of natural disasters, such as floods, famines, droughts. Poverty can also be the result of the indifference of those who are selfish and uncaring.

We Are Called to Reconciliation

Objectives ~~~~~~

To help the children

■ Discover the process of reconciliation.

■ Realize that God calls us to forgive one another.

■ Welcome the Holy Spirit, source of grace and forgiveness, into their lives.

■ Express sorrow for their sins.

■ Celebrate reconciliation in prayer and review the chapter.

Chapter Outline ~~~~~~~~~~~~~~

	Step 1 Learning About Our Lives	**Step 2** Learning About Our Faith	**Step 3** Learning How to Live Our Faith
Day 1	■ Introduce the chapter. ■ Study and interpret the illustrations. *ABOUT 10 MINUTES*	■ Discover reconciliation. ■ Present the new word. ■ Present the doctrine. *ABOUT 10 MINUTES*	■ Compare unforgiveness and reconciliation. *ABOUT 10 MINUTES*
Day 2	■ Remember reconciliation. *ABOUT 5 MINUTES*	■ Read and discuss a story. ■ Study an illustration. *ABOUT 15 MINUTES*	■ Complete an activity. ■ Pray together. *ABOUT 10 MINUTES*
Day 3	■ Introduce the chapter. ■ Read and discuss a story. *ABOUT 10 MINUTES*	■ Rely on God's grace. ■ Present the new word. *ABOUT 15 MINUTES*	■ Complete an activity. ■ Discover steps to reconciliation. *ABOUT 5 MINUTES*
Day 4	■ Explain sorrow. *ABOUT 10 MINUTES*	■ Pray for God's forgiveness. ■ Complete an activity. *ABOUT 10 MINUTES*	■ Pray together. *ABOUT 10 MINUTES*
Day 5	**Prayer** Find prayer partners and pray together a responsorial prayer of reconciliation. **Review** Find the hidden words and complete the chapter review.		

Correlation
to the
Catechism of
the Catholic Church

Paragraphs
845, 982, 1459, 1999, 2003, 2608

Plan Ahead

	Preparing Your Class	**Materials Needed**
Day 1	Read over the lesson prior to the sesion. Cut out small, red paper heats for each child.	■ pencils ■ red paper hearts
Day 2	Read over the lesson. Prepare a personal story of reconciliation and forgiveness.	■ pencils
Day 3	Read over the lesson. Write words on chalkboard.	■ pencils ■ blindfold
Day 4	Read over the lesson. Make sad/ smiling faces out of cardboard and yellow construction paper. Cue up song recording of "God Loves Me and You."	■ round piece of cardboard ■ colored construction paper ■ crayons or markers ■ tape recorder and cassette
Day 5	Read over the lesson. Prepare discovery table. Make sad/smiling faces in matching colors. Cue up instrumental recording of "God Loves You and Me."	■ construction-paper smiling/sad faces ■ candle, matches ■ tape recorder and cassette

Additional Resources

As you plan this chapter, consider using the following materials from The Resourceful Teacher Package.

■ *Classroom Activity Sheets* 7 and 7a

■ *Family Activity Sheets* 7 and 7a

■ *Chapter 7 Test*

■ *Prayers for Every Day*

■ *Projects: Grade 2*

You may also wish to refer to the following Big Books.

■ *We Celebrate the Sacraments*, pages 13–15

■ *We Celebrate God's Word*, page 8

In preparing the children for the Sunday readings, you may wish to use Silver Burdett Ginn's *Getting Ready for Sunday* student and teacher materials.

BOOKS FOR THE JOURNEY

Schnitzel Is Lost. Hans Wilhelm. Simon & Schuster, 1994. Schnitzel ignores advice, wanders off, and becomes hopelessly lost. He finds his way back to his forgiving friend.

The Quarreling Book. Charlotte Zolotow. HarperCollins, 1982. Meanness as well as goodness has a spiraling effect.

MORE BOOKS FOR THE JOURNEY

The Red Balloon. Albert Lamorisse. Doubleday, 1978. The story of the healing thing that all the balloons of Paris do for a little boy, Pascal, after a gang of boys breaks his friend, a magical balloon.

Sometimes I Get Mad. Elspeth Campbell Murphy. Chariot Family, 1981. A child prayerfully reflects on the emotion of feeling hurt and being angry about it.

REDUCED CLASSROOM ACTIVITIES

Name _____

We Are Called to Reconciliation

Reconciliation happens when we make up and become friends with someone again. Read each problem. Circle the number of the sentence that tells how you would make things right.

When someone makes fun of me,
1. I will forgive the person and try to be friends again.
2. I will say mean things to the person.
3. I will talk about the person.

When I lie about breaking a lamp at home,
1. I will tell another lie.
2. I will blame someone else.
3. I will say "I'm sorry."

When someone takes my favorite toy,
1. I will take one of his or her toys.
2. I will forgive the person and ask for my toy.
3. I will stop being the person's friend.

When someone is mean to my friend,
1. I will talk about that person.
2. I will be mean to others.
3. I will forgive the person and help him or her to like my friend.

To the Teacher: This activity will help explain the process of reconciliation.

Chapter 7   We Are Called to Reconciliation   THIS IS OUR FAITH 2   **7**

Name _____

A Story About Reconciliation

Color and cut out the puppets. Glue each puppet to a craft stick. Use the puppets to act out "A Story About Reconciliation."

To the Teacher: This activity follows "A Story About Reconciliation."

7a   THIS IS OUR FAITH 2   Chapter 7   We Are Called to Reconciliation

RECONCILIATION AND CONVERSION

Jesus taught us to pray: "Forgive us our trespasses as we forgive those who trespass against us." We know that we will receive God's forgiveness to the degree that we forgive others. If we have hurt another person, we must decide to admit our actions and to ask forgiveness. If we have been hurt, we must be willing to put aside the pain and offer forgiveness to the person who has hurt us. To refuse to reconcile is to refuse friendship, personal growth, and God's grace.

The *Catechism of the Catholic Church* states: "Jesus calls us to conversion. This call is an essential part of the proclamation of the kingdom: 'The time is fulfilled, and the kingdom of God is at hand; repent, and believe in the gospel'" (#1427). We are the witnesses to the gospel today, the disciples called to forgiveness and conversion.

Jesus' command to love God and neighbor demands a turning away from selfishness and sin and a willingness to turn from sin towards God's mercy. This conversion is motivated by a contrite heart. While conversion is interior, it also has an exterior dimension. Conversion happens when we experience God's presence in the Church, in the Eucharist, in doing charitable works, and in loving relationships. Strengthened by these experiences, we find the grace to make difficult choices. God's grace helps us

begin anew. When we repent of our sins, we give up our past life and look to the future with "the firm purpose of sinning no more . . . nourished by hope in God's mercy." (*Catechism of the Catholic Church,* #1490)

THE RECONCILIATION PROCESS

Second graders have experienced reconciliation. They can recall experiences of making up with friends or family, and times when differences were settled with an apology, a handshake, or a hug. These experiences provide you with the opportunity to help the children appreciate the unlimited forgiveness God offers us.

The chapter's parable "A Story About Reconciliation" highlights a father's forgiveness of his repenting son. By telling us this parable, Jesus invites us to look at our relationships. When we choose to act selfishly, God the Father waits for our return. His generous forgiveness draws us to sorrow for our sins and calls us to respond by forgiving others.

Emphasize the importance of reconciliation with God and with others. Remind the children that God loves us and is always ready to forgive our wrongdoings when we are sorry for them. Also, help the children learn the Prayer of Sorrow.

Day 1

Doctrine

Objective

This lesson helps the children discover the process of reconciliation and God's call to reconciliation.

Step 1 / Introduction

Learning About Our Lives

Reviewing Chapter 6

Invite the children to explain the differences between mistakes, accidents, and sins. Ask them how they can make good choices.

Introducing the Chapter

Have the children open their books to page 82. Instruct a volunteer to read aloud the focus question. Invite the children to share their experiences. Conclude by pointing out that we call the process of making up *reconciliation.* Have the children repeat the word a few times.

Interpreting the Illustrations

Read aloud the opening paragraph. Tell the children to look at the two illustrations on page 82 and decide who is feeling angry and who is feeling hurt. Continue by asking:

- Do you think Kelly will stay mean and angry?
- What do you think will happen between Kelly and her friend? (*They won't remain friends, or they'll make up and remain friends.*)

Step 2 / Development

Learning About Our Faith

Discovering Reconciliation

Ask the children to describe what has to happen between Kelly and her friend for them to remain friends. Record their responses on the chalkboard. Explain that there are a variety of ways for us to reconcile, to become friends again. Instruct the children to look at the two pictures on page 83 and follow the directions above the pictures. (*Circle the second picture that shows Kelly trying to be friends again.*)

7

Tell a story about a time when you hurt someone or they hurt you. What did you do to make up?

We Are Called to Reconciliation

Forgiving Friends

Sometimes we say or do things that hurt someone. We may be feeling angry, or we may be acting selfishly.

Look at the pictures.
Who is feeling angry?
Who is feeling hurt?

Hi, Kelly! Look what I found.

Who cares? I don't
to see it.

Teaching Tips

Role-playing can help reinforce a concept. Having the children act out real-life situations followed by a discussion offers an opportunity to clarify, to enrich, and to question. Keep the atmosphere flexible and help the children feel at ease. Have the children role-play scenarios demonstrating two responses: (a) the selfish response where the persons do not make up; and (b) the reconciliation response where the persons become friends again.

Enriching the Lesson

Gather the children around the prayer table and proclaim John 15:9, "As the Father has loved me, so I have loved you. Live on in my love." Explain that we live in Jesus' love when we forgive one another. Invite the children to think of someone who has forgiven them. Then pray together: *Dear Jesus, we thank you for the people who have forgiven us. Help us to be forgiving of others. We ask this because we want to live in your love. Amen.*

Activity

Circle the picture that shows Kelly trying to be friends again.

Forgiving Friends

Friends say, "I forgive you" and "I'm sorry." Our words can help others or hurt others. Kelly's words hurt her friend's feelings. Only when she said, "I'm sorry" were they able to make up and become friends again. Kelly's friend showed that he forgave her when he said, "I forgive you."

Making up and becoming friends again is called **reconciliation**.

We Believe

God always loves us, even when we hurt others and do wrong. God will always forgive us when we are sorry. God wants us always to be willing to forgive others, too.

New Word

reconciliation   making up and becoming friends again

Doctrine   83

CURRICULUM CONNECTION

Art Collaborate with the art teacher to make storybooks based on the biblical stories of forgiveness. Use an illustrated children's Bible as a resource. Describe the scenes for each story. Let children work with partners to design them. The storybooks can consist of drawings, paintings, or collages. Use various collage techniques. The collages can be folded accordion-style and unfolded as each story is told.

Ask the children to identify how Kelly and her friend made up. Circle words on the chalkboard that match the illustration responses. Then ask a volunteer to read "Forgiving Friends" on page 83. Restate that this process of making up is called *reconciliation*.

Presenting the New Word

Direct the children's attention to the New Word box on page 83. Have the class read the definition of *reconciliation* aloud with you. Explain that "re" means *again, anew, once more*. Discuss how in reconciliation we begin again. We begin anew by putting aside the hurt and trying to be helpful. We have the opportunity once more to be friends.

Presenting the Doctrine

Point to the title of Chapter 7 on page 82. Explain that God wants us to reconcile with those we have hurt. We are called to make up when we have acted selfishly. Present the We Believe statements on page 83, stressing that God always loves us, even when we sin. The Lord always forgives us and invites us to be sorry for our sins. God calls us to forgive others.

Step 3 / CONCLUSION

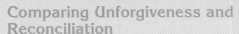

Learning How to Live Our Faith

Comparing Unforgiveness and Reconciliation

Draw a large, broken heart divided into three segments on the chalkboard. Explain that the broken heart represents the times we refuse to make up, when we stay angry, and when we continue to hurt another person. Ask the children to say aloud words we speak when our hearts do not forgive (*Stupid; dumb; no, go away; don't bug me.*) Write the children's responses in the heart segments. Now distribute a small, red paper heart to each child. Explain that the whole heart represents the time when we reconcile with others. What words show that we want to make up? (*Let's be friends. I'm sorry. I forgive you. We can help one another. Let's share. I like you.*) Instruct the children to write on their paper hearts the name of one person who has forgiven them.

DAY 2
SCRIPTURE

Objective

This lesson helps the children discover how God calls us to forgive one another through the Scripture story of the forgiving father.

Step 1 / INTRODUCTION

Learning About Our Lives

Remembering Reconciliation

Tell the children a personal story about reconciliation and forgiveness. Then invite the children to remember and share their own stories. Point out *how* the people in the stories became friends again, forgave one another, and were reconciled to one another.

Step 2 / DEVELOPMENT

Learning About Our Faith

Reading and Discussing a Story

Explain to the children that Jesus told his followers a story about reconciliation between a father and his son. Ask volunteers to read aloud "A Story About Reconciliation." After they have finished, ask the following questions as you discuss the story with the children.

- Why did the son want his father to give him money? (*He wanted to leave home.*)
- How did the father feel? (*Sad*)
- How did the son spend his money in the city? (*Foolishly*)
- How did the son feel when he had no more money? (*Unhappy and lonely*)
- What did the son decide to do? (*To go back home*)
- How did the son apologize? (*He told his father that he was sorry.*)
- How did his father answer him? (*"I forgive you. The important thing is that you've come back to the family. How happy I am to see you."*)

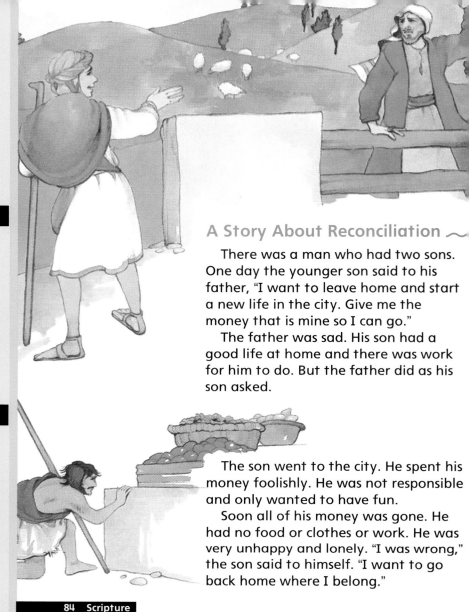

A Story About Reconciliation

There was a man who had two sons. One day the younger son said to his father, "I want to leave home and start a new life in the city. Give me the money that is mine so I can go."

The father was sad. His son had a good life at home and there was work for him to do. But the father did as his son asked.

The son went to the city. He spent his money foolishly. He was not responsible and only wanted to have fun.

Soon all of his money was gone. He had no food or clothes or work. He was very unhappy and lonely. "I was wrong," the son said to himself. "I want to go back home where I belong."

84   Scripture

★ ★ ★ ★ Enriching the Lesson ★ ★ ★

Invite volunteers to act out the forgiving father story as you narrate it. Give the children a few directorial cues and a quick run-through about where to stand and where to move before they begin. Encourage the children to interpret their characters through their actions. When appropriate, the "actors" can speak the words of their characters. After acting out the story, interview the "characters." The children stay in character while answering your questions about their actions.

At home the father worried about his son. He watched for him every day. When he saw his son walking up the road, the father ran to meet him.

"I'm sorry for what I've done," the son said. "I know I did wrong. I want to take my place at home again."

The father hugged and kissed his son. "It's all right," the father said. "I forgive you. The important thing is that you've come back to the family. How happy I am to see you."

Based on Luke 15:11–24

Activity

1. In this story, find the word **home**. Circle it each time you find it.

2. Now find the words of sorrow that the son said. Draw a line under them.

3. Find the words of forgiveness that the father said. Draw two lines under them.

4. Trace over the words below.

I'm sorry.

I forgive you.

Scripture   85

Teaching Tips

Seven-year-olds sometimes can find it hard to forgive. Praise their efforts at trying to forgive others. Encourage the children to try again if they fail. Build self-esteem.

Eight-year-olds can be exuberant, cocky, and have short attention spans. Provide them with opportunities to reflect on their actions, to experience quiet time, and to slow down.

Studying an Illustration

Ask the children what is happening in the picture on page 85. Help the children understand that the father and the son needed to speak out loud what they each were feeling inside. They did this through words (*"I'm sorry." "It's all right."*) and actions (*The father hugged and kissed his son.*). Explain that if the son had felt sorry but had not come home, reconciliation would not have happened. If the father had not had the chance to show that he forgave his son, reconciliation would not have been possible.

Step 3 / CONCLUSION

Learning How to Live Our Faith

Completing an Activity

Read the directions aloud for the activity on page 85. Allow sufficient time for the children to do the work. Have the children read aloud each of the sentences with the word *home* in it. Connect the actions in this biblical home with how we live and act in our homes today. Speak aloud the words of sorrow and forgiveness from the story. Explain how we need to speak these words to one another today in our families. Have the class say aloud the words "I'm sorry" and "I forgive you."

Praying Together

Invite the children to gather for prayer. Tell them to pray "Thank you, Jesus" after each line you say. Pray the following.

■ For calling me to reconciliation, . . .

■ For teaching me about forgiveness, . . .

■ For inviting me to be sorry for my sins, . . .

■ For forgiving me, . . .

■ For calling me to forgive others, . . .

Objective

This lesson invites the children to welcome the Holy Spirit into their lives by learning to trust in God, to accept others, and to make peace with everyone. Through these actions we welcome God's grace into our lives.

Step 1 / INTRODUCTION

Learning About Our Lives

Introducing the Chapter

Before the class begins, write these words on the chalkboard: *Trust, Accept, Reconcile.* Ask: Who can recall what we talked about in our last chapter? (*Reconciliation, making up*)

Continue with the concept that to make up, or to reconcile, we must learn to trust and accept one another and God.

Reading and Discussing a Story

Turn the children's attention to the story "Nathan, the Magnificent," on page 86. Tell the class that this is a story about two friends, hurt feelings, reconciliation, and the Holy Spirit.

Ask for a volunteer to read the story aloud. After the story is read, ask the following questions.

- Describe the feelings of Nathan. (*Felt good that he played soccer well*)
- Describe the feelings of Tony. (*Felt angry that he didn't play soccer as well as Nathan*)
- Have you ever experienced feelings like Nathan or Tony? (*Answers will vary*)
- What did Nathan do to help stay friends with Tony? (*Practiced together*)
- Can you remember a time when a friend helped you and you felt less angry? (*Answers will vary*)

Nathan, the Magnificent!

All the kids said Nathan was the best player on the school soccer team. His teammates called him Nathan, the Magnificent! But Nathan's friend, Tony, felt angry and jealous inside because he wasn't as good a player as Nathan. Sometimes Tony had to sit on the bench the whole game without ever getting to play.

Somehow Nathan knew how sad Tony felt. He could tell by the way Tony looked on those days when he had to sit out the whole game. After all, Tony was his best friend.

It took a lot of the fun out of soccer, knowing that Tony was feeling left out. But Nathan didn't know what he could do about it.

Then one day, Nathan had an idea. He asked Tony to practice with him after school without any of the other kids. The two friends passed and headed and kicked the soccer ball. Nathan and Tony had a great time! Whenever they could, the two boys practiced together.

Tony began to feel less angry. He was glad he had a friend like Nathan.

86   Doctrine

Grace   People of faith believe that they are not alone in this imperfect world. People of faith believe that God's very life has been infused into our beings, our Church, and our world. This infusion of God's very self is called grace. Grace calls us out of ourselves toward God. Grace brings us to repentance and gives us the strength we need to live as Jesus lived. The great gift of grace makes it possible for us to live in relationship with God.

CURRICULUM CONNECTION

Language Arts   The following stories deal with the theme of reconciliation. You may wish to read one to the class.

Be Good to Eddie Lee. Virginia Fleming. Philomel Books, 1993.

The Big Book for Peace. Lloyd Alexander. Dutton Children's Books, 1990.

Hannah. Gloria Whelan. Knopf, 1992.

Babushka Baba Yaga. Patricia Polacco. Books of Wonder, 1993.

Discovering God's Grace

We know that the Holy Spirit helps us say we're sorry whenever we've hurt someone. God also gives us a wonderful gift called **grace** to help us. Grace is God's loving presence in our lives.

God's grace helps us to become friends again. Grace makes us strong so that we can make good choices. The grace of God helps us say we're sorry. Grace helps us know how others are feeling.

Activity

1. Read again the story, "Nathan, the Magnificent!" on page 86.

2. Draw one line under the sentence in the story that tells how God's grace helped Nathan know that Tony was feeling angry.

3. Circle the sentence that tells how the grace of God helped Tony feel better about Nathan.

4. Draw a box around the sentence that tells what the boys did to show that they were friends again.

New Word

grace   God's loving presence in our lives

Doctrine 87

CURRICULUM CONNECTION

Music   You might wish to invite the school music specialist or the parish music director to teach the first two verses of "Amazing Grace!" to the class. The music can be found in the THIS IS OUR FAITH Music Program Director's Manual, page 16.

Teaching Tips

Often some children do not feel comfortable asking questions or we don't allow sufficient time to consider their questions. Encourage the children to put questions into a question box in your classroom. Designate a weekly time to respond to the questions. Remember the successful, time-tested methodology of Socrates: he often answered a question by asking another question. The process encourages the child to think harder and reflect more deeply on issues.

Step 2 / DEVELOPMENT

Learning About Our Faith

Relying on God's Grace

Explain that the presence of the Holy Spirit helps us to reconcile. Read aloud "Discovering God's Grace," at the top of page 87. Then help the children name times when they feel that God's grace helped them become friends again with someone with whom they were angry.

Presenting the New Word

Explain that the new word is *grace*. Invite the children to say the word *grace* aloud. Read the definition aloud and discuss its meaning. Then invite a child to read aloud the top paragraph on page 87. Discuss the meaning of the paragraph. Ask the children to list all the things that we do with the help of God's grace.

Step 3 / CONCLUSION

Learning How to Live Our Faith

Completing an Activity

Direct the children's attention to the activity on page 87. Give them sufficient time to complete the activity. When the children have completed the activity, take time to review their responses.

Discovering Steps to Reconciliation

The following scenario reinforces the concept that the Holy Spirit and God's grace help us to trust, to accept others, and to make peace. Discover the steps in the process that leads the children in the scenario to reconciliation.

David's class had worked long and hard to create a clay statue of a dinosaur. It was three-feet high and painted a bright, glossy green. Everybody said it was great! David was fooling around. His teacher corrected David and asked him to return quietly to his seat. David didn't like being corrected. He became angry and walked over to the dinosaur and purposely knocked it off the table. The statue broke into pieces. Everyone was upset with David. How could David's class trust, accept, and make peace with him?

Guide the children to the realization that every day we have opportunities for reconciliation. It is through the grace of the Holy Spirit that we forgive and say we're sorry to one another.

DAY 4
MORALITY

Objective

This lesson helps the children welcome God's gift of forgiveness and to express their sorrow for having sinned.

Step 1 / INTRODUCTION

Learning About Our Lives

Explaining Sorrow

Cover a round piece of cardboard with yellow paper on both sides. On one side, draw a sad face and on the other side, a smiling face. Show the class the sad face. Ask them to tell you what they think of when they see this face.

Introduce the word *sorrow*. Ask: What do you think *sorrow* means? Discuss its various meanings—sadness, grief, regret. It is what we feel when we are sorry for our sins. Hold the sad face up and invite the children to join you at the prayer table.

Step 2 / DEVELOPMENT

Learning About Our Faith

Praying for God's Forgiveness

Introduce the Prayer of Sorrow on page 88. Teach the prayer line by line, helping the children understand the meaning. Tell them that reconciliation gives us a new start in our relationship with God and with others.

Help the children understand that God's mercy and goodness make it possible for our sins to be forgiven. Then pray the Prayer of Sorrow with them. Encourage the children to pray this prayer daily.

To help the children memorize the Prayer of Sorrow, help them make prayer cards. Distribute white construction paper and crayons or felt-tip markers. Instruct the children to copy the prayer on the cards and then add decorations. Suggest that they place the cards in a convenient place at home so that they can pray the Prayer of Sorrow every night.

A Prayer of Sorrow

Lord God,
I trust in your goodness and mercy.
I am sorry
for all the wrong things I have done.
I am sorry
for all the good things I have not done.
I want to love you with all my heart.

Activity

Draw a picture of yourself making friends again with someone you have hurt and who has forgiven you.

Teaching Tips

Here are some ways to help a child build self-esteem.

Espouse encouraging influences.

- Build on a child's strengths.
- Show confidence in the child.
- Value the child in your words and actions.
- Stimulate independence.

Avoid discouraging influences.

- Don't focus on mistakes.
- Don't expect perfection.
- Don't have negative expectations.
- Don't nurture dependence.

o reconcile with our friends, we put one action on
op of another. Number the blocks to show the steps
of reconciling. Decide which block to start with.
Number it with the number **1**. Number each of the
other blocks with the numbers **2**, **3**, **4**, or **5**.

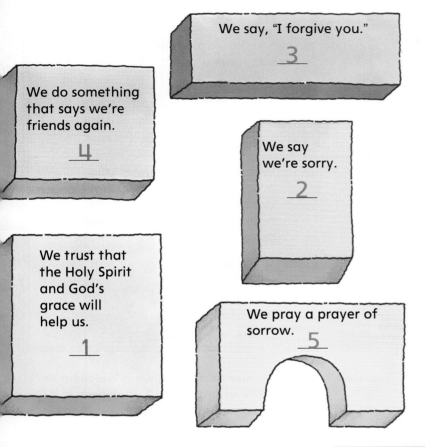

We say, "I forgive you."

3

We do something
that says we're
friends again.

4

We say
we're sorry.

2

We trust that
the Holy Spirit
and God's
grace will
help us.

1

We pray a prayer of
sorrow.

5

Cultural Awareness

Teach the children how to say
"peace" in many languages. Use
the peace greetings throughout
the day. If celebrating liturgy, use
these languages during the Sign
of Peace.

Latin	*Pax*
French	*Paix*
Hebrew	*Shalom*
Hmong	*Kev sib haum xeeb*

(Pronounced: Ck see ho seng)

German	*Frieden*
Polish	*Pokój*
Vietnamese	*Hoà-bình*
Swahili	*Amani*
Spanish	*Paz*

If time permits, ask the children to suggest
gestures to accompany each sentence of the
Prayer of Sorrow. For example, for the first
sentence you might have them extend both
arms up over their heads as they say the words
Lord God. As they pray the words *goodness
and mercy*, direct them to cross their arms
gently over their chests.

Conclude by singing "God Loves Me and You"
from THIS IS OUR FAITH Music Program, Grade
2. Turn the sad face to the other side and show
the children the smiling face. While holding up
the smiling face, lead the children back to their
desks.

Completing an Activity

Read aloud the directions to the activity on
page 89. Allow the class as a group to arrange
the blocks in the order of the steps of
reconciling.

Step 3 / CONCLUSION

Learning How to Live Our Faith

Praying Together

Light a candle on the prayer table and place
the sad face near it. Remind the children that
this face reminds us of those times when we
are sad because we have hurt or have not
helped another person. Enthrone the Bible.
Invite a child to proclaim Colossians 3:13, "as
the Lord has forgiven you, so must you also
do." Ask the children to tell you what those
words mean. Cite the words "Forgive us our
trespasses as we forgive those who trespass
against us" from The Lord's Prayer. Ask how
the words are similar. Invite the children to
share by asking what happens inside us when
we tell God we are sorry. (*We feel better. We
become peaceful.*) Remind the children that
God wants us to forgive others when they
hurt us.

PRAYER/REVIEW

Objective

This lesson helps the children celebrate reconciliation in a "We Come Home to Jesus" prayer.

Finding a Prayer Partner

Distribute to the children circles on which you have drawn either a sad or a smiling face. (Use various colors of paper. The idea is to partner each sad face with a smiling face of the same color.) Invite the children to scatter around the classroom, holding a paper circle. Play the instrumental recording of "God Loves Me and You" from THIS IS OUR FAITH Music Program, Grade 2. When the music starts, all should seek a partner who has the matching color circle and the opposite face. When the music stops, all freeze. On finding a partner, the child with the sad face says, "I'm sorry." The other child replies, "I forgive you." After this exchange, the partners move to the prayer circle. Demonstrate the process. Ask if there are any questions. If not, begin the music. Continue the process until everyone has moved to the prayer circle.

Praying Together

Light the candle and invite the children to place all the smiling faces on the discovery table. Explain that reconciliation means coming home to Jesus. Then read the introductory passage under "Praying to Come Home to Jesus." Ask the children to respond to each invocation with "We come home to Jesus." To vary how this prayer is said, assign several readers to pray the teacher's part. The rest of the class will join in the response. On another day, teach the children to sing the response on any easy six-note melodic pattern.

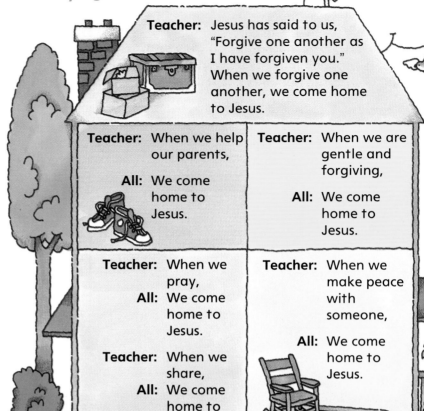

Praying to Come Home to Jesus

Teacher: Jesus has said to us, "Forgive one another as I have forgiven you." When we forgive one another, we come home to Jesus.

Teacher: When we help our parents,
All: We come home to Jesus.

Teacher: When we are gentle and forgiving,
All: We come home to Jesus.

Teacher: When we pray,
All: We come home to Jesus.

Teacher: When we share,
All: We come home to Jesus.

Teacher: When we make peace with someone,
All: We come home to Jesus.

Teacher: Jesus, we know that you always welcome us to your home of grace and forgiveness. It is so good to come home to you!
All: Amen.

90 Prayer

Focus on

Asking Forgiveness Remind the children that there are many ways we can ask God's forgiveness. We can ask the Father to forgive us in private prayer, or we can join our prayer with others. We can use official prayers of the Church, or we can speak to God in our own words. Stress to the class that the only words we need to use are the words *I'm sorry*. Assure the children that the Lord always forgives us. All we need do is ask.

Enriching the Lesson

Ask the children to stand and place their hands over their hearts. Invite them to echo you as they make the following promises.

Dear Jesus,
I promise to trust you.
I promise to forgive others when they hurt me.
I promise to make up when I hurt others.

I make these promises in the name of the Father, and of the Son, and of the Holy Spirit. Amen.

90

Chapter Review

Circle the word hidden in each line.

```
P F R I E N D
H U R T B G W
B K U G O D B
F O R G I V E
H M S O R R Y
```

. What does God want us to do when others hurt us?

forgive them

. What do we call the process of making up and being friends again?

reconciliation

. Talk about how we can make up with someone when we have hurt them.

> **Forgive each other just as the Lord has forgiven you.**
> **Based on Colossians 3:13**

Finding the Hidden Words

Tell the children that words about reconciliation are hidden in the puzzle tree. Point out the words listed on the chalkboard and encourage the children to check them over for clues. Read aloud the puzzle directions and have the children complete the puzzle on their own. Afterward, invite sharing.

Reviewing the Chapter

Have the children respond orally to the review questions, then allow them sufficient time to write their answers to questions 1 and 2 on the lines provided. Be supportive of each child who participates in the discussion of item 3. Write the class's suggestions on the chalkboard. Select one thing for the children to do at home and in school to forgive others. State the choice and have the class repeat it aloud with you.

Teaching Tips

Write "Thoughts for the Day" on the chalkboard, visual reminders about the need to be gentler and kinder to one another.

1. Teasing hurts others.
2. Learn to walk in someone else's shoes.
3. Sometimes what we say and do to others is unfair.
4. Don't be unkind to people just because they are different.
5. Girls are as important as boys.

We Celebrate Reconciliation

Objectives ~~~~~~~~~~

To help the children

- Realize that Jesus gives us the sacrament of Reconciliation.
- Learn how to make an examination of conscience.
- Understand the process of the sacrament of Reconciliation.
- Understand the Rite of Reconciliation.
- Pray for forgiveness and review the chapter.

Chapter Outline ~~~~~~~~~~

	Step 1 **Learning About Our Lives**	**Step 2** **Learning About Our Faith**	**Step 3** **Learning How to Live Our Faith**
Day 1	■ Review Chapter 7. *ABOUT 5 MINUTES*	■ Introduce the chapter. ■ Read a poem. ■ Learn about forgiveness. ■ Present the doctrine. ■ Introduce the new word. *ABOUT 20 MINUTES*	■ Pray together. *ABOUT 5 MINUTES*
Day 2	■ Gather at the discovery table. ■ Think about choices. *ABOUT 10 MINUTES*	■ Make an examination of conscience. *ABOUT 10 MINUTES*	■ Complete an activity. *ABOUT 10 MINUTES*
Day 3	■ Review Day 2. *ABOUT 5 MINUTES*	■ Describe the sacrament of Reconciliation ■ Present the new words. ■ Present the doctrine. *ABOUT 20 MINUTES*	■ Review the Prayer of Sorrow. *ABOUT 5 MINUTES*
Day 4	■ Review the vocabulary. *ABOUT 5 MINUTES*	■ Explain the rite. ■ Continue to explain the rite. *ABOUT 15 MINUTES*	■ Review the process. ■ Understand reconciliation. *ABOUT 10 MINUTES*

Day 5 **Prayer** Prepare for a prayer experience and pray together for forgiveness.
       Review Review the chapter and read the Scripture verse.

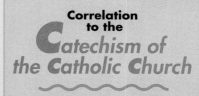
**Correlation
to the
Catechism of
the Catholic Church**

Paragraphs
986, 1465, 1486, 1490, 1491

Plan Ahead

	Preparing Your Class	Materials Needed
Day 1	Review Chapter 7 and read over the lesson.	■ pencils
Day 2	Read over the lesson. Gather items for the discovery table, such as a stethoscope, microscope, magnifying glass, scale, and so on.	■ stethoscope, microscope ■ magnifying glass ■ postal or health form ■ scale, eye glasses ■ crayons, markers, drawing paper
Day 3	Read over the lesson prior to the session. Prepare the prayer table.	
Day 4	Read over the lesson. Review the Rite of Reconciliation. Make arrangements for guest speakers and for the reconciliation room.	
Day 5	Read over the lesson. Prepare prayer table. If enriching the lesson, make hinged paper hearts for each child.	■ pencils ■ candle, matches ■ hinged paper heart for each child

Additional Resources

As you plan this chapter, consider using the following materials from The Resourceful Teacher Package.

■ *Classroom Activity Sheets 8 and 8a*

■ *Family Activity Sheets 8 and 8a*

■ *Chapter 8 Test*

■ *Prayers for Every Day*

■ *Projects: Grade 2*

You may also wish to refer to the following Big Book.

■ *We Celebrate the Sacraments,* pages 13–15

In preparing the children for the Sunday readings, you may wish to use Silver Burdett Ginn's *Getting Ready for Sunday* student and teacher materials.

BOOKS FOR THE JOURNEY

The Hurt. Teddi Doleski. Paulist Press, 1983. How to deal with hurt feelings.

The First Strawberries: A Cherokee Story. Retold by Joseph Bruhac. Dial Books for Young Readers, 1993. A Cherokee legend of a gift of strawberries reconciling and reuniting a couple who have quarreled.

MORE BOOKS FOR THE JOURNEY

Coat of Many Colors. Dolly Parton. HarperCollins, 1994. The author's own story of being laughed at by the children in her school and how she tries and fails to help them understand.

The Rag Coat. Lauren Mills. Little, Brown, 1991. Another story of a child who is laughed at and scorned but is able to help her classmates understand and appreciate the love and stories in the rags of her coat.

REDUCED CLASSROOM ACTIVITIES

Name _____

We Celebrate Reconciliation

Underline the sentences that show reconciliation.

1. You tell your brother that you forgive him.
2. You tell someone that he is not your friend anymore.
3. You smile and hug your dad.
4. You help a friend you have hurt.
5. You make your mother a card to ask forgiveness.
6. You are mean to a classmate you don't like.
7. You call a friend to ask her to come to your house.
8. You try to fix your sister's toy that you broke.

To the Teacher: This activity will help explain reasons for reconciling with others.

Chapter 8   We Celebrate Reconciliation   THIS IS OUR FAITH 2   **8**

Name _____

The Sacrament of Reconciliation

Draw a line to match the words and their meanings. One word does not have a meaning given. Discuss that word with your classmates.

1. confess
2. penance
3. reconciliation room
4. contrition
5. absolution
6. priest

- a leader of the Christian community who forgives us in God's name and in the name of the Christian community
- the words of forgiveness that the priest prays over us
- to tell our sins to the priest
- another word for sorrow
- a prayer or good action to show God that we are sorry and want to be more caring

To the Teacher: This activity reviews the vocabulary words presented in the chapter.

8a   THIS IS OUR FAITH 2   Chapter 8   We Celebrate Reconciliation

THE SACRAMENT OF RECONCILIATION

In the sacrament of Reconciliation, Catholics have a special way to express sorrow for sin and to celebrate God's forgiveness. This sacrament gives us great cause for rejoicing because through it we may choose to restore our friendships with God and with others. Therefore, as the *National Catechetical Directory* states: "Frequent participation in this sacrament, even though one has not committed a serious sin, is a highly desirable way of celebrating ongoing conversion and making progress in holiness" (#124).

Some of the children in your group may be celebrating the sacrament of Reconciliation for the first time this year. This session is not intended to prepare them for their first reception of the sacrament. They will need more immediate and formal preparation. However, the steps are explained in story form to familiarize the children with the ritual and its meaning.

THE RITE OF RECONCILIATION

The Church has traditionally taught that the essential elements of the sacrament are confession, purpose of amendment, contrition, absolution, and satisfaction.

According to the revised rite, the priest, acting in Christ's name, warmly greets the penitent and then proclaims a Scripture reading about conversion and reconciliation. Having previously examined his or her conscience, the penitent then confesses sins and expresses sorrow for the offenses by saying a prayer of contrition. The priest, in Jesus' name, and in the name of the Christian community, forgives and absolves the penitent and extends a gesture of peace as a sign of God's mercy and love. During the celebration, the priest gives the penitent a penance to do to make satisfaction for sin. After the celebration of the sacrament, the penitent performs the penance. The penance is a sign of the penitent's willingness to continue the healing process and of the penitent's acceptance of God's transforming love, peace, and forgiveness.

As the teacher, you should try throughout the session to emphasize the sacrament's celebration aspect. Remind the children that God loves us and forgives us even when we have been selfish in our friendships with him and with other people.

Objective

This lesson helps the children recognize that Jesus gives us the sacrament of Reconciliation.

Step 1 / INTRODUCTION

Learning About Our Lives

Reviewing Chapter 7

Help the children recall what they have already learned about the process of reconciliation. Remind them that reconciliation is the process of making up and becoming friends again.

Step 2 / DEVELOPMENT

Learning About Our Faith

Introducing the Chapter

Ask the children to turn to page 92. Ask a volunteer to read the chapter title and focus question aloud. Remind the children that they have learned that when we hurt someone on purpose, we sin. Invite the children to respond to the question. Possible answers may include *sorry, guilty, ashamed, sad.* Emphasize that we do not have to live with these feelings after we have confessed our sin. Help the children recall that God always forgives us when we say we are sorry for our sins.

Reading a Poem

Ask the children to study the photograph on page 92. Ask volunteers to tell a story about the two friends in the photograph. Then read the poem "Asking Forgiveness." Speak with the children about ways they can act to show that they are sorry, as well as by using words.

Learning About Forgiveness

Have the children follow in their books as you read aloud the paragraph "Jesus Teaches Us to Forgive" on page 93. Ask:

- With whom is Jesus speaking? (*His friend Peter*)

- What does Peter ask Jesus? (*He asks how often must he forgive someone who does him harm; he asks if seven times is enough.*)

8

We Celebrate Reconciliation

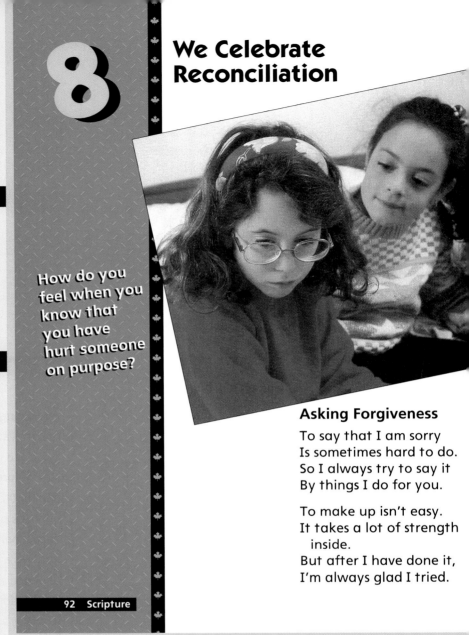

How do you feel when you know that you have hurt someone on purpose?

Asking Forgiveness

To say that I am sorry
Is sometimes hard to do.
So I always try to say it
By things I do for you.

To make up isn't easy.
It takes a lot of strength inside.
But after I have done it,
I'm always glad I tried.

Focus on

Praying for Forgiveness   Lead the class in a prayer of forgiveness. Teach them to pray, "Jesus, forgive us" after each prayer statement.
For fighting with friends . . .
For hurting others . . .
For being mean to those we don't like . . .
For making fun of others . . .
For not listening to our parents . . .
Jesus, you have called us to grow in your love. Forgive us for the times we have hurt others by being selfish. Help us to learn to say "I'm sorry."

Jesus Teaches Us to Forgive

Jesus teaches us about forgiveness. This story about forgiveness is found in the Bible.

A friend of Jesus, whose name was Peter, came to Jesus and asked, "Lord, when someone hurts me, how often must I forgive? Is seven times enough?" "No," said Jesus, "not seven times, but seventy times seven times."

Based on Matthew 18:21–22

The Sacrament of Reconciliation

Catholics have a special way of showing sorrow and asking God's forgiveness. We call it the **sacrament of Reconciliation**. In this sacrament we tell God we are sorry for our sins. In this sacrament the priest brings us God's forgiveness.

Activity

Underline the name of the sacrament in which we show sorrow for our sins and ask God's forgiveness.

New Word

sacrament of Reconciliation	the sacrament in which we say we are sorry for our sins and celebrate God's forgiveness

Scripture 93

- What does Jesus reply? (*Not seven times, but seventy times seven times*)
- What do you think Jesus meant when he told Peter to forgive "seventy times seven times"? (*Answers will vary.*)

Explain that Jesus did not mean for Peter to forgive a certain number of times, such as seven times, or four hundred ninety times, but rather to forgive over and over again, without limit.

We must always forgive one another. Remind the children that just as Jesus invited his friend Peter to seek forgiveness always, Jesus, who loves us as friends, invites us to ask pardon for our sins and to seek forgiveness. God's forgiveness is without limits. It's always there for us.

Presenting the Doctrine

Invite a volunteer to read aloud "The Sacrament of Reconciliation" on page 93. Have the children repeat the words *sacrament of Reconciliation* together aloud a few times.

Introduce the sacrament of Reconciliation as an opportunity to celebrate God's mercy and forgiveness in our lives. Ask: How do you think this happens? (*Answers will vary.*)

Introducing the New Word

Have the children repeat after you as you read the new term *sacrament of Reconciliation* and its definition. Break up the definition into phrases no longer than six words so that the children will be able to echo you without stumbling.

Step 3 / CONCLUSION

Learning How to Live Our Faith

Praying Together

Invite the children to join you at the prayer table. When the children are quiet, pray: "God, we thank you for Jesus, who teaches us about forgiveness. We thank you too for the Church, which gives us a special way to show our sorrow and ask for God's forgiveness in the sacrament of Reconciliation. Stay with us, God, as we continue to learn about forgiveness. We ask this in Jesus' name. Amen."

Focus on

The Role of the Priest Help the children understand the role of the priest in the sacrament of Reconciliation. Priests are ordained members of the Catholic community who have chosen to follow Jesus in a special way by serving God's people. One way a priest serves is to forgive sins on Jesus' behalf. The priest reminds us that Jesus always loves us. Through the words of the priest, Jesus forgives our sins.

Teaching Tips

Recall the meaning of the word *sacrament* from Unit 1, Chapter 3. (Print the word *sacrament* on the board or, if you have made one, use the poster from Chapter 3.) Ask: What are the sacraments we have studied already? (*Baptism and Confirmation*) Invite the children to share what they remember about these sacraments.

93

DAY 2
MORALITY

Objective

This lesson helps the children learn how to make an examination of conscience.

Step 1 / INTRODUCTION

Learning About Our Lives

Gathering at the Discovery Table

Place on the discovery table items that help us to examine things: stethoscope, microscope, magnifying glass, postal or health form, scale, eye glasses, and so on.

Invite the children to tell you how each of these items helps us to examine something. Explain that when we examine something, we study it. Draw them to the conclusion that when we examine something, we learn more about it. By knowing more about something, we can understand it better.

Tell the children that our conscience is a sense we have of what is right and good, and also of what is wrong and sinful. Explain that when we examine our conscience, we study how well we are living as followers of Jesus.

Thinking About Our Choices

Explain to the children that we have to examine our choices in life in order to see how we are doing and to plan how we might grow better and improve. This is called an examination of conscience. Tell them that our conscience is that part of us that helps us determine right from wrong. Give the children this example: When your mom says, "No cookies before dinner," and you sneak some cookies when your mom isn't around, you know that you have chosen to do something wrong. This is your conscience talking to you.

Read aloud "Thinking About Our Choices" on page 94. If the children have any questions about this paragraph, take the time to answer them.

Thinking About Our Choices

It is good to ask ourselves questions about the choices we make every day. We can think about how we have chosen to hurt others, ourselves, and the earth on purpose. We call this an examination of conscience. Examining our consciences helps us grow into more caring and loving persons. It is something Catholics do carefully before they celebrate the sacrament of Reconciliation.

An Examination of Conscience

Use these questions to help you think about your everyday words and actions.

Caring for God

● Do I listen and talk with God?
● Do I thank God for making me special?
● Do I thank God for all my gifts and talents?
● Do I tell God I'm sorry when I am selfish and don't share my gifts and talents with others?

Caring for Myself

● Do I take care of my health?
● Do I try to learn new things from my family, my teachers, and my friends and neighbors?

🍎 Teaching Tips

Praying a litany of sorrow at home could engage the parents in helping their child sort out the things he or she does to show care and love or to hurt or damage someone or something. Also, encourage the parents to read through the examination of conscience. Invite them to write a comment in the book after praying with their child.

★ Enriching the Lesson ★

Pray with the class this litany of sorrow, asking Jesus' forgiveness. Remind the children that Jesus came to save all people. Our response is, *Forgive us, Lord.*

Jesus, Son of the Father, *R.*
Jesus, Child of Mary, *R.*
Jesus, who loves us, *R.*
Jesus, who hears our prayers, *R.*
Jesus, who forgives our sins, *R.*
Jesus, who healed the sick, *R.*
Jesus, who died on the cross, *R.*
Jesus, who rose from the dead, *R.*
Jesus, who is with us now, *R.*

Caring for Others

- Do I tell the truth?
- Am I kind to other people, especially to people who are different from me?
- Do I help others?
- Do I listen to others?
- Do I forgive people who hurt me?
- Do I obey my parents and others who care for me?
- Do I thank other people for what they do for me?

Caring for Things

- Do I take care of what I have?
- Do I share my things?
- Do I respect what belongs to others?
- Do I treat animals and the earth with care?

 Activity

Draw yourself making a good choice.

Morality 95

Cultural Awareness

You might wish to take some time to speak with the children about the sin of prejudice, especially prejudice against people of other cultures. Be sure to explain what prejudice is and how it affects people's lives. Discuss with the children some concrete ways of combating prejudice, such as making friends with children in school or in the neighborhood who are from different cultures.

Step 2 / DEVELOPMENT

Learning About Our Faith

Making an Examination of Conscience

Tell the children that an examination of conscience will help us to feel proud of the good things we have done and it will help us to be sorry for the wrong things we have done.

To prepare the children to experience an examination of conscience, invite them to close their eyes and take slow, deep breaths. Tell them that they should listen to each question and answer it silently, in their hearts. Make clear to them that their answers are between God and themselves and that you will not ask them to share their responses. Read the examination questions under "Caring for God," "Caring for Myself," "Caring for Others," and "Caring for Things" on pages 94–95. Read slowly and reflectively to the group, pausing briefly after each question. Encourage the children to examine their consciences often as a way of becoming more caring and loving people.

or . . .

Ask the children to sit quietly in a prayerful position. Explain that you will be praying a litany of sorrow. Change the questions in the examination of conscience to statements of sorrow such as the ones below. Tell the children to respond to each statement of sorrow with the words *Lord, forgive us.*

For the times when we didn't listen and talk with God, _____.

For the times when we didn't tell the truth, _____.

Step 3 / CONCLUSION

Learning How to Live Our Faith

Completing an Activity

In the space provided on page 95, help the children draw themselves making a good choice. Praise all efforts.

DAY 3
DOCTRINE

Objective

This lesson introduces the children to the process for the sacrament of Reconciliation: confession, penance, contrition, and absolution.

Step 1 / INTRODUCTION

Learning About Our Lives

Reviewing Day 2

Remind the children that yesterday they reflected on an examination of conscience, the process that helps us know how we have been selfish in word and in deed. Review also the meaning of the new term from Day 1, *sacrament of Reconciliation*. Ask if there are any questions. Respond to the children's questions.

Step 2 / DEVELOPMENT

Learning About Our Faith

Describing the Sacrament of Reconciliation

Ask for volunteers to read aloud "José Asks Questions," on pages 96 and 97. Ask:

■ What is the special way the Church gives us to say we are sorry for our sins? (*The sacrament of Reconciliation*)

■ What does this sacrament give us? (*Forgiveness and peace*)

■ What is the name of the room where we confess our sins? (*Reconciliation room*)

■ What does the priest give after the sins are confessed? (*A penance*)

■ How does God know we are sorry for our sins? (*We say a prayer of contrition, or sorrow, for our sins.*)

■ What does the priest give after the prayer of contrition? (*Absolution*)

Presenting the New Words

Repeat each new word and ask a child to read aloud its definition. The entire class should repeat each definition aloud. Here are some ideas for clarifying the meaning of the new words.

José Asks Questions

"Why do Catholics celebrate the sacrament of Reconciliation?" José asked his mother.

"Because, José," Mrs. Ríos said, "the Church gives us this very special way of saying that we're sorry for our sins. The sacrament of Reconciliation also gives us God's forgiveness and peace."

José thought about that for a moment. Then he asked, "What happens when you go into that little room?"

"Well, we call that room the reconciliation room. When we go in, the priest welcomes us. Then we read together from the Bible," answered Mrs. Ríos.

"When do you **confess** your sins?" asked José.

"That comes next. I tell the priest how I may have hurt myself or others on purpose. Then the priest gives me a **penance**. A penance is something we do that shows that we are really sorry for being selfish and unloving," answered Mrs. Ríos.

96   Doctrine

🍎 Teaching Tips

How should I react when a child tells me that he or she does not want to receive the sacrament of Reconciliation? Remembering that children mature and develop at individual rates and have different needs and personalities, try to respond to such a statement with calm assurance and acceptance. Listen closely as the child explains his or her reasons. Reassure the child that it is okay to have such feelings. Never react in a way that shows annoyance or impatience.

José had another question. "How does God know that you are sorry for your sins?"

"God knows I'm sorry because next I say a prayer of **contrition**. Contrition means to be sorry. I also promise to try not to sin again."

"Then you go home, right, Mom?" José asked.

"Not yet, José," said Mrs. Ríos. "Before I leave the reconciliation room, the priest gives me **absolution**. He forgives me and blesses me in Jesus' name and in the name of the Christian community. I can now leave in peace."

José's mother smiled at him. José could sure ask a lot of questions!

New Words

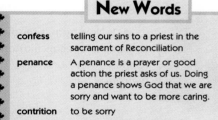

confess	telling our sins to a priest in the sacrament of Reconciliation
penance	A penance is a prayer or good action the priest asks of us. Doing a penance shows God that we are sorry and want to be more caring.
contrition	to be sorry
absolution	the words of forgiveness the priest prays over us in the sacrament of Reconciliation

We Believe

In the sacrament of Reconciliation, we tell God we are sorry. We ask God to forgive us for our sins. We promise to try not to sin again. God forgives us through Jesus Christ and the Church.

Doctrine 97

1. *confess* We tell our sins to the priest; for instance, "I have hit my brother many times. I get angry with him when he takes my toys without asking. He bugs me when I watch TV. I really get angry with him, so I hit him."

2. *penance* The priest now asks us to do some good action that will help us overcome the sin; for instance, "Because you're often angry at your brother, be kind and gentle to him. Do something helpful for him at least once each day. Tell your brother that you love him. These two actions are your penance."

3. *contrition* We show we are sorry by what we say and what we do. We will do kind acts to make up for our sins, but we also tell God through a prayer of sorrow that we are sorry; for instance, I say a prayer of sorrow.

4. *absolution* A sign helps us to understand what is happening when we celebrate a sacrament. Remember that in Baptism, the water reminded us of new life; in Confirmation the oil reminded us that we are strengthened; in Reconciliation the priest speaks words of forgiveness on God's behalf. While he is speaking, the priest often lays his hands on our heads, another sign that we are celebrating God's forgiveness.

Presenting the Doctrine

Read aloud the We Believe statements with the children. Write the four steps on the chalkboard.

1. We tell God we are sorry for our sins.
2. We ask for God's forgiveness.
3. We tell God we will not sin again.
4. God forgives us.

Ask the children to read the four steps.

Step 3 / CONCLUSION

Learning How to Live Our Faith

Reviewing the Prayer of Sorrow

Invite the children to bring their books to the prayer table. In a quiet voice, ask them to open their books to page 88. Explain that whenever they pray the Prayer of Sorrow to pray it gently and with sincerity. Then begin to pray together.

Objective

This lesson helps the children recognize the process and understand the Rite of Reconciliation.

Step 1 / INTRODUCTION

Learning About Our Lives

Reviewing the Vocabulary

Ask the children to name each of the four new words presented yesterday and to define what each word means. Then continue by explaining that today we are going to look at what we actually say and do when we enter the reconciliation room and greet the priest.

Step 2 / DEVELOPMENT

Learning About Our Faith

Explaining the Rite

Read aloud the first two paragraphs of "Samantha Celebrates the Sacrament of Reconciliation" on page 98. Ask one of the children to read the picture caption for step 1 of the rite. Direct the children to look at this photograph. Ask: What words might Father Connor use to welcome Samantha? How might Samantha respond?

Direct the children's attention to step 2, on page 99. Read aloud step 2 of the rite. Explain that Father Connor and Samantha are reading a Scripture story about God's forgiveness.

Read step 3 aloud. Remind the children that a sin is a selfish or uncaring action. Explain that when Samantha talks about such actions, she is confessing her sins. Review the meaning of the new word *confess*.

Direct the children's attention to step 4 of the rite and read it aloud. Explain that we can show God that we are truly sorry for our sins by doing a kind act or by saying a prayer. Identify some penance a priest may ask of us.

Now that you better understand what takes place in the sacrament of Reconciliation, follow Samantha as she celebrates the sacrament with Father Connor.

Samantha Celebrates the Sacrament of Reconciliation

Before Samantha goes into the reconciliation room, she thinks about how much God loves her. She knows God will forgive her sins. Sam thinks about how she chose to hurt her friendship with God, others, herself, and the earth. She thinks about times when she ignored her responsibilities. Sam knows some of her choices were wrong.

◀ **1.** Now Sam is ready to go to the reconciliation room. Father Connor welcomes her.

Enriching the Lesson

To reinforce what the children have learned about the Rite of Reconciliation, invite some students who have already celebrated the sacrament to share their experience with the class. Be sure to speak with the older students before the session regarding the content you wish for them to share. Another option is to use puppets to review the rite.

CURRICULUM CONNECTION

Art Invite the art teacher to help the class design and draw a project that reinforces the idea that acts of kindness can be symbolized by beams of light in a world darkened by hurtful actions. In each beam have the students name those acts of kindness that they can do to let the light of goodness shine in the world.

◀ **2.** Father Connor and Samantha read together from the Bible. They read about how good God is and how God is always ready to forgive.

▼ **3.** Samantha confesses her sins. She tells Father Connor that she has done things she knows were wrong and has hurt other people on purpose.

▶ **4.** Father Connor talks to Sam for a few minutes. He helps her find ways to love others as Jesus wants us to love them. Then Father Connor gives Samantha a penance. He asks Sam to say a prayer or to do a kind act to show her love for others and sorrow for her sins.

▲ **5.** Sam tells God that she is sorry and that she will try not to sin again. She asks forgiveness. She says a prayer of contrition.

◀ **6.** Father Connor gives Samantha absolution. He forgives and blesses her in Jesus' name and in the name of the Christian community. Father Connor then offers Sam a sign of peace. She can leave in peace.

Doctrine 99

⭐ **Enriching the Lesson** ⭐

Visit your parish reconciliation room. You might have one or more of the children role-play the celebration of the sacrament, with you taking the part of the priest. To avoid any embarrassment or invasion of privacy, suggest a few sins for the children to confess, such as fighting with a brother or sister or telling a lie.

Continuing to Explain

Read aloud step 5 of the rite. Explain that the word *contrition* is another word for "sorrow." Tell the children that an act of contrition is a prayer of sorrow. Review with them the Prayer of Sorrow on page 88.

Read aloud step 6. Explain that the word *absolution* means "a washing away of sins." Tell the children that the priest absolves us in Jesus' name and in the name of the Christian community. The priest gives us a sign of peace as an assurance of God's forgiveness.

Step 3 / CONCLUSION

Learning How to Live Our Faith

Reviewing the Process

Read through the six steps of the rite once again. To ascertain the children's comprehension of the rite, ask:

■ What do we say in the sacrament of Reconciliation? (*We say that we are sorry.*)

■ What do we celebrate? (*God's loving forgiveness and peace*)

Understanding Reconciliation

Invite the children to recall the story of the forgiving father on page 84. Ask them to recall how the son felt when he was welcomed home by the father. (*Happy, joyful*) Explain that we too feel good when we are welcomed home to Jesus in the sacrament of Reconciliation.

DAY 5
PRAYER/REVIEW

Objective

This lesson invites the children to pray for forgiveness in a responsorial prayer experience.

Preparing for a Prayer Experience

Darken the room by turning off the overhead lights and adjusting the window shades or blinds. (Readers still need to be able to read from the text.) Have available on the prayer table a candle and matches, if fire regulations allow.

Praying Together

Ask the children to join you at the prayer table. Keep the candle unlit for the first part of the prayer experience. When the children are seated and quiet, tell them that today's prayer experience will be a time to remember God's love and forgiveness. Remind them that when we sin, it is like living in darkness. Explain to the class that the room is darkened to remind them of the darkness of sin.

Begin the prayer experience by asking the children to repeat after each statement you read, *We live in darkness.* Now read the first four statements on page 100, pausing after each statement for the children's response.

Then light the candle. Allow sufficient time for the candle's light to brighten the room. Ask: Whose light fills our lives? (*Jesus'*) Help the children realize that Jesus is the Light of the World. Continue by saying that the followers of Jesus are asked to let the light of Jesus shine in their lives.

Read the next four statements, allowing time after each statement for the children to respond *Jesus' light shines.*

Complete the prayer experience by reading the closing prayer. Encourage the children to respond *Amen.*

Praying for Forgiveness

Teacher: When we hurt others,
All: We live in darkness.

Teacher: When we don't share,
All: We live in darkness.

Teacher: When we cause trouble in school,
All: We live in darkness.

Teacher: When we don't pray,
All: We live in darkness.

Teacher: When we care for others,
All: Jesus' light shines.

Teacher: When we share our things,
All: Jesus' light shines.

Teacher: When we cooperate at school,
All: Jesus' light shines.

Teacher: When we pray,
All: Jesus' light shines.

Teacher: We are forgiven.
We are at peace.
Let us live this day
in the light of Jesus.
All: Amen.

100 Prayer

Teaching Tips

Make it a habit to point out to the children occasions when you have observed them living peacefully with each other. When children are often praised for acting kindly and cooperatively, they grow as human beings and as Christians. They can begin to see the connection between *learning* their faith and *living* their faith.

CURRICULUM CONNECTION

Music Invite the music specialist or parish music director to teach "This Little Light of Mine" to the children. The children need only sing the repeated chorus section: *This little light of mine, I'm gonna let it shine* (repeat three times); *Let it shine, let it shine, let it shine.* Have the class listen as a soloist sings the verse. This gospel song is recorded on CD 1-10, Grade 5, THE WORLD OF MUSIC, 1991, Silver Burdett Ginn.

100

Chapter Review

Draw a line to match the words with their meanings.

confess your sins — telling the priest how you have hurt others

a penance — thinking about things you did or said that you know were wrong

an examination of conscience — a prayer or good action the priest asks of you to show God that you are sorry

absolution — a prayer that tells God you are sorry and asks forgiveness

a prayer of sorrow — a blessing of forgiveness

1. What is another word for sorrow?

contrition

2. What do we ask God for in the sacrament of Reconciliation?

forgiveness

3. Talk about ways we can make up with other people and with God.

> Let us always ask God to forgive us.
>
> Based on Hebrews 4:16

Reviewing the Chapter

Invite a child to read aloud the directions for the review on page 101. Instruct the children to write their answers on the lines provided. Assist them as needed. When all are finished, say each match aloud. Help the children check their work.

Allow enough time for the children to write their answers to questions 1 and 2. Be supportive of each child who participates in the discussion of the third item.

Reading the Scripture Verse

Direct the children to read aloud the Scripture verse. Remind them of God's love and forgiveness. Encourage them to ask the Lord each day to forgive them for anything wrong or hurtful they might have done.

★★★ Enriching the Lesson ★★★

Distribute hinged paper hearts. Invite the children to print their names on the outside of their hearts. On the inside of the hearts, have them write one thing they will do to become a more forgiving person. Tell the children to take their hearts home and pray each morning and evening for the Holy Spirit to help them live in God's love and forgiveness.

101

Using the Unit Organizer

Completing a graphic organizer such as a chart or table can help the children to organize information that has been presented in the unit. Organizers can enable the children to visualize their thinking and recognize relationships among ideas. This will give the children that opportunity to understand more completely the materials they have been studying.

Completing the Organizer

Have the children turn to page 102 in their books. Read aloud the directions to the Unit Organizer activity. Point out where to start. Then ask the children to complete the activity independently. If necessary, tell them that they may look back through the previous four chapters for help. When everyone has finished, have the children compare their responses with the class.

Looking Back: Self-Assessment

The critical reflection questions below give the children an opportunity to sharpen their thinking skills. The questions can be used as a class discussion or independent writing activity.

- What did you learn in this unit that could help you make good choices?

- Which person in this unit would you like to learn more about?

- What have you learned in this unit that you are glad you learned?

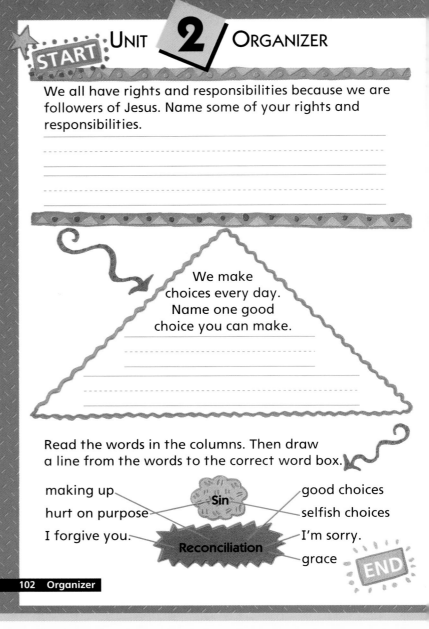

START UNIT 2 ORGANIZER

We all have rights and responsibilities because we are followers of Jesus. Name some of your rights and responsibilities.

We make choices every day. Name one good choice you can make.

Read the words in the columns. Then draw a line from the words to the correct word box.

making up — Sin — good choices

hurt on purpose — selfish choices

I forgive you. — I'm sorry.

Reconciliation — grace

END

102 Organizer

UNIT 2 REVIEW

Circle the correct word to finish each sentence.

1. In a community everyone has a _____ to care.

(responsibility)   need

2. In Jesus' story the poor woman gave more than the rich people because she gave _____.

silver and gold   (all she had)

3. Jesus says, "People will know you are my friends by your _____ one another."

(love for)   sadness

4. When we hurt someone on purpose, we _____.

forget   (sin)

5. The _____ _____ helps us to say, "I'm sorry."

Holy Bible   (Holy Spirit)

Reviewing the Unit

The purpose of the Unit Review is to reinforce concepts presented in the preceding four chapters and to check the children's understanding. After explaining the directions, give the children sufficient time to complete the two-page review. Answer any questions they may have as you check their work.

Testing

After the students have completed the Unit Review, you may wish to distribute copies of the Unit 2 Test from the Test Booklet.

Project

If time permits, you may wish to do the following project with the children.

Invite a priest who is comfortable with children to visit the class. Before the session, inform him carefully of the chapters in this unit. Ask him to speak from his own experience of his faith in Jesus' forgiveness and mercy and in the sacrament of Reconciliation. Encourage the children to question the priest about anything concerning sin and sorrow, God's forgiveness, and the celebration of Reconciliation. After Father and the children are finished with their discussion, ask Father to lead the children in spontaneous prayer.

UNIT **2** REVIEW

Think about "A Story About Reconciliation."
Put an **X** by the true sentences.

6. _____ When we are mean and hurt someone, we can never make up with them.

7. __X__ Reconciliation is the process of making up and being friends again.

8. __X__ God always forgives us when we are sorry.

9. _____ In the story, the father did not forgive his younger son.

10. Number these parts of the sacrament of Reconciliation in their right order. Use the numbers **1** through **4**.

__4__ receive absolution

__1__ confess your sins

__2__ accept a penance

__3__ pray an act of sorrow

RESPONDING TO WHAT I'VE HEARD

When people talk to us, they tell us about their feelings or about things they want us to know. I can let someone know I have heard what he or she has said by saying back, or restating, the message.

Activity

Look at the pictures below. Tell if the person who is listening in each picture is restating a feeling message or an information message.

SO HAPPY. MY G HAD FOUR PPIES LAST NIGHT.

YOU SOUND REALLY HAPPY.

GUESS WHAT I DID ON SATURDAY! MY DAD TOOK ME FISHING. I CAUGHT A FIVE-POUND TROUT!

WOW! YOU CAUGHT A FIVE-POUND TROUT!

Feeling Message   Information Message   Feeling Message   Information Message

AN'T BELIEVE YOU O CALLY THE SECRET I O YOU. I TOLD YOU T TO TELL ANYONE.

I GUESS YOU'RE REALLY MAD AT ME.

I'M INVITING FOUR KIDS OVER TO MY HOUSE AFTER SCHOOL. I WANT YOU TO COME OVER.

YOU WANT ME TO COME OVER TO YOUR HOUSE. SURE I CAN COME.

Feeling Message   Information Message   Feeling Message   Information Message

Day to Day   105

Objective

This lesson helps the children increase their awareness of how to respond to a speaker in ways that indicate the message has been heard.

Introducing the Lesson

Review with the children what had been studied in the previous lesson about being a good listener. Remind them that when we listen it is important to use eye contact, pay attention, and remain quiet while the other person is speaking. This helps assure that we will hear what the person is trying to tell us. Explain that today's lesson shows us how to let the speaker know we have heard his or her message.

Read with the children the title of the lesson "Responding to What I've Heard" and the introductory paragraph at the top of page 105. Then write the word *restating* on the chalkboard and ask what the term means. Elicit from the children that *restating* means "repeating" or "saying again what someone has said." Ask the children to underline the term *restating* in the first paragraph.

Further clarify that when we listen we hear two kinds of messages: messages about how the speaker feels and messages about information that the speaker wants us to know. The first is called a *feelings message* and the second, an *information message*.

Completing the Activity

Have a volunteer read aloud the directions for the activity on page 105. Have the children take turns reading the dialogue boxes for each picture. Identify with the class who the speaker is and who the listener is for each picture. Have the children circle whether or not they think the listener's response is restating a feeling message or an information message. If the children need further clarification on the difference between feelings and information, have them go back to the dialogue boxes and underline the feeling words with a red marker, and the information words with a blue marker. Tell the children that when we restate how someone feels, the words we say back to the person must contain a feeling word.

Lesson continues on page 106.

Practicing Restating Messages

Allow the children to begin practicing the skill of restating feeling and information messages. Read aloud with the children the directions on page 106. Ask:

- What kind of word must be in our restatement of what we think a speaker is feeling? (*A feeling word*)

- What are some words that tell about feelings? (*Mad, sad, happy, proud, disappointed, and so on*)

Have a volunteer read aloud the dialogue box in the first picture on page 106. Note that the character does not explicitly state his feelings. Ask the children to guess how the character might be feeling. (Clues to how someone may be feeling include how they look, what they say, and how they say it. The children may guess that the child is angry, mad, disappointed, sad, or lonely. Affirm all responses.) Have the children write their responses in the blank dialogue box. Then share them with the group.

Read the directions for completing the information message box. Remind the children that restating an information message means repeating back to the speaker the things he or she said. Have the children write their answers in the space provided. (*"Play ball."*)

Following Jesus

Invite a volunteer to read aloud the sentences in the Following Jesus box. Then ask: Why are listening and restating what has been said good things to be able to do? (*These skills let people know the listener cares about them; shows respect; lets the other person know the listener is interested in what they have to say.*)

Concluding the Lesson

Explain that sometimes the speaker talks about both feelings and information. A good listener can hear and restate both kinds of messages. Ask: When would be a good time to try to use this skill? (*When someone is telling us something important; when someone is filled with emotion; when someone is especially happy, sad, upset, excited, and so on; when someone asks us to listen*)

Select four volunteers to lead the class in praying the closing prayer. Ask each volunteer to read one of the lines of the prayer. Have the class echo each line.

106

Activity

Pretend you are the person listening to what is being said. Restate the feeling message. Write your response in the box.

Now restate the information message. Write your response in the box.

Following Jesus

Jesus wants us to show respect for others. Restating what has been said tells the speaker that I am listening and that I understand the message. Restating is one way to show respect.

A Prayer

Jesus, help me care about others. Help me listen. Help me hear. Help me respond in a way that says to the other person, "You are important." Amen.

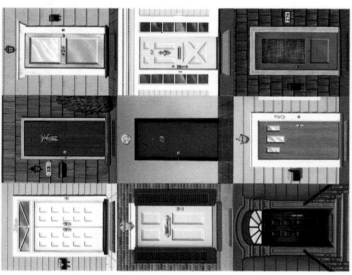

OPENING DOORS
A Take-Home Magazine™

Growing Closer

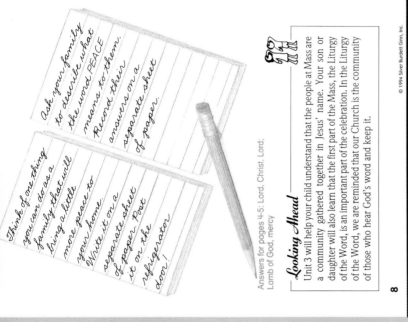

Think of one thing you can do as a family that will bring a little more peace to your home. Write it on a separate sheet of paper. Post it on the refrigerator door!

Ask your family to describe what the word PEACE means to them. Record their answers on a separate sheet of paper.

Answers for pages 4-5: Lord, Christ, Lord; Lamb of God, mercy

Looking Ahead

Unit 3 will help your child understand that the people at Mass are a community gathered together in Jesus' name. Your son or daughter will also learn that the first part of the Mass, the Liturgy of the Word, is an important part of the celebration. In the Liturgy of the Word, we are reminded that our Church is the community of those who hear God's word and keep it.

8

Opening Doors ~~~

Sending the Magazine Home

As you complete Unit 2 with your class, assist the children in carefully removing *Opening Doors: A Take-Home Magazine* (two pages) from their texts by separating the pages from the book along the perforations. Demonstrate how to fold the two pages, forming an eight-page booklet. Ask the children to take the magazine home and encourage their families to read it with them and participate in the suggested activities.

MODELS OF FORGIVENESS

The central message of Jesus beckons all Christians to provide for others the same unconditional forgiveness modeled in Jesus. As Christians we believe that the very life of Jesus shows us the limitless love of God the Creator and Father, the God who continuously seeks us out, even when we have turned away. When assured of this truth, we can confidently learn to trust God's goodness and seek God's mercy without fear.

Children, too, need this kind of assurance. Only when they are confident that they will be loved and forgiven—in spite of anything they have said or done—will they initiate or respond to any kind of peacemaking effort. This confidence comes first and foremost from a nurturing relationship at home.

According to the revised rite, there are different ways to celebrate the sacrament of Reconciliation.

* *anonymously* (behind a screen)
* *face to face* (sitting next to or across from the priest)
* *during a communal Reconciliation service* (celebrated with other members of the parish, with the opportunity for private confession)

Each of these ways of celebrating the sacrament has the following common elements:

* *a Scripture reading telling of God's mercy*
* *a confession of sins*
* *a discussion of ways to improve*
* *an act of contrition*
* *absolution given by the priest in the name of Jesus and the Catholic Christian community*
* *a penance as a sign of the person's desire to change for the better*

If it's been a while since you celebrated this sacrament, now may be a good time to try again. Chances are, you'll be pleasantly surprised!

The Sacrament of Reconciliation

Many Catholic children celebrate the sacrament of Reconciliation sometime during the second grade year. If your son or daughter is preparing for first Reconciliation you may find yourself examining the value of this sacrament and what it really means.

The sacrament of Reconciliation may have been called *Confession* or *Penance* when you were a child. You may still hear the sacrament referred to by those titles. The emphasis in years gone by, however, was on confessing the sins you had committed and doing penance. On December 4, 1963 the bishops of the Second Vatican Council issued the "Constitution on the Sacred Liturgy," calling for a revised rite of Penance that "more clearly expressed the nature and effects of this sacrament." Instead of emphasizing sin, the revised rite would emphasize the real meaning of the sacrament: God's mercy and redeeming love.

To understand this shift in emphasis, consider Jesus' parable of the Prodigal Son. In the story, the son demands his inheritance, then leaves home and squanders it on immoral living. The point of the story, however, is not the son and how sinful he is but rather the father's mercy and forgiveness.

Likewise, the revised *Rite of Penance* emphasizes God's forgiving love for us. No matter what sin we may have committed or how long we've been away, God always welcomes us back! Through the sacrament we are not only reconciled to God, we are also reconciled with the other members of the Christian community.

for their children. Just as the first disciples knew the Father through Jesus, our children come to know God through us. By experiencing a loving and forgiving relationship with their parents or guardians, children can begin to believe in a loving and forgiving God. Gradually, then, our children will freely join us in praying "Lord, have mercy," trusting that a compassionate God loves them and invites them to come closer to Jesus, our Reconciler, both in the eucharistic celebration and in all the grace-filled moments of their lives.

Jesus, Our Reconciler

Remind your child that Jesus came among us to tell us how much God loves us. We call Jesus our Reconciler because he brought us back to God, our loving Father. Review with your child the following Mass prayers. Help him or her fill in the missing words. Then discover with your son or daughter the meaning of the Sign of Peace.

At Mass we remember Jesus, our Reconciler. We remember God's love and forgiveness. We pray these prayers.

_____, have mercy.

_____, have mercy.

_____, have mercy.

_____, you take away the sins of the world, have _____ on us.

have _____ on us.

4

Jesus asks us to make peace with everyone. We show that we forgive one another when we share a sign of peace at Mass. We show that we care for one another when we say, "Peace be with you."

Check the ways your family shares a sign of peace with others at Mass.

____ Shaking hands   ____ Saying "Peace be with you"

____ Hugging   ____ Waving at others

____ Giving a family member a kiss   ____ _____

Pray these prayers the next time you go to Mass. Greet everyone around you with a sign of peace.

5

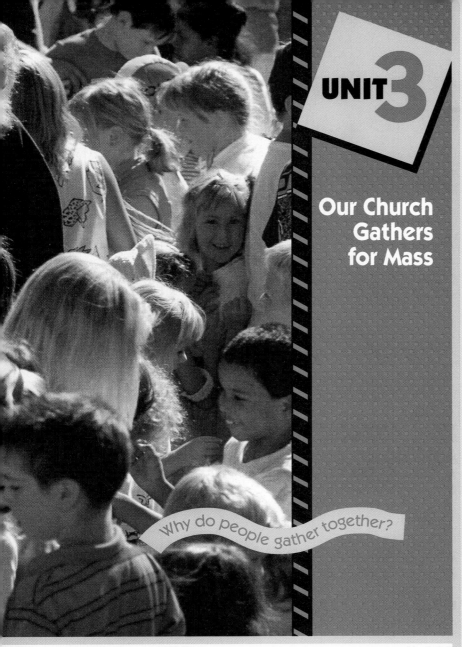

UNIT 3

Our Church Gathers for Mass

Why do people gather together?

To help the children understand that the Liturgy of the Word is the first part of the Mass, during which we listen to God's word in the readings and in the homily.

Doctrinal Summaries

CHAPTER 9

The Catholic Church gathers to celebrate a special meal with Jesus. This celebration is a sacrament called the Eucharist.

CHAPTER 10

Jesus speaks God's word to us at Mass, especially during the Liturgy of the Word.

CHAPTER 11

We are called to respond to God's word. At Mass we respond with songs, prayers, and actions. In our lives we respond by doing what Jesus asks of us.

CHAPTER 12

Jesus wants us to pray for ourselves and for people everywhere. We can do this in many ways.

Note:

As you prepare this unit and the remaining units, you might wish to refer to the reference section, *Our Catholic Heritage,* beginning on page 327.

Additional resources for Unit 1 include a Unit Test and a Family Letter as well as a video and selections from THIS IS OUR FAITH Music Program. You might also find it helpful to preview *Saints and Other Holy People* and *Prayer Celebrations* for possibilities to enhance the unit.

Introducing the UNIT

Ask the children to study the photograph on page 111. Invite them to speculate on what the children in the picture might be doing. Then ask a volunteer to read aloud the focus question. List the children's answers on the chalkboard. Tell the group that in Unit 3 they will learn why Catholics gather at Mass.

New Words

Mass
procession
Liturgy of the Word
Old Testament
responsorial psalm
New Testament
gospel
homily
respond
Prayer of the Faithful

We Gather Together for Mass

Objectives

To help the children

- Recognize Sunday as a gathering of the Catholic Christian community.
- Read in the Scriptures that people gathered around Jesus.
- See how we gather as a Catholic community for Sunday Mass.
- Learn the greeting dialogue at Mass.
- Pray to and praise God in a procession and review the chapter.

Chapter Outline

	Step 1 **Learning About Our Lives**	Step 2 **Learning About Our Faith**	Step 3 **Learning How to Live Our Faith**
Day 1	■ Name gathering times. ■ Discuss Sunday gatherings. *ABOUT 5 MINUTES*	■ Read and discuss a story. ■ Define the new word. ■ Present the doctrine. *ABOUT 15 MINUTES*	■ Complete an activity. ■ Pray together. *ABOUT 10 MINUTES*
Day 2	■ Extend hospitality to children. ■ Reflect on hospitality. *ABOUT 10 MINUTES*	■ Read a Scripture story. ■ Read about Nicodemus and discuss. ■ Read about the Last Supper. *ABOUT 15 MINUTES*	■ Complete an activity. *ABOUT 5 MINUTES*
Day 3	■ Introduce the chapter. ■ Role-play the greeter at Mass. *ABOUT 10 MINUTES*	■ Greet those who gather. ■ Introduce the new word. *ABOUT 10 MINUTES*	■ Complete an activity. ■ Pray together. *ABOUT 10 MINUTES*
Day 4	■ Welcome a guest. ■ Discuss ways to welcome others. ■ Complete an activity. *ABOUT 10 MINUTES*	■ Learn the greeting at Mass. *ABOUT 10 MINUTES*	■ Complete an activity. *ABOUT 10 MINUTES*

Day 5   **Prayer**   Prepare for procession; prepare for prayer; process to the prayer table; and pray together.

            Review   Review the chapter and explain the Scripture verse.

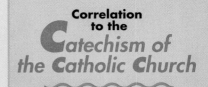

Correlation
to the
**Catechism of
the Catholic Church**

Paragraphs
1140, 1193, 1348

Plan Ahead

	Preparing Your Class	Materials Needed
Day 1	Read over the lesson prior to the session. If enriching the lesson, prepare the discovery table with objects that recall family gatherings.	■ pencils
Day 2	Read over the lesson. Prepare invitations for a snack. Prepare snack. Decorate room for the special snack.	■ recording of soft music ■ invitations ■ special table cloth, napkins ■ centerpiece or candles ■ cookies, fruit, drink
Day 3	Read over the lesson. If you have opted to make New Word posters, prepare poster. Become familiar with gathering practices.	■ felt-tip markers or crayons
Day 4	Invite a host or hostess to speak. If enriching the lesson, prepare videotape of opening greeting at Mass.	■ guest speaker ■ pencils
Day 5	Assemble materials for the procession. Prepare prayer table. Choose an entrance song and prepare song sheets.	■ processional cross and stand ■ lectionary or Bible ■ Bible stand, two candles, taper ■ colored cloth, vase, flowers ■ song and song sheets

Additional Resources

As you plan this chapter, consider using the following materials from The Resourceful Teacher Package.

■ *Classroom Activity Sheets 9* and *9a*

■ *Family Activity Sheets 9* and *9a*

■ *Chapter 9 Test*

■ *Prayers for Every Day*

■ *Projects: Grade 2*

You may also wish to refer to the following Big Books.

■ *We Celebrate the Mass,* pages 1–23

■ *We Celebrate the Sacraments,* pages 7–9

In preparing the children for the Sunday readings, you may wish to use Silver Burdett Ginn's *Getting Ready for Sunday* student and teacher materials.

BOOKS FOR THE JOURNEY

Who Will Miss Me If I Don't Go to Church? Susan Heyboer O'Keefe. Paulist Press, 1992. The creative wonderings of a child about the importance of her presence at Mass.

The Bread and the Wine. Denise Ahern. Concordia, 1979. An imaginative rhyming version of the Last Supper story.

MORE BOOKS FOR THE JOURNEY

My Big Family at Church. Helen Caswell. Abingdon Press, 1989. Each parish is like a big family of God's children and each has a role to play in the mission of the Church.

Sunday's Children. "Sunday Is Gathering Day," p. 1. James Bitney. Resource Publications, 1986. A poem about the special gathering of Christians on Sunday.

REDUCED CLASSROOM ACTIVITIES

Name

We Gather Together for Mass

When you decode the sentence below you will discover what Catholic Christians do as a community each Sunday. Write the words on the banner when you finish.

1	2	3	4	5	6	7	8	9	10	11	12	13
A	B	C	D	E	F	G	H	I	J	K	L	M

14	15	16	17	18	19	20	21	22	23	24	25	26
N	O	P	Q	R	S	T	U	V	W	X	Y	Z

C a t h o l i c s
3 1 20 8 15 12 9 3 19
c e l e b r a t e
3 5 12 5 2 18 1 20 5
a t M a s s .
1 20 13 1 19 19

To the Teacher: This activity follows the We Believe section of the chapter.

Chapter 9 We Gather Together for Mass   THIS IS OUR FAITH 2   **9**

Name

Jesus Is with Us

Use the following code to complete Jesus' words below.

When you see a △, fill in the letter **e.**

When you see a ☐, fill in the letter **a.**

When you see a ♡, fill in the letter **o.**

When you see a ◇, fill in the letter **i.**

"Wh△ r △ tw♡ ♡ r
thr△ △ g☐ th△ r ◇ n
my n☐ m△ , ◇ ☐ m
th△ r △ w ◇ th th△ m."

Matthew 18:20

To the Teacher: This activity follows the end of the chapter and will help students become more familiar with the Scripture reference.

9a THIS IS OUR FAITH 2   **Chapter 9** We Gather Together for Mass

A DAY OF CELEBRATION

Sunday is a day of celebration. For the Church, from the time of the apostles until now, Sunday has been the "Lord's day" (Revelation 1:10). One glorious Sunday, Christ rose from the dead; therefore, every Sunday we gather to celebrate his victory over death.

THE GATHERING OF THE CATHOLIC COMMUNITY

The celebration of the Eucharist is the source of our life as a community. "It is the culmination both of God's action sanctifying the world in Christ and of the worship men offer to Christ and through him to the Father in the Holy Spirit." (*Catechism of the Catholic Church*, #1325) The Greek word *eucharistein,* or "Eucharist" means a blessing or thanksgiving to God for creating the world, for redeeming it, and for sending the Spirit to sanctify it. The word "Mass" comes from the Latin word *Missa,* which means sending forth the people to continue God's saving work.

The Mass begins with our gathering. Gathering is more than merely assembling with others in a place. In our gathering, we are hospitable to one another in words of welcome, in a smile, and in polite conversation. Greeters begin the process of gathering at the entrance of the church, and the assembly continues this hospitality in the pews. A time of welcoming

is essential. Before we can pray together, we need to feel welcomed and comfortable with one another. The hospitality of the community reminds us that we are all equal in the sight of God and we are all welcomed into the family of Jesus. Extending hospitality exemplifies the meaning of being Catholic. *Catholic* means "universal." God's gift of Jesus is extended to all regardless of age, race, economic situation, or physical or mental limitations.

HOSPITALITY IN OUR LIVES

The children are invited to remember family gatherings and gatherings of the Catholic community. Second graders are old enough to make the connection between these types of gatherings. Some of the same principles of hospitality and welcoming apply to both situations. Basic hospitality is learned at home through experiences of welcoming guests, being attentive to them, and extending to them the warmth of friendliness.

Feeling at home during the Mass requires that the children become comfortable with their surroundings and their participation. Practice and role-playing can help achieve a level of familiarity that enriches participation. This chapter begins the study of the celebration of the Mass, which helps prepare the second graders for their first reception of the Eucharist.

Day 1

DOCTRINE

Objective

This lesson helps the children recognize the Mass as a Sunday gathering of the Catholic community.

Step 1 / INTRODUCTION

Learning About Our Lives

Naming Gathering Times

Invite the children to open their books to page 112. Ask: What does it mean to gather together? (*To come together as a group in one place*) Invite a volunteer to read the focus question. Have them name their favorite gathering times.

Discussing Sunday Gatherings

Have the children study the three photographs on page 112 and answer the activity question. (*The people in the photographs have come together at church to pray.*) Invite the children to share their experiences of coming to church to pray. Be sensitive to those children who do not experience Sunday as a special day. Probe their awareness of different customs when the Catholic community gathers to pray. For example, if it is the custom in your parish for people to join hands when praying The Lord's Prayer, ask the children why the people in the photograph to the right are holding hands. Then ask the children if they have ever prayed with your parish community out-of-doors, as shown in the photograph to the left. Tell the children that Sunday is special for Catholics because we gather together at church. Explain to them that many Catholics gather for Sunday Mass on Saturday evening because the Church considers Saturday evening the beginning of the Lord's Day, or Sunday.

Step 2 / DEVELOPMENT

Learning About Our Faith

Read and Discuss a Story

Read aloud "Friends of Jesus Gather" on page 113 as the children follow along in their books.

112

---

9 We Gather Together for Mass

 Activity

These are pictures of Sunday gatherings of people. What have they come together to do?

▲ Mass at San Jose Mission, San Antonio, Texas

▲ Mass at San Jose Parish, Austin, Texas

▲ Mass at a Canadian Eskimo village

People often gather to do things together. What are your favorite gathering times?

112 Doctrine

Cultural Awareness

Call attention to the diversity of the people and to the different types of churches in the photographs on page 112. Point out the walrus tusks on the altar in the photograph of a Mass in an Inuit (Eskimo) Catholic community. Help the children appreciate that the Catholic Church is made up of many groups of people, all of whom contribute to the richness of our community. Point out signs of your parish's history or tradition.

Enriching the Lesson

Gather the children around the discovery table on which are displayed various objects that remind the children of times of family gatherings. (Thanksgiving napkin, Christmas decoration, Easter eggs or candy, birthday card, picnic basket, Mother's Day card, and so on) Ask a volunteer to choose an object and explain the family celebration that it recalls. Some children may have had more gathering experiences than others because of family size and make-up.

Friends of Jesus Gather

Jesus loved his friends. People felt special when they were with Jesus. He really listened to them.

Jesus' friends also loved to listen to his stories. They often gathered around him at mealtimes and other times to hear his wonderful stories and teachings.

We come together as friends and disciples of Jesus when we gather at Mass. At Mass we pray together and listen to Jesus' stories and other readings from the Bible. We also share a special meal with Jesus.

Activity

Who gathers with you for Mass? Write their names here.

New Word

Mass — The Mass is a special meal with Jesus. At Mass we pray together and listen to God's word from the Bible.

We Believe

The Catholic community gathers to celebrate a special meal with Jesus. We come together as friends and disciples of Jesus when we gather at Mass.

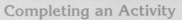
Doctrine 113

Focus on

Sunday The *Catechism of the Catholic Church* states, "Sunday, the 'Lord's Day,' is the principal day for the celebration of the Eucharist because it is the day of the Resurrection. It is the preeminent day of the liturgical assembly, the day of the Christian family, and the day of joy and rest from work. Sunday is 'the foundation and kernel of the whole liturgical year' " (SC 106) (#1193).

Teaching Tips

Some children may be worried that they attend Mass on Saturday evening instead of Sunday. Explain that the Sabbath (the seventh day) in the Jewish religion begins on Friday evening at sunset. The Sabbath is celebrated from sundown to sundown. So, too, we begin the Sunday celebration on Saturday evening, or the vigil of Sunday.

Ask:

■ How did Jesus make his friends feel special? (*He loved them, listened to them, and told them stories.*)

■ When did Jesus' friends like to gather with him to hear his stories? (*Often at mealtime*)

■ When do we gather as friends and disciples of Jesus? (*On Sunday, at Mass*)

Defining the New Word

Have the children repeat the word *Mass* and its definition. Explain that at Mass we gather in church around the table or altar to celebrate a special meal with Jesus.

Presenting the Doctrine

Read aloud the We Believe statement with the children. To help reinforce the statement, ask: What community gathers to celebrate a special meal with Jesus? (*The Catholic community*)

Step 3 / CONCLUSION

Learning How to Live Our Faith

Completing an Activity

Have the children look at the pictures on page 112 again. Explain that when we gather as a Catholic community on Saturday evening or Sunday, we see people we know. Then ask: Who gathers with you for Mass? (*Answers will vary.*) Print their answers on the chalkboard. Encourage the children to use the names of brothers, sisters, friends, and so on, as they write their answers on the lines provided.

Praying Together

Invite the children to gather around the prayer table and join hands as brothers and sisters in Jesus. Ask each child to name someone who attends Mass with him or her. Have the children echo each phrase as you pray a gathering prayer.

We come together to the table of the Lord.

We come together to greet each other in the name of Jesus.

We come together to praise God for all God's gifts.

We come together to meet our Living God.

Amen.

Objective

This lesson presents three Scripture stories that reveal how people liked to gather around Jesus.

Step 1 / INTRODUCTION

Learning About Our Lives

Extending Hospitality to the Children

Early in the school day, distribute simple invitations to the class: You are invited to have a snack with Mrs. (*name*) at (*time*) in the (*place*).

Decorate this special place with tablecloths, napkins, and a centerpiece. Place name cards on the table to designate where each child is to sit. Dim the lights and play soft music to create an atmosphere. Arrange for another teacher or aide to walk with your class to the place for the snack. Greet each child at the door, invite him or her to enter and sit at their assigned places. Serve the children cookies, fruit, and a drink on special plates. Be sure to treat them as "company."

Reflecting on Hospitality

When the snack is finished, invite the children into a sharing circle. Talk about the experience of sharing food, being a guest, or being the host or hostess. Ask: When you are a guest, how are you treated? (*Invited, welcomed, given a place to sit, given food*) What should you do as a host or hostess to make your guest feel welcome? (*Pay attention to him or her, prepare a special table, fix special food, listen to and talk with him or her*) We call these actions *hospitality*. Christians are known for their hospitality and their willingness to pay attention to the needs of others and to welcome them into their community.

Step 2 / DEVELOPMENT

Learning About Our Faith +

Reading a Scripture Story

Have a volunteer read the introductory sentences before reading aloud the story "Jesus Welcomes a Child" on page 114.

People liked to gather around Jesus. These gospel stories tell about some of those times.

Jesus Welcomes a Child

One day Jesus' disciples and many other people were gathered around him, listening to Jesus' teachings and stories.

The disciples asked him, "Jesus, who is the greatest in the kingdom of heaven?"

Jesus called a little child over and said, "Look at this child. Unless you change your hearts and become like little children, you will not have a place in my Father's kingdom."

Everyone was surprised by Jesus' answer. Then Jesus said, "Anyone who welcomes a little child such as this one, also welcomes me."

Based on Matthew 18:1-

A Man Named Nicodemus

Another time, a man named Nicodemus came to Jesus at dinner time. He had heard that Jesus was a good teacher and Nicodemus wanted to talk with him.

"Teacher," Nicodemus said. "We know that you are a teacher who has come from God. No one can do such wonderful things unless God is with him."

Based on John 3:1-2

114   Scripture

Enriching the Lesson

Emphasize that living like Jesus means being kind to everyone. The word *hospitality* comes from the same root word as *hospice*, which means to provide a resting place or shelter for pilgrims or strangers. Review the kinds of courtesy we need to show others to make them feel at home with us. We welcome all, we treat all with respect, we listen when others speak, we care about their needs, we keep their secrets, we do not make fun of others, and we respect their culture.

Cultural Awareness

Read a story that stresses hospitality from another culture. Possible stories are *Almond Cookies and Dragon Well Tea* by Cynthia Chi-Lee, Polychrome Publishing Corp., 1990; *Nobiah's Well: A Modern African Folktale* by Donna W. Guthrie, Ideals, 1993; and *One Round Moon and a Star for Me* by Ingrid Mennen, Orchard Books, 1994.

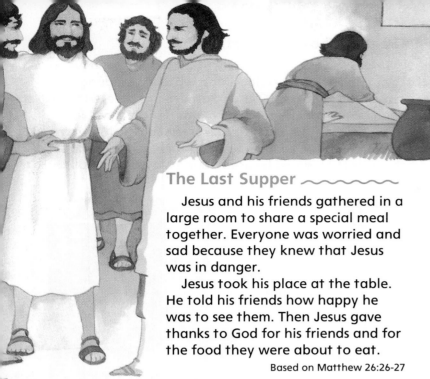

The Last Supper

Jesus and his friends gathered in a large room to share a special meal together. Everyone was worried and sad because they knew that Jesus was in danger.

Jesus took his place at the table. He told his friends how happy he was to see them. Then Jesus gave thanks to God for his friends and for the food they were about to eat.

Based on Matthew 26:26-27

Activity

Draw a picture of Jesus telling a story to friends who have gathered around him. Put yourself in the picture.

CURRICULUM CONNECTION

Art Invite the children to draw figures of Jesus and his friends. Cut out these figures and glue them to craft sticks. Use these simple puppets to retell the story of Jesus thanking God for his friends and the food they were about to eat at the Last Supper. Invite the children to reenact this story with their puppets in small groups.

Ask:
- Why were people gathered around Jesus? (*To hear him teach and tell stories*)
- What must people do in order to enter his Father's kingdom? (*Change their hearts and become like little children*)
- If someone welcomes a little child, who is also welcomed? (*Jesus*)

Reading About Nicodemus

Tell the children that Nicodemus was a Jewish leader and teacher. Then read the story of Nicodemus to the class. Ask: Why did he come to eat dinner with Jesus? (*To talk to him, because he had heard that Jesus was a teacher who came from God*)

Discussing the Story

Explore with the children times when they were invited to eat with someone special. Ask: Who was that person? How did you feel? (*Affirm all answers.*) Make the connection that Nicodemus felt that Jesus was someone very special. He came to eat with Jesus to get to know him better and to find out more about his teachings. Stress that we get to know others better when we gather and share a meal with them. Recall the story in Chapter 2 about Jesus eating with Mary, Martha, and Lazarus. These people ate often with Jesus because they were his friends.

Reading About the Last Supper

Ask for volunteers to read aloud the story "The Last Supper" on page 115. Ask: Why did Jesus and his friends gather together? (*To share a special meal*) For what did Jesus give thanks? (*For his friends and for the food*)

Step 3 / CONCLUSION

Learning How to Live Our Faith

Completing an Activity

Assist the children in drawing a picture of Jesus telling a story to his friends. Tell the children that Jesus' stories touched the hearts and lives of those who gathered to listen to him. Ask the children to put themselves into the picture. Encourage them to share what they have drawn.

DAY 3
DOCTRINE

Objective

This lesson helps the children see how we gather as a Catholic community for Sunday Mass.

Step 1 / INTRODUCTION

Learning About Our Lives

Introducing the Chapter

Begin this lesson by asking the children:

- What happens before Mass begins? (*Altar servers light candles, people come into church, the priest puts on vestments.*)

- Have you noticed people at church who greet others as they enter? (*Affirm any answer.*)

  In some parishes, the ushers are the official greeters. In other parishes, families assist the ushers with this responsibility.

- Where do the greeters in our parish stand to welcome the people? (*In the gathering space in the rear of church*)

Role-playing the Greeter at Mass

Call on several volunteers to show how greeters welcome people into church on Sunday mornings. Invite other members of the class to role-play families coming to Mass. Be sure to have the children reach out to shake hands and to introduce themselves and members of their families.

Step 2 / DEVELOPMENT

Learning About Our Faith

Greeting Those Who Gather

Have the children read along silently as you read aloud the first paragraph of text on page 116. Ask: What color vestments does Father Jerry wear? (*Green*) Explain that the priest wears different color vestments according to the liturgical season of the year. Explain that green is the color of Ordinary Time. (*See "Focus on" box.*) Ask:

- Who are the altar servers who arrive early? (*John, Michelle, and Diana*)

116

Greeting Those Who Gather

It was the Flanagan family's turn to greet and welcome the people to the 9 o'clock Mass. When the Flanagans arrived at Saint Paul Church, Father Jerry greeted them. Then he put on his green vestments. Before long, John, Michelle, and Diana, the altar servers for the Mass arrived. They lighted the candles on the altar. Then they placed the gifts that would be used during Mass on a small table near the entrance of the church.

"The Riós family is bringing up the gifts today," Mr. Scanlon, the usher, told Father Jerry. Soon it was time to greet the people who were coming to Mass. Erin and her family smiled and said, "Good morning!" to everyone.

When it was nine o'clock, the ministers lined up. John carried the cross and led the **procession**. The other altar servers followed. Mrs. Santini carried God's word in the lectionary high so that everyone could see it. Then came Father Jerry.

As the procession started down the aisle, all the people stood to sing and praise God.

Focus on

Liturgical Colors The colors of the priest's vestments are green, rose, purple, red, and white. They symbolize the seasons of the liturgical year. Green is for Ordinary Time. Purple for Advent symbolizes our waiting for the Messiah. Purple, for repentance, is worn during Lent. White, for joy, is worn on Easter and Christmas. Red reminds us of Jesus' blood shed on Good Friday. On Pentecost, red recalls tongues of fire. Rose is sometimes worn on the third Sunday of Advent and the fourth Sunday of Lent to sym

overset from Focus On

bolize relieved repentance and subdued joy.

Activity

Draw a picture that shows what the Sunday gathering looks like at the church where you go to Mass.

New Word

procession   people walking in line for a special reason

- What do they do? (*Light candles on the altar*)

Invite a volunteer to read the last three paragraphs. Ask the following questions:

- Who are the greeters? (*Erin and her family*)
- How do they greet those gathering for Mass? (*They smile and say, "Good morning" to everyone.*)
- Who carries the cross and leads the procession? (*John, the cross bearer*)
- What does Mrs. Santini carry? (*The lectionary*)
- What do the people do as the procession begins? (*They stand, sing, and praise God.*)

Introducing the New Word

Introduce the word *procession* and its definition from the New Word box on page 117. Have the children repeat it after you. If you have opted to create a new word poster, show the poster depicting a line of people led by the cross bearer, the lector holding a book, the servers, and the priest. Identify each person in the line.

Step 3 / CONCLUSION

Learning How to Live Our Faith

Completing an Activity

Read aloud the directions to the drawing activity. Distribute crayons or felt-tip markers to the children. Encourage them to include as many details as possible in the space provided. As they are working, move from child to child and ask each one to tell you about his or her drawing.

Praying Together

In many parishes, the priest prays with the ministers before the entrance procession. Ask your parish priest for a copy of the prayer that he says with the ministers. Use that prayer as your prayer for this day. If your parish priest does not use such a prayer, pray the following: We praise you, God, for calling us to minister to your people today. Help us to do our part to make this Mass a prayer. May our hearts be moved to love you and each other more. Amen.

Teaching Tips

Before teaching this chapter, familiarize yourself with the gathering customs of your parish and other parishes in the diocese. In some churches the priest vests in the sacristy located next to or behind the altar. People entering the church would not see the priest vesting. Learn how formal greeters are used. Check if the Eucharistic ministers are included in the entrance procession. Ask if there are formal or informal prayers of the ministers before Mass. Tailor the lesson to the children's experience.

Objective

This lesson helps the children learn the greeting dialogue at Mass.

Step 1 / INTRODUCTION

Learning About Our Lives

Welcoming a Guest

Read to the class the story on page 118 of the Dawson family welcoming a special dinner guest. Ask the class to demonstrate how the family welcomed Mr. Parker. Select five children to be Mr. and Mrs. Dawson, Michael, Lisa, and Mr. Parker, the guest. Reenact the welcoming of Mr. Parker.

Discussing Ways to Welcome Others

Ask the following questions.

■ What are the ways we welcome others into our classroom? (*We say "good morning" or "good afternoon," we get extra chairs for the visitors, we share our books.*)

■ How do you welcome someone into your home? (*Meet them at the door, invite them in*)

■ Does your mother or father remind you to use your best manners? (*Answers will vary.*)

■ What are your best manners? (*Being polite, listening to the guest, paying attention to him or her, observing good table manners, and so on*)

or . . .

Invite one of the parents or grandparents to speak to the class about preparing for a guest. Request the speaker to bring pictures of his or her family entertaining a guest. Ask him or her to remind the children to greet a guest warmly and to be polite. Encourage the speaker to talk about special foods that are served to his or her guests and special table decorations or dishes he or she may use. If there are special ethnic family celebrations, encourage the speaker to describe these to the children.

Welcoming a Guest

Mr. Dawson was bringing home a special dinner guest. Everyone in the family was reminded to be friendly and polite.

"When Mr. Parker gets here," Mrs. Dawson said, "be sure to say hello and tell him your name."

When their dinner guest arrived, the Dawson family greeted him at the door.

Mrs. Dawson said, "It's so good to see you, Mr. Parker. Come in and sit down in the living room."

Mr. Dawson took the guest's coat and hung it up. Michael brought Mr. Parker a cold drink. Lisa showed him her new kitten. Everyone tried to make Mr. Parker feel welcome.

Activity

How does your family welcome guests? Write about it here.

Answers will vary.

118   Doctrine

Cultural Awareness

Mexican Christians have a special procession on the Feast of Our Lady of Guadalupe, December 12. Led by a mariachi band, four men carry a statue of Our Lady of Guadalupe through the streets surrounding the church. Children, in traditional costume, and their families follow. If Mass is to be celebrated, servers and the priest follow the families. After Mass, a dramatization retells the story of Our Lady's appearance to Juan Diego. A feast of enchiladas, tostadas, beans, and rice completes the celebration.

Enriching the Lesson

Teach the song "Be Our Guest" from the Walt Disney film *Beauty and the Beast* to demonstrate the steps of hospitality. The servants dust themselves off and prepare to give a lavish feast to the heroine. We also make preparations for our guests: we cook something special. We clean the house. We get dressed up. We welcome the guest.

The Priest Welcomes Us

When the people have gathered and the procession is finished, the priest turns to the people and greets them by saying, "The Lord be with you."

The people return the greeting with the words, "And also with you."

This greeting reminds us that Jesus is present with us in a special way as we gather at Mass.

The priest then welcomes us to the celebration of the Mass. He tells us that it is good that we have gathered together to listen to God's word and to share the gift of Eucharist.

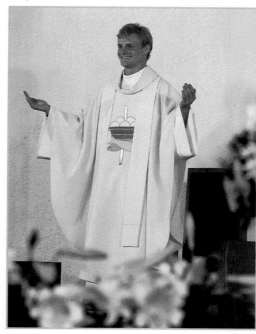

Activity

Practice the greeting used at Mass by tracing over the letters below.

The Lord be with you.

And also with you.

Doctrine   119

Completing an Activity

Read the directions to the activity. Help the children write their answers on the lines provided.

Step 2 / DEVELOPMENT

Learning About Our Faith

Learning the Greeting at Mass

Explain to the children that the entrance procession is over when the procession reaches the sanctuary of the church. The cross bearer bows, places the cross in a stand and stands by his or her designated seat. The lector bows, places the book on the ambo, and takes the seat designated for the lector. The servers bow and stand by the chairs designated for servers. The priest bows, walks to the altar and kisses it, and then stands at the presider's chair. He faces the assembly and says the greeting "The Lord be with you." Invite a volunteer to read "The Priest Welcomes Us" on page 119.

Explain to the children that the priest reminds us in the greeting that Jesus is present with us. We respond that we also believe Jesus is present with the priest. Practice the greeting and response several times.

Step 3 / CONCLUSION

Learning How to Live Our Faith

Completing an Activity

Instruct the children to practice the greeting used at Mass by tracing over the letters in their books. Then practice the dialogue orally with the class. Say, "The Lord be with you," and encourage the children to respond, "And also with you."

Objective

This lesson helps the children pray a prayer of praise to God in a procession.

Preparing for the Procession

To prepare for today's procession and prayer, you will need a cross, and a lectionary or Bible (with Psalm 122 in it). Drape a colored cloth on the prayer table; on it place a vase with flowers, a Bible stand, and two candles. Have at hand a taper to light the candles and matches, if fire regulations allow.

Prepare song sheets with the words for the song you have chosen for the procession. Assign a reader (lector) for Psalm 122. Review with the cross bearer, the lector, and the children where they are to move and where the cross and lectionary will be placed.

Preparing for Prayer

Explain to the children that a procession is a kind of prayer. By processing they will praise God and remember that the Lord is present with them. Ask the children to practice saying the responses found on page 120.

Processing to the Prayer Table

Assemble the children in the back of the room and distribute song sheets if needed and the items to be used in the procession. Pause for a moment of quiet. Then pray aloud the introductory prayers on page 120, with the children responding. The procession moves slowly while the song is sung. Enthrone the lectionary or Bible on the prayer table. When the procession is over, motion for the children to sit during the reading of the psalm. After the reading, ask for spontaneous prayer intentions. Invite the children to speak their intentions. At the conclusion of the prayers, have the children in the procession recess in the same order they processed to the prayer table.

Praying with a Procession

Teacher: Today we will have a procession to praise God. Let us process to the prayer table, remembering that God is here with us.

Teacher: The Lord be with you.

All: And also with you.

Teacher: O great and wonderful God, you always listen to our prayers. Let our procession today be our prayer. May it give you glory. We pray this prayer and all our prayers in the name of Jesus, your Son.

All: Amen.

120   Prayer

 **CURRICULUM CONNECTION**

Art Enlist the help of the art teacher to show your class examples of processions depicted in works of art. Works of art could include paintings, friezes, or historical photographs.

Ask the art teacher to explain where and on what occasion the procession depicted takes place and who the artist, sculptor, or photographer is.

 ***Cultural Awareness***

In Mexico, the Christmas season begins on December 16 with *Las posadas,* a series of nine nightly processions that reenact the journey of Joseph and Mary to Bethlehem. The word *posada* means "lodging." A child dressed as an angel leads the candle-lit procession from house to house. Each night the pilgrims seek lodging in an "inn" and are denied. On the ninth evening, the child leading the procession carries a statue of the infant Jesus to place in the manger in the last "inn," where they are welcomed.

Chapter Review

Choose a word to fill in each blank.

family	Jesus	friends

Thank you, God, for giving us Sundays!

On Sundays we share a special meal with

__Jesus__ We gather with __family__ and

__friends__ to say thank you for sending us __Jesus__.

Thank you, God, for giving us Sundays!

1. What do we call the special meal we share with Jesus?

__Mass__

2. Who gathers to share a special meal with Jesus?

__Catholic Christians__

Jesus says,
"Where two or
three gather in my
name, I am there
with them."
**Based on Matthew
18:20**

3. Talk about ways that sharing in the Mass can help us to be kinder and more helpful in our other gatherings.

Completing the Chapter Review

Read the directions for the review to the children. Ask them to fill in the blanks with the words provided. Then correct the children's answers.

Continue with the three items. Check each child's written answers to questions 1 and 2. Lead a discussion of item 3. Encourage all children to take part in the discussion.

Explaining the Scripture Verse

Have the children read aloud the Scripture verse on page 121. Ask them to explain what happens when two or three persons gather in the name of Jesus. (*Jesus is there with them.*) Make the connection between God's people gathering for Mass and Jesus' presence there. Ask: Is Jesus with us when we gather for Mass? (*Yes, because he promised to be where two or more are gathered in his name.*)

★ ★ ★ ★ Enriching the Lesson ★ ★ ★

Provide magazine photographs of small groups of people or of large crowds. Display one picture at a time. Invite the children to tell you a story about each photograph. Also ask them to point out the reason for the gathering. Then have the children compare and contrast each pictured gathering with the gatherings for Sunday Mass found on page 112.

10 We Listen to God's Word

Objectives

To help the children

- Learn to listen to the stories of Jesus.
- Share Bible stories from the Old and New Testaments.
- Discover the Liturgy of the Word.
- Relate favorite Bible stories to life.
- Pray God's word and review the chapter.

Chapter Outline

	Step 1 Learning About Our Lives	**Step 2** Learning About Our Faith	**Step 3** Learning How to Live Our Faith
Day 1	■ Greet one another. ■ Introduce the chapter. ■ Listen to a story. ■ Complete an activity. *ABOUT 10 MINUTES*	■ Listen to a gospel story. ■ Discuss the story. *ABOUT 15 MINUTES*	■ Share how to listen to God. *ABOUT 5 MINUTES*
Day 2	■ Review Jesus' request to listen well. ■ Introduce Bible stories. *ABOUT 5 MINUTES*	■ Read the story of Noah. ■ Read about the mustard seed. ■ Introduce the gospel reading. *ABOUT 15 MINUTES*	■ Complete an activity. ■ Sing together. ■ Connect to home. *ABOUT 10 MINUTES*
Day 3	■ Share favorite Bible stories. ■ Introduce the lesson. *ABOUT 5 MINUTES*	■ Discover Liturgy of the Word. ■ Complete an activity. ■ Define the new words. ■ Present the doctrine. *ABOUT 15 MINUTES*	■ Make a word tree. ■ Pray together. *ABOUT 10 MINUTES*
Day 4	■ Share Bible stories from home. ■ Review the Liturgy of the Word. *ABOUT 10 MINUTES*	■ Continue with Liturgy of the Word. ■ Study the photographs. ■ Learn from the readings. ■ Review the new words. *ABOUT 15 MINUTES*	■ Complete an activity. *ABOUT 5 MINUTES*
Day 5	**Prayer** Prepare for prayer and pray God's word. **Review** Review the chapter; complete the chapter review; and read the Scripture verse.		

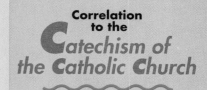

Plan Ahead

	Preparing Your Class	**Materials Needed**
Day 1	Read over the lesson prior to the session. Learn "The Noise Song." Think of a story to share.	■ recording and song sheets for "The Noise Song"
Day 2	Assemble books for discovery table. Learn Bible stories. Practice song "We Hear God's Word." If enriching the lesson, prepare necessary materials.	■ music for "We Hear God's Word" ■ pencils
Day 3	Prepare space to display Bible story drawings. Prepare prayer table. Gather recording and song sheets for "We Hear God's Word."	■ pencils
Day 4	Read over the lesson prior to the session. Prepare for sharing Bible stories.	■ children's drawings of favorite Bible stories ■ candles
Day 5	Read over the lesson prior to the session. Prepare food items and music prior to class. Prepare for prayer.	■ basket of rolls ■ bowl of honey ■ recording of "We Hear God's Word" ■ plates, knives, napkins ■ Bible, cross or crucifix

Additional Resources

As you plan this chapter, consider using the following materials from The Resourceful Teacher Package.

■ *Classroom Activity Sheets 10* and *10a*

■ *Family Activity Sheets 10* and *10a*

■ *Chapter 10 Test*

■ *Prayers for Every Day*

■ *Projects: Grade 2*

You may also wish to refer to the following Big Books.

■ *We Celebrate the Mass,* pages 1–23

■ *We Celebrate the Sacraments,* pages 7–9

In preparing the children for the Sunday readings, you may wish to use Silver Burdett Ginn's *Getting Ready for Sunday* student and teacher materials.

BOOKS FOR THE JOURNEY

I Have a Sister, My Sister Is Deaf. Jeanne Whitehouse Peterson. Harper & Row, 1977. Reveals that there are many ways to listen.

City Noise. Karla Kuskin. HarperCollins, 1994. A poetic story of a child listening to city noises through a tin can held up to her ear like a conch shell.

MORE BOOKS FOR THE JOURNEY

The Random House Book of Poetry for Children. Selected by Jack Prelutsky. "Foghorns," p. 98, Lillian Moore; "Mountain Wind," p. 26, Barbara Kunz Loots; "They're Calling," p. 139, Felice Holman. Random House, 1983. Poems to deepen children's appreciation of listening.

REDUCED CLASSROOM ACTIVITIES

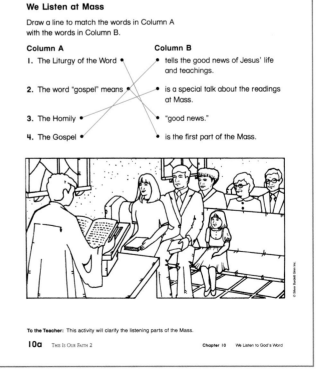

Name

We Listen to God's Word

Every day we hear wonderful sounds. It is important for us to listen to them. Think about some of your favorite sounds. Then complete the sentences below.

1. A person's voice I like to listen to is

2. A sound in nature I like to listen to is

3. A sound in my neighborhood I like to listen to is

4. A sound in my school I like to listen to is

To the Teacher: This activity introduces the chapter. A discussion of the difference between *hearing* and *listening* will enhance student responses on this page.

Chapter 10   We Listen to God's Word   THIS IS OUR FAITH 2   **10**

Name

We Listen at Mass

Draw a line to match the words in Column A with the words in Column B.

Column A	Column B
1. The Liturgy of the Word •	• tells the good news of Jesus' life and teachings.
2. The word "gospel" means •	• is a special talk about the readings at Mass.
3. The Homily •	• "good news."
4. The Gospel •	• is the first part of the Mass.

To the Teacher: This activity will clarify the listening parts of the Mass.

10a   THIS IS OUR FAITH 2   Chapter 10   We Listen to God's Word

Background for the Teacher

THE LITURGY OF THE WORD

One of Jesus' major tasks was preaching God's word. The Catholic Church teaches that Jesus continues to speak to God's people through the Liturgy of the Word at Mass. The sacred readings and the homily are regarded as an integral part of the eucharistic celebration.

In the Scriptures, we hear the story of our ancestors in their struggle for fidelity to the covenant. We listen to the good news and God's promises renewed in the gospels. This faith story mirrors our life struggles. The word of God is a living reality. God's word nourishes us like bread. God's word calls us to conversion and faithfulness. As a community we celebrate at the Sunday liturgy God's word in the Scriptures and in our lives. We hear the message proclaimed and explained in the homily. We challenge one another to hold firmly to the word of God and keep it. Each week the seeds of Scripture grow and blossom in Christian action and prayer. Because we experience God's word and intervention in our lives, we believe he is present in the Scriptures.

LISTENING TO GOD'S WORD

Children of this age can learn the importance of listening to God's word during the celebration of the Eucharist. Second graders have begun to develop and refine their listening skills. Most of the time, they know when it is important to listen at home and at school. They like to hear stories that can spark their imaginations, and they respond well when they sense that someone is speaking directly to them.

You, as a teacher, can encourage the children to listen well to the readings and to the gospel at Mass. During this session and throughout the year, provide a good example by listening attentively to each child who responds or speaks to you. Speak in a tone that invites the children to listen. When you read a story aloud, put expression in your voice. Also, when you read a verse from Scripture, proclaim it in such a way that the children realize that God is speaking to them through you. All these points will help you teach the importance of listening to the readings from Scripture proclaimed during the Liturgy of the Word. Throughout the year, remind the children often that the readings from Scripture have life and meaning for us today.

Objective

This lesson helps the children learn to listen to the stories of Jesus.

Step 1 / INTRODUCTION

Learning About Our Lives

Greeting One Another

Welcome the children by saying, "The Lord be with you." Have them answer with the response they learned in Chapter 9: "And also with you."

Introducing the Chapter

Teach the children "The Noise Song" from THIS IS OUR FAITH Music Program, Grade 2. Use the recording. Ask the following questions.

- What sounds do you hear without listening closely? (*Possible responses are sirens screeching, dogs barking, drums beating.*)

- What sounds do you have to listen to closely so that you can identify them? (*Possible responses are people whispering, forest animals moving, people walking.*)

Direct the children's attention to the focus question on page 122. Ask: When are you asked to listen? (*In school, at home, when someone gives directions, when the coach tells how to play*) When do you listen without being asked? (*When watching TV, when someone is telling a good story*) Invite responses to the question about best listening. (*Affirm all answers.*)

Listening to a Story

Direct the children's attention to the picture of the storyteller telling a story to a group of children. Ask: Can you describe how your storyteller tells a story? (*Gathers listeners around, speaks in a slower, more dramatic manner*) How do we become good listeners? (*By paying attention to the storyteller*)

Share with the children one of your favorite stories. When finished, give the story a title (for instance, "Grandpa's Day at the Fair").

10 We Listen to God's Word

 Activity

1. Who's the best storyteller you know?

_____

2. What's your favorite story?

_____

3. What story do you like to listen to again and again?

_____

When do you do your best listening?

 ***Cultural Awareness***

Some individuals cannot hear with their ears and some others, especially the elderly, can hear only loud sounds. Discuss ways these people are helped to understand what is being said. Many people who are deaf or hearing-impaired use a special language called sign language. Others have learned how to read the lips of people who are speaking.

 **Teaching Tips**

Learning to listen is a sign of growing self-discipline. Practice to develop good listening skills. Assist the children in exercises that focus attention and blot out distractions. Compliment the children when they show evidence of good listening skills. Allow time to process what has been heard before calling on a child. Affirm answers that are evidence of good listening skills.

Jesus was a wonderful storyteller. This is a gospel story that tells about a time when Jesus asked people to listen carefully to what he was telling them.

Jesus Teaches the People

One day, Jesus was walking along the seashore. A large crowd of people gathered to listen to him.

Jesus wanted everyone to be able to see him and hear him. He climbed into a fishing boat. He welcomed the people, sat down in the boat, and began teaching those who had gathered on the shore.

"Listen carefully," Jesus said. Then he told them many things about God. He told them how God wants them to live.

When he finished teaching, Jesus said, "Whoever has ears to hear me, listen well!"

Based on Mark 4:1-2, 9

Scripture 123

Teaching Tips

In native cultures, the storyteller had the serious responsibility of teaching the young children about the tribe's cultural myths, values, and vision. As you share your faith with the children, the art of storytelling becomes unique and effective. To sharpen your skills, apprentice yourself to a good storyteller. Learn the techniques and resources. How does the storyteller describe actions and make the characters come alive? What symbols does the storyteller use to intrigue the listener?

Enriching the Lesson

Invite a storyteller to visit your class. Ask him or her to invite the children to sit on a rug around a chair designated for the storyteller. Allow enough time for the storyteller to use his or her gifts to captivate the children. Thank the storyteller for helping the class learn how to listen better. Invite the children into a sharing circle to retell the stories. Affirm and compliment the children for listening well.

Completing an Activity

Invite the children to name their favorite storytellers and stories. Assist them in printing the names on the lines provided. Ask the children to name a story in their books.

Step 2 / DEVELOPMENT

Learning About Our Faith

Listening to a Gospel Story

Ask a volunteer to read the text at the top of page 123 that introduces Jesus as a wonderful storyteller. Challenge the children to sit still and listen very carefully. Direct them to close their eyes and imagine that they are walking along the seashore with Jesus. Challenge their listening by softening and slowing your speech as you read the story "Jesus Teaches the People" on page 123.

Discussing the Story

Pause to allow the children to think about what they just heard. Ask:

- What did Jesus do so that everyone could see and hear him well? (*He climbed into a boat.*)
- What did Jesus teach the people? (*How to live as God wants them to live*)
- What did Jesus say when he finished teaching? (*"Whoever has ears to hear me, listen well."*)

Explain to the children that Jesus wanted people to listen to his teaching. He also wanted them to put his words into action in their lives.

Step 3 / CONCLUSION

Learning How to Live Our Faith

Sharing How to Listen to God

Invite the children to become quiet. Direct them to invite God to speak to their hearts. (Pause.) Allow a few moments of quiet. Encourage the children to practice listening to God even when they do not feel or hear any response. Tell them that to sit still and wait is also prayer.

Objective

This lesson introduces the children to Bible stories from the Old Testament and the New Testament.

Step 1 / INTRODUCTION

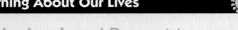

Learning About Our Lives

Reviewing Jesus' Request to Listen Well

Ask the children to repeat Jesus' request to his followers, "Whoever has ears to hear me, listen well." Invite the children to share how they are becoming good listeners in school and at home.

or . . .

Invite the children to do the actions in this story: "Once upon a time the children of the kingdom were sleeping. They had slept for a long time. One morning a brilliant rooster crowed at dawn. The crowing of the rooster was so beautiful, it woke the children. They stretched and stretched and yawned and yawned. They began to shake their arms and hands. They stretched their legs and wiggled their toes. They rubbed their sleepy eyes. They looked around and noticed their friends. They waved to one another and said, 'Good morning!'" Applaud the children for following the story with the correct actions. Stress that good listening made this story fun.

Introducing Bible Stories

Assemble various books—a Bible, dictionary, math textbook, library book, song book, photo album, book on CD-Roms—on the discovery table. Invite the children to choose a book and describe its purpose to the class (for instance, a dictionary gives the meanings of words, a math book shows us how to use numbers, a song book gives us songs to sing, a photo album reminds us of good times with friends and family, and so on). Emphasize that the Bible tells us stories of God's love for us. We believe that we hear God's word when we listen to stories from the Bible.

The Bible is full of wonderful stories about God and God's people. Here is a story from the first part of the Bible.

Noah

A long time ago, there lived a man named Noah. Noah had a wife and three sons. Noah and his family were good people. They loved God very much, and God loved them.

The Lord asked Noah to build a large boat called an ark. On the ark, Noah's family and some animals would be safe from the flood waters that were to come.

It rained for forty days and forty nights. The land became flooded. Inside the ark Noah, his family, and the animals were safe.

Noah's family gave thanks to God for saving them and all the animals from the flood. A rainbow in the sky is a sign of God's promise not to flood the earth with water again.

Based on Genesis 6-9

124 Scripture

★ ★★★ ★
Enriching the Lesson ★

Invite the children as a class to pretend they are Paul and are writing a letter to their second-grade class. On newsprint print "A Letter of Paul to the Second Graders." Ask: What Christian behaviors would Paul remind us to live? Compose several sentences from the children's responses. When finished, invite a volunteer to read "Paul's letter" to the class.

Focus on

The Liturgy of the Word The *Catechism of the Catholic Church* states, "*The Liturgy of the Word* is an integral part of sacramental celebrations. To nourish the faith of believers, the signs which accompany the Word of God should be emphasized: the book of the word . . . its veneration . . . the place of its proclamation . . . its audible and intelligible reading, the minister's homily which extends its proclamation, and the responses of the assembly . . ." (#1154).

Here is a story that Jesus told his disciples. It is from the second part of the Bible.

The Mustard Seed

The kingdom of heaven is like a mustard seed. The farmer plants a mustard seed in a field. It is the smallest seed but it grows into the largest tree of all. It becomes a tree so large that birds come and build nests in its branches.

Based on Matthew 13:31-32

Activity

Draw a picture of your favorite Bible story.

Scripture 125

CURRICULUM CONNECTION

Art Distribute star patterns cut out of file folders. Give each child two sheets of shiny silver or gold paper, glue, glitter, and string or yarn. Have them trace two stars and decorate each. Tape the two stars together. Attach a piece of yarn to hang the stars from a string stretched above the chalkboard. These stars will remind the children to shine and hold firmly to God's word.

Focus on

Self-Esteem Encourage the children to invite an older family member to relate stories about the children's birth and early childhood. Also ask them to tell stories about family gatherings or traditions. Several children may be assigned a day of the week to share stories and pictures of themselves and their families. Display these pictures on a wall or bulletin board. Affirm how important each person is as an individual and as a member of a family.

Step 2 / DEVELOPMENT

Learning About Our Faith

Reading the Story of Noah

Invite the children to open their books to page 124. Read the opening paragraph to introduce them to the story of Noah and the ark. Ask the children to read silently as you read the story aloud. When you have finished reading, ask:

- Who was Noah? (*A good man*)
- Why did Noah build the ark? (*To be safe from the flood that was to come*)
- Who went into the ark? (*Noah, his wife and three sons, and two of every kind of animal*)
- Why did Noah's family give thanks to God? (*For saving them and the animals from the flood*)

Reading About the Mustard Seed

Ask a volunteer to read aloud the story about the mustard seed on page 125. As you explain the meaning of the reading, emphasize that Jesus also explained the meaning of readings from Scripture to his disciples. Explain that the mustard seed was very small, but grew into a great tree. Explain that this story applies to us, because even though we are small, we are great in God's eyes.

Step 3 / CONCLUSION

Learning How to Live Our Faith

Completing an Activity

Read the directions and assist the children in drawing a picture of their favorite Bible story.

Singing Together

Teach the song "We Hear God's Word" from THIS IS OUR FAITH Music Program, Grade 2. Concentrate on singing verses 1 and 2 with the children.

Connecting to Home

Invite the children to ask a family member to share a favorite Bible story. Provide paper for the children to draw the stories. Assure them that there will be time in class to share these stories and drawings.

125

DAY 3
DOCTRINE

Objective

This lesson helps the children to discover the Liturgy of the Word.

Step 1 / INTRODUCTION

Learning About Our Lives

Sharing Favorite Bible Stories

Invite the children to bring their drawings of favorite family Bible stories to a sharing circle. Encourage them to use the drawings to recall the stories. If some of the families have not yet shared a story, assure the children that they may share their stories on another day.

Introducing the Lesson

Recall Mark's story on page 123 about Jesus teaching the people on the seashore. Ask the children to complete Jesus' request, "Whoever has ears to hear me . . . (*listen well.*")

Step 2 / DEVELOPMENT

Learning About Our Faith

Discovering the Liturgy of the Word

Invite a volunteer to read the first paragraph on page 126. Ask: What do we learn at Mass when we listen to the readings? (*About God and ourselves*) What do we call this part of the Mass? (*The Liturgy of the Word*)

Invite another child to read the second paragraph about the first reading. Ask: From what part of the Bible does the first reading come? (*The first section*) What do we call this section? (*The Old Testament*) What are all the first readings about? (*God's people who lived before Jesus was born*)

Invite another child to read the third paragraph about the responsorial psalm. Tell the children that this reading is also from the Old Testament. Ask: How do we participate in this part of the Liturgy of the Word? (*We respond to God's word that we heard in the first reading.*)

Read aloud "The Second Reading" as the children follow in their books. Write *New Testament* and *Old Testament* on the chalkboard.

126

The Liturgy of the Word

Jesus spoke God's word to the people on the seashore. We believe that Jesus speaks God's word to us, too, each time we listen to the readings at Mass. We call this part of the Mass the **Liturgy of the Word**.

The First Reading

The first reading is usually taken from the first section of the Bible, called the **Old Testament**. It tells about God and God's people who lived before Jesus was born.

The Responsorial Psalm

The next part of the Liturgy of the Word is called the **responsorial psalm**. The song leader and the parish community sing this special prayer song together.

The Second Reading

The second reading is taken from the second section of the Bible called the **New Testament**. It tells about Jesus, his disciples, and the first Christian communities. The second reading is usually a reading from one of Paul's letters to the first Christians.

126 Doctrine

Teaching Tips

Try this method for "breaking open the word" or interpreting the gospel with the students. Using missalettes or the lectionary, read the Liturgy of the Word for Sunday. Ask: What did Jesus say or do in this story? How did the people respond? How do you feel about what Jesus said or did? How can we be more like Jesus was or as Jesus said to be?

The Responsorial Psalm The responsorial psalm consists of a series of verses from a psalm interspersed by a response that remains unchanged throughout the prayer. The response is repeated by the community at the beginning of the responsorial psalm and after each verse is said or sung. You might want to offer an example of a responsorial psalm from the Sunday liturgy. Ask the children to repeat the response after you read it and after each verse of the psalm.

Activity

Use the words on the scroll to finish part of a letter that Paul wrote to one of the first Christian communities.

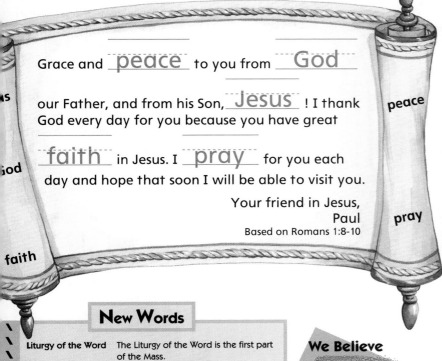

Grace and **peace** to you from **God** our Father, and from his Son, **Jesus** ! I thank God every day for you because you have great

faith in Jesus. I **pray** for you each day and hope that soon I will be able to visit you.

Your friend in Jesus,
Paul
Based on Romans 1:8-10

Words on scroll: peace, pray, God, faith

New Words

Liturgy of the Word	The Liturgy of the Word is the first part of the Mass.
Old Testament	The Old Testament is the first section of the Bible. It tells about God and God's people who lived before Jesus.
responsorial psalm	a psalm we sing after the first reading
New Testament	The New Testament is the second section of the Bible. It tells about the life and teachings of Jesus, his disciples, and the first Christians.

We Believe

Jesus speaks God's word to us at Mass, especially during the Liturgy of the Word.

Doctrine 127

Cultural Awareness

In some parishes, the readings are proclaimed in more than one language. This allows all of the congregation to participate. Invite a pastor and parish leader from a bilingual parish to visit your class. Invite them to proclaim the Scripture readings in both languages spoken in their parish.

Ask:

- From what part of the Bible does the second reading come? (*New Testament*)
- What does the New Testament tell us about? (*About Jesus, his disciples, and the first Christian communities*)

Completing an Activity

Read the directions for the activity. Have the children fill in the blanks to complete the sentences. Allow sufficient time for the children to print their answers. Correct the answers with the children.

Defining the New Words

Direct the children's attention to the New Words box. Invite them to read aloud the definitions and to define the terms in their own words.

Presenting the Doctrine

Read aloud the We Believe statement. Encourage the children to study the doctrine by reading the sentence aloud three or four times.

Step 3 / CONCLUSION

Learning How to Live Our Faith

Making a Word Tree

Distribute lined paper to the children. Ask them to make a word tree by writing the words *Liturgy of the Word* horizontally across the middle of the page. Then instruct them to add the other new words to the tree by fitting them in vertically.

You might have them add these words also: *listen*, *Bible*, and *Jesus*.

Praying Together

Gather the children around the prayer table. Light the candle and say, "Listen, all you lands; listen, all you people. The Lord called me from my birth and gave me my name. You are my disciples. Through you will my glory shine." Ask the children to repeat after you: "We believe in God's word. (echo) God's word speaks to our hearts. (echo) God's word lives in our lives." (echo) Conclude the prayer by singing "We Hear God's Word," verses 3 and 4.

Objective

This lesson helps the children relate favorite gospel stories to their lives.

Step 1 / INTRODUCTION

Learning About Our Lives

Sharing Favorite Bible Stories from Home

Invite the children who had not yet presented their drawings and favorite family Bible stories to do so. Display all pictures about the room as a reminder for us to hold firmly to God's word.

Reviewing the Liturgy of the Word

Review the parts of the Liturgy of the Word: the first reading from the Old Testament, the responsorial psalm, also from the Old Testament, and the second reading from the New Testament. Tell the children that today they are going to continue learning about the Liturgy of the Word.

Step 2 / DEVELOPMENT

Learning About Our Faith

Continuing with the Liturgy of the Word

Invite a volunteer to read the first two paragraphs on page 128. Ask: What is the most important reading in the Liturgy of the Word? (*The gospel*)

Then ask another child to read the third paragraph. Ask: What do we call the talk the priest or the deacon gives? (*The homily*)

What is the purpose of the homily? (*To explain the readings proclaimed at Mass*)

Studying the Photographs

Have the children look at the two photographs on page 128. Ask: What is the reader reading in the first photograph? (*The first or second readings*) What is the priest doing in the second photograph? (*Giving a homily*)

The Liturgy of the Word Continues

We have already learned about some of the Scripture readings read at Mass. Now we will read about two more important parts of the Liturgy of the Word.

The Gospel

The third reading is called the **gospel**. It is the most important reading because it tells the story of Jesus' life and teachings. Gospel stories help us know how to love and care for others. When we listen to the gospel, we stand as a sign of our love for Jesus.

The Homily

Then the priest or deacon gives a special talk that helps us understand what the gospel and the other readings mean. We call this talk the **homily**.

128   Doctrine

 Focus on

Deacons   Deacons serve their parishes in many different ways, often visiting the sick or working on committees. One of the privileges of a deacon is to preach homilies. Deacons may baptize and witness marriages. A deacon may be a transitional deacon, a person who will later be ordained a priest, or a permanent deacon, a person ordained as a deacon for life. Invite a deacon to visit your class and describe the deacon's role.

Activity

Share what you think the gospel stories pictured below are telling you about how to live as a follower of Jesus.

New Word

gospel   The gospel is the third reading we hear at Mass. It tells about Jesus' life and teachings.

homily   A homily is a special talk by a priest or deacon that explains the readings we listen to at Mass.

Doctrine   129

CURRICULUM CONNECTION

Reading   Naming, understanding, and applying the moral of a story is an important reading skill. Request the assistance of a librarian to collect children's stories emphasizing children who profit from listening, telling the truth or making peace with each other. Invite the children to share their story's moral (lesson) and how to live it.

Learning from the Readings

Ask the following questions: What do we learn when we listen well to the readings? (*We learn about God and ourselves, we learn about Jesus' life and teachings.*) How do we learn how to love and care for others? (*By listening to the gospel stories*)

Reviewing the New Words

Direct the children's attention to the New Words box on page 129. Repeat each new word and its definition. Have the children repeat the words and their definitions after you. Invite the children to say in their own words what *gospel* and *homily* mean.

Step 3 / CONCLUSION

Learning How to Live Our Faith

Completing an Activity

Read the directions to the activity on page 129. Allow the children time to look at the four pictures and think about each story. Divide the class into small sharing groups. Encourage each group to retell one of the gospel stories pictured. Circulate to assist the storytellers. Explore what each story teaches and how it applies to the daily life of the Christian. Then ask the children to explain the message of each story and how the story tells them to live as followers of Jesus.

or...

Invite the children to dramatize some of the stories pictured on this page. Divide the class into groups and have each group select the gospel story they will act out. You might arrange, in advance, for the children to perform their dramatizations for children in another class or grade.

DAY 5

PRAYER/REVIEW

Objective

This lesson helps the children pray God's word in the Scriptures and allow themselves to be fed by the word of God.

Preparing for Prayer

Assemble the following items beforehand: music for "We Hear God's Word," a lighted candle (for safety, use a large votive candle), a Bible, a small cross or crucifix, a bowl of honey, a basket of small bread rolls, small paper plates, plastic knives, and napkins.

Choose children for the procession: two readers and a candle bearer, a cross bearer, and two volunteers to carry the basket of bread and the bowl of honey.

When the preparations are completed, explain to the class that today's prayer celebration will focus on the word of God in the Scriptures. Tell the children that the word of God is often thought of as food or nourishment for people who listen carefully to it.

Line up the children in procession. When everyone is ready, begin the procession to the prayer table, singing "We Hear God's Word."

When the procession reaches the prayer table, the items carried should be placed on the table and you and the children should gather around.

Praying God's Word

Begin the prayer by reading aloud the first paragraph found on page 130. Next, ask the first reader to read his or her designated reading. After the reading, speak with the children about the Scripture reading. Help the children understand that it is God's word that helps to keep us healthy and alive in God's love.

Ask the second reader to read his or her reading. Then talk with the class about the different ways that God's word in the Scriptures can be like honey for those who listen carefully.

Complete the prayer by reading aloud the final paragraph at the bottom of page 130.

When the children have returned to their seats, allow sufficient time for the class to enjoy a small treat of bread and honey.

130

Praying God's Word

Teacher: We gather in prayer today to listen to God's word. Let us listen carefully with our ears and with our hearts.

Reader 1: A reading from the Gospel of Matthew. Jesus said, "It is written in the Scriptures 'We do not live on bread alone, but on every word that comes from God.' "

Based on Matthew 4:4

Reader 1: The word of God is like honey in our mouths. It is sweet and it is good for us.

Teacher: Whenever we read the Bible or listen carefully when it is read to us, we are fed with the word of God.

130 Prayer

Focus on

The Bible The Bible is a collection of sacred writings—the Holy Scriptures of Christianity and Judaism. It is comprised of books of the Old Testament and the New Testament. The total number of books in the Roman Catholic Bible is seventy-three.

Emphasize that the Scriptures are the word of God.

Chapter Review

Put an **X** next to each reason below that tells why you listen carefully. Then add one more reason why you listen well.

_____ I listen to learn new things.

_____ I listen to enjoy stories.

_____ I listen to have fun.

_____ I listen to share ideas.

_____ I listen to be a good friend.

_____

1. What is the first part of the Mass called?

Liturgy of the Word

2. Which reading tells of the life and teachings of Jesus?

gospel

3. Talk about some things we can do to help us listen more closely to God's word at Mass.

> **We are happy when we hear God's word and obey it.**
> **Based on Luke 11:28**

Review 131

★ ★★★ ★
Enriching the Lesson

Help the children make a banner. On a large poster, print in large letters the Scripture verse at the bottom of page 131. Lay the poster flat on the floor or on a large table. Distribute crayons or felt-tip markers. Direct each child to write his or her name on the poster. After the banner is completed, display it in a prominent place.

Reviewing the Chapter

Invite the children to play a game. Contestants will complete a Scripture verse or definition. Appoint two moderators to call on the first children to raise their hands. Invite a volunteer to be the person to give stars or stickers as prizes to those who answer correctly. Use the following statements for review.

"Whoever has ears . . . (_to hear me, listen well._") The first part of the Mass is . . . (_the Liturgy of the Word_). The first part of the Bible is . . . (_the Old Testament_). The second part of the Bible that tells about the life and teachings of Jesus is . . . (_the New Testament_). A special talk given by the priest or deacon that explains the readings at Mass is . . . (_a homily_). "Hold firmly . . . (_to the Word of God_"). The good news of Jesus' life is called the . . . (_gospel_). "The kingdom of heaven is like . . . (_a mustard seed_"). "It becomes a tree so big that . . . (_birds come and build nests in its branches_"). The readings for Mass are found in a book called the . . . (_lectionary_).

Completing the Chapter Review

Read the directions for the review on page 131 to the children. Give them sufficient time to mark their answers and write one reason on the line provided. Then read aloud questions 1 and 2. Ask the children to write their answers on the lines provided. Then read aloud item 3 and encourage all children to contribute to the discussion.

Reading the Scripture Verse

Ask the children to read aloud the Scripture verse. Encourage them to conclude that listening to and obeying God's word will make us truly happy.

131

11 We Respond to God's Word

Objectives

To help the children

- Explore the various ways we respond to one another.
- Discover how some of Jesus' listeners responded to him.
- Encounter Mary who responded "yes" to God's call.
- Experience the responses used in the Liturgy of the Word.
- Pray together to express their belief in God and review the chapter.

Chapter Outline

	Step 1 **Learning About Our Lives**	**Step 2** **Learning About Our Faith**	**Step 3** **Learning How to Live Our Faith**
Day 1	- Role-play scenarios. - Review Chapter 10. - Introduce the chapter. *ABOUT 10 MINUTES*	- Read and discuss the call to respond. - Review the new word. *ABOUT 15 MINUTES*	- Complete an activity. *ABOUT 5 MINUTES*
Day 2	- Review Day 1. *ABOUT 5 MINUTES*	- Read and discuss the story. - Understand Peter's responses. - Discover Jesus' call to respond. *ABOUT 15 MINUTES*	- Complete an activity. - Sing together. *ABOUT 10 MINUTES*
Day 3	- Learn to listen and respond to God's word. *ABOUT 5 MINUTES*	- Read about God's messenger. - Understand Mary's response. *ABOUT 15 MINUTES*	- Complete an activity. - Pray together. - Represent Mary in art. *ABOUT 10 MINUTES*
Day 4	- Learn different ways to respond. *ABOUT 5 MINUTES*	- Recall the Liturgy of the Word. - Discover our responses at Mass. - Complete an activity. - Present the doctrine. *ABOUT 20 MINUTES*	- Share things learned. *ABOUT 5 MINUTES*
Day 5	**Prayer** Share together a prayer experience of faith. **Review** Do chapter review; discuss questions; review responses to God's word and read the Scripture verse.		

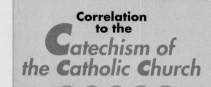

Correlation
to the
Catechism of
the **C**atholic **C**hurch

Paragraphs
1157, 1190, 1348, 1548

Plan Ahead

Preparing Your Class

Day 1 Read over the lesson prior to the session. Gather items and prepare discovery table. Review Chapter 10.

Day 2 Read over the lesson prior to the session. Gather rhythm instruments to accompany song.

Day 3 Read over the lesson. Prepare puppet. If enriching the lesson, gather tape recording, recorder, and map of the Holy Land found on page 329.

Day 4 Read over the lesson prior to the session.

Day 5 Read over the lesson prior to the session. Prepare prayer table.

Materials Needed

Day 1
- pencils
- play telephone
- thank-you note
- interactive game
- Bible or lectionary

Day 2
- pencils
- recording of "We Hear God's Word"; Music Program Director's Manual, Grade 2
- rhythm instruments

Day 3
- puppet
- white cloth and blue cloth
- art resource books
- drawing paper

Day 4
- pencils

Day 5
- pencils
- candle, matches
- Bible or lectionary

Additional Resources

As you plan this chapter, consider using the following materials from The Resourceful Teacher Package.

- *Classroom Activity Sheets 11* and *11a*
- *Family Activity Sheets 11* and *11a*
- *Chapter 11 Test*
- *Prayers for Every Day*
- *Projects: Grade 2*

You may also wish to refer to the following Big Books.

- *We Celebrate the Mass,* pages 1–23
- *We Celebrate the Sacraments,* pages 7–9

In preparing the children for the Sunday readings, you may wish to use Silver Burdett Ginn's *Getting Ready for Sunday* student and teacher materials.

BOOKS FOR THE JOURNEY

Praise for the Singing. "This Little Light," pp. 46–47. Madelaine Gill. Little, Brown and Co., 1993. A song in which a promise is made to be a light to others.

The Seeing Stick. Jane Yolen. A blind man teaches a child how to live a happy and giving life even if she is blind.

MORE BOOKS FOR THE JOURNEY

Sunday's Children. "Sunday Is a Storytelling Day," p. 15; "Stories," p. 18. James Bitney. Resource Publications, 1986. Prayer poems about listening to and hearing God's word.

Say It. Charlotte Zolotow. Greenwillow Books, 1992. An ongoing dialogue between a child and her mother that climaxes with the mother using the words, "I love you."

REDUCED CLASSROOM ACTIVITIES

Name

We Respond to God's Word

Every day we respond to other people. Circle all the ways you responded to someone today.

I listened carefully to a story.

I answered a question.

I laughed at a joke.

I talked with my classmates.

I prayed for someone who is sad.

I forgave someone.

Now think of ways you responded to God today.
Write two ways on the lines below.

To the Teacher: This activity will affirm different ways of responding. Discuss how we respond to others in word and gesture.

Chapter 11   We Respond to God's Word   THIS IS OUR FAITH 2   **11**

Name

We Respond to Jesus

We respond to Jesus when we tell him that we believe in him. Trace over the letters on the lines below. Then pray these words often.

Lord your words give me
lf e and hope.
I believe in you I will not
leave you. Amen.

To the Teacher: This activity follows "Jesus Talks with His Friends."

11a   THIS IS OUR FAITH 2   Chapter 11   We Respond to God's Word

THE WORD OF GOD

The word of God is food for our soul. Rather than "eat and run" we pause to savor it. We allow it to warm us. We delight in its subtle flavors. Because God's word in the Scriptures is a living word, it is always new, with new meanings for each person, each day. To savor the Scriptures, we need a prayerful attitude, an attitude of openness. Only then can we listen to the homily and digest God's word, letting it seep through us and compel us to action. Ours is a world filled with many conflicting values. We hunger for direction, for clarity, for assurance that our lives have purpose. By connecting God's word to our daily lives, we are nourished and can, in turn, feed others by sharing his word with them.

RESPONDING AT MASS

In the Scriptures, Jesus asks his followers to make choices based on friendship with him, trust in the Father, and openness to the Holy Spirit. Jesus' words are words of challenge and of comfort. He challenges us to make sacrifices, to risk everything, and to be obedient. He comforts us with the knowledge that in him we will find peace and harmony. As disciples, we see and hear God's word at Mass. The call is to follow Jesus. At Mass, we respond in prayer and song.

RESPONDING TO GOD IN OUR LIVES

God's word nourishes us to live our response through honesty, compassion, and love wherever we may be—in offices, factories, classrooms, our homes, and the marketplace.

God's repeated expressions of love invite us to respond with gratitude and love. Daily we are challenged to be a sign of God's word for others. In this lesson's Scripture readings, some people listened to Jesus and thought his teachings too radical. They chose to walk away and reject Jesus' message. Jesus' close friends renewed their belief in him through the words of Peter, "We have come to believe and are convinced that you are the Holy One of God" (John 6:69).

Second graders spend many hours listening to parents and teachers. Too often their only response is supplying expected answers to adult questions. Yet second graders are capable of creative thinking and of dialogue. They can genuinely express their feelings and, with encouragement and patience, state their beliefs.

Help the children develop confidence in themselves as believers. Affirm their faith responses. Help them to value active participation in the celebration of the Eucharist. Learning the responses so that they can be engaged in the prayer of the community is vital to their faith development.

DAY 1
DOCTRINE

Objective

This lesson helps the children explore the various ways we respond to one another.

Step 1 / INTRODUCTION

Learning About Our Lives

Role-playing Scenarios

Gather the children around the discovery table, where you have placed a play telephone, a thank-you note, and an interactive game. Demonstrate receiving and answering a telephone call. Tell the children that we *respond* to the person calling us when we answer. We often have to make a decision about something. Role-play with the class one of the following scenarios.

1. It is late, and you are not home from school. Your mother is worried. She phones the principal of your school.

2. You and your mom are planning your birthday party. You want to invite the new girl in your class. Show how using the telephone can be helpful.

3. Someone is hurt in an accident in front of your home. Your dad stays to help the injured person. He instructs you to go inside and phone for an ambulance.

Read the thank-you note on the discovery table to the class. Invite the children to share responses on why they think writing and receiving a thank-you note is important. What does it say to the gift giver?

Using the interactive game, demonstrate how one game move determines your next selection. Show how the game continues or ends based on your decisions.

or...

Have the children play the game Simon Says. Then discuss how they responded to the leader's words with an action. They listened, interpreted what the leader said, then responded.

Reviewing Chapter 10

Invite the children to look at the Bible or lectionary. Ask the children to say what they

132

11
We Respond to God's Word

Our Response

We talk with each other in many ways. We invite people to celebrations. We teach each other. We ask questions. We tell stories. We ask for help.

Name one time when it was easy for you to answer someone who asked you a question and one time when it was hard.

We answer or **respond** to each other in many ways, too. Sometimes we answer with words or by nodding our heads. Sometimes we smile or clap our hands. And sometimes we respond by being silent and still.

What might the people in the pictures on this page be saying to each other? How are they responding to each other?

132   Doctrine

🍎 Teaching Tips

When doing something creative, take time to do the activity yourself before you instruct your class to do it. Do exactly what you will be asking your class to do. Notice what happens inside you. Be aware of how you feel as you do the activity. Avoid criticism of your work. Notice what you like about it. This experience can ensure success for you and a satisfactory response from your students when you bring the activity to the children in the classroom.

Focus on

Jesus' Call to Listen There are many passages in Scripture that emphasize the importance of listening well to God's word. Read aloud to the class some of the verses cited here.

Matthew 11:15; 13:9; 13:43

Mark 4:9; 4:23; 7:14

Luke 21:38

John 18:37

Revelation 2:11

Jesus Calls Us to Respond

Jesus responded to people in many ways. He told stories to help people understand God's love and forgiveness. His stories helped people believe in him and change their lives.

Jesus wants us to listen to him, too. We can respond to Jesus by treating others with kindness and respect. We can also respond by spending time each day talking with Jesus in prayer.

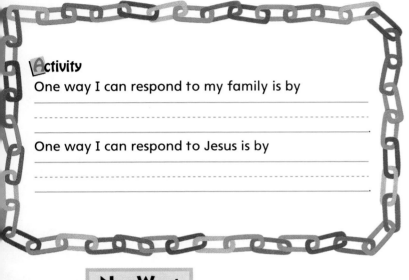

Activity

One way I can respond to my family is by

_____

_____

One way I can respond to Jesus is by

_____

_____

New Word

respond to answer with words or actions

Doctrine **133**

can remember about the Liturgy of the Word at Mass. (If you have opted to make and use new word posters for each lesson, display the new word poster for Chapter 10 for the review.) Explain to the children that they will look at ways of responding to God's word at Mass. These responses help the community of worshipers to participate by singing, gesturing, and praying together.

Introducing the Chapter

Ask a volunteer to read aloud the chapter-focus statement on page 132. Encourage all the children to tell about when it was easy and when it was difficult to answer someone's questions.

Now ask a volunteer to read aloud the paragraph at the top of page 132. Encourage each child to study the photographs and participate in the discussion. Remind the children of Jesus' call to "Listen well!"

Step 2 / DEVELOPMENT

Learning About Our Faith

Reading and Discussing the Call to Respond

Read aloud the text "Jesus Calls Us to Respond" on page 133. Discuss by asking:

- Who can remember a story of God's love or forgiveness?
- How could Jesus' story "A Story About Reconciliation" (Chapter 7) help people change their lives?
- How can we respond to Jesus? (*By doing what he does*)

Reviewing the New Word

Say the word *respond* and its definition found in the New Word box on page 133. Ask the children to repeat the definition several times.

Step 3 / CONCLUSION

Learning How to Live Our Faith

Completing an Activity

Have the children write their responses on the lines provided. Invite volunteers to read aloud their responses.

133

Objective

This lesson helps the children discover how some of Jesus' listeners responded to him as he proclaimed God's word.

Step 1 / INTRODUCTION

Learning About Our Lives

Reviewing Day 1

Ask the children to remember what *respond* means. Be sure the children realize that a response can be a word or an action. Explain that today they will read a story about the way some people responded to Jesus.

Step 2 / DEVELOPMENT

Learning About Our Faith

Reading and Discussing the Story

Read aloud the introductory paragraph at the top of page 134. Then ask four volunteers to read "Jesus Talks with His Friends." After the readers finish, ask the following questions.

- What were some of the things Jesus told the people? (*Stories about God and about how to live good lives*)

- Why did Jesus ask questions? (*To make people think*)

- Why didn't some people believe Jesus? (*Some things were too hard to do.*)

- What did these people do? (*They went away.*)

- What did Jesus ask his friends? (*"Do you want to leave me, too?"*)

- How did Peter answer Jesus? (*He told Jesus what he and his friends believed.*)

Understanding Peter's Responses

Challenge the children to identify and list on the chalkboard Peter's responses to Jesus.

- "Your words give us life and hope."
- "We believe you."
- "We believe God sent you."
- "We will not leave you."

This is a story about Jesus speaking to a group of people. Discover how the people respond to him in different ways.

Jesus Talks with His Friends

Jesus had much to tell people who came to listen to him. He told them stories about God. He told them how to love and care for all people. He told them they were special. And to make them think, he asked them many questions.

Some people who listened to Jesus asked, "How can anyone believe all he says? What he says is too hard to do." So they went away.

One day Jesus asked his friends, "Do you want to leave me, too?" Everyone was silent for a minute.

134   Scripture

Teaching Tips

Help the children recognize and deal with their negative feelings that may prompt inappropriate responses. Ask how they respond when they are upset with other people or with themselves.

- Do you stay calm and try to work things out?

- Do you shout and blame others when you feel unhappy?

- Do you feel discouraged when you see other children's work after having completed a task?

Participation The *Catechism of the Catholic Church* states, "*All gather together.* Christians come together in one place for the Eucharistic assembly . . . *All* have their own active parts to play in the celebration, each in his own way: readers, those who bring up the offerings, those who give communion, and the whole people whose 'Amen' manifests their participation" (#1348).

Then Peter answered for them all. "Lord, to whom shall we go? Your words give us life and hope. We believe in you. We believe God sent you. We will not leave you."

Based on John 6:60-69

Activity

Choose a word from the clover leaf to fill in each blank.

Jesus, we **believe** in you and want to

stay with you.

Jesus, we **love** you.

We will try to **live** your word.

clover leaf words: stay, live, believe, love

Have the children prayerfully read each of Peter's responses. Tell them that Peter's responses can be their responses to the story from Scripture they just heard.

Discovering Jesus' Call to Respond

Explain that during the Liturgy of the Word, we hear God's call. We respond to God's call during Mass and in our daily lives.

Invite discussion from the children about what they would choose to do in response to Jesus' call. Avoid being judgmental. Point out that sometimes to follow Jesus is difficult, risky, and demands sacrifice.

Step 3 / CONCLUSION

Learning How to Live Our Faith

Completing an Activity

Read the directions on page 135 aloud. Allow the children to fill in the blanks. Then have the children read their answers aloud.

Singing Together

Play the recording of "We Hear God's Word" from THIS IS OUR FAITH Music Program, Grade 2. Stress verses 2, 3, and 5, in which the words *keep, share,* and *live,* signify our responses to hearing God's word. Follow the suggestions on page 202 of the Music Program Director's Manual, Grade 2, for movement and for using instruments as you play the song a second time.

135

Objective

This lesson introduces Mary, the Mother of God, as someone who responded "yes" to God's call.

Step 1 / INTRODUCTION

Learning About Our Lives

Learning to Listen and Respond to God's Word

Gather the children in a sharing circle. Using a puppet, ask each of the questions individually, allowing the children to respond to the puppet. Encourage the children to share more by having the puppet say "I don't understand" or "Tell me more" or "Paint me a word picture of what you saw and heard." Conclude with the concept that our actions toward self and others reflect our responses to God's word.

Step 2 / DEVELOPMENT

Learning About Our Faith

Reading About God's Messenger

Narrate the story on page 136 about Gabriel and Mary. Invite two children to read the words of Gabriel and Mary. After the first reading, instruct the children to close their eyes. Read the story a second time, very softly. Now invite the children to open their eyes and answer the following questions.

How do you think Mary felt having the angel Gabriel visit her? (*Answers will vary.*) What was Gabriel's message? (*God wanted Mary to be the mother of God's Son.*) What do you think Mary thought about before she made her choice? (*Answers will vary.*) What was Mary's answer to God? (*Yes, she would be the mother of Jesus.*)

or . . .

Have a boy and a girl role-play the story using two props, a white cloth for Gabriel and a blue cloth for Mary. Gabriel holds the white cloth in front of his face and lowers it when he appears to Mary. Mary wears the blue cloth as a veil. These two children can pantomime the parts of Gabriel and Mary as the rest of the children read each character's words.

136

God Sends a Messenger

One day God sent an angel as a messenger to a young woman named Mary. The angel's name was Gabriel.

"Mary," Gabriel said, "God wants you to be the mother of a special baby boy. The baby's name will be Jesus. He will be called the Son of God."

Mary wondered how she could become the mother of God's Son. Mary decided to trust God.

"Yes," Mary told Gabriel. "I will do what God wants. I will be the mother of Jesus."

Based on Luke 1:26-38

Mary Listens and Responds

Mary listened to God's call to be the mother of Jesus. At first Mary didn't understand what God was asking her to do.

Mary prayed. She decided to trust God. She listened carefully to what God was telling her. She said, "Yes, God. I will do what you ask."

136 Scripture

★ ★ ★ ★
Enriching the Lesson ★

Teach "Hail Mary," the song found on page 16 in the Program Director's Manual, Grade 2, of THIS IS OUR FAITH Music Program. Use the directions on page 71 to teach the song to the children. Follow the suggestions for movement and using instruments.

Focus on

Mary We know little about the life of the Blessed Virgin Mary. Tradition teaches us that Mary's parents were Joachim and Anna. It is believed that Mary was a young teenager when she accepted God's call to become the mother of God's Son. The Church teaches that Mary was conceived without original sin, and lived and died as an all-holy, sinless virgin. She is the model of holiness for Catholics.

Activity

We are asked to respond to God's love for us.
Draw lines to match ways we can respond. Then
draw matching pictures.

1. God gives us
parents who
love and care
for us.

We can respond
by listening to
them, obeying
them, and helping
them.

2. God gives us
the beautiful
earth and all
the good things
that grow on it.

We can respond
by recycling
aluminum cans
and by using only
the water we
need.

3. God gives us
wonderful
animals.

We can respond
by treating our
pets and all
animals with care
and kindness.

4. God gives us
our friends to
make us happy.

We can respond
by caring about
them and by
treating them
fairly.

Enriching the Lesson

Display a map showing Naza-reth, Bethlehem, and Jerusalem. Place cut-out figures of Mary, Joseph, and the boy Jesus. (Move the cut-out figures to each town at the appropriate time.) To begin, explain to the children that Mary and Joseph traveled together to Bethlehem where Jesus was born. Then they returned to Nazareth to live as a family. When Jesus was about 12 years old, Joseph, Mary, and Jesus traveled to Jer-usalem to visit the Temple.

Understanding Mary's Response

Direct the children's attention to "Mary Listens and Responds" on page 136 as you read the paragraph aloud. Ask: Did Mary understand at first what God was asking her to do? (*No.*) After she prayed and trusted in God, what did she respond? (*"Yes, God. I will do what you ask."*) Comment that because Mary listened and responded "yes" to God, she became Joseph's wife and the mother of Jesus.

Step 3 / CONCLUSION

Learning How to Live Our Faith

Completing an Activity

Read aloud the directions for the activity on page 137. Have the children read along with you as you read each item and the responses to be matched. Allow sufficient time for the children to complete the matches. Discuss the correct matches with the class.

Praying Together

Invite the children to name some special people or special animals in their lives. After all the children have had an opportunity to speak, say, "Thank you, Jesus, for all the people and pets who continue to love us. They are a sign of your word in our lives. Amen." Conclude by praying the Hail Mary together.

Representing Mary in Art

Tell the children that Mary has been represented in many works of art. Select some art books from your public library that depict Mary in paintings and sculpture. Show them to the children. Explain that many of these pictures interpret special titles of honor for Mary. Write some Mary titles on the chalkboard, such as Mother of Jesus, Mother of the Church, Mary Immaculate (Patroness of the United States), Our Lady of Guadalupe (Patroness of the Americas), Mother of Mothers, Wife of Joseph, Faithful Follower of Jesus, Comforter of the Sick, and Guide for the Young. Distribute a sheet of drawing paper to each child. Direct the children to select one Mary title, print it on their paper, and draw pictures of Mary as they think she would look for the particular title they have chosen. When all have finished, pray a litany by having each child hold up his or her picture and say the title. All respond, "Pray for us."

DAY 4
DOCTRINE

Objective

This lesson helps the children experience the responses used during the Liturgy of the Word.

Step 1 / INTRODUCTION

Learning About Our Lives

Learning Different Ways to Respond

Explore with the children different ways we can respond to one another. Demonstrate by saying "Hello"; "How are you?"; "Good morning"; or "Let's go out and play." Encourage the children's responses. Since not all responses are verbal, demonstrate gestures for which actions are appropriate responses, such as waving hello or goodbye.

Step 2 / DEVELOPMENT

Learning About Our Faith +

Discovering Ways to Respond at Mass

Ask a volunteer to read aloud the explanatory paragraph "Responding to God at Mass" on page 138. Tell the children that we can respond to God's word just as Peter responded to Jesus in the story they read in their session on Day 2. Stress that by expressing our belief in the teachings of Jesus through words and deeds of thanks and praise, we respond to Jesus.

Recalling the Liturgy of the Word

Write the phrase *Liturgy of the Word* on the chalkboard. Underneath it write the parts introduced thus far: *first reading, responsorial psalm, second reading, gospel, homily.* Ask:

- Where does the first reading generally come from? (*Bible, Old Testament*)
- Where does the second reading come from? (*Bible, New Testament*)
- Who reads the gospel and preaches the homily at Sunday Mass? (*Priest or deacon*)

Responding to God at Mass

We can hear Jesus speak to us when we listen to the readings and homily during the Liturgy of the Word. We are called to respond with songs, prayers, and actions. And we are called to respond by living in a caring and responsible way.

Activity

Trace over the letters on the lines below.
Then read our responses to God's word.

The word of the Lord.

Thanks be to God.

The gospel of the Lord.

Praise to you,
Lord Jesus Christ.

Enriching the Lesson

Use the *We Celebrate the Mass Big Book,* pages 5–11, to introduce or review parts of the Liturgy of the Word during this chapter. (The Profession of Faith will be taught at the intermediate level.)

CURRICULUM CONNECTION

Music Explain that responding to a call occurs in songs that have a group of singers answering or responding to a soloist. Many call-and-response songs are spirituals. Play two songs from Silver Burdett Ginn's THE MUSIC CONNECTION: "Mary Had a Baby," Grade K, CD 3-9 and "Michael, Row the Boat Ashore," Grade 2, CD 2-9. Ask the children to raise their hands when they hear the response to the soloist's call. Teach them to sing the response in each song along with the recording.

At Mass we respond to God's word after each reading. We also thank Jesus for teaching us about life and about God. We praise God through songs, prayers, and actions.

Activity

Learn these gestures based on Psalm 19 as one way of responding to God's word.

The heavens tell of your glory, O God!

And all creation shouts with joy and praise.

Come, children, play on your instruments and dance.

And sing glory to our God!

We Believe

We are called to respond to God's word. At Mass we respond with words, songs, and prayers. In our lives we respond by doing what Jesus asks of us.

Doctrine 139

Teaching Tips

Audio or video-taping one of your parish liturgies would be helpful to introduce or reinforce the components of the Liturgy of the Word.

Remind the children that the Liturgy of the Word is God's word for us in our lives and that it invites us to respond.

Discovering Our Responses at Mass

When the children have finished the tracing activity on page 138, tell them that by using these words they respond to God's word each time they attend Mass. Point to the appropriate part of the Liturgy of the Word on the chalkboard and explain that *Thanks be to God* is our response after the first and second readings and *Praise to you, Lord Jesus Christ* is our response to the gospel.

Completing an Activity

Read the explanatory passage at the top of page 139 about responding to, thanking, and praising God through songs, prayers, and actions. Give the directions for completing the activity.

Encourage the children to repeat each phrase of the psalm along with you and then show you the appropriate gesture.

Presenting the Doctrine

Ask a volunteer to read the We Believe statements. Then read the statements again as the children echo you.

Step 3 / CONCLUSION

Learning How to Live Our Faith

Sharing Things Learned

Invite the children to share the responses and gestures they have learned in class with their parents at home tonight.

DAY 5
PRAYER/REVIEW

Objective

This lesson helps the children to express their faith in God through prayer.

Praying with Faith

Invite the children to gather around the prayer table with their books. Enthrone the Bible and light the candle. Begin the prayer experience by reading the invitation to prayer at the top of page 140. Have the children read together the eight belief statements of the prayer.

At the conclusion of the prayer, direct the children to return to their seats for the chapter review.

Praying with Faith

Teacher: We come to our prayer table with great faith in God, our Creator, and in Jesus, our Friend. Let us pray together about some things we believe as children of God.

All: We believe in you, God!

We believe that you made us in your own image and that we are like you.

We believe that you sent us Jesus, your greatest gift. And we believe that Jesus shows us who you are.

We believe in the Holy Spirit, who is your Spirit. And we believe that the Holy Spirit helps us each day to make good choices.

We believe that your love will never leave us.

We believe in you, God!

Amen.

140 Prayer

Enriching the Lesson

Ask the children to close their eyes. Ask them to remember a time when they prayed and how they prayed. Ask: What words did you say to God? How did you feel as you prayed?

Now invite the children to open their eyes. Encourage them when they pray to remember to

- PRAISE God.
- tell God they are SORRY.
- ASK God for something.
- say THANK YOU to God.

Chapter Review

The five words hidden in the puzzle tell of ways we can respond to God in our lives. Circle each word you find.

L	T	H	A	N	K	S
F	E	O	M	I	L	U
A	P	K	F	M	O	Z
I	C	A	R	E	V	P
T	Z	P	O	L	E	D
H	G	O	T	U	C	N
T	P	R	A	I	S	E

1. What word describes what we do when we answer someone with words or actions?

respond

2. How can we respond to God's word at Mass?

with songs, prayers,

and actions

3. Talk about some things we can do to respond to Jesus and his teachings.

"Lord, you have the words of life."
Based on John 6:68

Review 141

Reviewing the Chapter

Explain the directions to the hidden words puzzle. Allow the children sufficient time to complete the puzzle. After they have finished, check their responses. Take time to go through the three review items now. Walk around the room offering help to any child that may need assistance in writing responses to items 1 and 2 on the lines provided. Be supportive of each child who participates in the discussion of the third item.

Reading the Scripture Verse

Read the Scripture verse at the bottom of page 141. Explain that God's word is life-giving. Remind the children that reading and responding to the Scriptures will help us to live good and happy lives. Help the children memorize the verse.

★ Enriching the Lesson ★

Second-grade children are often comfortable praying "Thank-you" prayers to God. Pray this litany to give thanks for the blessings of creation. The response is, "We thank you, God."

For sunshine and flowers, *R.*
For the sounds of birds, *R.*
For sparkling water, *R.*
For crackling campfires, *R.*
For the smell of fresh air, *R.*
For all your gifts, *R.*

141

We Pray for People

Objectives ~~~~~~~~

To help the children

■ Realize that God invites them to pray for everyone.

■ Learn that Jesus prayed for others.

■ Experience the Prayer of the Faithful.

■ Realize that praying for others is part of the vocation of religious sisters.

■ Celebrate with a community prayer chain and review the chapter.

Chapter Outline ~~~~~~~~

	Step 1 Learning About Our Lives	**Step 2** Learning About Our Faith	**Step 3** Learning How to Live Our Faith
Day 1	■ Play a game to introduce prayer. ■ Introduce the chapter. *ABOUT 10 MINUTES*	■ Read and discuss a poem. *ABOUT 10 MINUTES*	■ Identify those for whom we pray. ■ Pray together. *ABOUT 10 MINUTES*
Day 2	■ Discuss community prayer. *ABOUT 5 MINUTES*	■ Read and discuss a story. *ABOUT 18 MINUTES*	■ Complete an activity. ■ Pray together. *ABOUT 7 MINUTES*
Day 3	■ Introduce the chapter. *ABOUT 5 MINUTES*	■ Pray to show that we care. ■ Role-play. ■ Review the new word. ■ Present the doctrine. *ABOUT 20 MINUTES*	■ Write and pray a prayer of the faithful. *ABOUT 5 MINUTES*
Day 4	■ Introduce the chapter. *ABOUT 5 MINUTES*	■ Learn about religious life. ■ Recall a visit to a convent. ■ Read about a religious sister. *ABOUT 15 MINUTES*	■ Complete an activity. ■ Pray for the needs of others. *ABOUT 10 MINUTES*

Day 5 **Prayer** Prepare to make a prayer chain; make a prayer chain and pray together as a community.

Review Review the chapter and read the Scripture verse.

Correlation
to the
**Catechism of
the Catholic Church**

Paragraphs
1346, 1349, 2634

Plan Ahead

	Preparing Your Class	**Materials Needed**
Day 1	Read over the lesson. Prepare verbal game. Prepare personal prayer experiences to share. Select and cut out magazine/newspaper pictures.	■ pencils ■ magazine and newpaper pictures ■ parish Book of Intercessions
Day 2	Read over the lesson prior to the session. Select appropriate instrumental music. Get tape recorder. Prepare prayer table.	■ pencils ■ crayons or felt-tip markers ■ tape recorder ■ recording of instrumental music
Day 3	Read over the lesson prior to the session. Videotape a televised Mass (optional).	■ pencils ■ video of Prayer of the Faithful at Mass (optional)
Day 4	Read over the lesson prior to the session. Gather books about and pictures of nuns and convents. Prepare discovery table. Gather pictures of needs.	■ parish Book of Intercessions ■ pictures of nuns in a convent ■ pictures of rural, urban, and global needs
Day 5	Prior to the session, invite older students to help children make a community prayer chain. Gather necessary craft materials to make paper chain.	■ construction paper ■ 11" × 3" paper links ■ paste, glue, or stapler ■ black markers, masking tape

Additional Resources

As you plan this chapter, consider using the following materials from The Resourceful Teacher Package.

■ *Classroom Activity Sheets 12* and *12a*

■ *Family Activity Sheets 12* and *12a*

■ *Chapter 12 Test*

■ *Prayers for Every Day*

■ *Projects: Grade 2*

You may also wish to refer to the following Big Books.

■ *We Celebrate the Mass,* pages 1–23

■ *We Celebrate the Sacraments,* pages 7–9

In preparing the children for the Sunday readings, you may wish to use Silver Burdett Ginn's *Getting Ready for Sunday* student and teacher materials.

BOOKS FOR THE JOURNEY

What Can I Say to You, God? Elspeth Campbell Murphy. David C. Cook, 1980. A child meditatively dialogues with God about prayer.

Praise God. pp. 30–55. Gunvor Edwards and Joan Brown. Liturgical Press, 1994. Prayers of the Mass, including a prayer for all God's holy people.

MORE BOOKS FOR THE JOURNEY

Goodnight Blessings. Karen Mezek Leimert. Word Publishing, 1994. Prayers thanking God for all things, especially the people in a child's life.

Anytime Prayers. Madeleine L'Engle. Harold Shaw Publishers, 1994. A collection of prayers for children that are ideal for the whole family.

REDUCED CLASSROOM ACTIVITIES

Name

We Pray for People

Make your own prayer wheel. In each section, write the name of a person you would like to pray for often. Cut out your prayer wheel and keep it in a special place.

I remember
_____
today in prayer.

Cut out the arrow above. Use a metal brad and attach the arrow at the dot to the center of your prayer wheel.

To the Teacher: This activity will encourage students to pray often for specific people.

Chapter 12   We Pray for People   This Is Our Faith 2   **12**

Name

Prayer of the Faithful Garden

Help God's love grow. Plant the prayer of Jesus by choosing the correct words to write on the signs below.

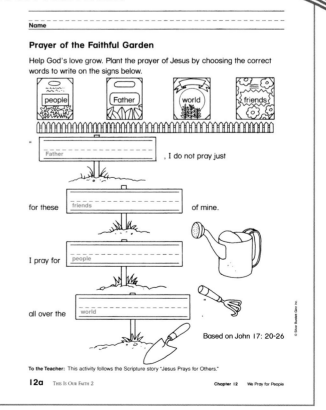

people   Father   world   friends

"_____Father_____, I do not pray just

for these _____friends_____ of mine.

I pray for _____people_____

all over the _____world_____

Based on John 17: 20-26

To the Teacher: This activity follows the Scripture story "Jesus Prays for Others."

12a   This Is Our Faith 2   Chapter 12   We Pray for People

ABOUT PRAYER

Prayer can help us feel comfortable and safe. Prayer is rooted in who we are. It reflects how we were formed by our families. If our families prayed together, we may feel comfortable in shared or community prayer. We are led to prayer by praying. Prayer doesn't change God, but it can change us. We can feel more intimate with God through prayer. In the home, prayer is best nurtured as the day begins, at meals, and at bedtime. Sustaining prayer rituals at those times is an ongoing sign of God's presence in our lives.

As teachers we can nurture children in the habit of praying by providing them with significant rituals, memorable experiences, and by using rich symbols. Through prayer, we remind the child that he or she is not alone. God is a constant companion. Community prayer offers the child a supportive and caring presence. A child can feel that prayer makes a difference in his or her life, in the life of families, in the classroom, and parish communities.

As teachers we also must help our children become friends with silence. Silence invites the child on an inner journey. It offers a quiet place for reflection and growth. It can provide a meaningful way for the child to discover who he or she is. Discovering the God within offers the child forgiveness, comfort, and acceptance.

PRAYER OF THE FAITHFUL

Jesus prayed for everyone, especially for people in need. As Christians we are called to pray for all people. At Mass we say the Prayer of the Faithful. The intercessions reflect the Christian community's concern for those in need. They include prayers for the world and its leaders, for the Catholic Church, for people far away, for those who live in our neighborhoods, and for persons who live in our parish community. The Prayer of the Faithful concludes the Liturgy of the Word at Mass.

LEARNING TO PRAY FOR OTHERS

It is important for the children to recognize that during the Prayer of the Faithful at Mass, they can respond in prayer to the needs that others have voiced. Provide opportunities in your classroom and in your parish community for the children to offer spontaneous prayer for others. Help the children formulate petitions that include people and events that are meaningful and tangible to them. Your affirmation and encouragement will help the children become comfortable engaging in active, spontaneous, intercessory prayer.

Objective

This lesson helps the children realize that God invites them to pray, especially for others, and that they join in prayer with others at Mass.

Step 1 / INTRODUCTION

Learning About Our Lives

Playing a Game to Introduce Prayer

Invite the children to sit in a circle around the discovery table. Begin by saying, "We are going to praise God by playing a game. God has given us many gifts. We are going to say, 'Thank you, God' for our gifts. We will practice together. Let's begin with our hair. Do you have hair? Show me your hair." (Explain that each child should point to or touch his or her hair now.) Then the children say together, "Thank you, God, for my hair." Continue with "Do you have eyes? Show me your eyes. (Pause as they touch their eyes.) Then all say, "Thank you, God, for my eyes." Ask if anyone has any questions. Begin again with hair, eyes, and continue with mouth, arms, heart, stomach, legs, feet, and toes. (Play and pray as long as the children are engaged.) Conclude by asking, "Who are you?" Each child responds, "I am (*Name*). I thank you, God, for me."

Introducing the Chapter

Direct the children to return to their seats and open their books to page 142. Read aloud the chapter-focus question. Help the children consider some reasons why people ask for prayers. Invite volunteers to tell about times when knowing that people were praying for them helped them. You may want to share two or three personal experiences to begin the discussion.

Step 2 / DEVELOPMENT

Learning About Our Faith

Reading and Discussing a Poem

Read aloud the title of the poem "Praying for Others." Divide the class into two groups. Direct the groups to alternate reading the lines of the poem. Use the following questions.

12

We Pray for People

 Many people need or want us to pray for them. What are some reasons why they ask us to pray for them?

Praying for Others

I know that someone's hungry.
I know that someone's sad.
I know that I have much more
Than many ever had.

I know that I should share my things.
I know that I should care.
And one thing I can do right now
Is help someone with prayer.

 Teaching Tips

For young children, praying with a symbol helps them to connect tangible objects to prayer. Some symbols you might share at your prayer table for spontaneous prayer are sheaves of wheat, a globe, seeds, evergreen branches, soil, water, rocks, stones or pebbles, seashells, colored eggs, food, fruit or vegetables, and pictures.

Enriching the Lesson

Invite the children to offer prayers for people who need us or want us to pray for them. Begin the prayer with an invocation: "God, our Creator, you call us to pray for other people. We now offer you these prayers for them." Invite spontaneous petitions from the children. Ask the class to echo the response *We pray to the Lord* after each petition. Give them a pattern such as, "For my little sister who is sick, we pray to the Lord. For my friend who lost a pet, *R*."

God Asks Us to Pray

God wants us to pray for the world and its people. When we pray for people, we show our love for them.

We can pray alone or with others. God says that when we pray with others, our prayer is strong. When we pray at Mass, we pray with others.

This family is praying ▶ together. When do you pray with your family?

◀ This class is praying for the earth. How can your class pray for God's creation?

◀ This Christian community is praying for those who are sick. Whom does your Christian community pray for?

Prayer 143

- How do you know when someone is sad or hungry? (*By looking at their expression, by things they say or do*)
- What do you want to do when you see someone who is hungry or sad? (*Help them.*)
- What is one way mentioned in the poem that we can help someone? (*Pray for them.*)

Step 3 / CONCLUSION

Learning How to Live Our Faith

Identifying Those for Whom We Pray

Invite the class to read aloud the introductory paragraph on page 143. Ask the children to look at each photograph and then give a response to each question. Write *Family, Class, Parish Community* on the chalkboard. Place the children's responses under the appropriate category.

or...

Place on the discovery table a variety of magazine or newspaper pictures that depict situations or events about which the children could pray. Invite the children to read aloud together the introductory paragraph on page 143. Ask the children to each select a picture. Then have them say a prayer for the people in the picture. Ask them to share how they feel when they pray.

Praying Together

Ask your parish leadership if the parish has a Book of Intercessions in which people write their prayer requests. If your parish has such a book, ask permission to borrow it. Read each intention from the latest entry. Have the children respond to each intercession, "Lord, hear our prayer." You might create a few intentions from the responses on the chalkboard to write in the Book of Intercessions. Respond aloud to these intentions as well. If your parish does not have such a book, help the children to name a few intentions of their own. List them on the chalkboard.

143

Objective

This lesson helps the children learn that Jesus prayed for others.

Step 1 / INTRODUCTION

Learning About Our Lives

Discussing Community Prayer

Invite the children to recall times when they joined people in prayer. You may want to offer the following suggestions.

- Saying grace at mealtimes.
- Praying in Religion class.
- Praying during Mass.
- Praying during a sacramental celebration.

Remind the children that we can pray in many different ways.

Step 2 / DEVELOPMENT

Learning About Our Faith

Reading and Discussing a Story

Ask the children to look at the illustration on pages 144–145. Tell them that Jesus often prayed with his family and friends. Ask for five volunteers to read aloud the story "Jesus Prays for Others," each child reading one of the five paragraphs.

After they have finished reading, discuss the story. Use the following questions.

- When did Jesus and his friends gather together? (*On the night before Jesus died*)
- Why were they together? (*To share a special meal*)
- What did Jesus do after the meal? (*He prayed.*)
- For whom did Jesus pray? (*For his friends and for people all over the world*)
- What did Jesus ask for in prayer? (*That people would live as sisters and brothers*)

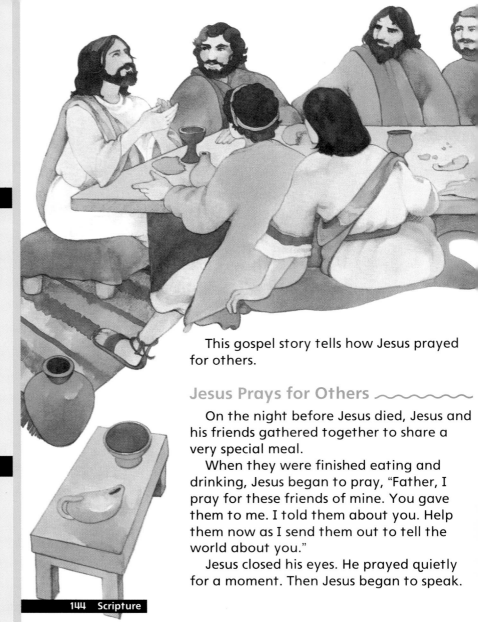

This gospel story tells how Jesus prayed for others.

Jesus Prays for Others

On the night before Jesus died, Jesus and his friends gathered together to share a very special meal.

When they were finished eating and drinking, Jesus began to pray, "Father, I pray for these friends of mine. You gave them to me. I told them about you. Help them now as I send them out to tell the world about you."

Jesus closed his eyes. He prayed quietly for a moment. Then Jesus began to speak.

144 Scripture

CURRICULUM CONNECTION

Music and Art Find a song that is prayerful and tells a story, such as "Garden Song" from THIS IS OUR FAITH Music Program, Grade 2. Help the class to create a pantomime or body movement to interpret the song. Another activity to do on another day is to have each child select a phrase from the song and draw or paint a picture suggested by the phrase. Have the class learn the song and perform it with movements for another class. Display the artwork that the song inspired.

Focus on

Prayer of Petition The *Catechism of the Catholic Church* states, "Intercession is a prayer of petition which leads us to pray as Jesus did. He is the one intercessor with the Father on behalf of all men, especially sinners. He is 'able for all time to save those who draw near to God through him, since he always lives to make intercession for them.' The Holy Spirit 'himself intercedes for us . . . and intercedes for the saints according to the will of God' " (#2634).

"Father," Jesus said, "I do not pray just for these friends of mine. I pray for people all over the world. Help them live like brothers and sisters. Love them as you love me. Be with them as you are with me."

Based on John 17:1-26

Activity

Complete this picture of a place where Jesus might have prayed. Draw yourself and Jesus at this place.

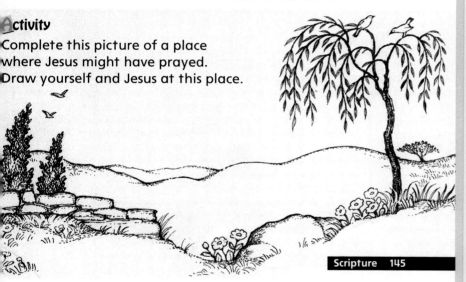

Scripture 145

Enriching the Lesson

Explain that the Berakah is an ancient Hebrew prayer of blessing. Incorporated in the eucharistic prayer at Mass, its purpose is to bless God for all the goodness shown to us. In the following Berakah the children echo each line after you.

Blessed are you, Lord, our God.

You have given us all the earth.

We praise you, God.

Completing an Activity

Explain that Jesus often prayed with his followers on mountaintops, at the seashore, in a garden. Ask: What scene do you see? Does it look finished? What's missing? Instruct the children to draw themselves and Jesus praying in the scene.

Praying Together

After the children have completed their pictures, invite them to the prayer table. Invite the children to close their eyes. (Play quiet instrumental music here.) When everyone is still, speak quietly the following narration: "Jesus is in your picture. Try to remember what he looks like. Jesus is speaking to you. He invites you to pray with him. Jesus is quiet. Silently pray your prayer with Jesus now. (Pause) Listen as God speaks to you. Silently say, 'Thank you, God.'" (Briefly pause in silence before inviting the children to open their eyes. Then instruct the children to return to their desks.)

Objective

This lesson introduces the children to the Prayer of the Faithful at Mass as the community's prayer for people everywhere.

Step 1 / INTRODUCTION

Learning About Our Lives

Introducing the Chapter

Ask the children if they have ever prayed for someone they do not know. Tell them that today they are going to learn about the special prayer at Mass in which we pray for people everywhere, even those people we do not know. Explain to the class that the Catholic community prays together for people's needs, responding to the intercessions read by the lector.

or . . .

Show a video that you have taped prior to this class of a priest introducing the Prayer of the Faithful, a reader saying the intercessions, the community responding, and the priest saying the concluding prayer. After the viewing, invite the children's comments. Play the video again without sound. Invite the children to recall what the priest said, some of the needs prayed for, how the community responded, and how the priest concluded the Prayer of the Faithful. Affirm the children's attentiveness and participation.

Step 2 / DEVELOPMENT

Learning About Our Faith

Praying Shows That We Care

Explain to the children that just as Jesus prayed for everyone, he wants us to pray for people everywhere.

Invite the children to follow in their books on page 146 as you read aloud "Praying Shows That We Care." Ask: When do we pray for others at Mass? (*During the Prayer of the Faithful*) What part of the Liturgy of the Word is the Prayer of the Faithful? (*The last part*)

▲ This person is leading the Prayer of the Faithful at Mass.

Praying Shows That We Care

Jesus prayed for his friends and for all people in need. Jesus prays for us, too. He wants us to show that we care by praying for one another.

We can pray for others at Mass during the **Prayer of the Faithful**. This prayer is the last part of the Liturgy of the Word. In the Prayer of the Faithful, we pray for the Church, for our country and its leaders, and for all God's people.

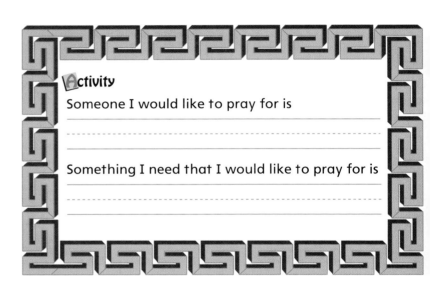

Activity

Someone I would like to pray for is

_____

Something I need that I would like to pray for is

_____

CURRICULUM CONNECTION

Social Studies Display a map of the world. Ask the children to share the names of the people they pray for who live far away. Help the children find on the map the countries where these relatives or friends live. Point out that we can pray for people whether they are near or far, relatives or friends, known or unknown to us. Tell the children that they show concern for others when they pray for them.

Prayer of the Faithful

During the Prayer of the Faithful, we can pray for people everywhere. We can pray for ourselves, too.

Leader: We pray for world leaders. Help them make good choices so that all people may live in peace.

People: Lord, hear our prayer.

Leader: We pray for those who are hungry and poor.

People: Lord, hear our prayer.

Leader: We pray for our families and friends. Help us live in peace.

People: Lord, hear our prayer.

New Word

Prayer of the Faithful The Prayer of the Faithful is the last part of the Liturgy of the Word. During this prayer we pray for ourselves and for people everywhere.

We Believe

Jesus wants us to pray for people everywhere. We can do this any time and in many ways. At Mass we do this during the Prayer of the Faithful.

Prayer 147

★ Enriching the Lesson ★

Make a paper jigsaw-puzzle heart from red construction paper. Help the children write something they want to ask God for on the puzzle pieces. Draw another heart on posterboard. Place the jigsaw pieces in a basket. Each day the children select and glue some puzzle pieces onto the poster-board heart and pray these petitions. When the puzzle is complete, display it or use some of the petitions at Mass during the Prayer of the Faithful.

Cultural Awareness

Jesus wants us to pray for all people, whatever their color, race, or religion. To help the children realize that all people are children of God, invite a few children each morning to pray aloud for another child in the world. Conclude the prayer with, "Help us to live as brothers and sisters. Amen."

DAY 4
PRAYER

Objective

This lesson helps the children realize that praying for others is part of the vocation for women called religious sisters, or nuns.

Step 1 / INTRODUCTION

Learning About Our Lives

Introducing the Chapter

Have displayed on the discovery table your parish's Book of Intercessions and some pictures of nuns praying, living, and working in a convent. Invite the children to gather around the discovery table. Show the Book of Intercessions. Ask the children what they remember about this special book. (*People write their prayer requests in it.*) When is the book used for prayer? (*For the Prayer of the Faithful at Mass*) Read a few of the intentions aloud. Have the children respond, "Lord, hear our prayer." Explain that while our community prays for these intentions, there are women who pray all day, every day, for all the people of the world.

Step 2 / DEVELOPMENT

Learning About Our Faith

Learning About Religious Life

Show pictures of a convent. (Your diocesan vocation office or the school library are good resources.) Explain that there are women who pray daily for the needs of all the world and its people. These women are called religious sisters, or nuns. Explain that not all religious sisters do the same work—some are teachers, some are doctors and nurses, and some visit the sick or elderly. Tell the children that some sisters don't work outside the convent. They spend most of their day in prayer.

Recalling a Visit to a Convent

Invite a volunteer to read the opening paragraph. Ask if anyone has ever visited a convent. If a child responds "Yes," invite that child to tell about the visit. If you have visited a convent, share that experience.

148

Here is a story about a friend of Jesus who spends her whole life praying for God's people.

A Special Kind of Prayer

My name is Sister Anna. I am a religious sister, or nun. I live in a convent with eight other sisters. Our convent is on a farm. We have come here to live because God asked us to pray in a special way for all God's people. That's a lot of people!

Very early each morning, we get up and go into our chapel to pray. We pray for everyone who needs our prayers that day. Then we eat breakfast and begin our work.

My special job is to care for the farm animals. We have lots of cows on our farm. We also have goats, pigs, and chickens. I feed the animals and milk the cows. I make sure that the animals are clean and healthy.

Even while I work, I never stop praying. I praise God for the wonderful animals on the farm that I enjoy so much. I ask God to help parents care for their children and to heal those who are sick or hurt.

148 Prayer

Enriching the Lesson

Explain that in certain convents special prayers are said every hour of the day. To experience praying the hours in class, ring a bell or chime each hour, stop any activity, and pray together. Some suggested prayer topics are

10 A.M. Praise God for the new day.

11 A.M. Pray for safety on the playground.

12 P.M. Pray a meal prayer.

1 P.M. Pray for the sick and lonely.

2 P.M. Thank God for the school day.

The other sisters and I eat dinner together and return to the chapel. Again we pray for people everywhere. We ask God to keep everyone safe through the night.

I like to pray as Jesus must have prayed—for everyone and at all times. I am grateful that God asked me to live as a sister of prayer.

Activity

Not everyone is asked to spend their whole lives in prayer in the same way as Sister Anna. But we are asked to pray often. Put a [✔] in front of those special times when you pray.

_____ when I get up in the morning

_____ before I eat a meal

_____ when I'm at Mass

_____ when I'm alone

_____ when I'm with others

_____ when I'm with my family

_____ before I go to bed

CURRICULUM CONNECTION

Music Invite the music teacher to tell about the ancient musical tradition of the Church called *Gregorian chant*. Ask the specialist to play some short examples of chant for the class.

Examples can be found on *Chant,* an Angel CD, CDC 7243 5 55138 2 3, sung by the Benedictine monks of Santo Domingo de Silos (men who devote their lives to praying for others). They sing Gregorian chant seven times a day in their monastery in Spain every day of the year.

Enriching the Lesson

Display the other resources about convent life that you have brought to the discovery table. Tell the children that they can visit the discovery table and look at the books during free time. Encourage the children to pause after looking at the books and thank God for the nuns who pray for us always.

Reading About a Religious Sister

Read aloud the first three paragraphs of the text on page 148 about Sister Anna. Ask:

- Where does sister Anna live? (*In a convent*)
- Where is the convent? (*On a farm*)
- Why does she live there? (*To pray with other nuns for all of God's people*)
- What is the first thing the nuns do each morning? (*Go to the chapel to pray*)
- What is Sister Anna's special job? (*To take care of the animals*)

Continue reading aloud the final three paragraphs.

Step 3 / CONCLUSION

Learning How to Live Our Faith

Completing an Activity

Read the directions to the activity on page 149. Allow sufficient time for the children to put a check by those times when they pray. Go over the responses orally with the class.

Praying for the Needs of Others

Show some pictures that depict contemporary urban, rural, and global needs. Instruct the children to look at the pictures. Ask them individually to identify orally the needs of those in the pictures.

Pray with the children, "Generous God, we know many people pray for us. We want to pray for others in need." Invite each child to say, "I will pray for _____," describing the person or persons and their needs in one of the photographs studied above.

DAY 5
PRAYER/REVIEW

Objective

This lesson helps the children create a community prayer chain.

Preparing to Make a Prayer Chain

You may wish to invite older students to join your class as helpers. Place the needed materials (11" × 3" strips of construction paper in various colors, black markers, stapler, glue, paste, or rubber cement) on the discovery table. The prayer chain can be created by your class community, with the help of older students, or can become an all-school or all-parish chain. Be sure that when the chain is completed it is used for community prayer and displayed for the parish community to enjoy.

Making a Prayer Chain

Read aloud "Praying with a Prayer Chain" on page 150. Follow the steps for making a prayer chain given in the textbook.

Praying Together

When the children are ready for prayer, pray "Dear God, today we gather together as people who pray, who care about one another, and who want peace in the world. We bring our prayers together as we join the links of this chain. We pray for the Church." (Allow the children to present aloud the intentions for those links.)

Continue with, "We pray for all people." (Allow the children to present aloud the intentions for those links. Join them together. Continue with each topic until all the prayers have been joined together.)

Conclude by praying, "Hear these prayers, O Lord, as we pray for all people. We display our chain as a sign of our ongoing love and care for one another. Amen."

Praying with a Prayer Chain

There are many ways we can join our prayers together. We can pray together at Mass. We can pray with our families. We can pray with our friends and classmates.

Another way we can join our prayers together is by making prayer chains.

Make a prayer chain with your classmates or invite the other classes in your school to join you in making a school prayer chain. Follow these directions.

Step 1
Cut strips of construction paper about 11" long and 3" wide.

Step 2
On each paper strip, write the name of a person or a need that you would like to pray for. You might want to use a felt-tip marker.

Step 3
Staple or glue the strips together so that the names of the people or needs you want to pray for can be seen.

Step 4
Join your prayer chain to your classmates chains. Hang the finished prayer chain on your classroom prayer table or in another place where it can be seen by others.

🍎 Teaching Tips

To set a quiet, contemplative mood while the children pray the intentions printed on the community prayer chain, play the recording of "Emmanuelle" by Michel Columbier, a listening selection from Silver Burdett Ginn's THE MUSIC CONNECTION, Grade K, CD 5-26.

Enriching the Lesson

Have the children find a small, flat, smooth pebble. Tell them that this will be their prayer stone. Tell the children to carry it in a pocket. Each time they hold it, they should pause and say a silent prayer for someone in the world.

Chapter Review

Circle the word hidden in each line. Then write these words on the lines below the puzzle.

Z	M	X	F	A	T	H	E	R
P	M	I	Z	H	J	M	B	T
C	L	E	P	R	A	Y	Y	S
F	O	R	N	D	J	R	B	I
J	T	H	E	S	E	N	P	T
Q	U	F	R	I	E	N	D	S
S	U	L	O	F	L	A	Z	N
C	D	M	I	N	E	I	M	B

Father, I pray for these

friends of mine.

1. How can we help people who are in need?

pray for them

2. Who taught us that we should pray for others?

Jesus

3. Talk about the many ways we can pray for ourselves and for other people.

> **Pray always for all God's people.**
> **Based on Ephesians 6:18**

Review   151

Enriching the Lesson

Before the session, write special prayer intentions such as the following, on slips of paper.

- For a child in the hospital
- For someone who is lonely
- For a newborn baby

Allow each child to pick one slip of paper from the box and read aloud the intention written on the slip of paper. Encourage each child to pray for that intention during the week, especially during the Prayer of the Faithful at Mass.

Reviewing the Chapter

Read aloud the directions for the hidden word puzzle on page 151. Allow sufficient time for the children to write their answers on the lines provided. Continue with the three review items. When the children have finished writing their answers to questions 1 and 2, correct their responses. Then encourage all children to particiate in the discussion of item 3.

Reading the Scripture Verse

Ask the children to read aloud the Scripture verse at the bottom of page 151. Help the children understand that God wants us to pray for all people, not just our relatives and friends. Allow the children time to practice memorizing the verse.

Using the Unit Organizer

Completing a graphic organizer such as a chart or table can help the children to organize information that has been presented in the unit. Organizers can enable the children to visualize their thinking and recognize relationships among ideas. This will give the children that opportunity to understand more completely the materials they have been studying.

Completing the Organizer

Have the children turn to page 152 in their books. Help the children identify each illustration. Read aloud the parts of the Liturgy of the Word. Then ask the children to match the parts of the Liturgy of the Word with the pictures by printing the names of the parts on the appropriate lines. Point out where to start. Then ask the children to complete the activity independently. If necessary, tell them that they may look back through the previous four chapters for help. When everyone has finished, have the children compare their responses with the class.

Looking Back: Self-Assessment

The critical reflection questions below give the children an opportunity to sharpen their thinking skills. The questions can be used as a class discussion or independent writing activity.

- Which was your favorite Scripture story in this unit? What did you like most about it?
- What did you learn in this unit that you think you will always remember?
- Which activity in this unit did you most enjoy? Why?

Unit 3 Organizer

start

Prayer of the Faithful   second reading   homily

Liturgy of the Word

gospel   responsorial psalm   first reading

finish

152   Organizer

152

Unit 3 / Review

Complete each sentence below by circling the correct answer. Then use these answers to fill in the puzzle.

1. The _____ tells of the life and teachings of Jesus.

(gospel)   first reading

2. The _____ celebrates a special meal with Jesus.

Reconciliation   (Eucharist)

3. The first part of the Mass is called the Liturgy of the _____ .

(Word)   Altar

4. On Sunday we _____ together for Mass.

listen   (gather)

5. Fill in the puzzle. Use the words you circled above.

```
1.
G
O
S              3.        4.
P              W         G
2.
E  U  C  H  A  R  I  S  T
L              D         A
                         T
                         H
                         E
                         R
```

Reviewing the Unit

The purpose of the Unit Review is to reinforce concepts presented in the preceding four chapters and to check the children's understanding. After explaining the directions, give the children sufficient time to complete the two-page review. Answer any questions they may have as you check their work.

Testing

After the students have completed the Unit Review, you may wish to distribute copies of the Unit 3 Test from the Test Booklet.

Project

If time permits, you may wish to do the following project with the children.

Plan a prayer celebration with the children. Help them write five or six petitions, including prayers for our leaders, our Church, the poor, parish needs, and our personal concerns.

Before you begin, choose two volunteers to be candle bearers and a third child to hold the Bible. Then ask the children to stand and form a prayer circle. Begin the celebration by singing together a song with which the children are familiar. Then read the following passage. "Let the words of Jesus live in you. Sing thankful prayers and songs to God. Let your words and actions be done in Jesus' name. Give thanks to God through Jesus" (based on Colossians 3:16–17).

Invite the children to discuss the words and actions they can say and do in Jesus' name. After the discussion, ask a volunteer to read the petitions you wrote together. Invite the children to respond *Lord, hear our prayer* to each petition. End the celebration with a spontaneous prayer, thanking God for Scripture and for being with us always.

Unit 3 Review

6. How can we respond to God's word at Mass?

with songs, prayers, and actions

7. How can we respond to God's word in our lives?

by doing what Jesus asks of us

Circle the correct answer.

8. We should only pray for people in need.
   Yes (No)

9. We can pray for people during the Prayer of the Faithful.
   (Yes) No

10. God wants us to pray for people everywhere.
    (Yes) No

11. In the story "Jesus Prays for Others," Jesus only prayed for his close friends.
    Yes (No)

12. The Liturgy of the Word ends with the Prayer of the Faithful.
    (Yes) No

XPRESSING MY FEELINGS

Using "I" messages
ets me share my
eelings in a helpful way.

My feelings are an
mportant part of me.
Sharing my feelings is a
jood way for others to
now more about me.
When I feel sad, angry,
r upset, others can
lelp me feel better if I
et them know how I
eel. An "I" message
tells how I feel and what
as caused the feeling.

feel

_____

_____ ,

vhen

_____

_____ .

Activity

Read the
story. Write a
word that tells how
each child might be feeling.
Then decide what "I" messages they
might use.

Stacy is bothering Tim. Tim is trying
to finish his work. Stacy keeps asking
Tim questions.
Tim is beginning to feel

_____

_____

_____ .

What "I" message might Tim use?
I feel

_____

_____ ,

when Stacy

_____

_____ .

Day to Day   155

Day to Day

Objective

This lesson helps the children to learn to use "I" messages as a way of expressing feelings verbally.

Introducing the Lesson

Read aloud with the children the paragraphs in the box on page 155 about using "I" messages to communicate feelings. Emphasize that an "I" message has two important components: the "I feel" part, which tells how the person is feeling, and the "when" part, which tells what happened to cause the particular feeling.

Provide these examples.

I feel happy *when* my children are kind to each other.

I feel excited *when* we have a field trip planned.

I feel nervous *when* I have to give a speech.

Ask the children to complete the "I feel" sentence in the box. Have them share their sentences with the class.

Completing the Activity

Ask the children to read together the story about Stacy and Tim on page 155. Ask: How is Tim feeling? (*Accept a variety of feeling words, such as "annoyed", "mad", "irritated", "angry", "frustrated", "sad".*) Encourage the children to be creative in choosing adjectives that describe feelings rather than just using the word *bad*.

As the children generate a list of feelings, write them on the chalkboard. Have the children write how Tim is feeling on the line provided.

Ask the class to decide what "I" message Tim might use to let Stacy know how he is feeling. Write the message on the chalkboard and have the children copy it into their books.

Completing Another Activity

Repeat this same process for completing the activity to the second story about Alex, found on page 156.

Lesson continues on page 156.

Reviewing How to Be a Good Listener

Ask the children if they can remember what they have learned about being a good listener. (*Eye contact, paying attention, being quiet, restating feeling or information messages*) Read aloud with the children the paragraph on page 156 under the heading "What Should I Do When I Hear an 'I' Message?"

Responding to an "I" Message

Direct the children's attention to the drawing, then read aloud the paragraph under "How would you respond to Alex?" Allow some discussion of possible responses.

Have the children write a response in the box that tells how they might respond to Alex's "I" message.

Following Jesus

Read aloud with the class the paragraph under "Following Jesus." Ask: What is one way to follow Jesus? (*Listen well to others*)

Concluding the Lesson

Ask the children to think about kindness as an important part of what it means to be a good person. Ask: How many of you would like others to describe you as a kind person? Reinforce that being kind is something that Jesus asks of us.

Pray the prayer at the bottom of page 156 together with the class.

156

Activity

Alex is at recess. Alex wants to play ball with the other kids. When Alex asks to play, the others tell him, "No, we already have our teams."

_____

_____

Alex is feeling _____

What "I" message might Alex use?

_____   _____

I feel _____ when you _____

What should I do when I hear an "I" message?

When someone tells me how he or she feels, I need to remember to be a good listener. A good listener uses eye contact, pays attention, and remains quiet while the speaker is talking. A good listener restates the feeling or information given by the speaker.

How would you respond to Alex?

Fill in the box with what you would say to Alex.

I FEEL LEFT OUT WHEN I DON'T GET TO PLAY.

Following Jesus

Jesus always cared about people's feelings. He spent much time listening to people and speaking with them. Jesus asks us to care about other people's feelings, too. When we listen well to others, we follow Jesus.

A Prayer

Jesus, help us to be open to telling each oth how we feel. Help us to more willing to listen to feelings of others. Amer

Sending the Magazine Home

As you complete Unit 3 with your class, assist the children in carefully removing *Opening Doors: A Take-Home Magazine* (two pages) from their texts by separating the pages from the book along the perforations. Demonstrate how to fold the two pages, forming an eight-page booklet. Ask the children to take the magazine home and encourage their families to read it with them and participate in the suggested activities.

Opening Doors

A Take-Home Magazine™

Growing Closer

EVERY FAMILY HAS stories to tell! Share some favorite family stories at mealtime or whenever the family is together. Enjoy listening to one another—if only for a few brief moments.

ASK EVERYONE in your family to listen carefully to the gospel reading the next time you go to Mass. Later at home, talk with one another about what the story might mean for your family. Encourage everyone to share their feelings about the story. Listen carefully to one another and accept everyone's ideas.

Looking Ahead

In Unit 4 your child will learn that the Eucharist is a thanksgiving celebration. At Mass we praise and thank God for many gifts, especially for the gift of God's Son, Jesus. Your son or daughter will learn that the Eucharist is a sacrificial meal. Jesus not only gave himself to us in the Eucharist but gave his life for us after much suffering.

8

Responding to the Word

"Glory to you, Lord." —Roman Missal

When those we love speak meaningful words to us, we often feel a need to respond appreciatively. God's word proclaimed at Mass can inspire in us a similar response. During the Liturgy of the Word as we listen to the story of our salvation, what more grateful replies can there be than "Thanks be to God" and "Praise to you, Lord Jesus Christ"?

Praying words of thanks and praise, then, is a natural response to the good news of our salvation. The real challenge, perhaps, lies in the way we respond to the Scriptures *with our lives.*

We are challenged each time we hear a Scripture reading to hear more than words we may have heard many times before. We are encouraged to hear the God of love speaking endearing and meaningful words to each of us, and we are challenged to find ways of responding appreciatively with our lives.

the Canticle of Mary (Luke 1:46–55); night prayer includes the Canticle of Simeon (Luke 2:29–32). In addition, the prayer contains quiet times for silent meditation.

The Liturgy of the Hours stems from our Jewish heritage. In the time of Jesus, Jews assembled each morning and evening in the synagogue to recite the Shema (shuh MAH) (Dt. 6:4–9; 11: 13–21; Numbers 15:37–41) and the eighteen blessings. Early Christians continued the practice of meeting for prayer each morning in the synagogue and for the Eucharist each evening in their homes.

If you are interested in finding out more about the Liturgy of the Hours, check with your Catholic bookstore for the revised English version, entitled *The Liturgy of the Hours According to the Roman Rite,* or ask for one of the many published versions that have been simplified for general use. You may wish to pray this prayer by yourself at home or you may choose to pray it with others at church.

Christian Prayer, Morning and Evening

Prayer is an important part of Christian living. As you probably realize, there are many different ways to pray. There are memorized prayers, spontaneous prayers, individual prayers, group prayers. One kind of prayer that is growing in popularity again in some sections of our country is the Liturgy of the Hours. Many parishioners are beginning to practice this prayer, especially during the liturgical seasons of Advent and Lent.

What is the Liturgy of the Hours? Basically, it is a Scripture-based group prayer. Parts of the prayer are prayed at certain hours of the day: morning, midmorning, midday, midafternoon, evening, and night. This prayer is the official prayer of the Church for praising God and sanctifying the day. For centuries, priests and men and women religious had been required to pray the Liturgy of the Hours. But many lay people have prayed this prayer, too.

In today's Church, morning prayer (Lauds), evening prayer (Vespers), and night prayer (Compline) are the three most popular forms of the Liturgy of the Hours. The principal parts of these prayers consist of a hymn, two psalms, a brief Scripture reading, responses, intercessions, and a concluding prayer. Morning prayer includes the Canticle of Zechariah (Luke 1:68–79); evening prayer includes

6

The word of God always meets us where we are and beckons us to live the message in and through the particular circumstances of our daily lives. Some of us are called to respond to God's word in extraordinary ways, such as with lives of service to the poor. Most of us, however, are called to respond in more ordinary ways. Each time we forgive our spouse or child, each time we let another ahead of us in line, each time we give up an evening to help someone in need, we respond to Jesus' command to "love one another." This is good news, indeed!

3

Responding with Love

Read through these pages with your child. Discover together some ways of responding to the readings at Mass. Encourage your child to complete the activity. Ask others in your family to participate.

Stories are fun to hear! Sometimes we clap our hands when we hear a good story. Sometimes we just smile and feel good inside.

At Mass we listen to God's stories. We feel happy. We know God loves us.

4

We want to thank God for loving us.

Here are some ways we can respond to God's stories of love. Try a different way each day. Then color that part of the caterpillar.

Do your homework carefully.

Be kind. Look for signs of God's love.

Take a walk. Help your family.

Thank God for your family, family and friends.

Say a prayer. Smile!

Write a letter to someone you don't like.

Prepare prayer dinner.

Listen carefully to your teacher.

Clean your room without being told.

Tell your favorite Bible story to a younger brother or sister.

For someone who misses you.

Listen carefully to God's stories the next time you go to Mass. Try to find some ways to respond to God's love for you.

5

160

UNIT 4

Our Church Celebrates the Eucharist

What's the best present you have ever received?

Introducing the UNIT

Ask a volunteer to read aloud the unit-focus question on page 161. Invite the children's responses. Tell the children that in Unit 4 they will learn about Jesus' greatest gift to us.

New Words

Liturgy of the Eucharist
Eucharistic Prayer
sacrifice
Communion

To help the children understand that the Liturgy of the Eucharist is the second part of the Mass, during which our gifts of bread and wine are changed into the body and blood of Christ.

Doctrinal Summaries

CHAPTER 13

The second part of the Mass is called the Liturgy of the Eucharist. At the Preparation of Gifts, we prepare the altar and bring our gifts for our special meal. We offer the gift of ourselves.

CHAPTER 14

During the Eucharistic Prayer, we praise and thank God for all creation and for God's greatest gift, Jesus.

CHAPTER 15

On the cross, Jesus gave his life for all his friends. At Mass we remember his sacrifice and celebrate it. The bread and wine become Jesus' body and blood.

CHAPTER 16

Jesus gives us himself in the Eucharist. He fills our hungers and unites us in peace and love. Jesus gives us himself, the Bread of Life.

Note:
As you prepare this unit and the remaining units, you might wish to refer to the reference section, *Our Catholic Heritage,* beginning on page 327.

Additional resources for Unit 4 include a Unit Test and a Family Letter as well as a video and selections from THIS IS OUR FAITH Music Program. You might also find it helpful to preview *Saints and Other Holy People* and *Prayer Celebrations* for possibilities to enhance the unit.

13 We Present Ourselves to God

Objectives

To help the children
- Recognize the Liturgy of the Eucharist as the second part of the Mass.
- Identify the offering of the bread and wine as the Preparation of Gifts.
- Understand that Jesus wants us to share our gifts with others.
- Discover what it means to offer one's self and one's day to God in prayer.
- Pray together and review the chapter.

Chapter Outline

	Step 1 **Learning About Our Lives**	Step 2 **Learning About Our Faith**	Step 3 **Learning How to Live Our Faith**
Day 1	■ Present a gift. ■ Read a poem. ■ Talk about gifts. ■ Discuss photographs. *ABOUT 15 MINUTES*	■ Introduce Liturgy of the Eucharist. ■ Present the doctrine. ■ Review the new word. *ABOUT 10 MINUTES*	■ Complete an activity. ■ Celebrate the gift of ourselves. *ABOUT 5 MINUTES*
Day 2	■ Review Liturgy of the Eucharist. ■ Remember ourselves as gifts. *ABOUT 5 MINUTES*	■ Learn about the offertory gifts. ■ Discuss eucharistic bread and wine. ■ Role-play offering gifts. *ABOUT 15 MINUTES*	■ Complete a drawing activity. *ABOUT 10 MINUTES*
Day 3	■ Discover the need to share. *ABOUT 5 MINUTES*	■ Read and discuss the story. ■ Dramatize the story. *ABOUT 15 MINUTES*	■ Complete an activity. ■ Offer ourselves in prayer. *ABOUT 10 MINUTES*
Day 4	■ Review the Scripture story. *ABOUT 5 MINUTES*	■ Introduce sharing of self. ■ Complete an activity. ■ Learn to give the gift of ourselves. *ABOUT 15 MINUTES*	■ Complete a story. ■ Pray together. *ABOUT 10 MINUTES*
Day 5	**Prayer** Prepare for prayer; pray together and pray a morning offering. **Review** Review the Scripture story; review the chapter and read the Scripture verse.		

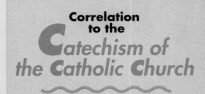

Correlation
to the

Catechism of
the Catholic Church

Paragraphs
1346, 1350

Plan Ahead

Preparing Your Class

Day 1 Read over the lesson prior to the session. Wrap gift of treats. Prepare prayer table. Gather recording and music.

Day 2 Read over the lesson prior to the session. Prepare gift tags. Prepare offering table.

Day 3 Read over the lesson prior to the session. Prepare bowl of fruit. If enriching the lesson, contact service agencies.

Day 4 Read over the lesson and print prayer on chalkboard prior to the session. Prepare prayer table.

Day 5 Read over the lesson. Prepare prayer table. Gather materials for hand activity.

Materials Needed

- gift box of treats
- song sheets
- recording of "My Hands Belong to You"

- gift tags (5" × 7")
- curling ribbon
- hosts, wine, offering table
- recording of "My Hands Belong to You"

- apples, oranges
- Scripture prop box
- 5 buns and 2 cut-out fish

- pencils
- paper
- candle and Bible

- colored construction paper
- hosts, wine, basket
- scissors, pencils
- recording of "My Hands Belong to You"

Additional Resources

As you plan this chapter, consider using the following materials from The Resourceful Teacher Package.

- *Classroom Activity Sheets 13* and *13a*
- *Family Activity Sheets 13* and *13a*
- *Chapter 13 Test*
- *Prayers for Every Day*
- *Projects: Grade 2*

You may also wish to refer to the following Big Books.

- *We Celebrate the Mass,* pages 1–23
- *We Celebrate the Sacraments,* pages 7–9

In preparing the children for the Sunday readings, you may wish to use Silver Burdett Ginn's *Getting Ready for Sunday* student and teacher materials.

BOOKS FOR THE JOURNEY

Not So Fast Songolo. Niki Daly. Puffin, 1987. Story about a gift given with great love to a grandchild.

Chicken Sunday. Patricia Polacco. Philomel Books, 1992. Some children find a way to get a special hat as a gift for someone they love.

MORE BOOKS FOR THE JOURNEY

Santa's Favorite Story. Hisako Aoiki and Ivan Gantschev. Picture Book Studio, 1991. The forest animals worry that there won't be Christmas any more until Santa helps them discover what the real gift of Christmas is.

Tomie dePaola's Book of Bible Stories. "Jesus Feeds the Five Thousand," pp. 96–97. G. P. Putnam's Sons, 1990. The Bible story of Jesus feeding a large crowd of people.

REDUCED CLASSROOM ACTIVITIES

Name _____

We Present Ourselves to God

Reread the story from Scripture "Sharing with Others." Color the picture on page 13 and cut along the heavy black lines. Glue or tape the picture to the bottom of a box to use in a play. The figures for the play are on page 13a.

To the Teacher: This activity and page 13a follow the Scripture story "Sharing with Others."

Chapter 13 We Present Ourselves to God   THIS IS OUR FAITH 2   **13**

Name _____

Sharing with Others

Color each figure below. Cut along the heavy black lines. Then use the figures with the picture you colored on page 13 to tell the story "Sharing with Others."

13a THIS IS OUR FAITH 2   Chapter 13   We Present Ourselves to God

Background for the Teacher

GIFTS OF BREAD AND WINE

The Liturgy of the Eucharist begins with the Preparation of the Altar and the Gifts. At this time we bring to the altar the bread and wine that will be used for the eucharistic meal. The setting for the sacrificial meal is prepared.

The early Christians donated bread and wine. In time, the offerings included other foods and goods, and then money. From these donations, the bread and wine were supplied for Mass, and the other donations were given to the needy in the community. Today the people who bring the gifts to the altar are our representatives. Through them we present the bread and wine and ourselves to God. The lesson's Scripture story about the boy with the loaves and fish provides an example of sharing gifts. The boy presented food to Jesus for the good of the community. Jesus models the response for gifts shared when he gives thanks for these gifts. As disciples, we are called to name, develop, and share our gifts with the community for the common good. As teachers, we name and affirm the giftedness of our students. We encourage them to develop their gifts so that the community might benefit. The greatest gift we can offer is the gift of ourselves.

When the bread and wine are brought to the altar, the priest takes the bread and wine, blesses them, and offers them to God. Our response is "Blessed be God forever." This is one of the most ancient forms of prayer found in the Liturgy of the Eucharist. It is the beginning of the Hebrew prayer of thanksgiving called the Berakah. It is similar to the Shabbat prayer over the bread and wine prayed weekly in Jewish homes. The bringing of the gifts to the altar and the blessing of these gifts is called the Preparation of Gifts.

OUR SPECIAL OFFERINGS

Bringing food or gifts to a gathering is a familiar experience to most second graders. They have seen parents preparing food to take to a potluck supper or to a holiday meal at a relative's home. Many have brought a gift for a friend whose birthday party they were attending.

The children are beginning to understand the meaning behind these offerings of gifts and sharing of food. They are starting to realize that these times are opportunities to share with others and to show love. Therefore, the children can begin to grasp the symbolism of this part of the Mass.

While teaching this lesson, point out to the children that at the presentation of the gifts, we offer ourselves to God. Explain that during the Preparation of the Altar and the Gifts, we say to God, "We want to be with you. We want to share ourselves with you."

DOCTRINE

Objective

This lesson introduces the children to the Liturgy of the Eucharist as the second part of Mass.

Step 1 / INTRODUCTION

Learning About Our Lives

Presenting a Gift

Prior to the class, wrap a box of small packaged treats—candy or wrapped fruit treats. Display this box on the discovery table. Invite volunteers to come forward and shake the box. Allow the class to guess its contents. Ask: What is exciting about receiving a gift? Emphasize the element of surprise and mystery. Tell the children that the package contains a surprise for them, which they will receive at the end of class. Leave the wrapped package on the table and form a sharing circle.

Reading a Poem

Invite the children to read aloud the poem "We Bring Gifts" on page 162. Explain that the thought and care that go into making or choosing a gift is also a sign of our love.

Talking About Gifts

Read aloud the chapter-focus sentence on page 162. Give each child an opportunity to tell about when he or she gave someone a special gift. Help the children appreciate that the gifts we give are special because they are a sign of how we feel about the other person.

Discussing the Photographs

Direct the children's attention to the photographs on page 162. Invite volunteers to tell a story about each one. Ask: Have you had experiences similar to those in the photographs?

Step 2 / DEVELOPMENT

Learning About Our Faith +

Introducing Liturgy of the Eucharist

Review with the children the meaning of the Liturgy of the Word. (If you have opted to make new word posters, use the poster from the last unit for review.) Remind the children that in the

162

---

13 We Present Ourselves to God

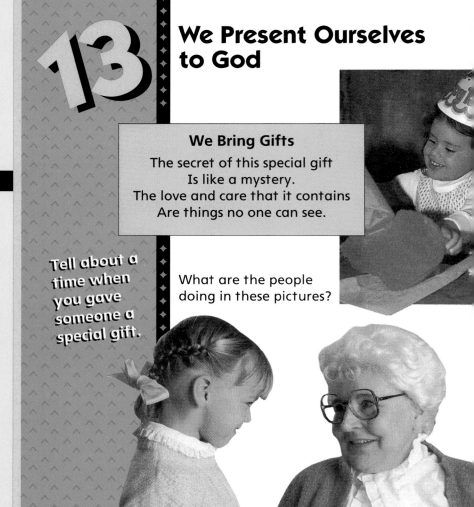

We Bring Gifts
The secret of this special gift
Is like a mystery.
The love and care that it contains
Are things no one can see.

Tell about a time when you gave someone a special gift.

What are the people doing in these pictures?

Cultural Awareness

Help the children understand that in other cultures people often give gifts for different reasons than we are accustomed to. You might tell them that although we usually receive gifts on our birthdays, in some countries, birthday children give their parents a gift instead of receiving gifts themselves. Tell the class that this gift says thank you to the parents for giving their children the gift of life.

Teaching Tips

Children are gifts in themselves. Their unique and special qualities add something to each family and classroom. Children need to be affirmed and told how special they are. Personal gifts and talents are sometimes self-evident—such as athletic ability or artistic talent. Other gifts are recognized and named by others—such as a gift for hospitality, inclusion, and warmth; the gift of patience, humor, or delight. Look for and name the gifts you see in the children. Encourage them to develop these gifts.

Gifts to Share

There are many times when we give gifts. A special time when Catholics bring gifts to share is during the **Liturgy of the Eucharist,** the second part of the Mass. The gifts we bring to the altar are bread and wine. We also bring money and sometimes other gifts for people in need. Most of all, we bring ourselves. The Liturgy of the Eucharist begins as we prepare the altar and bring gifts for our special meal with Jesus.

Activity

Fill in the missing words.

1. We call the second part of the Mass the _Liturgy_ of the _Eucharist_.

2. The best gift that I can give to God is the gift of _myself_.

We Believe

The second part of the Mass is called the Liturgy of the Eucharist. It begins as we prepare the altar and bring gifts for our special meal.

New Word

◆ **Liturgy of the Eucharist** The Liturgy of the Eucharist is the second part of the Mass. It begins as we prepare to share a special meal with Jesus.

Doctrine 163

Liturgy of the Word, we listen to God's word and respond in praise and prayer. Now explain that the second part of the Mass is called the *Liturgy of the Eucharist.*

Invite a volunteer to read the first three sentences of the paragraph "Gifts to Share" on page 163. Have the class recall the people who carried the gifts at the last school Mass. Invite another volunteer to read the remainder of the paragraph. Ask: What else do we bring to the altar? (*Money, other gifts for people in need, ourselves*)

Singing Together

Light the candle on the prayer table. Direct the children to close their eyes and hold their hands open, palms up. Say, "Think of yourself as a gift to God." Invite the children to raise their hands as an offering as they listen to the song "My Hands Belong to You" from THIS IS OUR FAITH Music Program, Grade 2. Then teach the song and have the children sing it.

Presenting the Doctrine

Invite a volunteer to read the We Believe statements at the bottom of page 163. Ask: What do we call the second part of Mass? (*Liturgy of the Eucharist*) When does it begin? (*As we prepare the altar and bring our gifts*)

Reviewing the New Word

Print on the chalkboard the term *Liturgy of the Eucharist.* Have the children repeat the term and its definition.

Step 3 / CONCLUSION

Learning How to Live Our Faith

Completing an Activity

Before the children complete the activity, direct them to reread the paragraph "Gifts to Share." After they have written their answers on the lines provided, correct their responses.

Celebrating the Gift of Ourselves

Invite the children to the discovery table. Invite a child with a recent birthday to open the gift. Explain that the treats inside are to remind us to give the gift of ourselves today. Pass a treat to each child. Before dismissal, have the children recall some of the ways they gave the gift of self today.

CURRICULUM CONNECTION

Language Arts Make an alphabetical list of gifts on the chalkboard; for instance, *A*—actor, good appetite; *B*—ballplayer, biker; *C*—caring person, and so on. Invite each child to pick a name from a basket and print it at the top of a sheet of paper. Have the children choose words from the chalkboard that best describe the gifts of the person they selected. Assist the children in making good choices and printing these under the child's name. Present all papers to those named on the sheets.

★ Enriching the Lesson ★

Divide the class into small groups. Designate a leader, a recorder, a reporter, and a checker. The leader keeps the group on task and within the time allotted. The recorder prints the group's response. The reporter reads the response. The checker makes sure that everyone participates in the project. After explaining the roles, direct the children to list the gifts of their class. Circulate around the room to affirm the strengths and cooperation skills of each group.

Objective

This lesson helps the children learn the community's responses at the offering of bread and wine.

Step 1 / INTRODUCTION

Learning About Our Lives

Reviewing the Meaning of Liturgy of the Eucharist

Print ad̲Ber and e̲niW on the chalkboard. Ask the children to work in pairs to unscramble these words. The capital letter begins the word; the last letter of the word is underlined. Direct the pairs to stand quietly when they recognize the words. Ask: What do we do with bread and wine at Mass? (*Bring them as gifts*)

On the chalkboard, print gtiuyrL and cas̲tuEhir. Direct the teams to unscramble the words and define *Liturgy of the Eucharist.*

Remembering Ourselves as Gifts

Distribute to each child a large gift tag (5" × 7" card with a hole punched and curling ribbon attached). Invite the children to print "To God" on one side and "To Mom" or "To Dad" (or both) on the other side. Instruct the children to make a border around the cards by printing words that describe good things about themselves. Use the curling ribbon to make a necklace with the gift tag. Say, "Today we will wear this gift tag to remind ourselves that each of us is a gift to God and to our families." Ask: How will we treat each other if we are God's treasured gifts? (*Affirm all answers.*)

Step 2 / DEVELOPMENT

Learning About Our Faith ✚

Learning About the Gifts We Offer at Mass

Direct the children to page 164 in their books. What is happening in the photograph? (*A family is bringing up the gifts to the priest.*) Invite a volunteer to read "Blessed Be God" on page 164. Ask: Why does the Catholic community offer these gifts to God? (*To give thanks to God*)

Blessed Be God

At Mass we bring gifts of bread and wine to the altar to say thanks to God. The gifts may seem ordinary, but through them Jesus unites us with himself and with one another.

▲ The family in this picture is bringing up the gifts of bread and wine. Has your family ever brought up the gifts at Mass?

These are the gifts that ▶ the Catholic Christian community offers as thanks to God.

🌐 *Cultural Awareness*

Tell the children that in some regions of our country and in some cultures, Catholics bring more than bread and wine to the altar as gifts. Tell them that in farming communities, for instance, where people depend on the land to help them earn a living, farmers sometimes bring to the altar the first vegetables and fruits they have harvested from their land. Explain that this is how the farmers thank God for creating our earth.

★ Enriching the Lesson ★

Invite the children to wear their gift tags home. Instruct them to say "I am giving you a wonderful gift. I am giving you myself." Encourage them to explain to their families their choice of the words around the border. Invite members of the family to add more gift words. Encourage the children to think of some other ways they can be a gift for each member of the family.

Then the priest holds up the paten. He asks God to bless the bread that will become Jesus, the Bread of Life. We respond, "Blessed be God forever."

Next, the priest holds up the chalice. He asks God to bless the wine that will become Jesus. Again we respond, "Blessed be God forever."

Activity

Draw the gifts we bring at Mass.

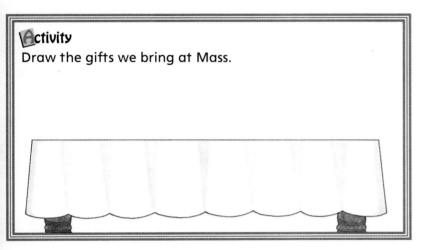

Doctrine **165**

Focus on

Blessings A blessing is an ancient form of prayer taken from the Berakah, an ancient Hebrew prayer. It is a custom to pray a blessing over things of the earth that remind us of God and of our relationship to God. As part of the Jewish Sabbath celebration, the mother of the family blesses the bread and the father blesses the wine. The children are also blessed at this time. In the Catholic faith, we are accustomed to the priest blessing people and things. Informal family blessings are also appropriate.

Teaching Tips

In your classroom, you might begin a custom of blessing the children at the end of the day. Ask the children to sit quietly. Extend your hands over them and pray, *May God bless you as you go home to your families. May you be kept safe and feel the warmth of their love.* Invite the children to respond *Amen.* Touch each child's head or shoulder gently as he or she leaves the room at dismissal.

Read aloud the captions under the photograph. Tell the children that families are called by the liturgist or invited by the usher to bring up the gifts. Discuss whether any child's family has brought up the gifts.

Responding at the Offering of Gifts

Ask another volunteer to read the paragraphs on page 165. Discuss the paragraphs by asking the following questions.

- What do we respond when the priest blesses the bread? (*"Blessed be God forever."*)
- What do we respond when the priest blesses the wine? (*"Blessed be God forever."*)

Discussing Eucharistic Bread and Wine

Gather around the discovery table. Explain that the type of bread used at Mass is called *hosts*. It looks very different from sandwich bread or breakfast toast. Ask: Why do you think we use such small, flat pieces of bread? (*Easier to eat at Communion, easier to store, does not get moldy. Accept any reasonable answer.*) Tell the children that this bread has not been blessed yet; it is not Jesus, the Bread of Life. Allow them to feel and touch a host.

Hold up the cruet of wine, the other gift that is offered. Invite the children to describe the color and the aroma of the wine. Refer to the photos on page 164. Ask: How does the family know when to bring up the gifts? (*The priest comes to a spot to receive the gifts.*)

Role-playing Bringing the Gifts

Invite volunteers to role-play the bringing of gifts to the altar. Choose children to role-play parents, several children, the priest, and altar servers. The class may sing "My Hands Belong to You" as the gifts are brought forward.

Step 3 / CONCLUSION

Learning How to Live Our Faith

Completing a Drawing Activity

Direct the children to draw the gifts of bread and wine on the illustration of an altar. Tell them that they may refer to the photographs on page 165 showing the gifts being offered. Allow the children to add to their drawings any other gifts they might like to offer.

Objective

This lesson helps the children understand that Jesus wants us to share our gifts with others.

Step 1 / INTRODUCTION

Learning About Our Lives

Discovering the Need to Share

Invite the children to sit around the discovery table. Indicate the bowl of apples and oranges. Ask the children: Who likes apples? Who likes oranges? Note that there are not enough apples and oranges to go around. Ask: What can we do? (*Share*) How can we share apples and oranges? (*By cutting them in pieces*) Cut the oranges and apples and ask several students to pass them on napkins to the others.

Step 2 / DEVELOPMENT

Learning About Our Faith

Reading and Discussing the Story

Ask a volunteer to read aloud each paragraph of the story "Sharing with Others." When the children have finished reading, ask the following questions.

- Why did the people follow Jesus? (*To be with him and to listen to him*)
- How long did Jesus talk to the people? (*All day*)
- How did the people feel in the evening? (*Hungry*)
- What did the young boy have? (*Five loaves of bread and two fish*)
- What did the boy want to do? (*Share them*)
- What did Jesus do? (*He shared the food with all the people.*)
- How many people ate the bread and fish? (*Five thousand*)

Help the children appreciate the boy's willingness to share the bread and fish.

Sharing with Others

One day, Jesus and his friends wanted to go up into the mountains. Many people began to follow them. They wanted to be with Jesus and listen to him.

Jesus talked to them all day. By evening everyone was hungry. Jesus wanted to feed them. "There is a young boy here," Andrew told Jesus, "who has five loaves of bread and two fish. Although it's not much, he is willing to share them."

166 Scripture

Enriching the Lesson

Check with the local St. Vincent De Paul Society or food pantry about donating items to needy families in the community. Write a note to the children's parents explaining the plan to donate items to the needy. Suggest that the children bring in boxes of cereal or canned foods for hungry children. You might also encourage the children to contribute a used toy or game that is in good condition. Invite the children to include a note with their gifts.

Teaching Tips

Explain to the class that sharing can be difficult when it means having to give up something we want now or want to use. Give a specific example: two children are sharing when they take turns playing with a game or toy; if both children have toys and play together they are not sharing. One child allowing another to play with his or her computer game is sharing. Sharing means taking turns, cheering the other on, and waiting one's turn. Give other examples of real sharing.

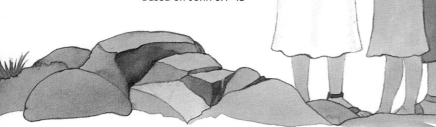

The boy gave his bread and fish to Jesus. Jesus thanked the boy. Jesus thanked God for the boy's gift. Then something wonderful happened. Jesus had enough food to share with all the people. There was even food left over. More than five thousand people were fed with the bread and the fish the boy had given to Jesus.

Based on John 6:1–13

Activity

Think about some of the gifts you have to share with others. Name these gifts on the pictures below.

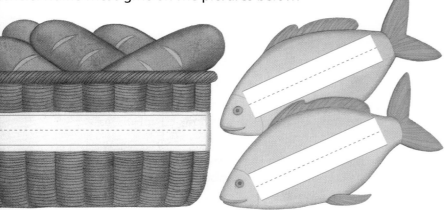

Scripture   167

Focus on

The Symbol of a Fish   In the early Church, it was dangerous to be known publicly as a Christian. The disciples would identify themselves as Christians by drawing a fish in the sand. Draw a simple fish on the chalkboard. Explain to the class how it was used as an identity symbol. Ask: Where have you seen a fish like this drawing or symbol? (In church windows, on bumper stickers, as a necklace, and so on) Use face paints to paint a simple fish on the faces or hands of the children.

Dramatizing the Story

Invite the children to dramatize the story. Ask a volunteer to play Jesus. Invite "Jesus" to choose "Andrew" and eleven apostles. Direct him or her to include girls as apostles. Invite "Andrew" to choose the young boy with five loaves and two fish. Use buns or rolls for the bread loaves. Use cut-out shapes for the two fish. Direct the rest of the class to be the thousands of hungry followers of Jesus. Invite the children to choose props and costumes from the Bible prop box. Coach "Jesus" to break apart the rolls to share with the class. When the class has finished eating, ask the leading characters the following questions.

"Jesus, how did you feel when you realized that you talked all day and the people might be hungry?"

"Andrew, how did you notice the young boy with the loaves and fish?"

"Young boy, how did you feel when Andrew asked if you would share your bread and fish?"

Encourage the children to be imaginative in their answers. Stress that the boy offered to share. Jesus thanked him. Jesus would like us all to share what we have with others who are in need.

Step 3 / CONCLUSION

Learning How to Live Our Faith

Completing an Activity

Invite a volunteer to read the introduction to the activity. Discuss possible answers to things we have to share with others. Ask: How does Jesus use our gifts? (*Jesus said that whatever we do for others, we do for him. Jesus thanks God for our gifts.*) Ask the children to name the gifts in the pictures in their books.

Offering Ourselves in Prayer

Ask the children to pause for a few minutes of private prayer. Then instruct them to repeat the words *Jesus, I bring myself to you* after you read aloud each line below.

Jesus, I want to be with you at Mass.

I thank you for your gifts.

Jesus, I want to share my gifts with others.

Jesus, I want to be with you always.

167

Objective

This lesson helps the children discover what it means to give of self.

Step 1 / INTRODUCTION

Learning About Our Lives

Reviewing the Scripture Story

Invite the children to tell the story of the boy who shared his loaves of bread and fish. Jesus thanked the boy for sharing. Ask: How did you share with others yesterday?

Step 2 / DEVELOPMENT

Learning About Our Faith

Introducing Sharing of Self

Invite a volunteer to read the story of Jessie and Grandpa on page 168. To discuss the story ask the following questions.

- What did Grandpa want to share? (*Peanut butter*) What did Jessie share? (*Herself—she found the peanut butter for Grandpa.*)
- How do you share yourself with others? (*Affirm all answers.*)
- How does that show love? (*Affirm all answers.*)

Completing an Activity

Invite the class to complete the activity. When the children are finished, discuss their responses.

Learning to Give the Gift of Ourselves

Ask a volunteer to read "We Offer Gifts of Love" on page 169. Explain that the gifts we cannot buy come from ourselves. Ask:

- What are some of the gifts we can give to one another? (*Gifts of laughter, friendship*)
- Why are these called gifts of love? (*They show that we care.*)

168

Peanut Butter Sunday

Grandpa was bending down, looking into the cupboard when Jessie arrived.

"Jessie, I need your help," he said. "Can you find the new jar of peanut butter?"

"Here it is, Grandpa!" Jessie said as she reached into the back of the cupboard.

"Thank you, Jessie. I'm taking this to church for Peanut Butter Sunday," explained Grandpa.

"On Peanut Butter Sunday, we collect peanut butter for people in our community who don't have enough money to buy groceries."

"That's a great idea, Grandpa," answered Jessie. "Here's a jar of jelly to go with it."

Grandpa smiled at Jessie. Then they both hurried off to church.

Activity

1. Circle the sentence in the story above that shows how Grandpa showed his care for those who were hungry.

2. Draw a line under the sentence that tells how Jessie showed she cared about Grandpa.

168 Morality

★ ★ ★ ★ Enriching the Lesson ★

Traditionally in the Catholic Church, following a religious vocation was one way of offering one's life for the sake of God and the Church. Invite a priest, a deacon, or a religious sister or brother to speak to the class about his or her choice of religious vocation and how he or she sees that vocation as a gift of self.

Focus on

Giving of Self To give of self means to place one's needs second to another. To give of self is to be attuned to the needs of others. Giving of self is a Christian virtue that needs to be developed in most Christians. Sometimes it is difficult and demands sacrifice. Point out the times when you have asked the children to give something of themselves for the sake of another or for the common good. Affirm their positive attitude toward giving to others.

We Offer Gifts of Love

In the story, "Peanut Butter Sunday," we learn that not all gifts are gifts we buy. Some gifts come from within us.

We have many opportunities to give gifts to one another. When someone is sad, we can give the gift of our laughter. When someone needs a friend, we can give the gift of our friendship.

Activity

Finish these stories about two children who want to give the gift of themselves.

Michelle's little brother Joey didn't get to play at all in the soccer game. He said, "I never want to play soccer again!" Joey is sitting on the front steps, looking sad and disappointed. What gift could Michelle give to Joey?

_____

_____

Julio's teacher, Mrs. Sanchez, is ill and will miss school for several days. Julio really misses her. What gift could Julio give to Mrs. Sanchez?

_____

_____

Morality 169

Cultural Awareness

Intergenerational sharing is considered a gift among many cultures. The oldest generation relates stories of identity and values to children. Host a grandparent sharing time. Invite older people of the parish to assist as "foster grandparents" to those whose relatives live at a distance. Invite these elders to share some stories of their childhood and the values they were taught. The children may offer a handmade gift as a thank-you.

Learning How to Live Our Faith

Completing a Story

Read the directions to the activity on page 169 together. Invite a volunteer to read the story of Michelle and Joey. Invite oral answers to the question. Allow time for the children to complete the story. Invite another volunteer to read the story of Julio and Mrs. Sanchez. Again discuss possible ways that Julio could let Mrs. Sanchez know she was missed. Assist students in completing the story. Give them sufficient time to write their answers on the lines provided. Discuss with the children the answers they have written. (*Answers will vary. Praise the children for their effort.*)

Praying Together

Distribute paper and pencils. Invite the children to think of one way they can give the gift of themselves at school and at home. Print on the chalkboard: *Dear Jesus, Today I will give the gift of myself by _____ .* Encourage the children to complete this prayer by adding how they would give of themselves. When all have completed their prayers, invite the children to gather around the prayer table. Light the candle. Read this simple passage based on Psalm 116: 12,17: *What can I offer the Lord for all God's goodness to me? I will give an offering of thanksgiving and offer my prayers to God.* Invite the children to place their prayers on the prayer table. Conclude the prayer by singing "My Hands Belong to You," THIS IS OUR FAITH Music Program, Grade 2.

Objective

This prayer celebrates the offering of oneself and one's day to God.

Preparing for Prayer

We need to think about the gifts that we will bring to prayer. Invite the children to remember a recent occasion when they gave the gift of themselves. Distribute colored construction paper. Invite the children to trace and cut out the outline of one of their hands. Have them print one thing on the hand that was a gift of self. Circulate to give assistance. Invite the children to bring their paper handprints and their books to the prayer table.

Praying Together

Hold up the bread and wine and an empty basket that are displayed on the prayer table. Remind the children that each day Mass is celebrated by Catholics all over the world. Tell them that each day Catholics offer the gifts of bread, wine, and themselves to God. Pick up the basket. Say, "Today we offer the gift of ourselves to God." Pass the basket and invite the children to read aloud their gift and place their paper handprints in the basket.

Praying a Morning Offering

Say, "Yesterday we offered ourselves to God. Let us pray together the morning offering on page 170 and offer ourselves and our day to God." Invite the children to read together the Morning Offering prayer with you. Say, "We will now pause to think of how we will give ourselves to God today." After a few moments, close the prayer by singing "My Hands Belong to You" from THIS IS OUR FAITH Music Program, Grade 2. You might wish to use the suggestions for movement given in the Program Director's Manual on page 130.

Praying a Morning Offering

Teacher: Jesus, as we begin this day,

All: We offer you our hands.
Teacher: May our work and our caring give you praise.

All: We offer you our feet.
Teacher: May we play fairly and follow you

All: We offer you our eyes.
Teacher: May we see ways we can show our love for others.

All: We offer you our ears.
Teacher: May we listen and learn well today

All: We offer you our mouths.
Teacher: May our words be kind and gentle

All: We offer you our whole day.
Teacher: May everything we say and do tell others that we are your friends.

All: Amen.

CURRICULUM CONNECTION

Science Children look to others as models of giving. Famous scientists devote much time to their work for the good of others. They give of their skills and talents so that society might benefit. Challenge the children to find stories in the library about famous scientists or inventors whose talents or gifts of their life work have made our lives easier.

Chapter Review

Write a **T** if the sentence is true. Write an **F** if the sentence is false (not true).

__T__ 1. There are many times when we give gifts.

__F__ 2. Catholics offer gifts at Mass during the Liturgy of the Word.

__F__ 3. The gifts we bring to the altar are bread and milk.

__T__ 4. Most of all we bring ourselves as gifts at Mass.

__T__ 5. At Mass, Jesus unites us with himself and with one another.

1. What do we call the second part of the Mass?

Liturgy of the Eucharist

2. What gifts are brought to the altar?

bread and wine

3. Talk about what we can do to show thanks for all God's gifts.

> **Bring gifts and come to the Lord.**
> **Based on Chronicles 16:29**

Focus on

Community Gifts Every community—be it a small town or large city—has distinctive attributes. The location or environment of the town or city may be a gift. Industry there may produce products that enhance our lives. The community may be especially hospitable or hard-working. Perhaps the community works together to be a desirable place for children to be reared because of its excellent schools. Invite the mayor or a city council member to speak to the class about the gifts of your community.

Reviewing the Scripture Story

Review with the children the Scripture story for this chapter. Ask:

■ What did Jesus need to do? (*Feed the hungry people*)

■ Who helped Jesus feed the hungry people? (*The young boy*)

■ How did the young boy help? (*He shared five loaves of bread and two fish.*)

■ What does Jesus want us to do? (*Share what we have with others*)

Reviewing the Chapter

Take time to go through the true-false statements and the two review questions. Be supportive of each child who participates in the discussion of the third item.

Reading the Scripture Verse

Direct the children's attention to the Scripture verse from 1 Chronicles on page 171. Invite the class to read it together. Ask: Who is to bring gifts and come to the Lord? (*All of us*) What gifts are we supposed to bring? (*Gifts of the earth and of ourselves*) Encourage the children to learn the verse from memory.

171

We Thank God for Many Gifts

Objectives ～～～～～

To help the children

■ Appreciate the Eucharistic Prayer as a special time during Mass to thank God.

■ Become thankful in their daily lives.

■ Learn that Jesus encourages his followers to be thankful.

■ Learn the responses to the Eucharistic Prayer.

■ Pray with gestures and review the chapter.

Chapter Outline ～～～～～～～

	Step 1	**Step 2**	**Step 3**
	Learning About Our Lives	**Learning About Our Faith** ✚	**Learning How to Live Our Faith** ✚
Day 1	■ Review Chapter 13. ■ Introduce the chapter. ■ Say thank you. ■ Complete an activity. *ABOUT 10 MINUTES*	■ Present the new word. ■ Present the doctrine. ■ Learn about the Eucharistic Prayer. *ABOUT 15 MINUTES*	■ Complete an activity. *ABOUT 5 MINUTES*
Day 2	■ Review the meaning of the Eucharistic Prayer. ■ Introduce the lesson. *ABOUT 10 MINUTES*	■ Learn the Preface responses. ■ Discuss the photograph. *ABOUT 10 MINUTES*	■ Read about giving thanks. ■ Pray together. ■ Complete an activity. *ABOUT 10 MINUTES*
Day 3	■ Be grateful for favors. ■ Discover times we say thank you. *ABOUT 10 MINUTES*	■ Read and discuss the story. ■ Dramatize the story. *ABOUT 10 MINUTES*	■ Complete an activity. ■ Pray our thanks. *ABOUT 10 MINUTES*
Day 4	■ Introduce the lesson. ■ Read and discuss a story. *ABOUT 10 MINUTES*	■ Present Eucharistic Prayer II for Children. *ABOUT 10 MINUTES*	■ Complete an activity. ■ Sing a prayer of praise. *ABOUT 10 MINUTES*
Day 5	**Prayer** Prepare for prayer and pray together. **Review** Complete the chapter review and read the Scripture verse.		

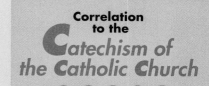

Correlation
to the
**Catechism of
the Catholic Church**

Paragraphs
293, 1360, 1361, 2637

Plan Ahead ∼∼∼∼∼∼∼∼∼

	Preparing Your Class	**Materials Needed**
Day 1	Read over the lesson prior to the session. Mark place in missalette or in the Sacramentary. If enriching the lesson, gather magazine pictures.	■ Sacramentary ■ missalette ■ pencils
Day 2	Read over the lesson. Arrange for parish music ministry member to teach sung responses. Prepare prayer table.	■ index cards ■ Bible ■ family picture, animal book ■ class roster, plant
Day 3	Read over the lesson prior to the session. Provide Bible prop box.	■ Bible prop box ■ felt-tip markers
Day 4	Read over the lesson. Bring jar of pennies. Prepare discovery table. Prepare Eucharistic Prayer II for Children.	■ jar of pennies ■ Sacramentary
Day 5	Read over the lesson. Prepare prayer table. Practice melody for song.	■ Sacramentary ■ pencils

Additional Resources

As you plan this chapter, consider using the following materials from The Resourceful Teacher Package.

■ *Classroom Activity Sheets 14* and *14a*

■ *Family Activity Sheets 14* and *14a*

■ *Chapter 14 Test*

■ *Prayers for Every Day*

■ *Projects: Grade 2*

You may also wish to refer to the following Big Books.

■ *We Celebrate the Mass,* pages 12–16

■ *We Celebrate the Sacraments,* pages 7–9

In preparing the children for the Sunday readings, you may wish to use Silver Burdett Ginn's *Getting Ready for Sunday* student and teacher materials.

BOOKS FOR THE JOURNEY

He Remembered to Say Thank You. Victor Mann. Concordia, 1976. The story of a grateful man told in rhyme.

A Child's Book of Prayers. Edited by Linda Yeatman. Workman Publishing, 1992. A book of prayers and poems of which the whole second part, pp. 22–31, is "Saying Thank You to God."

MORE BOOKS FOR THE JOURNEY

The Beginner's Bible. "The Man Who Remembered," pp. 427–431, as told by Karyn Henley. Questar, 1989. The story of Jesus healing the ten lepers.

Praise God. Gunvor Edwards and Joan Brown. Liturgical Press, 1994. Prayers of the Mass, including prayers of thanks that are part of the Eucharistic Prayer, pp. 36–39.

REDUCED CLASSROOM ACTIVITIES

Name _____

We Thank God for Many Gifts

Use your favorite color to color all the spaces marked with an **X**. Color all the spaces marked with an **O** in another color. You will discover God's greatest gift to us. If you cut along the outside heavy black lines, you will have a banner to hang or give away.

To the Teacher: This activity will remind students that Jesus is a gift to us.

Chapter 14   We Thank God for Many Gifts   THIS IS OUR FAITH 2   **14**

Name _____

Showing Our Thanks

Color the front and back covers of the card below. Cut along the heavy black lines. Then fold the card along the dotted line. Write a message inside the card to thank someone who has given you a gift or has done something kind for you.

To the Teacher: This activity emphasizes the importance of thanking people for things given to us or things done for us.

14a   THIS IS OUR FAITH 2   Chapter 14   We Thank God for Many Gifts

Background for the Teacher

GIVING THANKS

The word *Eucharist* is derived from a Greek word meaning "to give thanks." From the beginning of Christianity, the Mass has been a special celebration of praise and thanksgiving. During the Eucharistic Prayer, we praise and thank God for the gifts of creation and for our redemption in Jesus Christ. During this celebration, we thank God for the gifts of creation, especially for Jesus' gift of himself in the Eucharist.

THE EUCHARISTIC PRAYER

The prefaces to the Eucharistic Prayer stress the rightness of thanking God. The preface for each Eucharistic Prayer, liturgical season, or feast day helps us recall a specific event or gift for which we are thankful. The words are repeated in each preface to remind us that we should thank God not only at Mass but constantly in our thoughts and prayers.

The Eucharistic Prayer has five distinct parts: the preface—the prayer of thanksgiving before the Holy, Holy, Holy; the epiclesis—in which the Church asks God the Father to send the Spirit on the bread and wine so that they may become the body and blood of Jesus; the words of institution—Jesus' words over the bread and wine prayed at the Last Supper; the anamnesis—the remembrance of the passion, resurrection, and return of Jesus—and finally the intercessions for the whole Church in heaven and on earth. (See *Catechism of the Catholic Church*, #1352–1354.)

In the Eucharistic Prayer, we are reminded about who we are as a people of God. We are called to be a people who gives thanks and praise to God. The choices of Eucharistic prayers attest to the various ways in which we can praise God and remember the deeds of salvation. The response to the preface—the Holy, Holy, Holy—is usually a sung prayer of praise. Liturgists tell us that even if nothing else is sung, the Holy, Holy, Holy; the Memorial Acclamation; and the Great Amen are to be sung. This emphasizes the people's affirmation of this powerful prayer of praise offered on behalf of the community by the priest.

EXPRESSING GRATITUDE

From a very young age, children learn to say thank you for a present they have received, a kindness shown to them, or a favor done for them. In many cases these words are automatic social responses. Yet children of this age are becoming more reflective. They are more appreciative of the people and things in their lives.

As a teacher, you have the opportunity to help the children develop an appreciation for all God's gifts. You can remind them that each day is a time to praise and thank God. If this attitude is nurtured at home and in your class, the children will grow in appreciation of the Eucharist as a special celebration for giving thanks to God.

Objective

This lesson introduces the Eucharistic Prayer as a special time to give thanks to God at Mass.

Step 1 / INTRODUCTION

Learning About Our Lives

Reviewing Chapter 13

Review the previous chapter. Ask:

- What do we call the second part of Mass? (*The Liturgy of the Eucharist*)
- What gifts do we bring to the altar? (*Bread, wine, and ourselves*)
- What do we respond when the priest holds up the gifts of bread and wine? ("*Blessed be God forever.*")
- What is the best gift we can give? (*The gift of ourselves*)

Introducing the Chapter

Ask a volunteer to read aloud the chapter title and the chapter-focus sentences. Give the children an opportunity to recall a time when they remembered to thank someone. Then invite them to share their stories with a partner. As the children do this, move around the room, listening to and commenting on their stories.

Saying Thank You

Ask a volunteer to read aloud the first paragraph on page 172. Point out to the children that, no matter how we say or show our thanks, it always means, "I'm glad you did what you did."

Help the children understand the importance of expressing thanks. Then discuss with them reasons why we should thank others for gifts and kind actions. Ask:

- How do you feel when someone thanks you? (*Good*)
- How can you thank others? (*By telling them thank you; by doing something for them*)

Completing an Activity

Encourage the children to have fun with this activity as they become sensitized to a few different languages. Help the children pronounce *thank you* in the languages listed.

We Thank God for Many Gifts

Saying Thank You

Everyone knows how important it is to say thank you. We can say it in every language and in many different ways. But no matter how we say thank you, it always means "I'm glad you did what you did!"

Activity

The children below are showing you words that mean "thank you" in different languages. Circle the picture that shows the words *thank you* in a language you can speak or would like to learn.

Remembering to say thank you is very important. Tell a story about a time when you remembered to say thank you.

172 Doctrine

★ ★ ★ ★
Enriching the Lesson ★

Invite the class to list the things in creation for which they would like to give thanks. Print these on the chalkboard. Distribute old magazine and calendar pictures. Group the children into small groups. Invite each group to make a picture booklet of the things in creation for which they are thankful.

Focus on

Giving Thanks According to the *Catechism of the Catholic Church*, The Eucharist is a sacrifice of thanksgiving to the Father, a blessing by which the Church expresses her gratitude to God for all his benefits, for all that he has accomplished through creation, redemption, and sanctification. Eucharist means first of all 'thanksgiving'" (#1360)

Thanking God

God gives us many gifts. At Mass, we can thank God for all the gifts we have been given. A special prayer at Mass for thanking God is prayed during the **Eucharistic Prayer**.

The word <u>eucharistic</u> means "giving thanks." In the Eucharistic Prayer, the priest thanks God for our many gifts. We join the priest in a prayer of praise and thanks to God for all creation. We are especially thankful for God's greatest gift, the gift of Jesus.

Activity

What does the word <u>eucharistic</u> mean? To find out, circle every other letter. Begin with the second letter. Write the letters you circled on the lines below.

giving thanks

New Word

Eucharistic Prayer — The Eucharistic Prayer is a special prayer at Mass for praising and thanking God, especially for the greatest gift, Jesus.

We Believe

During the Eucharistic Prayer, we praise and thank God for all creation and for God's greatest gift, Jesus.

Doctrine 173

CURRICULUM CONNECTION

Social Studies Explore with the children some of the gratitude customs in various world cultures. A Thai family might wish to thank someone by making and offering a gift of a money tree or a jewel tree. Some Native American tribes give thanks by offering gifts, hosting a dance or powwow, or adopting a person into the tribe. An Hispanic family shows gratitude by hosting a fiesta in someone's honor.

Ask the children if they know how to say thank you in any other language. (*Danke,* German; *grazie,* Italian; *dziekuje,* Polish) Emphasize that in all cultures, saying thank you is important.

Step 2 / DEVELOPMENT

Learning About Our Faith

Presenting the New Word

Present the new term *Eucharistic Prayer* from the New Word box on page 173. Ask the children to repeat the term. Read the definition together. The *Eucharistic Prayer* is a part of the Liturgy of the Eucharist, the second part of Mass. Invite a volunteer to read the paragraph "Thanking God" at the top of the page. Ask:

- What kind of prayer is the Eucharistic Prayer? (*A prayer of praise and thanks to God for all of creation*)
- What is the greatest gift? (*The gift of Jesus*)
- Who are we thanking in the Eucharistic prayer? (*God*)

Presenting the Doctrine

Invite a volunteer to read the We Believe statement on page 173. Ask: For what do we praise God during the Eucharistic prayer? (*All creation and for Jesus*) Invite the class to read the We Believe statement together.

Learning About the Eucharistic Prayer

Show the children a copy of the Eucharistic Prayer in a Sacramentary or missalette. Explain that it is a long and important prayer. The first part of the Eucharistic Prayer is a prayer of thanksgiving. Because we have so many things for which to give thanks, the Church has more than one Eucharistic Prayer.

Step 3 / CONCLUSION

Learning How to Live Our Faith

Completing an Activity

Encourage the children to solve the puzzle on page 173 by circling the letters that spell out *giving thanks.* Then have the children write the two words on a sheet of paper.

DAY 2
DOCTRINE/MORALITY

Objective

This lesson encourages the children to become thankful in their daily lives.

Step 1 / INTRODUCTION

Learning About Our Lives

Reviewing the Meaning of the Eucharistic Prayer

To review yesterday's lesson, ask:

■ What does the word *Eucharist* mean? (*"Giving thanks"*)

■ What do we call the prayer in which the priest thanks God for our many gifts? (*Eucharistic Prayer*)

Introducing the Lesson

Explore with the children ways to become more grateful. Ask: How can we become more aware of the things for which we should be grateful? (*We need to notice the good things of the earth. We need to pay attention to other people who do good things for us.*) Conclude by saying, "Thankful people take time to think of all their blessings."

Step 2 / DEVELOPMENT

Learning About Our Faith

Learning the Preface Responses

Read aloud the prayers and responses, found on page 174, that are said at the beginning of the Preface. Then read the prayers of the priest and instruct the children to respond by reading aloud the community's responses. Summarize by reminding the children that we participate during Mass by thanking and praising God. Tell them that by responding at Mass, they are expressing thanks both as individuals and as a community.

If time permits, tell the children that our responses at Mass are often sung. Practice singing the responses on page 174 with them or invite someone from your parish music-ministry team to practice the responses with the children.

174

Prayers and Responses

Thanking God during the Eucharistic Prayer can help us become more thankful people in our everyday lives.

Read the prayer below. These are some of the prayers and responses that we say before the Eucharistic Prayer.

Priest: The Lord be with you.
All: And also with you.

Priest: Lift up your hearts.
All: We lift them up to the Lord.

Priest: Let us give thanks to the Lord our God.
All: It is right to give him thanks and praise.

CURRICULUM CONNECTION

Art Distribute magazines and pictures from calendars. Invite the children to look for pictures of things, people, events for which they would like to thank God. Ask the children to work in groups to make mobiles. Cut out large letters from posterboard that spell the things the children are thankful for. Encourage them to glue pictures on both sides of each letter. Use string to attach the letters at different heights to a wire hanger. Display the mobiles from the ceiling of the classroom.

Focus on

The Eucharistic Prayer The Eucharistic Prayer is patterned on an ancient Jewish prayer called the Berakah. It is a prayer of thanks to God the Creator, the one who sustains life; thanks for the land, for the sanctuary (the holy place of Jerusalem and its Temple); and thanks for everything that is good.

Give Thanks Everyday

Bernard came from a large family in Wisconsin. When he grew up, he became a religious brother and later a priest. Brother Solanus, as he was called, answered the monastery door and greeted people. He thanked them for the gifts they brought. When hungry people knocked, he gave them food. Often people asked him to listen to their stories or to pray with them for healing. Brother Solanus taught people how to thank God in their daily lives.

Activity

Every day we can thank God for all the good things we have been given. Fill in the schedule below with pictures or words that show what you will thank God for at each time of day.

in the morning		
at noon		
in the afternoon		
in the evening		
at bedtime		

Point out that in the photograph on page 174, the priest has his arms spread out and his palms raised up. Explain that we often fold our hands to pray, but some people choose to hold their palms up as the priest does when they pray The Lord's Prayer. This position of the hands shows that one is open to the graces and gifts of God. Encourage the children to say The Lord's Prayer with hands raised and open to God.

Step 3 / CONCLUSION

Learning How to Live Our Faith

Reading About Giving Thanks

Invite a volunteer to read the story of Brother Solanus on page 175. Then ask:

- What did Brother Solanus do at the monastery? (*He greeted the people, thanked them for gifts, gave them food, listened to their stories, prayed for healing.*)
- How can we be like Brother Solanus? (*We can be grateful for gifts and thank God.*)

Praying Together

Invite the children to write on index cards one thing for which they are thankful. Have them gather around the prayer table, on which are displayed a picture of a family, a plant, a book about animals, a Bible, and a class roster. Ask the children to identify the objects on the table. Invite volunteers to tell how these objects remind them to be thankful. Instruct the children that you will begin the Eucharistic Prayer and they will respond. Now invite the children to read the things for which they are grateful from their cards. After each child's statement of gratitude, all respond together, "Let us give thanks to the Lord our God."

Completing an Activity

Read aloud the directions for the activity on page 175. Circle the room, assisting the children as they complete the schedule in their books with drawings or words thanking God.

or . . .

Invite the children to make an acrostic for the word *thankful*. Distribute lined paper for this purpose. Encourage the children to decorate the margins of their papers with pictures of the objects and persons spelled out in their acrostics.

Cultural Awareness

In the southern part of Chile, a tribe of Mapuche Indians observes a fourth of the year as Rimugen, a season of thanks. This is celebrated during the months of March, April, and May. It is a time of harvest. Fruit, corn, wheat, and honey are placed in the center of a circle. Musicians and dancers circle the gifts to celebrate the beginning of a new year.

Teaching Tips

Teach the children to write a simple prayer of thanks or praise. Use this prayer formula: (1) Begin with a greeting. (2) Tell where you are. (3) Tell what you are doing. (4) Thank or praise God for something. (5) Close in the name of Jesus. (6) End with Amen. For example: "Dear God, I am at school. I am learning religion. Thank you for being my friend. I pray this in Jesus' name. Amen."

Objective

In this lesson, the children learn that Jesus encourages his followers to be thankful.

Step 1 / INTRODUCTION

Learning About Our Lives

Being Grateful for Favors

Begin the lesson by asking volunteers to do specific tasks to help you prepare the class. Be emphatic in your gratitude. Thank the children with emphasis, for instance, "Thank you so much, Susan, for distributing the felt-tip markers so quickly." Ask: Do you see what is happening? (*Children are doing tasks for the teacher, and she or he is thanking them.*)

Think of a time when someone did a favor for you. How did you thank that person? (*Affirm all answers.*) Remember a time when you were asked to do something for someone else. How did that person thank you? (*Encourage specific answers.*)

Discovering Times We Say Thank You

Invite the children to close their eyes and imagine all that has happened to them in the school day. After a brief pause, ask: Who are some persons you could have said thank you to today? (*Parent or the bus driver for taking me to school, brother or sister for helping me find something I needed for school, friend who showed me where to find the place in the book, and so on*) As the occasions are mentioned, ask if they are the same or similar to the experiences of the other children in class. Ask for a show of hands of those who remembered to say thank you. Encourage those who forgot to say thank you to do so later today.

Step 2 / DEVELOPMENT

Learning About Our Faith +

Reading and Discussing the Story

Ask volunteers to read aloud the story "Only One Said Thanks." After they have finished, use the following questions for discussion.

Only One Said Thanks

One day, Jesus was walking toward a small village. Ten men and women called out to Jesus. They stood far away from him. These people had a skin disease called leprosy.

"Jesus, help us!" they begged. Jesus felt sorry for them. He could see how sick they were. He understood how much they were hurting.

"Go up to the Temple in Jerusalem," Jesus told them. They did what Jesus said. On their way to Jerusalem, all ten of them were completely healed.

176 Scripture

★ ★★★ ★ Enriching the Lesson ★

Help the children prepare a mural to illustrate the story on pages 176–177. Tape butcher paper to the floor and distribute crayons or felt-tip markers. Assign two or three children to work on each scene. When the mural is completed, make arrangements to display it in the church, the parish hall, or your religious education center.

Focus on

Building Self-Esteem Expressing gratitude results from a positive experience of having one's needs met. Children who are hurting may identify with the lepers in the chapter's Scripture reading. The lepers asked for help and received it. (Encourage the children who appear to be hurting or who are setting themselves apart from others to express their concerns by confiding in you.) Assure the children that you will always be willing to listen to them and help them.

One man ran his hand over his face and arms. He felt how smooth his skin was. All the sores were gone. He praised and thanked God.

Then the man went back to find Jesus. When he saw Jesus, he ran over to him and thanked him.

Based on Luke 17:11–17

▲ What words do you think the man used to thank Jesus? What did Jesus say to him?

Activity

On the lines below, list some of the people and things you are thankful for.

Scripture 177

★ ★★★ ★
Enriching
the Lesson

Encourage the children to ask their families to tell them about a person in their lives for whom they are grateful—a relative, a former teacher, a coach, a co-worker, a boss, and so on. Invite the children to retell their parents' stories. Or you might wish to invite some of the adults who volunteer in the school to share a story with the class about someone who made a difference in their lives and for whom they are grateful.

- What did the people ask Jesus to do? (*To help them*)
- How did Jesus feel when he looked at them? (*He was sorry for them.*)
- What did Jesus tell them to do? (*To go to the Temple in Jerusalem*)
- What happened to them on the way to Jerusalem? (*They were healed.*)
- What three things did one of the men do? (*He praised and thanked God and returned to find Jesus.*)
- What did he say to Jesus? ("*Thank you.*")

Dramatizing the Story

Invite the children to dramatize the story "Only One Said Thanks." Choose a narrator and select other children to take the parts of Jesus, the grateful man, and the other nine who were healed. Encourage the child who plays the part of the grateful man to use his or her own words to praise and thank God.

Step 3 / CONCLUSION

Learning How to Live Our Faith

Completing an Activity

Distribute two felt-tip markers in different colors to each child. Invite the children to list people and things on the lines provided in the activity box. Have them print the names of people in one color and the names of things in another. Ask them to share their responses.

Praying Our Thanks

Invite the children to close their eyes again. Guide them in saying a thank-you prayer to God for all the people who helped them today. Pray: Dear Jesus, I thank you now for all those who helped me get to school this morning. (Pause.) I thank you for those who helped me here at school. (Pause.) I thank you now for all those who will help me later today. (Pause.) Please help me to remember to say thank you to all who will help me each day. Amen.

or . . .

Ask the children to stand and form a prayer circle. Then ask each child to name a person or thing for which he or she is thankful. Encourage the other children to respond with the words *God, we give you thanks and praise* after each child speaks.

177

Objective

This lesson helps the children learn the responses to the Eucharistic Prayer.

Step 1 / INTRODUCTION

Learning About Our Lives

Introducing the Lesson

Gather the children around the discovery table. Place a jar of pennies and some loose pennies in the center of the discovery table. Ask the children to guess how many pennies there might be in the jar. Accept all their guesses. Tell the children that sometimes people use the expression "a penny for your thoughts." Ask what this means. Explain that today they will place a penny into the jar of pennies each time they are thankful.

Reading and Discussing a Story

Invite a volunteer to read the story "One Way to Say Thanks" on page 178. Tell the children that Pauline Jaricot was the founder of the Society for the Propagation of the Faith—an organization that is concerned about telling all people about Jesus. Explain that Pauline founded this group, which still contributes money, food, clothing, and so, on to people in need who live in faraway countries. Ask the children:

- How did Pauline know that certain people needed many things? (*Her brother Pierre worked with people who were very poor.*)
- What did Pauline do to help? (*She saved a penny a week and her friends did, too.*)
- Why did Pauline do that? (*To thank God and to help others*)
- What other things can we do to show God that we are thankful? (*Affirm all answers.*)

One Way to Say Thanks

A long time ago in France, Pauline received a letter from her brother Pierre. Pierre worked with people in a faraway country who were very poor. He told her how the people were starving and how they had so few clothes and no money.

Pauline encouraged her friends to save a penny a week to share with those who had nothing.

"A penny of thanks for those in need is my way of saying thank you to God!" exclaimed Pauline. How do you remember to thank God?

We Give Thanks to God

During the Liturgy of the Eucharist, we gather to give thanks. Our special meal with Jesus is a time to thank and praise God for all creation. We give thanks for all God's gifts, especially for the greatest gift of all—Jesus.

At the top of the next page is a part of one of the great prayers of praise we pray during the Liturgy of the Eucharist.

Teaching Tips

The word *Hosanna* is a joyful exclamation of praise to God. It would be similar to saying *hooray!* and clapping for a good performance. Encourage the children to say the responses with an expression of joy. Choose a simple musical arrangement so that the children may concentrate on making the song joyful. An echo version may be most appropriate.

Enriching the Lesson

Invite a parish priest to come to visit the classroom. Explain that the class is studying the Eucharistic Prayer and you would like him to explain the prayer to the children. Request that he bring the Sacramentary to show the children the choices that he makes. Invite the priest to practice with the children a Eucharistic Prayer for Children and their responses.

Priest: Because you love us, you give us this great and beautiful world. With Jesus we sing your praise.

People: Hosanna in the highest.

Priest: Because you love us, you sent Jesus your Son to bring us to you and to gather us around him as the children of one family.

People: Hosanna in the highest.

Priest: For such great love we thank you with the angels and saints as we sing.

Priest and People: Holy, holy, holy Lord, God of power and might, heaven and earth are full of your glory.
Hosanna in the highest.
Blessed is he who comes in the name of the Lord.
Hosanna in the highest.

Activity

Color and decorate these words of praise and thanks to God who saves us.

Doctrine 179

CURRICULUM CONNECTION

Language Arts Invite the children to write thank-you notes to those who volunteer to make their school day easier, such as crossing guards, playground supervisors, lunch room monitors, and so on. Assist them in printing the names correctly and in composing their notes. Encourage the children to include other professionals who add to their learning experience, such as the principal, counselor, art and music specialists, physical education teachers and coaches, and so on.

Focus on

Sung Response Invite the school musician or liturgist to your class to teach the sung responses to the Eucharistic Prayer. Encourage him or her to teach both the arrangements for the Eucharistic Prayers for Children as well as the responses used for the parish Sunday Liturgies. Such a practice will allow better participation by your students at Mass.

Step 2 / DEVELOPMENT

Learning About Our Faith

Presenting Eucharistic Prayer II for Children

As a Catholic community, we thank God together in the Eucharistic Prayer. The Eucharistic Prayers for Children are presented because of their simple wording and involvement of the children in the responses. Invite a volunteer to read the introduction "We Give Thanks to God." Tell the children that you will read the priest's part and encourage them to read the responses on page 179.

Step 3 / CONCLUSION

Learning How to Live Our Faith

Completing an Activity

Distribute crayons or felt-tip markers. Read aloud the directions for the activity on page 179. Encourage the children to show their classmates how they decorated the words of praise and thanks used at Mass.

Singing a Prayer of Praise

Review the melody for "Make new friends, but keep the old, some are silver and the others gold." Teach and sing the following words to this melody: "For the sun that rises in the east, we give praise and thanks to God.

For the birds that fly from the south, . . .

For the wind that blows from the west, . . .

For the stars that twinkle in the north, . . ."

Gather the children in a circle. Begin by facing the east. After singing the tune about the east, join hands and walk a quarter of the circle to face the south. Sing the words about the south. Walk a quarter of the circle to the west and sing about the wind. Walk in the circle to the north to complete the song.

Objective

This lesson helps the children praise God by praying with words and gestures.

Preparing for Prayer

Assemble any art projects on giving thanks that the class has completed this week. Gather any responses to thank-you notes the class has written or thank-you notes yet to be delivered. Arrange these objects on the prayer table. Place a Sacramentary opened to the Eucharistic Prayer in the center of the table.

Praying Together

Invite the children to gather around the prayer table with their books. Practice the response found on page 180 with the children: *We bless you and thank you, God, for you are great indeed!* Then practice the gestures shown in the illustrations. When the children are familiar with the gestures, have them match the gestures to the words of the response. Do the first gesture on *We bless you;* the second on *and thank you;* the third on *God;* and the fourth on *for you are great indeed!* Practice the response and gestures with enthusiasm and expression. When the children are ready, pray the prayer on page 180 with them.

Praying with Gestures

Teacher: We can pray with words and songs and gestures. Let us praise and thank God today by using words and gestures.

All: We bless you and thank you, God, for you are great indeed!

Teacher: You make springs in the mountains to provide water for your people.

All: We bless you and thank you, God, for you are great indeed!

Teacher: You created the birds of the sky that sing their songs from the trees.

All: We bless you and thank you, God, for you are great indeed!

Teacher: You made the moon and the sun to show us the time and the seasons.

All: We bless you and thank you, God, for you are great indeed!

Teacher: You make our hearts glad and our faces shine with joy.

All: We bless you and thank you, God, for you are great indeed!

Based on Psalm 104

180 Prayer

Cultural Awareness

As a nation, we celebrate the holiday of Thanksgiving. Ask the children to describe this holiday and tell why it is celebrated. In many cultures, the observance of the New Year is another time to reflect on the blessings of the past year. Ask how the Fourth of July and the observance of Martin Luther King, Jr. Day in the United States could also be celebrations for giving thanks.

Enriching the Lesson

Invite the children to bring to class a picture (or an object) of something that they are thankful for. Encourage each child to show the picture and tell his or her story of thanks. Cover large cardboard boxes with craft paper. Distribute felt-tip markers and invite the class to print "thankful" graffiti on the boxes, for instance, "Thanks, God. Tommy." Arrange on the covered boxes the children's pictures or objects. Invite another class to view the display.

hapter Review

alk about how these people are saying thank you.

. Whom can we thank for all the good people and things in our lives?

God

. What prayer do we pray at Mass to praise and thank God?

Eucharistic Prayer

. Talk about your favorite ways of showing thanks.

Give thanks
to God
for everything
in the name of
Jesus Christ.
Based on
Ephesians 5:20

Review   181

Completing the Chapter Review

Instruct the children to turn to page 181 in their books. Ask the class to look at the pictures and discuss how the people are saying thank you. Then ask a volunteer to read the first question. Allow time for the children to print *God* or *Jesus*, or both, as a response. Invite another volunteer to read the second question. Assist the children in the spelling of *Eucharistic*. Invite a volunteer to read item 3. Be supportive of each child who participates in the discussion of the third item.

Reading the Scripture Verse

Direct the children's attention to the Scripture verse from Ephesians on page 181. Invite the class to read it together. Ask: To whom must we give thanks for everything? (*God*) In whose name do we give thanks? (*Jesus*) Encourage the children to learn the verse from memory.

181

15 We Celebrate the Sacrifice of Jesus

Objectives

To help the children

- Begin to understand the concept of personal sacrifice.
- Understand the greatness of Jesus' sacrifice on the cross for us.
- Remember Jesus' sacrifice and understand that we celebrate it during Mass.
- Recognize the cross as a sign of the sacrifice of Jesus.
- Celebrate the Sign of the Cross prayerfully and review the chapter.

Chapter Outline

	Step 1 **Learning About Our Lives**	Step 2 **Learning About Our Faith**	Step 3 **Learning How to Live Our Faith**
Day 1	■ Decide to share. ■ Sacrifice by giving of ourselves. ■ Read stories about sharing. ■ Retell stories about sharing. *ABOUT 12 MINUTES*	■ Read about Jesus' sacrifice. ■ Present the new word. ■ Present the doctrine. *ABOUT 10 MINUTES*	■ Complete an activity. *ABOUT 8 MINUTES*
Day 2	■ Review the meaning of *sacrifice*. *ABOUT 5 MINUTES*	■ Read about the great sacrifice. ■ Dramatize a Scripture story. ■ Explain the new life of Jesus. *ABOUT 20 MINUTES*	■ Complete an activity. *ABOUT 5 MINUTES*
Day 3	■ Consider sacrifices. *ABOUT 5 MINUTES*	■ Remember Jesus' love for us. ■ Complete an activity. ■ Sing the Acclamation. ■ Read a poem. *ABOUT 20 MINUTES*	■ Complete an activity. *ABOUT 5 MINUTES*
Day 4	■ Recall where crosses may be seen. ■ Pray together. *ABOUT 5 MINUTES*	■ Recognize the cross as a Christian sign. ■ Recognize the cross as a reminder of Jesus' sacrifice. *ABOUT 15 MINUTES*	■ Complete an activity. ■ Pray together. *ABOUT 10 MINUTES*
Day 5	**Prayer** Pray the Sign of the Cross. **Review** Decorate a banner; review the chapter; play a game and read the Scripture verse.		

Plan Ahead 〜〜〜〜〜〜〜〜

	Preparing Your Class	**Materials Needed**
Day 1	Read over the lesson. Assemble objects for discovery table. Cut out letters for *sacrifice*.	■ juice box, video game, deck of cards ■ picture of a lonely person ■ clock or watch, crucifix or cross ■ cut-out letters for *sacrifice*
Day 2	Read over the lesson prior to the session. Gather props for Scripture dramatization.	■ pencils ■ triangle and rod ■ loaf of bread ■ cup of juice
Day 3	Read over the lesson. Select melody for the Memorial Acclamation. Select a familiar "Alleluia."	■ pencils
Day 4	Read over the lesson. Prepare prayer table. If enriching the lesson, prepare story sheet for family crosses.	■ pencils ■ crayons, felt-tip markers ■ recording of quiet instrumental music ■ cross
Day 5	Read over the lesson. Prepare for prayer experience in the church. Make game cards for Liturgy of the Eucharist review.	■ pencils ■ cross, felt-tip markers ■ recording of quiet instrumental music ■ game cards and markers

Additional Resources

As you plan this chapter, consider using the following materials from The Resourceful Teacher Package.

■ *Classroom Activity Sheets 15* and *15a*

■ *Family Activity Sheets 15* and *15a*

■ *Chapter 15 Test*

■ *Prayers for Every Day*

■ *Projects: Grade 2*

You may also wish to refer to the following Big Books.

■ *We Celebrate the Mass,* pages 1–23

■ *We Celebrate the Sacraments,* pages 7–9

■ *We Celebrate God's Word,* page 16

In preparing the children for the Sunday readings, you may wish to use Silver Burdett Ginn's *Getting Ready for Sunday* student and teacher materials.

BOOKS FOR THE JOURNEY

The Legend of the Blue Bonnet. Tomie dePaola. G. P. Putnam's Sons, 1993. A retelling of the Comanche legend of how a little girl's sacrifice brought the bluebonnet flower to Texas.

Sunday's Children: Prayers in the Language of Children. p. 40. James Bitney and Suzanne Schaffhausen. Resource Publications, 1986. A prayer poem about sharing.

MORE BOOKS FOR THE JOURNEY

With Love at Christmas. Mem Fox. Abingdon Press, 1988. A story of a woman who gave away to poor people the gifts she had planned to give to relatives and who is rewarded in a miraculous way.

Days with Frog and Toad. "The Hat," pp. 42–51. Arnold Lobel. Harper & Row, 1979. A story in which a friend gives a gift that doesn't fit and then secretly and lovingly does something to it so that it does.

REDUCED CLASSROOM ACTIVITIES

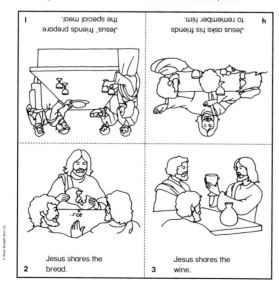

Name _____

We Celebrate the Sacrifice of Jesus

Color the pictures of the Last Supper. Cut along the heavy black lines. Then fold along the dotted lines to make a booklet. Read the story aloud.

1 Jesus' friends prepare the special meal.

4 Jesus asks his friends to remember him.

2 Jesus shares the bread.

3 Jesus shares the wine.

To the Teacher: This activity follows the Scripture story "The Great Sacrifice."

Chapter 15   We Celebrate the Sacrifice of Jesus   THIS IS OUR FAITH 2   **15**

Name _____

Showing Our Love

To sacrifice is to give up something out of love. Read the sentences below. Decide which children are choosing to sacrifice something special to them. Circle their names.

(Roberto)   My brother and I are watching TV. I let him choose his favorite show.

Anne   My little sister would like to wear my ring. I never let her wear it.

Maria   Mrs. White asks me to pick up papers in her yard. I want to ride my bike instead.

(Mark)   My mom doesn't feel well today. I will stay home after school and take care of my baby sister.

To the Teacher: This activity will help students examine the meaning of sacrifice in concrete situations.

15a   THIS IS OUR FAITH 2   Chapter 15   We Celebrate the Sacrifice of Jesus

A SACRIFICIAL MEAL

Before Jesus died and rose again from the dead, he asked us to celebrate the Eucharist in his memory. Each week the parish community gathers to remember and participate in Christ's sacrifice of his life for us. As the *National Catechetical Directory* states: "The Eucharist is a memorial of the Lord's passion, death, and resurrection. This holy sacrifice is both a commemoration of a past event and a celebration of it here and now. Through, with, and in the Church, Christ's sacrifice on the cross and the victory of his Resurrection become present in every celebration" (#120). We give thanks and remember.

The Memorial Acclamation we say after the bread and wine are changed into Christ's body and blood is a statement of belief. We proclaim that we believe that Jesus sacrificed his life to save us from our sin. We state our belief in Christ's death and resurrection and our hope in his coming again.

JESUS' PRESENCE AT MASS

As we gather to celebrate the Eucharistic Liturgy, Jesus is present in four ways. Jesus is present through the worshiping community that has gathered for prayer, through the priest and other ministers, through the word of God proclaimed, and through the consecration of the sacred bread and wine into his body and blood. As

Catholics, we believe that the bread and wine are truly changed into the body and blood of Jesus Christ by the power of the Holy Spirit.

In the *Catechism of the Catholic Church*, we learn that at Mass we respond to the command of the Lord on the eve of his Passion, "'Do this in remembrance of me'" (#1356). We carry out this command by celebrating the memorial of his sacrifice. We offer to God the Father "what he himself has given us: the gifts of God's creation, bread and wine which, by the power of the Holy Spirit and by the words of Christ, have become the body and blood of Christ" (#1357).

SACRIFICING FOR OTHERS

The concept of sacrifice may be difficult for the children to grasp at first. But they have had experiences of different types of giving or sharing: giving time or things, giving up things, giving of themselves. To explain Jesus' great sacrifice, emphasize that Jesus gave his life out of love for his friends.

Throughout the chapter, remind the children of Jesus' great love for them. Help them understand that one way of showing gratitude to Jesus is by giving of themselves to others. Encourage the children to look for opportunities to make loving sacrifices at home, at school, and with their friends.

Objective

This lesson helps the children begin to understand the concept of personal sacrifice.

Step 1 / INTRODUCTION

Learning About Our Lives

Deciding to Share

Prior to the session, place the following on the discovery table: a juice box, a video game, a deck of cards, a picture of a lonely person, a watch or clock, and a crucifix. Have the children bring their books to the discovery table.

Hold up the juice box. Say to the children, "Pretend that it is a hot afternoon. You and your sister are both thirsty. Only one juice box is left in the refrigerator. What would you do?" (*Share the juice box*) Explain that sometimes we must *sacrifice* by sharing something we want with another person.

Hold up the video game and the playing cards. Now say, "Your friend is coming to your house after school. You have your new video game ready to play. Your friend arrives, but he wants to teach you a new card game. What would you do?" (*Answers will vary. Establish that in order to make that friend feel welcomed, the plans for playing the video game ought to be put off.*) Explain that when we give up something because of love, we make a *sacrifice.*

Sacrificing by Giving of Ourselves

Hold up the picture of a lonely person. Then set it next to the watch or clock. Show the clock or watch. Talk about how time is spent playing with friends or enjoying some hobby. Ask the children to describe what they see in the picture. Ask: What could you do to help this person feel less lonely? (*Visit the person, tell the person a story, and so on*) Remind them that often making such a sacrifice is not easy, but it can be rewarding.

Reading Stories About Sharing

Invite a volunteer to read aloud the story on page 182 about Felipe. Discuss the story, focusing on Felipe giving the glove to his brother José because he loves him more than the glove. Then have the children write their responses on the lines provided.

---

15 We Celebrate the Sacrifice of Jesus

Tell a story about a time when you didn't want to share but you did it anyway because you loved the person.

Sharing Ourselves

Sometimes we give away things that are special to us. To give up a favorite thing is hard to do.

Felipe has a baseball glove that is very special to him. His little brother José needs a baseball glove. What do you think Felipe might do?

_____

_____

Cathy's class is going on a special field trip. Everyone needs a partner. Cathy likes to sit with Beth, but Cathy knows that no one ever chooses Jennifer as a partner. What do you think Cathy might do?

_____

_____

When we give up a favorite thing out of love, we make a **sacrifice**. When we give our time and help out of love, we are also making a sacrifice.

🍎 Teaching Tips

As you teach this chapter, consider arranging the class in the shape of a cross when the children stand and pray together. This will reinforce the children's understanding of the cross of Jesus. Repeat the cross arrangement for prayer as often as possible.

★★★★ Enriching the Lesson ★

Select and retell some hero's and heroine's stories that uphold our Catholic traditions of personal sacrifice, fidelity to God, and commitment to local and global justice issues from the following books: *Girls and Young Women Leading the Way.* Frances A. Karnes and Suzanne M. Bean, Free Spirit Publishing, 1993; *Kids with Courage.* Barbara A. Lewis, Free Spirit Publishing, 1992; *Kid Stories, Biographies of 20 Young People You'd Like to Know.* Jim Delisle, Free Spirit Publishing, 1991.

Jesus' Love for Us

At Mass we remember how much Jesus loves us. We remember how Jesus gave his life for us on the cross. He made this sacrifice for us because he loves us.

Jesus gave his life for all his friends, including us. At Mass, we celebrate the love Jesus has for us.

Activity

Think of someone in your family who has made a sacrifice for you. What did this person sacrifice? Write it on the lines below.

_____

_____

_____

_____

_____

_____

_____

_____

We Believe

On the cross, Jesus gave his life for all his friends. At Mass, we remember his sacrifice and celebrate it.

New Word

sacrifice   to give something out of love

Doctrine   183

CURRICULUM CONNECTION

Language Arts   Help the children recall that they have already learned the importance of saying thank you for gifts. Point out that when someone makes a sacrifice for us, they are giving us a loving gift. Distribute writing paper and invite the children to write a thank-you note to a person who has sacrificed for them. Consider inviting older students to help your students write their notes. Encourage the children to deliver or mail the note to the person who sacrificed for them.

Invite another volunteer to read aloud the story about Cathy. Ask: What do you think Cathy can do to help Jennifer feel loved? (*Cathy could choose Jennifer as her partner.*) Explain that when you give of yourself to another, you help that person feel loved. Help the children write their responses on the lines provided.

Retelling Stories About Sharing

Invite the children to return to their desks. Ask a child to read aloud the focus statement on page 182. Emphasize that it is not always easy to sacrifice for others. Invite each child to think of a story in which another person sacrificed for him or her. Have a few of the children share their stories with the class.

Step 2 / DEVELOPMENT

Learning About Our Faith

Reading About Jesus' Sacrifice

Read aloud to the class the paragraphs at the top of page 183. Hold up a crucifix. Explain that Jesus showed his love for us by dying on the cross and sacrificing his life for us. Jesus wants us to sacrifice for one another. Ask: How can we show our love for others? (*By giving up something for another person and spending time with someone who needs help*)

Presenting the New Word

Place cut-out letters for the word *sacrifice* scrambled on the chalkboard ledge. Invite a child to unscramble them. Say *sacrifice* and its definition aloud. Invite the children to repeat.

Presenting the Doctrine

Have a volunteer read aloud the We Believe statements. Ask the class to repeat the sentences. Remind them that Jesus asked us to celebrate his sacrifice in his memory. Emphasize that at Mass we do as Jesus asked.

Step 3 / CONCLUSION

Learning How to Live Our Faith

Completing an Activity

Read aloud the directions for the activity on page 183. Invite the children to write on the lines provided what a family member sacrificed for them.

DAY 2
SCRIPTURE

Objective
This lesson helps the children understand the greatness of Jesus' sacrifice on the cross for us.

Step 1 / INTRODUCTION

Learning About Our Lives

Reviewing the Meaning of *Sacrifice*
Ask: How can you tell when someone loves you? How do you show love for others? Help the children realize that loving is not always easy, but when we really love someone, we show our love no matter how difficult. Write *Sacrifice* on the chalkboard. Write *Love* vertically so that it intersects with the *e* in sacrifice. Point out that when we love, we are willing to give of ourselves to show our love.

Step 2 / DEVELOPMENT

Learning About Our Faith

Reading About the Great Sacrifice
Explain to the children that because of his love for us, Jesus made the greatest sacrifice of all. Then ask volunteers to read the story on pages 184–185 aloud. After they have finished, use the following questions to discuss the story.

- Why were Jesus and his friends together? (*For a special meal*)
- Why was Jesus in danger? (*Some people were plotting to kill him.*)
- What did Jesus say was the greatest love? (*To give your life for your friends*)
- As he broke the bread, what did Jesus say? (*"Take this and eat it. This is my body. I give it up for you."*)
- As he took the cup of wine, what did Jesus say? (*"This is the cup of my blood. I am ready to shed it for all of you."*)
- After everyone ate and drank, what did Jesus say? (*"Do this in memory of me."*)
- What happened the next day? (*Jesus died on the cross.*)
- What was Jesus' sacrifice? (*He gave his life for all his friends.*)

The Great Sacrifice
The night before he died, Jesus and his friends came together for a special meal, the Last Supper.

Jesus was happy to be with his friends. But everyone knew that Jesus was in danger. Some people were even plotting to kill him.

At the meal, Jesus told them, "You are my friends. The greatest love you can show is to give your life for your friends."

184 Scripture

Enriching the Lesson
Invite the children to echo your words in prayer to Jesus.

Dear Jesus, (echo)
Thank you for loving us. (echo)
Thank you for giving your life for us. (echo)
We remember your sacrifice. (echo)
Help us to make sacrifices for one another. Amen. (echo)

Focus on
Eucharist as Sacrifice The *Catechism of the Catholic Church* states, We carry out this command of the Lord by celebrating the *memorial of his sacrifice*. In so doing, *we offer to the Father* what he has himself given us: the gifts of his creation, bread and wine which, by the power of the Holy Spirit and by the words of Christ, have become the body and blood of Christ. Christ is thus really and mysteriously made present" (#1357).

184

Jesus then took bread into his hands. He thanked God for it. He broke the bread and gave it to his friends. "Take this and eat it," Jesus said. "This is my body. I give it up for you."

Then Jesus took a cup of wine. He thanked God for it. He gave the cup to each of his friends. "This is the cup of my blood," Jesus said. "I am ready to shed it for all of you."

They all ate and drank. "Do this in memory of me," Jesus said.

The next day, Jesus died on a cross. He gave his life for all his friends, including us. There is no greater gift than that.

Based on Matthew 26:20–30; 27–50

The New Life of Jesus

On the third day after Jesus died, God raised Jesus to new life. The risen Christ shares himself and his new life with us and all people.

Activity

Fill in the missing words for each sentence.

Jesus gave the gift of his <u>life</u> for us.

We remember his <u>sacrifice</u> and give thanks.

Scripture 185

Teaching Tips

Engage the children actively in the learning process by
1. Offering the children choices.
2. Using movement, gesture, and action often.
3. Doing physical exercises when the children become lethargic.
4. Engaging the children with hands-on items.

Dramatizing the Story

Ask for volunteers to act out the Scripture story on pages 184–185. Use the following technique to enhance the dramatization.

Use the sound of a triangle as a cue for the narrator to begin reading and for the children to "freeze" (not to move, to hold their positions still). Whenever the triangle sounds, everyone "freezes." When Jesus speaks, everyone "unfreezes" (comes to life, moves and acts as if eating and drinking at the Last Supper). Explain that the words of Jesus gave life to his apostles. The words of Jesus are spoken at Mass to give us life in the Eucharist. Strike the triangle. Narrator begins and all freeze until Jesus says, "You are my friends. . . ." (Players nod and smile at Jesus' comments.) Strike the triangle for all to freeze. Narrator continues until Jesus says, "Take this and eat it . . ." (All look confused at Jesus' words.) Strike the triangle. All freeze. Narrator continues until Jesus holds up the cup and says, "This is the cup of my blood. I am ready to shed it for all of you. Do this in memory of me." (The class shares the bread and the "wine" [use juice].) When all have eaten and drunk, strike the triangle. All freeze. Narrator concludes the story.

Explaining the New Life of Jesus

Read aloud the paragraph on page 185. Explain how Jesus was raised from the dead to new life on the third day after he died.

Step 3 / CONCLUSION

Learning How to Live Our Faith

Completing an Activity

Read aloud the directions on page 185. Allow sufficient time for the children to fill in the missing words on the lines provided. Go over the children's responses, making corrections where necessary.

185

Objective

This lesson helps the children remember Jesus' sacrifice and understand that we celebrate it during Mass.

Step 1 / INTRODUCTION

Learning About Our Lives

Considering Sacrifices

Ask the children to name a sacrifice they are willing to make out of love for another person. Tell the children that each time they give of themselves, they are being a sign of Jesus for others.

Step 2 / DEVELOPMENT

Learning About Our Faith

Remembering Jesus' Love for Us

Invite a child to read aloud the explanatory paragraph on page 186. Help the children to realize that we remember three things in the Liturgy of the Eucharist: Jesus loves us; Jesus died for us; Jesus rose to new life for us. Explain that at Mass the priest repeats the words and actions of Jesus at the Last Supper:

- takes bread —"This is my body."
- offers a cup of wine —"This is my blood."

Emphasize that the bread and wine and the words of the priest are signs of Jesus' sacrificial love. Remind the children that when the priest says these words, the bread and wine become Jesus' body and blood for us. When we speak or sing our response we witness our belief in Jesus' sacrificial love for us.

Completing an Activity

Repeat the priest's words, "Let us proclaim the mystery of faith." Invite the children to trace over the letters to discover their response, *Christ has died. Christ is risen. Christ will come again.* Afterward, have the children memorize the response by reading aloud each line several times.

186

Signs of Love

At Mass we remember how much Jesus loves us. We remember how Jesus gave his life for us. We remember how he rose to new life. We celebrate his gift of himself to us in the Eucharist.

We remember Jesus' sacrifice during the Liturgy of the Eucharist. The priest says, "Let us proclaim the mystery of faith."

Activity

Trace over the letters of the words below to discover our response.

186   Doctrine

CURRICULUM CONNECTION

Music Invite the music specialist or parish choir director to teach "Jesus, You Love Us," found in THIS IS OUR FAITH Music Program, Program Director's Manual, page 101. Focus the children's attention on the words of the song that speak of the gift of love and the sacrifice Jesus made for us on the cross. When the class has learned the melody, invite an older student to perform the instrumental descant to the song.

Teaching Tips

Research suggests that a child's memory of being cared for helps him or her become a caring person. A child needs to feel that there is an adult who loves him or her dearly. Enable caring in your class by

1. Sharing the responsibility of caring with the parish.
2. Treating everyone fairly.
3. Committing to the child first, then to the subject matter.
4. Presenting caring as a joyful ideal to cherish.
5. Giving children hands-on caring opportunities.

By remembering and celebrating Jesus' sacrifice, we can become more willing to make sacrifices for others.

For You

You didn't ask me for the shell,
But I gave it to you anyway.
It was my very favorite thing,
I found it near the bay.

It may not seem like very much,
But it means a lot to me.
I gave this gift to show my love,
And I gave it willingly.

Activity

Think of something special that you could sacrifice to show your love for someone. Draw yourself offering the gift to the person.

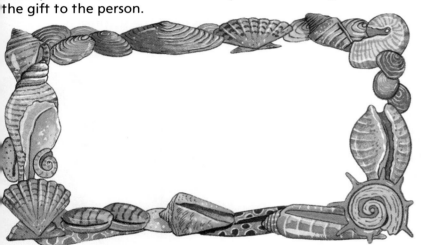

Doctrine   187

Say, "Let us each silently thank Jesus for his sacrifice of love on our behalf. Let us sing our acclamation together: *Christ has died. Christ is risen. Christ will come again.*" After the singing, say, "The risen Jesus shares himself and his new life with us every day." Then lead the class in singing a familiar "Alleluia."

Reading a Poem

Together with the children read aloud the poem "For You" on page 187. Then encourage the children to share examples of sacrifices they have made for others. Accept all comments. Compliment the children especially on their gifts of time and help. Explain that sacrifices are signs of our love for others.

Step 3 / CONCLUSION

Learning How to Live Our Faith

Completing an Activity

Read aloud the directions for the activity on page 187. Distribute pencils or crayons to the children and have them draw in the space provided in their books.

Objective

This lesson helps the children recognize the cross as a sign of the sacrifice of Jesus.

Step 1 / INTRODUCTION

Learning About Our Lives

Recalling Where Crosses May Be Seen

Read aloud the directions for completing the activity on page 188. Read aloud with the children the possible choices. After the children have put checks in the spaces provided, discuss their answers with them.

Praying Together

Invite the children to kneel and to make the Sign of the Cross. Explain that kneeling is a small sacrifice we make to remind us of Jesus' sacrifice for us. Invite the children to echo the following words and gestures.

We pray the Sign of the Cross (extend arms wide).

We pray to God, our Father (extend arms above head).

We pray to Jesus, God's Son (cross arms over chest).

We pray to the Holy Spirit (sweep right arm in arc from left to right).

We pray Amen (sweep left arm in arc from right to left).

Amen (place hands together in front of body pointing outward).

Step 2 / DEVELOPMENT

Learning About Our Faith

Recognizing the Cross as a Christian Sign

Read aloud with the children the paragraph in the middle of page 188. Discuss with the class those times when they have seen and heard the Sign of the Cross spoken (at Mass; at the celebration of a sacrament; at the blessing of a home or religious objects such as rosaries, medals, holy pictures; in the prayer experiences held in class, and so on).

188

Activity

Put a check [✔] in front of the names of places where you have seen a cross.

_____ in your home

_____ in your parish church

_____ in your classroom

_____ on a chain around someone's neck

_____ in a car

_____ in someone else's house

_____ on a building

_____ (other) _____

The Cross Is a Christian Sign

The cross is a sign that reminds us of the sacrifice of Jesus. It marks us as followers of Jesus. Christians all over the world place the cross in their homes and in their churches. We use the cross in gesture and in prayer. We pray the **Sign of the Cross** when we give and receive special blessings.

CURRICULUM CONNECTION

Art Collaborate with the art teacher to help the children create crosses. They could be a collage of different style crosses, such as small crosses used for bookmarks or Bible covers, paperweights or bead necklaces. Consider the following materials for a cross project: felt, construction paper, posterboard, fabric, baker's clay, yarn, wallpaper, beads, or shells.

Focus on

Saint John of the Cross John lived out Jesus' words "Whoever wishes to come after me must deny himself, take up his cross, and follow me." (Mark 8:34) John was ordained a Carmelite priest in 1567. He worked hard to reform the Carmelite order but was imprisoned. In prison, John began writing poetry. Today many people learn from his writings that to become Jesus' disciple means to experience sacrifice and darkness before realizing the joy of living in the light of the resurrected Christ.

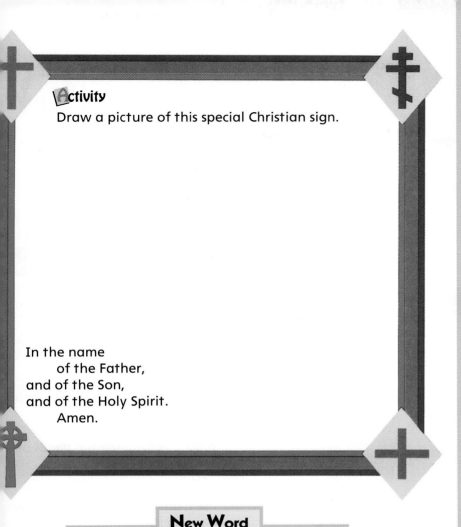

Activity

Draw a picture of this special Christian sign.

In the name
of the Father,
and of the Son,
and of the Holy Spirit.
Amen.

New Word

★
★
★ **Sign of the Cross** the prayer and gesture that marks us as
★   followers of Jesus

Doctrine 189

Enriching the Lesson

Invite the children to bring a cross or crucifix from home to display on the discovery table. You might prepare a story sheet for the parents to complete about the cross or crucifix they send to school. For example:
Family Name _____ .
This cross/crucifix has been in our family since (*year*) _____ . It came from (*name person or place*) _____ and was given to our family because _____ . Our family uses this cross/crucifix when we _____ .

Recognizing the Cross as a Reminder of Jesus' Sacrifice

Review with the children that a cross is a Christian sign and that it helps us remember Jesus' sacrifice, made for us out of great love. Invite the children to look at the crosses in the border on page 189. Draw attention to the four different styles of crosses. Explain that Christians from other lands and nations also show their belief in Jesus by having special crosses to honor Jesus. These crosses show that people of the world are joined together in following him.

Step 3 / CONCLUSION

Learning How to Live Our Faith

Completing an Activity

Distribute crayons or felt-tip markers. Read aloud the directions for drawing a cross in the space provided in the children's books. Share the children's drawings with the class. Complete the activity by saying aloud and making the Sign of the Cross.

Praying Together

Play quiet instrumental music during this prayer experience. Process to the prayer table following a leader who carries the cross. The leader continues to hold the cross as the children all face it. Say, "God our Creator, Redeemer, and Sanctifier, by the cross and resurrection of Jesus Christ you have given life to your people." Each child is invited to bow to the cross. Conclude by saying, "We, your disciples, have bowed to the cross. Help us to be living proof of its saving power. Help us to walk in the footsteps of Jesus. We ask this through Christ, our Lord." All respond, "Amen." This lesson helps the children recognize the cross as a sign of the sacrifice of Jesus.

DAY 5
PRAYER/REVIEW

Objective

This lesson helps the children celebrate the Sign of the Cross prayerfully.

Praying the Sign of the Cross

Explain to the children that today they are going to celebrate the Sign of the Cross as a prayer that marks them as the followers of Jesus. Demonstrate for the children how the sign of the cross is to be traced on their foreheads, ears, eyes, and hands as you read each invocation of the prayer. Begin the prayer and lead the children in praying the Sign of the Cross and responding *Amen* after each gesture is made.

or . . .

Remind the children that the sign of the cross is one of the signs that welcomed us into the Catholic Church. Tell them that you are going to church to gather around the baptismal font to pray the Sign of the Cross. If that setting is not available, gather the children around the prayer table, where a large cross is displayed.

Say: "Today we are going to sign ourselves with the sign of the cross. We are going to sign our foreheads, ears, eyes, and hands to remind us to serve God and others." Demonstrate each gesture. Explain that the children will echo the words and do the sign after you. Pray slowly, saying,

Let us trace the sign of the cross (echo)

on our foreheads (echo)

on our ears (echo)

on our eyes (echo)

on our hands. (echo)

May this sign of Jesus' love (echo)

give us the strength (echo)

to follow him. (echo)

To enhance the prayer experience, you might wish to play quiet instrumental music in the background.

190

Praying the Sign of the Cross

Teacher: The cross of Jesus is a sign that marks us as followers of Jesus. The cross reminds us that we should be willing to sacrifice for others. When we sacrifice to help someone, we celebrate the life, death, and rising of Jesus.

We trace the sign of the cross on our foreheads.
May this sign of Jesus' love help us understand his teachings and follow him.

All: Amen.

Teacher: We trace the sign of the cross on our ears.
May we hear the voice of Jesus calling us to help others.

All: Amen.

Teacher: We trace the sign of the cross on our eyes.
May Jesus, the Light of the World, help us see the needs of others more clearly.

All: Amen.

Teacher: We trace the sign of the cross on our hands.
May we use our hands to help others.

All: Amen.

190   Prayer

Teaching Tips

Before beginning the prayer experience, you might want to model for the children the small gesture for tracing the sign of the cross. Allow sufficient time for the children to practice tracing the shape of a small cross with the tip of the right-hand thumbnail on their foreheads, ears, eyes, and hands.

CURRICULUM CONNECTION

Music The following are suggestions of instrumental pieces that would serve as quiet background music for the prayer experience. All are available from Silver Burdett Ginn, THE MUSIC CONNECTION, 1995.

"Berceuse" from *Firebird Suite,* Stravinsky, Gr. 3, CD 2-24; "Largo" from *Concerto for Flute in G Minor,* Vivaldi, Gr. 2, CD 2-14; "Adagio" from *Sospiri,* Elgar, Gr. 1, CD 4-12; "By the Still Waters" from *Dark Garden,* Beach, Gr. 1, CD 4-15; *Zuni Song,* Nakai, Gr. 5, CD 8-18.

Chapter Review

Decorate and color the banner.

1. What word describes what we do when we give something out of love?

sacrifice

2. When do we remember and celebrate the sacrifice of Jesus?

at Mass

3. Talk about one sacrifice that you will make this week to show your love for someone.

Forgive each other just as the Lord has forgiven you.
Based on Colossians 3:13

Review 191

Decorating a Banner

Ask a volunteer to read the directions for the activity. Then ask everyone to read aloud the words on the banner. Distribute crayons or felt-tip markers. Encourage the children to work independently.

Reviewing the Chapter

Take time to go through the two review questions now. Be supportive of each child who participates in the discussion of the third item.

Playing a Game

Using a bingo format, create a Eucharist game that reinforces the children's understanding of the Liturgy of the Eucharist. The goal of the game is to complete any four squares in a row or to complete the entire card. When a child gives a correct response, the child places a marker in the appropriate square. Some suggested statements and questions follow.

First Row: Pray aloud the following prayers: The Lord's Prayer; the Sign of the Cross; the Hail Mary; a meal prayer.

Second Row: Say aloud the responses to each of the following.
The Lord be with you.
Let us proclaim the mystery of faith.
(3 responses)

Third Row: Explain the meanings of the following words: *sacrifice, Amen, Last Supper, sharing.*

Fourth Row: Tell what is important about each of these symbols: cross, bread, wine, altar.

Reading the Scripture Verse

Direct the children's attention to the Scripture verse from Galatians on page 191. Invite the class to read it together. Ask: What does Jesus do for you because he loves you? (*Gives his life for me.*) Encourage the children to learn the verse from memory.

★ ★★★ ★
Enriching the Lesson
★

In Matthew 25:35-46, Jesus gives us the Corporal Works of Mercy. To live these works of mercy, the children must be willing to sacrifice. Create six large posters, each representing a single work of mercy. For example, title one poster *I Was Hungry*. Then paste magazine or newspaper pictures of people feeding the hungry on it. Or the children may write ways they can feed others. When completed, host an all-school prayer service, inviting each grade to take a poster and do the services described.

Jesus Is the Bread of Life

Objectives

To help the children

■ Recognize that they have many needs and hungers that Jesus can fulfill.

■ Understand that Jesus, the Bread of Life, satisfies their hungers in Communion.

■ Learn how to respond to God's fulfilling love at Communion.

■ Discover how ordinary bread and eucharistic bread (hosts) differ.

■ Celebrate in prayer God's gift of bread and review the chapter.

Chapter Outline

	Step 1 Learning About Our Lives	**Step 2** Learning About Our Faith	**Step 3** Learning How to Live Our Faith
Day 1	■ Pray The Lord's Prayer. ■ Introduce the chapter. ■ Read and discuss the story. ■ Discuss needs. *ABOUT 15 MINUTES*	■ Learn about Communion. ■ Introduce the new word. ■ Present the doctrine. *ABOUT 10 MINUTES*	■ Pray together. *ABOUT 5 MINUTES*
Day 2	■ Discuss being fed. *ABOUT 10 MINUTES*	■ Read and discuss the story. ■ Understand the Bread of Life. *ABOUT 15 MINUTES*	■ Complete an activity. *ABOUT 5 MINUTES*
Day 3	■ Introduce the lesson. *ABOUT 5 MINUTES*	■ Learn the response at Communion. ■ Role-play. *ABOUT 10 MINUTES*	■ Complete a writing activity. ■ Complete a drawing activity. ■ Pray together. *ABOUT 15 MINUTES*
Day 4	■ Introduce the chapter. ■ Read about how ordinary bread is made. *ABOUT 10 MNUTES*	■ Discover how eucharistic bread is made. *ABOUT 10 MINUTES*	■ Sing together. *ABOUT 10 MINUTES*
Day 5	**Prayer** Prepare for a prayer experience and pray about the gift of bread. **Review** Find a hidden message; review the chapter and read the Scripture verse.		

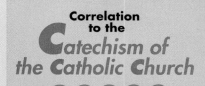

Correlation
to the
Catechism of
the **C**atholic **C**hurch
~~~~~~~
Paragraphs
1377, 1380, 1384, 1406

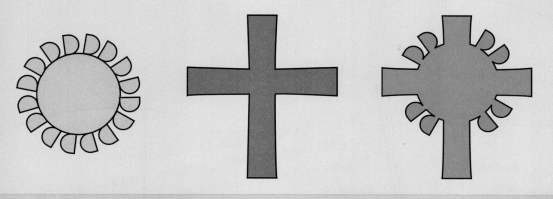

Plan Ahead ~~~~~~~~~~~~~

Preparing Your Class	Materials Needed	Additional Resources

Preparing Your Class

Day 1 Read over the lesson. Prepare discovery table. Cut out letters for word *Communion*.

Day 2 Read over the lesson prior to the session. Cut out pictures from magazines. If enriching the lesson, bring bread and juice.

Day 3 Read over the lesson. Gather hosts and juice for role-playing.

Day 4 Read over the lesson prior to the session. Prepare song sheets and gather recording of song.

Day 5 Read over the lesson. Prepare for prayer experience. Prepare prayer table. If enriching the lesson, gather materials for preparing food baskets for needy.

Materials Needed

Day 1
- drawing paper
- crayons, felt-tip markers
- paten, unconsecrated hosts
- cup/chalice of wine or juice
- cutout letters for *Communion*

Day 2
- pencils
- magazine pictures of foods
- pictures of people eating/celebrating

Day 3
- pencils
- unconsecrated hosts

Day 4
- pencils
- large host, small host
- song sheets and recording of "Jesus, You Are Bread for Us"

Day 5
- pencils
- loaf of bread
- cutouts in shape of a loaf

Additional Resources

As you plan this chapter, consider using the following materials from The Resourceful Teacher Package.

- *Classroom Activity Sheets 16* and *16a*
- *Family Activity Sheets 16* and *16a*
- *Chapter 16 Test*
- *Prayers for Every Day*
- *Projects: Grade 2*

You may also wish to refer to the following Big Books.

- *We Celebrate the Mass,* pages 13–21
- *We Celebrate the Sacraments,* pages 7–9

In preparing the children for the Sunday readings, you may wish to use Silver Burdett Ginn's *Getting Ready for Sunday* student and teacher materials.

BOOKS FOR THE JOURNEY

My New Mom and Me. Betsy Pen Wright. Raintree, 1993. A young girl has a problem with her new mother after her father remarries, and healing takes place after they save a cat together.

Sometimes I Get Lonely. Elspeth Campbell Murphy. David C. Cook, 1981. A child prayerfully reflects on loneliness and how her belief in God's love helps.

MORE BOOKS FOR THE JOURNEY

Why Did Grandma Die? Trudy Madler. Raintree, 1993. After her grandmother dies, a child deals with grief and loss.

Everett Anderson's Goodbye. Lucille Clifton. Holt, Rinehart, and Winston, 1983. A small child longs for his father, who has died, and is finally able to let go.

REDUCED CLASSROOM ACTIVITIES

Name _____

Jesus Is the Bread of Life

During Communion, Jesus gives himself to us in a special way. Make a booklet that shows the order in which things happen at Communion time. Cut along the heavy black lines of the pictures on this page and page 16a. Put the pictures in the correct page order. Talk it over with a classmate to be sure you agree. Then number the pages and finish the booklet.

We answer, "Amen."

We receive Jesus in our hands or on our tongues.

To the Teacher: This two-page activity will help students retell the sequence of events at Communion time.

Chapter 16   Jesus Is the Bread of Life   THIS IS OUR FAITH 2   **16**

Name _____

The priest or eucharistic minister says, "The Body of Christ."

We return to our seats and thank Jesus for the gift of himself.

We walk up to the priest or eucharistic minister.

16a   THIS IS OUR FAITH 2   Chapter 16   Jesus Is the Bread of Life

191c Chapter Organizer

THE BREAD OF LIFE

The Catholic Church teaches that Jesus, in the Eucharist, gives himself to his friends as food. This teaching is expressed in the theological term *transubstantiation*, meaning that without being changed in appearance, the bread and wine actually are changed into the body and blood of Christ.

Through the Eucharist, Jesus is intimately united with each of us. Jesus, the Bread of Life, gives himself to us as nourishment for our whole person. The *National Catechetical Directory* states: "Catechesis recognizes the Eucharist as the heart of human life. It helps people understand that celebration of the Eucharist nourishes the faithful with Christ, the Bread of Life, in order that, filled with the love of God and neighbor, they may become more and more a people acceptable to God and build up the Christian community with the works of charity, service, missionary activity, and witness" (#122).

THE COMMUNION RITE

Our understanding of the Eucharist grows as we mature as believing persons. Children in the second grade can begin to understand that Jesus, the Bread of Life and Cup of Promise or Salvation, fills our hungers and thirsts for life's fullness. Participating in this sacrament can help us grow in holiness. The *National Catechetical Directory* states: "Children should be taught that the Holy Eucharist is the real body and blood of Christ, and what appear to be bread and wine are actually His living body" (#122).

As a teacher you have the opportunity to awaken the children's desire to be united with Jesus in the Eucharist. You can help them understand that Jesus fulfills our needs in the Eucharist meal. Remind them that when we receive Communion we are united in a special way to Jesus, to our parish community, and to God's Church throughout the world.

Objective

This lesson helps the children recognize that they have many needs and hungers that Jesus can fulfill.

Step 1 / INTRODUCTION

Learning About Our Lives

Praying The Lord's Prayer

Begin the session by praying The Lord's Prayer together. After you have finished, call attention to the words *Give us this day our daily bread.* Ask the children what these words mean.

Introducing the Chapter

Ask a volunteer to read aloud the chapter-focus question on page 192 and encourage the children to answer the question. Help the children appreciate that although we need nourishment to stay healthy, we have other needs as well. After this discussion, tell the children that in today's lesson they will learn about other kinds of needs and hungers.

Reading and Discussing the Story

Ask several volunteers to read the story "Hungry for Comfort" on pages 192–193. After they have finished, encourage the children to retell the story in their own words. Ask the children if they, like Rita, have ever hungered for things they couldn't see. Help them think about the needs and hungers they may have. (*We need to feel loved. We need to be at peace. We need other people, and so on.*)

Discussing Needs

Ask: What do you need when you feel afraid, lonely, or sad? (*Answers will vary. Seek words such as love, care, peace, understanding, forgiveness.*)

Now invite the children to write two words that express a hunger or need that they have experienced. Assist those children needing help with spelling.

or . . .

Distribute drawing paper and crayons or felt-tip markers. Invite the children to draw pictures of foods and beverages that help them grow and be

192

16 Jesus Is the Bread of Life

Sometimes we feel hungry but nothing we eat or drink helps. What are some of the things we need besides food?

Hungry for Comfort

Rita's class at school had a pet hamster named Squeaky. Every morning, Rita made sure that Squeaky had enough food and fresh water. Rita and Squeaky were good friends.

One morning Squeaky's cage was empty. Rita's teacher explained, "When I cleaned the cage last night, Squeaky escaped. I'm sorry, boys and girls, I know how much you loved Squeaky."

After school that day, Rita went home and sat in the kitchen. She was very quiet. "What's wrong, Rita?" her mother asked. "Do you need something to eat?"

🍎 Teaching Tips

Create flash cards for the various invocations and responses used in the Communion Rite. You might want older students to help the children print an invocation on one side and the response on the other side. Number the cards to help the children learn the correct sequence. Allow time for the class to practice responding with the cards.

★ Enriching the Lesson ★

Distribute writing paper. Tell the children that they are to write a new ending to the story "Hungry for Comfort." Encourage them to think about the thing that Rita needs most. Then have them write an ending to the story that shows her need being met by someone other than her mother. Let the children work individually. Afterward, invite volunteers to share their endings to the story with the class. Compliment the children on their imaginations.

Rita answered slowly, "No, thanks. I'm not hungry."

Then Rita told her mother about Squeaky. "Rita, now I understand," she said. "You don't need a snack. You need someone to comfort you."

Mother gave Rita a hug. After that, Rita felt better.

Jesus Gives Himself to Us

Everyone needs to feel special and to belong. At Mass, Jesus gives himself to us in the **Eucharist**. We feel special because Jesus is with us in this special way. At **Communion**, we receive Jesus.

New Words

- ✦ **Eucharist** — Jesus' gift of himself to us at Mass
- ✦ **Communion** — Communion is a part of the Liturgy of the Eucharist. At Communion, Jesus gives himself to us in the Eucharist.

We Believe

Jesus gives us himself in the Eucharist. The Eucharist we receive at Communion is more than ordinary food and drink. In the Eucharist, Jesus gives us himself, the Bread of Life.

Doctrine   193

★ ★ ★ Enriching the Lesson ★

Help the children answer these questions regarding needs. What do you need

- ■ when you are not chosen for a team and you feel left out?

- ■ when you have forgotten your homework at home and the teacher is collecting the assignment?

- ■ when your classmates see a hole in your sock and laugh at you?

- ■ when you have to visit the doctor to get a flu shot?

Cultural Awareness

Explain to the children in age-appropriate language that at Communion, we are called to the table of diversity. All people share in common the need to eat and be nourished. The cuisines of different cultures have unique flavors and satisfy particular tastes. At Eucharist, when we come to the Lord's table, we are nourished by the presence of Jesus. At this table all people are welcome—all nationalities, female and male, all races, poor and rich. Communion unites all Catholics.

---

healthy. Then ask them to add to their drawings other things they need to be happy and healthy. When the children are finished, invite them to share their pictures with the class. Help the children appreciate that we all have needs that cannot be satisfied merely with food and drink.

Step 2 / DEVELOPMENT

Learning About Our Faith

Learning About Communion

Place on the discovery table a paten with hosts on it and a chalice of wine or grape juice. Invite the children to join you at the discovery table. Explain that the bread and wine on the table will become the body and blood of Jesus at Mass. Have a volunteer read aloud "Jesus Gives Himself to Us" on page 193. Ask: When do we receive Jesus at Mass? (*At Communion*) Have the children sing along with the recording of "Jesus, You Are Bread for Us" from THIS IS OUR FAITH Music Program, Grade 2.

Introducing the New Word

Direct the children to return to their seats. Place the scrambled letters for the word *Communion*, which you cut out prior to the session, on the chalkboard ledge. Invite the children to help you place the letters in the correct order. Say aloud with the class the new word and its definition. If you have opted to make new word posters, paste the letters to spell out *Communion* on one side of posterboard and print the definition on the other side.

Presenting the Doctrine

Ask a volunteer to read aloud the We Believe statements. Help the children study the material by listing the three statements on the chalkboard.

Step 3 / CONCLUSION

Learning How to Live Our Faith

Praying Together

Invite each child to name now one of the feelings written in today's writing activity. (Encourage the children who are comfortable with this sharing to speak aloud the words they wrote.)

Thank you, Jesus, the Bread of Life, for giving us all these feelings. Thank you for being with us every day of our lives. Amen.

Objective

This lesson helps the children recognize that Jesus, the Bread of Life, satisfies their hungers in Communion.

Step 1 / INTRODUCTION

Learning About Our Lives

Discussing Being Fed

Gather the children around the discovery table to see a variety of pictures from magazines of food and of people sharing food, especially at a table. Discuss the pictures with the children. Mention in your discussion that at meals we share conversation and companionship in addition to food. Explain that we talk and share words with one another as we share food with each other. Discuss what it feels like to be hungry. Ask if they have ever shared food with someone who was very hungry. Explain that they will now read a story about Jesus and a crowd of his followers who were very hungry.

Step 2 / DEVELOPMENT

Learning About Our Faith

Reading and Discussing the Story

Invite a volunteer to read aloud the story "The Bread of Life" on pages 194–195. After the story is read, use the following questions for discussion.

- Why did Jesus give the people bread and fish? (*They were hungry.*)
- What happened the next day when the people asked for more food? (*Jesus spoke to them about other kinds of hunger and other kinds of food.*)
- What does God's bread give to the world? (*Life*)
- Who is this bread? (*Jesus*)
- What happens to us when we come to Jesus? (*Jesus fills all our hungers and thirsts.*)

194

The Bread of Life

Remember the crowd of people who listened to Jesus all day and by evening was very hungry? On that day, Jesus gave them bread and fish.

The next day the crowd was still following Jesus. They asked him for more food, but Jesus did not feed them. He spoke to them about other kinds of hunger and about other kinds of food.

Jesus said, "You should be looking for God's bread. This bread gives life to the world."

194 Scripture

Enriching the Lesson

Invite the class to respond "Thank you, Jesus, the Bread of Life" after you pray each invocation.
For giving us many different feelings, R.
For hearing our needs and hungers, R.
For being with us when we feel sad or lonely, R.
For being with us when we are afraid or unsure of ourselves, R.
For helping us to be kind and respectful to others, R.
For helping us to learn about Communion, R.

Focus on

Jesus According to the *Catechism of the Catholic Church*, "It is highly fitting that Christ should have wanted to remain present to his Church in this unique way. Since Christ was about to take his departure from his own in his visible form, he wanted to give us his sacramental presence; since he was about to offer himself on the cross to save us, he wanted us to have the memorial of the love with which he loved us 'to the end,' even to the giving of his live" (#1380).

Jesus knew how important bread is in our lives. He is the Bread of Life. Here is the story of how hosts are made.

3. When the flat sheet of dough is baked, Sister removes it from the machine. ▶

▲ **1.** Sister is mixing the ingredients in a very large mixing bowl. An electric mixer is helping her mix together the flour and water.

◀ **4.** Now it is ready to be placed in another machine. This machine puts moisture into the crisp sheet of dough.

▲ **2.** Sister is spreading the thin batter on a machine that will bake the batter into a flat sheet of dough.

▲ **5.** The next morning, Sister cuts both large and small hosts with a cutting machine.

Doctrine 199

★ ★ ★ ★
Enriching the Lesson
★ ★ ★

Read aloud the following Scripture verse based on Matthew 26:26: "As they were eating, Jesus took a small loaf of bread and blessed it and broke it apart and gave it to the disciples and said, 'Take it and eat it, for this is my body.'" Pause here to answer any questions the children may have.

Learning About Our Faith

Discovering How Eucharistic Bread Is Made

Hold up two hosts (one large host and one small host). Tell the children that they are going to discover how these hosts are made, often as the ministry of nuns. Invite a volunteer to read the introductory sentences on page 199 and the caption to the first photograph. Ask:

■ What is another name for eucharistic bread? (*Hosts*)

■ What is Sister doing? (*Mixing the ingredients for the hosts*)

■ What are the ingredients? (*Flour and water*)

Invite several other volunteers to continue reading aloud the captions to each photograph. Check the children's understanding of the process by asking appropriate questions. Conclude by asking how eucharistic bread (hosts) and ordinary bread differ. (*Answers could include the following. Ordinary bread is made with yeast, hosts have none; bread is kneaded before baking, host batter is spread thinly on sheets; loaves of bread are sliced, hosts are cut out in large and small sizes in a machine, and so on.*)

Step 3 / CONCLUSION

Learning How to Live Our Faith

Singing Together

Distribute the song sheets to "Jesus, You Are Bread for Us," found on page 98 in the Director's Manual of THIS IS OUR FAITH Music Program, Grade 2. Use the recording to help the children learn the song. When the children know the song, have them sing it together with the recording.

Objective

This lesson helps the children celebrate with grateful hearts God's blessings, especially the gift of bread.

Preparing for a Prayer Experience

Prior to the session, place a loaf of bread on the prayer table.

Ask the children to recall what the word *Eucharist* means. ("*Giving thanks*") Explain that we are thankful for the blessings God has given us. Distribute paper cutouts in the shape of a loaf of bread to the children. Invite them to write one thing for which they are thankful. (*Answers will vary. Appropriate responses would include peace; hope; joy; family; friends; a favorite pet; ability to read, think, feel, speak, hold, touch; the eucharistic bread and wine.*) Emphasize that we are thankful for the gift of bread, especially for the gift of Jesus in the Eucharist.

Have the children process to the prayer table and gather in a circle around it with their paper loaves of bread and their books.

Praying About the Gift of Bread

Before leading the prayer experience on page 200, invite each child to read aloud what he or she has written on his or her paper loaf of bread. Then begin the prayer experience.

Praying About the Gift of Bread

Teacher: God has blessed us with the gift of bread. Bread fills our hunger for food. The Eucharist fills our hunger for Jesus. Let us pray together about this special gift.

Reader 1: May this loaf of bread remind us to share our bread with those who have none.
All: Blessed be God forever!

Reader 2: May this dish of unblessed hosts remind us to come often to the table of the Lord to receive Jesus, the Bread of Life.
All: Blessed be God forever!

Teacher: God, our Father, you give us everything that is good. Thank you for the gift of bread and especially for Jesus, your greatest gift.
All: Amen.

200 Prayer

★ ★★★ ★ Enriching the Lesson

Distribute blank sheets of stationery and pencils or pens. Ask the children to think about what receiving Jesus in the Eucharist means to them. Invite the children to write a letter to their families expressing their feelings. After the children have completed the letters, send the letters home.

Chapter Review

Circle the word hidden in each line. Then write these words on the lines below the puzzle.

P	X	J	E	S	U	S
I	S	R	Y	M	N	T
P	T	H	E	L	B	T
J	O	B	R	E	A	D
X	I	N	D	M	O	F
G	L	I	F	E	S	U

Jesus is the Bread of Life.

1. Who is the Bread of Life?

   Jesus

2. In the Mass, when does Jesus give himself to us?

   at Communion

3. Talk about what we can do to help another person who is sad, worried, or lonely.

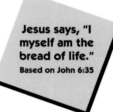

Jesus says, "I myself am the bread of life."
Based on John 6:35

Review   201

Enriching the Lesson

Have the children draw fish and loaves of bread on lunch bags. Have them use the bags to bring nonperishable food items to school. Prepare a food basket as a gift to the hungry in the community. The basket can be given to the parish for distribution, to a local food pantry, to the St. Vincent de Paul Society, or to the Salvation Army. Suggest that families save money to donate to the needy by eating less expensive and smaller meals at least once a week.

Finding a Hidden Message

Read aloud the directions for the hidden-word puzzle on page 201. Allow the children to complete the activity independently. After they have finished, ask them to read aloud the message. Help the children appreciate that Jesus fills our hungers and helps us grow in holiness.

Reviewing the Chapter

Take time to go through the two review questions now. Be supportive of each child who participates in the discussion of the third item.

Reading the Scripture Verse

Direct the children's attention to the Scripture verse from John on page 201. Invite the class to read it aloud together. Ask: Who is the Bread of Life? (*Jesus*) Encourage the children to learn the verse from memory.

Using the Unit Organizer

Completing a graphic organizer such as a chart or table can help the children organize information that has been presented in the unit. Organizers can enable the children to visualize their thinking and recognize relationships among ideas. This will give the children the opportunity to understand more completely the materials they have been studying.

Completing the Organizer

Have the children turn to page 202 in their books. Tell the children that they will complete the organizer by first drawing pictures that illustrate each part of the Liturgy of the Eucharist. Secondly, instruct the children to write the response we pray at each part. Point out where to start. Then ask the children to complete the activity independently. If necessary, tell them that they may look back through the previous four chapters for help. When everyone has finished, have the children compare their responses with the class.

Looking Back: Self-Assessment

The critical reflection questions below give the children an opportunity to sharpen their thinking skills. The questions can be used as a class discussion or independent writing activity.

- Which was your favorite story in this unit?
- Which picture in this unit did you like best? What did you like about it?
- What have you learned in this unit that you are glad you learned?

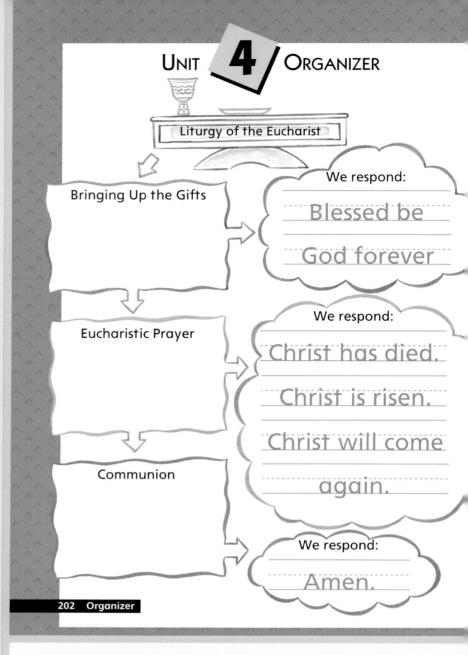

UNIT **4** ORGANIZER

Liturgy of the Eucharist

Bringing Up the Gifts

We respond:
Blessed be
God forever

Eucharistic Prayer

We respond:
Christ has died.
Christ is risen.
Christ will come
again.

Communion

We respond:
Amen.

202   Organizer

202

UNIT 4 REVIEW

Look at the words in the box. Use the correct word to finish each sentence.

| wine | altar | praise | thanks | ourselves |

1. The Liturgy of the Eucharist begins as we prepare the

   altar_____.

2. We bring bread and wine_____ to be used in our special meal.

3. When we bring our gifts to the altar, we also bring

   ourselves_____.

4. The Eucharist is a celebration of thanks_____.

5. At Mass we praise_____ and thank God for many gifts.

Reviewing the Unit

The purpose of the Unit Review is to reinforce concepts presented in the preceding four chapters and to check the children's understanding. If you have opted to make and use new word posters, they can be included in an oral review. After explaining the directions, give the children sufficient time to complete the two-page review. Answer any questions they may have as you check their work.

Testing

After the students have completed the Unit Review, you may wish to distribute copies of the Unit 4 Test from the Test Booklet.

Project

If time permits, you may wish to do the following project with the children.

Before the session, cut out two waxed-paper circles, six inches in diameter, for each child. Also bring an iron, two pressing cloths, and a supply of colored tissue paper to the session.

Explain to the children that they are going to make "stained-glass" crosses. Distribute the waxed-paper circles and tissue paper. Direct the children to tear the tissue paper into small pieces and place the pieces in the shape of a cross on one of the waxed-paper circles. When they have finished making the crosses, have each child place the other waxed-paper circle over the crosses.

Ask the children to bring their crosses to the area where you have set up the iron. Place the project between two pressing cloths. Use a warm iron to press the project until the two pieces of waxed paper have fused together. Then allow the projects to cool. Encourage the children to place their crosses in a window at home to remind them of Jesus' sacrifice.

Match the priest's prayers at Mass with our responses. Draw a line from the prayer to the correct response.

Priest	**All**
6. Let us give thanks to the Lord our God.	Christ has died. Christ is risen. Christ will come again.
7. Let us proclaim the mystery of faith.	Amen.
8. The Body of Christ.	It is right to give him thanks and praise.

Circle the correct answer.

9. To sacrifice is always easy.

      Yes   (No)

10. At Mass we remember Jesus sacrificing his life for us.

      (Yes)   No

11. We can be hungry for something that is not food.

      (Yes)   No

12. At Communion, Jesus gives himself to us in the Eucharist.

      (Yes)   No

WHEN SHOULD I EXPRESS MY FEELINGS?

good time to express my feelings is when the other person is able
to pay attention to what I am saying. The other person is able to pay
attention when he or she is feeling calm and is not too busy doing
other things. A good time to express feelings is when the other person is
ready to listen.

Activity

Look at the pictures and tell if the person in each picture is
ready or not ready to listen to someone's feelings.

Ready to Listen   Not Ready to Listen

Ready to Listen   Not Ready to Listen

Ready to Listen   Not Ready to Listen

Ready to Listen   Not Ready to Listen

Day to Day   205

Day to Day

Objective

This lesson helps the children appreciate when
to express feelings.

Introducing the Lesson

Ask volunteers to read aloud the opening
paragraph on page 205. Ask the children why
they think it is important to pay attention when
someone is trying to tell us about their feelings.
(*Communicates respect, assures that we hear
the message*) Ask them to share times when
they tried to tell someone something important
but the person was too upset, or too busy
to listen.

Completing the Activity

Direct the children to look carefully at the
picture on page 205. Ask them to tell you what
is happening in each picture. Have the children
circle whether they think the person in the
picture is ready to listen or not ready to listen.
Share their responses with the class.

Discussing What to Do When Someone Isn't Ready to Listen

Direct the children to look at pictures #1, #3,
and #4, which show people not ready to listen.
Ask the children to tell what they would do to
get their feeling message heard. (*Picture #1,
talk on the phone when the mother is less
busy; picture #3, wait until the friend is less
angry, or calmer; picture #4, wait until the
teacher is finished writing*)

Read together with the children the statement
on page 206 that answers the question "What
should I do if someone is not ready to listen to
my feelings?" Have the children circle the two
answers with their pencils.

Expressing Feelings When There Is a Problem

Read aloud "Expressing Feelings When I Have
a Problem" on page 206. Emphasize that the
children should tell their feelings to the person
who is causing the problem. Taking this positive
step is one way to begin to solve the problem.

Let the children know that sometimes when
the other person hears how you feel, that

Lesson continues on page 206.

205

person may try to correct the problem. Sometimes that person might not care or be unable to do anything about it. If the problem continues to be upsetting, it is best to ask a trusted adult for help.

Recalling a Past Problem

Before asking the children to print the name of a trusted person in the space provided, have them close their eyes and think about a time when they had a problem. It could be a time when they felt left out because others wouldn't let them play, when they felt afraid that they wouldn't be able to finish all of their homework, or they had a fight with a friend, or felt worried because they broke something that didn't belong to them. Ask them to think silently about this problem and their feelings that went with it. (Allow a few minutes of quiet time.) Now ask them to think about someone they trust, such as a friend, a parent, a big sister or brother, an aunt or uncle, a teacher. Have them imagine themselves sharing their problem with that person. (Allow a brief period of silence.)

Have the children write the name of the trusted person in the space provided. Now ask them to think about what that person could say or do to help them feel better.

Following Jesus

Ask a volunteer to read aloud the sentences in the Following Jesus box. Emphasize that we can share our feelings with Jesus just as we would tell our feelings to a trusted person.

Concluding the Lesson

Have the class pray together the prayer at the end of the lesson. Allow time for the children to tell Jesus silently their feelings and their problems.

What should I do if someone is not ready to listen to my feelings?

If a person is not ready to listen to my feelings, I can wait until the person is ready, or I can tell someone else.

Activity

Expressing Feelings When I Have a Problem

It is important to express my feelings when I have a problem. By sharing my feelings with someone I trust, I can get help to solve my problem. I can also tell the person who is causing the problem how I feel.

Print the name of a person you can trust on the line below.

_____

_ _

Following Jesus

Jesus is always ready to listen to my feelings. Telling Jesus about my feelings is a way of praying.

A Prayer

Jesus, I love you. You are my friend. I know I can always tell you my feelings. I can always tell you my problems. You are always ready to listen. Thank you, Jesus, for loving me. Amen.

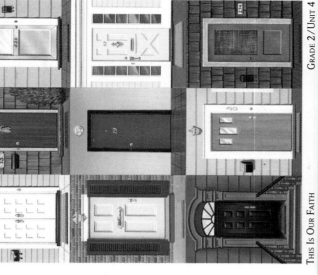

OPENING DOORS
A Take-Home Magazine™

Growing Closer

Make a special effort this week to be grateful to one another. Remember to say thanks for every kindness you experience.

Write a family prayer of thanks for all of the special people, places, and times you have shared together. Pray this prayer at meals or bedtime.

Answers for pages 4-5: family, snow, friend, God, church, Jesus; sacrifice

Looking Ahead

In Unit 5 your child will be introduced to the concept of the mystery that is the sacramental presence of Jesus in the Eucharist. He or she will focus on the Eucharist as communion—union with Jesus and others in him. Unit 5 will emphasize that those who are united to Jesus in the Eucharist are called to live according to his example.

8

Opening Doors ~~~

Sending the Magazine Home

As you complete Unit 4 with your class, assist the children in carefully removing *Opening Doors: A Take-Home Magazine* (two pages) from their texts by separating the pages from the book along the perforations. Demonstrate how to fold the two pages, forming an eight-page booklet. Ask the children to take the magazine home and encourage their families to read it with them and participate in the suggested activities.

The Generosity of God

*"If you come to me,
I will fill all your hungers and thirsts."*
(Adapted from John 6:34)

People who expect nothing will never be disappointed, so the saying goes. But one needs only to look at Jesus in the gospels to see that our God is a God of surprise and often gives us more than we could ever ask for or expect.

Jesus' ability to transform our simple requests into miracles and the gifts we bring to the altar into lifegiving gifts calls for more than a simple "thank you."

In the gospel accounts, we witness a few loaves and fishes multiplied to feed thousands, lepers not only helped but also completely healed, and hunger and thirst satisfied so completely that one will never again be hungry or thirsty.

Such generosity calls us to a much larger response. While we know that Eucharist means "to give thanks," we observe that the Eucharistic Prayer is more than this. When

learn that people and their needs are more important than rules, customs, and proper etiquette. Finally, the Last Supper and the resurrection meal show the sacramental dimension of meals: *when people share a meal of love and friendship, Jesus himself is present.*

Jesus understood the significance of a meal and all its implications. Giving himself under the appearances of bread and wine—made real for his followers then, and for us now, the presence of the One in whose memory this special meal was to be shared.

Forgiveness and understanding, sharing and generosity, listening to others and attending to their needs—these are all expressions of Christian spirituality. It's no wonder that the Mass, the eucharistic meal, is the center of Catholic life. We praise God when we gather in love around the altar. Jesus lives in us when we are truly present to one another; we are nourished, nurtured, and filled with new life.

Meals in the Bible

Eating a certain amount of food each day is essential to human existence. Meals, however, have always provided more than basic nourishment for those who shared them.

In biblical times, the Jews ate only two meals a day. The chief meal was eaten between 3 and 4 P.M., but it often lasted until nightfall. The most important meal of the year was the Passover meal—the ritual meal of lamb, bitter herbs, wine, and unleavened bread, which commemorated the flight of the Jews from Egypt.

Here are a few of the meals recorded in the gospels.
- Jesus shares a meal at Simon's house (Mt. 26:6–13).
- The multiplication of loaves (Mt. 14:19; 15:35).
- Jesus eats a meal with Zacchaeus (Lk. 19:1–10).
- Jesus eats a meal with Martha and Mary (Lk. 10:30–42).
- Jesus works his first miracle at a wedding banquet (Jn. 2:1–11).
- The Emmaus meal (Lk. 24:13–35).

From these examples, it is clear that meals can have more than a physical or social function. Meals can have a spiritual dimension as well.

At the suppers with Simon and Zacchaeus, Jesus forgives someone. In the stories about the multiplication of loaves and the wedding feast of Cana, sharing and generosity emerge as important virtues. From the meal with Martha and Mary, we

6

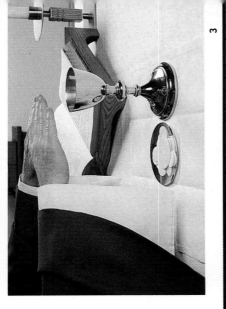

3

the priest prays, "Let us give thanks to the Lord our God" we respond, "It is right to give him thanks *and praise*." Knowing just how generously God provides for us, we recognize that God deserves more than mere thanks and we acknowledge our need to praise God for everything that is good.

There can be no greater investment than to bring our needs and our gifts to the Lord as we do in each eucharistic celebration. When we do this, our needs are filled and our gifts are returned to us many times over. Most especially, the gifts of bread and wine come back to us as the Bread of Life and the Cup of Salvation. In expressing our gratitude in the Eucharistic Prayer, we acknowledge the generosity of our God and confidently expect to be renewed and transformed into the Body of Christ.

God's Great Gifts

Recount with your child the many gifts and blessings your family has enjoyed. Teach your child the prayer response from the Mass, "It is right to give you thanks and praise." Enjoy the riddles on these pages with your child.

At Mass we praise and thank God for many gifts. We remember Jesus and the new life he shares with us. We thank Jesus for the wonderful gift of Eucharist.

Try these riddles. Discover some of God's gifts to you.

We love you more than anyone else. We take care of you every day. You made us very happy the day you were born. Who are we?

m (a) f (y) (i) l
o (s) w n

I make the earth look beautiful in winter. I lay a soft, fluffy blanket of white everywhere. I am fun to play in. What am I?

4

spend fun times together. We help one another and share secrets. Who am I?

n d (i) e (r) (f)

I made you because I love you. I give you everything you need and people who take care of you. Who am I?

o d G

We are the people of God. We are followers of Jesus. Our building has the same name as us. Who are we?

r h (c) u (c) h

I give myself to you in the Eucharist. I died on the cross for you. I share new life with you. Who am I?

(e) s J s u

Now unscramble the circled letters to complete the sentence below.

At Mass we remember the _____ of Jesus and give thanks.

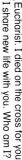

Thank Jesus for the gift of Eucharist the next time you go to Mass. Pray the prayer of thanks and praise you learned today. Celebrate God's love for you!

5

UNIT 5

The Eucharist Is Jesus with Us

Who is one person you always like to be with?

To help the children learn that the Eucharist calls us to lead lives of Christian peace, love, and hope.

Doctrinal Summaries

CHAPTER 17
The Eucharist is a sacrament of unity and peace. Jesus taught his disciples to say The Lord's Prayer and pray for unity. During the Mass, we offer one another a sign of peace. We are called to be peacemakers in our families and in our world.

CHAPTER 18
In the Eucharist, Jesus calls us to love and serve one another. We are called to follow the example of Jesus and to serve with love. The Christian community serves the needs of all.

CHAPTER 19
Jesus rose from death to new life. He promises that those who eat the bread of life will live with him forever. The Eucharist is a sacrament of new life.

CHAPTER 20
The Eucharist is the sacrament of the presence of Jesus. Jesus is present in the world, in other people, in the word of God, and in the Eucharist. We celebrate the presence of Jesus in our lives.

Note:
As you prepare this unit and the remaining units, you might wish to refer to the reference section, *Our Catholic Heritage,* beginning on page 327.

Additional resources for Unit 1 include a Unit Test and a Family Letter as well as a video and selections from THIS IS OUR FAITH Music Program. You might also find it helpful to preview *Saints and Other Holy People* and *Prayer Celebrations* for possibilities to enhance the unit.

Introducing the UNIT

Direct the children's attention to the photograph on page 211. Ask the children to tell what is happening in the picture. Read aloud the unit-focus question. Give each child an opportunity to respond. When they have finished, read with them the Unit 5 title. Help the children understand that in this unit, they will discover how Jesus continues to be with his friends and followers.

New Words

unity
serve
resurrection
Emmaus

The Eucharist Unites Us

Objectives

To help the children

- Recognize experiences of working together in peace.
- Share in Jesus' prayer for unity.
- Recognize The Lord's Prayer and the Sign of Peace as prayers of peace.
- Celebrate peace and unity in the world, in the parish, and in the family.
- Pray for peace in their lives and review the chapter.

Chapter Outline

	Step 1 **Learning About Our Lives**	Step 2 **Learning About Our Faith**	Step 3 **Learning How to Live Our Faith**
Day 1	■ Introduce the chapter. ■ Read the story. ■ Study an illustration. *ABOUT 10 MINUTES*	■ Discuss working together in peace. ■ Present the doctrine. ■ Define the new word. *ABOUT 10 MINUTES*	■ Draw together. ■ Pray together. *ABOUT 10 MINUTES*
Day 2	■ Introduce the lesson. *ABOUT 5 MINUTES*	■ Read and discuss the story. *ABOUT 10 MINUTES*	■ Complete an activity. ■ Pray together. ■ Make suggestions for unity. *ABOUT 15 MINUTES*
Day 3	■ Role-play a family scenario. *ABOUT 5 MINUTES*	■ Read and discuss The Lord's Prayer. ■ Pray the Prayer of Jesus. ■ Learn about the Sign of Peace. *ABOUT 15 MINUTES*	■ Complete an activity. ■ Pray together. *ABOUT 10 MINUTES*
Day 4	■ Complete an activity. *ABOUT 10 MINUTES*	■ Read the story. *ABOUT 10 MINUTES*	■ Complete an activity. ■ Pray together. *ABOUT 10 MINUTES*

Day 5   **Prayer**   Prepare to dance a prayer and pray with dance.
              Review   Review the chapter and explain the Scripture verse.

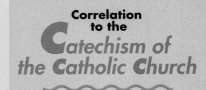

Correlation
to the
**Catechism of
the Catholic Church**
Paragraphs
1325, 1396, 1416

Plan Ahead ～～～～～～～

	Preparing Your Class	**Materials Needed**
Day 1	Read over the lesson. Assemble samples of class work. Prepare materials for drawings. If enriching the lesson, gather materials for weaving project.	■ samples of class work ■ basket, candle ■ drawing paper ■ felt-tip markers in different colors
Day 2	Read over the lesson. Make or locate a jigsaw puzzle.	■ jigsaw puzzle ■ candle ■ paper slips ■ pencils
Day 3	Read over the lesson. Create scenarios for role-playing. Select musical setting of The Lord's Prayer.	■ music for The Lord's Prayer ■ pencils
Day 4	Read over the lesson. Prepare slips of student names. Prepare prayer table. Practice new lyrics to "Peace Is Flowing Like a River."	■ pencils ■ name slips
Day 5	Read over the lesson prior to the lesson. Practice steps for dance of peace.	■ recording of "Prayer for Peace" ■ pencils

Additional Resources

As you plan this chapter, consider using the following materials from The Resourceful Teacher Package.

■ *Classroom Activity Sheets 17* and *17a*

■ *Family Activity Sheets 17* and *17a*

■ *Chapter 17 Test*

■ *Prayers for Every Day*

■ *Projects: Grade 2*

You may also wish to refer to the following Big Books.

■ *We Celebrate the Mass,* pages 17–18

■ *We Celebrate the Sacraments,* pages 7–9

In preparing the children for the Sunday readings, you may wish to use Silver Burdett Ginn's *Getting Ready for Sunday* student and teacher materials.

BOOKS FOR THE JOURNEY

Abuela's Weave. Omar S. Castaneda. Lee & Low Books, 1993. A story of a child and her grandmother who together weave their goods and sell them at the market.

The Mountain That Loved a Bird. Alice McLerran. Picture Book Studio, 1991. The story of a bird and a mountain that promised to reunite every year.

MORE BOOKS FOR THE JOURNEY

The Patchwork Quilt. Valerie Flournoy. E. P. Dutton, 1985. A story about a quilt that is begun by one member and finished with the help of others in the family.

Praise for the Singing. "We Shall Overcome," pp. 28–29. Collected by Madelaine Gill. Little, Brown, and Co., 1993. A song in which union is necessary for overcoming wrong.

REDUCED CLASSROOM ACTIVITIES

Name _____

The Eucharist Unites Us

Cut out the puzzle pieces. Ask a friend to help you put the puzzle together. Read the message from Jesus.

To the Teacher: This activity will make the message of working together peacefully a concrete experience.

Chapter 17   The Eucharist Unites Us   THIS IS OUR FAITH 2   **17**

Name _____

Be at Peace!

Put an **X** by the pictures that show people at peace with each other. Talk with your classmates about how the people are making peace.

To the Teacher: This activity illustrates a variety of ways the students can model peace.

17a   THIS IS OUR FAITH 2   Chapter 17   The Eucharist Unites Us

A SACRAMENT OF UNITY

The sacrament of the Eucharist calls us to unity. We are united as we listen to the word of God. We unite in offering our prayers, songs, and gifts in community. We receive Jesus in the Eucharist, making us one with him, the Father, and the Spirit. Together we go forth to share our gifts and faith with others. The Eucharist symbolizes and renews the unity that Jesus prayed for at the Last Supper.

As we begin the Communion Rite, we pray The Lord's Prayer. This prayer summarizes our relationship (covenant) of unity with God and with the community of believers (see *Catechism of the Catholic Church,* #2787, 2790). We call God *Abba* ("Daddy") and look to forgive and be forgiven as family. We ask for our daily needs and pray to be free of temptation. We express our hope that the kingdom of God will come. Whenever we pray this prayer taught by Jesus, we model his relationship with the Father and with others (see *Catechism of the Catholic Church,* #2701).

A Christian relationship with others is one of peace. Achieving peace is an ongoing effort. Because some persons may be in conflict with one another, the priest prays that the peace of the Lord may be with us. We are invited to turn to one another and extend a sign of peace, a gesture of peace and unity. This ritual symbolizes our efforts in the daily struggle for unity and harmony as we live and work together.

EXPERIENCING UNITY AND PEACE

Children at this age have had many opportunities to observe and experience unity and disunity in their daily lives. They have enjoyed being with others at home, in school, and at play. They have also suffered the pain of division, fighting, and hostility. They recognize that arguments between family members tend to upset the entire family. They are also aware that when family members are cooperating and working well together, the family is happy and at peace. These experiences can help the children appreciate that the Eucharist is a sacrament of unity and peace.

In this chapter, the children will consider opportunities in their lives to work together in peace. The Lord's Prayer will be reviewed as a prayer that calls us to unity through forgiveness of others and a hope for the kingdom of God to come. They will have the opportunity to practice the ritual for extending a sign of peace. As a teacher, you might want to spotlight each child's efforts to bring about peace and unity in the classroom. You may take the opportunity to encourage others to reach out to those who are hurting or who are alone. This chapter is an appropriate time to learn how to solve problems peacefully and to develop skills that contribute to unity.

Objective

This lesson helps the children experience working together in peace.

Step 1 / INTRODUCTION

Learning About Our Lives

Introducing the Chapter

On the discovery table, assemble samples of class work that show evidence of working together (a group chart, a thank-you card with notes from each student, an art or science project). Ask:

- Who can tell me about this project or object?
- Who worked on it?
- Can you name some other projects that you worked on together?

Invite a volunteer to read aloud the chapter-focus sentence on page 212. Encourage the children to tell about as many projects as they can recall. Then ask: What would have happened to your project if everyone did not help? (*The project would not have been done as well or have had as much variety.*) Help the children appreciate that a project can be better if the talents of many people are used to make it.

Reading the Story

Read aloud the first paragraph of the story "A Class Project" on page 212. Invite the children to guess what Mr. Jackson's project might be. Invite volunteers to read the other paragraphs.

Studying an Illustration

Direct the children's attention to the illustration of the finished quilt on page 213. Ask them to name the objects on the patches. Emphasize that each child contributed to the quilt's beauty and the project's success.

or . . .

Assemble the materials to make a felt and paper quilt. Distribute 6" × 6" squares of polyester blend craft felt pieces in three colors (primary colors or complementary colors). Encourage the children to draw and cut simple

212

17

The Eucharist Unites Us

A Class Project

One day, Mr. Jackson carried a large box into the second-grade classroom. He put the box on his desk and began to pull out small pieces of cloth. He told the class, "This week we are going to work together on a class art project."

Mr. Jackson explained what they were going to do. "I'm going to give each of you a large cloth patch," he said. "I'm also going to give you scissors, glue, and some smaller pieces of cloth. Each of you can cut out a shape. Then I'll help you glue it on the large patch. When you have finished your patches, we will sew them together to make one big quilt."

The children worked on their patches for two days. Then it was time to work together to form all the patches into a quilt. The children worked together peacefully and helped one another.

Tell about a project you worked on with other people.

★ Enriching the Lesson ★

To weave a banner with crepe paper and ribbon or yarn, tie vertical strips of yarn or ribbon about an inch apart on an old wooden picture frame. Help the children weave colored strips of crepe paper horizontally through the vertical ribbons. Complete the project by stapling the edges of the crepe-paper strips to the back of the frame. Ask the children to name their weaving and decide where to hang it in the classroom. Stress that working together in peace produced a beautiful class project.

🍎 Teaching Tips

Remind the children that working together may be difficult. When a conflict arises, designate a special place in the classroom where the conflict may be resolved peacefully. Use the following simplified conflict-resolution process.

1. Name the disagreement.
2. Listen to both sides.
3. Look at solutions.
4. Decide together what to do.

When the quilt was finished, Mr. Jackson hung it on the classroom wall.

"What a beautiful quilt we've made," Mr. Jackson said. "Because we worked together, all the individual patches now form one special quilt."

We Can Work Together

To make the quilt, everyone in Mr. Jackson's second grade class had to work together peacefully. Each person helped make the project special.

Jesus wants us to work together and live together in peace. This is not always easy. Jesus gives himself to us in the Eucharist to help us live together in peace and **unity**.

We Believe

The Eucharist is a sacrament of peace and unity. In this sacrament, Jesus helps us to become friends with all people and to be united in peace and love.

New Word

* **unity**   joined together in peace

Doctrine   213

Teaching Tips

Help the children see the value of working together, even though it may take time and effort. After the children have completed the Step 3 drawing activity, have them evaluate themselves on how well they worked together and the benefit of sharing their markers with other groups. Invite the children to bring their drawings to a sharing circle. Ask the groups to show and tell about the group's drawings. Compliment the children on the beauty and message that the drawings portray.

Cultural Awareness

Individuals are unique and may have values, attitudes, ideas, and emotional needs that may be different from our own. Yet we all have in common basic human needs. Having a healthy respect for people's differences fosters appreciation for all cultures in our society. Two stories from different cultures that would highlight our differences and commonalities are *Mufara's Beautiful Daughters*, John Steptoe, Lothrop, Lee, and Shepard, 1987; and *The Legend of Bluebonnet*, Tomie dePaola, Scholastic, 1983.

---

designs from colored construction paper—use colors that will contrast with the colors of the felt squares. Glue the paper designs to the felt squares. Instruct each child to print his or her name on the paper design. Invite the children to assemble their completed squares on a table. Glue or sew the felt squares together. Emphasize that the cooperation of each child was needed to complete the quilt.

Step 2 / DEVELOPMENT

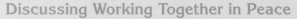

Learning About Our Faith

Discussing Working Together in Peace

Invite a volunteer to read "We Can Work Together" on page 213. Ask: What does it mean to live in peace and unity with others? (*To get along, to play fairly, to do things together*)

Presenting the Doctrine

Present the We Believe statements. Ask the children to read them aloud. Then ask the children to express in their own words how the Eucharist helps them work together in peace.

Defining the New Word

Draw the children's attention to the New Word box. Ask a volunteer to read the word *unity* and its definition. Then have the children repeat the word and definition together with you.

Step 3 / CONCLUSION

Learning How to Live Our Faith

Drawing Together

Form groups of four children. Distribute a large sheet of drawing paper to each group. Instruct the children to draw a school-day activity that shows children working or playing together in peace. Distribute to each group four felt-tip markers in four different colors. Encourage each child to share his or her marker with the other three children in the group and with other groups.

Praying Together

Invite the children to offer their drawings by placing them in a large basket on the prayer table. As each picture is presented, say, "We offer this experience of drawing together." Instruct the children to respond, "Jesus unites us in peace and love."

213

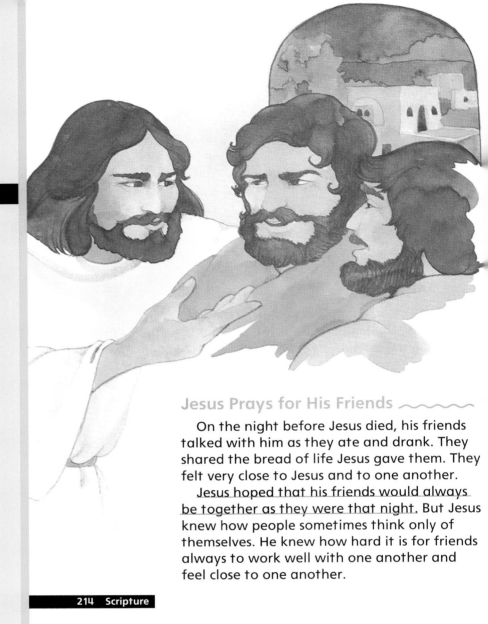

DAY 2
SCRIPTURE

Objective

This lesson helps the children pray with Jesus for unity.

Step 1 / INTRODUCTION

Learning About Our Lives

Introducing the Lesson

Locate or make a simple jigsaw puzzle. Distribute one or two pieces of the puzzle to each child. Invite the children to the discovery table to assemble the puzzle. Encourage them to work together to complete it. Review the benefits of working together peacefully. Tell the children that Jesus knew that it would be important for his disciples to work together in peace, so he prayed that they would be united in peace and love.

or...

Invite the children to think of times when people gathered to do something together. (*Affirm all answers.*) Review the word *unity*—joined together in peace. Ask: What do we do together that shows our unity as a class? (*We learn together, we pray together, we play at recess together.*) When we do things together without arguing or holding back, we are united in peace and love.

Step 2 / DEVELOPMENT

Learning About Our Faith

Reading and Discussing the Story

Ask for volunteers to read the story "Jesus Prays for His Friends" on pages 214–215. Then discuss the story's meaning, using the following questions.

- What did Jesus and his friends do on the night before he died? (*They shared a special meal.*)

- How did the friends of Jesus feel? (*Very close to Jesus*)

- What did Jesus hope? (*That his friends would always be together*)

- What did Jesus pray for his friends? (*That they would be united in peace and love*)

214

Jesus Prays for His Friends

On the night before Jesus died, his friends talked with him as they ate and drank. They shared the bread of life Jesus gave them. They felt very close to Jesus and to one another.

Jesus hoped that his friends would always be together as they were that night. But Jesus knew how people sometimes think only of themselves. He knew how hard it is for friends always to work well with one another and feel close to one another.

214   Scripture

Cultural Awareness

Ask the children if they think Jesus' friends all looked alike or if they all liked to do the same things. Help them understand that Jesus' followers were all unique, with different looks, interests, jobs, and friends. Explain that although they were all different, they were one because of their love for Jesus. Emphasize that we, too, although different are one in Jesus.

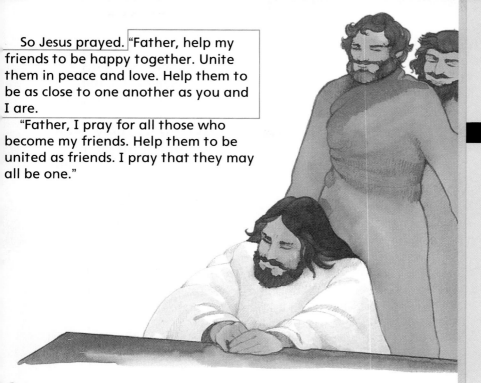

So Jesus prayed. "Father, help my friends to be happy together. Unite them in peace and love. Help them to be as close to one another as you and I are.

"Father, I pray for all those who become my friends. Help them to be united as friends. I pray that they may all be one."

Activity

1. Underline the sentence that tells what Jesus hoped for his friends.

2. Draw a box around the prayer Jesus prayed for his friends.

3. Write a short prayer for your friends. Use the lines below.

_____

- -

_____

_____

- -

_____

Scripture 215

Focus on

Building Self-Esteem Invite the children to form an affirmation circle when their names are called one by one. Invite each child to share one thing he or she likes about himself or herself. The class will assist by naming things they like about this child. For example, "Anna, come join our circle. What do you like about yourself?" (I'm the tallest girl in the class.) "Class, name one thing we like about Anna." (Her smile, she's a good rope jumper, she reads well.) Continue until all are called to the circle.

- What did Jesus pray for those who would become his friends? (*That they would be united as friends*)

Step 3 / CONCLUSION

Learning How to Live Our Faith

Completing an Activity

Read aloud the directions for the three-step activity on page 215. Assist the children in composing their own prayers on the lines provided. Remind them to begin by addressing God or Jesus and to close the prayer with *Amen*. Circulate in the classroom to assist with composition and spelling.

Praying Together

Gather the children at the prayer table with their books. Light the candle and say, "Jesus is our Light. Jesus shows us how to live and to pray for one another." Invite volunteers to read the prayers they have composed for their friends.

Making Suggestions for Unity

When all prayers are read, invite the children to close their eyes to think about how they, as followers of Jesus, can contribute to unity among classmates and family members. Ask volunteers to share their suggestions. Distribute small slips of colored paper and pencils. Invite each child to write what he or she would do to promote unity at school or at home. Collect these slips and attach them to the quilt or banner, if one was made, as suggested in the previous lesson.

DAY 3
DOCTRINE

Objective

This lesson helps the children recognize The Lord's Prayer and the Sign of Peace as prayers of peace at Mass.

Step 1 / INTRODUCTION

Learning About Our Lives

Role-playing a Family Scenario

Present the following scenario: Bobby has forgotten to take out the garbage. Amanda did not put away the clean dishes. When their mother came home from work, she was upset. Ask the class to guess what the mother might say. Then ask: What can Bobby and Amanda do to bring peace back into the home? Invite volunteers to role-play the situation. Stress that besides doing the neglected chores, the children should extend to their mother some gesture of peace. Have volunteers repeat the role-playing with alternate suggestions for gestures of peace.

Step 2 / DEVELOPMENT

Learning About Our Faith

Praying the Prayer of Jesus

Read aloud the introductory paragraph of "The Prayer of Jesus" on page 216. Teach the children to pray The Lord's Prayer. Invite the children to repeat as you say each line of the prayer. Then say The Lord's Prayer together in its entirety.

Reading and Discussing The Lord's Prayer

Invite a volunteer to read "Together in Peace." Discuss the following questions.

■ How do we show our unity at Mass? (*By singing and praying together; standing, kneeling, and sitting together; praying The Lord's Prayer*)

■ What is another name for The Lord's Prayer? (*The Our Father*)

216

The Prayer of Jesus

Jesus' first friends and followers knew that Jesus often prayed to God, our Father. They noticed, too, that Jesus prayed in a very special way. He called God "Abba." In the language Jesus spoke, Abba means "Daddy." They asked Jesus to teach them to pray. Jesus taught them the prayer that we now call The Lord's Prayer. All Christians pray the prayer that Jesus taught.

The Lord's Prayer

Our Father, who art in heaven,
  hallowed be thy name;
thy kingdom come;
thy will be done on earth
  as it is in heaven.
Give us this day our daily bread;
and forgive us our trespasses
  as we forgive those
  who trespass against us;
and lead us not into temptation,
  but deliver us from evil.
Amen.

Together in Peace

Jesus asks all who receive the Eucharist to live together in unity and peace.

At Mass we show our unity by singing and praying together and by standing, sitting, and kneeling together. Before we receive the Eucharist, we show our unity by praying the prayer that Jesus taught us.

216   Doctrine

CURRICULUM CONNECTION

Music   You might want to use the African American spiritual "Peace like a River" to reinforce the concepts of peace, joy, and love. The music is found in Silver Burdett Ginn's THE MUSIC CONNECTION, Book 3, page 56. Use the recording (CD 2-29) to help you teach the song.

After we pray The Lord's Prayer at Mass, we pray:

Priest: The peace of the Lord be with you always.
All: And also with you.
Priest: Let us offer each other a sign of peace.

Then we reach out to those around us, shake their hands, kiss or hug them, and wish them peace.

Activity

Tell how you wish peace to others at Mass.

_____

_____

_____

Focus on

The Lord's Prayer Tell the children that when the priest raises up his hands as he leads us in praying together The Lord's Prayer at Mass, we are reminded to open our hearts to God and to each other. When praying The Lord's Prayer—the prayer that Jesus taught us to pray—we may wish to raise up our hands as does the priest, join hands with those near us, or we may fold them in prayer.

Explain the meaning of the prayer. Help the children understand that *Our daily bread* refers to all our needs; the word *trespass* means any wrong that we do to others; we ask God to forgive us in the same way that we forgive others; we ask God to help us avoid temptation and keep us free and safe from harm, from sin. Explain that *temptation* is not a sin, but is a desire or thought to do what we know is wrong.

Learning About the Sign of Peace

Continue by reading aloud the text on page 217 about the Sign of Peace at Mass. Practice the response with the children. Then role-play the giving of a sign of peace.

Step 3 / CONCLUSION

Learning How to Live Our Faith ✦

Completing an Activity

Ask the children to describe on the lines provided how they wish peace to others at Mass.

Praying Together

Invite the children to the prayer table. Remind them that Jesus taught us to ask God for all that we need. Invite the children to name persons for whom they wish to pray and anyone or anything for which they are thankful. Then join hands and sing together a familiar musical setting of The Lord's Prayer. You might want to consider using the plainchant setting in the Sacramentary; "The Our Father" by Carey Landry in *Young People's Glory and Praise*; "The Lord's Prayer" from *Mass of Creation* by Marty Haugen, found in *Gather*; or "Our Father" by Juliana Garza, S.P., found in *Communion Muse*, Oregon Catholic Press.

Objective

This lesson helps the children understand that Jesus calls everyone to be a peacemaker.

Step 1 / INTRODUCTION

Learning About Our Lives

Completing an Activity

Discuss with the children their ideas of peace. Then ask them to draw in the space provided on page 218 what they think peace looks like.

or . . .

Invite the children to assemble around the discovery table. Display the Bible, an invitation to a wedding or an anniversary party, a parish bulletin, and a picture of Pope John Paul II. Invite the children to give their ideas about how each item is related to peace.

Step 2 / DEVELOPMENT

Learning About Our Faith

Reading About Uniting Our World in Peace

Explain to the children that as Catholics, we celebrate peace every time we gather together for Eucharist. Tell the children that when the pope arrives in any country, he brings with him the message of peace that the Church teaches throughout the world.

Invite a volunteer to read aloud the first paragraph of "Uniting Our World in Peace" on page 218. Ask:

■ Who traveled to different countries of the world spreading the message of peace? (*Pope John Paul II*)

■ Who calls us to be peacemakers? (*Jesus*)

Invite another volunteer to read aloud the paragraph at the top of page 219. Discuss by asking:

■ With whom did the pope celebrate Mass? (*With young people*)

ctivity
What does peace look like to you? Draw it here.

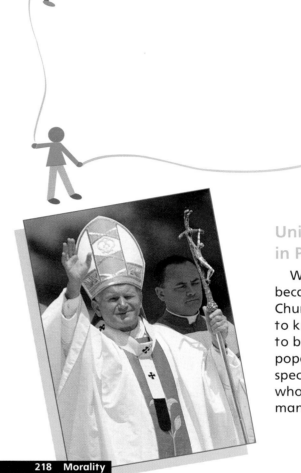

218 Morality

Uniting Our World in Peace

When Pope John Paul II became head of the Catholic Church, he wanted everyone to know that Jesus calls us to be peacemakers. The pope decided to take that special message to the whole world by visiting as many countries as he could.

Enriching the Lesson

Provide mission magazines or calendars for the class to cut out pictures of children from different places in the world. Distribute glue and felt-tip markers. Ask the children to draw a picture of a parish community celebrating or praying. Invite the children to glue the cut-out pictures to their drawings in a collage. Encourage the children to share their drawings. Affirm all the different world peoples celebrating their unity as Catholics.

Focus on

Peace   Peacemaking includes finding peace within ourselves, making peace with others, and working for peace in our world. We can foster inner peace by replacing selfish thoughts with generous, caring thoughts. Skills for making peace with others include learning to use words rather than fists to settle disagreements and by sharing our possessions. We must learn to care for the world, appreciate people from different cultures, and seek cooperative, nonviolent solutions to problems.

On one of his trips to the United States, the pope met with thousands of young people. The young people were from all over the world. The pope celebrated Mass with them. He asked them to be followers of Jesus. He asked them to take peace and unity back to their families and parishes.

Activity

Put a ✔ in front of some ways you might choose to bring peace and unity to your home, neighborhood, and school.

_____ Cooperate in school

_____ Do my chores without being reminded

_____ Let others have their way sometimes

_____ Play fairly on my sports team

_____ Respect my brothers' and sisters' things

_____ Pray for people who make me angry

_____ Not fight with my friends or family

- Where were they from? (*From all over the world*)
- What did he ask them to do? (*To be followers of Jesus and to take back peace and unity to their families and parishes*)

Step 3 / CONCLUSION

Learning How to Live Our Faith

Completing an Activity

Read aloud with the children the choices for bringing peace and unity to their world. Then have the children complete the activity independently. When all have finished, have the children share their choices with the class.

Praying Together

Gather the children to the prayer table. Review aloud Jesus' prayer for unity and peace for his friends on page 215. Pass the name of a classmate on a folded slip of paper to each child. Be sure no one receives his or her own name. Invite the children to pray quietly that the person whose name appears on the slip of paper will be at peace and will experience peace in his or her family. Pass a basket to collect the names. Place the basket on the prayer table. Conclude by teaching the children to sing the following lyrics to the melody of "Peace Is Flowing Like a River" by Carey Landry: *Peace I pray for you, my sister. Peace I pray for you, my brother. Peace I pray for you, my special friend. Peace I pray for everyone.*

★ Enriching the Lesson ★

Place a large kettle on the table. Put on an apron. Tell the children you are going to make "peace soup." Ask: What are the ingredients for peace soup? As each child mentions an ingredient (such as love, unity, fairness, and so on), invite the child to print that ingredient on a sheet of paper and put the sheet of paper into the kettle. Distribute recipe cards. Invite the children to write their own recipes for making peace soup.

Focus on

Building Self-Esteem Select a peacemaker for the week. Place that child's photograph along with photographs of the child's family on a special bulletin board. Invite the children to print on 3" × 5" cards the ways the child showed that he or she is a peacemaker. Add the cards to the bulletin board.

Objective

This lesson helps the children pray by dancing a dance of peace.

Preparing to Dance a Prayer

Tell the children that they will pray today by dancing a dance of peace based on a Navaho Indian prayer. Move the classroom desks to clear a space for dancing. Teach the dance movements for the simple peace dance. Instruct the children to form a circle and join hands. (Imitate the dance movements as given in each photograph in the student text. Directions for the dance movements follow each sentence of the prayer below.)

Peace before us. (All move to the center of the circle, hands joined.)

Peace behind us. (Move back to original position.)

Peace under our feet. (With hands still joined, lift the right foot and then the left foot.)

Peace within us. (Walk in a circle slowly to the left.)

Peace over us. (Walk in a circle to the right, slowly raising joined hands.)

Let all around us be peace. (Drop hands, turn in individual circles in place, join hands again.)

Practice the dance movements before dancing the prayer to the music of "Prayer for Peace" by David Haas, found in *Gather*, GIA Publications, 1987.

Praying with Dance

Play the recording of the music and begin the prayer experience by dancing the dance of peace. Repeat the dance three times.

Praying with Dance

Teacher: Let us pray today by dancing a dance of peace.

Peace before us.
Peace behind us.

Peace under our feet.
Peace within us.

Peace over us.
Let all around us be peace.

220 Prayer

★ ★ ★ Enriching the Lesson ★

Divide the class into groups of three or four. Give each group a large sheet of drawing paper and crayons or felt-tip markers. Have each group make a sign that expresses the chapter's theme. Then have the children use their books to find a slogan for their signs, for example, "The Eucharist Makes Us One" or "The Eucharist Unites Us." Help the children decorate their signs. Afterward, arrange to display the signs in the back of the church.

Cultural Awareness

Native Americans have several customs associated with peace-making. Powwows are held to unite Indian nations for special occasions—honoring the living, remembering the dead, celebrating adulthood, renewing friendships, and celebrating peace. Dances, songs, speeches, games, gift-giving, and pipe-smoking are included in a powwow. Smoking the peace pipe is believed to have power to unite people in friendship. In the past, tomahawks were buried as part of the ceremony.

Chapter Review

Put a **T** by each sentence below that is true.

___T___ Jesus prayed that his friends would be happy and always united.

_____ Jesus does not want us to work together in peace and love.

___T___ In the Eucharist, Jesus helps us to be united and to work in peace.

_____ We should not pray for our friends.

1. What did Jesus pray for on the night before he died?

that all his friends

would be one

2. What word means "joined together in peace"?

unity

3. Talk about what we can do as friends and followers of Jesus that shows we care about other people and are ready to be peacemakers.

All who eat the bread of life are one.
Based on
1 Corinthians 10:17

Review   221

Focus on

The Peacemaker Some people have been gifted with the ability to listen well and bring about peace. Among the Inuits in Alaska, the oldest hunter in a tribe was often called upon to settle conflicts. Invite the class to focus on people who are good listeners and peacemakers. Present them with a "Blessed Are the Peacemakers" award.

Recalling What Jesus Wants

Call attention to the true-false exercise on page 221. Read aloud the directions. Then ask a volunteer to read aloud each statement and have the children mark it accordingly. Afterward, share answers.

Reviewing the Chapter

Direct the children's attention to the three-part review. Have a volunteer read the first two questions aloud. Then give the children time to write their answers on the lines provided. Afterward, check answers. Conclude the review by reading aloud and discussing the third item. Be supportive of each child who participates in the discussion.

Reading the Scripture Verse

Ask the children to read the Scripture verse based on Corinthians 10:17 at the bottom of page 221. Remind the children that we are united because we share the Eucharist. Encourage the children to memorize the verse.

The Eucharist Calls Us to Serve

Objectives

To help the children

■ Name ways in which they can serve others.

■ Recognize that at Mass they are sent forth to serve the Lord.

■ Learn that Jesus gave us an example of service.

■ Learn about a contemporary couple who serves others.

■ Pray so as to learn how to serve Jesus, and review the chapter.

Chapter Outline

| | Step 1
Learning About Our Lives | Step 2
Learning About Our Faith | Step 3
Learning How to Live Our Faith |
|---|---|---|---|
| **Day 1** | ■ Introduce the chapter.
■ Study the photographs.
ABOUT 5 MINUTES | ■ Discover how to help.
■ Introduce the new word.
■ Make a ways-to-serve chart.
■ Present the doctrine.
ABOUT 15 MINUTES | ■ Discuss how we can serve.
■ Complete an activity.
■ Pray together.
ABOUT 10 MINUTES |
| **Day 2** | ■ Listen to a guest speaker.
■ Complete an activity.
ABOUT 10 MINUTES | ■ Discuss the photograph.
■ Explain the responses.
ABOUT 10 MINUTES | ■ Complete a prayer activity.
■ Pray together.
ABOUT 10 MINUTES |
| **Day 3** | ■ Recognize symbols of service.
■ Make a symbol of service.
ABOUT 5 MINUTES | ■ Read and discuss the story.
ABOUT 15 MINUTES | ■ Complete an activity.
■ Make action prayer beads.
ABOUT 10 MINUTES |
| **Day 4** | ■ Meet a search and rescue team.
ABOUT 5 MINUTES | ■ Read about search and rescue.
ABOUT 10 MINUTES | ■ Complete an activity.
■ Pray together.
ABOUT 15 MINUTES |
| **Day 5** | **Prayer** Prepare for prayer and pray about serving Jesus.
Review Review the chapter orally; review ways to serve others; complete the chapter review and read the Scripture verse. | | |

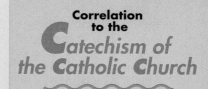

Plan Ahead

	Preparing Your Class	Materials Needed
Day 1	Read over the lesson. Prepare a ways-to-serve chart. Prepare prayer table. Invite speaker for next session. If enriching the lesson, select newspaper/magazine pictures.	■ pencils ■ Ways-to-Serve chart ■ felt-tip markers ■ candle
Day 2	Read over the lesson prior to the session. Prepare prayer table. Prepare for speaker. If enriching the lesson, arrange to visit a collection site.	■ Ways-to-Serve chart ■ candle ■ pencils
Day 3	Read over the lesson prior to the session. Gather and assemble symbols of service. Make apron-shaped badges. Collect beads and shoelaces for action prayer beads.	■ apron-shaped badges ■ dusting spray, apron, bowl, and towel ■ felt-tip markers ■ shoelaces, beads
Day 4	Read over the lesson prior to the session. Bring collection basket. Prepare prayer table. Practice song "We Come to Share."	■ collection basket from church ■ recording and music for "We Come to Share"
Day 5	Read over the lesson prior to the session. Prepare items for prayer. Practice song "We Come to Share." If enriching the lesson, gather materials for certificates.	■ candle ■ pencils ■ recording and music for "We Come to Share"

Additional Resources

As you plan this chapter, consider using the following materials from The Resourceful Teacher Package.

■ *Classroom Activity Sheets 18* and *18a*

■ *Family Activity Sheets 18* and *18a*

■ *Chapter 18 Test*

■ *Prayers for Every Day*

■ *Projects: Grade 2*

You may also wish to refer to the following Big Books.

■ *We Celebrate God's Word,* pages 16 and 17

■ *We Celebrate the Mass,* page 22

■ *We Celebrate the Sacraments,* pages 7–9

In preparing the children for the Sunday readings, you may wish to use Silver Burdett Ginn's *Getting Ready for Sunday* student and teacher materials.

BOOKS FOR THE JOURNEY

The Beginner's Bible. "Washing Feet," pp. 470–475. As told by Karyn Henley. Questar Publishers, 1989. The story of Jesus washing the feet of his special friends as a way of teaching them to be kind and helpful to each other.

Rechenka's Eggs. Patricia Polacco. Philomel Books, 1988. The kindness of an old woman is richly rewarded.

MORE BOOKS FOR THE JOURNEY

Best Friends. "The Telephone Call," by Jack Prelutsky. Selected by Lee Bennett Hopkins. Harper & Row, 1986. A poem about a telephone call that cheers up a friend.

One Small Blue Bead. Byrd Baylor Schweitzer. Macmillan, 1992. The story of the only person in an entire tribe—a young boy—who shares an old man's belief and is willing to do the old man's work.

REDUCED CLASSROOM ACTIVITIES

Name _____

The Eucharist Calls Us to Serve

Color the picture. Share with your family the story of how Jesus served his friends before he died.

To the Teacher: This activity follows the Scripture story "To Love and Serve."

Chapter 18   The Eucharist Calls Us to Serve   THIS IS OUR FAITH 2   **18**

Name _____

Serve One Another

Think of ways you can serve others at home, at school, or in your neighborhood. Write one way on each line inside the hand.

To the Teacher: In this activity, students demonstrate caring. You may wish to display the completed hands on a bulletin board.

18a   THIS IS OUR FAITH 2   Chapter 18   The Eucharist Calls Us to Serve

CHRIST'S CALL TO SERVE OTHERS

The Eucharist is the sacrament of Christ's total self-giving. We share in the Eucharist and are called to give of ourselves out of love and service toward others. This call is a responsibility we share and an invitation to follow Jesus' example.

Jesus' washing of the disciples' feet at the Last Supper dramatizes the love and service that should characterize those who share the bread of life. Jesus' words after the washing are a clear statement of our responsibility. "I have given you a model to follow, so that as I have done for you, you should also do." (John 13:15). We need only look around us to find opportunities to answer Jesus' instruction. From its beginning the Church has taught that the fruit of Eucharist is love, leading to a life of service to others.

SERVICE IN THE CHRISTIAN COMMUNITY

As Catholics, we are called to serve others, especially those in great need. We need to work together to achieve the common good; that is, meet the conditions necessary for people to be able to enjoy a good life. Three of these essential conditions are respect, social well-being, and peace (see *Catechism of the Catholic Church,* #1906–1909). All service arises from a deep respect and concern for people. We desire to help people better themselves or their situations. Peace results when those who serve and those who receive help are valued by the community. Those who are served may become for the community examples of humility, hospitality, and gratitude. Those who serve are models of generosity, sacrifice, and dedication. Service is the sharing of our gifts as experienced within the eucharistic community.

LEADING LIVES OF SERVICE

The children have experienced receiving service from others. Second graders are able to see and identify the needs of others. With assistance, they can arrive at possible ways in which they can show caring for others. Stories about those who dedicate themselves to helping others may encourage, inspire, and teach the children concrete ways to serve. The children realize how important it is to follow Jesus' example of service. Prayer for others is presented as another way of recognizing need and increasing a desire for service. This chapter stresses the sense of reaching out to others with care and love, prayer, and kind acts.

In this chapter, the children will be encouraged to find opportunities to serve others at home and in school. The desire to serve may be in answer to the invitation at the Eucharist to go forth to love and serve the Lord. We serve the Lord through service to others. Service is distinct from general goodness because it is motivated by the love of God and the example of Jesus. Christian service expects no rewards and is often done in anonymity.

Objective

This lesson helps the children name ways in which they can serve others.

Step 1 / INTRODUCTION

Learning About Our Lives

Introducing the Chapter

Begin the session by reading aloud the chapter title and the chapter-focus sentence on page 222. Invite the children to share their experiences of helping others. List their responses on the chalkboard. Read aloud the list. Reinforce the idea that there are many ways to help. Praise the children for their willingness to serve others.

Studying the Photographs

Read aloud the directions for the activity on page 222. Call attention to the photographs that show how the people are helping in each situation. Assist the children in appreciating that there are many ways in which we can serve other people.

Step 2 / DEVELOPMENT

Learning About Our Faith

Discovering How to Help

Invite a volunteer to read aloud "Jesus Wants Us to Help" on page 223. Now ask: What word did Jesus use for helping others, especially those who are hurting? (_Serve_)

Introducing the New Word

Invite the children to brainstorm words that mean _help_. Write the responses in a column on the chalkboard. Remind the children that Jesus had a special word for helping others: _serve_. Invite the children to look at the New Word box at the bottom of page 223. Ask: What does _serve_ mean? (_To help others and to be kind to them_) Have the children repeat the word _serve_ and its definition aloud after you. Ask: How does Jesus want us to treat other people? (_The way Jesus treated others, by helping and being kind to them._)

222

The Eucharist Calls Us to Serve

Activity

Read the sentences near the pictures. Talk about the different kinds of help we can give to other people.

◄ The children are welcoming a new student. They want him to feel a part of their class.

Devon enjoys spending time with his grandfather. Devon's grandfather likes teaching him how to hit a baseball. ►

◄ Linda, Tracy, and Maria are [helping] each other with a school pr[oject]

Tell a story about something you said or did that helped another person.

★★★★ Enriching the Lesson ★

Before the session, select several pictures from newspapers or magazines that show people helping or serving others. Show these pictures to the children one at a time. Discuss with them why they think the people in the pictures decided to be of help to others. Lead the children to the understanding that people make decisions to help because they believe that they have a responsibility to love and care for others. Emphasize that we, too, can make decisions to help others.

Focus on

Building Self-Esteem Children like to be useful. They need affirmation that their perceptions of the world are correct. Invite the children to describe needs they see. Affirm that these needs are real and should be addressed by caring Christians. Help them brainstorm ways in which children their age can do something about these needs. In their direct ways, children often call attention to what adults could do to help. Involve the families in the ideas for service that are generated in this chapter.

Jesus Wants Us to Help

Jesus wants his friends always to love and **serve** all people. He wants us to treat other people the way he treated them. At Mass we remember that Jesus asked us to serve one another. The Eucharist helps us reach out with love and kindness to other people, especially to those who are in need.

Activity

Think about the different kinds of help you give to others every day. List them here.

_____

_____

_____

Think about the kinds of help others give you every day. List them here.

_____

_____

_____

We Believe

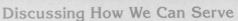

The Eucharist is a sacrament of love and service. Those who share the Bread of Life are asked to care for everyone.

New Word

serve to help others and to be kind to them

Doctrine **223**

Teaching Tips

At first, the children will need affirmation and a response for their acts of service. Your example of quiet, dedicated service and involvement in the community will help the children see the generosity and caring that motivates those who respond to Jesus' call to serve.

Focus on

Caring About Animals To young children, animals are sometimes as important as humans. Take time to discuss with the children the benefits and responsibilities of owning a pet. Because domesticated animals are dependent upon humans, the children can experience direct service in caring for pets at home and in school. Encourage the children to create a bulletin board as a class project featuring photographs or their own drawings of their pets and those who care for them.

Making a Ways-to-Serve Chart

Print the new word *serve* and its meaning in the center of a sheet of posterboard. Invite the children to choose words from the help synonym list on the chalkboard and then write a phrase on the posterboard about how they can serve others.

Presenting the Doctrine

Invite a volunteer to read aloud the We Believe statements at the bottom of page 223. Ask the children to circle the words *Eucharist, love,* and *service* in the first sentence. Explain that because we share in the Eucharist and have received God's blessing, we have a responsibility to serve others.

Step 3 / CONCLUSION

Learning How to Live Our Faith

Discussing How We Can Serve

Direct the children's attention to the photograph on page 223. Ask: How is the child in the photograph serving another? Ask the children to name the ways they can serve in school. (*Distribute papers, do classroom chores, help classmates.*) Ask: What are some ways that you can serve at home? (*Affirm all answers.*) Invite the children to refer to the words on the chalkboard for ideas.

Completing an Activity

Read the directions to the activity on page 223. Ask the children to respond orally to each statement before writing their answers on the lines provided.

Praying Together

Invite the children to the prayer table. Light the candle. Ask: How can you show respect to others? (*Speak politely, listen to others, give them your time and attention.*) Ask the children to close their eyes and pretend that Jesus is sitting next to them. Say, "Tell Jesus about someone whom you did not treat with respect. (Pause) Ask Jesus' forgiveness for not treating this person with respect. (Pause) Tell Jesus how you will treat this person with respect the next time. (Pause) Now tell Jesus how you treated someone with love today. (Pause) Thank Jesus for this time together. (Pause) When you have finished talking with Jesus, open your eyes and sit quietly."

223

DAY 2
DOCTRINE

Objective

This lesson helps the children recognize that at Mass they are sent forth to serve the Lord.

Step 1 / INTRODUCTION

Learning About Our Lives

Listening to a Guest Speaker

Invite an older student to speak to the class about ways in which he or she serves others. Ask the speaker to identify ways in which he or she was inspired to serve by the stories of the caring actions of others.

or . . .

Invite a parent or grandparent to talk to the class about ways in which family members serve others.

Completing an Activity

Direct the children's attention to the illustration on page 224. Discuss how the children and adult are helping each other. Then have the children write an answer to the question on the line provided.

Step 2 / DEVELOPMENT

Learning About Our Faith +

Discussing the Photograph

Read aloud the paragraph "Love and Serve" on page 224. Invite a volunteer to explain what is happening in the photograph on page 224. (*The priest is blessing the people.*) Ask: When does this blessing take place at Mass? (*At the end of Mass*) Have a volunteer read the priest's words of blessing and have the class read the responses. Ask:

- What are we told to do at the end of Mass? (*Go in peace to love and serve the Lord.*)

- How do we love and serve the Lord? (*By loving and serving others*)

- Who remembers what it means to serve? (*To help others and to be kind to them*)

224

Activity

How are these people helping others?

_____

- -

Love and Serve

At the end of Mass, the priest sends us forth with a blessing. He reminds us that what we just celebrated together strengthens us to love and serve God. We do this by helping and caring for all God's people.

Priest: May almighty God bless you, the Father, and the Son, ✠ and the Holy Spirit.

All: Amen.

Priest: Go in peace to love and serve the Lord.

All: Thanks be to God.

224 Doctrine

★ ★★★ ★
★ **Enriching the Lesson** ★

If your parish or school has a collection site, arrange for your class to visit it. Demonstrate the quiet and regular way the parish serves people in need by showing the children the place in the parish church, school, or other parish facility where food or clothing is collected for the needy. Explain to them how the items are distributed to the poor.

🌐 **Cultural Awareness**

Children recognize those who are physically, mentally, or emotionally challenged as people in need. When discussing persons with disabilities, stress that the children must first show respect for the person before showing concern for the disability.

Explain that all people are sensitive and need to be considered as whole people. Encourage the children to serve the physically challenged with the same respect they afford others.

Activity

When we leave Mass, we can begin to love and serve others at home, at school, and in our neighborhoods. Choose a word from the picture to complete the prayer below.

When someone is sad,
Lord Jesus, help me to bring **joy** .

When someone hurts me,
Lord Jesus, help me to **forgive** .

When someone feels lonely,
Lord Jesus, help me to be a **friend** .

When someone fights,
Lord Jesus, help me to bring **peace** .

Doctrine 225

Focus on

Prayer and Service As Christians, we believe in praying for all people. But prayer alone does not excuse us from our responsibility to assist others in need. Prayer with action is the best way to show our care and concern for others. Point out to the children that in the prayer activity in today's lesson, we pray that we may take action to serve others.

Explaining the Responses

Read aloud the words of the priest again. Remind the children to make the sign of the cross as the priest blesses them. Encourage them to respond *Amen* in a strong voice. Explain to the children that *Amen* means "I agree" and saying this response means "I want God's blessing." Explain that *Thanks be to God* means that we are grateful for the special meal we just shared and we agree it's a good thing to love and serve others in peace. Practice the responses several times with the class. Help the children memorize them.

Step 3 / CONCLUSION

Learning How to Live Our Faith

Completing a Prayer Activity

Read aloud the directions on page 225 for completing the activity. Assist the children by reading aloud each phrase of the prayer and allowing sufficient time for the children to look at the picture and then write the correct word to complete the prayer on the lines provided. Invite the children to bring their books with the completed prayer to the prayer table.

Praying Together

Gather the children around the prayer table. Light the prayer candle. Ask a volunteer to bring the Ways-to-Serve chart created in the previous lesson. Read some of the phrases about helping others that the class wrote on the posterboard. Ask the children to raise their hands if they served someone in a similar way today. Now invite the children to read the completed prayer on page 225. Assign the first part of each phrase to a reader. Instruct all the children to respond *Lord Jesus, help me to . . .* All respond *Amen* at the end of the prayer.

DAY 3
SCRIPTURE

Objective
This lesson helps the children learn that Jesus gave us an example of service.

Step 1 / INTRODUCTION

Learning About Our Lives

Recognizing Symbols of Service
Invite the children to the discovery table. Display a can of dusting spray, a work apron or coveralls, a bowl of water, and a towel. Invite the children to tell how these items represent service. Ask: Who uses them? When are they used?

Making a Symbol of Service
Distribute paper apron-shaped badges to each child and one for yourself. Distribute felt-tip markers. Invite the class to print "We are servants of Jesus" on the front of their badges. Ask the children to join you in wearing the badges all day as a symbol of service and as a reminder of being servants of Jesus.

Step 2 / DEVELOPMENT

Learning About Our Faith

Reading and Discussing the Story
Direct the children's attention to the illustration on pages 226–227. Ask them what they think Jesus is doing. Read aloud the story's title and have volunteers read aloud each paragraph of the story. Then use the following questions to discuss the story with the children.

- What did Jesus do during the meal? (*He washed the feet of his friends.*)
- Why was Peter upset? (*He thought he should be washing Jesus' feet.*)
- How did Jesus explain what he was doing? (*He said that he was giving an example of how to serve others.*)

or . . .

Dramatize the story "To Love and Serve" with the group. Instead of washing the children's feet, wash their hands. Then invite the children to share their feelings about this experience.

226

To Love and Serve

It was the night before Jesus died. He and his friends were gathered together to share a very special meal. Jesus had many things to teach his friends that night.

At the meal, Jesus stood up and walked across the room. He picked up a bowl of water and a towel. He carried them back to the table.

Jesus knelt down in front of his friends. He began to wash their feet. When he came to Peter, Peter said, "Jesus, I should be washing your feet. You should not be washing mine."

226   Scripture

Focus on

Washing of Feet   Relate the Scripture story of the washing of the disciples' feet to the liturgical service on Holy Thursday. Ask: How does our parish or school celebrate this event? (*Wash hands; wash feet of a representative group; priest washes feet of adult ministers or teachers.*) Tell the children that since we no longer wash the feet of travelers, we perform similar ritual actions of service by providing refreshments for visitors, washing the hands of small children before meals, and so on.

Cultural Awareness

Saint Lawrence of Brindisi, whose feast is celebrated on July 21, learned eight different languages so that he could help people. A missionary, or one who serves in the missions, must be willing to learn the language and customs of another culture to do God's work. Challenge the children to learn a few words in a language of the people of another culture in your area. Invite a member of that group to teach something interesting and appropriate about the culture.

No one in the room understood why Jesus was doing what servants always did for guests. So when Jesus was finished washing his friends' feet, he explained. "I have given you an example," he said. "You must serve others, as I have served you."

Based on John 13:1–17

Activity

Use the code to find a message from Jesus.

a	e	h	x	o	r	s	t	v	m	p	d
1	2	3	4	5	6	7	8	9	10	11	12

g	i	n	y	f	l
13	14	15	16	17	18

M y   f r i e n d s ,   s e r v e   o n e
10 16   17 6 14 2 15 12 7 ,   7 2 6 9 2   5 15 2

a n o t h e r   i n   l o v e .
1 15 5 8 3 2 6   14 15   18 5 9 2 .

Scripture 227

Teaching Tips

To assist children in becoming aware of the service they do, encourage them to make a list of the usual ways in which they serve. Suggest that they check things on the list or add items to the list. Invite them to keep records for a week of the way they serve. Remind the children that service is not always something that is fun or convenient. It may mean giving up something we would rather do. Service may also mean surprising someone with an act of kindness or helping someone complete a task.

Call attention to the feelings Peter and the other disciples had as Jesus washed their feet. Challenge the children to compare their own feelings to those of the disciples. Help the children understand that Jesus wants us, like Jesus' friends, to follow his example of loving and serving others.

Step 3 / CONCLUSION

Learning How to Live Our Faith

Completing an Activity

Instruct the children to use the numerical code to find the hidden message from Jesus.

Circulate to assist those who are having difficulty. When all have finished, write the message on the chalkboard so that the children may correct their work.

Making Action Prayer Beads

Provide each child with a brightly colored shoelace with a plastic tip on one end. Knot the other end. Display four dishes of plastic beads that may be threaded on the shoelace. Invite the children to think of four simple ways they can serve one another during the school day. (*Say a kind word, help with simple tasks, assist another at recess, respond politely to others, and so on.*) Instruct the children to add a bead each time they serve during the day so as to make action prayer beads.

Objective

This lesson helps the children learn about a contemporary couple who serves others.

Step 1 / INTRODUCTION

Learning About Our Lives

Meeting a Search and Rescue Team

On the discovery table, place a picture of two dogs, an ambulance, and rescue equipment. Explain to the children that these are symbols of the people they will meet in today's lesson. Ask them to guess what these people do to serve others.

Step 2 / DEVELOPMENT

Learning About Our Faith

Reading About Search and Rescue

Invite a volunteer to read aloud the first two paragraphs of the story "Search and Rescue" on page 228. Ask:

- How do Darryl and Peggy serve others? (*They search for and help find people who are missing because of earthquakes or disasters.*)

- Where do they look for trapped or injured people? (*Inside buildings or under bridges*)

- Whom do they help in their search efforts? (*Local police and firefighters*)

Invite two volunteers to finish reading aloud the story on page 229. Continue the discussion by asking the following questions.

- Do Darryl and Peggy do their work alone? (*No*)

- What help do they have? (*Two specially trained search dogs*)

- How do the dogs help? (*They pick up a human scent, and bark or scratch the ground when they find an injured person.*)

- In what special way do Darryl and Peggy serve others? (*They use their time and talents to rescue people all over the world.*)

Search and Rescue

Darryl and Peggy know what it means to serve others. This husband and wife are rescuers—persons who search for and rescue people who are missing because of earthquakes or other disasters.

Darryl and Peggy have been rescuing injured or missing people since they first met each other ten years ago. They have traveled around the world, helping local police officers and firefighters find people who may be trapped or badly injured inside buildings or under bridges.

Darryl and Peggy have two search dogs named Molly and Duffy. The dogs have been specially trained to sniff their way through a fallen building or other dangerous area until they pick up the scent of a child or grown-up who is trapped.

228 Morality

Enriching the Lesson

Call the local food pantry to find out what items are needed. Send a letter home with each child suggesting that the family contribute one item from the list of needed things. Give a collection date and ask adult volunteers to help deliver the food items. Invite the class to decorate the boxes that will be used to collect and deliver the food to the needy.

Focus on

Angels According to Scripture, angels are messengers sent by God to bring good news or to give assistance to us on earth. We believe that our guardian angels watch over us. We can also act like angels by bringing good news to others or assisting them. Brainstorm with the class some special things second graders might do to assist others in school. (Play safely on the playground and keep others from hurt or harm; be a friend to someone who is alone; help find what is missing or lost.)

When Molly and Duffy find an injured person, they let Darryl and Peggy know that someone is trapped by barking and scratching at the ground. Darryl and Peggy then let the rescue people know where to start digging so that the person can be brought to safety.

Darryl and Peggy serve many, many people by using their time and their talents to help others in a very special way. They show us that all Jesus' followers can serve others by using the gifts and talents God has given us.

Activity

Draw a picture of or write about one special way you can serve others by using your gifts and talents.

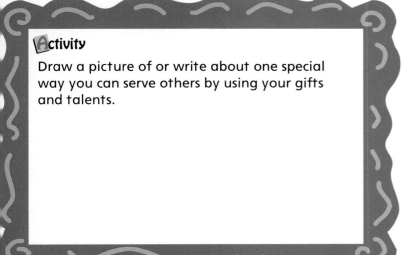

Cultural Awareness

Missionaries generally appreciate any school supplies, paper, photographs for teaching, and so on. With permission from your principal and the assistance of parent helpers, have a cookie sale in school to raise shipping money to send extra school supplies at the end of the year to the missions supported by your diocese. Encourage the children to collect pictures from calendars and used greeting cards that could be used for art projects by children in the missions.

Learning How to Live Our Faith

Completing an Activity

Read aloud the directions for the activity at the bottom of page 229. In the space provided, ask the children to either draw a picture of or write about using their talents to serve others.

Praying Together

Gather the children at the prayer table. Display a collection basket from church. Explain that at Sunday Mass, we pass the basket to collect the money offerings for the parish needs and for the poor. This action reminds us to be aware of the needs of others and to help them.

Read aloud this passage based on Sirach 7:32–33: "To the poor extend your hand that your blessing may be complete; Be generous to all the living and do not withhold your kindness."

Ask: How many of you have a bank in which you save extra coins? Why are you saving? (*To buy something special*) Explain that God asks us to be generous and kind to those who are in need. Ask: Do you remember to put some of your money in the collection basket on Sunday? Suggest that the children offer the price of one special treat each Sunday. Close the prayer with the song "We Come to Share" from THIS IS OUR FAITH Music Program, Grade 2.

PRAYER/REVIEW

Objective

This lesson helps the children pray so as to learn how to serve Jesus.

Preparing for Prayer

Gather the children around the prayer table with their books. Ask the children to open their books to page 230. Assign four readers to read the parts for Child #1, #2, #3, and #4. The rest of the class will read the parts for All.

Praying About Serving Jesus

Light the candle and begin the prayer experience. When the prayer is concluded, have the children sing along with the recording of "We Come to Share" from THIS IS OUR FAITH Music Program, Grade 2.

Praying About Serving Jesus

All: Jesus, how can we serve you?
Child #1: You can serve me by visiting those who are sick or old.

All: Jesus, how can we serve you?
Child #2: You can serve me by giving food to those who are hungry.

All: Jesus, how can we serve you?
Child #3: You can serve me by welcoming people to your home or school.

All: Jesus, how can we serve you?
Child #4: You can serve me by using your gifts and talents to help others.

Teacher: Jesus, help us to see you in all those we serve.
All: Amen.

230 Prayer

★ Enriching the Lesson ★

Invite the children to make service gift certificates. Give each child a half-sheet of construction paper and crayons or felt-tip markers. On the chalkboard write: *Out of love, I will do an act of service for _____.* Instruct the children to copy the message onto their certificates and write the names of the persons they will help. Ask them to sign their names. Help the children decorate the certificates. Invite them to deliver the certificates and complete the act of service promptly.

CURRICULUM CONNECTION

Science Explore ways that the children can show their concern for the earth. Stress the importance of caring for the environment. Receive permission to have the children plant flowers to beautify the school grounds. If there are no places to plant flowers outside, have the children plant window boxes for the classroom. Begin with starter plants, since children like to see their planting efforts progress quickly. Assign chores, such as watering and turning the plants prior to the planting day.

Chapter Review

We can love and serve other people every day.
We can help people wherever we are.
Finish each group of words below by naming
one way you can serve other people.

In school, I can

_____

_____ .

At home, I can

_____

_____ .

1. What word means to help people and to be kind to them?

serve

2. In the gospel story we just read, how did Jesus serve his friends?

washed their feet

3. Talk about those people in your community who give service to other people or who help care for the earth.

Out of love, place yourselves at one another's service.
Galatians 5:13

Focus on

Sharing with the Elderly With the permission and assistance of parents, arrange a spring visit to a nursing home. Prepare a singing and poetry reading program. Have the children make simple door decorations to be shared. Thread yarn or string handles on colored plastic coated cups to make a hanging decoration. Place a small circle of styrofoam in the bottom of each cup. Attach paper flowers to straws and push these into the styrofoam. Print a happy message on the cup.

Reviewing the Chapter Orally

Invite the children to review what they have learned about serving others. Ask the following questions.

- What does *serve* mean? (*To help others and to be kind to them*)
- What is the sacrament of love and service? (*The Eucharist*)
- When are we sent forth to serve the Lord in peace and love? (*When the priest blesses us at the end of Mass and says, "Go in peace to love and serve the Lord."*)
- How did Jesus give us an example of service? (*He washed his disciples' feet.*)
- Who are two people who give of themselves by serving others? (*Darryl and Peggy*)
- How does Jesus want us to treat others? (*As we would like to be treated*)

Reviewing Ways to Serve Others

Read aloud the directions at the top of page 231. Allow sufficient time for the children to write their answers on the lines provided. Have the children share their responses.

Completing the Chapter Review

Take time to go through the review items. Read aloud the first two questions. Have the children write their answers on the lines provided. Check their answers. Then read aloud the third review item. Be supportive of each child who participates in the discussion.

Reading the Scripture Verse

Ask a volunteer to read aloud the Scripture verse at the bottom of page 231. Then ask the children to stand and respond to each invocation with the words *You are our example, Jesus.*

Lord Jesus, you washed your friends' feet. *R.*

Jesus, you call us to serve others. *R.*

You give yourself to us in the Eucharist and ask us to care for others. *R.*

The Eucharist Is a Promise of New Life

Objectives

To help the children

- Recall experiences of life changes and discover Jesus' promise of new life.
- Understand that everything that is alive grows and changes.
- Begin to understand that we will rise to new life and be forever with God.
- Realize that after death there is life with Jesus.
- Celebrate God's presence throughout their lives and review the chapter.

Chapter Outline

	Step 1 Learning About Our Lives	**Step 2** Learning About Our Faith	**Step 3** Learning How to Live Our Faith
Day 1	■ Review Chapter 18. ■ Introduce the chapter. ■ Discuss changes in nature. ■ Complete a drawing. *ABOUT 15 MINUTES*	■ Understand changes in our lives. *ABOUT 5 MINUTES*	■ Complete an activity. ■ Pray together. *ABOUT 10 MINUTES*
Day 2	■ Introduce the chapter. ■ Complete an activity. *ABOUT 10 MINUTES*	■ Discuss growth and change. *ABOUT 10 MINUTES*	■ Complete an activity. ■ Pray together. *ABOUT 10 MINUTES*
Day 3	■ Experience the unexpected. *ABOUT 5 MINUTES*	■ Read a Scripture story. ■ Believe in the resurrection. ■ Present the new word. ■ Present the doctrine. *ABOUT 20 MINUTES*	■ Pray together. *ABOUT 5 MINUTES*
Day 4	■ Remember those who have entered new life. *ABOUT 5 MINUTES*	■ Study an illustration. ■ Read and discuss a story. ■ Celebrate new life. ■ Complete an activity. *ABOUT 20 MINUTES*	■ Pray together with gestures. *ABOUT 5 MINUTES*
Day 5	**Prayer** Prepare for prayer and celebrate the prayer experience. **Review** Fill in sentences; review the chapter and explain the Scripture verse.		

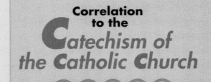

Plan Ahead ~~~~~~~~~~~~~

	Preparing Your Class	**Materials Needed**
Day 1	Read over the lesson prior to the session. Prepare discovery table. Prepare song sheets and get recording for "Garden Song."	■ pencils ■ pictures of a cocoon, butterflies, mother and baby kangaroos ■ seeds and plants ■ music for "Garden Song"
Day 2	Read over the lesson prior to the session. If enriching the lesson, gather materials for making a changing life banner.	■ pencils
Day 3	Read over the lesson prior to the session. Prepare discovery table.	■ small doll, white sheet ■ pencils
Day 4	Read over the lesson prior to the session. Prepare discovery table.	■ pencils ■ candle
Day 5	Read over the lesson prior to the session. Prepare discovery table. Prepare for prayer experience.	■ pencils ■ dead plant ■ blooming plant ■ packets of seeds

Additional Resources

As you plan this chapter, consider using the following materials from The Resourceful Teacher Package.

■ *Classroom Activity Sheets 19* and *19a*

■ *Family Activity Sheets 19* and *19a*

■ *Chapter 19 Test*

■ *Prayers for Every Day*

■ *Projects: Grade 2*

You may also wish to refer to the following Big Books.

■ *We Celebrate God's Word,* page 19

■ *We Celebrate the Mass,* pages 17–18

■ *We Celebrate the Sacraments,* pages 7–9

In preparing the children for the Sunday readings, you may wish to use Silver Burdett Ginn's *Getting Ready for Sunday* student and teacher materials.

BOOKS FOR THE JOURNEY

Grandpa Loved. Josephine Nobesso. Green Tiger Press, 1991. The story of a boy and his grandfather who share a unique relationship that doesn't end with the grandfather's death.

Annie and the Old One. Miska Myiles. Little Brown, 1985. A grandmother uses things in her Indian culture to help her granddaughter appreciate and accept death and its promise of new life.

MORE BOOKS FOR THE JOURNEY

The Beginner's Bible. "Surprise!" pp. 486–490. As told by Karyn Henley. Questar Publishers, 1989. The story of Mary at the tomb meeting Jesus who is no longer dead, but alive.

Sophie and Lou. Petra Mathers. HarperCollins, 1991. A story of a very shy woman who experiences new life because of a dance studio and someone who asks her to dance.

Working Cotton. Sherley Anne Williams. Harcourt, Brace, Jovanovich, 1992. A story of the hardships endured by a migrant family.

REDUCED CLASSROOM ACTIVITIES

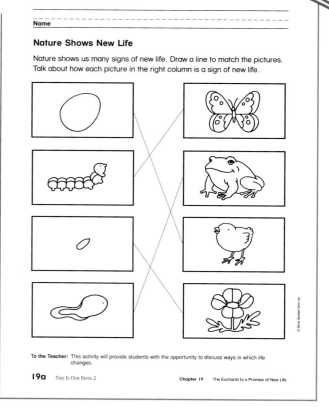

Name _____

The Eucharist Is a Promise of New Life

Choose one of the words from the box to complete each sentence. Then fill in the puzzle.

Easter	Resurrection	Easter candle	new life

Across

1. ___ means rising from death to new life.

Down

2. We celebrate Jesus' Resurrection on ___ Sunday.
3. Jesus rose to ___ ___.
4. The ___ ___ reminds us that we will share new life after we die.

To the Teacher: This activity reviews important concepts from the chapter.

Chapter 19   The Eucharist Is a Promise of New Life   THIS IS OUR FAITH 2   **19**

Name _____

Nature Shows New Life

Nature shows us many signs of new life. Draw a line to match the pictures. Talk about how each picture in the right column is a sign of new life.

To the Teacher: This activity will provide students with the opportunity to discuss ways in which life changes.

19a   THIS IS OUR FAITH 2   Chapter 19   The Eucharist Is a Promise of New Life

Background for the Teacher

THE RESURRECTION IS A HISTORICAL AND A TRANSCENDENT EVENT

The *Catechism of the Catholic Church* explains that "The mystery of Christ's resurrection is a real event, with manifestations that were historically verified, as the New Testament bears witness" (#639). We learn from Paul that Christ died for our sins in accordance with the Scriptures, that he was buried, and that he was raised on the third day. When the women, including Mary of Magdala, arrived at the tomb, the angel said, "Why do you seek the living among the dead? He is not here, but has risen" (Luke 24:5). The empty tomb is a sign of the resurrection of Jesus. Eventually through touch and the sharing of meals, the risen Jesus establishes direct contact with his disciples. He invites them to recognize that he is not a ghost, but now possesses the new properties of a glorious body. Christ has passed from the state of death to another life beyond time and space. One day this new life that Jesus experiences will be imparted to our bodies as well.

THE PROMISE OF NEW LIFE

For Christians, death is not the end but a new beginning. As the *National Catechetical Directory* states: "The Lord's resurrection signals the conquest of death, thus we have reason to live and face death with courage and joy" (#110).

And Christ's words in the Gospel of John likewise promise life after death to all who eat the bread of life. We see the transformation of nature at the change of seasons. We can watch a caterpillar spin a cocoon and then break out of the cocoon as a butterfly. We can bury a seed and then watch in wonder as it blooms into a beautiful plant.

DEATH AND RESURRECTION

Throughout this chapter be sensitive and careful in helping the children understand that death is a part of life. Pointing out the signs of life in the natural world helps children begin to deal with the notion of death and resurrection. The story of Christ's appearing to Mary of Magdala at the empty tomb will also help them. Since the story emphasizes the friendship between Jesus and Mary, the story helps the children identify both with Mary's sadness and also her great joy.

In this chapter, work to help the children develop an attitude of hopefulness and gratitude for the gift of new life. This attitude may be hard for the children to attain, especially if they have experienced great sadness at the loss of a family member or friend. However, the story of Jesus' resurrection and your expressions of hope and faith can reassure them. Throughout the chapter be aware that you are laying the foundation for the children's understanding that death is not an end but the beginning of a new and lasting life with God.

Objective

This lesson helps the children recall experiences of life changes and discover Jesus' promise of new life.

Step 1 / INTRODUCTION

Learning About Our Lives

Reviewing Chapter 18

Begin the session by asking the following review questions.

■ What are some of the ways we have learned to serve others at home and at school? (*Affirm all answers.*)

■ How did Jesus give us an example of service? (*At the Last Supper he washed his friends' feet.*)

■ Name some people you know who serve those in need. (*Answers will vary.*)

Introducing the Chapter

Invite the children to read aloud the chapter title and focus question on page 232. Encourage each child to respond. Remind the children that they first received Jesus' new life at Baptism. Help them appreciate that in addition to the things they may have named, being alive means growing and changing.

Discussing Changes in Nature

Place on the discovery table samples of new life from nature; for instance, pictures of a cocoon, butterflies, a kangaroo in its mother's pouch; seeds, and growing plants. Invite the children to touch and feel the items. Discuss how each of them changes. Then read "The Changing Seasons" on page 232. Discuss what Brian's oak tree should look like in the summer.

Completing a Drawing

Read aloud the directions for the drawing activity on the bottom of page 232. Distribute crayons or felt-tip markers. In the space provided, have the children draw a picture of the tree in summertime. (You might want to have some oak tree pictures or samples of oak tree leaves to help the children visualize the tree.) Afterward, have the children share their drawings.

232

19 The Eucharist Is a Promise of New Life

The Changing Seasons

Brian can see his favorite oak tree from his bedroom window. The leaves turn colors, die, and fall from the trees in the autumn.

What does being alive mean to you?

In the winter, snow covers the bare branches, and squirrels scamper for buried food.

The birds return in the spring and perch on the budding limbs.

Activity
What will Brian see when he looks at his oak tree in the summer? Draw it here.

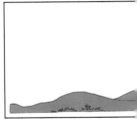

232 Doctrine

 **CURRICULUM CONNECTION**

Science Involve the science teacher in helping your class to create a garden. Plan it now but plant it only when the danger of frost has passed. Be sure to choose flowers that will bloom or vegetables that will be ready before school ends. Celebrate outdoors the new life God has given you and your students. Suggest that the children share some of their bounty with others: the elderly, the homebound, or family members.

 *Focus on*

Life Everlasting The *Catechism of the Catholic Church* states that by death the soul is separated from the body, but in the resurrection God will give incorruptible life to our body, transformed by reunion with our soul. Just as Christ is risen and lives forever, so all of us will rise at the last day. (#1016).

Changes in Our Lives

Life changes every day. After Jesus died, he rose to new life. Someday our lives will change in a very special way. Jesus promises that those who receive him in the Eucharist will share in his life.

Activity

Complete the message from Jesus. Use the words in the box.

life	bread	forever	eats	live

Jesus says,

"Whoever eats the bread

of life will live

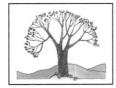

forever ."

Doctrine 233

Learning About Our Faith

Understanding Changes in Our Lives

Read aloud "Changes in Our Lives" on page 233. Help the children appreciate that after his resurrection Jesus had a totally new kind of life. Jesus shares that new kind of life with us in the Eucharist. Remind the children that we often call the Eucharist *the bread of life* or *the cup of promise* or *the cup of salvation*. Explain that as we share the Eucharist, we are reminded that someday we will live with God forever in heaven.

Learning How to Live Our Faith

Completing an Activity

Tell the children that they will use symbols to discover the message that tells what Jesus says about the bread of life. Read aloud the directions for the activity on page 233. Assist the children in decoding the message. Write the completed message on the chalkboard so that the children may check their work.

Singing Together

Distribute song sheets for "Garden Song" from THIS IS OUR FAITH Music Program, Grade 2. The music can be found in the Music Program Director's Manual, page 48. Use the recording to help teach the song. After practicing the song, have the class sing it together.

DAY 2
DOCTRINE

Objective

This lesson helps the children understand that everything that is alive grows and changes.

Step 1 / INTRODUCTION

Learning About Our Lives

Introducing the Chapter

Talk with the group about changes in nature. Review Day 1 with the children by citing the example of the oak tree changing through the different seasons. You may want to explain how a catepillar changes into a butterfly or how a seed that is buried in the ground grows into a beautiful flower or plant. Human beings also change. Emphasize that change is a natural and normal part of life.

Completing an Activity

Read aloud the directions for the activity on page 234. Allow the children sufficient time to complete their written responses on the lines provided. Discuss with the children ways they have changed.

Step 2 / DEVELOPMENT

Learning About Our Faith ✝

Discussing Growth and Change

Ask for volunteers to read aloud the paragraphs of "We Grow and Change" on page 234. Lead a class discussion on how people grow and change. Continue the discussion by asking:

■ What other living things grow and change? (*Plants and animals*)

■ Who made all living things special? (*God*)

■ Are people or animals or plants the most special of all? (*People*)

234

Activity

Your grandparents live far away. You haven't seen them for two years. Name two ways you have changed since their last visit.

_____

_____

_____

_____

We Grow and Change

God makes each of us special. No two people are exactly the same. Yet every person grows and changes.

As we grow, we change in many ways. We grow taller. We learn to walk and to talk. We change from babies into toddlers and then into children. In the years ahead, we will continue to grow. We will change into teenagers and finally, into adults.

Just as people grow and change, animals and plants grow and change. God has made all living things special. God has made people most special of all.

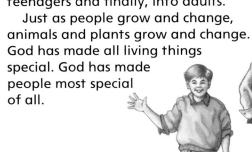

234 Doctrine

 **CURRICULUM CONNECTION**

Language Arts Find the poem "Our Tree" by Marchette Chute in Silver Burdett Ginn's THE MUSIC CONNECTION, Book 1, on page 285. Read the poem aloud to the children. Then talk with them about how an apple tree looks and changes its appearance from season to season—spring, summer, autumn, and winter. See if the children can identify words from the poem which help paint pictures of how the tree looks throughout the year.

 **Teaching Tips**

Refer to Silver Burdett Ginn's SCIENCE DISCOVERYWORKS, Teacher Edition / K, pages A48–A55 and A64–A79 for additional information on plants and animals, including their life cycles of growth, development, reproduction, and death.

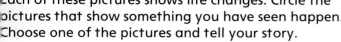

Activity

Each of these pictures shows life changes. Circle the pictures that show something you have seen happen. Choose one of the pictures and tell your story.

Learning How to Live Our Faith

Completing an Activity

Invite the children to look at the four pictures on page 235. Encourage the children to tell what life changes they see in each picture. Instruct them to choose one of the pictures that shows changes they have seen happen. Ask the children to write a story about it. Their stories should be short, having only three sentences— a beginning, a middle, and an end. Take time to share some of the stories aloud with the class.

Praying Together

Gather the children at the prayer table. Invite them to repeat the response "We praise you, God." Instruct the children to say the response aloud after each statement of the prayer.

Blessed are you, O Lord, the God of all creation.

Bless the Lord for bright and sunny days. *R.*

Bless the Lord for twinkling stars and dark, clear nights. *R.*

Bless the Lord for blue skies and fluffy white clouds. *R.*

Bless the Lord for gentle breezes. *R.*

Bless the Lord for flowers and fruits. *R.*

Bless the Lord for lakes, ponds, and rivers. *R.*

Bless the Lord for animals, wild and tame. *R.*

Bless the Lord for birds in the air. *R.*

Bless the Lord for baseball and soccer. *R.*

Bless the Lord for bicycles, wagons, and skate-boards. *R.*

Bless the Lord for picnics and parties. *R.*

Bless the Lord for our vacation from school. *R.*

Bless the Lord for the gift of Jesus. *R.*

Filled with God's praises, we prepare to enjoy our summer. We look forward to becoming third graders. May peace be with us. (Invite the children to exchange a greeting of peace.)

Enriching the Lesson

Make a changing life banner with the class. Roll out a large sheet of butcher paper on which, prior to class, you have drawn a large butterfly. Explain to the children that a butterfly is a good sign of changing life. What was once a caterpillar has become a whole new creature. Distribute sheets of different-colored tissue paper. Have the children tear the paper into odd-sized pieces and then glue them onto the butterfly. Make sure each child has a chance to add to the banner. Display the banner in class.

235

DAY 3
SCRIPTURE

Objective

This lesson helps the children begin to understand that just as Jesus rose to new life, we, too, will rise to new life and be forever with God.

Step 1 / INTRODUCTION

Learning About Our Lives

Experiencing the Unexpected

Place a small doll covered by a small white sheet on the discovery table. Make sure that the children notice that the doll is there. Gather the children in a circle with their backs to the discovery table. Talk about how sometimes we expect things to happen in a certain way and then we are surprised when they don't. As you are talking, slip the doll out from under the sheet being careful that your action is not noticed. Conceal the doll so the children cannot see it. Now invite the children to all turn around. Ask:

- What is under the sheet? (*A doll*)

- Can you explain how you know this? (*Probable response: We saw you put it there.*)

Lift the sheet up to show that the doll is gone.

- What is there now? (*Nothing*)

- How did this happen? (*Answers will vary.*)

Conclude with the concept that sometimes we experience something other than what we expect. Something new occurs.

Step 2 / DEVELOPMENT

Learning About Our Faith

Reading and Discussing a Scripture Story

Tell the children that they are going to hear a story from Scripture which tells how after Jesus died, Mary of Magdala went to the place where he had been buried expecting to find Jesus, but found that it was empty. She discovered something new.

Direct the children's attention to the illustration. Tell them that the woman is Jesus' friend, Mary of Magdala. Help the children recall that after Jesus died on the cross, he was buried in a tomb. Explain that on the Sunday after Jesus

New Life

Mary of Magdala was crying as she stood in front of the place where they had buried Jesus. When she looked inside, she found that it was empty.

A man was standing a few feet away from Mary. "Why are you crying?" he asked. "Whom are you looking for?"

Mary turned around. She thought the man was a gardener. "Please tell me where you have taken Jesus," Mary begged.

The man called her name again. Mary wiped her tears and saw that it was Jesus! Now Mary recognized him. "Teacher!" she shouted. She was so glad he was alive!

236   Scripture

Teaching Tips

To help the children focus on the new word *resurrection,* print it horizontally on the chalkboard. Print various words from the story vertically, so that common letters will overlap. As you write each vertical word, invite the children to locate the word in the story and explain how it is used; for instance, Mary (the woman who went to the place where Jesus was buried to find him). Continue until all the words that follow have been printed and identified: standing, gardener, empty, teacher, good.

Enriching the Lesson

Create a mural retelling the story "New Life." Place four panels of butcher paper on the floor. Divide the class into four groups. Assign one part of the story to each group.

1. Mary finds the empty tomb.
2. Mary talks with the gardener.
3. Mary recognizes Jesus.
4. Mary runs back to the other disciples to share the good news.

Display the completed mural in the church or parish hall.

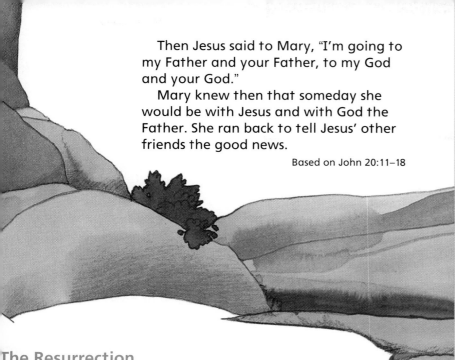

Then Jesus said to Mary, "I'm going to my Father and your Father, to my God and your God."

Mary knew then that someday she would be with Jesus and with God the Father. She ran back to tell Jesus' other friends the good news.

Based on John 20:11–18

The Resurrection

We, like Mary of Magdala, believe that Jesus rose to new life after his death on the cross. We call that rising to new life Jesus' **resurrection**. We also believe that we share in Jesus' resurrection. Jesus promised that all who eat the bread of life will live forever. When we die, we will share a new life with Jesus and with all who love God.

New Word

resurrection   Jesus' rising from death to new life

We Believe

Jesus rose from death to new life. He promises that those who eat the bread of life will live with him forever. The Eucharist is a sacrament of new life.

Scripture   237

Prayer   Invite the children to echo this prayer about Jesus' resurrection.

Resurrection,

New life.

Alleluia, alleluia!

Easter excitement;

Shout and sing,

spin and dance.

Be happy.

Alleluia, alleluia!

---

was buried, Mary of Magdala went to his tomb. Then read aloud "New Life," beginning on page 236. After the reading, ask:

■ Why was Mary crying? (*The tomb where Jesus was buried was empty.*)

■ What happened when the man spoke to Mary? (*Mary recognized Jesus.*)

■ What did Jesus tell Mary? (*"I'm going to my Father and your Father, to my God and your God."*)

■ Where did Mary go? (*To tell the good news to the other friends of Jesus*)

Believing in the Resurrection

Read aloud "The Resurrection" on page 237. Help the children appreciate that after Jesus' death on the cross, he rose to new life, which he shares with us. Ask the children to identify when Catholics eat the bread of life. (*At Communion, when we receive Eucharist*)

Presenting the New Word

Present the new word *resurrection* by writing it on the chalkboard. Help the children study the definition.

Presenting the Doctrine

Ask a volunteer to read the We Believe statements. Explain Jesus' promise that those who eat the bread of life will share a new life with God after they die. Acknowledge the fact that this teaching is a mystery and may be difficult to understand. Explain that it is all right to be sad when someone dies, but we should be comforted in knowing that death is the beginning of a new life forever with God.

Step 3 / CONCLUSION

Learning How to Live Our Faith

Praying Together

Invite the children to echo the following prayer as you pray it.

Dear Jesus,
When we feel empty, fill us with your love.
When we cry, help us to know that after sadness there is joy.
When we have good news, inspire us to run and share it with others. Amen.

DAY 4
DOCTRINE

Objective

This lesson helps the children realize that after death there is life with Jesus.

Step 1 / INTRODUCTION

Learning About Our Lives

Remembering Those Who Have Entered New Life

Invite the children to name persons they know who have died recently. List the names on the chalkboard. (You also might check with the parish secretary for names of recently deceased parishioners.) Explain to the children that the class will now pray for all of these people. Gather the children at the prayer table. Light the candle; then explain that you will say each name aloud. After each name is said aloud the children should respond, "Jesus promises us new life."

Leader: We pray for the following men and women who have died and now live with Jesus. (Name the individuals and invite the children to respond.)

We trust that all of these people have found new life in Jesus. Amen.

Step 2 / DEVELOPMENT

Learning About Our Faith

Studying an Illustration

Invite the children to look at the story illustration on page 238. Point out that the family looks sad. Explain that sometimes sad things happen and those sad things are difficult for us to understand.

Reading and Discussing a Story

Invite the children to listen as you read aloud the story "Alive with Jesus" on page 238. After you have finished reading, ask:

- What happened to Josh's grandpa? (*He died.*)
- Why did Mr. Ríos and the children hold each other? (*It helped them to be together.*)
- How did Mr. Ríos explain that death is not the end? (*He told Josh that his grandfather was alive with Jesus and that death is a part of living and we all will die someday.*)

238

Alive with Jesus

The phone rang just as they sat down to eat dinner. Melissa got to it first, as she always did.

"Hi, Grandma!" Melissa smiled as she heard her grandmother's voice. But soon Melissa began to cry and quickly handed the phone to her mother.

"Grandpa died," she said softly as she threw her arm around her dad's neck. Josh got out of his chair and climbed up on his father's lap.

Mr. Ríos and the children held each other tight. It helped so much to be together now.

"Why did he have to die?" Josh asked.

"Grandpa had been sick for a long time. The doctors did everything they could to help him get well, but he was just too sick," Mr. Ríos said.

"Death is a part of life, and we all will die someday. But death is not the end. Grandpa is alive with Jesus."

"I will miss him so much," Melissa cried. Josh said nothing, but he thought about Grandpa and about what his dad had told them.

238 Doctrine

Teaching Tips

If a child should ask you, "Will my pet go to heaven?" you might want to answer that the child's pet and all animals are created by God and reflect God's goodness and love. As Catholics we believe that we will share in that goodness and love forever.

Focus on

Christian Death According to the *Catechism of the Catholic Church,* because of Christ, Christian death has a positive meaning: "For to me to live is Christ, and to die is gain." "The saying is sure: if we have died with him, we will also live with him." (#1010)

Remember and Celebrate

When those we love die, we are sad. But we know they are alive with Jesus. At Mass we remember them and celebrate their new life. On Easter we celebrate Jesus' resurrection.

The large Easter candle that stands near the altar reminds us that all who die will live a new life with Jesus.

Activity

At Mass we express our belief in Jesus' resurrection and in his promise of new life when we say this prayer. Use the words below to complete the prayer.

| resurrection | cross | world | savior | free |

Lord, by your **cross** and

resurrection,

you have set us **free**.

You are the **savior**.

of the **world**.

Doctrine 239

Teaching Tips

Work toward culturally relevant teaching. See yourself and all your students as part of the human family created by God. Structure social relations in order to promote a shared-power model rather than an authoritarian model. Use cooperative learning principles. Conceive knowledge so as to empower the children to bring knowledge into the classroom. Relate the learning situation to their experiences and so celebrate diversity.

Celebrating New Life

Invite two volunteers to read aloud the paragraphs of "Remember and Celebrate" on page 239. Point out the photograph of the Paschal candle on page 239. Ask the children if they have seen the Paschal candle in the sanctuary of the church, near the altar. Suggest that they notice it the next time they attend Mass. Stress that the candle is there to remind us of the new life we will share with Jesus when we die.

Completing an Activity

Read aloud the directions to the activity and the activity text on page 239, pausing briefly at each blank. Now say the five words beneath the directions with the class. Instruct the children to fill in the blanks with the correct words. Check the children's work and make corrections as necessary. Practice saying the prayer aloud with the class.

Step 3 / CONCLUSION

Learning How to Live Our Faith

Praying Together

Explain to the children that often we use our hands to help others and to create new life. Say, "As we pray together, let's show with our hands how we help God take care of creation." Then begin the prayer.

Our hands
shake in friendship. (Everyone shakes hands.)

Our hands
plant seeds for gardens to grow. (Everyone pantomimes planting seeds.)

Our hands
care for our pets. (Everyone pantomimes petting an animal.)

Our hands
help our parents at home. (Everyone does a helping motion.)

Our hands
pray to God. (Everyone folds hands for prayer.)

Our hands
clap with joy at new life. (Everyone claps hands together.)

Clap with joy,
clap with joy. Alleluia!

DAY 5
PRAYER/REVIEW

Objective

This lesson helps the children celebrate God's presence with us throughout the various stages of our lives.

Preparing for Prayer

Place on the discovery table a dried up plant, a blooming plant, and small packets of seeds. Gather the children around the table. Invite the children to comment about what they see on the table. Explain that it takes time for a seed to grow into a plant, for a plant to bloom and then, later, wither and die. Emphasize that all life changes evolve over a period a time. We, too, grow, mature, and then die. Tell the children that in all our past life changes God was there and God will be there in the future. Teach the children the two responses needed for the prayer experience about time. For past events the children should respond, "You were there, God, giving us life," and for future events the children should respond, "You'll be there, God, giving us life."

Celebrating the Prayer Experience

Invite the children to bring their books with them as they gather around the prayer table. Light the candle. Then begin the prayer experience on page 240 that celebrates the various stages in our lives and God's presence with us.

Praying About Time

Teacher: When we were born,
All: You were there, God, giving us life.

Teacher: When we learned how to walk,
All: You were there, God, giving us life.

Teacher: When we made our first friend,
All: You were there, God, giving us life.

Teacher: When we become teenagers,
All: You'll be there, God, giving us life.

Teacher: When we get our first jobs,
All: You'll be there, God, giving us life.

Teacher: When we die and go home to you,
All: You'll be there, God, giving us life.

240 Prayer

★ ★ ★ ★ ★
Enriching the Lesson

Distribute writing paper. Have the children write a letter to persons they know are sad because someone they loved has died. Encourage the children to show in their letter how the promise of new life offered by Jesus can help the sad person.

240

Chapter Review

Choose a word to complete each sentence.

Jesus rose from death to new life.

When we die, we will be with Jesus.

The Easter candle reminds us of Jesus' resurrection.

1. What do we call Jesus' rising from death to new life?

resurrection

2. What does Jesus promise those who eat the bread of life?

life forever

3. Talk about how we can help those who are sad because someone has died.

> Jesus says,
> "Whoever eats the bread of life will live forever."
> John 6:51

CURRICULUM CONNECTION

Art Reinforce the concept of new life with the following art projects. Bring seeds into the classroom. Have the children paste a seed on drawing paper, then using chalk or felt-tip markers create what that seed might grow and become—an apple tree, a corn stalk, and so on. Invite the children to draw themselves when they received the "seed" of faith at Baptism. Then have the children draw how they have grown through love, prayer, and good works.

Filling In Sentences
Draw attention to the fill-in exercise at the top of page 241. Read aloud the directions and let the children work on their own. When they finish writing, check answers.

Completing the Chapter Review
Ask a volunteer to read aloud the two review questions on page 241. Tell the children to write their answers on the lines provided. Afterward, check the answers. Then read aloud item 3 and discuss it. Encourage all the children to participate in the discussion and offer suggestions as to what to say and do for people who are saddened by the death of someone they love. Conclude by reminding the children that because of Jesus' resurrection, death is not the end of life but the door to a new life with God in Jesus.

Explaining the Scripture Verse
Invite the children to read aloud together the Scripture verse based on John 6:51. Ask: What does Jesus say? (*Whoever eats the bread of life will live forever.*) Help the children memorize the verse.

241

The Eucharist Celebrates the Presence of Jesus

Objectives

To help the children

- Explore and celebrate experiences of presence.
- Remember Jesus' presence is with us in the Eucharist.
- Know that Jesus is with us at Mass.
- Realize that images of Jesus are symbols of his constant presence.
- Pray about the presence of Jesus and review the chapter.

Chapter Outline

	Step 1 Learning About Our Lives	**Step 2** Learning About Our Faith	**Step 3**  Learning How to Live Our Faith
Day 1	■ Review Chapter 19. ■ Introduce the chapter. ■ Study the photographs. *ABOUT 10 MINUTES*	■ Share stories of presence. ■ Present the doctrine. *ABOUT 10 MINUTES*	■ Complete an activity. ■ Learn to pray with gestures. *ABOUT 10 MINUTES*
Day 2	■ Introduce a Scripture story. *ABOUT 5 MINUTES*	■ Read and discuss the Scripture story. ■ Interpret the story. *ABOUT 15 MINUTES*	■ Complete an activity. *ABOUT 10 MINUTES*
Day 3	■ Complete and activity. *ABOUT 5 MINUTES*	■ Know that Jesus is present at Mass. ■ Respond to Jesus' presence. ■ Review the doctrine. *ABOUT 15 MINUTES*	■ Pray together. *ABOUT 10 MINUTES*
Day 4	■ Complete an activity. *ABOUT 10 MINUTES*	■ Recognize Jesus with us. ■ Complete a drawing activity. *ABOUT 10 MINUTES*	■ Discuss symbols of Jesus' presence. ■ Pray together. *ABOUT 10 MINUTES*

Day 5   **Prayer**   Review symbols of Jesus' presence and pray about the presence of Jesus.
            Review   Review presence; complete the chapter review; read the Scripture verse; and celebrate an anointing ceremony.

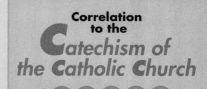

**Correlation
to the
Catechism of
the Catholic Church**

Paragraphs
1088, 1358, 1373

Plan Ahead

	Preparing Your Class	**Materials Needed**
Day 1	Review Chapter 19. Read over the lesson prior to the session. Decide on personal experience of presence to share.	■ pencils
Day 2	Read over the lesson prior to the session. Assure correct pronunciation of *Cleopas* and *Emmaus*.	■ pencils ■ prop box ■ Bible
Day 3	Read over the lesson prior to the session.	■ pencils
Day 4	Read over the lesson prior to the session. Gather pictures of sanctuary lamp, crucifix, candle, Bible.	■ pencils, felt-tip markers, crayons ■ picture of sanctuary lamp ■ crucifix ■ lighted candle ■ Bible
Day 5	Read the lesson plan. Gather bowl and oil for anointing ceremony. Get music recording of "Follow—A Round." Choose a familiar "Alleluia."	■ bowl, oil ■ instrumental and vocal recordings of "Follow—A Round" ■ a familiar "Alleluia"

Additional Resources

As you plan this chapter, consider using the following materials from The Resourceful Teacher Package.

■ *Classroom Activity Sheets 20* and *20a*

■ *Family Activity Sheets 20* and *20a*

■ *Chapter 20 Test*

■ *Prayers for Every Day*

■ *Projects: Grade 2*

You may also wish to refer to the following Big Books.

■ *We Celebrate the Mass,* pages 19–21

■ *We Celebrate the Sacraments,* pages 7–9

In preparing the children for the Sunday readings, you may wish to use Silver Burdett Ginn's *Getting Ready for Sunday* student and teacher materials.

BOOKS FOR THE JOURNEY

Time to Talk. "The Telephone," by Robert Frost, p. 17. Selected by Myra Cohn Livingston. Margaret K. McElderry Books, 1992. An exquisite poem describing a presence that is unseen but heard.

May I Visit? Charlotte Zolotow. HarperCollins, 1976. This story helps a child realize that her presence will always be wanted whether she's big or little.

MORE BOOKS FOR THE JOURNEY

Days with Frog and Toad. "Alone," pp. 52–54. Arnold Lobel. Harper & Row, 1979. The story of two friends who enjoy each other's presence although sometimes it's good to be alone.

A Child's Book of Prayers. "When God Talks to Me," p. 36; "Jesus, When I Am Afraid," by Janet Lynch Watson, p. 61; "Evening," by Thomas Miller, pp. 82–83. Edited by Linda Yeatman. Workman Publishing, 1992. Prayers remembering and acknowledging God's presence.

REDUCED CLASSROOM ACTIVITIES

Name

The Eucharist Celebrates the Presence of Jesus

Jesus is with us in the Eucharist and all the time. "Presence/Presents" is a card game to help you think about Jesus every day.

1. Color the game title, as well as the ribbon on each card.
2. Cut out the eight cards. Use a small box or an envelope to keep your cards together.
3. At home, pick out one card each day. Think of Jesus while you're doing the activity that is written on the card.

Presence Presents A Card A Day	I'll think of Jesus when I'm playing.
I'll think of Jesus when I get up in the morning.	I'll think of Jesus when I go to bed.
I'll think of Jesus when I'm bored.	I'll think of Jesus when I'm brushing my teeth.
I'll think of Jesus when I'm waiting.	I'll think of Jesus when I look out the window.

To the Teacher: In doing this activity, students can develop the habit of prayer. After a week, encourage the students to discuss their heightened awareness of Jesus' presence.

Chapter 20   The Eucharist Celebrates the Presence of Jesus   THIS IS OUR FAITH 2   **20**

Name

Being with You

It is always a good feeling to be with people who love us. Write the name of the person you would like to be with each time you have one of the feelings below. Then trace over the letters of Jesus' message to us.

1. sad
2. happy
3. lonely
4. frightened
5. sick

Jesus says,

I am with you always.

To the Teacher: In this activity, students examine times in their lives when Jesus is with them.

20a   THIS IS OUR FAITH 2   Chapter 20   The Eucharist Celebrates the Presence of Jesus

Background for the Teacher

CHRIST'S PRESENCE IN THE EUCHARIST

Catholics celebrate Christ's presence in the Eucharist, the sacrament of his presence. We believe that Jesus is with us in a unique way when we gather to celebrate the Eucharist. We also believe that through this sacrament, we celebrate Jesus' presence with us always.

As Christians we believe that God wanted to be with us so much that he became one of us. *Emmanuel,* the name foretold by the prophets, means "God with us." Jesus— God with us—loved us so much that he lived, suffered, died, and rose to new life for us. Jesus—God with us— loved us so much that he remains present with us through the power of the Holy Spirit.

The material in this chapter will help the children discover that Jesus is with us in a special way at Mass: in the gathered community, in the presider, in God's word proclaimed, and in his sharing of himself with us in the eucharistic meal. Through the Scripture verse and the words of Psalm 139, the chapter also helps the children recognize the presence of God with us always and everywhere.

CHRIST'S PRESENCE IN OUR LIVES

Children need to be with people who care for and about them. Most children have experienced at least one or two people who have fulfilled that need. However, an increasing number of children lack such experiences in an ongoing, predictable manner.

As a teacher, therefore, you should be alert and sensitive to the children's need for loving and caring relationships. Throughout this chapter help the children recognize and value Christ's loving and caring presence with us always and everywhere.

Objective

This lesson helps the children explore experiences of presence and invites them to celebrate presence.

Step 1 / INTRODUCTION

Learning About Our Lives

Reviewing Chapter 19

Invite the children to recall signs of new life in nature. Encourage them to share how they personally have grown and changed this past school year. (*Answers will vary. Affirm all answers.*) Remind the children that many people in their lives have helped them to grow and change this year. Pause to name some of those people. Explain that through nature, through these people helping us, and through celebrating at Mass, we come to know that Jesus is with us. Ask who remembers the special word learned early in the year that explains Jesus with us. (If you have opted to make new word posters, use the one for *presence* to help the children recollect.)

Introducing the Chapter

Invite a volunteer to read aloud the focus question on page 242. Encourage each child to share the name of at least one person who likes to spend time with him or her. Also encourage each child to name those with whom he or she likes to spend time. Ask the children to explain why they enjoy being with the persons they named. Possible responses: *They are fun or interesting; they are interested in others; they care about and love others.*

Studying the Photographs

Direct the children's attention to the photographs. Invite the children to read aloud together the sentences that accompany each photograph. Then ask them to tell a story about each one.

Step 2 / DEVELOPMENT

Learning About Our Faith +

Sharing Stories of Presence

Invite the children to think of a time when they were all alone but they felt as if others were

242

---

20 The Eucharist Celebrates the Presence of Jesus

Being with Others

It's good to spend time with those we love. It's good to be near people who love us.

Who are some people who enjoy spending time with you?

Sometimes we like to be alone. But we also want to know someone is near when we need him or her.

★ ★★★ ★ Enriching the Lesson ★

Visit the church to note signs and symbols that remind us of Jesus' presence.

The *sanctuary lamp:* Jesus is present in the consecrated hosts in the tabernacle.

The *Paschal candle:* all who die will live a new life with Jesus.

The *stained-glass windows:* scenes from Jesus' life are retold.

The *Bible:* stories help us to feel Jesus' presence.

The *Stations of the Cross:* Jesus' sacrifice is revealed to us.

Jesus Is Always with Us

Jesus is alive and with us. Jesus is with us always and everywhere. We celebrate the presence of Jesus with us in the Eucharist.

Activity

Read the prayer below. Then circle the names of some of the places where Jesus is with us.

O Lord,
Where can I go from your presence?
If I fly up into the sky,
You are there.
If I sink deep under the earth,
You are present there.
If I cross the widest ocean,
You are there to guide me.
Your right hand holds me tight.

Based on Psalm 139:7–10

We Believe

The Eucharist is the sacrament of the presence of Jesus. Jesus is with us in the Eucharist and always.

Doctrine 243

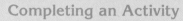

Enriching the Lesson

Distribute drawing paper and crayons or felt-tip markers. Invite the children to draw pictures of themselves doing something they enjoy with others. Then direct them to copy from the chalkboard the following sentence and complete it: *When I am with others, I feel _____.*

Allow time for the children to show their drawings to the group and share their feelings about being with others.

CURRICULUM CONNECTION

Art Create a "friendship basket" with the help of the art teacher. Fill a basket with sayings of Jesus printed as bookmarks. They can be created by the children, duplicated, and hand colored, then cut apart. Decorate the basket with a colorful ribbon. Fill it with the bookmarks. Have the children take the basket to another class, explaining that they bring the gift as friends of Jesus. The children then invite the class to keep the basket and to fill it with a gift of their choice to pass on to another grade.

---

with them. Invite the children to share such experiences. To begin the story sharing, you can tell of a personal experience in which you were alone but felt another's presence. The children can then draw from your concrete example. Next have a volunteer read aloud the sentences under "Jesus Is Always with Us" on page 243. Refer back to the new word poster (if you have taken this option) and review the meaning of *presence* and some ways Jesus is present with us today. (At Mass in the word, in the assembly, in the Eucharist, in the ministers; in our relationships, and in our life experiences) Remind the children that through Jesus' resurrection he is with us even when we are alone. Talk about times when they have felt the presence of Jesus.

Presenting the Doctrine

Read aloud the We Believe statements on page 243. Read the statements again as the children echo each phrase.

Step 3 / CONCLUSION

Learning How to Live Our Faith

Completing an Activity

Invite a volunteer to read aloud the directions for the activity on page 243. Before having the children circle their answers, read the prayer aloud together with the class. Then have the children work individually, circling the places where Jesus is with us.

Learning to Pray with Gestures

Invite the children to read aloud the prayer on page 243 again. Remind them that when the priest prays about God's presence at Mass, he uses gestures. Then teach the following gestures for this prayer.

O Lord, where can I go from your presence? (Outstretch arms.)

If I fly up into the sky, you are there. (Sweep both hands over head.)

If I sink deep under the earth, you are present there. (Genuflect.)

If I cross the widest ocean, you are there to guide me. (Stand, stretch both arms directly in front, pointing to the horizon.)

Your right hand holds me tight. (Sweep right arm out away from body and back again.)

243

Objective

This lesson helps the children remember that Jesus' presence is with us in the Eucharist.

Step 1 / INTRODUCTION

Learning About Our Lives

Introducing a Scripture Story

This lesson's Scripture story deals with welcoming a stranger. Since children are taught—with good reason—to be wary of strangers, invite the children to tell you what they have learned about talking to strangers. Then explain that they will be reading a story from the Bible about two friends of Jesus who meet and talk to a stranger. However, tell the children that in their hearts, Jesus' friends felt that the man they met really wasn't a stranger, that they knew him (Luke 24:32). Also point out that Jesus' friends were adults, and they were not alone. So, they were not afraid to talk to the stranger or have him join them. Make sure the children understand that it is different when strangers approach children. Finally, help the children focus on the fact that sometimes special people come into our lives, and we do not recognize them. Tell the children that this is what happened to the friends of Jesus in the story they are about to read.

Step 2 / DEVELOPMENT

Learning About Our Faith

Reading and Discussing the Scripture Story

Read aloud the first paragraph of the story "Jesus Is Here." Pronounce the name *Cleopas* and ask the children to repeat it. Then select volunteers to read the other paragraphs in the story. Use the following questions for discussion.

■ Where were Jesus' friends going? (*To a town named Emmaus*)

■ Why were Jesus' friends sad? (*They missed Jesus.*)

■ What did Cleopas tell the stranger? (*"We have lost our friend Jesus. He died on a cross two days ago."*)

Jesus Is Here

Two men were walking from Jerusalem to **Emmaus**. They were very sad. "I miss Jesus so much," Cleopas said, "I wish he was here with us."

A stranger came down the road and started walking with the two men. "Why are you so sad?" the stranger asked the two men.

"We have lost our friend Jesus," Cleopas answered. "He died on a cross two days ago."

"Don't be sad!" the stranger said. "Don't you understand what has happened? Jesus had to die to lead us all to new life." Then the stranger explained the stories in the Bible about the coming of the savior.

The two friends listened carefully. What the stranger said gave them hope. "It's getting late," Cleopas said to the stranger. "We are almost home. Please stay with us tonight." Soon they were home in Emmaus. They sat down to eat. The stranger took bread in his hands. He thanked God for it.

Teaching Tips

Give the children opportunities to do things together because

1. An emotional experience creates an emotional memory for the individual to recall and reexperience learning affectively.
2. An interpersonal relationship lingers within our psyche because a shared experience helps us to feel connected with others.
3. An informal setting invites more open sharing and produces lively discussion in a relaxed atmosphere.

He broke the
bread and gave it
to the other two.
Now they knew
that the stranger
was Jesus.

Later Cleopas ran to tell the
others, "He is alive! He is with us!"

Based on Luke 24:13–35

Activity

Draw a picture that shows a time when you were
sure that Jesus was with you.

New Word

✱
✱ **Emmaus** the place where Jesus shared a meal with two of
✱ his followers after he rose to new life
✱

Enriching the Lesson

Create a bulletin board that
shows the faith journey your class
has shared this year. Divide the
bulletin board space into five
areas, one area for each of the
five units of study. Assign one
team for each unit. Each team
should create art work or select
magazine photographs depicting
topics studied in the assigned
unit. Have the children include
the most important thing about
each unit and explain what they
have included as visuals and why
it has been significant.

- Why did the stranger tell Cleopas not to be
  sad? (*He said, "Jesus had to die in order to
  lead us all to new life."*)
- What did the stranger do with the bread?
  (*He broke it, thanked God for it, gave it to
  the two men.*)
- What did Cleopas say later? (*"Jesus is alive.
  He is with us."*)

or . . .

After reading the Scripture story, invite the
children to role-play the reaction Jesus' friends
might have had to the news that he had risen
from the dead. Encourage the children to have
a conversation about Jesus being alive.

Interpreting the Story

To help the children realize how the two men in
the story recognized Jesus alive with them, ask:

- How did the friends of Jesus recognize the
  presence of Jesus alive with them? (*In the
  breaking of the bread*)

Tell the children that just after the greeting of
peace at Mass, the priest breaks the host that is
Jesus' body for us so that we can share Jesus'
presence in Communion. Then help the children
recall the story "New Life" on pages 236–237.
Ask: How did Mary of Magdala recognize the
presence of Jesus alive with her? (*When Jesus
called her by name, Mary*)

Help the children appreciate that we recognize
and celebrate Jesus' presence through his
word and the breaking of the bread at Mass.

Presenting the New Word

Write the new word *Emmaus* on the chalkboard.
Pronounce the word for the children and have
them repeat it after you. Then direct their
attention to the New Word box. Ask a volunteer
to read the definition. Then have all repeat it.

Step 3 / CONCLUSION

Learning How to Live Our Faith

Completing an Activity

Read the directions for the activity on page
245. Allow sufficient time for the children to
draw their pictures in the space provided.
Encourage the children to share their pictures
and discuss them with the class.

DAY 3

DOCTRINE

Objective

This lesson helps the children know that Jesus is present with us at Mass.

Step 1 / INTRODUCTION

Learning About Our Lives

Completing an Activity

Invite a child to read aloud the directions for the activity on page 246. Point out the five different spots on the map where the children are to identify the names of the people usually present there. Instruct the children to look for the symbol of a pencil on the map where they are to write their responses on the lines provided. Ask several volunteers to read the names they wrote for each spot. Affirm the children for their good work.

Step 2 / DEVELOPMENT

Learning About Our Faith

Knowing That Jesus Is Present at Mass

Invite a volunteer to read aloud the paragraphs on page 247 about Jesus' presence at Mass. Help the children appreciate that Jesus is always with us and that the Eucharist is a special sacramental celebration of his presence. Ask the children to underline the ways in which Jesus is present with us at Mass. (*In the people and the priest, in the Bible readings, in the Eucharist*)

 ctivity

Pretend that this is a map of your neighborhood. Begin at the START sign and follow the arrows. Stop at each place along the way and write the name of a person who is usually present to you there.

246 Doctrine

★ ★ ★ ★ Enriching the Lesson ★

Help the children think of ways Jesus loved people and loves us now. Have the class echo each sentence descriptive of Jesus. *Jesus was gentle. Jesus forgave others. Jesus prayed to God the Father. Jesus shared meals with his friends. Jesus was kind to children. Jesus helped sick people. Jesus rose to new life.*
To pray responsorially, begin each response with "We can..." Change each verb to the present tense; for example: Jesus was gentle. We can be gentle.

We Celebrate the Presence of Jesus

We celebrate the presence of Jesus every time we gather as a community for Mass. The risen Jesus is present at Mass with the people and priest who gather.

Jesus is also present in the Bible readings. He is present in the Eucharist we share.

Activity

During Mass the priest reminds us that Jesus is present with us. Write our response on the line below.

Priest: The Lord be with you.

All:  And also with you.

Doctrine 247

Responding to Jesus' Presence at Mass

Ask a volunteer to read the directions for the activity on page 247. Instruct the children to write the response *And also with you* to the priest's greeting. Stress that the priest's words and the people's response are reminders of the presence of Jesus.

Reviewing the Doctrine

Read aloud together the We Believe statements at the bottom of page 243. Tell the children to study the sentences again by reading them quietly a few times. Then remind them that Jesus is with us in a very special way in the Eucharist and that Jesus is with us always and everywhere.

Step 3 / CONCLUSION

Learning How to Live Our Faith

Praying Together

Ask the children to stand and form a circle. Teach them the words and the gestures for each line of the following prayer.

We are one, Lord, in your name.
(Stretch arms out to include everyone in the circle.)

We serve others, Jesus, as you did.
(Turn and gesture out to the room and beyond.)

You give new life to us, Jesus.
(Turn to face one another and stretch arms overhead.)

We believe you are here with us, Jesus.
(Place hands on one another's shoulders and move closer together.)

Then lead the children in the prayer and gestures.

★ Enriching the Lesson ★

Explain to the children that at Mass we pray and sing together as we acknowledge Jesus' presence at Mass and as we remember the sacrifice of Jesus on the cross. Review the priest's words of greeting and the people's response by practicing the dialogue with the class. Say the words of the priest and have the class respond with the words of the assembly.

Priest: *The Lord be with you.*
Assembly: *And also with you.*

Focus on

The Presence of Jesus in the Eucharist Catholics believe that although the gifts of bread and wine at Communion still look like bread and wine, they are no longer bread and wine but the body and blood of Jesus. We believe this to be true through the gift of faith.

Day 4
DOCTRINE

Objective

This lesson helps the children imagine what Jesus looked liked and realize that images of Jesus are symbols of his constant presence.

Step 1 / INTRODUCTION

Learning About Our Lives

Completing an Activity

Read aloud the paragraphs about faces on page 248. Allow sufficient time for the children to picture the face they most like to remember and then write their responses on the lines provided.

As they share their responses with the class, have them tell why the remembered face is so special to them Then instruct them to draw the person's face in the box.

Step 2 / DEVELOPMENT

Learning About Our Faith

Recognizing Jesus with Us

Read aloud "Jesus Has Many Faces" on page 249. Ask the children to name the places where they have seen paintings or statues of Jesus. Explain that Jesus seems to have many different faces because no one really knows what Jesus looked like.

Direct their attention to the three images of Jesus. Ask the children to point to the image that they find most appealing. Ask volunteers to explain why the images they pointed to are appealing to them.

Completing a Drawing Activity

Distribute crayons or felt-tip markers. Explain the directions for the activity. Encourage the children to work independently to complete it. As they draw, move about the room talking with each child about the face of Jesus he or she has chosen to draw. Emphasize that although Jesus might look different to everyone, his presence with us is the same—loving and faithful.

or . . .

Invite the children to work together to make an altar cloth celebrating the presence of Jesus.

248

Faces! Faces! Faces!

Everyone has a face. Faces can be friendly, angry, mean, or sad. We like to remember the faces of people we love.

Activity

Whose face do you like to remember most?

Now draw that person's face in the box.

CURRICULUM CONNECTION

Art   Invite your school librarian or the art teacher to research pictures of representations of Jesus in various works of art. These works of art should be from different multicultural groups that reflect various ethnic depictions of the face of Jesus.

Invite the librarian to show the pictures to the class and give a little talk on the artists' conception of Jesus.

Jesus Has Many Faces

Christians around the world believe that Jesus is always with them. Many people paint pictures or make statues of Jesus to show that they believe that Jesus is always present. The paintings and statues show Jesus with many different faces, because no one really knows what Jesus looked like. Here are a few of those faces.

Activity

What do you think Jesus' face looks like? Draw it here.

You will need a large white cloth and fabric crayons. Spread the cloth on the floor in a large area and have the children work by moving around it. Encourage the children to draw pictures that show how Jesus is always with us.

Step 3 / CONCLUSION

Learning How to Live Our Faith

Discussing Symbols of Jesus' Presence

Have the children gather in a sharing circle around the discovery table on which you have placed a crucifix, a lighted candle, a Bible, and a picture of a sanctuary lamp. Discuss with the class how these items are symbols of Jesus' presence.

Praying Together

Take one or two symbols from the discovery table and use them in prayer. Pray with the children about the presence of Jesus. Thank Jesus for a time when you felt his presence in a special way. Allow the children to add to your prayer.

CURRICULUM CONNECTION

Art To prepare for the final procession which concludes religion class for the year, invite the art teacher to help your children prepare two ribbon banners. Select poles, holders, and ribbons appropriate for the season. Each child can be responsible for placing a ribbon on the pole. Select two children to be the banner carriers for the procession.

Objective

This lesson helps the children pray about the presence of Jesus.

Reviewing Symbols of Jesus' Presence

Begin the session by listing on the chalkboard some symbols of the presence of Jesus most frequently found in the children's homes, in church, and in the classroom (crucifix, picture of Jesus, Bible, religious calendar, songs, and so on). Discuss briefly how important it is to use these symbols to remind us of Jesus' presence.

Praying About the Presence of Jesus

Before beginning the prayer experience, tell the children that Jesus is also present within us. Ask the children to become still and very quiet so as to visit him in their hearts. Read the introductory sentences on page 250 and begin the prayer in a slow, soft voice, pausing briefly between sentences. At the conclusion of the prayer encourage all to respond *Amen.*

Praying About the Presence of Jesus

Teacher: Jesus is present in many ways. Let us think about Jesus' presence within us. Let us visit with him there.

Jesus, we know that you are always close to us. You are as close to us as the air we breathe. With each breath we thank you for being our friend.

Jesus, we know that you live in our hearts. The beating of our hearts reminds us that you stay with us every minute of every day.

Jesus, your love for us fills our minds. We can remember you. We can pray to you. We can speak to you. We can listen to you. We can love you.

Jesus, thank you for being so close to us. Even when we forget you, you never forget us. You never leave us. Help us stay close to you always.

All: Amen!

250 Prayer

Enriching the Lesson

Use some of the following questions to help the children review and summarize the year's experience in religion class.

What did you most enjoy about religion class this year? How would you describe Jesus? What do you like about praying and celebrating at Mass? When did you feel you reached out to help another child? Can you say aloud one Scripture verse?

Chapter Review

Read the sentences below.
Circle **YES** if a sentence is true.
Circle **NO** if a sentence is not true.

1. Jesus is with the Christian community.

   (YES)   NO

2. Presence means "being alone."

   YES   (NO)

3. Jesus is not with us anymore.

   YES   (NO)

4. Jesus is with us in the Eucharist.

   (YES)   NO

5. Jesus is with us in the Bible readings at Mass.

   (YES)   NO

6. In the story "Jesus Is Here," when did the two followers recognize Jesus?

   when he broke bread

7. When is Jesus, the risen Christ, with us?

   always

8. Talk about how we can help ourselves and others remember that Jesus is always with us.

Jesus says,
"I am with you
always."
Matthew 28:20

Review   251

Reviewing Presence

Read the directions for the Yes or No exercise at the top of page 251. When the children finish, check their answers.

Completing the Chapter Review

Read aloud the two review questions that follow. Then ask the children to write their answers on the lines provided. Correct the answers. Continue with the discussion topic in item 3. Encourage all the children to share in the discussion.

Reading the Scripture Verse

Invite the children to read together the Scripture verse from Matthew 28:20 at the bottom of page 251. Then ask: What does Jesus tell us? ("*I am with you always.*") Encourage the children to memorize the Scripture verse.

Celebrating an Anointing Ceremony

Play the instrumental recording of "Follow—A Round" from THIS IS OUR FAITH Music Program, Grade 3. Place a small bowl of oil on the prayer table. Gather the children around the prayer table. Begin the ceremony.

Leader: O God, source of strength, you have chosen us to follow your Son Jesus. As we leave our classroom for summer vacation, we ask you to strengthen us. Help us to be signs of your love in today's world.

(Dip into the bowl of oil and trace the sign of the cross on each child's forehead as you continue the prayer.)

Name, may God strengthen you.

(When all have been anointed, continue.)

We pray for God's blessings on each of us. Be strong. Follow Jesus in all that you do this summer.

Conclude by singing a familiar "Alleluia" or by singing "Follow—A Round."

Focus on

Anointing The *Catechism of the Catholic Church* explains that "The symbolism of anointing with oil . . . signifies the Holy Spirit, to the point of becoming a synonym for the Holy Spirit" (#695). The act of anointing the children with oil and invoking God the Holy Spirit to strengthen them as they leave for summer vacation is a fitting blessing at the conclusion of the school year.

Enriching the Lesson

Use the following review if you have opted to make new word posters.

Gather all of the new word posters from the five Grade 2 units. Put them in order. Seat the children in a sharing circle. As you hold up each poster, invite a volunteer to tell the story of the new word. Give the poster to the child who offers a response. When all the posters have been reviewed, invite the children to parade around the room with the posters.

251

Using the Unit Organizer

Completing a graphic organizer such as a chart or table can help the children organize information that has been presented in the unit. Organizers can enable the children to visualize their thinking and recognize relationships among ideas. This will give the children that opportunity to understand more completely the materials they have been studying.

Completing the Organizer

Have the children turn to page 252 in their books. Help the children complete the unit organizer by first reviewing the five senses: touch, taste, smell, sight, and hearing. Now read through each direction statement. Ask volunteers to give examples. Provide examples if the children are having difficulty using their senses to illustrate the chapter concepts. Point out where to start. Then ask the children to complete the activity independently. If necessary, tell them that they may look back through the previous four chapters for help. When everyone has finished, have the children compare their responses with the class.

Looking Back: Self-Assessment

The critical reflection questions below give the children an opportunity to sharpen their thinking skills. The questions can be used as a class discussion or independent writing activity.

- Which was your favorite prayer in this unit?
- Which person in this unit would you like to learn more about?
- What did you learn in this unit that you think you will always remember?

252

UNIT 5 ORGANIZER

The Eucharist Is Jesus with Us
Draw your pictures below.

This is my picture of what unity in Jesus <u>tastes</u> like.

This is my picture of what serving others <u>feels</u> like.

This is my picture of what new life in Jesus <u>sounds</u> like.

This is my picture of what the Emmaus meal <u>looks</u> like.

UNIT 5 REVIEW

Circle the correct answer.

1. Jesus wants us to work _____.

      apart   (together)

2. Jesus prayed for his friends to be _____.

      (united)   poor

3. At Mass we give each other a sign of _____.

      danger   (peace)

Look at the words in the box. Then write the correct word to complete each sentence.

| treat   example   peace |

4. Jesus washed his friends' feet to give us an

  example of how to serve others.

5. The Eucharist is a sacrament of love and **peace**.

6. Jesus wants us to **treat** others the way he did.

Reviewing the Unit

The purpose of the Unit Review is to reinforce concepts presented in the preceding four chapters and to check the children's understanding. If you have opted to make and use new word posters, they can be included in an oral review. After explaining the directions, give the children sufficient time to complete the two-page review. Answer any questions they may have as you check their work.

Testing

After the students have completed the Unit Review, you may wish to distribute copies of the Unit 5 Test from the Test Booklet.

Project

If time permits, you may wish to do the following project with the children.

Prepare an inventory sheet for each child to take home after completing the unit. Directions should stress that the sheet needs to be returned for the next day's class. The inventory sheet might use the following format:

Date _____

Child's name _____

Dear Family,

We have talked about how symbols remind us of Jesus' presence in our lives. Your child is bringing this sheet home to create an inventory of the symbols of Jesus present in your home. This is not a test. There is no scoring or assigning of grades. It is simply an aid to help your child discover symbols of Jesus in his or her life. Check off any of the items on the sheet that are present in your home. Be sure to have your child bring the completed inventory to class tomorrow. Thank you for your help and interest. Because of you, Jesus lives in the heart of your child!

_____ (*Teacher's signature*)

Inventory

____ cross or crucifix

____ picture of Jesus

____ statue of Jesus

____ rosary with a cross on it

____ a book about Jesus

____ holy water font

Project continues on page 254.

____ parish bulletin

____ a Bible

____ baptism candle

____ family prayer book

____ religious calendar

____ holy card(s)

____ holy medal(s)

____ religious magazine

____ meal blessing

____ blessing of children

____ prayer at meals

____ music or tape of sacred songs

____ words of forgiveness

____ blessing cup

____ other

Talk about the answers to the following questions.

7. What did Jesus promise those who eat the bread of life?
Possible answer: life with Jesus and God our Father forever

8. What do Christians believe happens after someone dies?
Possible answers: We share in the resurrection; We share the new life of Jesus; In heaven we will always be with Jesus and with God our Father.

9. What does the Easter candle remind us of at Mass?
Possible answer: the resurrection of Jesus, sharing a new life after we die

Think about the story "Jesus Is Here." Write your answer to each question.

10. What happened when Cleopas and his friend ate supper with the stranger?

Jesus broke bread.

11. When and where is Jesus with us?

always and everywhere

WHAT SHOULD I DO WHEN MY MESSAGE ISN'T HEARD?

Sometimes my message is not heard.
Sometimes my message is heard but not understood.

Activity

Meet Larry. Larry is a new student in the second grade. Larry is having a hard time fitting in. The other kids tease Larry. Larry feels

_____

Larry decides to tell his dad. His dad is watching a football game. Larry says, "Dad, I hate school. The kids are being mean." His dad says, "You'll like it after you're there a while. Wow! Look at that touchdown!"

Was Larry's message heard?

Yes   No

Was Larry's message understood?

Yes   No

What should Larry do?

Day to Day   255

Objective

This lesson helps the children increase their awareness of alternatives when a message is not heard or is misunderstood.

Introducing the Lesson

Let the children know that today's topic is what to do when you tell someone something important and they don't hear what you have said or have misunderstood what they have heard. Invite the children to share experiences when someone has not listened to them, or has not understood what they were trying to say. Ask how they felt and how they handled the situation.

Reading the Story

Read aloud with the children the introductory sentences on page 255. Direct the children's attention to the first picture that illustrates the story about a boy named Larry. Read aloud the story about Larry. Tell them that Larry is having a hard time getting his message heard. After reading the story ask, "How does Larry feel?" Have the children write their answers on the line provided. (*Sad, lonely, discouraged, mad, unhappy*)

Elicit ideas about what Larry should do. Encourage responses which suggest sharing his feelings. (A positive step in the direction of feeling better when upset, worried or sad, is to share feelings with someone who is able to help.)

Reading More of the Story

After reading this part of the story, have the children answer the questions by circling Yes or No. (*No, No*) Allow time for the children to share their responses. Elicit ideas for what Larry should do next.

Lesson continues on page 256.

Finishing the Story

Read aloud the final paragraph of the story at the top of page 256. Have the children tell what happened, and whether the message was heard and understood. (*Yes, Yes*)

Discussing the Story

Ask the class why it was a good thing for Larry to keep on trying until his message was heard and understood. Point out to the children that hurt feelings are important feelings to be shared. Once these feelings are heard and understood, someone can begin to help.

Concluding the Lesson

Read with the children the paragraph about sharing upset, scared or worried feelings on page 256. Ask them to reiterate what strategies Larry tried. (*Asking someone he thought would listen; asking again at a better time.*) Ask the children if there was anything else Larry could have done. (*Saying the message again; asking someone else to help him get his message heard.*)

Following Jesus

Invite a volunteer to read aloud the statements in the Following Jesus box.

Have the children silently ask Jesus for the courage to be persistent when asking others to listen to their feelings. Then together with the class pray aloud the prayer in the prayer box.

256

Larry decides to try again later. This time he waits for a time when his dad is ready to listen. Larry says, "Dad, I hate school. The kids are being mean." His dad says, "You sound really sad. Do you want to tell me more about it?"

Was Larry's message heard?

Yes   No

Was Larry's message understood?

Yes   No

Upset, scared, and worried feelings are important feelings to share with someone who will listen. Don't give up if your message isn't heard.

Following Jesus

Jesus understands what it feels like to be upset, scared, and worried. He sometimes felt those same feelings. Jesus wants us to share all our feelings with him and with someone else we trust.

A Prayer

Jesus, sometimes I need someone to listen to my feelings when I 'm upset or scared. I know you always listen to me. Thank you, Jesus! Amen.

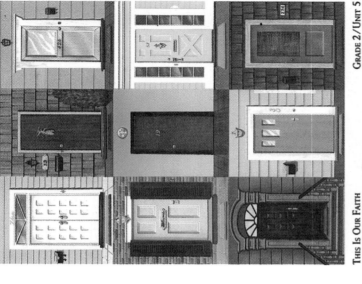

Opening Doors
A Take-Home Magazine™

GRADE 2/UNIT 5

THIS IS OUR FAITH

Growing Closer

TALK TOGETHER about what *sacrifice* means. Decide on one sacrifice your family could make this week. One example might be spending a few hours doing yard work for an elderly or handicapped person in your neighborhood or parish.

BE REALLY PRESENT to your family this week. Listen to one another. Spend some time together. Do something nice for your family for no reason at all!

Looking Ahead

However your family spends the summer, may it be a time of renewal and recreation, good health and happiness, joyful celebrations, and an opportunity to relax in the promise, "I am with you always" (Mt. 28:20).

8

Opening Doors ~~~

Sending the Magazine Home

As you complete Unit 5 with your class, assist the children in carefully removing *Opening Doors: A Take-Home Magazine* (two pages) from their texts by separating them from the book along the perforations. Demonstrate how to fold the two pages, forming an eight-page booklet. Ask the children to take the magazine home and encourage their families to read it with them and participate in the suggested activities.

257

A Builder of Unity

"Bring together in love and peace all who believe in you."
—Roman Missal

Today we understand the Mass as an important builder of unity among Catholics. It also stands as a sign of the unified body of Christ fully alive in the world today. As we are often reminded in the Mass, we not only gather to receive the body of Christ but we are also sent forth to be the body of Christ. Working together and making sacrifices for one another, we know that it is through our lives and the life of the Church that Jesus is made known to the people around us in a profound way. Without question, this is a great responsibility, but living and expressing our faith within a community of believers is a great gift, too!

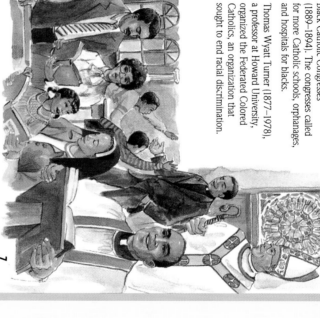

- Augustus Tolton was the first recognized black priest in the United States. He was ordained in 1886 and sent to work with black Catholics in Illinois.

- Lincoln Valle and Daniel Rudd, two prominent black newspapermen, founded a series of Black Catholic Congresses (1889–1894). The congresses called for more Catholic schools, orphanages, and hospitals for blacks.

- Thomas Wyatt Turner (1877–1978), a professor at Howard University, organized the Federated Colored Catholics, an organization that sought to end racial discrimination.

7

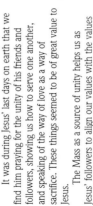

It was during Jesus' last days on earth that we find him praying for the unity of his friends and followers, showing us how to serve one another, and speaking of the way of love as a way of sacrifice. These things seemed to be of great value to Jesus.

The Mass as a source of unity helps us as Jesus' followers to align our values with the values of Jesus. We are challenged to serve one another. We are encouraged to walk the way of love, perhaps at great sacrifice to ourselves. And we are called to forgiveness and to faithfulness.

Through it all, the Mass reminds us that our faith journey is never a journey we take alone. Jesus is present to us throughout the journey, encouraging and guiding us through the Spirit and also by means of the community gathered around the eucharistic table.

3

Being Catholic

Black Catholic Contributions

Since the early years of the Church, black Catholics have embraced Catholicism with unswerving faith and dedication.

Did you know

- that North Africa was a flourishing center of the early Church?
- that many of the early monks and nuns were black?
- that one of these, Saint Moses the Black, was a great spiritual leader in the early fifth century?

Here is a brief list that will help acquaint you with some of the contributions black Catholics have made throughout the Church's history.

- Saint Benedict the Black (1526–1589) was a Franciscan friar and spiritual leader in Sicily, around Palermo.

- Saint Martin de Porres (1579–1639) was a Dominican friar who took care of the black slaves and the poor of Lima, Peru.

- Elizabeth Lange founded the Oblate Sisters of Providence for black women in Baltimore, 1829.

- Henriette Delille founded the Sisters of the Holy Family in New Orleans in 1842 to serve as teachers and guardians of black children.

- Pierre Toussaint (1766–1853) was a New York hairdresser who practiced remarkable charity. He is now a candidate for sainthood.

6

Jesus Is with Us

Every day your love and care make the presence of Jesus real for your family. At Mass we celebrate Jesus present in our lives and in the Eucharist. Help your child identify and celebrate all the moments when Jesus is present in your child's life.

Jesus is always with us. At Mass we gather together as friends. We celebrate Jesus with us. We remember how Jesus loved and served others.

When we leave Mass, we try to love and serve others as Jesus would. Jesus is always present when we care for one another.

Draw a picture on page 5 showing ways your family will try to make Jesus present to others this week.

At Mass, be aware of the special presence of Jesus in the scriptural readings and in the Eucharist. Bring that presence to everyone you live with, work with, and meet this week.

5

Celebrating the Journey

Leader: Many months ago we began a journey of faith together. Today we come here to recall all that we have learned and shared. We believe that Jesus is here with us and so we celebrate in the name of the Father, and of the Son, and of the Holy Spirit.

All: Amen.

Leader: Jesus, our Friend and our Savior, thank you for being with us on our journey of faith. Stay with us now as we listen carefully to your word. We ask this in your name.

All: Amen.

Reader: A reading from John's Gospel.
The gospel of the Lord.

All: Praise to you, Lord Jesus Christ.

Leader: Remembering that Jesus calls us his friends, let us offer each other a greeting of peace.

All: Amen.

Leader: Jesus, thank you for showing us God's love. Help us to share that love with one another. Keep us united with all our brothers and sisters.

All: Amen.

261

Introducing "Celebrating the Journey"

A vital dimension of Christian faith is the celebrations we experience at all the important moments of our lives. "Celebrating the Journey" is a special feature designed to help celebrate the completion of another important phase of the faith journey.

Using "Celebrating the Journey"

Plan a special time at the end of the year to use this celebration with your group. Select a child to read the suggested story from Scripture. Choose a few of the children's favorite songs to sing at various times during the celebration. You may wish to choose a song or acclamation from THIS IS OUR FAITH Music Program. Allow the children to participate as fully as possible. You may wish to invite others, such as the director of religious education or principal, the pastor, or the children's families to the celebration. End the celebration with a simple snack.

262

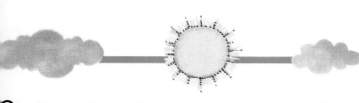

263

Our Church Celebrates Advent

Objectives

- LESSON 1: To help the children understand that Advent is a time of preparation.
- LESSON 2: To help the children appreciate Advent as a time to think about others.
- LESSON 3: To help the children prepare at home, school, and church for the coming of Jesus.
- LESSON 4: To help the children remember to prepare for the coming of Jesus.

Lesson Outlines

	Step 1 Learning About Our Lives	Step 2 Learning About Our Faith	Step 3 Learning How to Live Our Faith
Lesson 1	■ Discuss Christmas preparations. *ABOUT 5 MINUTES*	■ Read and discuss a story. *ABOUT 10 MINUTES*	■ Make Advent preparations. ■ Complete a banner. ■ Pray for help. *ABOUT 15 MINUTES*
Lesson 2	■ Discuss Church decorations. *ABOUT 10 MINUTES*	■ Read and discuss a story. ■ Listen to a Scripture story. *ABOUT 10 MINUTES*	■ Pray together. ■ Identify people in need of kindness. *ABOUT 10 MINUTES*
Lesson 3	■ Recall John's message. ■ Solve riddles. *ABOUT 10 MINUTES*	■ Read and discuss the text. ■ Listen to a Scripture verse. *ABOUT 12 MINUTES*	■ Complete a crossword puzzle. *ABOUT 8 MINUTES*
Lesson 4	**Project** Discuss the lessons of Advent. **Prayer** Prepare for a prayer service and participate in a prayer service.		

Plan Ahead

	Preparing Your Class	**Materials Needed**
Lesson 1	Read through the lesson plan.	■ pencils ■ crayons
Lesson 2	Read through the lesson plan.	■ pencils
Lesson 3	Read the lesson plan.	■ pencils
Lesson 4	Read the lesson plan and follow the directions to make a sample chalkboard to show the children. Cut yarn into 8" pieces, one for each child. Mark an aisle on the floor with tape or yarn.	■ craft sticks, four for each child ■ 4" squares of black construction paper ■ glue, yarn, and white crayons ■ masking tape ■ the song "Come to My Heart"

Additional Resources

As you plan these lessons, consider using the following materials from The Resourceful Teacher Package.

■ *Classroom Activity Sheets for Advent*

■ *Family Activity Sheets for Advent*

■ *Prayers for Every Day*

You may also wish to refer to the following Big Book.

■ *We Celebrate God's Word*, page 4

In preparing the children for the Sunday readings, you may wish to use Silver Burdett Ginn's *Getting Ready for Sunday* student and teacher materials.

REDUCED CLASSROOM ACTIVITIES

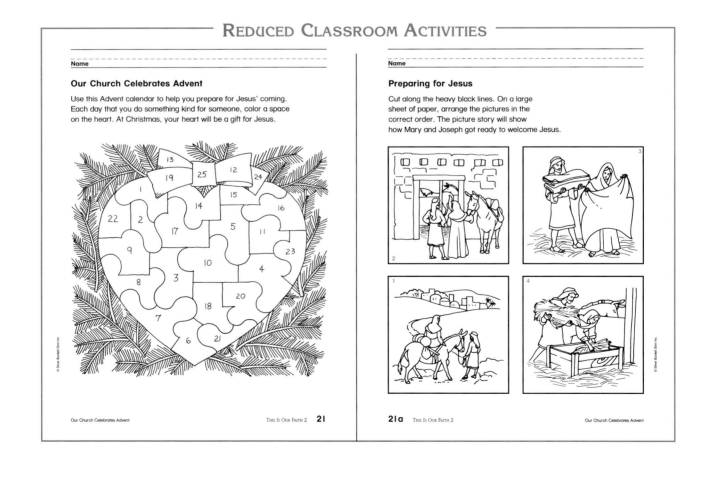

Name

Our Church Celebrates Advent

Use this Advent calendar to help you prepare for Jesus' coming. Each day that you do something kind for someone, color a space on the heart. At Christmas, your heart will be a gift for Jesus.

Name

Preparing for Jesus

Cut along the heavy black lines. On a large sheet of paper, arrange the pictures in the correct order. The picture story will show how Mary and Joseph got ready to welcome Jesus.

Our Church Celebrates Advent   THIS IS OUR FAITH 2   **21**

21a   THIS IS OUR FAITH 2   Our Church Celebrates Advent

JOHN THE BAPTIZER'S ROLE

Many times during the season of Advent, we hear about John the Baptizer's role of preparing the way of the Lord. John, in making immediate preparations for Christ's public ministry, "went about the entire region of the Jordan proclaiming a baptism of repentance which led to the forgiveness of sins" (Luke 3:3). He called the people to conversion so that their minds and hearts were open to listen and to follow Jesus Christ, the Savior.

PREPARING THE WAY OF THE LORD

Our attitudes and actions during Advent are very important. We can passively observe this season, merely waiting for the feast that helps us recall the historical event of Christ's birth. However, as Christians, we are called to participate actively in preparing for Jesus to come to us in mystery through the Eucharist and in majesty at the end of time. To prepare for Christ's coming, we must look within ourselves and ask, "How can I prepare myself to welcome the Lord?"

Children, at this age, maintain a high level of excitement and anticipation as they wait for the celebration of Christmas. They hold a trust that Christmas will come. This belief and anticipation provide a foundation upon which you, as the teacher, can build. During Advent we trust and hope that Jesus, our Savior, will come into our lives in a new way.

Every member of the Christian family longs for this event. We prepare ourselves so that we can celebrate it more joyfully. In these lessons, you can help the children see that we prepare not only to receive gifts but also to be gifts to others through our acts of love and kindness.

LESSON 1

Objective

This lesson helps the children understand that Advent is a time of preparation.

Step 1 / INTRODUCTION

Learning About Our Lives

Discussing Christmas Preparations

Take time to discuss with the children some of the traditional ways their families prepare for Christmas. You may want to share some of your family's traditional preparations. Conclude the discussion by explaining that the Church has a special time of preparation for Christmas. Explain that this special time is called Advent.

Step 2 / DEVELOPMENT

Learning About Our Faith

Reading and Discussing a Story

On the chalkboard, write the names *Elizabeth, Zechariah,* and *John.* Pronounce the names and have the children repeat them. Then have a volunteer read the first paragraph of "A Time to Prepare" on page 264. After the reading, ask the following questions.

- Why were Elizabeth and Zechariah lonely? (*They didn't have children.*)

- What did the angel tell Elizabeth and Zechariah? (*They were going to have a child.*)

Have a volunteer read the second paragraph. After the reading, ask all the children to underline John's message, "Make ready the way of the Lord."

Explain that John was the cousin of Jesus. Tell the children that when John was older, he was called John the Baptizer. He baptized many people with a baptism of sorrow for sin to prepare them for Jesus, the Savior.

264

Our Church Celebrates Advent

A Time to Prepare

Mary had an older cousin named Elizabeth. Elizabeth and her husband, Zechariah, were lonely because they did not have any children of their own. But one day God sent a messenger to Zechariah. The messenger said, "God will send you a son. Name him John. He will help prepare for God's Son, Jesus."

Based on Luke 1:5–17

When John grew up, he was a messenger for God. He told people to prepare their hearts and minds for Jesus. He went from town to town saying, "Make ready the way of the Lord."

Based on Matthew 3:3

Enriching the Lesson

Dramatize the story of John the Baptizer in three scenes: Elizabeth and Zechariah at home alone, longing for a child; God's messenger announcing the news to Zechariah that he and Elizabeth would soon have a child; and John preaching to the people and telling them to prepare for Jesus. Choose volunteers to play the parts of Elizabeth, Zechariah, the messenger, and John. The remainder of the children can act as the crowd listening to John preach.

Activity

During Advent we get ready for Jesus to come into our lives at Christmas. We prepare our hearts for Jesus by being loving and caring.

On the lines below, write ways you can be loving and caring during Advent. Then color the banner.

1. _____

2. _____

3. _____

4. _____

5. _____

Prepare your ♥ for Jesus

Focus on

Advent   The word *Advent* is taken from a Latin word that means "coming." During Advent we prepare to celebrate Christ's coming at Christmas. We recall the historical fact of Jesus' birth in Bethlehem, prepare to celebrate Christ's presence among us, and remember Jesus' promise to come again. Advent also marks the beginning of a new Church year, as we joyfully await our newborn Savior.

Step 3 / CONCLUSION

Learning How to Live Our Faith

Making Advent Preparations

Ask a volunteer to read the explanatory paragraph on page 265. Have the children sit quietly and speak to God with their minds and hearts. Encourage them to ask God to help them choose what they can do during Advent.

Completing a Banner

Distribute crayons. Have the children read aloud the directions for the activity. Then ask them to write what they have chosen to do during Advent. Have the children independently complete the writing and coloring activity.

Praying for Help

Have the children gather in a circle. Tell them that every day during Advent we should ask Jesus to help us prepare our hearts for Christmas. Then have them respond to each petition of the prayer below with the following response: *Prepare our hearts, Jesus.*

- Help us be kind to our family and friends.
- Help us share our time and love.
- Help us care for others.

265

LESSON 2

Objective

This lesson helps the children appreciate Advent as a time to think about others.

Step 1 / INTRODUCTION

Learning About Our Lives

Discussing Church Decorations

Ask the children to name some of the Advent and Christmas decorations they see in church, in school, and on the parish grounds. These may include Advent wreaths, Christmas trees, a crèche, bulletin boards, and so on. Explain that these decorations help us prepare for Jesus' coming at Christmas.

Step 2 / DEVELOPMENT

Learning About Our Faith

Reading and Discussing a Story

Direct the children's attention to page 266 and read with the children "The Church Prepares for Jesus' Coming." Discuss the story with the following questions.

- What did the Mead family see when they got to church? (*An Advent wreath; a tree decorated with paper tags*)

- What color vestments did Father Paul wear? (*Purple*) Explain to the children that the color purple is a sign of preparation and change. During Advent we prepare to welcome Jesus at Christmas by being more loving and caring.

- What was written on the tree tags? (*The names of families that needed food, clothing, and toys*)

- What did Father Paul ask the people? (*To take a name if they wanted to help another family*)

- What did Mrs. Mead tell Kana? (*That Advent was a special time to think about others*)

The Church Prepares for Jesus' Coming

"Hurry, Kara," called Mrs. Mead. "We have to get to church." Kara ran downstairs. Her family was waiting. "We're going to light the Advent wreath today," said David, Kara's brother.

When the Meads got to Saint John Church, it was quiet. The lights were dim. A big tree decorated with paper tags stood in the corner. An Advent wreath with tall candles was near the altar.

The Mass began. Father Paul was dressed in purple vestments. He prayed for Jesus to come into their lives during Advent. Mr. Mead helped Kara light a candle on the wreath.

Later, Father Paul talked about the tags on the tree. He said that the names of families who needed food, clothes, and toys for Christmas were written on the tags. Father asked the people of the parish to take a name if they wanted to help another family.

After Mass, David ran to take a tag from the tree. "Can we help?" asked Kara.

"What a wonderful idea!" said Mrs. Mead. "Advent is a special time to think of others."

★ ★★★ ★ Enriching the Lesson ★

Contact a parish organization that ministers to the needy to get information about a family in the parish that needs help. Work with the children to assemble a Christmas basket for the family. Enlist the parents' help in this effort. Include stocking stuffers and nonperishable food in the basket. Be sure to add a card signed by all the children.

During Advent we pray, "Jesus, you bring light and joy to our lives. Help us to be signs of your light by bringing happiness to others during Advent."

Activity

Write the names of some people you will be kind to this Advent. Use the tree tags.

Teaching Tips

Throughout the four weeks of Advent, take special note of the loving and caring acts the children perform. These actions may be as simple as holding open a door for someone, sharing their lunch with a student who has forgotten his or hers, or playing with a classmate who has few friends. Affirm the students' efforts by praising them and reinforcing that all of these actions help us prepare the way for Jesus.

Listening to a Scripture Story

Ask the children to listen carefully as you tell the following story about the first Christian community: *All of Jesus' followers met together often. They shared everything they had. They sold their property and the things they owned and gave the money to whomever needed it. They ate their meals together and shared their food happily, while praising God* (based on Acts 2:44–47). Note that the Christians showed their love by sharing with and caring for those who needed help.

Step 3 / CONCLUSION

Learning How to Live Our Faith

Praying Together

Read together the prayer at the top of page 267. Encourage the children to look for ways to bring happiness to others during Advent.

Identifying People in Need of Kindness

Ask the children to think about what groups of people are in need of special help and to whom they can show kindness, especially during Advent. Responses may include people who are poor, or homeless, or lonely, or sick. Explain the directions to the activity and have the children complete it. Afterward, encourage sharing.

LESSON 3

Objective

This lesson helps the children prepare at home, school, and church for the coming of Jesus.

Step 1 / INTRODUCTION

Learning About Our Lives

Recalling John's Message

Review the previous lesson with the class.

- What do we call the special time when we prepare for Christmas? (*Advent*)
- Who was John? (*The son of Elizabeth and Zechariah*)
- What was John's message? (*"Make ready the way of the Lord."*)

Help the children recall that John told people to prepare their minds and hearts for Jesus.

Solving Riddles

Point out the following three riddles you have written on the chalkboard. Invite the children to solve these three riddles by completing the rhyme: (1) I am a place, I never roam. You live in me, I am your (*home*). (2) I am easily found, You don't have to search. I am God's house, I am the (*church*). (3) I am a building, That's a rule. You come to learn, I am a (*school*). Tell the children that in today's lesson they will learn how they can prepare for Advent at home, at church, and at school.

Step 2 / DEVELOPMENT

Learning About Our Faith

Reading and Discussing the Text

Instruct the children to open their books to page 268. Read the first paragraph together. Have them suggest specific ways of being loving and caring to family members. You may want to print these suggestions on the chalkboard. The list might include helping a parent, being cheerful, and playing peacefully.

268

Advent in Our Lives

During Advent we prepare our hearts for Jesus. At home we can pray together. We can look for ways to be caring and loving to the people in our families.

At school we can do projects. We can collect toys for children who have none. We can secretly choose names of children in our class for whom we can do kind things during Advent.

In church we listen to God's word. We pray as people have prayed for many years while they have waited for Jesus.

At home, at school, and at church we celebrate Advent. Our words and actions say, "We are getting ready. Jesus is coming into our lives."

268   Advent: Lesson Three

 CURRICULUM CONNECTION

Art Distribute drawing paper and crayons. Invite the children to draw a picture of themselves being more loving and caring at home, at school, or at church. Encourage them to picture themselves doing some specific act that shows they are preparing their hearts for Jesus' birth at Christmas. When everyone has finished, allow time for volunteers to display their drawings and explain them to the group.

Activity

Circle the correct word to complete each sentence. Then use these words to fill in the puzzle below.

1. During Advent we can do _____ acts for our friends.

   (caring)   selfish

2. Advent is a time to _____.

   work   (pray)

3. During Advent we prepare our minds and hearts for _____.

   (Jesus)   Mary

4. We prepare for Christmas during _____.

   Lent   (Advent)

Read the second paragraph with the children. Have them suggest activities that can be done at school to prepare for Christmas. Be sure to include specific Advent preparations your class and/or your school are planning. This list might include a class Mass, prayer service, or service project.

Read the third paragraph. Invite the children to think of ways their parish community prepares for Christmas. Remind the children of the Advent wreath that is displayed and the songs that are sung at Mass.

Have the children read the fourth paragraph. Help them recognize that during Advent we get ready for Christmas by ourselves and with others.

Listening to a Biblical Verse

Tell the students that long ago, God told the people to begin to get ready for Jesus. God sent a holy man called Isaiah to give the people his message. Invite the students to listen as you read Isaiah's words, "Prepare the way for the Lord! Make a straight path for him" (based on Isaiah 40:3). Explain to the class that our loving and caring words and actions during Advent prepare us for Jesus. They help us make a straight path for Jesus to come into our lives.

Step 3 / CONCLUSION

Learning How to Live Our Faith

Completing a Crossword Puzzle

Explain the directions to the activity on page 269. Have the children complete the first part of the activity independently. When they have finished, read the completed sentences aloud together. Then, have each child fill in the crossword puzzle.

Conclude the lesson by praying with the children, "Help us prepare for you, Jesus. Help us find ways to be loving and caring at home, at school, and at church. Amen."

🍎 Teaching Tips

The four weeks of Advent can seem endless to a seven- or eight-year-old child and it is easy for the children to forget the resolutions they may have made for Advent. You may want to review, on a weekly basis, the choices they made to be more loving and caring during Advent. This weekly review will help the children focus on the true meaning of Advent and help them to follow through on their Advent plans.

269

LESSON 4

Objective

This lesson helps the children remember to prepare for the coming of Jesus.

Discussing the Lessons of Advent

Help the children recall their discussion from Lesson 2 of ways to celebrate Advent. Review the lists they made of ways to prepare at home, church, and school. Point out that one way to prepare for Advent at school is by doing projects together. Tell the children they are going to do a project to prepare for Advent.

Direct the children's attention to the Advent project on page 270. Read aloud the first two paragraphs. Show the children the sample you prepared before class.

Give the children step-by-step instructions on how to make the chalkboard. First, have them form a square with their sticks, gluing the top and bottom sticks over the two side pieces. Next, have them glue a piece of black construction paper to three sides of the square. Tell them not to put glue across the top section of the square yet. Next, show the children how to make a hanger for the chalkboard by tying the two ends of the yarn to the top stick of the chalkboard. Tell the children to slip the yarn between the paper and the stick gently so that the paper does not tear. Then have them glue the paper to the fourth side of the square.

Read with the class the second paragraph in the student text. Invite the children to use white crayons or chalk to write Advent messages on their chalkboards.

Read the last paragraph on page 270. Invite the children to identify where they will display their chalkboards.

An Advent Reminder

Make a chalkboard to remind yourself that Advent is a time to prepare for Jesus at home, at school, and at church. These are the things you will need.

- 4 craft sticks
- 1 square sheet of black construction paper
- a white crayon
- glue
- a piece of yarn

Follow the directions your teacher gives you to make your chalkboard. When you are finished, use the crayon to write an Advent message on your board.

You can hang your chalkboard on a doorknob or a mirror. It will remind you to get ready for Jesus.

Teaching Tips

During Advent, many feasts heighten our awareness of what it means to follow Jesus. On December 6, Saint Nicholas shows us the spirit of giving. The Immaculate Conception (December 8) reminds us that Mary was a special part of God's plan for the world from her first moment of life. Our Lady of Guadalupe (December 12) recalls Mary's care for all her children. On December 13, Saint Lucy teaches us to live always by Jesus' light. Share these special Advent days with your class.

Help Us Prepare, Lord Jesus

We can ask Jesus to help us get ready for his coming into our lives at Christmas.

Teacher: With our families we can pray and be helpful.

Children: Help us prepare at home, Lord Jesus.

Teacher: With our classmates we can share and be kind.

Children: Help us prepare at school, Lord Jesus.

Teacher: With our parish we can listen and learn.

Children: Help us prepare at church, Lord Jesus.

All: We want to get ready for you, Jesus. We want you to come into our hearts and minds at Christmas. Help us prepare for your coming.

Preparing for a Prayer Service

Choose an appropriate setting for your prayer service, and place long strips of tape or yarn on the floor to form an aisle in the area of the room you've selected. Have the class practice reading the closing prayer on page 271. Play a recording of "Come to My Heart" (Joe Pinson, *Young People's Glory and Praise,* NALR, page 12) and practice singing this song with the children.

Participating in a Prayer Service

Have the children bring their books and gather in the aisle you have marked. Ask them to make the sign of the cross together. Then begin the prayer service on page 271.

Before praying the closing prayer, invite the children to think silently of ways they can help clear a path for Jesus' coming through their words and actions. Ask them to quietly step out of the aisle when they have decided what they will do at home, school, and church. After all the children have moved out of the aisle, say, "We are clearing a path for Jesus. We are making our path with love and care for others." Then have the children pray the closing prayer aloud together. Conclude by having the children sing "Come to My Heart."

After the prayer service, encourage the children to remember and follow up on their decisions.

Our Church Celebrates Christmas

Objectives ~~~~~~~~

To help the children
- LESSON 1: To help the children respond to the good news that Jesus is our Savior.
- LESSON 2: To help the children appreciate Christmas traditions from around the world.
- LESSON 3: To help the children express their own Christmas stories.
- LESSON 4: To help the children give praise and thanks to God for Jesus.

Lesson Outline ~~~~~~~~

	Step 1 **Learning About Our Lives**	Step 2 **Learning About Our Faith**	Step 3  **Learning How to Live Our Faith**
Lesson 1	■ Discuss shepherds. ■ Study an illustration. *ABOUT 5 MINUTES*	■ Read and discuss a story. ■ Understand the message. *ABOUT 10 MINUTES*	■ Decode a message. ■ Draw a picture. ■ Respond in prayer. *ABOUT 15 MINUTES*
Lesson 2	■ Discuss a Christmas carol. *ABOUT 5 MINUTES*	■ Read about Christmas traditions. *ABOUT 15 MINUTES*	■ Write about Christmas traditions. ■ Pray together. ■ Sing together. *ABOUT 10 MINUTES*
Lesson 3	■ Share Christmas experiences. *ABOUT 5 MINUTES*	■ Read and discuss a story. ■ Listen to a Christmas legend. *ABOUT 20 MINUTES*	■ Complete a prayer. *ABOUT 5 MINUTES*
Lesson 4	**Project** Prepare to do a project; make story boxes; and recall the Christmas message. **Prayer** Prepare for a prayer service and participate in a prayer service.		

Plan Ahead

	Preparing Your Class	Materials Needed
Lesson 1	Read through the lesson plan. Have available some pictures of sheep and shepherds for Step 1.	■ pencils ■ crayons
Lesson 2	Read the lesson plan. Be prepared to teach "Joy to the World."	■ pencils ■ recording of "Joy to the World"
Lesson 3	Read the lesson, especially the legend of the poinsettia found in Step 2. Prepare to tell this legend in your own words.	■ pencils ■ recording of "Joy to the World"
Lesson 4	Read the lesson plan. Make a sample story box to show the class. If you decide to invite the children's parents, do so well ahead of time.	■ construction paper ■ craft sticks, string ■ glue, crayons, scissors ■ shoe boxes ■ song "Children, Run Joyfully"

Additional Resources

As you plan these lessons, consider using the following materials from the The Resourceful Teacher Package.

■ *Classroom Activity Sheets for Christmas*

■ *Family Activity Sheets for Christmas*

■ *Prayers for Every Day*

In preparing the students for the Sunday readings, you may wish to use Silver Burdett Ginn's *Getting Ready for Sunday* student and teacher materials.

REDUCED CLASSROOM ACTIVITIES

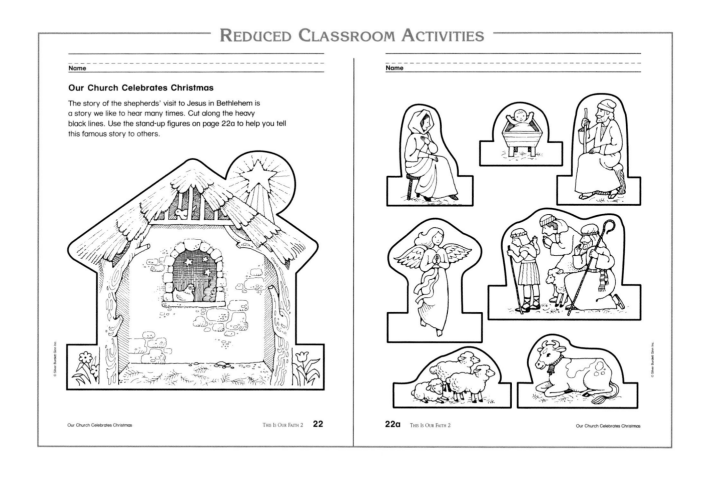

Name _____

Our Church Celebrates Christmas

The story of the shepherds' visit to Jesus in Bethlehem is
a story we like to hear many times. Cut along the heavy
black lines. Use the stand-up figures on page 22a to help you tell
this famous story to others.

Our Church Celebrates Christmas · THIS IS OUR FAITH 2 · **22**

Name _____

22a · THIS IS OUR FAITH 2 · Our Church Celebrates Christmas

Background for the Teacher

THE ROLE OF THE SHEPHERDS

Jesus, whose life has enriched and changed our lives drastically, was born in needy circumstances. His birth was first announced, not to royalty or public officials, but to a group of poor shepherds. Luke relates the story of the angel's announcement of Jesus' birth to the shepherds. Jesus was born into the world to save us all from sin.

The image of shepherd was a powerful one for Jesus. He spoke of himself as the good shepherd who cares for his flock and puts himself at risk to save his sheep. The image of the shepherd serves two purposes in the birth narrative: to identify Jesus as our shepherd; and to proclaim that Jesus was born to save all people, including the most humble, from sin.

JESUS, OUR SAVIOR

At this time of year, you may notice that children may seem to be overly concerned with the gifts they will be receiving for Christmas. They are probably responding to the commercialism that envelops them during this season. Yet, despite this concern, the children are capable of imagining the historical significance of the shepherds' visit to the child Jesus.

These lessons provide you, the teacher, with the opportunity to emphasize the important concept that Jesus was born as our Savior to save all people from the power of sin. In these lessons, the children can begin to realize that Jesus wants us to act as shepherds so that we may bring the good news of salvation to those around us. We can do this by showing our love and concern for others.

LESSON 1

Objective

This lesson helps the children respond to the good news that Jesus is our Savior.

Step 1 / INTRODUCTION

Learning About Our Lives

Discussing Shepherds

Begin class by showing the children pictures of shepherds tending their sheep. Discuss a shepherd's responsibilities.

Studying an Illustration

Remind the children that at Christmastime we see many cards that show pictures of shepherds. Then have the children look at the illustration for this lesson.

Step 2 / DEVELOPMENT

Learning About Our Faith

Reading and Discussing a Story

Have a volunteer read aloud "The Christmas Message" on page 272. Then ask the following questions.

- Why were the shepherds in the fields? (*They were tending their flocks.*)
- What news did the messenger give to the shepherds? (*That their Savior had been born*)
- Who was the Savior? (*Jesus*)

Understanding the Message

Explain to the children that God sent a messenger to the shepherds to show that Jesus came to earth to bring hope to all people. Tell the children that they can visit the Christmas crib when they go to church during the Christmas season. At this time, they can ask Jesus' help in showing love and help to those who are poor or needy.

272

Our Church Celebrates Christmas

The Christmas Message

Shepherds were caring for their sheep in a field near Bethlehem. An angel from God appeared to them and said, "Do not be afraid. I bring you good news. Today your Savior has been born. You will find him in a manger."

The shepherds were surprised and excited. They hurried to Bethlehem. There they found Jesus in the manger. They knew that what the messenger had said was true. Their Savior was born. They were happy and told everyone the good news about Jesus.

Based on Luke 2:8–18

272   Christmas: Lesson One

The Gospel Message In Jesus' time, shepherds were looked down on by society. They were poor and uneducated. That Jesus' birth was first announced to these lowly men and that they were the first to visit the newborn Savior gives us great insight into the message of Saint Luke's Gospel. The writer wants us to understand that Jesus has come to save all people, especially those who suffer from discrimination, poverty, and those who are most in need of God's love. Jesus is the Savior of all!

Cultural Awareness

Explore with the children the people in our world who are most in need of God's love today. Responses may include the homeless, the poor, people who are treated differently because of their skin color or culture, the elderly, or anyone whose country is at war. Discuss with the class how Jesus' birth is good news for the people they named. Invite the children to offer a special prayer for the people who need God's love in a special way today.

Activity

Use the following code to complete the Christmas message.

a	e	i	o	u	s	j	v	b	r	n
1	2	3	4	5	6	7	8	9	10	11

<u>J</u> <u>e</u> <u>s</u> <u>u</u> <u>s</u> , our <u>S</u> <u>a</u> <u>v</u> <u>i</u> <u>o</u> <u>r</u> ,
7   2   6   5   6   6   1   8   3   4   10

is <u>b</u> <u>o</u> <u>r</u> <u>n</u> .
  9   4   10   11

Draw a picture of the shepherds visiting the baby Jesus.

CURRICULUM CONNECTION

Art Invite the children to bring to class a variety of Christmas cards that show pictures of Mary and Joseph's journey to Bethlehem, the Holy Family in the stable after Jesus' birth, the angel's announcement to the shepherds, and the Magi. Also have available several art books that depict classic representations of these events. Invite the children's comments. Use the children's cards to make a Christmas bulletin board.

Learning How to Live Our Faith

Decoding a Message

Direct the children's attention to the good-news activity on page 273 and have them read aloud the directions. Distribute crayons. Have the children independently decode the message.

Drawing a Picture

Have the children complete the drawing activity on page 273. You may want to play Christmas carols while they are working.

Responding in Prayer

Conclude the lesson by asking the children to gather and form a circle. Invite them to join you in prayer by repeating each of the following sentences.

- Lord Jesus, the shepherds were the first to know of your birth.
- Help us to be like the shepherds.
- Help us to believe in you.
- Help us to share your love with all people.

Then have the children sing a Christmas carol.

Objective

This lesson helps the children appreciate Christmas traditions from around the world.

Step 1 / INTRODUCTION

Learning About Our Lives

Discussing a Christmas Carol

Print the words "Joy to the World" on the chalkboard. Ask the children if they have ever sung this Christmas carol. Sing the first two lines with the class. Then ask why we say that Jesus is "joy to the world." Explain to the class that Jesus came to teach everyone how to live and that in today's lesson, the children will learn how people all over the world celebrate Jesus' birth at Christmas.

Step 2 / DEVELOPMENT

Learning About Our Faith +

Reading About Christmas Traditions

Instruct the children to turn to page 274 in their books. Call on volunteers to read aloud "Christmas Around the World." Ask:

■ What does *tradition* mean? ("*Doing something the same way each year*")

■ Why do people in Mexico go from house to house carrying candles? (*To act out Mary and Joseph's search for a place to stay*)

■ How do Irish families welcome travelers during Christmas? (*By placing lighted candles in their front windows*)

■ Who started the tradition of the Christmas crib? (*Saint Francis*)

■ When do people in France put straw in an empty Christmas crib? (*Each time they do a good deed*)

■ How do people in Africa celebrate Christmas? (*By beating drums, sharing neighborhood meals, and singing and dancing*)

Explain that while people throughout the world celebrate Christmas in many ways, all these traditions have the same purpose: to help us joyfully remember that Jesus was God's gift to all the people of the world.

274

Christmas Around the World

Christmas is celebrated everywhere. There are many Christmas traditions. **Tradition** means doing something the same way every year.

In Mexico, <u>Las Posadas</u> is a Christmas tradition. The words <u>las posadas</u> mean "the inns." Families carry lighted candles from house to house, acting out Mary and Joseph's search for a place to stay on Christmas Eve. Two people act as Mary and Joseph. They knock on a neighbor's door and ask to come in. At first the person acting as the innkeeper will not let them in. Joseph asks again. Finally they are welcomed into the house. Inside, everyone sings Christmas carols. The children break open a piñata, a paper or clay decoration filled with candy.

In Ireland, families put lighted candles in their front windows to welcome travelers. This helps the people to remember Mary and Joseph's journey to Bethlehem.

Do you have a Christmas crib under your tree? Saint Francis began this tradition long ago in Italy. Francis used real people to tell the story of the shepherds, angels, and three kings coming to see the Holy Family. Then people began to make small wooden statues to put under their trees at home.

274   Christmas: Lesson Two

 Cultural Awareness

Arrange to share an International Christmas Feast with your class. Ask parents to prepare favorite ethnic Christmas foods for the children to taste and enjoy. You may also have the children make flags representing the different countries from which the foods originate. Encourage the children to be open to the holiday traditions of other people.

Enriching the Lesson

Before class, trace stockings on red construction paper, one for each child. Then talk with the class about family traditions they have regarding Christmas stockings. Where do they hang them? What kind of gifts do they find in them? Distribute the construction paper sheets and have the children cut out the stockings. Invite them to write their names on the stockings and one gift they want to give Jesus for his birthday. Hang the stockings on one of the parish Christmas trees.

Children around the world put pieces of straw in empty cribs each time they do a good deed. This tradition began in France. On Christmas the crib is filled with straw to keep Jesus warm in his bed.

In Africa, drums are used to announce important events. On Christmas Day the sound of drums can be heard in churches and neighborhoods. Later, neighbors eat a special meal. Every family brings a dish to share. The families sing and dance to welcome Jesus.

Christmas traditions help people all over the world celebrate Jesus' birth. Traditions help us remember that Jesus is "Joy to the World!"

Activity

How does your family celebrate Christmas? Write one or two of your family traditions on the lines below.

Learning How to Live Our Faith

Writing About Christmas Traditions

Invite the children to share some of their Christmas traditions with the class. These may include special foods, decorations, favorite television specials, and religious customs. Then explain the directions to the activity at the bottom of page 275. Have the children complete it independently.

Praying Together

Using the places named in this lesson—Mexico, Ireland, Italy, France, and Africa—pray a litany together. Pray: *Jesus, you came for all the people of the world. You are God's gift to the people of _____.* Add the places named in the lesson, one at a time. Invite the children to respond, "Jesus, you bring joy to the world." Include the United States and any other countries the children suggest.

Singing Together

Play a vocal recording of "Joy to the World." Lead the class in singing along with the recording.

📖 **CURRICULUM CONNECTION**

Social Studies With your help have the children use an atlas to locate the five places named in this lesson. Invite them to choose one of the places, draw a map outline of it, and illustrate the Christmas tradition celebrated in the place they chose.

275

Objective

This lesson helps the children recognize some Christmas traditions.

Step 1 / INTRODUCTION

Learning About Our Lives

Sharing Christmas Experiences

Talk with the children about their family traditions on Christmas morning. Use the following questions.

- Who usually wakes up first on Christmas morning?
- What do you do after everyone is up?
- Do you eat a special meal on Christmas morning?
- Do you open presents in any special order?
- Does your family go anywhere together on Christmas day?

As the children share their experiences, point out the variety of ways in which Christmas morning is celebrated. Ask them when their families attend Mass on Christmas. Some may attend on Christmas Eve; others on Christmas Day. Help the students appreciate that our celebration together at Mass is an integral part of our Christmas tradition.

Step 2 / DEVELOPMENT

Learning About Our Faith

Reading and Discussing a Story

Ask volunteers to read aloud "Christmas Morning" on page 276. Compare the Christmas traditions in the story with the family traditions the children discussed earlier. Ask:

- What did Michael's father call the poinsettias? (*The "flower of the holy night"*)
- What color were Father Bowman's vestments? (*White*)
- What did Michael and his family do after Mass? (*Prayed and thanked God for Jesus*)

Discuss the Christmas crèche and other specific traditions their parish may observe at Christmas.

276

Christmas Morning

On Christmas morning, Michael and his family were awake early. They opened gifts and sang songs. They called Nana and Granddad to say "Merry Christmas!" Then everyone hurried to get ready for Mass.

The church was very beautiful. Michael liked the poinsettia plants around the altar. Michael's father told a story about the flower. He called it the "flower of the holy night."

Father Bowman wore white vestments. He began Mass by saying, "Today our Savior is born! Joy to the world!"

After Mass, Michael's family knelt in front of the Christmas stable. They prayed and thanked God for Jesus.

Teaching Tips

Take time during the Christmas season to visit the parish church with your class to view the crèche. As the children stand near the crèche, retell the story of Jesus' birth. Then invite the children to kneel and offer spontaneous prayers, thanking God for our greatest gift, Jesus.

Activity

Unscramble the letters on each flower to form a word. Then use the words to complete the prayer. Pray the prayer aloud together.

Joy _____ to the world _____ !

Jesus _____ has come into our

lives _____ . Alleluia!

Cultural Awareness

In Latin America, it is traditional for every family, rich or poor, to build and display a Christmas scene in their homes. These scenes, called *nacimientos* or *portales,* may be small enough to fit on a table top or they may fill an entire room. The figures used in the scenes are often passed down from generation to generation. On Christmas Eve, neighbors visit one another's homes to view the scenes, sing carols, share traditional foods, and wish one another *Feliz Navidad.*

Listening to a Christmas Legend

In your own words, tell the children the following legend of the poinsettia: *One Christmas night in Mexico, a little boy wanted to bring a gift to Jesus in the manger of the crèche at his parish church. He was poor and could not afford to buy a gift. He began to walk to the church. As he walked, he noticed a green bush. He decided that at least he could bring Jesus a few of the green branches from the bush. As soon as he cut the branches, they sprouted beautiful, red, star-shaped flowers. The legend tells us that a star appeared in the sky over his church that evening as a sign that God was pleased with his gift of love.*

Step 3 / CONCLUSION

Learning How to Live Our Faith

Completing a Prayer

Explain the directions to the scrambled-letter activity on page 277. Instruct the children to complete the prayer. Afterward, check the children's responses by having them pray the prayer aloud together.

Praying Together

Pray with the children, inviting them to respond by saying the response *Joy to the world* after each line.

- Jesus, you were born on Christmas Day.
- Jesus, you are our Savior.
- Jesus, you teach us how to love.

Conclude this session by inviting the children to sing "Joy to the World."

277

LESSON 4

Objective

This lesson helps the children express their own Christmas stories.

Preparing to Do a Project

Read aloud the first paragraph on page 278. Show the children the completed story box you made before class. Then read the second paragraph aloud or have a volunteer read it. Discuss with the children what stories they want to tell in their story boxes.

Making Story Boxes

Distribute the art materials. Have the children cut and decorate a piece of paper for the background for their story. For example, if a child is creating the Nativity story, the background could show animals in the stable and stars in the sky. After they have decorated the background, have each child glue this piece to the inside bottom of his or her shoe box.

Next, have the children cut another piece of construction paper and glue it to one of the long inside panels of the box to serve as the floor or ground. Have the children draw and cut out construction-paper figures for their story. Instruct them to leave a half-inch margin at the bottom of the figures as they cut them out. They can then fold these flaps back and glue them to the story box so that the figures will stand up. Suggest that they glue sticks to the backs of the figures to reinforce them. Show the children how to use string to hang stars from the inside top of the box. Have the children cover the ends of the box with construction paper. Read the last paragraph in the student text aloud. Have the children write a Christmas message on the back of the box expressing why they like Christmas.

Recalling the Christmas Message

Ask the children to retell the story of the shepherds and the Christmas message. If necessary, have them turn to page 272 to review the details. Also, if time permits, have them recall the legend of the poinsettia, which you told them in Lesson 3. Look at page 277 and point out the Christmas prayer they made: "Joy to the world! Jesus has come into our lives. Alleluia!"

278

A Christmas Project

Make a Christmas story box for your room. Follow the directions given by your teacher to make your story box. These are the things you will need.

- construction paper
- craft sticks
- string
- glue
- crayons
- scissors

Think about a picture to draw on your box. You can draw Mary, Joseph, and Jesus in the stable. You can draw shepherds in the field. You can draw a picture of your family on Christmas.

Write a Christmas message on the back of the box.

Teaching Tips

The response in today's prayer service, "Glory to God and peace to all people," is based on the first line of the Glory to God (the Gloria). The Glory to God is prayed or sung on Sundays, solemnities, and feasts, except those celebrated during Advent or Lent. On Christmas and Easter, the Glory to God is often accompanied by the ringing of bells. Provide the children with bells, tambourines, and other rhythm instruments to use during the prayer service.

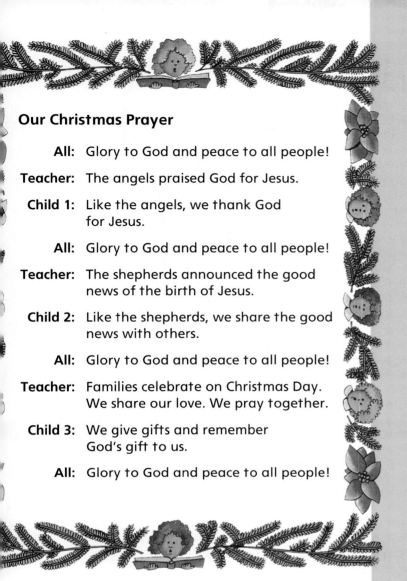

Our Christmas Prayer

All: Glory to God and peace to all people!

Teacher: The angels praised God for Jesus.

Child 1: Like the angels, we thank God for Jesus.

All: Glory to God and peace to all people!

Teacher: The shepherds announced the good news of the birth of Jesus.

Child 2: Like the shepherds, we share the good news with others.

All: Glory to God and peace to all people!

Teacher: Families celebrate on Christmas Day. We share our love. We pray together.

Child 3: We give gifts and remember God's gift to us.

All: Glory to God and peace to all people!

Preparing for a Prayer Service

Before the prayer service, divide the class into three groups. Ask one group to be the angels, one to be the shepherds, and one to be the families. Have the groups prepare pantomimes showing the angels praising God, the shepherds announcing the good news, and families celebrating Christmas. Give the children ample time to practice.

Select three volunteers and assign one of them to each of the three parts labeled **Child** on page 279. Have the children practice the response "Glory to God and peace to all people!" Play a recording of "Children, Run Joyfully" and practice singing it with the class. Also, practice a traditional carol.

Participating in a Prayer Service

Ask the children and the parent visitors to gather around you. Invite everyone to sing "Children, Run Joyfully." Afterward, make the sign of the cross together. Then begin the prayer service on page 279. At the appropriate points, ask the volunteers to read and the groups to perform their pantomimes. In conclusion, invite the children to thank God silently for the gift of Jesus. Discuss what gifts of love they can give to others at Christmas and encourage the class to share their ideas. Finally, sing a traditional Christmas carol together.

Our Church Celebrates Lent

Objectives ~~~~~~~

- LESSON 1: To help the children understand that Lent is a time of sacrifice.
- LESSON 2: To help the children understand that our Lenten sacrifices help us prepare for Easter.
- LESSON 3: To help the children learn about the tradition of Lenten prayer.
- LESSON 4: To help the children understand Lent as a time for fasting.
- LESSON 5: To help the children recognize the importance of making sacrifices and doing good deeds during Lent.

Lesson Outlines ~~~~~~~

	Step 1 Learning About Our Lives	**Step 2** Learning About Our Faith	**Step 3** Learning How to Live Our Faith
Lesson 1	■ Discuss changes. *ABOUT 5 MINUTES*	■ Learn about Lent. ■ Reflect on sacrifices. *ABOUT 12 MINUTES*	■ Make Lenten resolutions. ■ Complete a maze. *ABOUT 13 MINUTES*
Lesson 2	■ Identify sacrifices. *ABOUT 5 MINUTES*	■ Read and discuss a story. ■ Listen to a story about sacrifice. ■ Draw pictures. *ABOUT 15 MINUTES*	■ Complete an activity. *ABOUT 10 MINUTES*
Lesson 3	■ Recall the meaning of Lent. *ABOUT 5 MINUTES*	■ Read and discuss the text. ■ Listen to a Scripture story. *ABOUT 15 MINUTES*	■ Solve a coded message. *ABOUT 10 MINUTES*
Lesson 4	■ Review resolutions. *ABOUT 6 MINUTES*	■ Read and discuss the text. ■ Listen to a story about Jesus. *ABOUT 12 MINUTES*	■ Pray a prayer for Lent. ■ Complete an activity. *ABOUT 12 MINUTES*
Lesson 5	**Project** Review Lenten sacrifices and make a cross to color. **Prayer** Think about new hearts; prepare a prayer service and participate in a prayer service.		

Plan Ahead

	Preparing Your Class	**Materials Needed**
Lesson 1	Read through the lesson plan.	■ pencils
Lesson 2	Read the lesson plan. Bring to class several pictures of people doing good and kind things.	■ pencils ■ pictures of people doing kind things ■ drawing paper ■ crayons or markers
Lesson 3	Read the entire lesson plan.	■ pencils
Lesson 4	Read the lesson plan. Purchase pretzels to share in Step 3.	■ pencils ■ pretzels to share with the children
Lesson 5	Read the lesson plan. Obtain recording of "This Is My Commandment."	■ pencils, crayons ■ recording of "This Is My Commandment" ■ red construction paper ■ scissors

Additional Resources

As you plan these lessons, consider using the following materials from The Resourceful Teacher Package.

■ *Classroom Activity Sheets for Lent*

■ *Family Activity Sheets for Lent*

■ *Prayers for Every Day*

You may also wish to refer to the following Big Book.

■ *We Celebrate God's Word,* pages 12, 18

In preparing the children for the Sunday readings, you may wish to use Silver Burdett Ginn's *Getting Ready for Sunday* student and teacher materials.

REDUCED CLASSROOM ACTIVITIES

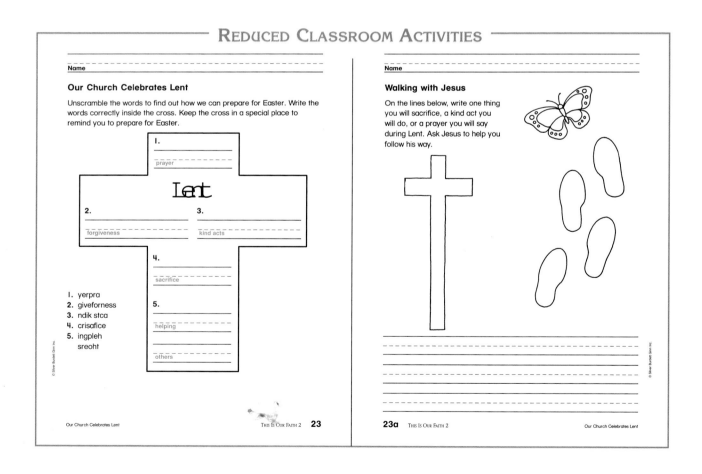

Name _____

Our Church Celebrates Lent

Unscramble the words to find out how we can prepare for Easter. Write the words correctly inside the cross. Keep the cross in a special place to remind you to prepare for Easter.

1. _____
   prayer

Lent

2. _____
   forgiveness

3. _____
   kind acts

4. _____
   sacrifice

5. _____
   helping
   _____
   others

1. yerpra
2. giveforness
3. ndik stca
4. crisafice
5. ingpleh sreoht

© Silver Burdett Ginn Inc.

Our Church Celebrates Lent   THIS IS OUR FAITH 2   **23**

Name _____

Walking with Jesus

On the lines below, write one thing you will sacrifice, a kind act you will do, or a prayer you will say during Lent. Ask Jesus to help you follow his way.

_____
_____
_____
_____
_____

© Silver Burdett Ginn Inc.

23a   THIS IS OUR FAITH 2   Our Church Celebrates Lent

Background for the Teacher

FASTING AND PRAYING

Before Jesus began his public life, he spent forty days in the desert. It was a time of fasting, temptation, and prayer. It was also a period of intense preparation for the ministry he was about to undertake. And it was, ultimately, a preparation for Jesus' death and resurrection. Jesus prepared for his redemptive acts during those forty days. Like Jesus, we also spend forty days in anticipation of what is to come. While we do not retreat to a desert, we do use this time to look inward—to examine what is keeping us from our own redemption. Based on this internal reflection, we perform acts of penance and reconciliation as a sign of our need for conversion. During Lent we respond to the possibilities of God's promise, "I will give you a new heart and place a new spirit within you" (Ezekiel 36:26). We prepare for Easter.

THE SEASON OF LENT

The Lenten season can seem like forever to second graders. Despite their enthusiasm to perform acts of love and sacrifice during this time, the children may forget the Lenten sacrifices they have promised to make. In these lessons, you, the teacher, will need to be mindful of the difficulty in sustaining even the best intentions for six weeks. Your task is to keep alive the children's incentive to perform good works during the season of Lent. Continuous praise and encouragement will help them as they prepare to celebrate Christ's resurrection.

LESSON 1

Objective

This lesson helps the children understand that Lent is a time of sacrifice.

Step 1 / INTRODUCTION

Learning About Our Lives

Discussing Changes

Begin class by thinking about some of the changes that the children have undergone since infancy. Then ask the children to think about changes they would like to make in themselves. Steer the children away from physical changes by suggesting that they might do things like study harder and read more books. Conclude the discussion by explaining that in today's lesson you are going to talk about a special season of change.

Step 2 / DEVELOPMENT

Learning About Our Faith +

Learning About Lent

Direct the students' attention to the illustration on page 280. Explain that before Jesus began teaching people about God, he spent forty days in the desert praying and fasting. Tell the children that the word *fasting* means "eating less food than we usually do."

Have a volunteer read the text for "A Time for Prayer and Sacrifice." On the chalkboard write the words *reconciliation* and *sacrifice*. Remind the children that reconciliation is the process of making up and being friends again. Also remind them God forgives our sins and asks us to be more loving and to forgive others.

Reflecting on Sacrifices

Explain that sacrifices are the good and kind acts we do to show that we are trying to live as God's children. Tell the children that Jesus made a sacrifice for us when he died on the cross. Invite them to share specific sacrifices they have made. Also share sacrifices you have made.

Our Church Celebrates Lent

A Time for Prayer and Sacrifice

During Lent we remember that Jes[us] prayed in the desert. He asked God t[o] help him show others how to live as God's children. Like Jesus, we pray during Lent. We ask God to help us ge[t] ready to celebrate Jesus' resurrection[.]

Lent is also a time of reconciliation[.] We ask God to forgive us. We also forgive others. We do good and kind acts to show God that we are sorry fo[r] our sins. We make sacrifices. We give [ ] something that is ours to help other people. Our sacrifices and kind acts he[lp] us prepare for Easter.

Teaching Tips

Decorate the classroom with symbols of Lent. You might place large, bare branches in a flower pot in the prayer area as a reminder that through the sacrifices we make, we are called to grow and change during Lent. During the Easter season, replace the bare branches with bouquets of spring flowers.

Activity

Find your way through the maze to Jesus. There are letters along the way. As you come to each letter, copy it on the line below. The letters will form a word to complete the sentence.

During Lent, God is pleased by our

<u>sacrifices</u> .

CURRICULUM CONNECTION

Science Lent is a perfect time to experiment with the growth of grasses, bulbs, or vegetables. In flower pots filled with soil, have the children seed different grasses. Label each type of grass and water often. You might also plant amaryllis bulbs or start a plant by putting the cut end of a sweet potato in a jar of water and placing it in the sun. Add water as needed. After the potato sprouts, plant it in soil. During Lent, comment on the growth you observe and compare it to the children's growth.

Learning How to Live Our Faith

Making Lenten Resolutions

Have the children think of good deeds they could perform during this Lenten season to prepare for Easter. Encourage the children to share their thoughts. Write each idea on the chalkboard or on a poster. Ask the students to consider the consequences of change. For example: If a child suggests that not fighting with a younger brother would be a good deed, ask the child, "How would not fighting change things at your house?" Guide the children in understanding that our sacrifices and good deeds during Lent will make our homes, our schools, and our communities happier and more loving places.

Completing a Maze

Have a volunteer read aloud the directions for the activity on page 281. Instruct the children to work independently. After they have finished, ask them to read aloud the sentence they have completed, "During Lent, God is pleased by our sacrifices." For a few minutes, have the children reflect quietly and ask God's help in sacrificing during Lent.

LESSON 2

Objective

This lesson helps the children understand that our Lenten sacrifices help us prepare for Easter.

Step 1 / INTRODUCTION

Learning About Our Lives

Identifying Sacrifices

Show the children several pictures of people doing good and kind things. Have the students identify what is happening in each picture. Discuss what the pictures have in common (*They show people being kind and good to others*). Review Sister Joan's definition of the word *sacrifice*. Also remind the children that sacrifices are the good and kind acts we do to show that we are trying to live as God's children. Have the children look again at the pictures you brought to class. Invite them to identify the sacrifice that is being made in each picture.

Step 2 / DEVELOPMENT

Learning About Our Faith

Reading and Discussing a Story

Ask a volunteer to read aloud "Preparing for Easter" on page 282. Ask:

■ What do sacrifices help us do? (*Prepare for Easter*)

■ How would Hal be making a sacrifice? (*He would give up eating dessert.*)

■ How would Lisa be making a sacrifice? (*She would let her brother watch his favorite TV show.*)

■ Why did Sister Joan's class pray together? (*To ask for God's help*)

Discuss with the children what other sacrifices Sister Joan's class may have suggested. Help the class focus on specific sacrifices that second graders can make.

Preparing for Easter

Sister Joan's class was talking about Lent. Sister wrote the word **sacrifice** on the board. She told the children that to sacrifice means to give something out of love. Making sacrifices helps us prepare for Easter.

"How can we sacrifice during Lent?" Sister Joan asked.

"I will give up dessert for Lent," said Hal.

"I will let my brother watch his favorite TV show," said Lisa.

The other children thought of sacrifices they could make. They prayed together, asking God to help them make the sacrifices they had chosen.

 *Focus on*

Lent The word *Lent* comes from a word with two meanings: "lengthen" and "springtime." During Lent, the hours of daylight lengthen as winter passes into spring. The primary color associated with the season of Lent is purple. The color purple represents sorrow, penitence, change, and preparation.

Activity

Circle the word hidden in each line.
The words tell how we can sacrifice
during Lent.

G	I	V	E	J	E	S
S	H	A	R	E	T	H
K	L	O	V	E	D	A
I	P	R	A	Y	L	O
E	C	A	R	E	G	N

Finish this letter about a sacrifice you will make to get
ready for Easter.

Dear Jesus, _____

_____

During Lent, I will _____

_____

_____

_____

_____

_____ .

Love,

_____

_____

⭐ ⭐ ⭐ ⭐
Enriching the Lesson ⭐

Distribute crayons and strips of
tagboard measuring 2" × 6". To
reinforce the importance of the
new word the children learned in
this lesson, have them print the
word *sacrifice* on the strip vertically and decorate it by making
small crosses on the top and bottom of the strip. Encourage the
students to use the strip as a
bookmark in any book that they
use frequently so that they will remember their Lenten resolutions.

Listening to a Story About Sacrifice

Tell the children the following story to help
them discover another way to sacrifice. *One
day Jesus was teaching in the Temple. He
saw a poor woman come into the Temple. He
watched her quietly put two small coins into
the collection. Jesus said, "This poor woman
has made a great sacrifice. Other people put
their extra money in the collection, but this
poor woman gladly gave the few pennies that
she had"* (based on Luke 21:1–4).

Drawing Pictures

Distribute drawing paper and crayons or felt-
tip markers. Invite the children to draw a
picture of the story of the poor woman in the
temple. At the bottom of the page, have the
children print the words "We make sacrifices
during Lent."

Step 3 / CONCLUSION

Learning How to Live Our Faith

Completing an Activity

Explain the directions to the hidden-word
activity on page 283. (The hidden words are
give, share, love, pray, and *care.*) Direct the
children's attention to the second half of the
activity at the bottom of the page. Talk with
the children about some of the sacrifices they
have thought about in the lessons on Lent. Ask
them to choose a sacrifice that they will make
during Lent and print it on the lines provided.
As the children are finishing their letters to
Jesus, move about the room and help them
with spelling and any other questions they
may have.

LESSON 3

Objective

This lesson helps the children learn about the Church's tradition of Lenten prayer.

Step 1 / INTRODUCTION

Learning About Our Lives

Recalling the Meaning of Lent

Review what the children know about Lent by asking the following questions.

- What do we prepare for during Lent? (*Easter; to celebrate Jesus' resurrection*)

- How do we get ready for Easter during Lent? (*Pray; express sorrow for our sins; make sacrifices*)

- What are sacrifices? (*Things we give out of love*)

Step 2 / DEVELOPMENT

Learning About Our Faith

Reading and Discussing the Text

Direct the children's attention to page 284 and have the children take turns reading "The Church Prays During Lent" aloud. Use the questions below to guide the discussion.

- Why do we pray during Lent? (*To ask God to help us be more like Jesus*)

- What do we call the first day of Lent? (*Ash Wednesday*)

- What do the ashes mean? (*That we want to follow Jesus more closely*)

- What do the Stations of the Cross help us remember? (*How Jesus showed his love for us*)

- Why do we celebrate the sacrament of Reconciliation during Lent? (*To tell God we are sorry for our sins; to ask God to help us grow in love*)

The Church Prays During Lent

Our Church has special ways of praying during the forty days of Lent. These prayers help us remember that Lent is a time to change. When we pray, we think about how we have been living. We ask God to help us be more like Jesus.

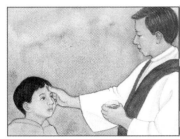

Ash Wednesday is the first day of Lent. When we go to church, the priest or another minister traces the sign of the cross on our foreheads with ashes. The ashes are a sign that we want to follow Jesus more closely.

During Lent we can pray the Stations of the Cross with our class or families. The Stations of the Cross tell us how Jesus died. In church we see pictures or statues that show Jesus going to Calvary, the place where he died. We call each picture a station—a place where we stop to pray. At each station we remember how Jesus showed his love for us.

Lent is also a time to celebrate the sacrament of Reconciliation. We think about the times we haven't acted with love. We tell God we are sorry for our sins. We ask God to help us grow in love so that we can share in Jesus' new life on Easter.

Enriching the Lesson

Take the children to church to see the Stations of the Cross. Then have them create a Stations mural. Divide the class into groups, one group for each station and one group for the resurrection. Distribute butcher paper panels, crayons, and index cards on which you have written the station titles. Share the mural with other classes by displaying it on a wall outside your classroom.

Activity

Solve this coded message. The message is a prayer that the Church prays during Lent. Copy each letter on the spaces below. As you do this, follow these directions.

- Change every A to E.
- Change every E to A.
- Change every O to U.
- Change every U to O.
- Change every S to T.
- Change every T to S.

DAER JATOT,
HALP OT SORN EWEY FRUM TIN. HALP OT SU LIVA SHA GUUD NAWT.

Dear Jesus,
Help us turn away from sin.
Help us to live the good news.

Invite the children to sit around you in a circle as you share the following Scripture story. *One day, Jesus' friends asked him to teach them how to pray. Jesus taught them to pray The Lord's Prayer. Then Jesus said, "If you forgive others for the wrongs they do to you, your Father in heaven will forgive you. But if you don't forgive others, your Father will not forgive your sins* (based on Matthew 6:14–15).

As you discuss this reading with the children, help them to grow in awareness that during Lent, Jesus asks us to do more than tell God that we are sorry for our sins. Jesus also tells us to make peace with those we have hurt and to forgive anyone who has hurt us.

Step 3 / CONCLUSION

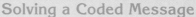

Learning How to Live Our Faith

Solving a Coded Message

Explain the directions to the activity on page 285. Caution the children to follow the instructions exactly. When they are finished, have the children read aloud the Lenten prayer together. Explain that the priest prays these words as he signs us with ashes on Ash Wednesday.

CURRICULUM CONNECTION

Music   Referring to the THIS IS OUR FAITH *Hymnal,* help the children learn one or more of the following songs for Lent.

- "Jesus, You Love Us" by Christopher Walker, page 75

- "Olive Trees" by Jack Miffleton, page 21

- "Psalm 89" by Christopher Walker, page 22

LESSON 4

Objective

This lesson helps the children understand Lent as a time for fasting.

Step 1 / INTRODUCTION

Learning About Our Lives

Reviewing Resolutions

Have the children recall the sacrifices they said they would make to prepare for Easter. Ask them to turn to page 283 in their books. Then ask the children how well they have been able to keep their resolutions. Remind them that Lent is not over and that they still have time to make the sacrifices they promised.

Step 2 / DEVELOPMENT

Learning About Our Faith

Reading and Discussing the Text

Instruct the children to turn to page 286 and read the title aloud. Write the word *fasting* on the chalkboard. Recall that in Lesson 1 the children learned that fasting means *eating less food than we usually do.* Tell the children that they will learn more about fasting in today's lesson.

Call on volunteers to read aloud "A Time for Fasting." Ask:

- How can children fast during Lent? (*By not eating between meals; by giving up a treat or dessert*)

- Why did people long ago make special breads during Lent? (*They could not eat regular bread.*)

- What do we call the special breads people made during Lent? (*Pretzels*)

- What does eating pretzels remind us of during Lent? (*That Lent is a time to pray and fast*)

A Time for Fasting

Fasting is one way we can sacrifice during Lent. Fasting is eating less food than we usually do. During Lent the Church asks grown-ups to fast in a special way.

Children can fast during Lent, too. We can decide not to eat between meals. We can give up candy or another treat. We may choose not to eat dessert for the forty days of Lent. God does not want us to stop eating healthy meals during Lent. God always wants us to keep our bodies strong.

Long ago, people fasted during Lent by not eating anything made with eggs, yeast, butter, or milk. Bread is made with all these ingredients, so the people did not eat regular bread. They made a special Lenten bread with flour, water, and salt. They twisted the bread into the shape of two arms crossed in prayer. Today, we call this special Lenten bread pretzels.

At meals during Lent we can eat pretzels. It will remind us that Lent is a time to pray and fast.

Teaching Tips

You may want to point out to the children that the shape of pretzels (two arms crossed in prayer) has another meaning. Traditionally, the three loops are a sign of the Blessed Trinity—the one God in the three persons of God the Father, God the Son (Jesus) and God the Holy Spirit. Remind the children that each time we make the sign of the cross, we also remember the Blessed Trinity: the Father, Son, and Holy Spirit.

A Prayer for Lent

Dear God,
Please accept our sacrifices during Lent.
Help us to follow Jesus always.
Amen.

Activity

How will you fast during Lent?
On the pretzel, write the name of a favorite food
or activity that you will give up during Lent.

Ask the children to listen carefully as you tell them the following story based on Matthew 6:16–18. *Jesus said to his friends, "When you fast, don't look sad like the showoffs do when they go without food. Instead, comb your hair and wash your face. Then other people won't know that you are fasting. But your Father in heaven sees what you are doing and your Father will reward you."*

Explain that God does not want us to brag about our Lenten sacrifices. God wants us to make our sacrifices quietly as a sign that we are trying to follow Jesus more closely.

Step 3 / CONCLUSION

Learning How to Live Our Faith

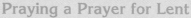

Praying a Prayer for Lent

Have the children read aloud together the Lenten prayer at the top of page 287. You may wish to add gestures or a simple melody line to the prayer.

Now ask the children to quiet their hearts. When the children are ready, pray the prayer together.

Completing an Activity

Read aloud the directions to the activity at the bottom of the page and have the children complete it. Afterward, invite them to read what they have written. Conclude the lesson by sharing with the children the pretzels you brought to class.

Enriching the Lesson

Point out to the children that Jesus himself fasted for forty days before he began his ministry. Christian tradition associates this act of Jesus with the forty-day fast of Moses during the giving of the Ten Commandments (see Exodus 34:28).

LESSON 5

Objective

This lesson helps the children recognize the importance of making sacrifices and doing good deeds during Lent.

Reviewing Lenten Sacrifices

Ask the children to define and discuss Lenten sacrifices. Use the following questions.

- Lent is a time for what three things? (*Prayer, sacrifice, and reconciliation*)
- What is a sacrifice? (*Giving up something that is ours to help others*)
- What are some words that tell how we can sacrifice during Lent? (Give, share, love, pray, care)

Making a Cross to Color

Have a volunteer read aloud the project directions on page 288. Invite the children to count the squares on the cross. Ask why they think there are forty squares on the cross. Help them realize that there are also forty days in the season of Lent.

Discuss with the children why keeping our Lenten promises is difficult. Emphasize that sometimes we forget our Lenten promises because Lent is so long. Explain that by working on this project every day, they will remember to do good and kind deeds all during Lent. Distribute crayons and invite the children to number the squares and color one square.

To make this project effective, call attention to it daily during Lent. Be sure to have the crosses available for the prayer service in Lesson 4 of the Easter lessons.

288

A Lenten Project

This cross will help you get ready for Easter. Make a sacrifice each day. Find ways to do good and kind things for others.

Number all the squares. Each day that you make a sacrifice, color a square.

Enriching the Lesson

Bring to class pictures or outlines of different crosses that have been used throughout the Church's history. These may include the Latin, Celtic, and Jerusalem crosses. The Latin, or Calvary, cross is thought to be like the cross on which Jesus was crucified. The circle on the Celtic cross is a sign that God's love for us is never-ending. The five crosses that make up the Jerusalem cross are a reminder of Jesus' wounds suffered during his sacrifice on the cross.

Our Prayer for Lent

Group 1: Lent is a time to pray.
Be with us, O God, as we pray.

Group 2: Lent is a time of reconciliation.
Forgive us, O God, and give us
forgiving hearts.

Group 1: Lent is a time of sacrifice.
Help us, O God, to be kind and good
to others.

Group 2: Lent is a time to prepare for Easter.
Make us ready, O God, for the resurrection
of Jesus.

Teacher: The Lord says, "I will give you a new heart.
I will put my spirit within you."

Based on Ezekiel 36:26–27

All: We pray,
Give us a new heart, O God!
Put your Spirit within us!

Lent: Lesson Five   289

Thinking About New Hearts

Ask the children to listen carefully as you read these words: "The Lord says, 'I will give you a new heart. I will put my spirit within you'" (based on Ezekiel 36:26–27). Ask the children what they think it means to have a new heart. Lead them to understand that when we make Lenten sacrifices, we are showing that we are sorry for our sins. When we try to live as Jesus teaches us, we have new, pure hearts.

Preparing for a Prayer Service

Divide the class into two groups. Have the groups practice the readings on page 289. Play a recording of the song "This Is My Commandment" and teach it to the class. Select a volunteer to proclaim the Scripture on page 289. Distribute red construction paper and scissors and have each child cut out a construction-paper heart. Have each child write his or her name on the heart.

Participating in a Prayer Service

Invite the children to bring their books and their construction-paper hearts and gather around you near the bulletin board or a poster you made prior to the session. Read the title *I Will Give You a New Heart,* which you have lettered on the poster or bulletin board. Ask the children to pray the Sign of the Cross together, then say, "Today we ask God's help in preparing for Easter. We ask God to be with us during the forty days of Lent." Begin the prayer service on page 289.

Ask each child in turn to tape his or her construction-paper heart to the bulletin board or poster as a sign of the child's willingness to prepare his or her heart for Easter. Have the children pray the closing prayer on page 289. Finally, invite them to sing "This Is My Commandment."

🍎 Teaching Tips

Throughout the six weeks of Lent, remind the children of Jesus' sacrifice on the cross and their Lenten promises by tracing the sign of the cross on their foreheads as you dismiss them each day. This silent ritual may replace the prayer you usually pray at the end of the day. The change in ritual may help the children recognize that Lent is a time of special preparation for Easter. As an alternative, you might pair up the students and have them sign one another's forehead.

Our Church Celebrates Holy Week

Objectives

- LESSON 1: To help the children prepare to celebrate Holy Thursday, Good Friday, and Holy Saturday.
- LESSON 2: To help the children understand that Jesus gave us the gift of himself in the Eucharist on Holy Thursday.

Lesson Outlines

	Step 1 Learning About Our Lives	**Step 2** Learning About Our Faith	**Step 3** Learning How to Live Our Faith
Lesson 1	■ Discuss Church celebrations. *ABOUT 5 MINUTES*	■ Read about three special days of prayer. *ABOUT 10 MINUTES*	■ Complete a matching activity. ■ Act out the liturgies. *ABOUT 15 MINUTES*
Lesson 2	■ Discuss celebrations. *ABOUT 5 MINUTES*	■ Explain the days of Holy Week. ■ Read about Holy Thursday. *ABOUT 15 MINUTES*	■ Complete a word puzzle. ■ Thank Jesus for the Eucharist. *ABOUT 10 MINUTES*

Plan Ahead

	Preparing Your Class	Materials Needed
Lesson 1	Read the lesson plan. Assemble the props needed in Step 3.	■ basin or bowl for washing the children's feet ■ towel, water ■ large crucifix ■ large candle ■ pencils
Lesson 2	Read through the lesson plan. Be ready to tell the children about what happened on Passion (Palm) Sunday and Holy Thursday.	■ pencils

Additional Resources

As you plan these lessons, consider using the following materials from The Resourceful Teacher Package.

■ *Classroom Activity Sheets for Holy Week*

■ *Family Activity Sheets for Holy Week*

■ *Prayers for Every Day*

You may also wish to refer to the following Big Book.

■ *We Celebrate God's Word,* page 19

In preparing the children for the Sunday readings, you may wish to use Silver Burdett Ginn's *Getting Ready for Sunday* student and teacher materials.

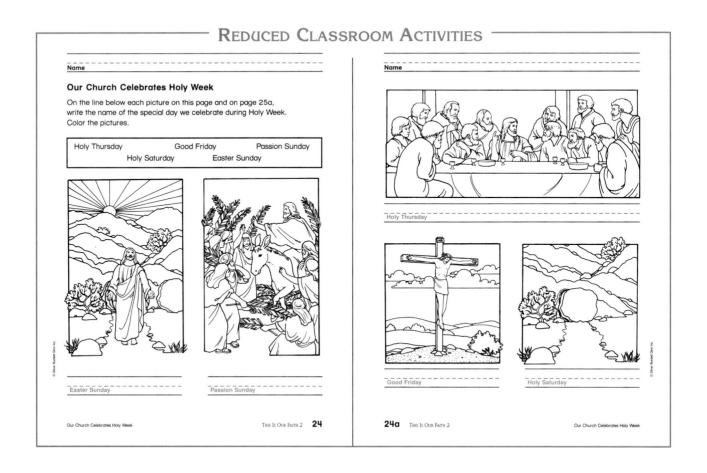

REDUCED CLASSROOM ACTIVITIES

Name

Our Church Celebrates Holy Week

On the line below each picture on this page and on page 25a, write the name of the special day we celebrate during Holy Week. Color the pictures.

Holy Thursday	Good Friday	Passion Sunday
	Holy Saturday	Easter Sunday

Easter Sunday

Passion Sunday

Our Church Celebrates Holy Week   THIS IS OUR FAITH 2   **24**

Name

Holy Thursday

Good Friday

Holy Saturday

24a   THIS IS OUR FAITH 2   Our Church Celebrates Holy Week

Background for the Teacher

THE TRIDUUM

During Holy Week the strands of past, present, and future seem to be drawn together. Our liturgies relive the events of Christ's last week on earth, beginning with his triumphal entry into Jerusalem on Passion Sunday, when we claim Jesus as our leader. At sundown on Holy Thursday, Lent ends and the three sacred days of the Triduum begin. The Triduum is at the very heart of our beliefs and the high point of the liturgical year. During these three days, we celebrate Christ's passage from death to new life. The Triduum is often called the Passover of the Lord.

HOLY THURSDAY

In studying the lessons about the Eucharist, the children have learned about the words and actions of Jesus during the Last Supper. While teaching Lesson 2, emphasize the importance of our participation during the Holy Thursday Mass. Emphasize that through our participation in the Eucharist, we, too, share the body and blood of Christ, we thank Jesus for his continuing presence, and we look to the future with hope.

TEACHING THE LESSONS

Seven-year-old children are familiar with holiday celebrations. Special days, special foods, and rituals mark their family traditions. In these lessons, you will have the opportunity to present to the children the traditional sacred celebrations of the Catholic community.

Lesson 1 focuses on the three days of the Triduum—Holy Thursday, Good Friday, and Holy Saturday; and the liturgies of these days—The Evening Mass of the Lord's Supper, The Celebration of the Lord's Passion, and the Easter Vigil. In teaching this lesson, keep in mind that the children might not participate in these liturgies due to the evening schedule and their length. For now, it is enough that the children recognize these days as holy and that they be aware of the central events that demonstrate Jesus' ultimate love for us and the life to which he invites us.

Objective

This lesson helps the children prepare to celebrate Holy Thursday, Good Friday, and Holy Saturday.

Step 1 / INTRODUCTION

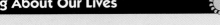

Learning About Our Lives

Discussing Church Celebrations

Invite the children to name special Church celebrations they have attended. These may include Mass, baptisms, First Eucharist liturgies, Christmas pageants, weddings, and school liturgies. Tell the children that when Lent is over, the Church community comes together to celebrate the three most important days of the Church year.

Step 2 / DEVELOPMENT

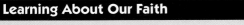

Learning About Our Faith

Reading About Three Special Days of Prayer

Read "Three Special Days of Prayer" on page 290 with the class. Discuss the reading with the following questions.

- What do we remember on Holy Thursday? (*Jesus' Last Supper*)

- Why does the priest wash people's feet during Mass? (*To remind us to serve others as Jesus did. Explain to the children that they will learn more about Holy Thursday in the next lesson.*)

- What do we remember on Good Friday? (*Jesus' death on the cross*)

- Why do we kiss or touch the cross? (*To show our love for Jesus*)

- Why is the Easter candle lighted on Holy Saturday night? (*To show that Jesus has risen*)

- When do we receive Jesus' new life? (*When we are baptized*)

Our Church Celebrates Holy Week

Three Special Days of Prayer

We celebrate the three holiest days of the year when Lent ends. They begin on Holy Thursday evening and end on Easter Sunday evening.

On Holy Thursday night we remember Jesus' Last Supper. During Mass, the priest washes the feet of twelve people. This is what Jesus did the night before he died. The washing of feet reminds us to serve others.

On Good Friday we go to church to hear the story of Jesus' death on the cross. We show our love for Jesus by kissing a special cross or by touching it with our hands. Then we all pray The Lord's Prayer together and receive Jesus in the Eucharist.

On Holy Saturday and Easter Sunday we remember that Jesus died to give us new life.

On Holy Saturday night the Easter candle is lighted. It shows that Jesus has risen. We hold lighted candles. They are a sign of our Baptism, when Jesus gave us new life. We welcome new members to our Church. We celebrate with joy.

During these three holy days, we pray, "Jesus, our Light. Thanks be to God!" (based on The Easter Vigil Procession, *Sacramentary*).

290   Holy Week: Lesson One

CURRICULUM CONNECTION

Art   Engage the children in creating a mural that begins with the Last Supper and concludes with the resurrection. Display the mural in your classroom or school hallway.

ctivity

Draw lines to match the three most holy days to their pictures.

Holy Thursday

Good Friday

Holy Saturday evening

Learning How to Live Our Faith

Completing a Matching Activity

Point out the matching activity on page 291. Explain the directions and have the children match the drawings on the right with the names of the celebrations on the left. Afterward, check the children's work.

Acting Out the Liturgies

Recall the important elements of the Holy Week liturgies by having the children reenact them, using the props you brought to class. Select volunteers for the washing of the feet. Have them remove one shoe and sock and sit on chairs in the front of the room. As you wash and dry the children's feet, say: "On Holy Thursday, we remember that Jesus told us to serve others, as he did."

Call the children forward individually to kiss the cross, as you say: "On Good Friday, we remember that Jesus showed his love for us by dying on the cross."

Light the candle you brought to class, praying: "Jesus, you bring light to the world by your life, death, and resurrection." Have the children respond, "Jesus, we want to share your new life always."

LESSON 2

Objective

This lesson helps the children understand that Jesus gave us the gift of himself on Holy Thursday.

Step 1 / INTRODUCTION

Learning About Our Lives

Discussing Celebrations

Discuss with the children days on which their families and friends gather to share special meals. For each day suggested, talk about what family members or friends are remembering in the celebration. You may want to provide the following examples: (1) birthday (day on which we remember the day someone was born); (2) Thanksgiving (day on which we remember God's goodness to us); (3) Easter (day on which we remember that Jesus rose to a new life). Remind the children that Jesus and his friends gathered for celebrations. Also explain that today the followers of Jesus gather to remember these celebrations.

Step 2 / DEVELOPMENT

Learning About Our Faith

Explaining the Days of Holy Week

On the chalkboard, write the words *Holy Week*. Tell the children that this week is a very special week in the Church. On the chalkboard, write the words *Passion Sunday* and tell the children that this is the first day of Holy Week. Tell the children about what happened on this day. (Jesus entered Jerusalem, and the people gathered to honor him as their leader.)

Write *Holy Thursday* on the chalkboard. Tell the children that we remember on this day the Last Supper, the special meal Jesus shared with his friends and followers.

Reading About Holy Thursday

Have a volunteer read "Holy Thursday" on page 292. After the volunteer has finished reading, have all the children underline the sentences in the last paragraph. Help the children study these sentences by repeating them aloud several times.

292

Holy Thursday

The week before Easter is Holy Week. It is a special time in the Church. We remember the words and actions of Jesus from the days before he rose from the dead. At Mass on Holy Thursday, we remember the Last Supper, the special meal Jesus shared with his friends.

During Mass the bread and wine become Jesus' body and blood. The priest reminds us that Jesus gave himself to us in the Eucharist.

On Holy Thursday we remember Jesus by celebrating the Eucharist. We thank Jesus for giving us the gift of himself.

<cite>292   Holy Week: Lesson Two</cite>

Focus on

Holy Thursday Holy Thursday used to be called "Maundy Thursday." This title was taken from the Latin word *mandatum,* which means "commandment." At the Last Supper, Jesus gave his followers the new commandment: "Love one another. As I have loved you, so must you love one another" based on (John 13:34).

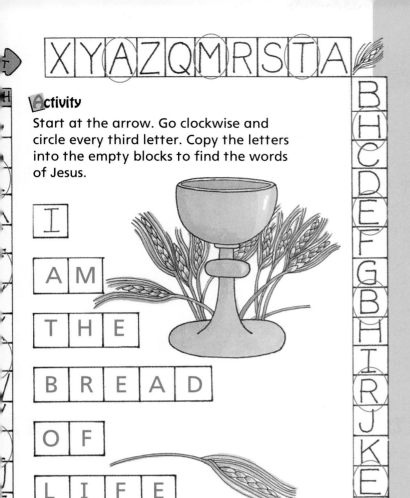

Activity

Start at the arrow. Go clockwise and circle every third letter. Copy the letters into the empty blocks to find the words of Jesus.

X Y A Z Q M R S T A
B H C D E F G B H I R J K E L
F S R O Q P D O N A M

I
A M
T H E
B R E A D
O F
L I F E

Learning How to Live Our Faith

Completing a Word Puzzle

Have a volunteer read aloud the activity directions on page 293. You may want to work through the puzzle with the children. When the children have filled in the empty blocks, have them read the words of Jesus.

Thanking Jesus for the Eucharist

Have the children gather in a prayer circle. Have them respond *Thank you, Jesus* to each of the following sentences.

- You have given us yourself in the Eucharist.
- You gave your life for us.
- You are the Bread of Life.

★ Enriching the Lesson ★

Share a meal celebration with the class in memory of Jesus' Last Supper. If possible, gather in the lunchroom or a room in which the children can sit around large tables. Ask several parents to help organize the celebration. You might serve pita bread, grape juice, and fruit. Remind the children that Jesus gave us the Eucharist at the Last Supper. Explain that the first Christians celebrated the Eucharist in their homes, gathered around their family tables.

Our Church Celebrates Easter

Objectives

- **LESSON 1:** To help the children understand the meaning of the empty tomb.
- **LESSON 2:** To help the children understand that Jesus rose to new life for us.
- **LESSON 3:** To help the children recognize that Jesus is with us.
- **LESSON 4:** To help the children share the joy of Easter.

Lesson Outlines

	Step 1 Learning About Our Lives	**Step 2** Learning About Our Faith	**Step 3** Learning How to Live Our Faith
Lesson 1	■ Talk about believing. *ABOUT 5 MINUTES*	■ Read and discuss the Scripture. ■ Read about Jesus' promises. *ABOUT 10 MINUTES*	■ Complete a maze. ■ Sing an Easter song. *ABOUT 15 MINUTES*
Lesson 2	■ Discuss meals. *ABOUT 7 MINUTES*	■ Read and discuss a story. ■ Appreciate Easter. *ABOUT 13 MINUTES*	■ Decode a message. ■ Pray a litany. *ABOUT 10 MINUTES*
Lesson 3	■ Share experiences. *ABOUT 5 MINUTES*	■ Read and discuss a story. ■ Compare two stories. *ABOUT 15 MINUTES*	■ Complete an activity. ■ Pray together. *ABOUT 10 MINUTES*
Lesson 4	**Project** Discuss Easter eggs; make Easter cards; and review the Easter message. **Prayer** Prepare for a prayer service and participate in a prayer service.		

Plan Ahead

	Preparing Your Class	Materials Needed
Lesson 1	Read the entire lesson plan. Prepare to teach the song suggested in Step 3.	■ seeds, an egg ■ pencils ■ music and recording of "Oh, Yes, Lord Jesus Lives"
Lesson 2	Read through the lesson plan and prepare to share your Easter joy with the class.	■ pencils
Lesson 3	Read the lesson plan.	■ writing paper ■ pencils ■ crayons or felt-tip markers
Lesson 4	Read the lesson plan and the prayer service on page 301. Make a sample Easter card to show the class. Collect props for the dramatization.	■ 9" × 12" sheets of pastel-colored construction paper ■ scissors, pencils, glue ■ colored tissue paper ■ crosses from Lesson 5 of Lent

Additional Resources

As you plan these lessons, consider using the following materials from The Resourceful Teacher Package.

■ *Classroom Activity Sheets for Easter*

■ *Family Activity Sheets for Easter*

■ *Prayers for Every Day*

You may also wish to refer to the following Big Book.

■ *We Celebrate God's Word,* page 19

In preparing the children for the Sunday readings, you may wish to use Silver Burdett Ginn's *Getting Ready for Sunday* student and teacher materials.

REDUCED CLASSROOM ACTIVITIES

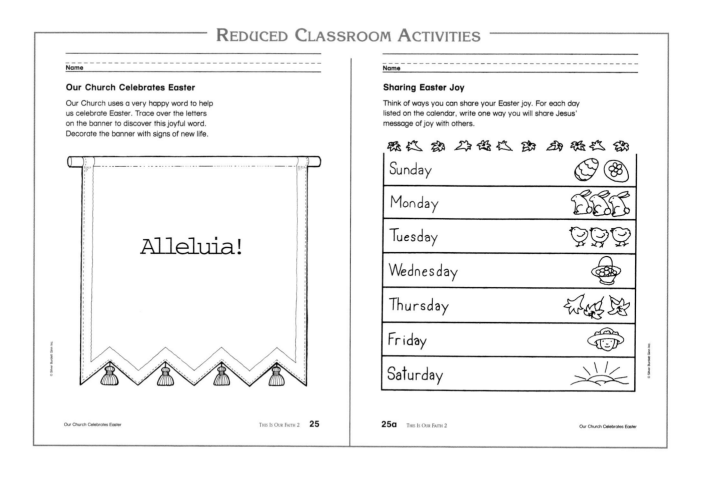

Name _____

Our Church Celebrates Easter

Our Church uses a very happy word to help us celebrate Easter. Trace over the letters on the banner to discover this joyful word. Decorate the banner with signs of new life.

Alleluia!

Our Church Celebrates Easter   THIS IS OUR FAITH 2   **25**

Name _____

Sharing Easter Joy

Think of ways you can share your Easter joy. For each day listed on the calendar, write one way you will share Jesus' message of joy with others.

Sunday	
Monday	
Tuesday	
Wednesday	
Thursday	
Friday	
Saturday	

25a   THIS IS OUR FAITH 2   Our Church Celebrates Easter

Background for the Teacher

THE EASTER SEASON

Easter is not just a one-day celebration. As the *National Catechetical Directory* states: "The fifty days from Easter Sunday to Pentecost are one long feast day" (#144).

The Scripture stories in these lessons relate to the discovery of the empty tomb on the first Easter. On the occasion of Jesus' third visit to his apostles following his resurrection, the apostles do not recognize him when he begins to speak. This can be attributed to the problem they had in grasping the full meaning of the resurrection of Jesus and the implications it had for them. We too are called to look at the implications of the resurrection for ourselves. We must move beyond the idea of the historical Christ who lived, died, and rose. We are called to live the life that Jesus has modeled for us—a life that reflects care and concern for others.

LEARNING ABOUT THE RESURRECTION

Children of this age are eager to know what Jesus was like after his resurrection. The image second graders have of the risen Jesus may only be one of a spirit. In this lesson, you can help the children understand that Jesus was very much alive following his death and resurrection. Jesus walked among his followers, showing the same care and concern that he exhibited before his death. Jesus passed on his mission to Peter and the apostles and, ultimately, to all of us.

Objective

This lesson helps the children understand the meaning of the empty tomb.

Learning About Our Lives

Talking About Believing

Show the children some seeds and an egg you have brought to class. Ask: What will happen to the seeds when they are planted and watered? (*Flowers will grow.*) Then ask what would happen to the egg on a farm. (*A baby chick would break out of the shell.*) Explore the children's reasons for believing these things. Help them recognize that we often believe things that we cannot see. Tell them that in today's lesson they will learn about something Jesus' friends believed in without seeing.

or . . .

Draw four columns on the chalkboard and label the columns *Passion Sunday, Holy Thursday, Good Friday,* and *Holy Saturday.* Ask the children what they know about Holy Week. Add a fifth column and ask the children what we call the day after Holy Saturday. Elicit from them that we call this great day *Easter Sunday.* Tell the children that in this lesson they will learn about the first Easter.

Learning About Our Faith

Reading and Discussing Scripture

Ask the children to open their books to page 294. Call on volunteers to read aloud the first Scripture story.

Discuss the story with these questions.

- What did Mary see when she got to the tomb? (*The stone had been rolled away.*)
- What did Mary tell Jesus' followers? (*That someone had taken Jesus' body away*)

Our Church Celebrates Easter

Jesus Is Risen

Early on Sunday morning, when it was still dark, Mary of Magdala went to Jesus' tomb. Mary was a friend and follower of Jesus. When Mary got to the tomb, she saw that the stone in front of it had been rolled away. She went to tell Jesus' followers.

Mary said, "They have taken Jesus' body away from the tomb. I don't know where they have put him."

Peter and a friend ran to the tomb. His friend ran faster than Peter. When they got to the tomb, they looked inside. Peter went into the tomb. He saw the cloths that had been used to wrap Jesus' body. Then Peter's friend went into the tomb. He too saw the cloths in which Jesus had been buried. He saw them and believed that Jesus had risen from the dead.

Later that day, Jesus appeared to his followers. He praised them for believing that he had risen. He said, "Blessed are you who believed."

(Based on John 20:1-9, 29)

On Easter we celebrate Jesus' new life. We remember that Jesus rose from the dead. Jesus promises us that we will share in his new life. Like Peter's friend, we believe in Jesus' promise to us.

Enriching the Lesson

To help the children remember that the empty tomb is a sign that Jesus had risen to new life, have them paint with water colors a symbol of new life (an egg, the sun, a flower, a rainbow, or a cross) on a small, flat rock. Afterward, set the rocks aside to dry. Encourage the children to keep the rocks as a reminder of Jesus' resurrection.

Activity

Follow the path from the empty tomb to the risen Jesus. Copy the letters you find along the way to complete the Easter prayer.

"We pray, __Alleluia__ Jesus is risen!"

- What did Peter see when he went into Jesus' tomb? (*The cloths that Jesus had been buried in*)
- What did Peter's friend believe when he saw the cloths? (*That Jesus had risen*)

Reading About Jesus' Promises

Read through the rest of the text on page 294 with the children. Help them understand that Jesus wants us to believe in him even though we cannot see him. Emphasize that Jesus promises us that if we follow him, we will share in his new life. Encourage the children to trust in Jesus' promises.

Step 3 / CONCLUSION

Learning How to Live Our Faith

Completing a Maze

Explain the directions to the activity on page 295. Instruct the children to complete the activity independently. Afterward, read the sentence aloud together.

Singing an Easter Song

Conclude the lesson by teaching the children the song "Oh, Yes, Lord Jesus Lives" by Carey Landry (*Young People's Glory and Praise*, NALR, available from OCP, 5536 N.E. Hassalo, Portland, OR). Point out that the verses retell the story of Jesus' followers at the empty tomb. Use the recording so that the children may join in on the chorus of the song.

Focus on

The Resurrection The *Catechism of the Catholic Church* calls Jesus' resurrection the "crowning truth of our faith in Christ, a faith believed and lived as the central truth by the first Christian community . . . preached as an essential part of the Paschal mystery along with the cross: Christ is risen from the dead! Dying, he conquered death; To the dead, he has given life" (#638). Help your students appreciate the risen Jesus' presence among us during this season.

LESSON 2

Objective

This lesson helps the children understand that Jesus rose to new life for us.

Step 1 / INTRODUCTION

Learning About Our Lives

Discussing Meals

Talk with the children about the times that they have shared meals with their friends. Guide them in a discussion of picnics or barbecues by first sharing some of your experiences. Encourage all the children to share their own experiences. End the discussion by explaining that, in today's lesson, they will read about a picnic breakfast Jesus shared with his friends after his resurrection.

Step 2 / DEVELOPMENT

Learning About Our Faith

Reading and Discussing a Story

Ask a volunteer to read each paragraph of "A Time of Great Happiness" on page 296. Discuss the story by asking the following questions.

- What were Jesus' friends doing when they saw him on the beach? (*Fishing*)
- What did Jesus do for his friends? (*Made breakfast*)
- Why were the friends of Jesus excited? (*Jesus was visiting them.*)

Appreciating Easter

Remind the children that we are like the friends of Jesus. We too share a special meal with him when we celebrate the Eucharist. Ask a volunteer to read "Celebrating Jesus' New Life" on page 297. Ask:

- What do we celebrate during the weeks following Easter Sunday? (*The resurrection of Jesus*)
- What do we remember at Mass when we gather with the parish community? (*What Jesus did for us*)
- What do we remember when we share the Eucharist? (*That Jesus is always with us*)

A Time of Great Happiness

One morning after Jesus had risen, his friends were fishing. Suddenly they saw Jesus standing on the beach. The brought their boat to shore so that they could visit with their friend.

Jesus had made a fire. He told his friends to bring some of the fish they had caught to cook for breakfast. Jesus shared cooked fish and bread with his friends.

They were excited. This was the third time that Jesus visited them after he rose to new life.

Based on John 21:8–

296 Easter: Lesson Two

296

Celebrating Jesus' New Life

In the weeks following Easter Sunday, we continue to celebrate Jesus' resurrection. At Mass we gather with the parish community to remember what Jesus did for us. We celebrate his rising to new life. By sharing the Eucharist we remember that Jesus is always with us.

Activity

Unscramble the letters on each fish to form a word. Then use the words to complete the prayer.

We praise you, <u>Jesus Christ</u>

<u>Son</u> of <u>God</u>.

Learning How to Live Our Faith

Decoding a Message

Have the children read aloud together the directions for the scrambled-word activity on page 297. Explain to them that the fish in the illustration are reminders of Jesus' picnic with his friends after he rose to new life. The picture will help the children remember to love and care for others just as Jesus did. You may want to help the children unscramble the words on the fish by writing on the chalkboard the correct spelling for each word. Then have the children complete the prayer.

Praying a Litany

After the children have finished the activity, have them stand to pray a litany. To each of the following sentences, encourage them to respond *We praise you, Jesus Christ, Son of God.*

- Jesus, you died for us.
- Jesus, you rose to new life for us.
- Jesus, you ask us to care for others.
- Jesus, you teach us to live.
- Jesus, you are with us always and everywhere.

Teaching Tips

After the children have completed the prayer on page 297, explain that a fish was an important sign to the first Christians. Each letter of the Greek word for *fish* had a secret meaning: Jesus Christ, God's Son, Savior. Distribute half-sheets of construction paper and have the children draw a fish and cut it out. Direct them to write their names and the words "I am a friend and follower of Jesus" on the fish. Use pins or masking tape for wearing these fish nametags.

297

Objective

This lesson helps the children recognize that Jesus is with us.

Step 1/ INTRODUCTION

Learning About Our Lives

Sharing Experiences

Talk with the children about experiences they may have had with moving to another town or having a close friend or relative move away. Invite them to share their feelings about these experiences. Then, ask them to identify ways that people can stay in touch with one another after one of them has moved away. Make sure the children recognize that letters, phone calls, and visits are among the ways people can remain friends after a move. End the discussion by telling the children that in today's session they will read about a girl whose best friend moved to another town.

Step 2 / DEVELOPMENT

Learning About Our Faith

Reading and Discussing a Story

Ask volunteers to read aloud "Waiting for a Letter" on page 298. Ask:

- What was Beth waiting for? (*A letter from her friend*)

- How did Beth feel? (*Sad and alone*)

- What did Beth say when she read Meg's letter? (*"Meg did not forget me!"*)

Invite the children to describe how Beth might have felt when she received Meg's letter. Help them appreciate that Beth felt joyful and happy. Affirm all responses.

Waiting for a Letter

Beth watched for the mail carrier every day. Beth was waiting for a letter from her best friend, Meg. Two weeks ago, Meg and her family had moved to another town. Beth missed Meg. She felt sad and alone.

Each day Debby gave Beth the mail. "No letter today, Beth," she said.

Beth kept hoping to hear from Meg. One day Debby took a letter from her pouch and asked, "Is this what you have been waiting for?"

Beth quickly opened the letter. It was from Meg. Beth smiled and said, "Meg did not forget me!" Then she went to share the news with her family.

298   Easter: Lesson Three

Enriching the Lesson

Invite the children to meditate on Jesus' presence by sitting quietly with their eyes closed. Read aloud the following, pausing after each sentence. *Imagine that you and Jesus are sitting together. Jesus is so close that you can touch him. Notice Jesus' eyes and his smile. Imagine that he is speaking to you alone. Jesus tells you that he loves you and that he is always with you. Repeat Jesus' words and then talk with Jesus about how it feels to have him with you always.*

Activity

Meg did not forget Beth. Like Meg, Jesus will not forget us. Jesus said, "I am with you always."

Choose a word from the box to complete each sentence.

Bible

people

Eucharist

1. Jesus is with us in the sacrament of the

Eucharist.

2. Jesus is with us in the

Bible.

3. Jesus is with us in other

people.

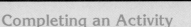

Comparing Two Stories

Ask the children to consider how Jesus' friends felt after he died. Have them compare Beth's feelings with those of Jesus' friends. Help them recognize that Jesus' followers, like Beth, felt sad and lonely. Have the children recall that after Jesus rose to new life, he visited his friends. Briefly relate Jesus' seaside appearance. (See Lesson 2, page 296.) Compare the Scripture story to the story about Beth and Meg. Remind the children that in the weeks following Easter we celebrate Jesus' new life and we remember that Jesus is always with us.

Step 3 / CONCLUSION

Learning How to Live Our Faith

Completing an Activity

Read to the class the first paragraph at the top of page 299. Explain the directions to the activity and give the children ample time to print the correct word in the sentence next to each picture. Afterward, check their answers and have the children discuss how each picture depicts Jesus' presence.

Praying Together

Distribute writing paper and pencils. Invite each child to write a prayer thanking Jesus for being with us always. If time permits, have the children use crayons or felt-tip markers to decorate their prayers.

Form a prayer circle with the children. After making the sign of the cross together, encourage them to share the prayers they have written. After each prayer, ask the children to respond by saying, "Jesus is with us, Alleluia!"

Teaching Tips

Ask the students to name the signs of Jesus' presence they see in their parish church. Responses may include the crucifix, the tabernacle, the Easter candle, and the sanctuary lamp. Stress that these symbols remind us that Jesus is with us always. Carry this theme out by bringing a large, fragrant white candle to class and keep it burning throughout the day when you are present. If fire regulations do not permit this, use an electric or battery-operated candle instead.

LESSON 4

Objective

This lesson helps the children share the joy of Easter.

Discussing Easter Eggs

Ask the children if they do anything special with eggs for Easter. You may want to tell the children that many years ago people *fasted* or went without special foods as a sacrifice during Lent. One of these special foods was eggs. When Easter came, people decorated eggs and gave them to their families and friends to celebrate the new life that Jesus shared with them.

Making Easter Cards

Invite the children to make Easter-egg cards as a sign of the new life of Jesus. Read aloud the directions on page 300. Distribute a 9" × 12" piece of pastel-colored construction paper, scissors, glue, colored tissue paper, and a pencil to each child. Demonstrate how to fold the paper in half so that it measures 6" × 9". With the fold of the paper to the left, have each child draw an egg shape on the paper. Instruct the children to begin drawing on the fold about 3" from the top of the paper and to finish on the fold about 3" from the bottom. Be sure to tell them to make their eggs as "tall" as the paper. Check to see that everyone has done this correctly. Have the children cut out the egg without cutting along the fold. (When they are finished, they will have two egg shapes, joined at the fold.) Hold the fold to the left and identify the top egg shape as the cover of the card. Instruct the children to cut random shapes in the cover, being careful not to cut on the edges or on the fold. When they have finished, have the children open their cards and glue small pieces of tissue over the cut-out shapes. Invite the children to write Easter messages on the inside of their cards. Offer suggestions and help with spelling as necessary. Afterward, encourage sharing.

Reviewing the Easter Message

Briefly relate the story, "A Time of Great Happiness," on page 296. Help the children appreciate that just as Jesus visited with his friends after he rose to new life he will be with us always. Jesus will not forget us.

An Easter Project

Follow the directions your teacher gives you to make a tissue paper Easter egg card. These are the things you will need.

- paper
- scissors
- glue
- tissue paper
- pencil

This is what you will do.

1. Fold a sheet of paper in half.
2. Cut a double egg out of the paper.
3. Cut shapes out of the cover of the card.
4. Glue pieces of tissue paper over the cutouts on the cover.
5. Write an Easter message inside the card.

CURRICULUM CONNECTION

Language Arts   Contact a senior citizen center and obtain a list of residents, one name for each child, who would enjoy hearing from your class. Point out that, like Beth in the story on page 298, many seniors feel lonely. Help the children write letters to the seniors, introducing themselves, and wishing them a happy Easter. Enclose the letters in the children's egg cards. As the seniors write back, display their letters for all to see.

Our Easter Prayer

Jesus died for us.
Alleluia!
Jesus is risen to new life.
Alleluia!
Jesus is always with us.
Alleluia!

Jesus,
teach us to know you better by doing good
for others. Help us grow in your love and
understand your new life.
Amen.

Based on the Opening Prayer
for Saturday, the Sixth Week
of Easter

Easter: Lesson Four 301

Preparing for a Prayer Service

Select volunteers to dramatize the story of Jesus' seaside appearance presented on page 296. Choose a child to narrate the story. Practice the dramatization several times with the children. Next, provide scissors and have the children carefully remove the Lenten project on page 288 from their books. Explain that they will present their crosses during the prayer service. Have the children practice the Alleluia litany and the closing prayer on page 301. Play a recording of the song "Oh, Yes, Lord Jesus Lives" by Carey Landry and, if it is unfamiliar to the children, teach it to them.

Participating in a Prayer Service

Ask the children to bring their texts and gather around you to sing "Oh, Yes, Lord Jesus Lives." Invite the children to make the sign of the cross. Then say, "Today we celebrate Jesus' resurrection. Let us rejoice and be glad." Pray the litany on page 301. Next, invite the volunteers to present their dramatizations of Jesus' seaside appearance.

Afterward, say, "All during the forty days of Lent we have looked forward to the celebration of Easter. We have sacrificed. We have tried to perform kind acts. We have prayed. We have done all these things to help us get ready to celebrate the resurrection of Jesus." Ask each child in turn to come forward and present his or her cross of sacrifices. Say to each child, "God is pleased with your sacrifices." After all the children have presented their crosses, conclude by singing "Oh, Yes, Lord Jesus Lives."

Enriching the Lesson

Using the diagram below, teach the children to sign the word *alleluia* as they pray it during the prayer service litany.

Our Church Honors Saints

Objectives

- **LESSON 1:** To help the children recognize Mother Frances Cabrini as a saint.
- **LESSON 2:** To help the children understand the special relationship between John the Baptizer and Jesus.
- **LESSON 3:** To help the children appreciate Saint Angela as a teacher who helped Catholic schools grow all over the world.
- **LESSON 4:** To help the children recognize Saint John Bosco as a model of joy and trust in God.

Lesson Outlines

	Step 1 Learning About Our Lives	**Step 2** Learning About Our Faith	**Step 3** Learning How to Live Our Faith
Lesson 1	■ Discuss occupations. *ABOUT 5 MINUTES*	■ Read and discuss a story. *ABOUT 12 MINUTES*	■ Complete a drawing activity. ■ Pray together. *ABOUT 13 MINUTES*
Lesson 2	■ Talk about relatives. ■ Discuss John the Baptizer. *ABOUT 7 MINUTES*	■ Read and discuss the text. *ABOUT 7 MINUTES*	■ Complete a prayer. ■ Make a mural. *ABOUT 16 MINUTES*
Lesson 3	■ Remember stories. *ABOUT 6 MINUTES*	■ Read and discuss the story. ■ Talk about Catholic schools. *ABOUT 12 MINUTES*	■ Complete an activity. ■ Pray together. *ABOUT 12 MINUTES*
Lesson 4	**Project** Discuss ways we learn; read and discuss a story; draw cartoons; and talk about saints. **Prayer** Prepare for a prayer service; participate in a prayer service.		

Plan Ahead

	Preparing Your Class	Materials Needed
Lesson 1	Read through the entire lesson plan for this lesson. Collect pictures showing people in many different occupations.	■ pictures of people in different occupations ■ crayons
Lesson 2	Read the lesson plan. Cut five panels of butcher paper for the mural in Step 3.	■ pencils ■ butcher paper ■ tape ■ crayons or felt-tip markers
Lesson 3	Read the entire lesson plan.	■ pencils ■ Bible
Lesson 4	Read the lesson plan. Make a recording of a phone ringing, a dog barking, water running, hands clapping, a person whistling, a car starting, and a baby crying.	■ drawing paper ■ crayons or felt-tip markers ■ tape recording of environmental sounds ■ tape recorder

Additional Resources

As you plan these lessons, consider using the following materials from The Resourceful Teacher Package.

■ *Classroom Activity Sheets for Saints*

■ *Family Activity Sheets for Saints*

■ *Prayers for Every Day*

You may also wish to refer to the following Big Book.

■ *We Celebrate God's Word,* pages 15–18

In preparing the children for the Sunday readings, you may wish to use Silver Burdett Ginn's *Getting Ready for Sunday* student and teacher materials.

REDUCED CLASSROOM ACTIVITIES

Name

Our Church Honors Saints

People become saints by loving God very much.
They try to love others as Jesus loves them.
Color the bubbles that name things we can
do to become saints.

Help at home.

Learn more about God.

Study hard.

Respect older people.

Visit the sick.

Pray often.

Talk Kindly to others.

Help the poor.

Don't fight.

Be kind to others.

Our Church Honors Saints

THIS IS OUR FAITH 2 **26**

Name

To God with Love

Write a letter to God. Name ways in which
you are trying to be like Mother Frances Cabrini.

26a THIS IS OUR FAITH 2

Our Church Honors Saints

Background for the Teacher

HONORING SAINTS

We all need people whom we can look up to, respect, and, to some extent, imitate. This need can be filled by the saints, those Christian men and women who have lived their lives in a way that is worthy of imitation.

SAINT FRANCES XAVIER CABRINI

The story of Mother Frances Xavier Cabrini is the story of a response to God's call. Frances was born in Italy on July 15, 1850. Due to illness, her childhood dream of becoming a missionary to China could not be realized. Despite ill health, she was founder of the Missionary Sisters of the Sacred Heart. She immigrated to the United States and established convents, schools, orphanages, and hospitals. Mother Cabrini died on December 22, 1917. She was canonized in 1946.

SAINT JOHN THE BAPTIZER

Saint John the Baptizer was born in a town of Judea about six months before Jesus was born. John was about thirty-two years old when he went to the desert to pray and fast. When he came back to preach in the villages of Judea, he made it clear that he was not the Messiah but was merely making a path for Jesus. Jesus once said that there was no greater prophet than John the Baptizer (Matthew 11:11). Saint John had lived his life in an attempt to get people to change their lives and prepare themselves for Jesus.

SAINT JOHN BOSCO

John Bosco was born in 1815, the youngest son of a peasant family in Italy. When he was two, his father died, and his mother was left alone to raise John and his two brothers. John was only nine years old when a dream led him to his lifelong vocation of caring for and teaching boys. John combined entertainment and learning and provided love to all in his care. Saint John Bosco, teacher of boys, writer of books for young people, builder of churches, and fund raiser, died on January 31, 1888. Pope Pius XI canonized him in 1934.

SAINT ANGELA MERICI

Angela Merici was born in Italy in 1474. Angela later joined the Third Order of Franciscans, which enabled her to devote herself to charity while remaining in her family home. There she took on the responsibility of educating the young girls of her village in the faith. In time she formed the Company of Saint Ursula, popularly known as the Ursulines. The Ursulines were the first order of religious teaching sisters. In teaching this lesson, help the children appreciate that in some way, their Catholic school's heritage is found in Saint Angela's leadership in the education of young people.

Objective

This lesson helps the children recognize Mother Frances Cabrini as a saint who answered God's call.

Step 1 / INTRODUCTION

Learning About Our Lives

Discussing Occupations

Discuss different professions and occupations with which the children are familiar. Also talk about how the people in these professions and occupations help other people. You may want to use the following examples.

- Doctors help people who are sick.
- Police officers keep our neighborhoods safe.
- Teachers help us learn about our world.

You may want to display pictures of people in various occupations. Have volunteers tell a story about each picture. Explain to the children that our dreams for the future help shape our lives.

Step 2 / DEVELOPMENT

Learning About Our Faith ✚

Reading and Discussing a Story

Direct the students' attention to page 302. Write the name *Mother Frances Cabrini* on the chalkboard. Pronounce the name and have the children repeat it. Then have a volunteer read aloud the story on page 302. After the reading, explain that Frances was a religious sister. Ask:

- What did a priest first ask Frances to do? (*Take care of children who did not have parents*)

- What did Frances do in the United States? (*She built schools and hospitals.*)

Tell the children that because Frances dedicated her life to doing God's work, we honor her as a saint. We celebrate a special day for her each year on November 13.

Our Church Honors Saints

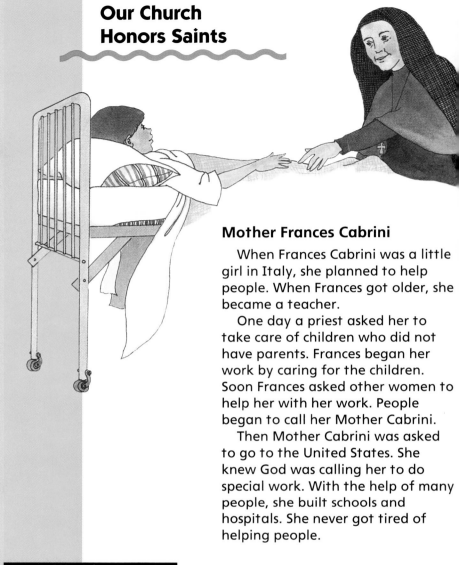

Mother Frances Cabrini

When Frances Cabrini was a little girl in Italy, she planned to help people. When Frances got older, she became a teacher.

One day a priest asked her to take care of children who did not have parents. Frances began her work by caring for the children. Soon Frances asked other women to help her with her work. People began to call her Mother Cabrini.

Then Mother Cabrini was asked to go to the United States. She knew God was calling her to do special work. With the help of many people, she built schools and hospitals. She never got tired of helping people.

 Focus on

Mother Frances Cabrini Mother Cabrini was the first United States citizen to be canonized a saint. During her life in America, she traveled back to Italy more than twenty times. Each time she returned, she brought with her new immigrant women, eager to share in her work. On Frances' feast day we pray, "May Saint Frances Cabrini's example teach us concern for strangers and those who are sick. Help us to see Christ in all the men and women we meet" (based on the Opening Prayer, November 13).

We honor Mother Cabrini on November 13. We pray, "God, help us live good lives. Help us to do your work."

Activity

Think about what work you want to do when you are older. Draw a picture of yourself doing that work.

Learning How to Live Our Faith

Completing a Drawing Activity

Distribute crayons. Allow a few minutes of quiet time for the children to reflect on what work they would like to do when they are older. Then have them draw a picture of themselves doing that work. Invite the children to share their drawings with the class.

Praying Together

Have the children quietly read aloud the prayer at the top of page 303. Encourage them to learn the prayer and say it often during the week.

Cultural Awareness

Mother Cabrini, an immigrant herself, felt special concern for those who were new to our country and for anyone who was treated as a stranger or an outsider. Invite the children to discuss how they welcome strangers and how they make new people feel at home in their new school or neighborhood. If you have a welcome ministry in your parish, you might also explain to the children how your parish welcomes new families.

LESSON 2

Objective

This lesson helps the children understand the special relationship between John the Baptizer and Jesus.

Step 1 / INTRODUCTION

Learning About Our Lives

Talking About Relatives

Begin by discussing family relationships. Ask:

- How many aunts, uncles, and cousins do you have? (*Answers will vary.*)

- How are relatives and friends different?

Help the students appreciate that family members can also be special friends. Tell them that in today's lesson they will learn about a very special relative of Jesus. This man's name was John the Baptizer.

Discussing John the Baptizer

Have the children relate what they already know about John the Baptizer. Refer them to the Advent story "A Time to Prepare" on page 264. Help them recall the following points: John was the son of Elizabeth and Zechariah; Elizabeth was Mary's cousin; and John told people to prepare for Jesus.

Step 2 / DEVELOPMENT

Learning About Our Faith

Reading and Discussing the Text

Have volunteers read aloud "John the Baptizer" on page 304. Ask:

- Where did John go when he was a young man? (*To live in the desert*)

- What did John do in the desert? (*Prayed and fasted*)

- What did John do when he left the desert? (*Baptized people*)

- Who was the most special person John baptized? (*Jesus*)

- What did Jesus say about John? (*That no man was greater than John*)

304

John the Baptizer

When John the Baptizer was a young man, he went into the desert. He wanted to discover God's plan for him. He prayed and fasted. God told him what to do.

John baptized many people. He told them, "Someone is coming who will baptize you with the Holy Spirit."

Jesus came to John to be baptized. Then Jesus began to do God's work in the world. He healed people. He brought them God's love and forgiveness.

Jesus said that no man was greater than John. People who follow Jesus can learn even more about God's love than John knew.

Based on Matthew 3:1–17, 11:4–11

Teaching Tips

Two feast days are set aside to honor John the Baptizer. On June 24 we celebrate John's birth and on August 29 we remember John's death as a martyr. John the Baptizer was put to death because he had the courage to tell even the most important officials that they had to change their lives and be baptized to help God's love grow in the world. Help the children remember the importance of the new life we received at Baptism by inviting them to use holy water to bless themselves.

Activity

We honor the birth of Saint John the Baptizer on June 24. This prayer can help us to be like Saint John.

Unscramble the letters below each line. Then fill in the words to complete the prayer.

Help us **tell** others
elHp   lelt

about **Jesus**. Help us **do**
seJus   od

God's **work** in the **world**.
korw   orldw

Cultural Awareness

Throughout the world, the name *John* is one of the most popular first names for boys. In Hebrew, the written language of the Jewish people in Jesus' time, John's name means "God is gracious." Write the following forms of John's names in different languages on the board and have the children guess their origin. Sean (Gaelic or Irish); Johann (German); Juan (Spanish); Evan (Welsh); and János (Hungarian).

Have the children turn to the map on page 329. Point out the Jordan River. Explain that it was in this river that John baptized people and prepared people for Jesus. Explain that the people walked into the water and were gently held under the water for a few seconds.

Step 3 / CONCLUSION

Learning How to Live Our Faith

Completing a Prayer

Read aloud the directions to the activity on page 305. Have the children unscramble the words to make a prayer. Check their responses by having them read aloud their answers. Then have the class pray the prayer aloud together.

Making a Mural

Have the children make a mural highlighting what they have learned about Saint John the Baptizer. Suggest that the mural have the following five panels: Elizabeth, Zechariah, and John as a family; John in the desert; John baptizing people in the Jordan River; John telling people about Jesus; and John baptizing Jesus.

Tape five large sheets of butcher paper on the floor. Divide the class into five groups and assign each group to one of the panels. Distribute crayons or felt-tip markers. When the children have finished, display the mural in a corridor or in the school hall. Conclude this session by calling attention to the special relationship between John and Jesus. Tell the children that as family members, John and Jesus loved, helped, and prayed for one another.

LESSON 3

Objective

This lesson helps the children appreciate Saint Angela as a teacher who helped Catholic schools grow all over the world.

Step 1 / INTRODUCTION

Learning About Our Lives

Remembering Stories

Encourage the students to recall how they first learned about God and Jesus. Ask: Who was the first person who told you about God or Jesus? Help the children recognize that most people first "meet" God and Jesus through the stories our parents tell. Tell the class that in today's lesson they will learn about a saint who helped many children learn about God and Jesus.

Step 2 / DEVELOPMENT

Learning About Our Faith

Reading and Discussing the Story

Direct the students' attention to page 306 and read the title. Call on volunteers to read the story aloud. Ask the following questions.

- Who taught Angela about God and Jesus? (*Her parents*)

- What did Angela want others to know about God? (*That God was good and loving*)

- Why did Angela begin to tell stories about God and Jesus to children? (*She saw that children were not learning about Jesus.*)

- What did the Ursuline sisters do? (*Began schools for poor children*)

- Why do we honor Saint Angela? (*She was a great teacher and leader.*)

Saint Angela

Angela learned about God from her parents. They told Angela many stories about God and Jesus. They taught her to pray every day.

When Angela was ten years old, her parents died. Angela went to live with her uncle. Angela grew closer to God every day. She wanted others to know about God's goodness and love.

When Angela grew up, she saw that many children were not learning how to follow Jesus. She began to tell the children the same stories her parents had told her.

Other women joined Angela. With Angela as their leader, they began schools for poor children. These women became known as the Ursuline sisters.

We honor Saint Angela on January 27 as a great teacher and leader. Like Saint Angela, we can pray, "Help us know and love you, O God!"

Teaching Tips

Saint Angela lived from 1474–1540. The order she founded was named after Saint Ursula, then the patron of university teachers. The Ursulines still teach children all over the world. If an order of nuns is affiliated with your school, invite one of the sisters to visit your class and talk about the founder of her order.

Activity

Print the name of your Catholic school on the banner below. Then in the cloud, write one thing you have learned about God or Jesus in your Catholic school.

Talking About Catholic Schools

Point out to the children that, like the schools Saint Angela and her Ursuline sisters began more than 400 years ago, their school is also a Catholic school.

Ask the children what makes their school special. Invite them to recall some of their experiences, such as Catholic Schools Week, special events, or other activities. Encourage the children to feel a sense of pride in being part of the Catholic school community.

Step 3 / CONCLUSION

Learning How to Live Our Faith

Completing an Activity

Explain the directions to the activity on page 307. Have the children print the name of their school on the banner.

Discuss with the children some of the things they have learned about God and Jesus in religion class. List their responses on the board. Have the children select one of the responses to copy into their books.

Praying Together

Explain that we learn about God through our religion lessons, families, priests and teachers, and the Bible. Have the children stand in a circle. Hold a Bible in your hands as you repeat Saint Angela's prayer from page 306 aloud. Have the children recite the prayer in turn, giving them each an opportunity to hold the Scriptures as they pray.

Objective

This lesson helps the children recognize Saint John Bosco as a model of joy and trust in God.

Discussing Ways We Learn

Ask the children what they like best about school. Accept all their answers. Then point out that most people learn best when they are having fun. Explain that in your class you try to provide a happy atmosphere and enjoyable activities to help the children learn.

Reading and Discussing a Story

Direct the children's attention to "Saint John Bosco" on page 308. Read the story aloud with the children. Ask:

- Why did Saint John do magic tricks for the boys? (*So they would have fun and want to listen to him*)

- What did Saint John do for the boys who had no homes? (*Built a school and home for them*)

- What did Saint John teach the boys? (*To love God, to sew clothes, and to make shoes*)

- When is Saint John Bosco's feast day? (*January 31*)

Drawing Cartoons

Distribute drawing paper and crayons or felt-tip markers. Have each child divide his or her paper into two horizontal panels. On one panel, have them draw cartoons that tell stories about how Saint John Bosco taught the boys for whom he cared. On the other panel, have them draw cartoons showing their favorite activities from this year's religion class. Encourage them to show what they learned from these activities.

Talking About Saints

Ask the children to name any saints the class has studied this year. Invite volunteers to tell what they know about these saints.

308

Saint John Bosco

The boys from the village watched the young man do magic tricks. They laughed and clapped and asked for more. Then the man took the boys to Mass. He taught them about Jesus.

The man was John Bosco, a priest who cared for poor boys. Some of the boys had no homes of their own. John Bosco asked rich people for money so that he could build a school and make a home for the boys.

John Bosco treated the children with love and kindness. He knew that children learned best when they could have fun. He taught the boys to love God. He taught them how to sew clothes and make shoes. When the boys grew up, they were able to find work because of all that John Bosco had taught them.

We remember Saint John Bosco on his feast day, January 31.

308   Saints: Lesson Four

Focus on

John Bosco   This saint's life is a prime example of accepting children for who they are, rather than for what they do or how well they learn. John believed that teachers must possess one important trait: kindness. He urged teachers to love their students as a parent does. Take time to demonstrate in words and actions your love for your students. Keep in mind the words of Jesus: "Whoever welcomes one child for my sake, welcomes me" (Matthew 18:5).

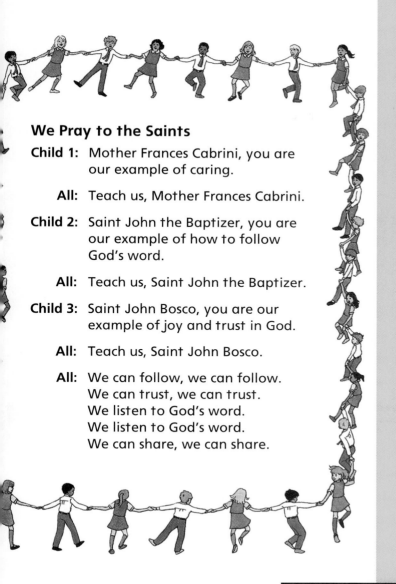

We Pray to the Saints

Child 1: Mother Frances Cabrini, you are our example of caring.

All: Teach us, Mother Frances Cabrini.

Child 2: Saint John the Baptizer, you are our example of how to follow God's word.

All: Teach us, Saint John the Baptizer.

Child 3: Saint John Bosco, you are our example of joy and trust in God.

All: Teach us, Saint John Bosco.

All: We can follow, we can follow.
We can trust, we can trust.
We listen to God's word.
We listen to God's word.
We can share, we can share.

Enriching the Lesson

Make ribbon banners honoring the saints in this chapter. Give each child an 18" ribbon or paper streamer and four 3" construction-paper circles. Invite the children to draw on the circles a symbol or picture for each saint; for example, a thermometer for Mother Cabrini, a picture of John baptizing people, and so on. When finished, help the children staple the circles to the ribbon. Have the children hang the ribbons on their doors at home.

Preparing for a Prayer Service

Ask three volunteers to read and practice the petitions on page 309. Teach the children to sing the words at the bottom of the page, beginning with "We can follow," to the tune of "Frère Jacques." Have ready the tape of environmental sounds, which you made before class. (See "Plan Ahead" for this lesson.)

Participating in a Prayer Service

Have the children bring their books and gather around you. Say, "Today we celebrate the saints we have learned about this year. Let us begin our prayer with the Sign of the Cross." Have the class participate in the prayer service on page 309. Before singing the closing song, invite the children to listen to the tape you made earlier. Have them identify the sounds, then ask them how their listening to the tape relates to Mother Cabrini, Saint John the Baptizer, and Saint John Bosco. Help them recognize that these holy people listened to God and responded. Point out that Mother Cabrini listened and then cared for those in schools and hospitals; Saint John the Baptizer listened to God and then prepared the way for Jesus; and Saint John Bosco listened and then cared for and taught homeless boys. Lead the children to appreciate that they too can listen and respond to God just as they listened to and responded to the tape. Say, "God speaks to us in our hearts when we pray. When God speaks to us, we can answer. We can follow, trust, and care just like Mother Cabrini, Saint John the Baptizer, and Saint John Bosco did." Next, invite the children to sing the closing song.

309

Our Church Honors Mary

Objectives

- **LESSON 1:** To help the children learn about the Feast of the Visitation.
- **LESSON 2:** To help the children understand that Mary and Jesus cared for each other and others.
- **LESSON 3:** To help the children learn that the Rosary honors the lives of Jesus and Mary.

Lesson Outlines

	Step 1	**Step 2**	**Step 3**
	Learning About Our Lives	**Learning About Our Faith**	**Learning How to Live Our Faith**
Lesson 1	■ Share experiences. *ABOUT 5 MINUTES*	■ Read and discuss a story. ■ Understand the message. *ABOUT 12 MINUTES*	■ Write a prayer. ■ Pray together. *ABOUT 13 MINUTES*
Lesson 2	■ Share experiences. *ABOUT 5 MINUTES*	■ Read and discuss a story. ■ Dramatize the story. *ABOUT 15 MINUTES*	■ Complete an activity. ■ Pray together. *ABOUT 10 MINUTES*
Lesson 3	■ Recall favorite ways of praying. *ABOUT 5 MINUTES*	■ Read about the Rosary. ■ Name the mysteries of the Rosary. *ABOUT 10 MINUTES*	■ Pray a decade of the Rosary. ■ Draw a rosary. *ABOUT 15 MINUTES*

Plan Ahead

	Preparing Your Class	**Materials Needed**
Lesson 1	Read through the lesson plan.	■ pencils
Lesson 2	Read the lesson plan and gather props for the dramatization in Step 2. Bring a wedding album to class.	■ pencils ■ wedding photos or a wedding album ■ simple props for the dramatization
Lesson 3	Read through the lesson plan. Have rosaries on hand for the children to use.	■ crayons ■ rosaries, one for each child ■ white art paper

Additional Resources

As you plan these lessons, consider using the following materials from The Resourceful Teacher Package.

■ *Classroom Activity Sheets for Mary*

■ *Family Activity Sheets for Mary*

■ *Prayers for Every Day*

You may also wish to refer to the following Big Book.

■ *We Celebrate God's Word,* page 4

In preparing the children for the Sunday readings, you may wish to use Silver Burdett Ginn's *Getting Ready for Sunday* student and teacher materials.

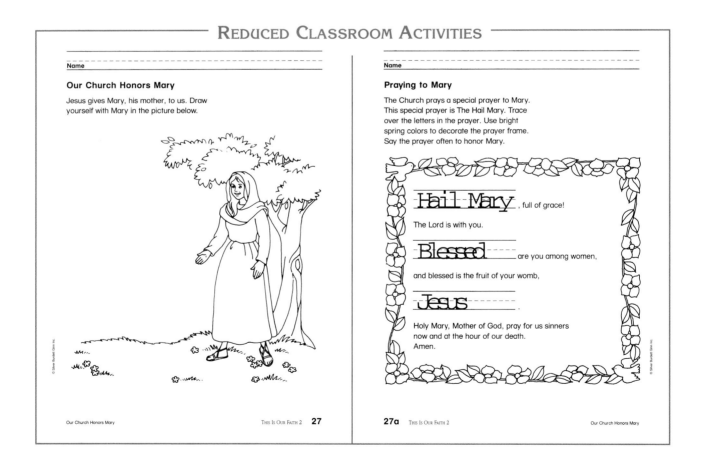

REDUCED CLASSROOM ACTIVITIES

Name _____

Our Church Honors Mary

Jesus gives Mary, his mother, to us. Draw
yourself with Mary in the picture below.

Our Church Honors Mary   THIS IS OUR FAITH 2 **27**

Name _____

Praying to Mary

The Church prays a special prayer to Mary.
This special prayer is The Hail Mary. Trace
over the letters in the prayer. Use bright
spring colors to decorate the prayer frame.
Say the prayer often to honor Mary.

Hail Mary, full of grace!

The Lord is with you.

Blessed are you among women,

and blessed is the fruit of your womb,

Jesus.

Holy Mary, Mother of God, pray for us sinners
now and at the hour of our death.
Amen.

27a THIS IS OUR FAITH 2   Our Church Honors Mary

Background for the Teacher

MARY'S VISIT

The Feast of the Visitation focuses on Mary in three ways. It shows her concern for her cousin, Elizabeth, her eagerness to serve, and the blessings bestowed on her. Mary used the occasion of her visit with Elizabeth to reflect on the great things God had done for her. On the Feast of the Visitation, we are also called to reflect on the gift that God has given us.

THE WEDDING AT CANA

At Cana Jesus worked his first miracle—changing water into wine. Mary was present when Jesus manifested his glory. At Mary's words of concern for the wedding couple and guests, Jesus asked the servants to fill stone jars with water. When they poured from the jars, the water had turned to fine wine. Through the ages, Catholics have prayed to Mary as an intercessor.

MARY'S EXAMPLE

As the teacher, you will be able to help the children identify Mary's virtues that can be imitated by people of any age. These virtues are the willingness to help others and the need to praise God. Mary went to Elizabeth's home because she saw an opportunity to serve Elizabeth. Through this example, the children can be challenged to look for occasions to help others. When Elizabeth greeted Mary and called her "blessed," Mary responded with humility. She praised God, calling herself his servant. Through Mary's example, the children can begin to develop an awareness that God does great things for all of us. And our response to God can be one of praise. Throughout these lessons help the children value the great example Mary has given us.

THE ROSARY

Originally, the Rosary consisted of 150 Hail Marys prayed daily by those too uneducated to read the psalms from the Liturgy of the Hours. The prayers were "counted" with a string of beads. The praying of the Rosary as a devotion to honor Mary was popularized by Saint Dominic in the thirteenth century. Pope Paul VI (1963–1978) is said to have called the Rosary the "Bible for those who cannot read and write." In this lesson, the children learn that the Rosary helps us remember the important events in the lives of Jesus and Mary. As you teach the children about the Rosary, you can encourage them to pray to Mary, who hears our prayers and brings them to Jesus.

Organizer 309d

Objective

This lesson helps the children learn about the Feast of the Visitation.

Step 1 / INTRODUCTION

Learning About Our Lives

Sharing Experiences

Talk with the children about trips they may have taken to visit relatives. Ask:

- Whom did you visit?
- Why did you visit them?
- Did you visit your relatives because they needed help?
- What kind of help did they need?

Step 2 / DEVELOPMENT

Learning About Our Faith

Reading and Discussing a Story

Help the children recall the following points: Mary is Jesus' mother; Mary is our mother, too; and God sent an angel to Mary to tell her that she was going to be the mother of God's Son. Have a volunteer read aloud "The Visitation" on page 310. Then help the children reflect on the story by asking the following questions.

- What did Elizabeth say to Mary? (*"Hail Mary! Blessed are you among women."*)
- What did Mary do after Elizabeth spoke to her? (*Thought about her words*)
- Why was Mary happy? (*She was going to be the mother of Jesus.*)

Explain that the words Elizabeth said are part of the Hail Mary.

Understanding the Message

Write the word *Visitation* on the chalkboard. Pronounce the word and have the children repeat it. Then have a volunteer read aloud "Thanking God for Jesus," the text following the story.

Our Church Honors Mary

The Visitation

One day, Mary went to visit her cousin, Elizabeth. When Elizabeth saw Mary coming, she ran out to meet her.

"Hail, Mary!" Elizabeth said. "Blessed are you among women." Elizabeth was telling Mary how very special she was to be the mother of God's Son, Jesus.

Mary thought about what Elizabeth said to her. Mary was so happy to be Jesus' mother that she began to thank and praise God.

Based on Luke 1:39–45

Thanking God for Jesus

Every year on May 31, the Church remembers Mary's visit to Elizabeth. W call this day the Feast of the Visitation. On this day we, like Mary, thank and praise God for the gift of Jesus.

310 Mary: Lesson One

CURRICULUM CONNECTION

Music The story of the Visitation invites us to reach out to others as Mary did. If the children wrote letters to senior citizens as part of the Language Arts activity on page 300, you might plan to visit their residence as a follow-up to today's lesson. Teach the children to sing a simple Marian hymn for their senior friends, such as "Hail Mary: Gentle Woman" (Carey Landry, *Young People's Glory and Praise*).

Activity

Think about all the things God has done for you. Below, write a prayer of thanks and praise to God. Share your prayer with your family and friends.

My Prayer

Focus on

Mary Mary is the greatest of all the saints and, as such, has more feast days and solemnities devoted to the events of her life as Jesus' mother and her role as Mother of the Church. In all, there are fifteen feast days set aside to honor Mary's great faith and love. Three of them are holy days of obligation in the United States: January 1, Mary, the Mother of God; August 15, the Assumption; and December 8, the Immaculate Conception.

Step 3 / Conclusion

Learning How to Live Our Faith

Writing a Prayer

Talk with the children about how Mary praised God's love and kindness. Tell the children that Mary loved God very much. She praised God for all the things that were about to happen to her. Help the children understand that we can praise God, too. Ask the children to think about how they can praise God. Explain that God shows love and kindness for us. This love and kindness makes us happy and helps us to live.

Have the children read the directions and write a prayer of thanks and praise on page 311. Assist the children with their writing if they need help.

Praying Together

After the children have finished writing, have them gather in a circle. Have each child pray his or her prayer of praise. Then invite the children to pray the Hail Mary together.

LESSON 2

Objective

This lesson helps the children understand that Mary and Jesus cared for each other and others.

Step 1 / INTRODUCTION

Learning About Our Lives

Sharing Experiences

Talk with the children about weddings. Ask:

- Have you ever attended a wedding?
- Who got married?
- What happened at the wedding?
- What was your favorite part of the wedding?

Show the children the wedding album you brought to class. Discuss all that happens at a wedding. Conclude the discussion by telling the children that in today's lesson they will learn about a wedding that Mary and Jesus attended.

Step 2 / DEVELOPMENT

Learning About Our Faith

Reading and Discussing a Story

Ask volunteers to read aloud "The Wedding at Cana" on page 312. Ask:

- How did Mary and Jesus spend time together at the wedding? (*They talked and visited.*)
- What happened at the wedding? (*The wedding party ran out of wine.*)
- Why was Mary worried? (*She didn't want the guests to leave.*)
- Why did Jesus want to help? (*He wanted to please his mother.*)

Help the children appreciate Mary's care and concern for others and Jesus' willingness to do what his mother asked. Point out that Mary and Jesus cared for each other and other people.

The Wedding at Cana

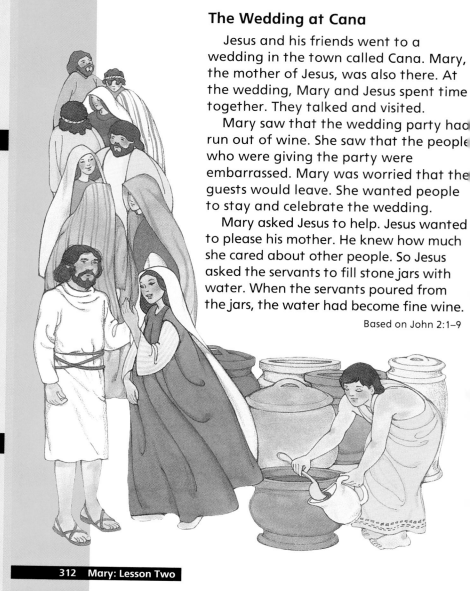

Jesus and his friends went to a wedding in the town called Cana. Mary, the mother of Jesus, was also there. At the wedding, Mary and Jesus spent time together. They talked and visited.

Mary saw that the wedding party had run out of wine. She saw that the people who were giving the party were embarrassed. Mary was worried that the guests would leave. She wanted people to stay and celebrate the wedding.

Mary asked Jesus to help. Jesus wanted to please his mother. He knew how much she cared about other people. So Jesus asked the servants to fill stone jars with water. When the servants poured from the jars, the water had become fine wine.

Based on John 2:1–9

312   Mary: Lesson Two

Focus on

The Miracle at Cana   Changing water into wine at Cana was Jesus' first public miracle. In John's Gospel, the writer calls Jesus' miracles "signs" and tells us that Jesus performed them "and so revealed his glory, and his disciples began to believe in him" (John 2:11). It is important that the children understand that the miracles Jesus performed were not magic. Instead, they were signs that revealed that Jesus was God's Son, who acted with God's power.

312

Activity

Find your way through the maze to Mary and Jesus. Use the words in the maze to complete the sentence below. Then write how you can show care for another person.

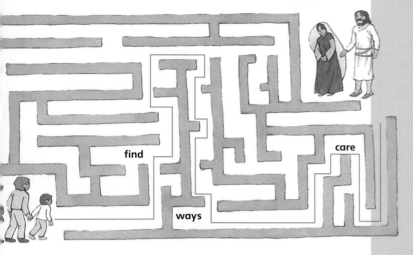

find

care

ways

Mary and Jesus help us learn to find

_____

ways _____ to care _____ for others.

I can show care for _____

by _____

Dramatizing the Story

Suggest that the children dramatize this story. Select volunteers to portray Mary, Jesus, the bridal couple, the parents, the guests, and a narrator. Encourage Mary and Jesus to make up a conversation. Do this by asking the children, "What do you think Mary (or Jesus) would say?" Provide tables, chairs, and a few large jars for props. You may want to have the children perform this dramatization for another class or for the children's parents at a special time.

Step 3 / CONCLUSION

Learning How to Live Our Faith

Completing an Activity

Read aloud the directions to the maze activity on page 313. Have the children solve the maze, copying the letters they discover on the lines. Check the children's responses by having them read the completed sentences. Discuss how Mary and Jesus showed care for others. Then brainstorm ways the children can show care for others. Have the children write one of these ways on the lines in their books.

Praying Together

Encourage the children to describe ways their mothers show care and concern for their families and others. Offer a short, spontaneous prayer thanking God for mothers, who teach us to care about others. Conclude by having each child say, "Thank you, God, for Mary and for my mother who cares for me by _____."

Enriching the Lesson

Set up a large flannelboard in the front of the classroom and have the children sit in a circle on the floor in front of it. Choose volunteers to help you retell the story of "The Wedding at Cana," using flannelboard figures and their own words. Encourage the students to tell the story in the first person, taking the parts of Mary, Jesus, the servants, and the wedding guests.

Objective

This lesson helps the children learn that the Rosary honors the lives of Jesus and Mary.

Step 1 / INTRODUCTION

Learning About Our Lives

Recalling Favorite Ways of Praying

Discuss with the children the different ways we can pray by asking the following questions.

- What is your favorite prayer?
- Which do you like better: prayers that you know by heart or prayers in which you use your own words?
- Which prayer did Jesus teach us? (*The Lord's Prayer or the Our Father*)
- Which prayer honors Mary? (*The Hail Mary*)

Tell the children that in today's lesson they will learn about another favorite prayer that Catholics pray to Mary.

Step 2 / DEVELOPMENT

Learning About Our Faith

Reading About the Rosary

Have the children turn to page 314 and call on volunteers to read aloud "The Rosary." As the children read, use rosary beads to help explain and demonstrate the different parts of the prayer. Discuss the following questions.

- What do we remember when we pray the Rosary? (*Jesus' and Mary's lives; Mary was the mother of Jesus; Mary always said yes to God.*)
- How can we pray the Rosary? (*Alone; together in school, at home, or in church; silently or aloud*)
- What do we ask Mary when we pray the Rosary? (*To pray for us that we may love and follow Jesus*)

314

The Rosary

The Rosary is a special prayer that honors Mary. When we pray the Rosary, we remember Jesus' and Mary's lives. We remember that Mary was Jesus' mother. We remember that Mary always said yes to God.

We can pray the Rosary alone. We can pray it together in school, at home, or in church. We can pray the Rosary silently or aloud. Mary always brings our prayers to Jesus. When we pray the Rosary, we ask Mary, "Pray for us that we may love and follow Jesus, your son."

Enriching the Lesson

While many of the Rosary's mysteries are beyond the children's comprehension, they will understand the Joyful Mysteries. Share one of these stories each day before praying: The Annunciation (Luke 1:30–33); The Visitation (Luke 1:50–53); The Nativity (Luke 2:10–11); The Presentation (Luke 2:29–32); and The Finding in the Temple (Luke 2:48–52).

Praying the Rosary

When we pray a decade of the Rosary, we think about an important time in Mary's and Jesus' lives. We call these important times **mysteries**. The mysteries are the special things that God has done for us through Jesus and Mary.

Activity

Pray a decade of the Rosary each day this week with your class or family. When you have finished praying the Rosary, draw your own rosary in the space below.

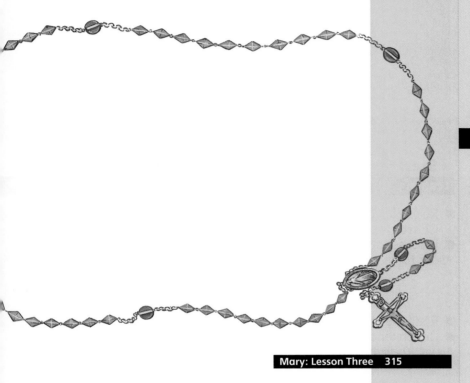

Teaching Tips

If you have an Altar and Rosary Society or a Legion of Mary group in the parish, ask them if they would be willing to donate rosaries to the children in your class. Arrange for a blessing ceremony in which the rosaries are formally presented to the children.

Naming the Mysteries of the Rosary

Point out the picture of the Rosary on page 315 and read aloud the text. Emphasize that the mysteries are stories about Jesus and Mary. Explain that each Rosary tells five stories about Jesus and Mary and that these stories are divided into three groups. Make three columns on the board and label them *The Joyful Mysteries, The Sorrowful Mysteries,* and *The Glorious Mysteries.*

Explain that the Joyful Mysteries tell the story of God's plan for Mary to be Jesus' mother, and Jesus' birth and childhood. The Sorrowful Mysteries tell stories about Jesus' death. The Glorious Mysteries tell us about Jesus' resurrection and how Jesus and Mary share in the glory of God's life in heaven.

Step 3 / CONCLUSION

Learning How to Live Our Faith

Praying a Decade of the Rosary

During the next five days, pray one decade of the Joyful Mysteries with the class daily. After praying, invite the children to color one decade of beads each day.

Drawing a Rosary

At the conclusion of the week, invite the children to draw their own rosary in the space provided in their books.

Our Church Celebrates Holy Days

Objectives ~~~~~~

- **LESSON 1:** To help the children understand that on the Feast of Corpus Christi we celebrate Christ's gift of himself in the Eucharist.
- **LESSON 2:** To help the children learn the story of Pentecost.
- **LESSON 3:** To help the children learn that Thanksgiving is a special time to thank God.

Lesson Outlines ~~~~~~

	Step 1 **Learning About Our Lives**	**Step 2** **Learning About Our Faith**	**Step 3** **Learning How to Live Our Faith**
Lesson 1	■ Discuss ways of showing honor. *ABOUT 5 MINUTES*	■ Read about the Feast of Corpus Christi. ■ Discuss the feast. *ABOUT 10 MINUTES*	■ Complete an activity. ■ Have a procession. *ABOUT 15 MINUTES*
Lesson 2	■ Talk about windy days. *ABOUT 5 MINUTES*	■ Read the story of Pentecost. ■ Understand the story. *ABOUT 10 MINUTES*	■ Fill in the missing words. ■ Review the story. ■ Pray together. *ABOUT 15 MINUTES*
Lesson 3	■ Look at Thanksgiving symbols. *ABOUT 5 MINUTES*	■ Read about Thanksgiving. *ABOUT 10 MINUTES*	■ Consider God's gifts. ■ Share Thanksgiving traditions. ■ Pray a picture prayer. *ABOUT 15 MINUTES*

Plan Ahead

	Preparing Your Class	**Materials Needed**
Lesson 1	Read through the entire lesson plan. Select a recording of a eucharistic song to play during the procession in Step 3.	■ pencils ■ recording of a eucharistic song ■ crayons ■ record or cassette player
Lesson 2	Read the lesson plan. Cut a flame for each child from red construction paper.	■ pencils ■ paper flames for each child ■ candle
Lesson 3	Read through the entire lesson plan. Gather Thanksgiving pictures or objects for use in Step 1.	■ Thanksgiving pictures

Additional Resources

As you plan these lessons, consider using the following materials from The Resourceful Teacher Package.

■ *Classroom Activity Sheets for Holy Days*

■ *Family Activity Sheets for Holy Days*

■ *Prayers for Every Day*

You may also wish to refer to the following Big Book.

■ *We Celebrate God's Word*, page 21

In preparing the students for the Sunday readings, you may wish to use Silver Burdett Ginn's *Getting Ready for Sunday* student and teacher materials.

REDUCED CLASSROOM ACTIVITIES

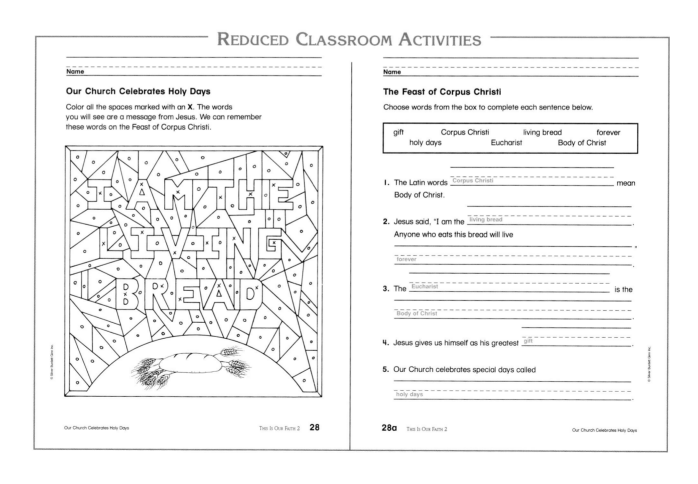

Name _____

Our Church Celebrates Holy Days

Color all the spaces marked with an **X**. The words
you will see are a message from Jesus. We can remember
these words on the Feast of Corpus Christi.

Our Church Celebrates Holy Days   THIS IS OUR FAITH 2 **28**

Name _____

The Feast of Corpus Christi

Choose words from the box to complete each sentence below.

gift	Corpus Christi	living bread	forever
	holy days	Eucharist	Body of Christ

1. The Latin words _Corpus Christi_____ mean
   Body of Christ.

2. Jesus said, "I am the _living bread_____.
   Anyone who eats this bread will live
   _forever_____"

3. The _Eucharist_____ is the
   _Body of Christ_____.

4. Jesus gives us himself as his greatest _gift____.

5. Our Church celebrates special days called
   _holy days_____.

28a THIS IS OUR FAITH 2   Our Church Celebrates Holy Days

315c Organizer

Background for the Teacher

THE FEAST OF CORPUS CHRISTI

The Feast of Corpus Christi, now called the Feast of the Body and Blood of Christ, seems to duplicate our celebration of Holy Thursday. But, in fact, the Corpus Christi feast is joy-filled and focused entirely on the Eucharist. The Holy Thursday liturgy carries with it the sorrow of Christ's impending crucifixion. The Feast of Corpus Christi celebrates our belief that Jesus is truly present in the Eucharist. This feast provides us with the opportunity to reflect on the mystery of the Eucharist and how that mystery makes us one with Christ. Corpus Christi is a movable feast; that is, it is not celebrated on the same Sunday each year. When the Solemnity of Corpus Christi is not observed as a holy day, as it is in some countries, it is assigned to the Sunday after Trinity Sunday, which is then considered its proper day in the calendar.

PENTECOST SUNDAY

Pentecost is often called the "birthday of the Church." Fifty days after Easter, we celebrate the outpouring of the Holy Spirit on Jesus' disciples and apostles, which filled them with courage to carry out the mission given to them by the risen Christ. The Acts of the Apostles records that Jesus' Spirit descended upon Jesus' followers in the form of fire and a mighty wind, enabling them to become "the Church,

which is the Body of Christ and the Temple of the Holy Spirit" (*Catechism of the Catholic Church*, #737). At Jesus' Baptism, the Holy Spirit appeared in the form of a dove that descended on Jesus. We, too, receive the Holy Spirit and the mission of Jesus at Baptism. As you teach the children about the great Feast of Pentecost, you can help them celebrate Jesus' presence among us through the Holy Spirit, who makes it possible for us to love and follow Jesus.

THANKSGIVING

The Mayflower arrived at the rocky shores of New England in November of 1620. The 100 Pilgrims were ill-equipped to deal with the hardships of the winter and almost half of them died within the first year. Native Americans provided seeds to plant and taught the Pilgrims how to survive. Together, they celebrated the fall harvest the following November. That first Thanksgiving feast lasted three days.

Today, Thanksgiving is a time for families to gather at their tables to offer thanks for the blessings of the year. In this lesson, you have the opportunity to help the children recognize that all good things come from God. You can also encourage them to be mindful of those who do not have enough to eat and those who, for one reason or another, do not experience the support and love of an extended family.

LESSON 1

Objective

This lesson helps the children understand that on the Feast of Corpus Christi we celebrate Christ's gift of himself in the Eucharist.

Step 1 / INTRODUCTION

Learning About Our Lives

Discussing Ways of Showing Honor

Discuss with the children different ways in which we thank people for doing something special or honor them because of their accomplishments. You may want to offer the following suggestions. We give people gifts; we give people awards or trophies; we hold special award ceremonies; and we honor them by having a parade. Explain that today the children will learn about a special way people thank Jesus for the gift of himself.

Step 2 / DEVELOPMENT

Learning About Our Faith

Reading About the Feast of Corpus Christi

On the chalkboard write the words *Corpus Christi*. Tell the children that these are Latin words for "the body of Christ." Also write the word *procession* on the chalkboard. Explain that a procession is like a quiet parade. Have a volunteer read aloud "The Feast of Corpus Christi" on page 316.

Discussing the Feast

After the reading, ask:

- What do the words *Corpus Christi* mean? (*The body of Christ*)

- What do we do on the Feast of Corpus Christi? (*Think about the Eucharist, thank Jesus for the gift of himself*)

- How do some people thank Jesus on this day? (*They have a procession.*)

- When do we celebrate this feast day? (*On a Sunday, nine weeks after Easter*)

316

Our Church Celebrates Holy Days

The Feast of Corpus Christi

The words <u>Corpus Christi</u> are Latin words that mean "the body of Christ." On the Feast of Corpus Christi, now called the Feast of the Body and Blood of Christ, we think about the Eucharist. We thank Jesus for the gift of himself.

In some parishes, people thank Jesus by having a procession. As they walk, they pray and honor the presence of Jesus in the Eucharist.

We celebrate the Feast of Corpus Christi on a Sunday that falls nine weeks after Easter. On this day we remember the words of Jesus.

"I am the living bread. Anyone who eats this bread will live forever."

Based on John 6:51

Teaching Tips

The gospel story on the Feast of Corpus Christi is the Feeding of the Five Thousand. This is the only miracle story told in all four gospels. The story provides us with a hint of how Jesus will nourish us through the Eucharist and helps us recognize how aware Jesus was of the human needs of others. Have the children look through news magazines and cut out pictures of people in need. Mount the pictures on posterboard and write the prayer, "Jesus, help us care about others" on the poster.

Activity

Use this code to color the stained-glass window.

yellow	**3**	green	**5**	blue	
brown	**4**	purple			

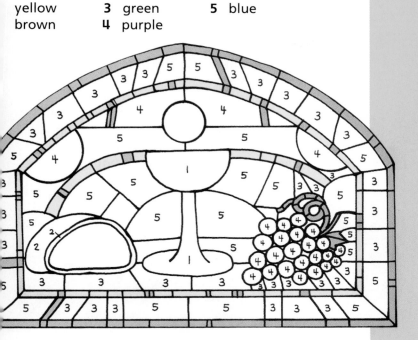

On the lines below, write a short prayer to Jesus.

Learning How to Live Our Faith

Completing an Activity

Distribute crayons. Have a volunteer read the directions for the coloring activity on page 317. Explain to the children that after they have finished coloring, they are to write a short prayer to Jesus on the lines provided at the bottom of the page. After the children have finished writing, ask volunteers to share their prayers with the class.

Having a Procession

Ask the children to stand and form a single line. Have them fold their hands in a prayerful position. Then lead the children in a prayerful procession around the room. Play a recording of a eucharistic song as the children process.

After the children have walked once around the room, have them form a prayer circle by joining hands. Have the children respond *Jesus, we honor you* to each of the following sentences.

- Jesus is the living bread.
- Jesus is with us always.
- Jesus is with us everywhere.
- Jesus is with us in a special way in the Eucharist.

Enriching the Lesson

With the help of parent volunteers, have the children bake loaves of bread, using commercial bread dough, to share with their families on the Feast of Corpus Christi. Direct the children to divide each pre-made loaf into three smaller loaves and place them on cookie sheets. Show the children how to brush the loaf with melted butter to make the crust crispy. As the bread bakes, invite the children to write a grace prayer to pray before eating the bread.

317

LESSON 2

Objective

This lesson helps the children learn the story of Pentecost.

Step 1 / INTRODUCTION

Learning About Our Lives

Talking About Windy Days

Encourage the children to talk about the things they notice on windy days. Responses may include *whistling, creaking, or blowing sounds, objects blowing outdoors, and the feeling of the wind "pushing" against them.* Then ask them to talk about activities they enjoy on windy days, such as flying kites, running, or blowing soap bubbles. Tell the class that in this lesson they will learn about a time that Jesus' friends heard the sound of a mighty wind.

Step 2 / DEVELOPMENT

Learning About Our Faith

Reading the Story of Pentecost

Direct the children to turn to page 318 and follow along as you read the story of the first Pentecost. Discuss the following questions.

- What did Jesus' friends hear? (*A loud noise like the wind*)

- What did they see? (*Flames of fire around them*)

- What happened to Jesus' friends? (*They were filled with the Holy Spirit.*)

- What did they begin to do? (*Praise and thank God in different languages; teach people about Jesus*)

- What did the people who listened do? (*They were baptized and became Jesus' followers.*)

Understanding the Story

Read with the children the next three paragraphs on page 319. Stress that the Holy Spirit is always with us to help us live with Jesus' love. Remind the class that we first receive the Holy Spirit at Baptism.

318

The Coming of the Holy Spirit

All of Jesus' friends were together. Suddenly they heard a loud noise that sounded like the wind. The sound filled the whole house. They saw flames of fire around them. All of Jesus' friends were filled with the Holy Spirit. They began to praise and thank God in many different languages.

Jesus' friends left the house and began to teach the people in the streets about Jesus, the Savior, who had risen to new life. Many people listened and believed in what Jesus' friends taught. Every day, new people were baptized and became followers of Jesus.

Based on the Acts of the Apostles 2:1–41

Enriching the Lesson

Have the students make Pentecost pinwheels by cutting 5" squares from stiff red paper. Draw lines from the corners to 1/4" from the center. Have the children carefully cut along the lines. Show them how to fold one point in each triangle to the center. Pin all four points to the eraser-end of an unsharpened pencil.

Pentecost

After Jesus rose to new life, he returned to God in heaven. He knew his followers would need help sharing the good news. Jesus promised that he would send the Holy Spirit.

The Holy Spirit came on **Pentecost**. We celebrate Pentecost fifty days after Easter. Pentecost is the birthday of the Church.

On Pentecost we pray, "Come, Holy Spirit, let your love shine brightly in us."

Activity

Find the word in the box that completes each sentence. Then put the story of Pentecost in order by numbering each sentence. Use the numbers 1 through 6.

teach	fire	Jesus'	baptized	wind	Holy Spirit

2. They heard a sound like w i n d.

4. They were filled with the H o l y   S p i r i t.

1. All of J e s u s' friends were together.

6. Every day new people were b a p t i z e d.

3. They saw flames of f i r e.

5. They began to t e a c h the people about Jesus.

Learning How to Live Our Faith

Filling in the Missing Words

Explain the directions to the first part of the activity on page 319. Direct the children to find the missing word in each sentence and write it in the space provided.

Reviewing the Story

Review the story of the first Pentecost by putting the story in order. Begin by asking, "What happened first?" Have the children put the number "1" next to the statement "All of Jesus' friends were together." Then ask what happened next. Continue this until each statement has been numbered.

Praying Together

Gather the children in a circle. Light a candle and explain that the flame is a sign of the Holy Spirit. Pray spontaneously, thanking Jesus for sending the Holy Spirit to help us live with love. Pray together the prayer at the top of page 319. Give the children the paper flames you prepared prior to class. Ask them to keep the paper flames as reminders that the Holy Spirit is always with us.

LESSON 3

Objective

This lesson helps the students learn that Thanksgiving is a special time to thank God.

Step 1 / INTRODUCTION

Learning About Our Lives

Looking at Thanksgiving Symbols

Show the children the objects or pictures related to Thanksgiving that you have brought to class: a turkey, Pilgrims, Native Americans, and so on. Ask the children what these things make them think of. Lead the class to recognize that these are objects or pictures that we associate with Thanksgiving. Tell the class that in this lesson they will learn about the first Thanksgiving and why Thanksgiving is a special time to thank God.

Step 2 / DEVELOPMENT

Learning About Our Faith

Reading About Thanksgiving

Read with the children "Thanksgiving" on page 320. Then discuss the reading with the questions below.

- What did the Pilgrims invite their friends to? (*A feast*)

- What is a feast? (*A special meal*)

- Why did the Pilgrims invite their new friends to the feast? (*The Native Americans gave them seeds to plant; they taught the Pilgrims how to grow food and hunt.*)

- What do we think about on Thanksgiving? (*All the good things God gives us*)

- How can we be like the Pilgrims on Thanksgiving? (*By sharing our food with hungry people*)

- How can we be like the Native Americans? (*By welcoming strangers*)

Have the children read aloud together the prayer from Psalm 100 that we pray on Thanksgiving Day.

320

Thanksgiving

Long ago the Pilgrims invited their Native American friends to a feast. These Native Americans had given them seeds to plant. They had taught the Pilgrims how to hunt and grow food. The Pilgrims thanked the Native Americans for helping them learn how to live in America. The friends celebrated together. Soon the celebration became known as Thanksgiving Day.

On Thanksgiving we think about all the good things that God gives us. We eat special foods. We celebrate with our families. We remember that some people are hungry. Like the Pilgrims, we share our food. Like the Native Americans, we welcome strangers to our land, churches, and homes.

On Thanksgiving Day we pray, "God, you are great and good. Your love lasts forever" (based on Psalm 100:5).

Enriching the Lesson

Distribute construction paper and crayons to the children. Have them each find a partner. Tell them to trace their partner's hand on the paper and cut it out. Turn the hand into a turkey by inserting an eye, mouth, and wattle on the thumb, and legs below the wrist. The children can color the fingers to make feathers. Have them write "Thank you, God" on the palm.

A Thanksgiving Picture-Story Prayer

Thank you, God, for making me.

Thank you for my

Thank you for the  and ,

for and and  that fly.

Thank you for the  we eat,

for and and fields of .

Thank you for a that mends,

for , our , and special .

Thank you most for , who sets us free.

O God, we praise you always, thankfully.

Learning How to Live Our Faith

Considering God's Gifts

Invite the children to each name a gift they have been given by God. Get this discussion started by naming several things or people for which you are thankful. Emphasize that all good things come from God.

Sharing Thanksgiving Traditions

Have the children discuss how their families celebrate Thanksgiving, naming what they eat, where they go, and with whom they celebrate. Then discuss how your parish observes Thanksgiving. Be sure to mention canned food drives or food basket projects, and your parish's efforts in welcoming strangers into the community. Help the children understand that at Thanksgiving, we try to imitate both the Pilgrims and the Native Americans by sharing food and welcoming newcomers.

Praying a Picture Prayer

Read through the picture-story prayer on page 321 with the children, having them supply the words for each of the pictures shown. Do this several times to fully acquaint the children with all the words and the rhythm of the prayer. Then ask the children to stand and pray the prayer with you.

In the Spirit of Jesus
Pope John XXIII

Objectives

- LESSON 1: To help the children learn about Pope John XXIII.
- LESSON 2: To help the children learn that Maryknoll priests and sisters share with others the good news about Jesus.

Lesson Outlines

	Step 1 Learning About Our Lives	**Step 2** Learning About Our Faith	**Step 3** Learning How to Live Our Faith
Lesson 1	■ Discuss qualities of leadership. *ABOUT 10 MINUTES*	■ Read and discuss a story. *ABOUT 10 MINUTES*	■ Complete a writing activity. ■ Pray together. *ABOUT 10 MINUTES*
Lesson 2	■ Identify special visitors. *ABOUT 5 MINUTES*	■ Read and discuss a story. *ABOUT 10 MINUTES*	■ Complete a map activity. ■ Make a poster. ■ Pray together. *ABOUT 15 MINUTES*

Plan Ahead

	Preparing Your Class	Materials Needed
Lesson 1	Read through the lesson plan.	■ pencils ■ crayons
Lesson 2	Read the lesson plan.	■ pencils ■ posterboard ■ Maryknoll magazines ■ glue, scissors, crayons

Additional Resources

As you plan these lessons, consider using the following materials from The Resourceful Teacher Package.

■ *Classroom Activity Sheets for In the Spirit of Jesus*

■ *Family Activity Sheets for In the Spirit of Jesus*

■ *Prayers for Every Day*

You may also wish to refer to the following Big Book.

■ *We Celebrate God's Word*, page 21.

In preparing the students for the Sunday readings, you may wish to use Silver Burdett Ginn's *Getting Ready for Sunday* student and teacher materials.

REDUCED CLASSROOM ACTIVITIES

In the Spirit of Jesus

Jesus gives us the Holy Spirit to be with us always. Some of those times are listed below. Complete each sentence by writing "the Holy Spirit is with us." Talk about other times when the Holy Spirit is with us.

1. When we share in the Eucharist,

2. When we listen carefully to God's word,

3. When we forgive others,

4. When we share happy times with our friends,

Pope John XXIII

Reread the story of Pope John XXIII. On the lines below, write ways in which Pope John XXIII showed that the Holy Spirit was with him.

HOLY SPIRIT

321c Organizer

Background for the Teacher ∿∿∿∿∿∿∿∿

IN THE SPIRIT OF JESUS

The Catholic Church teaches that God, our Father, and Jesus send the Holy Spirit into our lives to bring joy and happiness. The purpose of this lesson is to help us understand that Pope John XXIII gave the world an example of how to live the Christian way of life in a joyful, loving, and peaceful manner.

POPE JOHN XXIII

Angelo Joseph Roncalli (Pope John XXIII) was born on November 25, 1881, in Italy. Although he was pope for less than five years (from October 1958 to June 1963), his impact on ecumenism and the Church's role in the modern world is still being felt. Pope John was, perhaps, most loved for his effervescent charm. Pope John felt the need to be in touch with all people—world leaders, the poor, the sick, and the imprisoned. These contacts are what led Pope John to feel deeply the love that God has for each one of us. In this lesson, you, the teacher, have the opportunity to develop in the children the awareness that if we love one another, we will always have Jesus in our lives.

MARYKNOLL

Fathers James Walsh and Thomas Price founded the Catholic Foreign Mission Society of America, popularly known as Maryknoll. The Society was formally approved by the United States Bishops and Pope Pius X to recruit, train, and send missionaries devoted to apostolic ministry overseas. The following year, Father Walsh established the Maryknoll Sisters of Saint Dominic to minister to the catechetical, educational, medical, and social needs of people in non-Christian and Christian countries. Maryknoll's first work outside of the United States was done in the Orient and in 1918, a mission was established in South China.

During World War II, Maryknoll priests and sisters were formally expelled from the Far East. Many of those who were not expelled were interned by the government as prisoners of war. Maryknoll saw this as an opportunity to expand their mission to Latin America. Today, approximately 700 Maryknoll priests and 900 sisters minister to people in Africa, Latin America, the Far East, and virtually every corner of the world. As you teach this lesson, you can help the children appreciate how Maryknoll fulfills the command of Jesus to "teach all nations."

LESSON 1

Objective

This lesson helps the children learn about Pope John XXIII.

Step 1 / INTRODUCTION

Learning About Our Lives

Discussing Qualities of Leadership

Discuss with the children what leadership qualities someone would need to be a leader. Print these qualities on the chalkboard.

Explaining Church Leadership Roles

Explain that the Roman Catholic Church has leaders. Write the word *bishop* on the chalkboard. Tell the children that a bishop is the leader of many parishes.

On the chalkboard, print the word *pope*. Tell the children that the pope is the leader of the Roman Catholic Church. Then print *Pope John XXIII* on the chalkboard. Explain that XXIII means 23, but that we read XXIII after the pope's name as "the twenty-third." Tell the children that they are going to learn about Pope John XXIII, a leader who was special to many people throughout the world.

Step 2 / DEVELOPMENT

Learning About Our Faith

Reading and Discussing a Story

Read aloud "Pope John XXIII" on page 322. After you have finished reading, discuss the story by asking the following questions.

- Where did Father Roncalli work? (*In a school; in the army*)

- What did Bishop Roncalli always try to do? (*Lead others to Jesus*)

- What did Pope John do as a world leader? (*Talked to all people about peace*)

322

In the Spirit of Jesus

Pope John XXIII

Angelo Joseph Roncalli was a very good man. After he became a priest, he worked in a school. He also worked in the army, teaching the soldiers about Jesus.

He also taught them about the Catholic Church.

Father Angelo Roncalli became a leader in the Church. When he was a bishop, he cared for many people. He helped those who were in trouble. He invited many people without families into his home. Bishop Roncalli tried to lead others to Jesus.

After many years, Bishop Roncalli was chosen to be pope, the leader of the Roman Catholic Church. He chose the name Pope John XXIII (the twenty-third). As a world leader he talked to all people about peace. He wanted everyone to work together. He knew that when people love others, Jesus lives in their hearts.

🍎 Teaching Tips

Ask the children if they know what the word *pope* means. After allowing them a few moments to speculate on the correct answer, tell them that it comes from a very old Latin word. Write the word *papa* on the chalkboard and again ask the children to guess the meaning of the word. Once they see the Latin form of the word, they should have no trouble recognizing that *pope* means "father." Tell the children that we call the pope the "holy father" because he is the leader of the entire Church.

Activity

Look at the picture. Write your answers to the questions below. Then color the picture.

1. What is happening in the picture?

_____
_____
_____
_____

2. How can you be like Pope John XXIII?

_____
_____
_____
_____

Enriching the Lesson

Display pictures of Pope John Paul II and ask the children to identify him. Tell them that John Paul II has led the Church since 1978. Remind the class that when a new pope is elected, he chooses a new name. John Paul II chose the name in honor of the previous pope, John Paul I, who died shortly after being elected pope. Teach the children the chant the students of New York shared with the pope when he visited our country: "John Paul II, we love you!"

Learning How to Live Our Faith

Completing a Writing Activity

Have a volunteer read the directions for the activity on page 323. Allow the children to complete the activity independently by writing their answers on the lines provided. After they have finished writing, have volunteers share their responses. Then distribute crayons for the children to color the illustration at the top of the page.

Praying Together

Invite the children to join you in prayer. Ask them to repeat each of the following sentences after you.

- God, you give us many people to lead us.
- Thank you for Pope John XXIII.
- Help us remember his happiness in serving you.
- Help us find Jesus in others.

Objective

This lesson helps the children learn that Maryknoll priests and sisters share with others the good news about Jesus.

Step 1 / INTRODUCTION

Learning About Our Lives

Identifying Special Visitors

Ask the children to name special people who have visited their classroom during this and previous years. Responses may include the *principal, a priest or the parish pastor, Santa Claus, and others.* Tell the children that in today's lesson, they will read a story about a class of second graders who had a special visit from a very important person.

Step 2 / DEVELOPMENT

Learning About Our Faith

Reading and Discusssing a Story

Call on volunteers to read aloud "A Visit from Father Jim" on page 324. Afterward, discuss the reading.

- Who visited Sister Joan's class? (*Father Jim*)
- What was Father Jim? (*A missionary priest*)
- What do missionaries do? (*Travel to different lands to share the good news about God and Jesus*)
- How do Maryknolls share the good news? (*They teach people to pray; they talk about God and build churches and schools.*)
- How do Maryknoll priests and sisters live in the spirit of Jesus? (*They remember that Jesus wants us to share his good news; they believe that everyone has the right to hear about Jesus.*)

A Visit from Father Jim

"Boys and girls," said Sister Joan. "We have a special visitor today. Father Jim is a Maryknoll priest. He is going to tell us about his work."

"Hello, children," said Father Jim. "Does anyone know what a **missionary** is?"

Corey said, "A missionary tells people about God."

"That's right!" said Father. "A missionary travels to faraway lands to share the good news about God and Jesus."

"Where do you go?" asked Jorge.

"Maryknoll priests and sisters go all over the world," said Father Jim. He showed the children a globe. He pointed to the places he had gone. He showed them Africa, Central America, and South America.

"What do you do there?" asked Alexa.

"Maryknoll priests and sisters live with the people. We teach them to pray. We talk about God. We build churches and schools," said Father Jim. "We believe that everyone has the right to hear about Jesus."

CURRICULUM CONNECTION

Social Studies   Using a globe, help the children locate the countries in which Father Jim was a missionary. Explain that many people in these countries have never heard about Jesus and that in some places, the leaders do not want their people to know the good news of Jesus. Remind the class that Maryknoll missionaries believe that everyone has the right to hear about Jesus.

Activity

Follow Father Jim's journey from continent to continent. Unscramble the letters on each continent to form a word. Use the words to complete the sentence at the bottom of the page.

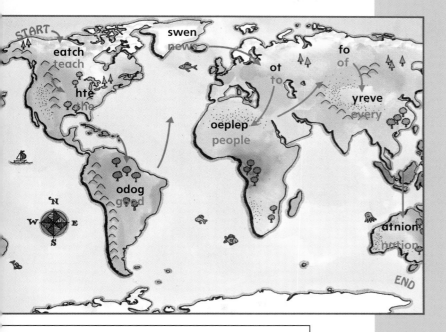

Jesus says,

"<u>T e a c h</u> <u>t h e</u> <u>g o o d</u>
<u>n e w s</u> <u>t o</u> <u>p e o p l e</u> <u>o f</u>
<u>e v e r y</u> <u>n a t i o n</u>."

Teaching Tips

Write a letter to the Maryknoll Missionaries or to The Society for the Propagation of the Faith. In your letter, ask for information about the missions and how your students can help in their work.

Maryknoll Educational Resources
Maryknoll, NY 10545

Society for the Propagation of the Faith
366 Fifth Ave.
New York, NY 10001

Step 3 / CONCLUSION

Learning How to Live Our Faith

Completing a Map Activity

Point out the activity on page 325 and explain the directions. Have the children work to complete it. Afterward, read the sentence aloud together. Then talk with the children about how they can be missionaries. Help them understand that they share the good news when they tell others about Jesus and help other people.

Making Posters

Divide the class into small groups and distribute Maryknoll magazines to each group, along with a sheet of posterboard, scissors, crayons, and glue. Direct the children to find pictures of missionary priests and sisters working to spread Jesus' good news by teaching and helping others. Have them glue the pictures onto the posterboard and print a title at the top. As the children work, offer suggestions and help each group think of a title, such as *Maryknolls Share the Good News; Missionaries Tell Others About God;* or *Maryknolls Live in the Spirit of Jesus.*

Praying Together

Have the children pray an echo prayer by repeating the following lines after you.

- Thank you, God, for sending Jesus to bring us good news.
- Thank you, God, for missionaries.
- Help me share Jesus' good news with others. Amen.

325

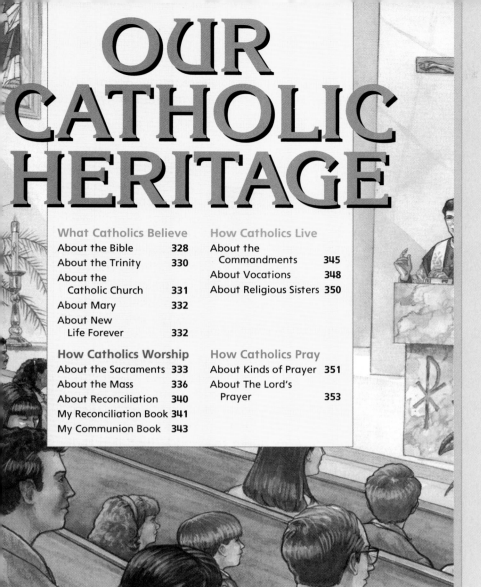

OUR CATHOLIC HERITAGE

Our Catholic Heritage

In June 1994, the *Catechism of the Catholic Church* was published in English and widely distributed throughout the United States. Bishops, pastors, and educators have used the *Catechism* as a basic resource in summarizing Catholic doctrine and for a better understanding of the theological background of the Church's teaching.

In this section, *Our Catholic Heritage,* there is a summary of Catholic belief, organized in the same way as the *Catechism.* It is meant as a ready reference for both you and your students to provide in summary fashion the basic teachings of the Catholic Church.

Over the course of the THIS IS OUR FAITH program, the *Our Catholic Heritage* section of each grade level is developmental in nature, and planned to complement the information presented in the lesson plans. These pages are most effectively used in conjunction with the student book pages that cover the topics in question.

You may want to read the Apostolic Constitution *Fidei Depositum* and the *Prologue* (paragraphs 1–25). These introduce the *Catechism* and provide a better understanding of its purpose in religious education.

What Catholics Believe

The *Catechism of the Catholic Church*, published in 1994, provides a clear and extensive statement of Catholic doctrine, divided into four parts or pillars of our faith. The first, "The Profession of Faith," develops the foundations of our creed, based on sacred Scripture and the tradition of the Church throughout the ages. As a Catholic Christian community, we renew our dedication to these beliefs each week at Sunday Mass, when we celebrate Baptism and Confirmation, and during the Easter Vigil. Our recitation of the creed reminds us of our unity in faith with Catholic Christians throughout the world.

About the Bible

TEACHER REFLECTION

Sacred Scripture is a source of nourishment and strength for the Church. The Church has accepted throughout history that certain books of both the Hebrew Scriptures and the New Testament were written under the inspiration of the Holy Spirit. The Church has recognized the importance of biblical scholarship for understanding the Scriptures. We are encouraged to study the Bible continually to be able to more deeply appreciate the Word of God.

You may want to review for yourself the teachings of the Church about the Bible in paragraphs 101–133 in the *Catechism of the Catholic Church*.

STUDENT REVIEW

Ask for volunteers to read "About the Bible" on page 328 on their books. Provide some examples of stories that are in the Old Testament. You may want to use the following.

- Story of Adam and Eve
- Story of Noah and the ark
- Story of Moses leading the people out of Egypt

Challenge volunteers to name some stories about Jesus that they have read. Remind the children that these stories are gospel stories. Write the names of the four gospels on the chalkboard or on a poster. Pronounce the names and have the children repeat them.

What Catholics Believe

Catholic Christians share many special gifts. We believe, live, and pray as one family.

ABOUT the Bible

The Bible is a book that is special to many people who believe in God. The book is divided into two parts: the Old and the New Testaments. The Old Testament includes many stories of God's people who lived before Jesus was born.

The New Testament is the second part of the Bible. The Holy Spirit helped some followers of Jesus write the books and letters in this section. Four of the books are the Gospels of Matthew, Mark, Luke, and John. In these books, the gospel writers wrote about the wonderful things that Jesus said and did. The gospel writers also tell us about the places where Jesus lived and visited.

The Gospel of Matthew tells about the birth of Jesus in Bethlehem. The Gospel of Mark tells about the baptism of Jesus in the River Jordan. The Gospel of Luke tells us that Jesus, Mary, and Joseph lived in Nazareth. The Gospel of John tells about the Last Supper in Jerusalem.

The Holy Land

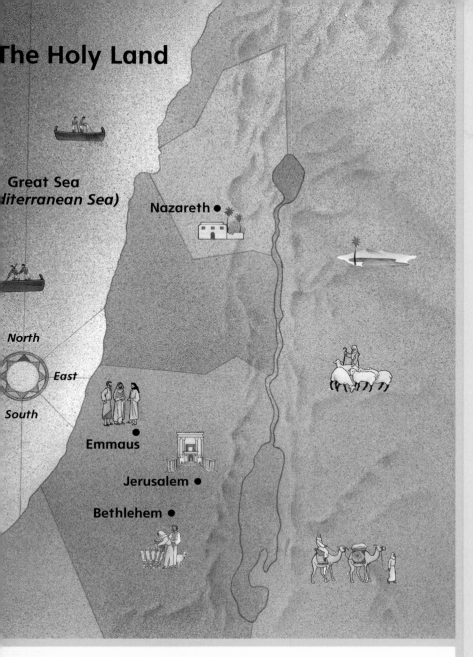

Great Sea
(Mediterranean Sea)

Nazareth ●

North

East

South

Emmaus ●

Jerusalem ●

Bethlehem ●

You may want the children to locate in their books a story from each gospel. Then direct the children to study the map on page 329. Help the children locate the four places named in the four gospels.

About the Trinity

TEACHER REFLECTION

Over the centuries the Church has come to an "understanding" of the Trinity as a result of reflection on the action of God in our lives. We have come to know God as love, creative and redemptive. This revelation of God, in whose image we are made, helps us understand both the meaning of our humanity and our calling to be part of a community. We believe that God reveals the work of the Trinity in the mystery of creation.

You may want to review for yourself the teachings of the Church about creation in paragraphs 279–412 in the *Catechism of the Catholic Church.*

STUDENT REVIEW

Ask for volunteers to read "About the Trinity" on page 330 in their books.

Review the major concepts about the one God in three persons, and the beliefs about God the Father; Jesus, God's Son; and the Holy Spirit. Point out to the children that God speaks to us in the Bible.

Write on the chalkboard the three vocabulary words printed in boldface on pages 330 and 331: *grace, Savior, and holy.* Review the meanings of these words with the class. Answer any questions the children may have.

ABOUT the Trinity

We Believe in God

There is only one God. God is three persons: Father, Son, and Holy Spirit.

God is our Creator. God made all things with love. Everything God made is good.

The Bible is a special book about God's love for us. God speaks to us in the Bible.

We share in God's life. **Grace** is God's life and love in us.

God loves and cares for us. God wants us to be happy. God gives us Jesus to help us.

We Believe in Jesus

Jesus is God's Son, who became a man and lived on earth with us. God sent Jesus to show us how to love.

Courtesy of the S.M.A. Fathers

Jesus is our brother and friend. Jesus is our teacher. Jesus teaches us how to live as children of God.

Jesus died on the cross and rose from the dead for us. Jesus is our **Savior**. He saves us from sin and death.

Jesus is always with us. Jesus shares his new life with us.

We Believe in the Holy Spirit

The Holy Spirit is the Spirit of God. God's Spirit helps us follow Jesus.

We receive the Holy Spirit at Baptism. The Spirit of God gives us gifts to help us live good lives. The Holy Spirit helps us to be **holy**. To be holy means to be like God.

ABOUT the Catholic Church

We are **Catholic Christians**. We follow Jesus. We belong to the Catholic Church. We celebrate the sacraments. We pray to God, and we help others.

The pope is the leader of the Catholic Church. We call the pope our Holy Father.

The Church is the people of God. We help God's love grow in the world.

About the Catholic Church

TEACHER REFLECTION

It is our belief as Catholic Christians that Jesus established the Church and set its course by forming the apostles and disciples as evangelizers and missionaries. We believe that at Pentecost the Holy Spirit revealed the Church to the world, and that the public mission of the Church began at that time. We profess in the creed that the Church is one, holy, catholic, and apostolic. These four marks describe essential features of the Church and her mission. We should be able to see and experience these characteristics of the Church in our parishes, in the Church in our nation, and in the work of the Church throughout the world.

You may want to review for yourself the teachings of the Church about the four marks of the Church in paragraphs 813–873 in the *Catechism of the Catholic Church*.

STUDENT REVIEW

Ask for volunteers to read "About the Catholic Church" on page 331 in their books.

Review with the children the main points about being Catholic Christians. Help them to remember that the Church is the people of God; the pope is the leader of the Church; and that as Catholic Christians we follow Jesus, celebrate the sacraments, and help love grow in the world.

About Mary

TEACHER REFLECTION

Mary has always been a sign of God's special love for us. Mary's willingness to be God's servant, her saying yes to God, began our salvation in Jesus Christ. We believe that Mary, from the first instant of her conception, was totally preserved from the state of original sin. The Church calls this doctrine the Immaculate Conception. The Church also teaches that, at her death, Mary was assumed, body and soul, into heaven, where she shares in the glory of her Son's resurrection. We honor Mary, the Mother of God, as Mother of the Church because she is the model of holiness for all of us.

You may want to review for yourself the teaching of the Church about Mary in paragraphs 963–972 in the *Catechism of the Catholic Church*.

STUDENT REVIEW

Ask for volunteers to read "About Mary" on page 332 in their books.

Explain to the children what a saint is. Help them understand that Mary is our greatest saint because she is the mother of Jesus and that she is our mother, also.

About New Life Forever

TEACHER REFLECTION

Our belief in new life forever, or life everlasting, has traditionally been described as the "last things"—the particular judgment, the realities of heaven, purgatory, hell, and the final judgment. We believe that, at the second coming of Christ, all people will be gathered in Christ's presence, and that the truth of each one's relationship with God will be revealed. At the same time, the Kingdom of God will come in its fullness, and humanity and the world will be transformed.

You may want to review for yourself the teaching of the Church about life everlasting in paragraphs 1020–1050 in the *Catechism of the Catholic Church*.

STUDENT REVIEW

Ask for volunteers to read "About New Life Forever" on page 332 in their books. Review with the children the meaning of heaven.

ABOUT Mary

God chose Mary to be Jesus' mother. Mary loved and trusted God. From the first moment of life, Mary was filled with grace.

Mary is our mother, too. Mary loves and cares for us.

Mary is our greatest **saint**. The **saints** are special people who show us how to follow Jesus. We honor the saints and ask them to pray for us.

ABOUT New Life Forever

Jesus teaches us that if we act with love, we will live forever. We will be happy with God in **heaven**. Heaven is unending happiness with God and all who love God. If we show love for God and others, we will be happy together in heaven.

How Catholics Worship

Worship is giving honor and praise to God. We worship God in the sacraments and prayer.

ABOUT the Sacraments

The **sacraments** are celebrations of God's love and signs of Jesus' presence with us now. There are seven sacraments.

Baptism is a sacrament of welcome into the Church. At Baptism we receive the Holy Spirit.

We are baptized with water. Water is a sign that we share Jesus' new life.

In the sacrament of Confirmation, we receive the Holy Spirit in a special way. God's Spirit helps us to tell everyone the good news about Jesus.

333

The liturgical life of the Church is the Catholic Christian community's way of celebrating what we believe. Through the signs of the sacraments and our participation in the liturgical celebrations, we renew our faith and gain an even greater share in the life of grace, God's life in us. Through the sacraments, we are challenged to follow ever more closely the way of Christ that leads to the realization of God's kingdom.

STUDENT REVIEW

Ask for a volunteer to read "How Catholics Worship" on page 333 in their books.

About the Sacraments

TEACHER REFLECTION

The whole life of the Church revolves around the Eucharist and the sacraments. In the sacraments we encounter Christ and are enabled to live the life of faith more deeply. The sacraments of initiation—Baptism, Confirmation, and Eucharist provide the building blocks for Christian life. Through them we are welcomed into the Church and are called to conversion and service.

The sacraments of healing—Reconciliation and Anointing of the Sick—recall the frailty of our human condition. The sacrament of Reconciliation provides us with an opportunity to acknowledge the reality of sin, to ask forgiveness, and to begin anew as disciples of Christ. Anointing of the Sick is a source of strength and consolation for those who are ill and those who are caring for them.

The sacraments in service to the community—Matrimony and Holy Orders—celebrate publicly the calling to family life and to ordained ministry in the Church. These vocations are sanctified in the sacramental rites in which we are called to build the Body of Christ through example and service.

You may want to review for yourself the teaching of the Church about the sacraments in Part Two of the *Catechism of the Catholic Church*.

Student Review

Ask for volunteers to read "About the Sacraments" on pages 333–335 in their books.

This special feature can be used at appropriate times throughout the year to help the children review the sacraments.

At Mass, we share a special meal with Jesus. The **sacrament of the Eucharist** celebrates the presence of Jesus in the Eucharist we share.

At Mass, we remember that Jesus died on the cross for us. At Mass, we thank God for giving us Jesus, the Bread of Life.

In the **sacrament of Reconciliation,** we say we are sorry for our sins. We celebrate God's forgiveness.

Anointing of the Sick brings Jesus' peace and help to people who are sick or elderly.

In the sacrament of **Holy Orders**, men become priests and join Jesus' work in a special way.

The **sacrament of Matrimony** celebrates the love of a man and a woman for each other.

About the Mass

TEACHER REFLECTION

Our celebration of the Mass is the primary source of renewal of our life in Christ. In the Mass we are once again welcomed into the community of the faithful, called to communion with others and service to others, and nourished by the Bread of Life. We are sent forth to exemplify the good news of the gospel in our everyday lives.

You may want to review for yourself the teaching of the Church about the Mass in paragraphs 1322–1405 in the *Catechism of the Catholic Church*.

STUDENT REVIEW

Ask for volunteers to read "About the Mass" on pages 336–339 in their books.

"About the Mass" is placed here as an easy-to-find reference for you and the children. This feature can be used throughout the year to

- review the Mass and its major parts.
- help the children prepare for First Eucharist.

You may wish to extend the use of these pages by inviting a parish priest to demonstrate and explain the various vestments and sacramentals used at Mass.

Note: For a more complete walk-through of the Mass, you may wish to use the Big Book, *We Celebrate the Mass,* available directly from Silver Burdett Ginn.

ABOUT the Mass

1. Our celebration begins. The priest and other ministers walk down the aisle in a procession. We stand and sing a gathering song.

2. The priest welcomes us. He says "The Lord be with you." We answer, "And also with you." We all make the sign of the cross.

3. We remember our sins and God's love and forgiveness. The priest prays an opening prayer.

4. We listen to God's word in readings from the Old Testament and the New Testament.

5. In the gospel story, we hear about Jesus' life and teachings. We stand to welcome Jesus in the gospel.

6. The priest or deacon explains the readings to us in a special talk called a homily.

7. We pray for the Church, for our country, and for all God's people. We call this prayer the Prayer of the Faithful.

8. We prepare the altar for the meal we are about to share. We bring our gifts of bread and wine. Sometimes we bring other gifts, too. We always bring ourselves, the most important gift of all.

9. The priest of
   our gifts of
   bread and w
   to God. They
   become the
   body and blc
   of Jesus.

10. We thank and
    praise God for all
    God's blessings,
    especially for the
    gift of Jesus.

11. Our gifts of
    and wine be
    for us the bc
    and blood o
    Jesus. We ca
    body and bl
    Jesus <u>Euchar</u>

12. The priest holds up th
    Eucharist and prays a
    prayer of praise to G
    We answer, "Amen!"
    Amen means, "Yes! W
    believe this is true."

13. We pray together The Lord's Prayer, the prayer that Jesus taught us.

14. We offer one another a sign of peace to show that we are all brothers and sisters in Jesus.

15. We come to the table of the Lord to receive Jesus in the Eucharist.

16. We receive God's blessing and say, "Amen." We sing a song of praise. Then we go in peace to love and serve all people.

About Reconciliation

TEACHER REFLECTION

The grace of the sacrament of Reconciliation or Penance gives us the courage to admit our failures and wrongdoing, to ask forgiveness, and to renew our dedication to the Christian life. The experience of the sacrament celebrated in community can give us a better appreciation of the social consequences of sin and the need for reconciliation as a whole people. Reconciliation makes visible the mercy of our loving God.

You may want to review for yourself the teaching of the Church about Reconciliation in paragraphs 1422–1484 in the *Catechism of the Catholic Church*.

STUDENT REVIEW

Ask for volunteers to read "About Reconciliation" on page 340 in their books.

"About Reconciliation" is placed here as an easy-to-find reference for you and the children. The special feature can be used at appropriate times throughout the year to

- review the steps of the sacrament of Reconciliation.
- help introduce children to the communal celebration of the sacrament.
- help prepare children for the sacrament of Reconciliation.

You may want to extend the use of this page by arranging a tour of your parish's reconciliation room. You may also want to use the material on this page in conjunction with Unit 2, pages 62–104.

340

How Catholics Worship

ABOUT Reconciliation

The sacrament of Reconciliation celebrates God's lo and forgiveness. Sometimes we celebrate the sacrame of Reconciliation with the Catholic community.

Opening Song   We sing a song of praise.

Greeting and Opening Prayer   The priest welcomes u and prays with us.

Readings and Gospel   We listen to stories from the Bi

Homily   The priest or deacon explains God's word to

Examination of Conscience think about our words and actions. Together we pray Th Lord's Prayer.

General Confession of Sins pray a prayer of sorrow.

Individual Confession   Now are ready to go one by one t the priest. We talk about the words and actions for which are sorry. We ask forgiveness receive absolution.

Prayer of Thanksgiving   We praise and thank God fo God's mercy.

Blessing and Dismissal   The priest asks God's blessing us. We sing a song of praise.

340

say a prayer of contrition.

A Prayer of Sorrow

My God,
I am sorry for my sins
with all my heart.

In choosing to do wrong
and failing to do good,
I have sinned against you
whom I should love
above all things.

I firmly intend, with your
help, to do penance,
to sin no more, and to avoid
whatever leads me to sin.

Rite of Penance

The priest reads a story from
the Bible.

The story reminds me that God is
always ready to forgive me.

3

The priest says, **Go in peace.**
I answer, **Amen.**

The priest and I thank God
for being forgiving.

**MY RECONCILIATION
BOOK**

Name

I

Making the Booklet

Assist the children in making the booklet "My Reconciliation Book." Each child will need a pair of scissors and you will need a stapler. After the children have separated the page from their books along the perforations, direct them to cut along the horizontal cut line indicated by the symbol of a pair of scissors. Direct the children to place the pages on top of each other so that page 1 is to the right and on top of page 3. Instruct them to fold the booklet on the fold line so that the fold is to the left and page 1 is facing them right side up. Ask the children to check to make sure all pages are in proper sequence. Staple the books for the children along the fold line.

This booklet has been designed for the children to use during the celebration of the sacrament of Reconciliation.

I confess my sins.

The priest listens as I talk about how I have turned away from God and hurt myself or others.

4

The priest gives me a penance.

The priest asks me to say a prayer or do a good act. This will show God that I am sorry and want to be more caring.

I examine my conscience.

I think about things I have said or done to hurt God, other people or myself.

2

The priest gives me absolution.

The priest says,
I absolve you from your sins in the name of the Father, and of the Son, and of the Holy Spirit.

Then we receive Communion,
the priest or special minister
says,

The body of Christ.

We respond, **Amen.**

After Communion, we thank Jesus.
We can say this prayer.

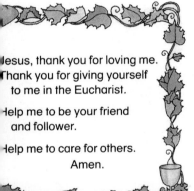

Jesus, thank you for loving me.
Thank you for giving yourself
to me in the Eucharist.

Help me to be your friend
and follower.

Help me to care for others.
Amen.

The priest shows us the chalice.

He says,
**Take this, all of you, and drink from it:
this is the cup of my blood,
the blood of the new and everlasting
    covenant.
It will be shed for you and for all
so that sins may be forgiven.
Do this in memory of me.**

3

MY COMMUNION BOOK

Name

_____

1

Making the Booklet

Assist the children in making the booklet "My Communion Book." Each child will need a pair of scissors and you will need a stapler. After the children have separated the page from their books along the perforations, direct them to cut along the horizontal cut line indicated by the symbol of a pair of scissors. Direct the children to place the pages on top of each other so that page 1 is to the right and on top of page 3. Instruct them to fold the booklet on the fold line so that the fold is to the left and page 1 is facing them right side up. Ask the children to check to make sure all pages are in proper sequence. Staple the books for the children along the fold line.

This booklet has been designed for the children to use during the second part of the Mass, the Liturgy of the Eucharist.

Then the priest says,
Let us proclaim the mystery of faith.

We respond,
**Christ has died,
Christ is risen,
Christ will come again.**

4

At Mass we remember Jesus' words and actions at the Last Supper. The priest shows us the bread.

He says,
Take this, all of you, and eat it: this is my body which will be given up for you.

2

Before we receive Communion, the priest says,
**This is the Lamb of God who takes away the sins of the wo
Happy are those who are called to his supper.**

We respond,
**Lord, I am not worthy to receive y
but only say the word and
I shall be healed.**

If we receive from the cup, the priest or special minister says,
The blood of Christ.

We respond, **Amen.**

How Catholics Live

Jesus teaches us how to live. The Holy Spirit and the Church help us live with love.

The Great Commandment

Jesus said, "Love God with all your heart, all your thoughts, and all your strength. Love your neighbor as yourself" (based on Mark 12:31).

Jesus teaches us to live the **Great Commandment**. The Great Commandment tells us how to show our love for God and our neighbor.

How Catholics Live

345

Morality is faith lived. To fully understand the demands of Christian morality, we need to recognize that it is based on the limitless love of God and the dignity of every human person as created by God. The focus of Christian morality is not rules, but relationships. The purpose of the Beatitudes and Commandments is to enable the relationship between God and ourselves to grow and to be expressed in our approach to our neighbor.

STUDENT REVIEW

Ask a volunteer to read the sentence under "How Catholics Live" and another volunteer to read "The Great Commandment" on page 345 in their books.

Help the children memorize the Great Commandment. Discuss with them its meaning.

About the Commandments

TEACHER REFLECTION

As the commandments were first given to the Israelites, so they are proclaimed today to the new people of God and to all men and women of faith. The commandments challenge us to deepen our relationship with God and to see the world around us from God's loving and caring viewpoint. Observing God's commandments is the first step to becoming followers of Christ and thus being called to greater holiness.

You may want to review for yourself the teaching of the Church about the commandments in paragraphs 2052–2557 in the *Catechism of the Catholic Church*.

STUDENT REVIEW

Ask for volunteers to read "About the Commandments" on pages 345–347 in their books.

Review God's laws in the chart on page 346 that show us how to love God and *our neighbor*. Explain to the children that our neighbor refers to other people, not just those who literally live near us. Explain that the Holy Spirit helps us to live out Jesus' new commandment. Help the children memorize Jesus' new commandment.

Answer any questions the children may have.

ABOUT the Commandments

We can find God's commandments in the Bible. God gave us the Ten Commandments to help us live the way God wants us to live.

We Live God's Laws

We show our love for God.	We believe in God and love God.
	We use God's name with love.
	We pray to God every day.
	We pray with our Church family at Mass on Sunday.
We show our love for our neighbor.	We obey our parents and those who care for us.
	We care for all living things.
	We tell the truth.
	We are careful with other people's things.
	We share with others.
	We are thankful for God's gifts.

Jesus' New Commandment

Jesus gave us a new commandment. He said, "Love one another as I love you" (based on John 15:12).

We can love like Jesus by being fair and kind. We can help others. We can be peacemakers.

When we do not act with love, we **sin**. Sin is choosing to do what we know is wrong.

The Holy Spirit Helps Us

We can choose to love. We can choose to sin. The Holy Spirit helps us choose to do what is good and to turn away from sin.

TEACHER REFLECTION

Every member of the Christian community is called by God to a particular role in the service of the Church. Although our vocation may be to serve as priest, religious or lay person; as teacher, missionary, or liturgical minister, we all derive our mission from our Baptism into the Church of Christ. Our vocation is strengthened by the Holy Spirit in Confirmation and encouraged by our participation in the Eucharist. Through prayer and our experience in the Christian community, we will be able to discern God's call to us and commit ourselves to our particular vocation in the Church.

You may want to review for yourself the teaching of the Church about vocations in paragraphs 871–945 in the *Catechism of the Catholic Church.*

STUDENT REVIEW

Ask for volunteers to read "About Vocations" on pages 348–349 in their books.

Make sure the children understand that everyone is called to help others in a special way. Help the children give examples of how Catholic Christians can help in their parish church (*Reading the Scriptures, leading the songs, giving Eucharist, and so on*). Point out that priests, religious brothers or sisters, and deacons have a special vocation to help in the Church.

348

ABOUT Vocations

When we were baptized, we began our new life as Catholic Christians. As we grow older, we know that we will be invited by God to live more and more as Jesus taught us. God calls each person to help others in a special way. This is called our **vocation**.

Many Ways of Helping

Most Catholics are called by God to help others as members of the parish church. They can help at Mass by reading the Scriptures, leading the songs, giving Eucharist, or by helping in other ways. They can teach others about God and Jesus' message found in the gospels. They can do many things to help others.

348

Sometimes God calls people to a special way of helping in the Church. There are priests who lead the parish community. There are religious brothers and sisters who teach, serve the poor, or help lead the parish. There are deacons who help in the parish by reading the gospel at Mass or by giving the homily. Deacons help in many other ways, too.

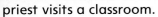
priest visits a classroom.

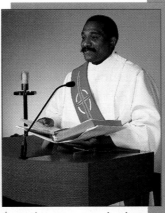
▲ A deacon reads the gospel.

As you learn more about God and the Church, you will discover in what special ways God is calling you to be a helper.

▲ A religious sister teaches a class.

349

TEACHER REFLECTION

Religious sisters are women who live in community, and who take the religious vows of poverty, chastity, and obedience. By promising to live simply, in community, and in accord with the wishes of their bishops and superiors, sisters are freed to serve the Church community and all those to whom the Church ministers. Religious sisters are involved in every aspect of Church life and mission, and often bring the message of Christ into the community at large through their presence in many different professional service organizations. The contribution of religious sisters to the life of the Church in the United States has been and continues to be essential.

You may want to review for yourself the teaching of the Church about religious sisters and other vocations in the Church in paragraphs 871–945 in the *Catechism of the Catholic Church.*

STUDENT REVIEW

Ask for volunteers to read "About Religious Sisters" on page 350 in their books.

Help the children review some of the ways religious sisters work for God's family, the Church. (*Teaching, working with the poor or in hospitals, working as missionaries, spreading the good news of the gospel to people around the world*)

ABOUT Religious Sisters

Religious sisters have a special vocation. They are women who live together in groups called communities. Religious sisters spend all of their time working for God's family, the Church.

Some sisters are teachers. They teach in elementary schools, high schools, and colleges. Other sisters work among the poor or in hospitals. Still others are missionaries who bring the good news of the gospel to people in many countries around the world. Religious sisters do the work of the Church in many different ways.

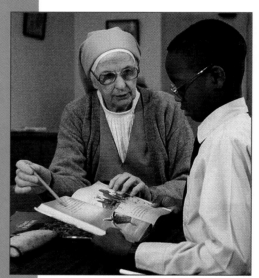

Every sister promises God and the other sisters that she will love God very much. She promises to live her life in a simple way. She hopes that people will see her goodness and try to live a better Christian life.

350

How Catholics Pray

Prayer is talking to and listening to God. God always hears our prayers. In prayer, we can thank and praise God. We can ask for God's help. We can pray alone or with others. The Mass is our greatest prayer.

ABOUT Kinds of Prayer

We can thank God for our wonderful world.

We can thank God for the gift of our families and friends.

We can ask God's help to live as Jesus taught us.

We can pray at morning and at bedtime.

We can pray with our families at mealtime.

We can pray in school with our teacher and classmates.

At Sunday Mass, we pray with our families and the whole parish community.

351

Regular prayer is conversation with our loving God, and is part of every believer's life and the life of the Church. Daily prayer and devotions, the liturgy of the hours, and the Sunday Eucharist all offer ways of celebrating and praising God. Growth in our life of prayer is nourished by taking every opportunity to listen and speak with God as individual believers and as members of the Christian community.

STUDENT REVIEW

Ask a volunteer to read the paragraph under "How Catholics Pray" on page 351 in his or her book.

About Kinds of Prayer

TEACHER REFLECTION

There is no preferred way to pray. God leads each person according to his or her needs. In Christian tradition, we find three major expressions or models of prayer—vocal prayer, meditation, and contemplation. Vocal prayer can be a recitation of formal prayers learned from others or as part of the liturgy. We can also speak our mind to God in our own words at any time. Meditation engages the mind, imagination, and emotions by focusing on a particular subject (a psalm, a Scripture passage, God's creation, the life of a saint). Contemplative prayer is attentiveness to God. It is active listening to the word of God, done in silence.

You may want to review for yourself the teaching of the Church about kinds of prayer in paragraphs 2650–2758 in the *Catechism of the Catholic Church.*

STUDENT REVIEW

Ask for volunteers to read "About Kinds of Prayer" on page 351 in their books.

Ask the children to think about all the ways we can pray. Ask:

- What is our greatest prayer? (*The Mass*)
- What are some of the ways we can pray? (*Thank and praise God; ask for God's help; pray alone or with others*)
- What are some of the places we can pray? (*At home, at school, in church*)

351

TEACHER REFLECTION

The Lord's Prayer teaches us that when we pray we are to be inclusive and mindful of the fact that we are connected to one another; it is the prayer of the community. The Lord's Prayer also teaches us that first we are to praise and adore God and then petition for our need for nourishment and healing. Since apostolic times, this prayer has been considered the most important prayer for the Christian community.

You may want to review for yourself the teaching of the Church about The Lord's Prayer in paragraphs 2759–2869 in the *Catechism of the Catholic Church.*

STUDENT REVIEW

Ask for volunteers to read "About The Lord's Prayer" on pages 352–353 in their books.

Discuss with the children what we pray for in The Lord's Prayer. Ask: What prayer did Jesus teach his friends and us? (*The Lord's Prayer*)

Pray The Lord's Prayer line by line with the children, reviewing the meaning of each phrase or sentence of the prayer. Then pray the entire prayer prayerfully with the class.

How Catholics Pray

ABOUT The Lord's Prayer

Jesus taught his friends **The Lord's Prayer**. All followers of Jesus pray the prayer Jesus taught. In this special prayer, we honor God. We pray that what God wants for us and for all people will be done. We ask God for the things that we need. We ask God to keep us safe from anything that may harm us. Then we pray, "Amen!"

Our Father, who art in heaven, **hallowed** be thy name.

God is our Father. We pray that everyone will remember how good God is.

Thy kingdom come,

Jesus told us about God's kingdom. We pray that everyone will live as Jesus taught us to live.

thy will be done on earth as it is in heaven.

We pray that everyone will obey God's laws.

Give us this day our daily bread;

We know that God cares for us. We pray for our needs and the needs of the poor.

and forgive us our trespasses as we forgive those who trespass against us;

We ask God to forgive us for the wrong things we have done.

and lead us not into temptation,

We ask God to help us always to choose what is right.

but deliver us from evil.

We pray that God will protect us from things that may harm us.

Amen.

Our "Amen" says that this is our prayer, too.

Using the Write-in Glossary

The write-in glossary provides a reference for the vocabulary and terms of the Catholic religion that have been introduced in the chapter lessons of Units 1–5, in the Amen lessons, and in the *Our Catholic Heritage* section.

After you have presented the New Words in each chapter, you may wish to have the children write each new word as part of its definition on the lines provided.

WRITE-IN GLOSSARY

absolution _____ is the words of forgiveness the priest prays over us in the sacrament of Reconciliation.

Advent _____ is the time before Christmas when we get ready for Jesus to come into our lives.

altar An _____ is the table at which the Mass is celebrated.

ambo An _____ is the reading stand where the word of God is read.

angel An _____ is a messenger from God.

anointing _____ means putting blessed oil on a person's body as a sign of love, respect, honor, or healing.

Ash Wednesday _____ is the first day of Lent.

Baptism _____ is a sacrament of welcome. At Baptism, our lives are joined to Jesus and the Church welcomes us as new members.

baptismal font A _____ is the water font where new members of the Church are baptized.

Catholic Church The _____ is the Christian community to which we belong.

celebrations _____ are special times when we show how important someone or something is to us.

chalice A _____ is the special cup that holds the eucharistic wine at Mass.

Christians _____ are friends and followers of Jesus Christ.

Christmas _____ is the time when we celebrate the birth of Jesus.

parish church A _____ is a place where Catholics gather to pray with other members of the Catholic Church.

Catholics _____ are followers of Jesus who belong to the Catholic Church.

Communion

_____ is a part of the Liturgy of the Eucharist. At Communion, Jesus gives himself to us in the Eucharist.

community

A _____ is a group of people who share something important together.

confess

_____ means to tell our sins to a priest in the sacrament of Reconciliation.

Confirmation

_____ is another sacrament of welcome into the Catholic Church through which the Holy Spirit makes us strong to live and share our faith in Jesus.

contrition

_____ means to be sorry.

crucifix

A _____ is a cross that holds the body of Jesus.

disciples

_____ are persons who live and love as Jesus did.

Easter

_____ is the time when we remember and celebrate Jesus' rising to new life.

Emmaus _____ is the place where Jesus shared a meal with two of his followers after he rose to new life.

Eucharist _____ is Jesus' gift of himself to us in the Eucharist we receive at Mass.

Eucharistic Prayer The _____ is a special time at Mass for praising and thanking God.

faith _____ in Jesus means that we have come to know him and trust him.

fasting _____ is eating less food than we usually do.

godparents _____ are two people chosen by our parents to help us grow as friends and followers of Jesus.

Good Friday _____ is the day when we remember Jesus' death on the cross.

gospel The _____ is the third reading we hear at Mass. It tells about Jesus' life and teachings.

grace

_____ is God's loving
presence in our lives.

**Great
Commandment**

The _____
tells us how to show our love for God and our neighbor.

guide

_____ means to show
the way.

hallowed

_____ means holy.

heaven

_____ is unending
happiness with God.

holy

_____ means to be like
God.

Holy Saturday

_____
is the day when we remember that Jesus died to give us new
life. We wait and watch for Jesus' rising to new life.

Holy Spirit

The _____ is the Spirit
of God who helps us follow Jesus.

Holy Thursday

_____ is the day when
we remember Jesus' Last Supper.

Holy Week

_____ is the week before Easter.

homily

A _____ is a special talk by a priest or deacon that explains the readings we listen to at Mass.

hosts

_____ are bread that becomes the Body of Christ at Mass.

lectionary

A _____ is the book where all the Bible readings used at Mass are found.

Lent

_____ is the time before Easter when we get ready to celebrate Jesus' resurrection.

Liturgy of the Eucharist

The _____ is the second part of the Mass. It begins as we prepare to share a special meal with Jesus.

Liturgy of the Word

The _____ is the first part of the Mass.

Lord's Prayer

The _____ is the prayer that Jesus taught us.

Mass

The _____ is a special meal with Jesus. At Mass, we pray together and listen to God's word from the Bible.

359

missionary   A _____ is a person who tells people about God.

mysteries   The _____ of the Rosary are special things that God has done for us through Jesus and Mary.

New Testament   The _____ is the second section of the Bible. It tells about the life and teachings of Jesus, his disciples, and the first Christians.

Old Testament   The _____ is the first section of the Bible. It tells about God and God's people who lived before Jesus.

parish   _____ is another name for our Christian community.

pastor   A _____ is the leader of a parish.

paten   A _____ is a special plate that holds the eucharistic bread at Mass.

penance   A _____ is a prayer or good action the priest asks of us. Doing a penance shows God that we are sorry and want to be more caring.

Pentecost

_____
_____ is the day when
we celebrate the coming of the Holy Spirit. It is the birthday of
the Church.

prayer

_____
_____ is talking to and
listening to God.

Prayer of the Faithful

_____
_____
The _____
is the last part of the Liturgy of the Word. During this prayer we
pray for ourselves and for people everywhere.

presence

_____
_____ means being
with someone.

procession

_____
A _____ is people
walking in line for a special reason.

reconciliation

_____
_____ means making up
and becoming friends again.

respond

_____
_____ means to answer
with words or actions.

responsibility

_____
A _____ is something we
are supposed to do as members of a community.

361

responsorial psalm

A _____ is a psalm we use at Mass to respond to God's word.

resurrection

_____ is Jesus' rising from death to new life.

right

A _____ is something we deserve to have as human beings.

Rosary

The _____ is a special prayer that honors Mary.

sacrament of Reconciliation

The _____ is the sacrament in which we say we are sorry for our sins and celebrate God's forgiveness.

sacrifice

_____ means to give something out of love.

saint

A _____ is a special person who shows us how to follow Jesus.

Savior

Jesus, the Son of God, is our _____ who saves us from sin and death.

serve _____ means to help
others and to be kind to them.

seven sacraments The _____
are special signs and celebrations of Jesus' love for us that make
him present to us now.

sin _____ means to hurt
someone on purpose or to do something we know is wrong.
When we don't do something we know we should do, we might
also sin.

sponsor A _____ is someone we
choose at Confirmation to help us live as a friend and follower
of Jesus.

tradition _____ means doing
something the same way every year.

unity _____ means joined
together in peace.

vestments _____ are special
garments worn by the priest during Mass.

worship _____ is giving honor
and praise to God.

The Resourceful Teacher

INTRODUCTION

Welcome to The Resourceful Teacher section of your teacher edition. Like the many other features of THIS IS OUR FAITH, the material in this section is designed to help you be successful in preparing for and teaching your religion class. Here you will find guidelines and practical ideas for your teaching and classroom management. This material enlarges on the instructions that accompany each chapter. Read through these pages thoughtfully as your year begins, and turn to them often throughout the year as a source of ideas and of answers to questions that may arise.

The questions teachers of religion ask—and we have sought them out and heard their inquiries—generally can be divided into three categories.

1. Questions about catechetics and the meaning of faith.
2. Questions about the psychological makeup of the child and the implications for teaching religion.
3. Questions about preparing and conducting a successful religious education class.

Answers to questions in these categories are in the Helps for the Teacher section. In some cases the question-and-answer format is used.

CATECHESIS

Catechesis refers to those actions that help people grow in their personal faith within a community of faith (*National Catechetical Directory*, 32–33).

As a teacher of religion, you should have a clear idea of what you are trying to accomplish with the children in your class. All of us want faith for our children. This faith, we know, is a gift from God. However, we can do much to help our children grow in faith. We can help them grow in knowing, loving, and serving God.

As adult Catholics, we have grown in faith over the years by being part of a community of believers. The children in our religious education classes will grow through the same interaction with people of faith.

Our first community of faith consists of those people who nurture and care for us in our earliest years. We grow in age and wisdom in a home setting, just as Jesus did. We learn first from people at home about what it means to love others.

This growth in faith continues in the course of our lives as we expand our horizons beyond the home to the school and to the larger community, including the parish. In the parish community, children meet those people who best exemplify what it means to love God and serve the needs of all people. In the parish, children learn how to pray, to worship, and to practice the love that Jesus asks of all of us.

Part of the children's religious experience today is your religion class. In fact, it may well be their most significant and meaningful experience in the Catholic Church. Here you have the opportunity to show the youngsters the joy of being a Catholic. You have the God-given chance to help them learn about their Catholic faith. You can help them discover ways in their own lives in which they can make the faith their own and put it into daily practice. Most of this learning will be from your example as a faith-filled catechist.

Faith

In talking about catechesis, we use the words *growing in faith*. But what is faith? As a catechist, you must understand what we mean by faith so that you can help the children grow in their faith.

It is important to remember that the Church understands faith in a twofold way: (1) Faith is that sound doctrine that teaches us about God and that has been passed down in the Church from age to age. (2) Faith is a relationship with God. It is a relationship that we grow in over the years. This growing relationship involves a faith based on believing and trusting in the providential care of God. Faith gives meaning to life and directs our actions in love of God and neighbor.

A major aspect of our relationship with God involves the fact that our faith is the *Catholic* faith. Here we have the heritage and tradition of the Church as it has evolved under the inspiration of the Holy Spirit down through the centuries. Here are the doctrines and principles that have come down to us as our inheritance from past generations of Catholic people. This inheritance includes Bible stories, practices of worship, moral positions, and a wide variety of customs.

THIS IS OUR FAITH aims at helping the children grow in their relationship with God. It also seeks to help the children learn the traditional beliefs and practices of the Catholic Church. In these ways, THIS IS OUR FAITH aims at helping our children know, love, and serve God. It seeks to help the faith of children become "living, conscious, and active, through the light of instruction" (*National Catechetical Directory*, 32).

Catechist

The term *catechist* is the name given to those people in the parish community who seek to help others grow in their Catholic faith through preaching and teaching. Thus, parents are the first catechists a child meets in life. The parish priests act as catechists because they help people know and love God more fully. Teachers of religion are catechists because they instruct children in the doctrines, principles, and customs of the Catholic religion. All catechists should have as their focus the desire to help people grow in their personal relationship with God.

CATECHISM OF THE CATHOLIC CHURCH

The *Catechism of the Catholic Church* is the document that contains the essential and fundamental beliefs of Catholic faith and morals.

It is organized into four parts: The Profession of Faith (what Catholics believe); The Celebration of the Christian Mystery (the Sacraments); Life in Christ (moral teachings); and Christian Prayer, with a concluding section on The Lord's Prayer.

The *Catechism* came about as a result of a recommendation of the bishops, recognizing the need for a compendium of the beliefs of the Church. The document, approved by Pope John Paul II in June 1992, is directed first and foremost to the bishops, who have the first responsibility for catechesis. It is directed also to those who prepare materials for catechesis, and through them, to all members of the faith.

The *Catechism of the Catholic Church* is the first such compendium of our faith since the Council of Trent and is therefore an important and historic document affecting future catechesis for generations to come.

A correlation of THIS IS OUR FAITH with the *Catechism of the Catholic Church* is available for teachers using the program.

National Catechetical Directory

The primary source for information about catechesis and your role as a religion teacher is the document of the National Conference of Catholic Bishops, titled *Sharing the Light of Faith: National Catechetical Directory for Catholics of the United States.* Approved in the late 1970s by the Bishops of the United States and the Sacred Congregation for the Clergy in Rome, the directory defines the goals and characteristics of quality religious education. The NCD, as it is called, sets forth what should be taught in a comprehensive program and explains how the religious formation of children should be approached.

THIS IS OUR FAITH is built on the foundation of the *National Catechetical Directory*. The program's goals and methods are the same as those that are set forth in the pages of the directory. THIS IS OUR FAITH presents the authentic and complete message of Christ and his Church in a way that is adapted to the capacity of the child.

PROFILE OF THE SECOND-GRADE CHILD

Bobby rushed into the room to show his new book to his mother. He was full of excitement as he talked about the first CCD class at Saint Ann Parish. "Here's my religion book! My teacher is Mrs. Johnson. She said we're going to do a lot of interesting things this year."

Bobby's mother listened with a sense of fascination. One short year ago, Bobby had begun regular school. Now, in second grade, he displayed the same curiosity and enthusiasm about life. He seemed more outgoing and sure of himself. He talked a mile a minute!

"How wonderful!" said Bobby's mother. "Were you good in class?"

"Yes," he beamed with a winning smile, "I did everything my teacher told me to do." Bobby paused for a moment and then turned to his mother. "Mom, what's a CCD?"

This simple account of Bobby's first CCD class shows us some of the characteristics of seven-year-old children. They are active, inquisitive, and full of life. Having been through one full year of school they are more sure of themselves. Yet they are still dependent on the guidance and approval of their parents, teachers, and other adults.

As a teacher of seven-year-old children, your aim should be to allow room for their enthusiasm for life to be expressed, while setting boundaries of respect and responsibility. The following questions, which come from second-grade teachers, should help in defining more clearly how this can be done. The answers to these questions will give you further insight into the makeup of the seven-year-old child. They will help you throughout the year.

The children in my class seem to lack focus at times. They pay attention one moment, then daydream the next. What can I do about this?

Try to adjust your lesson plan to the situation. The seven-year-old child has a short attention span and is easily distracted. Plan your lessons to include

- Activities of short duration, perhaps no more than eight to ten minutes.
- A variety of different kinds of activities.
- Brief periods of silence or prayer.
- Activities that involve doing something, such as drawing, singing, or acting out a play.
- A review of important points to remember.
- Lots of reminders throughout the class.

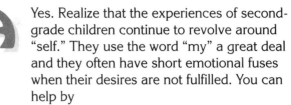

How can I help these children grow morally?

They need to be able to trust you as an adult who will accept them as they are, as someone who genuinely cares for them. Here are some suggestions.

- Be enthusiastic about God's love.
- Be patient, for children develop slowly.
- Assign simple tasks that the children can accomplish.
- When correcting the children, be gentle.
- Appreciate the children's need to feel that they belong to the group. Help them realize that you love them despite their mistakes. Dwell on their good actions.
- Accept the children's feelings of joy, fear, sadness, and anger.
- Help the children discover that Christians are happy people. Make humor and laughter part of each class whenever possible.
- Appreciate that each child is unique.

I tried being logical with these children and they looked at me with blank faces. What does this mean?

Seven-year-old children have difficulty thinking back logically to why something happened. They also have difficulty thinking abstractly. Try to involve the children with real objects and experiences. Allow them to smell, taste, and handle things as part of the class activities. Present one idea at a time and surround it with experiences that are real to the children.

I notice that the children in my second-grade class have difficulty at times sharing with each other. Is this self-centeredness normal?

Yes. Realize that the experiences of second-grade children continue to revolve around "self." They use the word "my" a great deal and they often have short emotional fuses when their desires are not fulfilled. You can help by

- Encouraging them to share.
- Being a model of someone who shares.
- Involving them in sharing activities, such as distributing materials for class, using supplies together, and cleaning up together.

DEVELOPING SOCIAL SKILLS

Teaching children self-discipline means equipping them with knowledge about socially acceptable customs in the world in which they live. It means, as well, helping them develop social skills such as showing respect for others and listening. The development of such skills of self-discipline are especially appropriate for second-grade children.

LISTENING

Explain to your children the steps of listening well.

- Stop whatever you are doing or saying.
- Look at the person who is speaking.
- Hear what the person is saying.

Print the three steps on a chart. Post the chart in the room so that the children can be reminded of their responsibility.

You can tell if your children are listening well if they are able to do one of the following.

- Ask questions of the speaker.
- Tell you in their own words what was said.
- Follow directions given.

You may wish to explore listening with the children by asking the following questions.

- In what places do you have to listen?
- How do you listen when you watch a movie?
- How do you listen when a parent is talking to you?
- How should you listen in class?

GETTING THE CHILDREN'S ATTENTION

Establish a procedure for getting everyone's attention during the session. Some children need to hear something. Others need a visual cue, such as a raised hand. You may want to employ a small bell or noisemaker to get their attention. You may decide simply to give an oral request such as, "I want everyone to stop talking and listen to me." Experienced teachers find that firmness and directness are the best ways to get attention.

GREETING PEOPLE

Another social skill children should learn is how to meet adults and new acquaintances. The following model might be used to teach the children this skill.

- Stand in front of the person to be greeted.
- Reach out your right hand.
- Take the hand of the other person and shake it.
- Say to the person, "My name is _____ ."
- Listen to what the person tells you his or her name is.
- Ask a question or answer a question the person may have.
- End by saying, "It was nice to meet you," or "I enjoyed meeting you."

USING PRAISE

You will often praise children for what they have said or done. Here are suggestions for making this praise-giving effective.

Remember that too much indiscriminate praise makes a child dependent on it. Focus on what the children have accomplished and give praise for specific instances of good work. It's best to provide specific information to children on their competence and the value of their accomplishments. For instance, you might say, "I liked your picture." Here are other examples of effective praise-giving.

- "Sue, your answer tells me that you have very special memories of the season of Advent. It makes me happy to learn that your Advent season has been so happy."
- "You were a very good reader. You spoke clearly and loudly enough for even the person in the back row to hear you."
- "Thank you for listening so well to the story that I just read. I noticed that no one spoke when I was talking. You asked questions when you did not understand something. You are good listeners!"

CLASSROOM ENVIRONMENT

Children learn best in an environment that is happy and secure. This environment should, of necessity, have the following characteristics.

First, there is reverence and respect for each individual in the group. The personal worth of each child is stressed when

- The teacher warmly welcomes each child to the session, calling each one by name.
- The teacher treats everyone fairly, showing no favoritism to particular children.
- The teacher praises a child for what he or she may have accomplished.
- The teacher sends home special notes to children who have missed a session because of sickness.
- The teacher enthusiastically responds to the children's ideas.

Second, a healthy environment is one in which there is a sense of caring among a cheerful community of people in the classroom. Such an environment is created when

- People share with each other.
- People cooperate as a group to get things done.
- People praise each other.
- Personal events such as birthdays and name days are remembered and celebrated.
- People are able to speak freely without fear of ridicule.
- People refrain from making judgments about each other.

Third, a healthy classroom environment is one in which there is a feeling that something of value is being accomplished. The children need to see that they have the opportunity to try new things and gain new skills as part of the experience of religious education. This happens in a practical way when

- Children take part in activities that allow each individual to be successful.
- Children enjoy working together.
- Children have a clear understanding of what is being taught.
- Children have their questions answered in a way that is meaningful.
- Children are presented with a variety of activities.

- A prayer life is cultivated and the children experience quiet time for reflection.
- Audiovisual material is a regular part of the class sessions.

Finally, a healthy classroom environment has a physical setting that is pleasant. Some factors that contribute to a setting conducive to learning are

- A room large enough to accommodate members of the class comfortably, allowing plenty of room for activities.
- A room with windows.
- A room that is well lit and comfortably heated.
- A room that is made visually appealing through the use of pictures, posters, banners, flowers, and the children's art work.
- Chairs that are comfortable.
- Desks or tables that are roomy and the right height.
- Background music at appropriate times.

PLANNING

One of the keys to a successful religion class is good planning. This involves taking the time to look ahead. It means being willing to put in work time before class. Such planning is one of the marks of a dedicated and concerned teacher.

There are three special planning times: before the year begins, before each unit, and before actual class time.

Before the Year Begins

Planning starts as soon as you receive copies of THIS IS OUR FAITH. Here are some suggestions for getting started.

- Open to the Contents pages in the student text, noting the major areas of Catholic faith being covered.
- Familiarize yourself with the organization of the book.
- Study the Teacher Edition. The beginning pages of the Teacher Edition provide valuable information on the organization of the program as well as the features of the student text and the Teacher Edition. There you will find a description of the three steps used in every lesson plan. You should become familiar with the features of the student text and this three-step plan.
- Study the Scope and Sequence Chart that also appears in the beginning pages of the Teacher Edition. This will familiarize you with the overall theme of the year as well as with the developmental strands that run through the grade levels.
- Make a program calendar for the year by first determining the number of religion classes you will have. Other activities might include service projects, planning for liturgies, field trips, and so on. Isolate the days on which you will be able to conduct a class using one of the lessons in the student text.

Next, decide what lessons you will cover during the year and on what days these lessons will be taken. Examine the Contents pages in the front of your Teacher Edition, noting that there are one introductory lesson, twenty core chapters, five unit review lessons, five Day to Day: Skills for Christian Living lessons and thirty-one supplementary lessons in the Amen section; and *Our Catholic Heritage,* a review section based on the *Catechism of the Catholic Church.* Each of the sessions is designed to provide you with at least a half-hour's worth of material to use with the children.

Before the Unit Begins

Each of the units of THIS IS OUR FAITH has four chapters that have been placed together because they cover related areas of Catholic faith. Become familiar with the overall development of each unit that you are about to begin teaching.

- Notice that in the Teacher Edition there is a page of information that begins each unit. This unit opener contains the unit aim, a doctrinal summary of each chapter, and the vocabulary. Reading these will give you a preview of the unit.
- For a more detailed overview of the unit, read through the chapters themselves, noting what they are seeking to achieve and the kinds of activities that are suggested.

Before the Class Begins

Experienced teachers have found it valuable to begin their preparation for next week's classes soon after the completion of this week's classes. Here are some steps they recommend.

- After your religion class is over and you have some time to sit and think, start asking yourself how the class went. What was successful? What did the children respond to most? What would you change if you could do the class over? Write down your observations on the pages of your Teacher Edition or in a separate notebook. You will also find this valuable when you teach the same lesson next year.

- Look ahead to the next lesson by turning to its *Chapter Organizer* in your Teacher Edition. Note the Objectives for the lesson.

- Review the *Chapter Outline.* This gives you an overview of the major activities that make up the lesson plan that appears in the book. Read through the lesson plan notes on the pages that follow. Make notes to yourself about what will work with your children and what will need to be altered or supplemented. Make any changes you feel necessary.

- Read the *Background for the Teacher* section of the Chapter Organizer. This will give you information about the theological content of the lesson as well as notes on the way the topic is approached in the lesson plan.

- Gather any supplies on the *Materials Needed* list that will not be readily available on the day of class. As you look through each lesson plan, you will find ideas for optional activities and additional information under Teaching Tips, Cultural Awareness, Curriculum Connection, Focus on, and Enriching the Lesson boxes that follow the basic lesson plan.

- During the days that follow this first preparation, review the lesson plan in your mind and in your heart. Ask yourself if you really understand what the lesson is trying to accomplish. Think about what you know about the topic and seek additional information if necessary. Pray to the Holy Spirit to guide you in your preparation.

- Finally, take time just before class (one-half day to a full day before) to review the lesson outline that you set down earlier in the week. Make any necessary changes. Make sure you have all the materials you will need for the class. Assign an approximate time that you will spend on each of the activities in the lesson plan. Mentally rehearse how you will conduct the class.

Try to make this procedure a part of your routine.

What does it mean to adapt the lesson plan to your needs?

Experienced teachers know that the lesson plans that appear in teacher manuals are only suggested ways to teach the chapter. They know their children and the kinds of activities they learn from best. They also know themselves and the kinds of things they do best in class. Experienced teachers take both of these into consideration when reviewing a lesson plan. They ask the following kinds of questions.

- What is really possible for me to accomplish in this lesson?
- What will the children be interested in?
- What is in this lesson that will work with my children?
- What do I have in my own experiences, interests, and talents that can complement or enrich this lesson plan?

Experienced teachers will make adjustments to the lesson plan that appears in the Teacher Edition, based on their answers to the above questions.

Is there anything that I can read during the year that will help me be a better teacher?

There are a variety of books and magazines available on becoming a better teacher. Two that should be read are *Sharing the Light of Faith: National Catechetical Directory for Catholics of the United States* and *The Creative Catechist* by Janaan Manternach and Carl J. Pfeifer, the authors of THIS IS OUR FAITH. Another helpful resource is the THIS IS OUR FAITH Program Director's Manual.

LEARNING ACTIVITIES

Storytelling

Children love stories. The sessions of THIS IS OUR FAITH contain many stories from the Bible and from contemporary life.

Be totally familiar with the story. While telling the story, look directly at the children. It is always a good idea to have visuals on hand to illustrate main points, attitudes, or feelings reflected in the story. Keep the storytelling short and simple, interrupting occasionally to ask the children how they would react in similar circumstances. Make sure that you distinguish Bible stories from other kinds of stories.

Drawing

Children do not have the vocabulary or the experience to express themselves in words the way we do as adults. They are able, however, to express themselves through drawing.

In order to use drawing effectively, maintain an atmosphere of order in the classroom. An art activity is not a play period. It helps to play appropriate background music. Explain clearly what the children are to do and have all materials ready.

Be sure that you do not make judgments about the artistic value of the children's drawings. Praise their work, allow them to show their work to others, ensure that specific insights they have expressed are respected. Above all, do not interpret meanings. Leave that to the individual.

Writing

Writing is a wonderful way for the children to gain insight into themselves and their faith. When we ask the children to write down their thoughts, they are forced to reflect on their ideas and feelings before putting their words on paper. Writing also brings up concerns and questions from the children's experiences that relate to your religion lesson.

In the THIS IS OUR FAITH program, such writing activity varies in the student text for each grade level. Generally, the activities include writing responses to questions, creating a story or poem, or writing personal prayers.

You should seek to create an atmosphere that encourages the children to write with openness and spontaneity. Don't indicate beforehand what you would write or what you expect them to say in their writing. Do not criticize their grammar and spelling, as you might in a language arts class.

Reading

In all the grade levels of THIS IS OUR FAITH, there are stories in the student text, both biblical and contemporary. There is also poetry to be read by the children. Each lesson contains some explanation of the teaching of Jesus or of various beliefs of the Catholic Church. All of these readings are set at the appropriate reading level for the children of that particular grade.

Reading is important because it is the primary way the children gain new information in their religious education class. Through the reading of the lesson, they are introduced to the vocabulary of the Catholic religion. They learn what the Church believes. They become familiar with the Scriptures through the reading of Bible stories and passages.

Listening to the Teacher

Often, the notes in the Teacher Edition will call upon you to explain something to the children, to add information to materials in the student text, or to clarify concepts that may be confusing to the children. The key advice in making such explanations is to keep them short and simple and avoid moralizing. Remember that explaining something to children in the form of a lecture has been cited in research as one of the least effective ways of teaching.

Memorizing

Memorization is an essential part of all education, including religious education. Two things should always be kept in mind, however. First, the children should not be required to memorize something they do not first understand. Second, the material they memorize should be important or relevant.

In THIS IS OUR FAITH, the children are asked to remember the We Believe statements and the essential vocabulary in the New Words boxes. These contain the key doctrinal concepts of the lesson as well as the new vocabulary.

You may also want the children to memorize the scriptural verse in particular lessons. Various traditional prayers that are valuable for the children to learn are introduced and others will be found in the Amen section.

Keep in mind that children are usually able to memorize only small amounts of information at any one time. Repetition and the use of memory games are often helpful.

Discussing

Good discussion is an important part of religious education. The children should be able to consider their experience, understanding, and questions about life and about what they have learned.

In planning a discussion, make sure that there is sufficient time. Plan a seating arrangement that lends itself to good discussion. Involve everyone in the group. Keep the discussion moving by asking probing questions. It is important that the children experience a freedom of expression, not fearing censure or ridicule. Make positive comments about their contributions and never allow them to interrupt a child who is speaking.

Questioning

There are four kinds of questions that children will be answering in THIS IS OUR FAITH. These questions can be found on the pages of the student text or in the lesson plans in the Teacher Edition.

The children will be asked *fact questions,* recalling information about the Catholic faith that has been presented.

After they have learned the given material, the children will be asked *meaning questions.* They will be asked what a particular concept or principle means and how they can put it into practice.

The children will be asked *value questions.* How do they feel about what they have learned or what is their attitude about various aspects of the Catholic faith?

They will also be asked to answer *faith questions.* "Why is it sometimes hard for me to do the right thing?" "What does God want me to do?"

Evaluating

There is no form of evaluation that precisely assesses a child's growth in faith. That would be making judgments about the relationship of faith between God and the children. There is, however, an opportunity for the teacher to evaluate what the children have learned as a result of the class sessions.

THIS IS OUR FAITH offers the opportunity to review with the children the content of the lessons of each chapter. A Chapter Review page that is part of the Day 5 lesson of each chapter includes fact questions that ask the children to recall the key doctrinal concepts of the lessons and, often, new vocabulary that is part of the chapter. The children are also asked to show how they will apply the teaching of the lessons to their daily lives.

At the end of every four chapters of THIS IS OUR FAITH, you will find a Unit Organizer and a two-page Unit Review. This review includes questions on the facts and concepts learned in the previous four chapters of the unit. It enables the teacher to evaluate what the children have learned and to give further clarification where needed. The suggested project allows for a practical application of the material taught in the unit.

Often, in the lessons themselves, the children are asked to examine their ideas and attitudes regarding some aspect of their life or faith. These are fine opportunities for the children to think critically, to reflect on the importance of possessing the Catholic faith, and to form the resolve to search always for deeper meaning in their relationship with God.

Prayer

Prayer is an important part of each religious education class in THIS IS OUR FAITH. The tasks of creating an environment for prayer in the classroom and of supplying various forms of prayer experience for the children are part of your role as a teacher. The children should have the opportunity to celebrate the Eucharist during the year. Those who are able to participate in the sacrament of Reconciliation should have the chance to do so. All the children should be able to experience the prayer services and informal prayers that are part of the lessons of THIS IS OUR FAITH. The children should learn firsthand as members of a community of faith and as persons of faith what it means to listen to and talk with God.

The Resourceful Teacher Package supplies you with prayer and liturgy supplements. This packet contains prayer services, and ideas for prayer for the entire year. It also provides you with guidelines and helpful hints for planning celebrations with the children.

INVOLVING THE COMMUNITY

Parish Involvement

Earlier in these Helps for the Teacher pages, you read that your role as a teacher is set within the community of faith that is your parish. You have people around you who influence the faith development of the children in your class. Involving these people in a partnership with you will do much to help our children grow as Catholics. There are three groups of people to think about when speaking of this partnership: parents or guardians, priests, and other parishioners.

Involving Parents

- At the beginning of the year, introduce yourself to the parents or guardians of each of the children in your class. You can do this by sending a letter home, making a friendly phone call, or inviting the parents or guardians to an open house. Explain what you are going to be studying with the children in religious education class. Help the parents feel that they are always welcome to talk to you about how their children are doing.

- Make sure that parents or guardians are aware of *Opening Doors: A Take-Home Magazine,* which can be found at the end of each unit in the student text.

- If a child misses a class, call the parents or guardians to let them know what they can do at home.

- Try to keep parents informed about what is happening in the class. Send home assignments for the children to do. Ask that they be returned with their parents' or guardians' signatures.

- Ask parents or guardians to help out with the class in a variety of ways. Try to have each parent do something for the class during the year.

- If a progress report is sent home during the year, see it as an opportunity to communicate with the family. Be willing to answer any questions that parents may have.

Involving Priests

The priests of the parish have a powerful influence on the children in your class. Try to involve the priests in ways other than the usual celebration of the sacraments of Eucharist and Reconciliation. Invite them to visit your class and talk about specific topics. Make them feel welcome at all class events by always extending a personal invitation.

Involving Parishioners

Challenge yourself to think of ways you can involve parishioners in your class. Invite people to share their talents and interests with the children. Ask the parish musicians who play for liturgical celebrations to help you bring music to the classroom. Ask the social service people of the parish to show you ways of involving the young in service activities.

TEACHER'S REFLECTIONS

Teacher's Reflections is a special resource for those who have the awsome responsibility of passing on the truths of our faith to young people. Its purpose is to provide a basis for reflections on the content of each chapter of THIS IS OUR FAITH.

This feature will give you the opportunity to grow in knowledge and faith so that you, in turn, can share that knowledge and faith with your students. As the *National Catechetical Directory* states, "Only men and women of faith can share faith with others, preparing the setting within which people can respond in faith to God's grace"(NCD, 207).

Each reflection consists of a question for each chapter of the text. This question is intended to be answered after you teach. There is also space to note what really worked in the chapter or what you would change the next time you teach this chapter.

In addition to the chapter reflections, there are sections for beginning-of-the-year and end-of-the-year entries. You can write your thoughts and concerns as you begin a new year of teaching the good news. And when classes come to a close, you can report your general reactions of the entire year along with suggestions for the following year.

Here is a chance to record your thoughts, feelings, beliefs, successes, and setbacks during the year. From time to time, you can look back at your entries and see how much you have really grown in faith and understanding.

Finally, note the "Teacher's Prayer Before Class" below. Pray for guidance and support before teaching your class. Thus, you will acquire the grace necessary to fulfill the mission on which you are sent: To go and teach all nations.

Teacher's Prayer Before Class

Loving God, I am about to share your word with my students. Allow me to awaken in the hearts of my students an awareness of your presence in their lives today.

As I share faith with these children, I ask you to help me

> *bring good news to them;*

> *proclaim your message of unconditional love to them;*

> *envision ways in which to bring your word into their lives.*

Help me listen to the needs of these children's hearts and respond to them with your gentle and compassionate spirit. I ask this in the name of Jesus, your gift to us. Thank you, gracious God, for calling me to be a teacher and for helping me to share your good news this day. Amen.

BEGINNING OF THE YEAR

How do I feel about teaching the truths of our faith to others this year?

What are my greatest doubts and fears as I begin the year?

What are my greatest strengths as I begin the year?

What do I hope to accomplish by the end of the year?

How do I hope to help my students grow in faith?

CHAPTER 1

How did I show my students that the Catholic community is different from other communities?

CHAPTER 2

What can I do to help my students feel at home in the Catholic Church?

CHAPTER 3

How did I help my students begin to see the sacraments as celebrations?

CHAPTER 4

What elements of Baptism did I help my students to learn about?

CHAPTER 5

In what ways did I help my students to learn to be responsible for others?

CHAPTER 6

How did I introduce the concept of free will to my students?

CHAPTER 7

How did I relate the concept of reconciliation to the lives of my students?

CHAPTER 8

How did I help my students to understand the sacrament of Reconciliation?

TEACHER'S REFLECTIONS

CHAPTER 9

How did I help my students to learn the importance of gathering for Mass?

CHAPTER 10

How did my students understand the importance of the Liturgy of the Word?

CHAPTER 11

How did my students learn to respond to God's word?

CHAPTER 12

How did I make the Prayer of the Faithful relevant to the lives of my students?

CHAPTER 13

How did I help my students to make the connection between the story of the loaves and the fish and the Liturgy of the Eucharist?

CHAPTER 14

How did I teach my students to be thankful to God, especially at Mass?

CHAPTER 15

How did I help my students to understand the Mass as a sacrifice?

CHAPTER 16

How well did my students comprehend that the Eucharist is really the body of Christ?

CHAPTER 17

How well did my students grasp the concept of the Eucharist as a sign of unity?

CHAPTER 18

How did I teach my students to "go in peace to love and serve the Lord"?

CHAPTER 19

In what ways did my students see the Eucharist as a sign of new life?

CHAPTER 20

How did I help my students understand that the Eucharist is a reminder of Jesus' presence with us now?

ADVENT

How did I help my students to be more loving and caring this Advent?

CHRISTMAS

How did I help my students' understanding of Christmas to grow this year?

LENT

How did I help my students to understand the meaning of prayer and sacrifice during Lent?

EASTER

How did I help my students to celebrate a joyous Easter season?

END OF THE YEAR

How have I been changed by teaching the truths of our faith to others this year?

How did I improve my teaching skills this year?

What do I feel I have accomplished this year?

How did I help my students grow in faith?

What would I have done differently?

RESOURCE GUIDE

This Resource Guide provides a list of recommended books, videos, and music recordings for use with the lessons in the student text. The guide follows the organization of the text into five units and the Amen section. The following is an explanation of the formats used in listing the different categories of resource material.

Books Books are listed by title, author or editor, publisher, copyright date, and description. The chapter number or section title in parentheses refers to the place in the student text where the material is recommended for use. For example:

> *I Got Community.* Dale Gottlieb. Holt, 1995. A celebration of various individuals' contributions to the community in first person narration. **(1)**

Videos Videos are listed by video title, length, series title if applicable, company, copyright date, description, and student text reference in parentheses. For example:

Zip Your Lip to Gossip. (25 min.) "Wooster Square" series. St. Anthony Messenger Press, 1990. Gossiping and telling things that are not true can hurt others and cause a lot of damage. **(14)**

Music Recordings Recordings are listed by title of the song or selection, title of the record album, company, copyright date, and student text reference in parentheses. For example:

> "Easter Rise Up." *Come Meet Jesus!* Pauline Books & Media, 1990. **(Easter)**

The Resourceful Teacher section ends with a list of frequently used publishers and media companies. An introductory note to this list, on page 392, offers advice about sources and scheduling.

Unit 1

Books

The Church. Carol S. Matthews. Concordia, 1983. Explains and describes the Church as people, as well as a building. **(1)**

I Got Community. Dale Gottlieb. Holt, 1995. A celebration of various individuals' contributions to the community in first person narration. **(1)**

Roxaboxen. Alice McLerran. Tambourine, 1991. The story of children in a desert who fashion an imaginary town and, in the process, learn what it is like to build a community. **(1)**

Rules and Mysteries of Brother Solomon. Sandol Stoddard. Paulist Press, 1987. Solomon, an elderly dog living on a Franciscan friary farm, lectures the younger dogs on how to conduct their lives. Special emphasis on five important mysteries that translate all aspects of the community of monastic life into doggy terms. **(1)**

Down the Road. Alice Schertle. Browndeer Press, 1995. An illustrated story about independence, making choices, experiencing the consequences of one's actions, and the love of family. **(2)**

Mouse's Birthday. Jane Yolen. Putnam Publishing Group, 1993. Many different animals and the farmer come to Mouse's tiny house to celebrate his birthday. **(2)**

Potluck. Anne Shelby. Orchard, 1991. Children whose names represent each letter of the alphabet bring an assortment of ethnic foods to a potluck supper. **(2)**

The Day We Met You. Phoebe Koehler. Macmillan, 1990. The book celebrates the great joy of welcoming an adopted baby into a household. **(3)**

I Love My Family. Wade Hudson. Scholastic, 1993. A yearly reunion of a large extended African family symbolizes the sense of belonging to a family larger than one's immediate family. **(3)**

The Child of God. Graci Evans. Multnomah, 1988. A simple depiction of the fruits of the Spirit with multi-ethnic children in everyday situations is presented in an eye-catching storyboard format. (**4**)

Heart of the Wood. Marguerite W. Davol. Simon & Schuster, 1992. A tree that is chopped down continues to give pleasure when it becomes a violin. Giftedness continues on in the heart of the wood of all things. (**4**)

Teach Me About the Holy Spirit. L. J. Sattgast and Jane Elkins. Multnomah, 1990. Flora and Flossie are identical twins who are very different. One wants to obey God, the other doesn't. Flora demonstrates the fruits of the Holy Spirit, while Flossie sulks, teases, and pushes, making herself and everyone else unhappy. She finally wants to be like Flora. (**4**)

Videos

The Church. (30 min.) "Sacred Heart Kids Club" series. Don Bosco, 1986. Christ loves and guides his people. The Church is more than a building; it is a community of persons called together to love, serve, and forgive as the Lord does. (**1**)

My Father's House. (10 min.) St. Anthony Messenger Press, 1983. Follow a seven-year-old as she explores her parish church as God's house and sees all that she has been told about the church. (**1**)

Sacraments for Children. (60 min.) Liguori, 1992. In eight vignettes the sacraments are explained. The first segment covers the concept of "sacrament." The seven sacraments are presented in the next seven segments. Explanations help children begin to learn and discuss how to see, hear, and touch Jesus through the sacramental life of the Church. (**2**)

Sacraments in General. (30 min.) "Sacred Heart Kids Club" series. Don Bosco, 1990. In the sacraments we see Jesus not only as a friend but as someone who shares divine life with us completely. (**2**)

Baptism. (30 min.) "Sacred Heart Kids Club" series. Don Bosco, 1990. This program highlights aspects of belonging to God's family, a genuine conversion experience, and the attractiveness of a joyful Christian community. (**3**)

Baptism: Sacrament of Belonging. (15 min.) St. Anthony Messenger Press, 1970. This classic true story tells of an orphaned Mexican boy who is alienated by others because of his scarred face. Explores Baptism as a sacrament of welcome when the other children ask him to join them. (**3**)

Celebrating the Church Year for Children: Pentecost. (15 min.) Paulist Press, 1989. This video shows children the liturgical practices and Christian family customs that convey the spirit of the first Pentecost. (**4**)

Confirmation. (30 min.) "Sacred Heart Kids Club" series. Don Bosco, 1990. We experience the Spirit in the ordinary events of our lives. The sacrament of Confirmation brings fullness to our initiation in God's life and love. (**4**)

Music Recordings

"Children of God." THIS IS OUR FAITH *Music Program.* Silver Burdett & Ginn, 1990. (**1–4**)

"God Is Building a House." ***Young People's Glory & Praise,*** Tape 1. NALR, 1984, available from Oregon Catholic Press. (**1**)

"God's Family." ***Joyful Noises.*** Brown-ROA, 1993. (**1**)

"Look Beyond." ***Young People's Glory & Praise,*** Tape 2. NALR, 1984, available from Oregon Catholic Press. (**2**)

"We Have Been Baptized in Christ." ***Young People's Glory & Praise,*** Tape 3. NALR, 1984, available from Oregon Catholic Press. (**3**)

"Everyone Moved by the Spirit." ***Young People's Glory & Praise,*** Tape 1. NALR, 1984, available from Oregon Catholic Press. (**4**)

"Spirit of God." ***Wake Up the Earth.*** NALR, 1983, available from Oregon Catholic Press. (**4**)

Unit 2

Books

Caring for My Home. Gwen Connelly. Child's World, 1991. A child describes how she and everyone in her

RESOURCE GUIDE

family acts responsibly by pitching in to get things done. (5)

The Giving Tree. Shel Silverstein. Harper, 1964. The story is old but the theme ever new. The tree in the story never gives up caring about the little boy who grew up under its leaves as it continues to care for him in various ways through the years. (5)

Now One Foot, Now the Other. Tomie dePaola. Putnam, 1981. This classic story follows a boy and his grandfather after the grandfather suffers a stroke and the grandson helps him to walk again. (5)

A Family That Fights. Sharon Bernstein. C. Whitman, 1991. A quiet story that deals with three children who live in a family in which the father hits the mother and threatens them all when he's angry. (6)

The Tantrum. Bobette McCarthy. Macmillan, 1993. Gracie tells about her terrible temper tantrum and how everyone responded to it. (6)

That's Exactly the Way It Wasn't. James Stevenson. Greenwillow, 1991. Two grandfathers who are brothers reminisce about their youth. They can't agree on anything that happened, lying unintentionally. Getting to the bottom of conflicting stories is the moral of this book. (6)

Even If I Did Something. Barbara Hazen. Macmillan, 1992. Mother still loves you even if you do something bad. (7)

I Hate My Sister Maggie. Crescent Dragonwagon. Macmillan, 1989. Everything Harry tries to do is spoiled by his pesky sister, Maggie. (7)

The Worst Person's Christmas. James Stevenson. Greenwillow, 1991. The worst person is at his worst when everyone else is brimming with good cheer. Some children try to overlook his attitude and give him a Christmas present, which changes his attitude on life. (7)

The Grandpa Days. Joan W. Blos. Simon & Schuster, 1989. A story of a ten-year-old who spends a week with his grandfather and has to learn the difference between wishing and good planning. (8)

Second Grade Pig Pals. Kirby Larson. Holiday House, 1994. Second-grader Quinn tries to earn a gold star on the bulletin board for National Pig Day and regain her friendship with a new student following a mix-up. (8)

You Make the Angels Cry. Denys Cazey. Bradbury Press, 1983. When rain begins to fall after his mother scolds him, Albert is convinced that he really made the angels cry. (8)

Videos

Honesty and Responsibility. (24 min.) "Character Builder Storybook" series. Oblate, 1988. Animated video with two segments in which children learn about being trustworthy and truthful, as well as responsible and reliable. (5)

The Promise. (17 min.) St. Anthony Messenger Press, 1988. Amy finds a job caring for an elderly man's guide dog while he is at the hospital. She carelessly leaves the gate open and the dog runs away. A story about responsibility, commitment, and forgiveness. (5–7)

Snap: How to Act Like a Responsible Adult. (30 min.) Oblate, 1994. Drea, a junior high school girl, agrees to baby-sit the neighbors' children and dog. The dog gets lost, so Drea dreams up an adventure to track down the dog and learns a lot about acting responsibly. (5–7)

The Basketball Game. (30 min.) Brown-ROA, 1988. The theme is good sportsmanship and the value of coping with anger through responsible behavior. (6)

Gertie, the Hungry Goldfish. (25 min.) St. Anthony Messenger Press, 1990. Sometimes things are forgotten and consequences occur because of forgetting. Learning responsibility is a part of growing up. (6)

Handle with Care. (10 min.) Twenty-Third Publications, 1989. Five open-ended stories involve students in problem solving and decision making, inviting the students to share their values. Caring attitudes and responsible behavior are emphasized. (6)

I Can Do It: Taking Responsibility. (16 min.) Sunburst, 1992. This program presents open-ended scenarios in which students are challenged to discuss each situation and decide on a responsible course of action. (**6**)

Forgive and Forget. (15 min.) St. Anthony Messenger Press, 1990. A kind king, a mischievous monkey, and a crooked crocodile will make viewers laugh and worry, but most of all, forgive and forget! (**7, 8**)

Integrity. (20 min.) "Gerbert" series. Evangelical Films & Video, 1990. Gerbert learns the consequences of taking what isn't rightfully his and attempts to make his wrong right by returning some money. (**7**)

Skateboard. (12 min.) St. Anthony Messenger Press, 1985. An adventurous eight-year-old disobeys her parents and takes her new skateboard onto the street. She rolls under a passing firetruck. She is unharmed, but her actions cause her to face other consequences. (**7, 8**)

Simon the Lamb. (25 min.) Oblate, 1993. Simon is shunned by the other lambs in the barnyard because he's different, but a winter storm strands the other lambs, and Simon's differences save the lambs. (**7, 8**)

The Stray. (14 min.) St. Anthony Messenger Press, 1978. A classic, creative retelling of the parable of the Lost Sheep, featuring thirteen first graders on a trip to the zoo. (**7, 8**)

Music Recordings

"Walk a Mile." ***Walk a Mile.*** Lovable Creature Music, 1989. (**5–7**)

"Kids' Peace Song." ***Peace Is the World Smiling.*** Music for Little People, 1986. (**5–8**)

"God Loves Me and You." T*HIS* I*S* O*UR* F*AITH Music Program.* Silver Burdett & Ginn, 1990. (**5–8**)

"Peace Is the World Smiling." ***Peace Is the World Smiling.*** Music for Little People, 1989. (**5–8**)

"He Forgives Me." ***Come Meet Jesus!*** Pauline Books & Media, 1990. (**7–8**)

"Jesus Is Light." ***Children of the Mountains.*** NALR, 1985, available from Oregon Catholic Press. (**8**)

Unit 3

Books

Going to a Party. Anne Civardi. Highgate, 1986. Explains what it is like to go a party for the first time. (**9**)

My Big Family at Church. Helen Caswell. Abingdon Press, 1989. Each church is like a big family of God's children, and each has a role to play in the mission of the Church. (**9**)

Just Listen. Winifred Morris. Atheneum, 1990. There's a difference in the sounds that Tara hears in the city and in the country. When she's with her grandma, she sometimes hears her own song. (**10**)

Listen to Me. Barbara Neasi. Children Press, 1986. When a little boy feels neglected because no one listens to him, his grandmother comes to the rescue. She spends time with him and carefully listens to everything the little boy says. (**10**)

"No!" Said Joe. John Prater. Candlewick Press, 1992. Joe's imaginative parents think of all the horrible things that might happen to him if he does not come shopping with them. (**11**)

My Mass. Piera Paltro. Pauline Books & Media, 1992. A colorful storybook that helps children learn and understand the basic prayers of the Mass. (**12**)

Thanks Be to God: Prayers from Around the World. Pauline Baynes. Macmillan, 1990. This is a collection of prayers, including prayers for giving thanks. (**12**)

Videos

Celebrating. (20 min.) "Table of the Lord" series. Our Sunday Visitor, 1992. Marco celebrates with his friends and expresses his appreciation for the gifts he has received. (**9**)

Eucharist. (30 min.) "Sacred Heart Kids Club" series.

RESOURCE GUIDE

Tabor, 1990. Jesus wants to be as close to us as the bread we eat. By sharing in the Eucharist, we become one in Christ. (9)

Mass and Me. (14 min.) Brown-ROA, 1994. A teacher helps two children preparing for first Eucharist to understand what is really going on in the Mass and how they can participate more fully. (9–12)

Breaking Open the Word Creatively. (124 min.) Resource Publications, 1994. In several segments the creative use of the arts—especially music, drama, and storytelling—is shown as a means to breaking open the word of God for young children. (10–12)

Let the Children Come to Me. (70 min.) Liguori, 1991. In twelve five-minute vignettes, Father Joe Kempf reads and explains Scripture passages, followed by children acting out each passage. Shows how the active involvement of the assembly can make the word of God come alive. (10, 11)

There's So Much to Do/So Many People. (20 min.) "Marvelous Mystery" series. Our Sunday Visitor, 1991. Explores the Liturgy of the Eucharist and the basic fact that liturgy is "people work." (10–11)

Prayer. (30 min.) "Sacred Heart Kids Club" series. Don Bosco, 1986. God speaks to and listens to us. When we interact with one another we sometimes overlook the obvious: simply talking and listening. (12)

Traditional Prayers for Children. (40 min.) Paulist Press, 1988. Features four ten-minute segments on The Our Father, Hail Mary, Glory Be, and Apostles Creed. Prayers are recited and appear on the screen. (12)

Music Recordings

Come Meet Jesus! Pauline Books & Media, 1990. All songs on this album would be appropriate for this grade level/topic. (9–12)

"Gathered as One." *Gift of Life.* "Sacred Heart Kids Club Music." St. Anthony Messenger Press, 1990. (9)

"We Hear God's Word." *This Is Our Faith Music Program.* Silver Burdett & Ginn, 1990. (9–12)

"Jesus Always Listens." *Joyful Noises.* Brown-ROA, 1993. (10–12)

Unit 4

Books

Chicken Sunday. Patricia Polacco. Putnam, 1992. Three youngsters of different races and religions unite to help Miss Eula have a good Easter Sunday. (13)

The Outside Inn. George E. Lyon. Orchard, 1991. All kinds of creatures seek their food, while in the foreground youngsters prepare a "pretend" meal. (13)

This Is the Bread I Baked for Ned. Crescent Dragonwagon. Macmillan, 1989. A rhythmic story in which Ned gets a nice surprise. (13)

And God Created Squash: How the World Began. Martha Hickman. C. Whitman, 1993. This is a fanciful retelling of the Creation story. (14)

I Sing for the Animals. Paul Goble. Macmillan, 1991. This book explores the relationship of humankind to the Creator and the natural world. (14)

The Story of Creation: Words from Genesis. Jane Ray. Dutton, 1993. The language of the first book in the Bible is used to tell the story of Creation. (14)

He Is Risen: The Easter Story. Elizabeth Winthrop. Holiday House, 1985. This is a retelling of Christ's crucifixion and resurrection. (15)

Gray Fox. Jonathan London. Viking, 1993. After Gray Fox is accidentally killed, his family carries his spirit into the future. (16, 17)

Mrs. Higgins and Her Hen Hannah. Lydia Dabcovich. Dutton, 1993. Mrs. Higgins is devastated when her hen falls and dies, until she discovers a new chick in Hannah's straw. (16, 17)

My Grandma Leonie. Bijou Le Tord. Macmillan, 1987. When Grandma dies, a child remembers all the wonderful times. (16, 17)

Videos

Eating. (20 min.) "Table of the Lord" series. Our Sunday Visitor, 1992. The story of a girl who shares a special meal with her grandmother and learns about her family. The Last Supper is explained through Scripture. **(13–16)**

Eucharist. (30 min.) "Sacred Heart Kids Club" series. St. Anthony Messenger Press, 1990. Jesus wants to be as close to us as the bread we eat. By sharing in the Eucharist, we become one body in Christ. **(13–16)**

Grandma's Bread. (15 min.) St. Anthony Messenger Press, 1985. A beautiful story about the friendship between a grandmother and grandson that stresses tradition, family, Easter, dying, and the Eucharist. **(13–16)**

Music Recordings

"Body of Christ." *I Like to Be with Jesus.* "Sacred Heart Kids Club Music." St. Anthony Messenger Press, 1990. **(13–16)**

"Come, Lord Jesus." *Wonderfully Made.* Our Sunday Visitor, 1990. **(13–16)**

"Jesus, You Are Bread for Us." *THIS IS OUR FAITH Music Program.* Silver Burdett & Ginn, 1990. **(13–16)**

"When We Eat This Bread." *I Like to Be with Jesus.* "Sacred Heart Kids Club Music." St. Anthony Messenger Press, 1990. **(13–16)**

Unit 5

Books

Peace Begins with You. Katherine Scholes. Little, 1990. The theme of this book is that courage, strength, and responsibility are needed to achieve peace in life. **(17)**

Rachel Parker, Kindergarten Show-Off. Ann M. Martin. Holiday House, 1992. Olivia's friendship with Rachel changes to rivalry, but an understanding teacher helps out. **(17)**

Rosie and the Yellow Ribbon. Paula DePaolo. Little, 1993. In this interracial story of friendship, two girls quarrel but later make up. **(17)**

Sycamore Street. C. B. Christiansen. Macmillan, 1993. When her best friend, Angel, goes on vacation, Chloe is forced to play with a newcomer. **(17)**

Loop the Loop. Barbara Dugan. Greenwillow, 1992. Anne visits her old friend, Mrs. Simpson, who is now in a nursing home. An engrossing book of intergenerational friendship. **(18)**

Miss Tizzy. Libba M. Gray. Simon & Schuster, 1993. Miss Tizzy is the one person the neighborhood people can count on for kind acts and expressions of concern and love. **(18)**

Mrs. Katz and Tush. Patricia Polacco. Bantam, 1992. A lonely Jewish widow is befriended by a black boy who brings her a kitten to love. **(18)**

The Dead Bird. Margaret Wise Brown. Harper, 1989. This book introduces the concept of death to young people. After finding a dead bird, children give it a solemn burial. **(19)**

Grandpa's Slide Show. Debbie Gould. Lothrop, 1987. Grandpa always runs the slide show and lets Sam help. Then Grandpa dies, but Sam helps the slide shows to continue. **(19)**

Jesus Comes to Me. Mary Therese Donze, A.S.C. Liguori, 1990. Jesus' presence in the sacrament of Eucharist is explained to youngsters. **(20)**

My First Communion: A Day to Remember. Nadia Bonaldo. Pauline Books & Media, 1991. Places for photos, quotes, and memories. Important moments in the life and teaching of Jesus. A simple and complete explanation of the Mass. **(20)**

My First Communion. Dorothy Haas. C. Whitman, 1987. Describes a little girl's preparation for her First Communion. **(20)**

Videos

Amanda Goes to Mass. (9 min.) Twenty-Third Publications, 1991. A seven-year-old girl explains what happens when she and her family worship with the parish family. Each part of the eucharistic celebration is shown and defined. **(17–20)**

A Child's First Communion. (20 min.) Liguori, 1987. A second-grade candidate for First Eucharist is confused about the meaning of Jesus being the "Bread of Life." A young priest uses simple explanations, analogies, and the child's imagination to respond to his questions. (**17–20**)

Come On In. Tapes I and II. (12 min. each) Twenty-Third Publications, 1995. This two-part series helps children feel right at home in church. Viewers learn about the significance of the baptismal font, altar, chalice, crucifix, reconciliation room, stations, statues, candles, and lecterns. (**17–20**)

Music Recordings

"Neighbors (Jesu, Jesu)." *Hi God! 3.* NALR, available from Oregon Catholic Press, 1986. (**17**)

"Peace Is Flowing." *Young People's Glory & Praise.* NALR, available from Oregon Catholic Press, 1984. (**17**)

"We Come to Share." THIS IS OUR FAITH *Music Program.* Silver Burdett & Ginn, 1990. (**17–20**)

"Helping Hands." *Wonderfully Made.* Our Sunday Visitor, 1990 (**18**)

"Love One Another." *Wonderfully Made.* Our Sunday Visitor, 1990. (**18**)

"Rise Up." *Joyful Noises.* Brown-ROA, 1993. (**19**)

"I Like to Be with Jesus." *I Like to Be with Jesus.* "Sacred Heart Kids Club Music." St. Anthony Messenger Press, 1990. (**20**)

AMEN

Books

Christmas. Alan Blackwood. Rourke, 1987. Various interesting and colorful celebrations and events associated with the holidays from Advent through the Epiphany, both past and present. (**Advent/Christmas**)

From Heaven Above: The Story of Christmas Proclaimed by the Angels. Patricia and Fredrick McKissack. Augsburg, 1992. Six short stories introduced by a quotation from the Gospels concerning angelic communication about forgiveness, love, kindness, and trust. (**Advent/Christmas**)

Hark! A Christmas Sampler. Jane Yolen. Putnam, 1991. Original stories, poems, adapted legends, traditional and new carols, a history and development of the holiday and its traditions, and a Nativity play about the shepherds all beautifully illustrated in this outstanding volume. (**Advent/ Christmas**)

Jesus Tree. Annette Dellinger. Concordia, 1991. Two sisters decorate the family Christmas tree while their parents remind them of the symbolism of each item. Blends religious meanings of Christmas with the secular. (**Advent/Christmas**)

Mary Had a Baby Amen! Mary Murphy. Liguori, 1993. Simple story that brings the birth of Jesus to life. (**Mary/Christmas**)

Simon and the Holy Night. Eve Tharlet. Picture Book Studio, 1991. A delightful telling of the Christmas story, with a new twist. (**Christmas**)

Petook: An Easter Celebration: Traditions and Customs from Around the World. Pamela Kennedy. Ideals, 1990. The pre-Christian background of spring festivals and goddesses; the symbolism of new birth and rebirth; the customs of Holy Week, Passover, and Easter are explained. (**Lent/Easter**)

Easter. Julian Fox. Rourke, 1989. Emphasis on the Christian aspect of Easter and the many unusual ways it is celebrated throughout the world. (**Easter**)

Easter. Gail Gibbons. Holiday House, 1989. Jesus' life and death are treated briefly but with detail to provide an excellent introduction for young children. The crucifixion is handled tastefully, and other traditional symbols and customs are discussed. (**Easter**)

Videos

Advent Roads. (8 min.) "Following Jesus Through the Church Year" series. Twenty-Third Publications, 1990. Krispin travels through the four weeks of Advent. Guided by signs along the way, and lighted by the Advent wreath, Krispin meets the prophets of old, who point the way to Jesus. (**Advent**)

Celebrating the Church Year for Children: Advent. (15 min.) "Celebrating the Church Year for Children" series. Paulist Press, 1989. This video looks at liturgical practices and Christian family customs that capture the hope for the Messiah. (**Advent**)

Celebrating the Church Year for Children: Christmas. (15 min.) "Celebrating the Church Year for Children" series. Paulist Press, 1989. Special lights on trees, nativity scenes, and other traditions at Christmas are explained. (**Christmas**)

Timmy's Special Delivery. (25 min.) Oblate, 1993. Two loving children have only one wish—that the other one will receive a gift. Timmy the angel is touched by their unselfishness and sets out to see that both are rewarded for their unselfishness. (**Christmas**)

Lenten Lane. (15 min.) "Following Jesus Through the Church Year" series. Twenty-Third Publications, 1990. Krispin travels to Nazareth and Jerusalem; he meets Bible figures along the way of his Lenten journey. (**Lent**)

Holy Week Crossing. (9 min.) "Following Jesus Through the Church Year" series. Twenty-Third Publications, 1990. Krispin meets people who walked the last days of Jesus' life as Jesus rode into Jerusalem, celebrated the Passover meal, and was crucified. Krispin's journey ends at the empty tomb. (**Lent/Holy Week/Easter**)

Easter. (30 min.) "Sacred Heart Kids Club" series. Don Bosco, 1986. The reasons why we celebrate Easter are explained. (**Easter**)

Easter Caterpillar. (13 min.) Don Bosco, 1987. David finds a caterpillar, later finds its empty cocoon, and discovers that it has been transformed into a butterfly. (**Easter**)

Saints and Heroes. (30 min.) "Sacred Heart Kids Club" series. Don Bosco, 1986. After Jeremy puts on "saint glasses," Sr. Jane points out other saints in the church. (**Saints**)

Mary. (30 min.) "Sacred Heart Kids Club" series. Don Bosco, 1986. Leads to a discussion about Mary, Jesus' mother, and our mothers. (**Mary**)

Mary, Our Friend. (15 min.) Brown-ROA, 1987. Five themes are emphasized in this video: Mary listens; Mary shares; Mary, the Mother of Jesus; Mary follows; and Mary cares. (**Mary**)

Pope John XXIII. (24 min.) "Famous Men and Women of the Church" series. Don Bosco, 1988. The story of a greatly loved man of the Catholic Church. (**In the Spirit of Jesus**)

Music Recordings

"Christmas Candle." *Wonderfully Made.* Our Sunday Visitor, 1990. (**Advent/Christmas**)

"Come Lord Jesus." *Young People's Glory & Praise,* Tape I. NALR, 1984, available from Oregon Catholic Press. (**Advent**)

Mary Christmas Album. Pauline Books & Media, 1992. (**Advent/Christmas**)

"I Will Follow." *I Like to Be with Jesus.* "Sacred Heart Kids Club Music." St. Anthony Messenger Press, 1990. (**Lent/Easter**)

"Easter Rise Up." *Come Meet Jesus!* Pauline Books & Media, 1990. (**Easter**)

"Saints Be Alive." *Saints Be Alive.* "Sacred Heart Kids Club" series. St. Anthony Messenger Press, 1990. (**Saints**)

"Hail Mary." I Like to Be with Jesus. "Sacred Heart Kids Club Music." St. Anthony Messenger Press, 1990. (Mary)

"Hail Mary, Gentle Woman." *Young People's Glory & Praise.* NALR, 1984, available from Oregon Catholic Press. (**Mary**)

"Jesus Cares for Everyone." *Big Steps for Little Feet.* Pauline Books & Media, 1991.

PUBLISHERS AND MEDIA COMPANIES

Many of the resources listed, beginning on page 383, are available from your school, parish, diocesan, regional, college, or university media center. Inquire there first. If you must seek further, the following partial list of publishers and or distributors will be helpful. In all cases where you plan to use free or rental materials, confirm availablity and make arrangements several weeks in advance of your scheduled use. Be sure to preview your selection before showing it to your class.

Abingdon Press
201 8th Ave., S, P.O. Box 801
Nashville, TN 37202-0801
(800) 251-3320

Atheneum
See Simon & Schuster Children's.

Augsburg Fortress Publishers
426 S. 5th St., Box 1209
Minneapolis, MN 55440
(800) 328-4648

Bantam Doubleday Dell
Publishing Group, Inc.
1540 Broadway
New York, NY 10036
(800) 223-6834

Brown-ROA
1665 Embassy West Dr.
Dubuque, IA 52002-2259
(800) 922-7696

Candlewick Press
(Div. of Walker Books)
2067 Massachusetts Ave.
Cambridge, MA 01240
(617) 661-3330

Children's Press
(Div. of Grolier Publishing)
Sherman Tpke.
Danbury, CT 06813
(203) 797-3500

Child's World, Inc.
505 N. Highway 169
Suite 295
Plymouth, MN 55441

(612) 797-0155
(800) 599-7323

Concordia Publishing House
3558 S. Jefferson Ave.
St. Louis, MO 63118-3968
(800) 325-3040

Dutton Children's Books
(Div. of Penguin USA)
375 Hudson St.
New York, NY 10014-3657
(212) 366-2000

Grace Products
1761 International Parkway
Suite 135
Richardson, TX 75081
(800) 527-4014

Harcourt Brace & Co.
6277 Sea Harbor Dr.
Orlando, FL 32887
(800) 543-1918

HarperCollins Publishers
100 Keystone Industrial Park
Scranton, PA 18512
(800) 242-7737

Highgate House Publishers
P.O. Box 683
Latham, NY 12110
(518) 785-0035

Holiday House, Inc.
425 Madison Ave.
New York, NY 10017
(212) 688-0085

Henry Holt & Co., Inc.
115 W. 18th St.
New York, NY 10011
(800) 488-5233

Ideals Publications
535 Metroplex Dr.
Nashville, TN 37211
(800) 558-4343

Liguori Publications
One Liguori Dr.
Liguori, MO 63057-9999
(800) 325-9521

Little, Brown & Co.
Time & Life Building
1271 Ave. of the Americas
New York, NY 10020
(800) 343-9204

William Morrow & Co., Inc.
1350 Ave. of the Americas
New York, NY 10019
(800) 843-9389

Multnomah Bible College &
Biblical Seminary
8435 NE Glisan St.
Portland, OR 97220
(503) 255-0332

Music for Little People
605 So. Douglas St.
El Segundo, CA 90245
(800) 727-2233

Oblate Media & Communications
7315 Manchester Rd.
Maplewood, MO 63143-9914
(800) 233-4629

Oregon Catholic Press
5536 NE Hassalo
Portland, OR 97213
(800) 548-8739

Our Sunday Visitor Publishing, Inc.
200 Noll Plaza
Hungtington, IN 46750
(800) 348-2440

Pauline Books & Media
50 St. Paul's Ave.
Boston, MA 02130
(800) 876-4463

Paulist Press
997 MacArthur Blvd.
Mahwah, NJ 07430
(201) 825-7300

Penguin USA
375 Hudson St.
New York, NY 10014
(800) 331-4624

G.P. Putnam & Sons
200 Madison Ave.
New York, NY 10016
(800) 631-8571

Resource Publications
160 E. Virginia St., Suite 290
San Jose, CA 95112-5848
(800) 736-7600

Rourke Publications, Inc.
P.O. Box 3328
Vero Beach, FL 32964
(407) 465-4575

Scholastic, Inc.
555 Broadway
New York, NY 10012-3999
(800) 325-6149

Simon & Schuster Children's
200 Old Tappan Rd.
Old Tappan, NJ 07675
(800) 223-2336

Simon & Schuster School Group
P.O. Box 2649
Columbus, OH 43216
(800) 848-9500

St. Anthony Messenger Press
(also Franciscan
Communications)
1615 Republic St.
Cincinnati, OH 45210
(800) 488-0488

Tabor Publishing
200 E. Bethany Dr.
Allen, TX 75002
(800) 822-6701

Twenty-Third Publications
P.O. Box 180
Mystic, CT 06355
(800) 321-0411

Whitman Pub.
(Devin-Adair Pubs.)
6 N. Water St.
Greenwich, CT 06830
(203) 531-7755

For further information you may
wish to consult the following
publishers and or distributors.

Alba House Communications
9531 Akron-Canfield Rd.
Box 595
Canfield, OH 44406-0595
(800) 533-2522

Argus Communications
P.O. Box 6000
Allen, TX 75013
(800) 527-4748

Ave Maria Press
Univ. of Notre Dame
Notre Dame, IN 46556-0428
(800) 282-1865

Ballantine Books, Inc.
201 E. 50th St.
New York, NY 10022
(800) 726-0600

Barr Media
12801 Schabarum Ave.
Irwindale, CA 91706-7878
(800) 582-2000

Benziger Publishing Co.
15319 Chatsworth St.
Mission Hills, CA 91345
(800) 551-8766

Billy Budd Films
235 E. 57th St.
New York, NY 10022
(800) 772-0380

Brethren Press
1451 Dundee Ave.
Elgin, IL 60120
(800) 441-3712

BridgeWater Books
(Div. of Troll Assocs.)
100 Corporate Dr.
Mahwah, NJ 07430
(800) 929-8765

Carousel Film & Video
260 Fifth Ave., Suite 405
New York, NY 10001
(800) 683-1660

Cathedral Films
Religious Film Corporation
P.O. Box 4029
Westlake Village, CA 91359
(800) 338-3456

Center for Media Literacy
4727 Wilshire Blvd., #403
Los Angeles, CA 90070
(213) 931-4177

The Christophers
12 E. 48th St.
New York, NY 10017
(212) 759-4050

David C. Cook Pub. Co.
850 N. Grove Ave.
Elgin, IL 60120
(800) 323-7543

Coronet/MTI Film & Video
4350 Equity Dr.
P.O. Box 2649
Columbus, OH 43216-2649
(800) 321-3106

Credence Cassettes (NCR)
115 E. Armour Blvd.
Kansas City, MO
(800) 444-8910

Crown Books for Young Readers
(Div. of Random House)
Columban Fathers
201 E. 50th St.
New York, NY 10022
(800) 733-3000

Crown Ministries Internat'l
9 Winstone Ln.
Bella Vista, AR 72714
(800) 433-4685

EcuFilm
810 12th Ave., S
Nashville, TN 37203
(800) 251-4091

Encyclopaedia Britannica
Educational Corp.
310 S. Michigan Ave.
Chicago, IL 60604-9839
(800) 554-9862

Family Films
(Div. of Concordia Publishing
House)
3558 S. Jefferson Ave.
St. Louis, MO 63118-3968
(800) 325-3040

Fawcett Book Group
(Div. of Ballantine Books)
201 E. 50th St.
New York, NY 10022
(800) 733-3000

Genesis Project
65 Bleecker St., 5th Floor
New York, NY 10012
(212) 979-2743

G.I.A. Publications, Inc.
7404 S. Mason Ave.
Chicago, IL 60638
(708) 496-3800
(800) 442-1358

Golden Books Publishing
1220 Mound Ave.
Racine, WI 53404
(800) 558-3291

Good Books
Box 419
3510 Old Philadelphia Pike
Intercourse, PA 17531
(800) 762-7171

Gospel Films
Box 455
Muskegon, MI 49443-0455
(800) 253-0413

Group Publishing Inc.
1515 Cascade Ave.
Loveland, CO 80538
(800) 541-5200

Harper San Francisco
1160 Battery St., 3rd Floor
San Francisco, CA 94111
(415) 477-4444

Hi-Time Publishing Corp.
Box 13337
Milwaukee, WI 53213-0337
(800) 558-2292

Houghton Mifflin Co.
222 Berkeley St.
Boston, MA 02116
(800) 225-3362

Hyperion Books for Children
(Div. of Disney Book Pub., Inc.)
114 Fifth Ave.
New York, NY 10011
(800) 343-9204

Ikonographics, Inc.
P.O. Box 801
Croton-on-Hudson, NY 10520
(800) 944-1505

Judson Press
P.O. Box 851
Valley Forge, PA 19482
(800) 331-1053

Kane/Miller Book Pubs.
P.O. Box 310529
Brooklyn, NY 11231-0529
(718) 624-5120

Light Records
3543 Old Conejo Rd., Suite 105
Newbury Park, CA 91320

Landmark Media
3450 Slade Run Dr.
Falls Church, VA 22042
(800) 342-4336

The Lerner Group
241 First Ave., N
Minneapolis, MN 55401
(800) 328-4949

J.B. Lippincott Co.
227 E. Washington Sq.
Philadelphia, PA 19106
(800) 777-2295

The Liturgical Press
St. John's Abbey
Collegeville, MN 56321
(800) 858-5450

Loyola University Press
3441 N. Ashland Ave.
Chicago, IL 60657
(800) 621-1008

Maranatha Music
31050 Laguna Hills
Laguna Hills, CA 92654

Mass Media Ministries
2116 North Charles St.
Baltimore, MD 21218
(800) 828-8825

The McGraw-Hill Cos.
1221 Ave. of the Americas
New York, NY 10020
(800) 262-4729

Media Guild
11722 Sorrento Valley Rd.
Suite E
San Diego, CA 92121
(800) 886-9191

Morehouse Publishing
871 Ethan Allen Hwy, Suite 204
Ridgefield, CT 06877-2801
(203) 431-3927
(800) 877-0012

Nest Entertainment
(Family Entertainment Network)
6100 Colwell Blvd.
Irving, TX 75039-9833
(800) 452-4485

Oliver-Nelson
(Div. of Thomas Nelson Pubs.)
Nelson Pl. at Elm Hill Pike
Nashville, TN 37214
(800) 251-4000

Paulist Productions
17575 Pacific Coast Hwy.
Pacific Palisades, CA 90272
(800) 624-8613

Peter Li Education Group
330 Progress Road
Dayton, OH 45449
(513) 847-5902

Prentice-Hall
113 Sylvan Ave., Rte. 9 W
Englewood Cliffs, NJ 07632
(800) 922-0579

Pyramid Media
P.O. Box 1048
Santa Monica, CA 90406-1048
(800) 421-2304

Random House, Inc.
201 E. 50th St., 22nd Floor
New York, NY 10022
(800) 733-3000

Raven Press Ltd.
1185 Ave. of the Americas
New York, NY 10036
(800) 777-2836

Red Hen Press
P.O. Box 419
Summerland, CA 93067
(805) 969-7058

William H. Sadlier, Inc.
9 Pine St.
New York, NY 10005-1002
(800) 221-5175

St. Mary's Press
702 Terrace Heights
Winona, MN 55987
(800) 533-8095

Standard Publishing
8121 Hamilton Ave.

Cincinnati, OH 45231
(800) 543-1301

Star Song Publishing Group
P.O. Box 150009
Nashville, TN 37215
(800) 835-7664

Sunburst Communications, Inc.
39 Washington Ave.
Pleasantville, NY 10570
(800) 431-1934

Treehaus Communications, Inc.
P.O. Box 249
Loveland, OH 45140
(800)638-4287

Troll Associates
100 Corporate Dr.
Mahwah, NJ 07430
(800) 526-5289

United States Catholic
Conference (USCC)
Publishing Services
3211 4th St., NE
Washington, DC 20017-1194
(800) 235-8722

Vision Media
P.O. Box 540
2030 Wentz Church Rd.
Worcester, PA 19490
(800) 523-0226

Franklin Watts
(Div. of Grolier Publishing Co.)
Sherman Tpk.
Danbury, CT 06813
(800) 672-6672

Word Records & Music
3319 W. End Ave.
Nashville, TN 37203
(800) 876-9673

ACKNOWLEDGMENTS

Excerpts from the English translation of *Rite of Confirmation, Second Edition* © 1975, International Committee on English in the Liturgy, Inc. All rights reserved.

Excerpts from the English translation of *Rite of Baptism for Children* © 1969, International Committee on English in the Liturgy, Inc. (ICEL); excerpts from the English translation of *The Roman Missal* © 1973, ICEL; excerpts from the English translation of *Eucharistic Prayers for Masses with Children* © 1975, ICEL. All rights reserved.

Scriptural texts used in this work are taken from the *New American Bible with Revised New Testament,* Copyright © 1970, 1986 by the Confraternity of Christian Doctrine, Washington, D.C. and are used by permission of the copyright owner. All rights reserved.

All adaptations of Scripture are based on the *New American Bible with Revised New Testament.*

Excerpts from the English translation of the *Catechism of the Catholic Church* for the United States of America Copyright © 1994, United States Catholic Conference, Inc.—Libreria Editrice Vaticana, are used with permission. All rights reserved.

Excerpts taken from *Sharing the Light of Faith: National Catechetical Directory for Catholics of the United States* Copyright © 1979 United States Catholic Conference, Washington, D.C. 20017. Used with permission. All rights reserved.

CREDITS

Cover art: Pamela Johnson
Helps for the Teacher art: Wendy Wassink Ackison
Photos: 368: Jo Browne/Tony Stone Images.